Remaking
Radicalism

Remaking Radicalism

A GRASSROOTS DOCUMENTARY READER OF THE UNITED STATES, 1973-2001

EDITED BY Dan Berger
AND Emily K. Hobson

The University of Georgia Press
ATHENS

Most University of Georgia Press titles are
available from popular e-book vendors.

Printed digitally

Library of Congress Cataloging-in-Publication Data

Names: Berger, Dan, editor. | Hobson, Emily K., 1975– editor.
Title: Remaking radicalism : a grassroots documentary reader
    of the United States, 1973–2001 / edited by Dan Berger and
    Emily K. Hobson.
Description: Athens : The University of Georgia Press, 2020.
    | Series: Since 1970: histories of contemporary America |
    Includes bibliographical references and index.
Identifiers: LCCN 2020028111 (print) | LCCN 2020028112 (ebook)
    | ISBN 9780820357263 (hardback) | ISBN 9780820357256
    (paperback) | ISBN 9780820357270 (ebook)
Subjects: LCSH: Radicalism—United States—History. | Right and
    left (Political science) | Social movements—United States.
Classification: LCC HN90.R3 R466 2020 (print) | LCC HN90.R3
    (ebook) | DDC 303.48/4—dc23
LC record available at https://lccn.loc.gov/2020028111
LC ebook record available at https://lccn.loc.gov/2020028112

CONTENTS

Part 1: Bodies and Lives   23

SECTION A. FEMINIST AND QUEER FLASHPOINTS

Part 2: Walls and Gates   **131**

SECTION A. RESISTING REPRESSION

SECTION B. UNDERMINING THE PRISON STATE

SECTION C. FIGHT FOR THE CITY, FREE THE LAND

Part 3: Borders and Maps   239

SECTION A. ANTI-IMPERIALISM BEYOND VIETNAM

Part 4: Utopias and Dystopias 345

SECTION A. STOPPING THE END OF THE WORLD

SECTION B. LEFT VISIONS IN TRANSITION

SECTION C. LAND, DECOLONIZATION, AND INTERDEPENDENCE

ILLUSTRATIONS

ACKNOWLEDGMENTS

Our thanks to Claire Potter and Renee Romano for first soliciting this project in 2011 and for providing consistent sounding boards in the intervening years. Lynn Itagaki proved strong support upon joining the Since 1970 editorial board, and Daniel Winunwe Rivers offered astute commentary just in the nick of time that helped us reorganize the final manuscript. We are grateful to Mick Gusinde-Duffy and everyone at the University of Georgia Press for their support and patience. Thanks also to the anonymous readers of the press who helped us shape the project at key intervals—both by opening our eyes to the enormity of the task involved in such an anthology and by posing thoughtful questions that, from beginning to end, sharpened our own approach.

This project would have taken at least a decade longer without the diligent labor of Grace Handy. We offer her our deepest gratitude for her invaluable assistance in researching and securing permissions for many of the items included here, as well as transcribing several items. Thanks also to Felicia Perez for creating the companion website to this book, www.remakingradicalism.org, where additional documents and resources can be found.

Our thinking about this time period owes to a large list of friends, comrades, colleagues, mentors, and associates—far too many people to name here. For their comments on the introduction and overall framing of the volume, we thank Denisse Andrade, Abena Asare, Michelle Commander, Brent Hayes Edwards, Jasmine Johnson, Kelly Josephs, and the anonymous readers for the press—both those who reviewed the initial book proposal and those who years later provided such astute feedback on the finished draft of the manuscript. For their research advice and help identifying many of the artifacts we have included, as well as many we were unable to include, and for assistance in locating permissions, we especially thank Frank Abe, James Allison, Sara Awartani, Rishi Awatramani, Arlen Austin, Charles Barragan, Dawson Barrett, Kate Boyd, Jenny Brown, Umayyah Cable, Elizabeth Castle, Tamar Carroll, Ryan Cartwright, Marisa Chappell, Merlin Chowkwanyun, Andy Cornell, Joe Courter, Manuel Criollo, Lincoln Cushing, Joseph Nicholas DeFilippis, Chris Dixon, Cindy Domingo, Roxanne Dunbar-Ortiz, Bradley Duncan, Nijmie Dzurinko, Max Elbaum, Mark Engler, Nick Estes, Max Felker-Kantor, Mary Gibson, David Gilbert, Craig Gilmore, David Goldberg, Harmony Goldberg, Deborah Gould, Trevor Griffey, David Gwynn, Estella Habal, Debra Harry, Glenn Hendler, Kevin Henderson, Kris Hermes, Rachel Herzing, Alec Hickmott, Charlie Hinton, Maurice J. Hobson, Daniel Horowitz de Garcia, Amanda Hughett, Naomi Jaffe, Cara Jennings, Naneen Karraker, LA Kauffman, Karl Kersplebedeb, Michael Kroll, Scott Kurashige, Sarah Loose, Joe Lowndes, Matthew Lyons, Josh MacPhee, Claude Marks, Donna Martinez, Austin McCoy, Daniel McGowan, Keith McHenry, Bernadine Mellis, Paul Messersmith-Glavin, Matt Meyer, Andrea Milne, Cindy Milstein, Isabell Moore, Bethany Moreton, Ryan Patrick Murphy, Ezra Berkeley Nepon, Tamara Nopper, Michelle O'Brien, Eric Odell, Edward Onaci, David Ostendorf, Vera Parham, David Pellow, Pamela Pennock, Victor Pickard, Steve Pitts, Tony Platt, Laurie Prendergast, Laura Pulido, Josh Reid, Dan Royles, Benjamin Shepard, Mira Shimabukuro, Michael Staudenmaeir, David Stein, Whit Strub, Suzy Subways, Coll Thrush, James Tracy, Alex Vitale, Erik Wallenberg, Kay Whitlock, Phil Wider, Danielle Wiggins, Todd Wolfson, Keith Makoto Woodhouse, Mary Yee, and Natasha Zaretsky. To anyone else who offered us advice or pointed us in the right direction who we may have forgotten to identify here: thank you, thank you.

While we have benefited greatly from the generosity of privately held collections (including those maintained by some of those mentioned above), this book would not have been possible without the diligence, support, and open access mission of libraries and archives. Our thanks especially to the staff at the following institutions: Amistad Research Center at Tulane University, Bancroft Library at the University of California, Berkeley, Cecil H. Green Library at Stanford University, Center for Southwest Research and Special Collections at the University of New Mexico, Freedom Archives, Center for Third World Organizing, Ethnic Studies Library at the University of California, Berkeley, Gay, Lesbian, Bisexual, Transgender Historical Society, Graduate Theological Union, Interference Archive, Labor Archives of Washington, Lesbian Herstory Archive, Paul K. Longmore Institute on Disability at San Francisco State University, ONE National Gay and Lesbian Archives, Puerto Rican Cultural Center, Southern California Library, Sallie Bingham Center at Duke University, San Francisco State University Labor Archives and Research Center, Swarthmore Peace Collection, Tamiment Collection at New York University, University of California, Los Angeles, Special Collections, University of California, San Francisco, Special Collections, University of Colorado, Boulder, Special Collections, University of Massachusetts, Boston, University of Nevada, Reno, Special Collections, University of Vermont Special Collections Library, and the Wisconsin Historical Society (Madison).

As with most scholarly works, this volume builds on our own passions, commitments, and experiences. Our respective partners, Dana Barnett and Felicia Perez, lived with us over the *longue durée* of this project, which meant that they lived with almost a decade of conference calls and complaints about the picayune nature of copyright. We thank them for their patience, wit, wisdom, and solidarity. We also offer our thanks, obliquely but no less sincerely, to the many organizations and individuals who have mentored and nurtured our own ability to make and remake radicalism over the years.

Remaking Radicalism

Usable Pasts and the Persistence of Radicalism

Dan Berger and Emily K. Hobson

History, it is often said, must be made looking forward but can only be understood looking backward. In considering the recent past, observers must look in front of and behind them simultaneously, for the events—and many of the principal actors—are still making their mark on the world. Radicalism animates both how people working for dramatic social change experience a given time period and how they remember it. The wholesale transformation of society is a rarity, accomplished through an imprecise and unpredictable combination of diligence and luck. Yet the struggle itself, its endurance and evolution, remains generative: as people work to remake the world, they remake the horizon of social change. The means to make change shift and adapt to circumstances, but people's commitment to transforming the world in equitable, sustainable, and fulfilling ways remains. Perhaps the most salient feature of the radical tradition is its ability to weather storms and generate new gusts of energy that can sustain hope in times of despair. Radicalism is persistent, and its persistence offers many lessons.

This book brings together the lessons of recent radical movements in the United States from 1973 through 2001. These years are typically viewed as having been dominated by conservative retrenchment and a realignment that saw both political parties move steadily to the right. An accelerating wave of policy undermined unions and social movements, diluted and revoked antiracist and feminist advances, limited government-guaranteed social supports, expanded police power and prison capacity, enlarged the scope of US imperialism through a series of direct and proxy wars, and enhanced the power and profits of multinational corporations and financiers. Many have dubbed this convergence of forces "neoliberalism."[1]

And yet activists from 1973 through 2001 proved tenacious in the face of upheaval, resourceful in developing new tactics, and dedicated to learning from one another. Persistent and committed, activists did more than just keep radical legacies alive. They remade radicalism—bridging differences of identity and ideology often assumed to cleave movements from one another and grappling with the eradication of liberal promises by turning to movement cultures as the source of a just future.

To speak of usable pasts is to adopt an active and pragmatic stance toward history. The usable past is an interpretive strategy that approaches history as a renewable resource in complex service of the present.[2] From painting street murals honoring movement ancestors, to sampling speeches or protest chants into music, to circulating readers like this one, activists routinely turn to the past to assert their movements' longevity, amplify their cultural resonance, and hone their strategies. In building links to past movements, radicals clarify their commitments and remind each other that other worlds are possible. This volume works in that spirit, bringing together 164 written documents, 20 images, and 32 short essays that reflect a wide mix of organizations, campaigns, tactics, and visions. Grouped into thematic sections that reflect multiple approaches to different sites of struggle and to struggle on different scales, the book's sources reflect the modes of thinking and organizing among left-wing US social movements from 1973 to 2001.

As the first reader to document radicalism writ large after the "long 1960s," this book moves against the received wisdom about the hegemony of conservatism between the decline of the war in Vietnam and the rise of war on terror. Dominant voices would have us believe that this period offers little in the way of a usable radical past. Certainly, the context of the last three decades of the twentieth century seems to be overdetermined by reaction: a decline in real wages and loss of union power; a rollback of gains by antiracist, feminist, and environmental movements; and unprecedented threats to the social and natural world as corporations and conservative politicians consolidated their power. Other discussions of this period focus almost exclusively on fragmentation and division. Some modern liberal critics maintain that radicals of the late 1960s and onward fractured the left by sacrificing a universal class- or nation-based political project on the altar of identity difference. Others argue that the political culture of the United States broke apart under the combined weight of right-wing resentment, a spectacle-driven media, and changing norms of race, gender, and sexuality, such that any victories were inseparable from losses. Though dominant narratives of recent history vary in their approaches, they share common ground in discounting the breadth and significance of radical movements.[3]

Reaction is only one part of the late twentieth-century story. Radicals in these decades mobilized in large numbers and took dynamic action at sites ranging from prisons to weapons facilities to the nation's capital. They worked creatively, developing new tactics and forging unexpected coalitions. Their histories give the lie to narratives that make activism invisible or that dismiss interventions against injustice and inequality. We approach the period from the position of grassroots radicalism, seeing these decades as a time both of social fracture and of movement coalescence. The country experienced not only breaks in consensus but also new kinds of political debate and exchange. Activists crafted new modes of activism to challenge forms of inequality and oppression enabled by the compromises of liberalism and the ravages of conservatism. We trace the remaking of radicalism that activists effected by forging interconnections among movements and by confronting the shifting political and economic order. The radical project remained the transformation of society, which activists maintained could only be accomplished by eradicating the root causes of inequality and injustice and by maximizing the conditions for healthy human solidarity, social expression, and interdependence with the nonhuman world. As conditions for the pursuit of liberation changed, radicals embraced new strategies, ideas, and networks—responses that won concessions, built power, and altered the terms of struggle. In this way, they defined the period.

The decades examined in this book saw the entrenchment of neoliberalism, a context in which activists had to struggle against the state but could not appeal to it in the ways they once had.[4] Thus, while activists still petitioned the government—often to maintain hard-fought protections like affirmative action or environmental safeguards—they did so to defend rather than advance a progressive mantle, and they did so with little faith in the promise of the US state. Under the auspices of neoliberalism, powerbrokers from both major parties dismantled social welfare and other commitments to public good in favor of the privatization of wealth and the restriction of democratic avenues for change.[5] From the 1970s forward, the US government and economics were shaped by a policy orthodoxy that distributed wealth upward at the expense of social programs and regulations while privatizing services and resources and undermining leftward challenges. Corporate power expanded while real wages stagnated, federal and state governments cut access to economic safeguards like welfare, civil rights and environmental protections were repealed, and the police became increasingly militarized, circumscribing people's ability to participate politically. More Americans were incarcerated than ever before, disenfranchising and actively removing millions of poor and working-class people, overwhelmingly people of color, from public life.[6] Simultaneously, neoliberalism demobilized the political language of race, gender, and sexuality, turning what had been a structural critique into superficial multiculturalism.[7]

After the 1960s, the ballot box, the legal system, and other means of pursuing liberal reform increasingly failed to win responses that would address structural inequality. They failed for many reasons. The legal system was too embedded in racial and gender domination to properly adjudicate disputes about racist sexism, a problem that led antiracist feminists to coin the term "intersectionality" as a way of articulating the nexus of multiple oppressions, particularly race, gender, and class. To be adequately addressed, new issues such as AIDS and nuclear waste required a boldness the major political parties lacked, and they could not be resolved at the ballot box either. In different but related ways, Indigenous sovereignty claims exceeded what traditional definitions of rights and citizenship could accommodate. The expansion of multinational business and free trade placed corporate decision makers at ever-increasing remove from worker or consumer influence, while increasing their authority over people's lives. The state hardly disappeared—in areas related to policing, incarceration, and militarization, it grew dramatically. But political elites of both major parties mobilized state power with a growing disregard for popular consent.[8]

As old roads to making change were closed down, change makers had to find or create other avenues. They had to pursue new strategies, build new coalitions, develop new tactics, rearticulate their goals, and establish new institutions to stay relevant in a changing world. Although the prospects for progressive change were bleak, they did not disappear. The disappointments of radical activism were themselves clarifying. The closing of traditional portals for achieving change sharpened a critique of how limited these outlets had *always* been. Radicals of the 1970s, 1980s, and 1990s often found themselves working to preserve vestiges of the liberal order even as they critiqued them. For example, the welfare rights movement opposed New Right cuts to social programs while objecting to the surveillance and miserly sums that had always structured benefits. Antiracists resisted efforts to cut affirmative action programs while noting that such programs did little to address the underlying problems of housing segregation, the racist distribution of school funding, or the immigrant poverty that US imperialism exacerbated. Feminists fought to preserve the right to abortion while also trying to expand access to it and while working against sterilization, coercive birth control, and other practices aimed at curtailing the reproduction of women of color. AIDS activists took care of each other in the face of deep neglect while demanding that the government respond to the crisis through concerted education, research, and treatment; viewing AIDS as a political rather than moral crisis, radicals advocated shifting military spending to health care, providing low-income housing to people with AIDS, and ending the criminalization of drug use and sex work.[9]

Working-class people of color, women, LGBTQ people, immigrants, and people with disabilities bore the brunt of the political and economic shifts of the era, and they faced the stiffest barriers to political power—including through previously influential outlets, such as unions. In one of the bitterest pills of the period, the hard-fought efforts to break Jim Crow's stranglehold on electoral power were undermined by the fact that most Black mayors found themselves managing if not pursuing the same neoliberal agendas as those of their white counterparts, cutting city services while enabling privatized development as federal resources dissipated.[10]

Complex realities required new and creative solutions. One key development came through the growth of intersectional feminism—that is, the effort to analyze the interdependent operation of racism, sexism, capitalism, and heterosexism, systems often summarized as race, gender, class, and sexuality. Reflecting the importance of this development, we have situated a foundational text of intersectional feminism—the Boston-based Combahee River Collective's call for an "integrated analysis and practice based upon the fact that the major systems of oppression are interlocking" (1977)—as the first source in this book, numbered 1.A.1. (1.A.1. indicates, as shown in the table of contents, part 1, section A, document 1. In this introduction, we use this numbering to reference where specific documents can be found in the book. We cite "snapshot" essays, or brief analyses by contemporary writers, by the author's last name and note their location in the book).[11]

Many other documents in the volume follow Combahee in applying the kind of "integrated analysis" by which the Black socialist feminists of the Combahee River Collective defined themselves. For example, the women signing the public statement "African American Women in Defense of Ourselves" (1.B.9.) speak from their position as Black women to challenge the appointment of conservative jurist and accused sexual harasser Clarence Thomas, a Black man, to the Supreme Court. Prison abolitionists from Critical Resistance and INCITE! Women of Color against Violence (1.A.15.) draw on intersectional analysis to highlight the need for nonprison solutions to gender violence. Activists for Inez Garcia, a Latina woman in California who was prosecuted for defending herself from rape, coined the term "racist sexism" to identify the nexus of oppressions facing women of color (1.A.4a. and 1.A.4b.), and Native activist Yvonne Swan describes the denial of her right to self-defense as part of an "undeclared war" against Native people (1.A.5.). In the late 1990s, the southern-based network SisterSong formulated the concept of reproductive justice as a way to integrate reproductive health with racial, economic, and environmental politics (Ross snapshot in part 1, section A). Among other contributions, intersectional feminism has offered a tool with which to confront the interplay between state marginalization, governmental abandonment of collective well-being, and the way social justice demands have been reduced to shallow conceptions of diversity.

As they remade radicalism, activists developed a complex argument about the US state. They recognized that the liberal welfare state was not bold enough to provide social, environmental, and economic justice. It was unable to support such radical aims both because it was being dismantled by neoliberalism and because it was a militaristic carceral state to begin with. The dismantling of the liberal welfare state opened the door to threats that demanded new coalitions and strategies of resistance. Radicalism rarely wins its full slate, and yet at their most productive, activists in this period experimented and collaborated to expand their visions even further. They questioned past assumptions, crafting what might be called (following New Left theorist Stuart Hall's insights into postwar Marxism) a radicalism without guarantees.[12]

Critiques of the US state propelled some radicals toward socialism, others toward anarchism (e.g., 4.B.3., 4.C.11.), and still others toward non-Western agendas of decolonial sovereignty (e.g., 3.A.4., 4.C.10). But perhaps most significantly, critiques of the state—and the overall context of attacks on liberalism, the rise of neoliberalism, and the deepening of racist and heteropatriarchal retrenchment—drew radicals together across disparate approaches. By the end of the Cold War, radicals around the world were reassessing the ideology of the left and responding to the decline of, as well as problems within, existing communist countries. Throughout the 1990s, critiques of state nationalisms and the growing power of corporations prompted expanded visions of solidarity, spurred on by the influence of the Zapatista rebels in southern Mexico and the rapid growth of the global justice movement.[13] Radicals came to synthesize multiple politics—anarchist, feminist, queer, antiracist, anti-imperialist, social-ist, environmental, abolitionist, Indigenous—into a shared, if at times incoher-ent, repertoire. *Remaking Radicalism* collects that repertoire together, making it the basis of a usable past.

The Neoliberal Order: Scarcity and Violence

All radicalism must be understood in the context of the barriers and forms of inequality it faces in a given period. The political-economic regime of the late twentieth century, often referred to as neoliberalism, was marked by scarcity and violence. The start of this period saw the withdrawal of US troops from Vietnam and the acceleration of economic restructuring signaled by deindus-trialization and recession. The beginning of the twenty-first century brought the September 11 attacks on the World Trade Center and Pentagon, which pro-duced a response from the United States that institutionalized the ongoing war on terror. *Remaking Radicalism* treats the boundaries of 1973 and 2001 as mo-ments of transition, clearest in retrospective, rather than a starkly defined be-ginning and end. These temporal markers situate the political-economic con-text that radicals of the era responded to and address and that the documents in this book likewise focus on.

The twentieth century concluded in chaos. The 1970s opened with a strong, militant rank-and-file labor movement leading powerful strikes. But global trends in trade and finance converged with deindustrialization and speedup practices, an alignment that had the effect of placing a growing number of American workers at risk.[14] Many began to lose their jobs, access to public ser-vices, and union power. During the mid-1970s, the country lost its war in Viet-nam, its president to resignation in the wake of massive corruption, and its here-tofore unquestioned access to natural resources, as the Arab nations of OPEC refused to export oil or gasoline products to the United States or other countries that backed Israel in the Yom Kippur War. As people searched for directions for-ward, conservative groups stoked racism, antifeminism, and homophobia.

Ronald Reagan's election in 1980 only intensified these trends. The Rea-gan presidency fused right-wing reaction to faith in US hegemony and the free market while empowering the Christian right. Reagan ushered in major cuts to taxes, antipoverty programs, and social services, and deregulated industry, at-tacked organized labor, and massively increased military and criminal justice spending. He aligned with antifeminist and homophobic forces, rolled back civil rights enforcement, backed apartheid South Africa, and both openly and covertly aided repressive regimes in Central America. His administration ex-panded the federal government's capacity to make war, but largely refused to do anything about the growing numbers of gay and bisexual men, IV drug users, African Americans, women, and poor people who were becoming ill and dying in the AIDS epidemic.[15] President George H. W. Bush called for a "kinder, gen-tler nation," while a decade later his son, George W. Bush, described his policies as "compassionate conservatism." Yet both administrations extended Reagan's policies of war making, racist antifeminism, hostility to unions and immigration, and an unchecked global pursuit of resource extraction and corporate profit.

Bill Clinton's 1992 election ended twelve years of Republican rule, but the "get tough" politics of austerity continued to govern the lives of marginalized Americans. Clinton's presidency further entrenched a neoliberal consensus that crossed party lines. This became especially apparent in policies enacted from 1994 through 1996, including the implementation of the North American Free Trade Agreement (NAFTA), a crime bill deepening systems of policing and mass incarceration, and the eradication of already minimal antipoverty supports through "welfare reform." The mid-1990s solidified many of the right's gains even as political and popular culture became superficially more open to people of color and LGBTQ people.[16] Amid this, many activists renewed their efforts to situate queer and feminist organizing in frameworks of anticapitalism and intersectional critique (e.g., DeFilippis snapshot in part 1, section A). Other radicalism that reflected these trends included organizing against censorship, against the policing of sex, and for the rights of sex workers (1.A.14., 1.B.5., 1.B.12.).

The politics of scarcity conjoined with targeted attacks on radicals, both from the government and from right-wing vigilantes. Throughout the country, states responded to prison rebellions by killing dissident prisoners or placing them in even more isolating conditions; at the same time, many journalists covering prison conditions lost either access or interest (or both). Such targeted repression was magnified by a bevy of expansions to criminal codes and sentencing policies that, together with emboldened police forces cracking down on poor communities of color in increasingly stratified urban areas, sent more people to prison and kept them there longer. Bipartisan crime bills in 1986 and 1994 rendered "law and order" the lingua franca of both parties, as successive waves of "get tough" and "zero tolerance" policies swept the country on everything from political activism and drug consumption to immigration and school discipline infractions.

This approach reached a particularly gruesome nadir on May 13, 1985, when the Philadelphia police department, under direction of the city's first Black mayor, dropped two military-grade bombs on a house occupied by the heterodox Black liberation organization MOVE and opted to "let the fire burn." Eleven MOVE members—six adults and five children—died in the attack, and more than sixty neighborhood homes were destroyed (ucker snapshot in part 4, section A).[17]

The MOVE bombing was the most severe example of a broader reactionary campaign. Several radicals were assassinated or attacked in state and corporate violence that melded the local and global. In 1974, Oklahoma union activist Karen Silkwood died in a mysterious car crash after working to expose dangerous and unsafe practices within the nuclear power industry; the energy company she worked for was later found guilty of contributing to her death. In 1990, Judi Bari, a prominent member of Earth First! who had been developing impressive coalitions between environmentalists and timber workers in an effort to stop clearcutting (4.A.12.), was paralyzed after a bomb exploded under the driver's seat of her car in Oakland; FBI officials strangely arrived on the scene in minutes to arrest Bari, though she was never prosecuted.

This political violence reflected the brutal configurations of US foreign policy. In two especially shocking incidents, right-wing authoritarian regimes supported by the US killed dissidents who were living in the United States. In 1976, Chilean and Cuban anticommunist militants planted a car bomb that killed Chilean dissident Orlando Letelier and US-born activist Ronni Moffit in Washington, DC. In 1981, the Marcos regime in the Philippines ordered the assassination of two Filipino American radicals in Seattle who had been organizing Filipino cannery workers to democratize their union and to oppose the Marcos dictatorship. And during an antimilitarism protest in 1987, Vietnam veteran and peace activist S. Brian Wilson was run over by a train carrying weapons destined for anticommunist paramilitaries in Central America. Wilson survived but suffered a skull fracture and lost both legs.

Finally, political violence demonstrated the growing significance of the carceral state. Working with police protection, members of the Klan and American Nazi Party murdered five Communist Workers Party members in North Carolina in November of 1979 (1.B.3.). That same year, Puerto Rican Socialist Party leader Angel Cristobal Rodriguez was found dead in a Florida prison, where he was serving six months for protesting US militarism in Vieques; his supporters allege he was murdered by guards. As Cristobal Rodriguez's death showed, attacks on militants in state custody continued well past the early 1970s, when the deaths of George Jackson, of participants in the Attica rebellion (2.B.1.), and of members of the Young Lords Party and Black Liberation Army—among others—dominated the headlines. The murders of incarcerated activists were the most extreme examples through which the criminal justice system bludgeoned dissent.

No less significantly, many of those who might otherwise have joined radical movements in working-class communities of color were among the thousands killed and millions incarcerated by increasingly armed and authorized police forces and prison guards (Ervin and Akinwole-Bandele and Kang snapshots in part 2, section A).[18] Several shocking acts of violence illuminated the increasingly punitive character of US public culture and the disparate application of punishment. Police faced no jail time, and often no charges, in numerous wrongful deaths or violent altercations. One of the few times they were charged came after four officers were videotaped in the beating of a Black motorist named Rodney King. The officers' acquittal sparked a massive uprising that highlighted persistent inequalities in Los Angeles (2.C.7.). The case stood in stark contrast to responses to the brutal rape of a white investment banker in New York's Central Park in the spring of 1989. Racist demagoguery saturated the case, promoted by voices including real estate developer Donald Trump. Prosecutors sent five Black and Latino teenagers to prison despite no evidence of their involvement in the crime; DNA evidence would later clear them but not until after their release.

Meanwhile, the two white men who admitted to beating Vincent Chin, a Chinese American man, to death in Detroit in 1982, and who tried to justify the murder by referring to their rage over the success of Japanese car manufacturers, were given probation and a $3,000 fine. Other targeted killings of people from minoritized groups—including Brandon Teena, a transgender man in Nebraska, with his friends Lisa Lambert and Philip Devine, a disabled Black man (1993), Matthew Shepard, a gay white man in Wyoming (1998), and James Byrd, a Black man in Texas (1998)—generated a rash of "hate crime" laws that allowed prosecutors to seek lengthier prison sentences in the name of opposing bigotry.[19]

Many radicals insisted that the criminal justice system could never solve the problems of social violence (1.A.7., 4.C.12.). For these critics, who would ultimately populate a self-professed movement for prison abolition, prison itself was a problem—a government mechanism to quash dissent and enforce marginalization. "We need to rid ourselves of prisons," the feminist journal *off our backs* declared in a prescient 1971 editorial (2.B.2.). "They are a danger to society not only because they are schools for 'crime' (70 percent of all 'crimes' are committed by ex-convicts) but because they try to erase from our consciousness people who could possibly bring about exciting changes in our social order."

This dialectic of scarcity and violence continued after US elites claimed success with the end of the Cold War, which wound down between the 1989 collapse of the Berlin Wall and the 1991 dissolution of the Soviet Union. Rather than, as some had hoped, turning to the task of creating a robust peacetime economy, the US adjusted its military targets toward Muslim-majority countries, declaring war on Iraq in 1991, then following that with twelve years of sanctions against Iraq that ended only after the second Gulf War in 2003. The discourse of US foreign policy slipped from an anticommunist focus to an anti-Islamic one. This shift was not wholly new, however, as it supported the long-standing role of the United States in the Middle East. The reorientation to antiterrorism recalibrated US imperialism and centered its racist long war on Muslim-majority countries in North Africa and South Asia.[20]

Amid this post–Cold War consolidation, the controversial presidential election in 2000 saw more than a million Floridians disenfranchised, as the Supreme Court—under the leadership of William Rehnquist, who was appointed to the court by Richard Nixon in 1971 and made chief justice by Ronald Reagan in 1986—halted a recount in that state and effectively appointed George W. Bush president. Mobilizing an agenda of Christian conservatism and white identity politics—pursued through the privatization of land, education, and public goods, restrictive assaults on abortion access and sexual freedom, and empire building—the George W. Bush administration culminated three decades of neoliberalism with a virulent neoconservative bluster. The attacks of 9/11 together with the brutal and blundered war on terror marked a new phase of US power, in the world and within its own borders.[21]

While responding to particular circumstances, each generation of radicalism points to as yet unknown futures, to worlds of what could be.[22] In facing the problems of the late twentieth century, radicals created new ways of organizing that exceeded the limitations of their historical context. The documents gathered in this book offer only some of the many historical examples of activism across the period, and demonstrate how radicals forged alternatives to the status quo and to new crises. In the last decades of the twentieth century, radicals saw a need to reimagine solidarity. They crafted a hybrid language of class, identity, land, democracy, coexistence, freedom, and sustainability. "It doesn't matter what they throw at us because *we* make the difference," Indigenous activist John Trudell told thousands of people assembled at the Black Hills International Survival Gathering in 1980 (4.B.1.). "*We* make the decision. *We* are power." Such affirmations of strength and vision carried radical social movements, uneasily but determinedly, through the dark days of neoliberalism. The documents activists left behind offer beacons, helping to bring to light struggles that might otherwise be forgotten.

Debates, Interventions, and New Formations

The political landscape shifted significantly from 1973 to 2001, but its transformations were not always evident at the time—in part because scarcity and violence ran alongside gains. What the democratic socialist scholar Michael Harrington said of the 1970s is likely true of the period overall: it was an era in which the country was moving "vigorously left, right, and center, all at once." Activists challenged or removed some of the institutional barriers and cultural norms that oppressed people of color as well as women, lesbians, and gay men of all racial and ethnic backgrounds. Yet more liberal social relationships did not ensure political democracy, contain state violence, or promote equality. In some ways, as we have seen, the country grew less democratic and more unequal.[23] It was not at all obvious how to win radical change in the political landscape of the late twentieth century. Activists had to search for and recruit like-minded people for their efforts, and they had to work to connect their efforts to a larger project of social transformation.

Radicals in this period debated many issues of tactics, strategy, and approach without resolution. Some found a way forward in a union, some in an underground cell, others in a mass march; some found it through cultural work, some through direct action, others through community organizing. Many moved between multiple formations or approaches at various points of their lives.

Expressions of radicalism change over both space and time. Organizing for immigrant rights, for environmental justice, or against the latest US war invariably look different in South Dakota (such as in the land and resource struggles documented in 4.C.1., 4.A.6., and 4.A.9.) than in South Central Los Angeles (where the problem of too much policing and too little public transit looms large, as documented in 2.A.10. and 2.C.8.). Activists make different demands depending on whether they are organizing homeless people (2.C.5., 2.C.10.), resisting gentrification (2.C.1., 2.C.2., 2.C.3. and Quizar and Rodriguez-Muñiz snapshots in part 2, section C), protecting Black and white farmers from both government malfeasance and right-wing militias (4.C.4., 4.C.5.), preserving public education (2.C.9. and Subways snapshot in part 2, section C), protecting communities of color from toxic dumping and environmentally racist zoning practices (4.A.7., 4.A.8., 4.A.9.), or safeguarding Indigenous land from tourism and extractive industry (4.C.3., 4.C.7, 4.C.8.). They likewise make different demands across the decades, as evident in welfare rights organizing in the 1970s versus the 1990s (compare 1.C.1. to 1.C.10 and 1.C.11, and see Chappell snapshot in part 1, section C). Efforts to stop prison construction likewise shifted and were varied (compare 2.B.5. and 2.B.7a. and 2.B.7b. to 2.B.10., and see Pelot-Hobbs and Gilmore snapshots in part 2, section B).[24]

Yet there are continuities in radicalism as well, and the basic questions are often the same. What issues are closest to home or motivate action? How can activists mobilize large numbers of people and which alternatives should they direct people toward? How do activists develop critical consciousness, find a political community, and build a larger movement? Answers differ by geography, community relationships, and local infrastructures for activism, yet common principles link people across movement sites.

We adopted a reading practice for this anthology that emphasizes process and aspiration—a framework through which major changes and features of activism over time can be traced. This tool guided our process in compiling the book: we used it as an invitation to look for types of activism that we did not already know about, to explore regions we had not previously researched, and to identify points of connection or divergence. Without imposing a uniformity that never existed, we track the rise, convergence, or dissipation of styles and approaches. As editors, we have cultivated key examples of how radicals approached political organization and social change in this time period.

We have organized the book in a way that demonstrates how radicals organized at different levels of politics, ranging from the body and home to urban and rural contexts and international and global levels. This way of organizing documents helps to show how activists understood their contexts and how they contested the political and economic relationships that brought those contexts into being. The book's organization enables the reader to compare organizing in locations that are conceptually similar but geographically distant. We hope, too, that it opens up questions not only about what has been but what might be—that it allows readers to use these pasts to imagine more just ways of organizing the world.

Remaking Radicalism maps thematic as well as physical geographies. Thinking through geography helps us to consider how designations we might take for granted, such as those of nations and citizenship, can be remade or unmade. It also can help us consider in what types of spaces movements take place. Some injustices are visited on the body, others within the family or extended kinship. Local, national, and global relationships are mutually embedded. The meanings of belonging and self-determination differ between cities and rural landscapes. Certain forms of violence and injustice displace people while others confine them. Likewise, people learn about radical politics and organizing techniques through many sources: fellow students, coworkers, neighbors, cellmates, flyers, community newspapers, neighborhood associations, protests, and cultural events. The relationships through which people move into activism are situated in racial, ethnic, religious, sexual, and economic communities. And these settings inflect the organizational forms that activism takes, from small collectives to large, structured unions.

We have sought to reflect the range of activist locations to the best of our ability. Some in the punk scene, for example, found radical politics by seeing members of the John Brown Anti-Klan Committee (1.B.2.) or Anti-Racist Action (1.B.8.) confront white supremacists at a music show or on the street. Many immigrant workers, isolated from formal unions by repressive labor laws, joined a broader movement through popular education workshops, hunger strikes, or solidarity marches (see, for example, 1.B.11., 3.B.11., Zavella snapshot in part 1, section C, and Kono snapshot in part 3, section B).

Several critical issues repeatedly come up across this time period: questions of organization, political process, and direct action. Radicals raised these questions both directly and implicitly as they sought to determine the best practices for social change. We leave it to readers to evaluate their answers. But we underscore that while versions of these questions have long been debated in US radicalisms, their inflection from 1973 to 2001 revealed the shrinking availability and relevance of liberal reform amid expanded corporate power and a determined conservatism across the two major political parties.

Questions of *organization* asked, above all, what vehicles were best suited to advance transformative social change. Many sought to control aspects of the state—to make government preserve or prohibit certain actions—yet disagreed over whether the government could confront injustices that were foundational to the US nation. At a more specific level, many debated whether the Democratic Party was a vehicle to be reformed for progressive change or an obstacle to achieving it. As a result of such debates, activists experimented with a host of organizing forms, including political parties, networks, collectives, federations, campaigns, affinity groups, coalitions, counterinstitutions such as co-ops, and more.

The different forms of organizing reflected differences of ideology, strategy, and power. Some national coalitions, such as the Rainbow Coalition, mobilized around presidential elections, yet others, such as Association of Community Organizations for Reform Now (2.C.4.), New Jewish Agenda (3.C.4.), the Black Student Leadership Network (Franklin snapshot in part 4, section B), or the Black Radical Congress (4.B.10.), bent their energy toward strategies and platforms of grassroots change. Local organizations like the Center for Third World Organizing (4.B.2.) or UPROSE (Sze and Yeampierre snapshot in part 4, section A) emphasized issue-based campaigns. Behind these debates, too, lay the broader changes of neoliberalism. Before 1970, many activists could advance social justice through government jobs in programs created through the New Deal or the War on Poverty. As those programs constricted or disappeared, nonprofit organizations became the primary place outside of unions to do paid social justice work. Yet many nonprofits focused more on providing services than community organizing or movement building. Further, regardless of their tactics, nonprofits risked prioritizing funder interests over community needs.

The reemergence of social justice unionism in the 1990s (as in 1.C.12. and 3.B.4.) offered some promise for overcoming these limitations, at least in several major cities.[25] But the dependence of unions on the Democratic Party and of nonprofits on foundations heightened radicals' desire for alternatives.[26] Many progressives, Marxists, and socialists debated whether to push the Democratic Party to the left or to build a third-party alternative. Pursuing the latter option gave rise to a number of Marxist and radical nationalist party formations; in the 1990s it generated the Green Party, Labor Party (4.B.9.), and New Party. Efforts to elect Black and other people of color fueled Jesse Jackson's Rainbow Coalition and his two presidential runs, which were replicated at the local level in several cities, such as Harold Washington's successful campaign for mayor of Chicago that upended the city's traditional political machine.

Yet critiques of state power, of flaws in socialist and national liberation projects, and of neoliberal and imperialist bipartisan consensus prompted many to turn away from investing in any future state. Radicals of many stripes—Marxist, socialist, revolutionary nationalist, anti-imperialist, anarchist, queer, feminist, or otherwise—prioritized community organizing, cultural work, or direct action protests over the electoral realm. Large numbers of radicals focused their energy on strategies of affinity group organizing and providing mutual aid (see, for example, 2.A.12., 4.A.1a–d., 4.A.5., 4.B.8. and Wood snapshot in part 4, section B).[27]

As radicals experimented with different organizational forms, they took up questions of how to organize in ways that did not reproduce the errors of the past. This led many to emphasize *accountability and political process*. With these concerns, activists sought to attend to questions of democracy and equity in how they worked together. Feminists and anarchists honed models of what Bruce Kokopeli and George Lakey describe as shared leadership (4.A.4.) and consensus decision making and brought these tools to settings ranging from mass mobilizations to tiny collectives (4.A.3.). Yet what tools of process worked best depended on context, as organizations sought to balance the greatest level of participation with rapid responses to each moment's urgency. Increasingly, many argued that transformative change demanded multiracial, mixed-gender, cross-class organizations guided by the emancipatory leadership and membership of working-class women of color, immigrants, and others who were commonly marginalized. They struggled with how to build such organizations while also drawing more privileged people into activism against oppression that centered the most affected.

These questions held particular weight in transnational activism, including efforts to oppose US military intervention and advance global economic justice. The vast majority of US activists, even in working-class and poor communities, had far greater access to money and media than most people in the global South. Yet most US activists lacked deep knowledge of sites or struggles outside the United States, and some suffered from a tendency to romanticize or exoticize non-Western leadership. Immigrants and refugees brought rich expertise into US-based organizing (e.g., 3.A.1., 3.B.5., 3.B.11., 3.C.1., 3.C.2.). Yet many born in the United States were unaware of such legacies. All these dynamics raised serious obstacles, and activists struggled to confront them, as for example in the Central American solidarity movement (3.A.7. through 3.A.14.), immigrant labor organizing (1.B.11., 3.B.12.), activism against US war in the Middle East (3.C.7a–b. through 3.C.12.), and movements pursuing the sovereignty that had been usurped by US settler colonialism (see especially part 4, section C, including Molina snapshot). Transnational organizing demanded confronting the legacies of empire within movements themselves. Yet it also opened up new means to build power—as by identifying diasporic sources for labor militancy, linking students of color and white students in campus anti-apartheid activism, or naming antiracism and queer liberation as central principles of global justice (see especially 3.A.9., 3.A.10., 3.C.8., and Cable snapshot in part 3, section C).[28]

As the traditional mechanisms of liberal reforms yielded fewer avenues for change, activists in this period took up diverse modes of *direct action*. Across the period covered in this book, the tactic of large-scale disruptive protest, particularly through mass convenings and efforts to interrupt the work of government and corporations, came into its own. Direct action secured especially high levels of participation in the antinuclear (part 4, section A), Central American solidarity (part 4, section A), anti-apartheid (part 3, section B), AIDS (1.A.9. through 1.A.12, 1.C.9., 2.B.10.), and global justice movements (part 3, section B). The majority of this direct action entailed nonviolent civil disobedience, as demonstrated by documents from the Clamshell Alliance and feminist campaigns against nuclear weapons (3.A.6., 4.A.1a.–d., 4.A.2a–b, 4.A.3) as well as efforts to secure abortion access (1.B.6., 1.B.7.). In the "Battle of Seattle," fifty thousand people from different social justice movements shut down the meeting of the World Trade Organization (3.B.8a–b.).

Major demonstrations increasingly featured direct action manuals outlining everything from which streets to block to legal, medical, and media advice for civil disobedience actions (4.A.1a–d.). Activists increasingly utilized spectacle, in the form of puppets, parody, and other creative disruptions. They made growing use of video to document actions and to seek a measure of safety (Cheng snapshot in part 1, section A). They also moved beyond the scripted pageantry of traditional marches and rallies and added long-term occupations of space to their tactics through encampments outside weapons manufacturers, nuclear power plants, campuses, federal agencies, and global meetings (Dixon snapshot in part 3, section B, Fulkerson snapshot in part 4, section A, Hall snapshot in part 3, section B, Wood snapshot in part 4, section B).[29]

Documents throughout *Remaking Radicalism* reflect struggles over means versus ends in direct action organizing. These questions were not new to the period, but they took on particular urgency as radicals contended with geopolitical shifts and nuclear or environmental annihilation. Some questions related to the tensions between movement culture and popular impact. While street theater drew media attention and buoyed activist energy, it was not always clear when it built political power. Other questions revolved around what kinds of actions were most strategically useful and morally defensible. Was nonviolence always necessary, or did it unethically preserve the state's monopoly on violence? Did property destruction count as violence, and was it worth the cost in potential harm or incarceration? Was violence a dead-end strategy that only alienated the left from popular support? What were the relationships and differences between self-determination, self-defense, and armed struggle?

Over the 1973 through 2001 period, some radicals continued deploying underground tactics against police and prison brutality (2.A.6., 2.B.4.), imperial aggression (3.A.2.), and the growing threat of ecological collapse (4.A.14., 4.A.15.). Violent action particularly continued in the 1970s and 1980s, typically through bombings of government or corporate buildings that were carried out after hours to avoid injuries while still drawing attention to specific issues. Organizers typically announced these actions with public messages that articulated their analyses of state and structural violence, targeting agencies ranging from the Department of Health, Education, and Welfare (1.C.4.) to the War College (3.A.7.). From policing to militarism, racist sterilization abuse to environmental destruction, seemingly every major issue generated an armed response. American guerrillas drew inspiration from armed struggle in socialist and national liberation movements worldwide. Some armed groups in the United States financed themselves through risky and at times fatal bank robberies; at least one, the Black Liberation Army, killed several police officers in targeted attacks in the 1970s. As many of the documents in sections A and B of part 2 demonstrate, armed struggle was linked to mass incarceration. Some radicals viewed the violence of incarceration as license for their own use of force. More generally, armed tactics resulted in lengthy or life sentences for many participants, often in newly designed isolation units (2.B.9., 2.B.10.).

The use of armed struggle on the left declined in the United States by the late 1980s. By the time of the Oklahoma City bombing and the September 11 attacks, nonstate political violence had become largely the province of right-wing militants, who adopted far more lethal forms of violence designed to cause maximal harm. By the 1990s, perhaps the only left-wing clandestine groups operating in the United States were the Animal Liberation Front and Earth Liberation Front (4.A.14., 4.A.15.), both of which caused millions of dollars in damage through sabotage and vandalism without causing human injury.[30]

Activists disagreed—often quite sharply—over many strategies and tactics. Yet even with these differences, radicals of this period shared a goal of drawing connections across issues, geographies, and communities without displacing the insights born of differing experiences and identities. This orientation, both strategic and aspirational, produced linkages between struggles as seemingly disparate as Indigenous sovereignty and prison abolition, reproductive justice and immigrant rights, queer liberation and movements supporting freedom in Central America, South Africa, and Palestine. As disarmament activist Joseph Gerson put it in 1986—responding, in part, to the peace movement's relative silence on Israel's invasion of Lebanon—"The lesson is being learned that focusing individual or organizational efforts on only the nuclear arms race or on only one manifestation of intervention often fragments and weakens the struggle for peace, justice, and survival" (3.C.5.). Forging solidarity through grassroots action generated movement power and radical possibility.

Organization of the Anthology

Remaking Radicalism is aimed at everyone interested in the recent history of radicalism and the radical history of the recent past. We have designed the book with the hope that it will be used in classrooms, study groups, and other sites where people study social movements and the issues that surround them. While treating the 1973 to 2001 period as a distinct era, we include a few documents from as early as 1970 and as late as 2003, using these to illustrate transitions that define the beginning and end of the book. The earliest sources help to illustrate shifts that accelerated after 1973; the last ones reveal activist responses to the context of the September 11 attacks and the start of the Iraq War (part 3, section C, especially 3.C.9. through 3.C.12. and Makhijani snapshot).

The book contains four parts (1–4), each divided into three sections (A, B, and C). These parts and sections are organized to draw attention to distinct spaces and levels of struggle. While each part highlights particular themes, our approach rejects rigid boundaries of identity and ideology. For example, LGBT/queer, Black, and Latinx radicalisms appear across all chapters, as do anarchist, socialist, and other approaches.

Part 1, "Bodies and Lives," examines struggles over bodily autonomy, reproductive labor, and the context of rising conservatism. Section A of part 1, "Feminist and Queer Flashpoints," documents the growth of intersectional feminisms and the expanding boundaries of gender and sexual politics. Issues illustrating these shifts include reproductive justice, sexual violence and the carceral state, HIV/AIDS, queer of color organizing, sex work, and trans activism. Section B, "Fighting the Right," shows how activists defended hard-won gains against conservative mobilization. Struggles represented include affirmative action, reproductive freedom, censorship, and alliances against racist, homophobic, and sexist attacks. Finally, section C, "Labors of Survival," addresses labor and social welfare, particularly as linked with health and disability, women and queer workers, and welfare rights.

Part 2, "Walls and Gates," focuses on activism challenging the punitive state, especially against political repression (section A, "Resisting Repression), mass incarceration (section B, "Undermining the Prison State"), and the privatization of urban space (section C, "Fight for the City"). In more practical terms, this section centers on activism confronting prisons, policing, and state containment of radical movements. It situates these forms of radicalism alongside organizing to win control of urban space and local economies, as the multiracial urban working class moved from activism that challenged urban renewal to activism that opposed gentrification. In the 1970s capital fled the city, deepening urban crises. By the 1990s it returned to gentrify the city, making room for wealthy elites at the expense of working-class residents.[31]

Antiwar, international solidarity, and global justice movements are featured in part 3, "Borders and Maps." The organization of part 3 reflects how major changes in world politics—from the Cold War to globalization to the war on terror—shifted radical frameworks. If previously Cuba, China, and the Soviet Union had stood as guiding models, now international solidarity became oriented around Chile, Nicaragua, South Africa, and Palestine. These sites reflected opposition to US intervention, but also offered more flexible modes of socialism and articulated resistance against occupation and white supremacy. Immigrant radicals played critical roles in forging labor, anticapitalist, and antiwar networks. US-born radicals, too, traversed borders and rewrote the maps of social change. A range of struggles are represented in part 3 but with varying emphasis. Section A, "Anti-Imperialism beyond Vietnam," focuses especially on Central American solidarity. Section B, "From Anti-Imperialism to Global Justice," illustrates anti-apartheid, immigrant, and global justice organizing. And section C, "Not in Our Name," documents opposition to successive US interventions in the Middle East.

The book closes with documents illustrating how radicals imagined the future. Part 4, "Utopias and Dystopias," devotes concentrated attention to Indigenous politics and environmental radicalism. It also features many sources on praxis, including how to organize direct action (section A, "Stopping the End of the World") and how to relate to electoral politics and build mass politics in a neoliberal context (section B, "Left Visions in Transition"). Through this range, part 4 illustrates how widely definitions of radicalism have varied, particularly since the end of the Cold War. Some documents reflect traditional Western and Marxist boundaries and others challenge those understandings. Some sources equate anti-imperialism with solidarity with national liberation, while those in section C, "Land, Decolonization, Interdependence," look at forms of sovereignty and social organization beyond nation-states.

Remaking Radicalism provides a representative sample of the many approaches to fundamental social change that defined the turn of the new millennium. We invite readers to engage the anthology as befits their own questions, analyses, needs, and uses of the past.

Editorial Considerations

Due to space considerations, many of the documents in the book are excerpted rather than reproduced in full. Ellipses note where we have cut portions of the original text, whereas the same in brackets—[. . .]—denotes ellipses that appear in the original. We have prefaced each document with brief contextual notes and corrected minor spelling or grammatical mistakes but left intact purposefully alternative spellings or capitalizations (such as "Amerika"). We retained emphasis from the originals but replaced bolded fonts, larger fonts, or other formats with italics for the sake of uniformity and space. The book also includes snapshot essays addressing important events, organizations, tactics, or net-works. Written by a wide range of contemporary scholars and activists and ar-ranged across the book, these snapshot essays offer a concise but focused look at special topics, often filling in gaps or narratives that cannot be explained by the documents themselves. Finally, we also include a handful of posters and graph-ics generated by and for activist campaigns. The book's bibliography provides a selected list of titles that directly informed our sense of the time period and that may be useful for further research.

We have prioritized documents for their accessibility—that is, documents that do not assume too much prior knowledge, that use minimal jargon, and that are not subsumed in debates that would be opaque to most contemporary readers. We have emphasized sources that demonstrate forms of action or that lay out political agendas rather than only explaining the forms of oppression they confront. We have emphasized breadth over depth, seeking to showcase a wide range of issues rather than drilling down into the nitty gritty of particular campaigns. With some exceptions, our focus on grassroots action has led us to deprioritize electoral politics, court rulings, and large nonprofits. Above all, we have sought to represent a wide mix of racial and ethnic communities, gender and sexual identities, geographic locations and political goals, and tactical ap-proaches and strategic orientations. Nonetheless, by virtue of population den-sity and our own research capacities, the book favors coastal hubs and existing archival sources and relies on sources originally published in English.

The format of a printed book has meant that we had to leave a lot out—in-cluding music, performance, graffiti, and most visual art. We feel these exclu-sions acutely; for us personally, as well as so many others, music and art were critical entry points into radical activism. However, we have found that written sources offer tremendous insight into the day-to-day work of movement build-ing, and we look forward to ways that other scholars and activists might place the book in conversation with histories of hip-hop, punk, poster art, or political theater, to name a few examples.[32] Similarly, because we prioritized grassroots practice, the collection largely omits works by major scholarly theorists of the time period. The bibliography cites some key scholarship.

Copyright law and reproduction costs posed certain limitations on the book. The copyright holder of some artifacts of radicalism is a corporate en-tity rather than the author or creator of the source; in some cases, such rights holders charge exorbitant reproduction fees. We lacked external funding for the book, and there were several items we were unable to include due to costs.

The internet makes a book such as this both less and more complicated: it has made some documents easier to find and enabled us to find many sources through email contacts with colleagues and comrades. But it has often made it difficult to correctly date sources or locate their origin, particularly in the con-text of collective and anonymous authorship. Activists in the 1990s left many sources online, while some of those in the 1970s and 1980s still barely register in the digital world. Observing these constraints, we have sought to mostly feature sources that are not available online. Exceptions primarily reflect documents' scale of impact or significance. Our website, *www.remakingradicalism.org*, offers links to other sources and to archives.

The 1973 to 2001 period is recent enough and activism in this period so decentralized that institutions are still physically locating documents and individuals are still determining what sources were most influential. Beyond collecting published materials, archives of radicalism generally depend on activists to donate their personal collections, and archivists may exert influence through their own political interests and relationships. Like people, archives can be eccentric and partial. They reproduce racial, gender, class, and other hierarchies in their funding, structures, and cultures. Whether activists save their materials and where they donate them are choices shaped by everything from storage space and housing access to perception of value. Countless activist materials are lost daily to the same structures of violence and inequality that radicals confront in their organizing.

We have aimed to locate a usable past amid chaotic times—or, more precisely, to curate one. We began developing this project during the tail end of the first Obama administration and completed it in the third year of the Trump administration. The years in between saw an array of fantastic scholarship that consistently revised our thinking. Even more influential to our approach were world events themselves. Any book is a product of the time it was created as much as the time it records. The 2016 election and its aftermath prompted us to turn greater attention to efforts at thwarting the vigilante right and its electoral power, while the activism of Indigenous water protectors at Standing Rock accentuated our focus on Native demands for ecological sustainability as a critical element of anticolonial sovereignty.[33]

These concerns were of more than passing interest. We would have completed the book faster had we not taken time to participate in protests against the expanded violence of deportation, incarceration, climate crisis, and privatization, and to build communities of resistance and support. Our efforts to trace the remaking of radicalism historically join our efforts, not only as historians but as human beings, to renew possibility in our contemporary moment. We claim no decisive victory in either effort. Yet we remain dedicated to the world of peace, justice, sustainability, and liberation that radicals of every generation pursue.

NOTES

1. Harvey, *A Brief History of Neoliberalism*; Duggan, *The Twilight of Equality?*.

2. Hall, "The Long Civil Rights Movement and the Political Uses of the Past"; Dixon, *Another Politics*; Zinn, *A People's History of the United States*.

3. Universalist critiques gained prominence among liberal critics in the 1990s reflecting on the 1960s; see, for example, Gitlin, *Twilight of Common Dreams* and Rorty, *Achieving Our Country*. Jefferson Cowie reanimated this critique in *Stayin' Alive*, his history of the white working class in the 1970s. It reappeared in the wake of the 2016 election, notably in the pages of the socialist journal *Jacobin*. For critiques of this approach, see Duggan, *Twilight of Equality*, Haider, *Mistaken Identity*, and Taylor, *From #BlackLivesMatter to Black Liberation*. For narratives of declension, reaction, and frac-

ture, see Rodgers, *Age of Fracture*, and Kruse and Zelizer, *Fault Lines*. For how transformations in capitalism anchored certain new intellectual horizons in this era, see Harvey, *The Condition of Postmodernity*.

4. Thanks to Jenna Loyd for helping us think through this particular phrasing.

5. See for example Harvey, *A Brief History of Neoliberalism*, 2.

6. Gilmore, *Golden Gulag*; MacLean, *Democracy in Chains*; MacLean, *Freedom Is Not Enough*; Hinton, *From the War on Poverty to the War on Crime*; Chappell, The *War on the Welfare Family*. On neoliberalism as an attack on politics, see Brown, *Undoing the Demos*.

7. See especially Duggan, The *Twilight of Equality?*, and Ahmed, *On Being Included*.

8. Cebul, Geismer, and Williams, *Shaped by the State*; Brown, *Undoing the Demos*.

9. Grandin, *Empire's Workshop*; Hudson, *Super Imperialism*; Kornbluh and Mink, *Ensuring Poverty*; Briggs, *How All Politics Became Reproductive Politics*; HoSang, *Racial Propositions*; Ross et al., *Radical Reproductive Justice*; Hobson, *Lavender and Red*; Brier, *Infectious Ideas*; Carroll, *Mobilizing New York*; Gould, *Moving Politics*.

10. Johnson, *From Revolutionaries to Race Leaders*; Taylor, *From #BlackLivesMatter to Black Liberation*.

11. Beal, "Double Jeopardy"; Crenshaw, "Mapping the Margins"; Taylor, *How We Get Free*; Anzaldúa and Moraga, *This Bridge Called My Back*; Collins and Bilge, *Intersectionality*; Hancock, *Intersectionality*. On the development of intersectional analysis in movement contexts, see Roth, *Separate Roads to Feminism*, Springer, *Living for the Revolution*, Hobson, *Lavender and Red*, and Bost, *Evidence of Being*, among others.

12. Hall, "The Problem of Ideology." For critiques of the liberal welfare state and liberal citizenship, see, for example, Murakawa, *The First Civil Right*, Hinton, *From the War on Poverty to the War on Crime*, and Cacho, *Social Death*.

13. Bookchin, *Anarchism, Marxism, and the Future of the Left*; Danaher, *Corporations Are Gonna Get Your Mama*; Dixon, *Another Politics*; Hardt and Negri, *Empire*; Khasnabish, *Zapatistas*; Mohanty, *Feminism without Borders*; Ponce de León, *Our Word Is Our Weapon*.

14. Brenner, Brenner, and Winslow, *Rebel Rank and File*.

15. Critical overviews of the Reagan years include Rossinow, *The Reagan Era*, and Martin, *The Other Eighties*.

16. On Clinton, see Bacevich, *American Empire*; Reed, *Without Justice for All*; Robinson, *Superpredator*.

17. Boyette and Boyette, *Let It Burn*.

18. Berger, *Captive Nation*; Felker-Kantor, *Policing Los Angeles*; Hinton, *From the War on Poverty to the War on Crime*; Vitale, *The End of Policing*; Schrader, *Badges without Borders*.

19. Whitlock and Bronski, *Considering Hate*.

20. Singh, *Race and America's Long War*.

21. Burbach and Tarbell, *Imperial Overstretch*; Finlay, *George W. Bush and the War on Women*; Maira, *The 9/11 Generation*.

22. Kelley, *Freedom Dreams*.

23. Michael Harrington, quoted in Cowie, "'Vigorously Left, Right, and Center,'" 76; Brick and Phelps, *Radicals in America*, 315. More broadly on this transformation, see Melamed, *Represent and Destroy*.

24. On the connections between welfare and incarceration in the 1970s, see Kohler-Hausmann, *Getting Tough*.

25. Clawson, *The Next Upsurge*.

26. INCITE!, *The Revolution Will Not Be Funded*; Beam, *Gay, Inc.*

27. Elbaum, *Revolution in the Air*; Epstein, Political Protest and *Cultural Revolution*; Cornell, *Oppose and Propose; Fithian,* Shut it Down.

28. The best-known discussion of antiracism in the global justice movement is Martinez, "Where Was the Color in Seattle?" We did not include this essay here due to reproduction costs, but it can be accessed at https://www.colorlines.com/articles /where-was-color-seattlelooking-reasons-why-great-battle-was-so-white.

29. Kauffman, *Direct Action*; Shepard and Hayduk, *From ACT UP to the WTO*; Solnit, *Globalize Liberation*; Fithian, *Shut it Down.*

30. Berger, *Outlaws of America*; Berger, *Captive Nation*; Burton-Rose, *Guerrilla USA*; Fernandez, *Prisoners of Colonialism*; Pickering, *The Earth Liberation Front.* For a look at how violence anchored the rise of the right-wing white power movement, see Belew, *Bring the War Home*; Berlet and Lyons, *Right-Wing Populism in America*; Burke, *Revolutionaries of the Right.*

31. Smith, *New Urban Frontier.*

32. For some examples of that work to date, see Greenwald, MacPhee, and Exit Art, *Signs of Change*; Martin, *The Other Eighties*; Chang, *Who We Be*; Bost, *Evidence of Being*; Cvetkovich, *An Archive of Feeling*; Duncombe, *Subcultures Reader.*

33. For other histories contextualizing Standing Rock as part of a long history of Indigenous resistance, see Cobb, *Say We Are Nations*, and Estes, *Our History Is the Future.*

PART 1

Bodies and Lives

In 1979, members of the Black lesbian and socialist feminist organization the Combahee River Collective marched to protest a series of recent murders of Black women in Boston. They carried a banner that read "3rd World Women: We Cannot Live without Our Lives." The banner's words point to the cutting edge politics that illuminated the time period and that are illustrated in this part of the book. To say that we cannot live without our lives is to acknowledge how many people live at risk of premature death and how many have been lost already. The causes of such deaths lie in racial, gender, and state violence, including systems of poverty and disease. To mark premature death is to value those living at risk. It is to insist on the freedom to make choices about our bodies and lives. In addition, it is to honor the unpaid or underpaid labor, typically assigned to women and people of color, that is required for daily survival in capitalism. Though our lives are sites of risk, radicals have redefined this vulnerability as the source of a transformative politics.

Combahee's banner illustrated the growth of intersectional feminism, not only because Black women created it but because in centering on radical women of color, Combahee challenged and expanded feminist thought. The group borrowed the phrase "we cannot live without our lives" from a 1974 book by white feminist writer Barbara Deming, who—adapting the line from Emily Brontë's *Wuthering Heights*—used it to think through the ways that sexism harms women's sense of self. Combahee expanded on Deming's analysis of the psychological costs of patriarchy by naming women of color as particularly vulnerable to both state and interpersonal violence. Through this, Combahee articulated sexism as interwoven with racism, capitalism, and empire.

Part 1 of *Remaking Radicalism*, "Bodies and Lives," explores how activists worked for liberation from the intimate scale of the body and through struggles to sustain everyday life. Feminist, queer, labor, and antiracist politics are the central frameworks reflected here. A host of activists grounded agendas for liberation in the body and the home, through work to secure sexual and reproductive freedom, rights and dignity on the job, and an end to poverty. As they did so, they fought back against deindustrialization, attacks on labor power, and the meticulous dismantling of social programs that often hit poor people of color the hardest. They faced down the rise of the

New Right, whose attacks on welfare and civil rights mobilized through the antifeminist, homophobic, and racist language of "family values." They worked to counter—and envision alternatives to—neoliberalism, which solidified through liberal-right consensus and which made some bodies and lives more vulnerable than others.

Section A, "Feminist and Queer Flashpoints," documents the growth of intersectional feminisms. Across the 1970s and early 1980s, feminist and LGBTQ politics grew dramatically and pushed well beyond frameworks of liberal civil rights. Many feminist and queer radicals crafted multi-issue politics in dialogue with antiracist, antiimperialist, and anticapitalist agendas. The first half of "Feminist and Queer Flashpoints" illustrates this through sources reflecting socialist and women of color feminisms, the gay and lesbian left, and the politics of reproductive justice and of rape. Many of the flashpoints here turn on the problem of how to conceptualize and respond to violence. Should feminists ally with police and prisons to address sexual and domestic violence? How is poverty itself a form of gendered and racialized violence? The second half of section A builds on the debates over these concerns, while also addressing the boundaries of identity in 1980s and 1990s feminist and LGBTQ politics. How can queer people of color, sex workers, and trans activists claim space in the face of marginalization? How are the politics of AIDS intertwined with feminism, antiracism, and antimilitarism? Debating these questions drove activists forward.

At the same time, radicals also faced down a growing threat: the rise of the right, in the form of both elected officials and social movements outside the government. From the 1970s forward, elements of the racist right joined forces, and Christian fundamentalists mobilized to influence policy. By 1980, conservatives claimed victory in the Reagan presidency, which shut down briefly held, mildly liberal gains. Bolstered by state repression, New Right politicians worked to turn back civil rights for people of color, women, and gay and lesbian people. Through the language of family values, it worked diligently to cut social programs, particularly welfare. A further measure of the New Right's power came as a growing number of Democrats joined in slashing cuts to social programs. Antiracist feminist and queer politics offered the clearest rallying cry against these threats.

This context is illuminated in section B, "Fighting the Right." Many of the documents here call for confronting a "common enemy" or for standing together against shared threats. Some address the racialization of gender and sexuality, the gender and sexual politics of race, or the class dimensions of these intersections. Key strategies reflected include opposition to the racist right, the defense of sexual and reproductive freedom, and efforts to maintain such policies as affirmative action. The documents here emphasize radical-liberal alliances that formed at the grassroots to challenge the right. These coalitions were especially significant in rural areas. This section also includes texts documenting feminist and queer debates over pornography, censorship, and the policing of sex. Among other contributions, the texts show how rising conservatism—in both its moralistic and free market faces—set much of the tone for debates over sexual freedom.

The 1970s through 1990s brought another threat into everyday life that was intertwined with the rise of the right. This was the accelerating concentration of wealth. Most people experienced this concentration through a loss of power on the job (or loss of the job itself), the deepening of poverty, the decimation of public services, and the narrowing worldview evident in a media environment dominated by just a handful of companies. Looking forward in 1970, many had been optimistic about radical, even revolutionary change. The decade kicked off with strong union power: 1970 saw 5,716 work stoppages involving over three million workers. Slowdowns, wildcat strikes, and efforts to democratize union leadership were frequent—targeting both unjust workplaces and corrupt union leadership. Socialist feminists, Black union activists, and other radicals appeared poised to win more rights on the job rather than to lose them and to be in a good position to push back against business unionism. Further, an array of activists pursued the radical community services, such as health clinics, that the Black Panther Party modeled through its survival programs.

By the mid-1970s, however, a recession arrived. Inflation took hold; union cutbacks hit full swing; and deindustrialization appeared relentless. Cuts to urban budgets and to public services shook communities across the country. Then Ronald Reagan became president. Campaigning on the promise of undoing decades of liberal and radical advances, Reagan ushered in a wholesale assault on welfare, health care, affirmative action, reproductive rights, and unions. These attacks amplified other crises, particularly that of AIDS, which Reagan—following hardliners in his administration—did very little to address. Reagan's successor, George H. W. Bush, continued his legacy, and Bill Clinton, the first Democratic president in twelve years, continued many of the fiscally austere policies of Reagan and Bush. Clinton's signature "welfare reform" bill of 1996 consigned millions to lifetime precarity by drastically cutting benefits and the length of time that people could receive them. Further, the policy allowed states to administer welfare funds through degrading tactics such as marriage promotion courses and "Dress for Success" programs rather than cash aid.

Despite all these onslaughts, radicals worked to sustain dignity, autonomy, and health in the face of deepening inequality and exploitation. Section C, "Labors of Survival," illustrates these efforts. Integrating labor, welfare, disability, and health activism, the section shows how radicals worked to win value both for work performed on the factory floor and for that done inside the home. It includes documents on welfare politics, texts from the 1970s for welfare rights and texts from the 1990s against welfare reform. It illustrates labor feminism in contexts ranging from food canneries to flight attendant unions. It touches on queer labor activism, notably through health care unions' responses to AIDS. More generally, the section considers how activists responded to the US economy's shift away from industrialized, unionized work toward a low-wage service economy and "right to work" laws. (Labor activism is also represented in the book in part 3, "Borders and Maps," which addresses immigrant worker organizing, international solidarity, and global justice movements.)

Throughout "Bodies and Lives," activists' breadth of vision appears in the ways they connect particular issues—whether a union contract fight, resistance to racist violence, or caring for people with HIV and AIDS—to broader contexts of repression and austerity. Activists across the 1970s, 1980s, and 1990s organized during a period of mounting loss and amid harsh threats to collective survival. By merging feminist and queer politics, participatory democracy, and traditions of radical labor organizing, they not only confronted neoliberalism but built toward an alternative society.

Feminist And Queer Flashpoints

1.A.1.

Combahee River Collective

From "A Black Feminist Statement" (1977)

The Combahee River Collective was a Black feminist and lesbian organization in Boston active from 1974 to 1980. Its 1977 statement is one of the founding documents of contemporary Black feminism and intersectional feminist thought. This edited version does not include the full statement's sections on the historical origins of Black feminism and on what Combahee saw as problems in Black feminist organizing.

We are a collective of Black feminists who have been meeting together since 1974. During that time we have been involved in the process of defining and clarifying our politics, while at the same time doing political work within our own group and in coalition with other progressive organizations and movements. The most general statement of our politics at the present time would be that we are actively committed to struggling against racial, sexual, heterosexual, and class oppression and see as our particular task the development of integrated analysis and practice based upon the fact that the major systems of oppression are interlocking. The synthesis of these oppressions creates the conditions of our lives. As Black women we see Black feminism as the logical political movement to combat the manifold and simultaneous oppressions that all women of color face. . . .

What We Believe

Above all else, our politics initially sprang from the shared belief that Black women are inherently valuable, that our liberation is a necessity not as an adjunct to somebody else's may because of our need as human persons for autonomy. This may seem so obvious as to sound simplistic, but it is apparent that no other ostensibly progressive movement has ever considered our specific oppression as a priority or worked seriously for the ending of that oppression. Merely naming the pejorative stereotypes attributed to Black women (e.g. mammy, matriarch, Sapphire, whore, bulldagger), let alone cataloguing the cruel, often murderous, treatment we receive, indicates how little value has been placed upon our lives during four centuries of bondage in the Western hemisphere. We realize that the only people who care enough about us to work consistently for our liberation are us. Our politics evolve from a healthy love for ourselves, our sisters, and our community which allows us to continue our struggle and work.

This focusing upon our own oppression is embodied in the concept of identity politics. We believe that the most profound and potentially most radical politics come directly out of our own identity, as opposed to working to end somebody else's oppression. In the case of Black women this is a particularly repugnant, dangerous, threatening, and therefore revolutionary concept because it is obvious from looking at all the political movements that have preceded us that anyone is more worthy of liberation than ourselves. We reject pedestals, queenhood, and walking ten paces behind. To be recognized as human, levelly human, is enough.

We believe that sexual politics under patriarchy is as pervasive in Black women's lives as are the politics of class and race. We also often find it difficult to separate race from class from sex oppression because in our lives they are most often experienced simultaneously. We know that there is such a thing as racial-sexual oppression which is neither solely racial nor solely sexual, e.g., the history of rape of Black women by white men as a weapon of political repression.

Although we are feminists and lesbians, we feel solidarity with progressive Black men and do not advocate the fractionalization that white women who are separatists demand. Our situation as Black people necessitates that we have solidarity around the fact of race, which white women of course do not need to have with white men, unless it is their negative solidarity as racial oppressors. We struggle together with Black men against racism, while we also struggle with Black men about sexism.

We realize that the liberation of all oppressed peoples necessitates the destruction of the political-economic systems of capitalism and imperialism as well as patriarchy. We are socialists because we believe that work must be organized for the collective benefit of those who do the work and create the products, and not for the profit of the bosses. Material resources must be equally distributed among those who create these resources. We are not convinced, however, that a socialist revolution that is not also a feminist and antiracist revolution will guarantee our liberation. We have arrived at the necessity for developing an understanding of class relationships that takes into account the specific class position of Black women who are generally marginal in the labor force, while at this particular time some of us are temporarily viewed as doubly desirable tokens at white-collar and professional levels. We need to articulate the real class situation of persons who are not merely raceless, sexless workers, but for whom racial and sexual oppression are significant determinants in their working/economic lives. Although we are in essential agreement with Marx's theory as it applied to the very specific economic relationships he analyzed, we know that his analysis must be extended further in order for us to understand our specific economic situation as Black women.

A political contribution which we feel we have already made is the expansion of the feminist principle that the personal is political. In our consciousness-raising sessions, for example, we have in many ways gone beyond white women's revelations because we are dealing with the implications of race and class as well as sex. Even our Black women's style of talking/testifying in Black language about what we have experienced has a resonance that is both cultural and political. We have spent a great deal of energy delving into the cultural and experiential nature of our oppression out of necessity because none of these matters has ever been looked at before. No one before has ever examined the multilayered texture of Black women's lives. An example of this kind of revelation/conceptualization occurred at a meeting as we discussed the ways in which our early intellectual interests had been attacked by our peers, particularly Black males. We discovered that all of us, because we were "smart," had also been considered "ugly," i.e., "smart-ugly." "Smart-ugly" crystallized the way in which most of us had been forced to develop our intellects at great cost to our "social" lives. The sanctions in the Black and white communities against Black women thinkers are comparatively much higher than for white women, particularly ones from the educated middle and upper classes.

As we have already stated, we reject the stance of lesbian separatism because it is not a viable political analysis or strategy for us. It leaves out far too much and far too many people, particularly Black men, women, and children. We have a great deal of criticism and loathing for what men have been socialized to be in this society: what they support, how they act, and how they oppress. But we do not have the misguided notion that it is their maleness, per se—i.e., their biological maleness—that makes them what they are. As Black women we find any type of biological determinism a particularly dangerous and reactionary basis upon which to build a politic. We must also question whether lesbian separatism is an adequate and progressive political analysis and strategy, even for those who practice it, since it so completely denies any but the sexual sources of women's oppression, negating the facts of class and race. . . .

Black Feminist Issues and Projects

During our time together we have identified and worked on many issues of particular relevance to Black women. The inclusiveness of our politics makes us concerned with any situation that impinges upon the lives of women [and] Third World and working people. We are of course particularly committed to working on those struggles in which race, sex, and class are simultaneous factors in oppression. We might, for example, become involved in workplace organizing at a factory that employs Third World women or picket a hospital that is cutting back on already inadequate heath care to a Third World community, or set up a rape crisis center in a Black neighborhood. Organizing around welfare and daycare concerns might also be a focus. The work to be done and the countless issues that this work represents merely reflect the pervasiveness of our oppression.

Issues and projects that collective members have actually worked on are sterilization abuse, abortion rights, battered women, rape, and health care. We have also done many workshops and educationals on Black feminism on college campuses, at women's conferences and most recently for high school women.

One issue that is of major concern to us and that we have begun to publicly address is racism in the white women's movement. As Black feminists we are made constantly and painfully aware of how little effort white women have made to understand and combat their racism, which requires among other things that they have a more than superficial comprehension of race, color, and Black history and culture. Eliminating racism in the white women's movement is by definition work for white women to do, but we will continue to speak to and demand accountability on this issue.

In the practice of our politics we do not believe that the end always justifies the means. Many reactionary and destructive acts have been done in the name of achieving "correct" political goals. As feminists we do not want to mess over people in the name of politics. We believe in collective process and a nonhierarchical distribution of power within our own group and in our vision of a revolutionary society. We are committed to a continual examination of our politics as they develop through criticism and self-criticism as an essential aspect of our practice. In her introduction to *Sisterhood Is Powerful* Robin Morgan writes:

> I haven't the faintest notion what possible revolutionary role white heterosexual men could fulfill, since they are the very embodiment of reactionary-vested-interest-power.

As Black feminists and lesbians we know that we have a very definite revolutionary task to perform and we are ready for the lifetime of work and struggle before us.

A Brief History of SisterSong
Loretta J. Ross

In 1997, sixteen women of color leaders of community-based organizations, including me, organized a reproductive health coalition called SisterSong. Four previous attempts over the past decade had floundered due to lack of funding, yet we were not deterred. We represented Native American, Latina, Asian Pacific Islander, and African

American women, four organizations from each group. We responded to a heartfelt need for women of color to organize our voices to collectively represent ourselves in policy debates on reproductive politics in the United States and Puerto Rico. Some of us were prochoice and others prolife. But all were impatient with the paralysis of the prochoice vs. prolife binary dominating reproductive health issues. We identified our common ground as women of color seeking to deliver services to our communities. Some worked as midwives, others on issues of HIV/AIDS, teen pregnancy, community health services, human rights, and abortion advocacy.

One of our founders, Juanita Williams (an AIDS survivor from Project Azuka), noticed that despite our differences, we were all saying the same thing about why our work was so hard. We faced inadequate funding, reluctance in our communities to talk about sex and sexuality, missing infrastructure like computers and fax machines, and a lack of support from the mainstream prochoice movement. Williams observed that if we sang our individual songs in harmony with each other, we could raise a powerful chorus for change. Thus, SisterSong was born, and our mission became our motto: "Doing collectively what we cannot do individually."

Luz Rodriguez, then the Puerto Rican director of the Latina Roundtable on Reproductive Rights, had a providential meeting in 1996 with Reena Marcello, then a program officer with the Ford Foundation. Reena, a Filipina nearing the end of her five-year term with Ford, sadly reported that she had never made a sizable grant to a women of color organization because many lacked institutional capacity. She asked what Luz would do with an opportunity from Ford, and Luz pulled out a cocktail napkin and drew a schema that would include sixteen organizations representing four major ethnic communities. After planning meetings in New York City and Savannah, the SisterSong Women of Color Reproductive Health Collective was born.

There were several critical issues facing the original founders. The first was that Ford wanted the organizations to pursue the foundation's agenda, which at that time centered on reproductive tract infections. SisterSong founders pushed back because they were familiar with funders demanding that women of color meet outside demands rather than building their infrastructures and reoriented the grant from a focus on programming and service delivery to longer-term capacity building.

Our second critical issue was developing a common focus. We decided to use the reproductive justice framework created in 1994 by African American women as our conceptual glue for strengthening a movement of women of color. Reproductive justice is built on three major pillars: 1) the right to not have a child, using birth control, abortion, and/or abstinence; 2) the right to have a child by resisting strategies of population control, including the right to use midwives and doulas; and 3) the right to raise children in safe and healthy environments. This intersectional framework expands the conversation about reproductive health to include environmental justice, gun control, quality schools, tax policies, police violence, and a host of other issues not addressed by the prochoice vs. prolife divide. Reproductive justice has grown to become the dominant framework of the women of color reproductive health movement and has exerted a profound influence on mainstream organizing as well.

Over time, SisterSong grew to include eighty women of color and allied organizations and changed its name to SisterSong Women of Color Reproductive Justice Collective. The group celebrated its twentieth anniversary in 2017 and has enlarged its membership base to include white allies, men, and LGBTQ members attracted to its radical politics. In its third decade, SisterSong proves that women of color, working together, can transform themselves and the entire landscape of reproductive politics.

The founding SisterSong organizations were the National Latina Health Organization, Women's House of Learning Empowerment, Casa Atabex Aché, and Grupo Pro-Derechos Reproductivos of Puerto Rico (Latina); SisterLove, the National Center for Human Rights Education, California Black Women's Health Project, and Project Azuka (African American); MoonLodge, the Native American Women's Health Education Resource Center, Wise Women Gathering Place, and Minnesota Indigenous People's Task Force (Native American); and Kokua Kalihi Valley Comprehensive Family Services, Asian Pacific Islanders for Reproductive Health, the National Asian Women's Health Organization, and THE (To Help Everyone) Clinic (Asian American/Pacific Islander).

1.A.2.

Iris Morales

"Sterilized Puerto Ricans" (1970)

Struggles for the right to bear and raise children, as well as to choose not to, have been fundamental to women of color feminism. Iris Morales served as minister of education in the Young Lords Party, a Puerto Rican radical organization in New York City and Chicago, and first published this essay in the Young Lords' newspaper *Palante*.

Genocide is being committed against the Puerto Rican women! In no other nation has sterilization been so prevalent as a means of genocide against an oppressed people. Why Puerto Ricans? First, the united states needs Puerto Rico as a military stronghold to maintain "political stability" and control in the rest of Latin America. Second, Puerto Rico is the fourth largest worldwide consumer of amerikkkan goods and yields massive profits to amerikkkan capitalists. Also, Puerto Rico supplies fighting men and a cheap labor pool, both necessary to u.s. capitalism. One way to control a nation of vital importance is to limit its population size. The u.s. is doing exactly this through sterilization.

The practice of sterilization in Puerto Rico goes back to the 1930s when doctors pushed it as the only means of contraception. As a result, throughout the island, Puerto Rican women of childbearing age were sterilized. In 1947–48, 7 percent of the women were sterilized; between 1953–54, four out of every twenty-five Sisters were sterilized; and by 1965, the number increased to one out of every three women. This system was practiced on Sisters of all ages. But, since 1965, the trend has been to sterilize women in their early 20s when they have had fewer babies. This is especially true among lower-class Sisters where future revolutionaries would come from. Committing sterilization on young Puerto Rican mothers with fewer children means that the u.s. is able to significantly reduce and limit the Puerto Rican population in a short period of time.

Genocide through sterilization is not only confined to the island of Puerto Rico. It is also carried out within the Puerto Rican colony in the u.s. In El Barrio, sterilization is still practiced as a form of contraception among women, especially young Sisters. One out of four sterilized women in El Barrio has the operation done when she's between twenty and thirty. But the system justifies the shit, saying the Sisters go to Puerto Rico to get it done. Yet the evidence says that over half the Sisters get the operation done right here in New York City and are strongly encouraged by their doctors to do so. Again, sterilization in the early reproductive years of a woman's life limits the Puerto Rican population substantially and permanently.

Sterilization is also a form of oppression against Puerto Rican women. We are oppressed by our own culture that limits us to the roles of homemaker, mother, and bearer of many children which measures male virility. We have been made dependent on family and home for our very existence. We are used by u.s. corporations to test the safety of birth control pills before placing them on the market for sale. Our bodies are used by capitalists for experimentation to find new moneymaking and genocidal gadgets. We are prevented from getting adequate birth control information and legal abortions. As a result, one out of every four Sisters who try it die from self-induced abortions, giving Puerto Ricans the notoriety of having the highest death rate casualties from abortion than any other group. Sterilization is just another form of oppressing us.

Sterilization is irreversible and as such the u.s. can control the Puerto Rican population. Sterilization once done cannot be undone. We must stop sterilization because we must leave the option open to ourselves to control the Puerto Rican population. Our men die in Vietnam, our babies are killed through lead poisoning and malnutrition, and our women are sterilized. The Puerto Rican Nation must continue. We must open our eyes to the oppressor's tricknology and refuse to be killed anymore. We must, in the tradition of Puerto Rican women like Lolita Lebron, Blanca Canales, Carmen Perez, and Antonia Marti-

nez, join with our Brothers and together, as a nation of warriors, fight the genocide that is threatening to make us the last generation of Puerto Ricans.

> *Stop the genocide! Off the pig!*
> *No more sterilization of Sisters!*
> *Que viva Puerto Rico libre!*

1.A.3.

United Front

"Forward Macho" (1973)

Feminist and gay politics, along with antiracism, made major inroads among
the radical soldiers and veterans who resisted the Vietnam War. This essay
comes from an underground newspaper, *Hansen Free Press*, that was produced by the United Front, an association of antiwar soldiers who were affiliated with Vietnam Veterans against the War and stationed in Okinawa, Japan.

Forward Macho! Perhaps that command best characterizes sexism in the military. The drill instructors in training are quick to call the gentle or soft-spoken
marine a "pussy" or some other lifer cliché. The recruit who fails in a task is
a "lady" or a "girl," while the gung ho recruit is praised as a "swinging dick."
The marine's personal relationships with women are put down, his wife or girl-
friend used for drill instructors' dirty jokes. Sometimes recruits are encouraged
to have their "old ladies" send "skin pics" which are put on display on "hog
boards" for public derision. Chauvinism is perpetuated by the attitude of those
pigs who train recruits, plus the two-month isolation period with no contact
with women. Women become dehumanized and objectified to a sickening degree. Shower-room walls tell the story with disgusting displays of graffiti and
smut. Barracks slang is well known for its disgusting content.

When a marine leaves training, he is an "American fighting man." He's been
taught to kill in a racist and sadistic fashion. He's been regimented to uphold
America's finest image. He has been programmed as an automaton for the military and taught to expect women to become automatons for him.

The attitude in the military towards women is similar to that in society at
large. Men fight, men win, men take. However, that attitude is intensified and
perpetuated in the military to such a degree that it is physically dangerous. (Ask
any woman who walks down the street in a military town on payday.) Because
the marine has now become a "man" through the military, it is hard for him
to understand why every woman he meets doesn't want to sleep with him. He
has been brainwashed to the point where he "knows" that women find him
sexually desirable because he is a tough, hard killer. He actually believes that
so much that when he is rejected or rebuffed by a woman, he blames her for

not acting as he has been told she would. This sometimes manifests itself not only in contempt, but in a genuine dislike for women. It is not unusual to see "pinup" nudes with breasts and crotches burned out by cigarettes and adorning walls and wall lockers.

The difference in attitude towards women at different duty stations is interesting, and of course, sick. In Germany, GIs may take their pleasure at bordellos, but don't go near a blonde German woman. In Vietnam, on the other hand, marines are systematically taught to see Vietnamese women as whores. Vietnamese women become not only sex objects, but subhumans, pieces of flesh in vaguely human form, suitable only for sexual outlet. A marine who displays any emotional attachment towards a Vietnamese woman is put down and ostracized by his comrades. It's no coincidence that US presence in South Vietnam has produced a generation of pimps and prostitutes. Crimes of rape in South Vietnam are too numerous to record.

The brass that conspires to turn out regimented robots understand machismo in much the same way that they understand racism. Machismo is considered the proper attitude for a marine. It pictures a strong man with a dumb blonde on each arm killing commie gooks in the shadow of old glory.

Like racism, machismo is used to divide and conquer. It produces troop "morale" instead of solidarity between people. By making enemies out of people who could be on the same side, it divides us and weakens our ability to fight back against the military.

1.A.4a. and 1.A.4b.

In March 1974 Inez Garcia, a Latina woman in Soledad, California, was charged with murder for defending herself against rape. Feminists, lesbians, and others organized to support her in court, linking her case to other women of color, such as Joan Little, Yvonne Swan (then known as Wanrow), and Dessie Woods, then facing similar charges. Garcia was convicted in 1974, then found not guilty on appeal in 1975. "Racist Sexism in the Trial" and the article that follows it, "We Need the Power to Defend Ourselves," were published in the Bay Area newspaper the *Feminist* during the campaign to overturn her conviction.

1.A.4a. *The Feminist,* "Racist Sexism in the Trial" (1974)

The possibility that the predominately white jury might be swayed by a racist attitude toward the defendants was obscured for some people at the beginning of the trial of Garcia and Medrano, because of the fact that not only were both the defendants members of an oppressed nationality, but the dead rapist was also, as was the prosecution's chief witness, Luis Castillo, who had committed the physical rape.

Garcia's defense lawyer, Charles Garry, when asked by a woman spectator why he did not question any of the prospective jurors on their racial attitudes, answered that racism had nothing to do with this case. "I know what I'm doing," he told the woman. "I'm an expert on racism."

The jurors were in fact not questioned on either racism *or* sexism, except for one question which was asked of only *some* of them—"Do you consider rape a violent crime?"

What was at work in that Monterey courtroom was *racist sexism*, which is a particularly virulent instrument of oppression against women of color and is something more than simply the sum of those two patriarchal poisons.

Judge Lawson led the pack, suggesting that the illiteracy of the defendant Inez Garcia must be a sign of being "a little retarded," and not a result of poverty, atrociously bad New York schools, neglect by American school systems toward Spanish-speaking children, and the lack of importance given to resolving learning difficulties for girls—in both the Anglo and Spanish cultures.

There was no attempt by the defense to tackle this view of illiteracy, thus leaving a wide gap for this suburban jury to fill in with its own prejudices, aided by Garry's painstaking reminders that Garcia had spent time in mental hospitals, "more than once."

There were several attempts on the part of the prosecution to insinuate that Garcia was "immodest" and tended to invite rape. This slur is used against all women, white included, who have been made objects of male depredations. But it is used with particular viciousness against women of color. The prosecutor's insinuations fell flat, but some residue of this attitude was left in the jury's minds, as indicated by a woman juror who believed, "It would not have happened to *me*!"—meaning, a woman who gets raped must have been doing something wrong. (And if she is not of *my* color or not of *my* class, then even more must she have been doing something wrong.)

The prosecution also tried to imply that the reason why Garcia killed Jimenez was not rape at all, but drugs. And here the emphasis was shifted to the other defendant, Fred Medrano. Without bringing in one shred of evidence to back up this charge, the prosecution was content to leave the impression in the jury's minds that Medrano, being nonwhite, was probably mixed up in something illegal. And that Garcia, being a woman, was probably helping "her man."

An Anglo woman would still have faced a mountain of tradition which says that a woman *never* meets violence with violence, that a woman must endure male violence and humiliation with stoicism and self-blame. (If she fights to the death, it must be *her* death, and not that of her attacker.)

But Inez Garcia, born in Spanish Harlem of Puerto Rican and Cuban parentage, faced several mountains.

This is not to say that the conviction was inevitable. But it does mean that it needed a real struggle, both in and out of the courtroom, to win justice for Inez.

And the struggle will be all the harder after the courtroom defeat that came down October 4.

1.A.4b. *The Feminist,* "We Need the Power to Defend Ourselves!" (1975)

There are no rights without power. We need the *right* and the *power* to do whatever is necessary to see that we are secure in our persons.

Physical and political weapons are inseparable—both of them indispensable to any oppressed group.

Without political struggle we will remain physically defenseless. Without *forcefully* proving that we value ourselves and will back up that self-value with whatever weapons are available, we will remain politically powerless.

We need economic power. We are expected to beg and grovel for the means to maintain life. They pour saccharin praises on our roles as mothers—but rob us of the means to carry out those roles with dignity.

Women make up the great majority of the "working poor." The work we are allowed or forced to do has been made a series of purgatories of monotony or degradation. Our wages make us nothing more than slaves.

We must attack the *sources* of our economic slavery.

We need political power. The federal, state, and city governments are nothing but instruments of the few rich men who keep us poor. As soon as women begin to fight for real gains—not tokens, not pretty phrases—we find ourselves up against the police, the courts, the jails.

There is no accommodation with this repressive apparatus nor with the politicians who cover for it. It is them or us!

Any "protection" which robs us of our autonomy is no protection at all. Any "protection" which uses white women as pawns in racist frame-ups is no protection at all. It is a deadly poison designed not only to undermine the struggles of Third World men, but to render women of all colors immobile, powerless, and terrorized.

We want no more of the protection racket.

We want self-determination.

Crimes against women will not cease until they are dealt with by *women,* whether they are in the street, in the bedroom, in the kitchen, in the jail, in the court, in the welfare building, in the plant, in the office, in the bank, in the governor's office, or in the White House.

1.A.5.

Yvonne Swan

Witness statement (1976)

Yvonne Swan, formerly known as Yvonne Wanrow, is a Native American woman from the Colville Indian Reservation who became a major figure in anticarceral feminism and Native activism through her insistence on her right to self-defense. In 1972, she killed a violent man who attempted to molest her children. Initially convicted of murder, she won a retrial in 1975, then faced delays as prosecutors sought to block her case. In this witness statement, which she gave as part of the first International Tribunal on Crimes against Women (held in Brussels in 1976), Swan describes the sexism and anti-Native racism of her first trial. In 1977, the Washington Supreme Court upheld Swan's right to a retrial in a ruling that helped expand women's access to self-defense against gender violence. Swan ultimately accepted a plea deal that allowed her to maintain her claim to self-defense and that kept her out of prison. Her case can be usefully compared to that of Inez Garcia (1.A.4a., 1.A.4b.) and Leonard Peltier (2.A.3.).

My name is Yvonne Wanrow. I am a Native American. I was born and raised on an Indian reservation. I left there to get an education, and I completed high school. I married young but got divorced right away. I have three children, aged twelve, five and twenty-two months, whom I have had to raise by myself. I live now in the state of Washington on the Colville Indian reservation with my mother, sister, two nieces, my children, and two other family members. Thirty-two years ago I was born into a defensive position. I was born to be oppressed, and I am fighting for my life.

Three and half years ago, I was arrested and charged with murder and assault. I was put in jail. I was brought before an all-white jury at the time of the Wounded Knee occupation in South Dakota, a time when all Native Americans were seen as militants and extremists. I was convicted by this all-white jury on Mother's Day, May 13, 1973, and sentenced to two twenty-year terms, and one five-year term for the use of a gun. Why? Because I had killed a man in defense of my child, my babysitter's child, and myself. William Wesler was a sixty-two-year old white man, six feet, two inches tall. He was known to the police as a child molester and rapist. He wasn't particular: he molested both boys and girls. He had previously raped the seven-year-old daughter of my babysitter and given her venereal disease. He had also attacked my son. He lured him into his home, locked the door, and picked up a knife. But my son was able to escape with only a lump on his arm. The next night when I was at my babysitter's home with my children, my babysitter, and her daughter, Wesler and another man broke into the house at five in the morning.

I had a broken leg at the time, and when Wesler headed towards one of the children, I screamed for help. Wesler, who was drunk out of his mind, turned, lurching toward me. So I shot him. I immediately called the police to report what had happened. They arrested me and put me in jail. I feel all I was guilty of was being a mother who loves her children.

At my trial the judge refused to allow evidence on Wesler's history as a child molester and rapist. He did not allow the babysitter's daughter, whom Wesler had raped, to testify because it was "irrelevant," and she was too young to be believed. It was said by the probation officer at my sentencing that I must be prone to violence because I had purchased a gun. But I had purchased the gun for self-protection, because my life had been threatened by white people, and I was living alone in a neighborhood known to the police as a troublesome area. I was told that I could pursue my career in art in prison and that I could teach other inmates art, and that I could counsel other Native American women in prison. And the probation officer said that as I come from a large family, there certainly would be no problem as to who would care for my children during my incarceration. He also implied he was an authority on Indians because he had spent two years on my Indian reservation. They really didn't care what happened to me. The judge said, "Hurry up. Let's get this over with. Let's wrap it up by the weekend!"

My tone of voice was used to convict me; they said I was calm because I was not screaming on the telephone when I reported what had happened to the police. And the prosecutor used my calmness in the courtroom against me, telling the jury: "Look at her, how cold blooded she is. How calmly she sits there!"

When they put down in their books, "the state of Washington vs. Yvonne Wanrow," they declared war on me as a person, and as a woman, and as an Indian woman, and as a mother. Since the Indians started to ask for their rights, there has been an undeclared war on Indians. My people are being killed every day, little children are being shot, their mothers are being shot in the back, in the head. And they are using the Bureau of Indian Affairs to train Indians to kill Indians. I am a political prisoner because the prosecutor is a political climber. He wants to have a higher position someday, and it's easy for him to get there by putting minority people in prison. It's easy to put minority people in prison because those who do not have money to hire an attorney, have to take a public defender, men who are paid by the state to defend poor people—and they talk you into pleading guilty.

I appealed my convictions and won the appeal, but the feeling of happiness was short lived. The prosecutor is now appealing that decision. The case rests now in the hands of nine white men in the state supreme court in Olympia, Washington. They are going to decide over the next few months whether or not I got a fair trial, or whether or not I deserve another trial. So, I wait, as I have been waiting for years, with the threat of being separated from my children, with the threat of a lifetime in prison. They want me to hand over the next twenty-five years of my life to satisfy a system that is dominated by men. By white men. But I decided not to sit back anymore and quietly watch the judge plan my destiny. I decided to make a stand because I had nothing to lose anymore. And I am asking you to stand with me, whether it be in spirit, or whether it be physically, by writing letters or doing whatever you can think of to help me raise money, to fight my case. I have been able to organize some defense committees in the States. I have one in Canada too. I would like to have one or more overseas. If there are any of you who are willing to help me establish some defense committees, please contact me later. If the men in the state supreme court know that the world is watching, they will be very careful in reaching their decision in the next few months. If I win a new trial, we will fight for a dismissal. If I lose, we'll fight for a change in sentence. This can go on for another two years.

But at least I am able to remain out on bond, to be with my family. Thank you for your kind attention.

1.A.6.

Lavender and Red Union

"Gay Liberation/Socialist Revolution" (1976)

Active from 1974 through 1977, Lavender and Red Union (L&RU) was a Los Angeles group of self-described "dyke and faggot communists." It located itself at the nexus of gay liberation and the New Communist Movement. This statement and other publications the group produced were widely circulated in the gay and lesbian left.

We would like to step back a moment and try to explain a slogan that is commonly used by L&RU: *Gay liberation is impossible without socialist revolution—socialist revolution is incomplete without Gay liberation.*

First, there can be no measure of real freedom for Gay people or any oppressed people in a capitalist society because all oppression is tied to the economic base of society and must be maintained in order to keep the capitalist system alive. How does antigayness reinforce capitalism?

Antigayness is a technique for dividing workers which has had awesome success.

In addition antigayness is necessary for the maintenance of the capitalist division of labor. By division of labor we mean that women are assigned the role of homemaker, wife, mother, servicer, etc., while the men are the producers, the providers, etc. Along with your particular function are supposed to come other characteristics like femininity and masculinity, passivity and aggressiveness, emotionality and intellect, etc. As well as models for how "woman" is supposed to relate to "man" and "man" to "man" and "woman" to "woman." The role of "woman" or wife is supposed to interlock with "man" to create a unit or complete whole. It is through this division of labor and the ideology that accompanies it that capitalism enslaves women and keeps them out of productive labor. It is through this division of labor that the subjugation of children is ensured. It is through the ideology of this division of labor that Gay people are deemed to be sick and perverted. It is through this division of labor that the capitalist maximizes consumption, since each family unit in this society must own their own stove and refrigerator and automobile.

Ultimately, the sexist division of labor is a necessity for the survival of capitalism. While the ruling class can accede to economic demands and legal reforms, the capitalists cannot agree to the most profound demands being put forward by women and Gay people for the overthrow of the sexist division of labor, the bourgeois nuclear family, and the ideology of sexism without cutting deeply into the very fabric of this system. The demands of Gay liberation and women's liberation cannot be granted to any large degree without playing havoc with the roles that are so necessary to maintaining capitalism. We are taught to look for support almost exclusively from our families rather than from coworkers, comrades, and friends. The family acts as an enormously conservatizing factor in organizing workers because a worker feels that any action she or he takes will also be suffered by her or his family. Women workers are discouraged in organizing because they believe that their jobs are only temporary or supplemental.

The ruling class seeks to repress Gayness as part of an overall assault on phenomena and ideas that do not fit within the sexist division of labor. Given that they have found it impossible to totally repress Gayness, they seek to contain it or rather to define it in terms of the same sexist roles. But much of what Gay people are flies in the face of these roles. Lesbians are capable of living and loving without the "protection" of a man, [and] faggots are able to do the cleaning and the cooking and satisfy each other sexually and emotionally without the presence of a woman as a service station. Likewise the struggle for women's liberation, the independence and power being displayed by women and for that matter by all oppressed people, refutes the lies and myths.

Why is socialist revolution incomplete without Gay liberation? Socialism by definition is a transitional stage of history. A bridge between the capitalist system of private ownership of the means of production and communism or classless society. Under socialism the workers consolidate their victory over the bourgeoisie, the rule of the proletariat over the capitalist class. Having achieved this the workers seek to destroy the system of classes and class rule itself. The destruction of the divisions that exist among the people like sexism and racism, which derive from class rule, are critical to the destruction of class society, and indeed one cannot really be said to be practicing socialism if one is not working to overthrow them. Inevitably, if the working class is not seeking to destroy these divisions they will revert to supporting them. We cannot proceed in the revolutionary process when we are borrowing heavily in our theory and practice from the bourgeoisie. When communist organizations or socialist countries uphold sexism they are doing the work of the capitalists, not of the workers.

If one defines victory for the workers only in terms of economic gains or only in terms of taking state power you are ignoring the heart of socialism, its fundamental goal—human freedom.

1.A.7.

Robin McDuff, Deanne Pernell, and Karen Saunders

From "An Open Letter to the Antirape Movement" (1977)

This statement offers an early expression of anticarceral feminism and reveals how debates over police, prisons, and the legal system helped to moti-

vate and ground the development of intersectional analysis. Written by three
members of Santa Cruz Women Against Rape, it was published in a feminist
magazine called *The Second Wave*.

We, the members of Santa Cruz Women Against Rape, are concerned about the
direction the antirape movement is taking, in particular in its relationship to
the criminal justice system.

When the organized movement against rape first started about five years
ago, most antirape groups were collectives of feminists, brought together
by their anger at the way the police and the courts treat rape victims. These
groups (including ours) were primarily political. We were critics of the police,
the courts, and the hospitals, the institutions that traditionally deal with rape
victims. Their dreadful treatment of women became a topic of interest to the
media, largely due to the efforts of the women's movement against rape. In a
snowballing effect, many other antirape groups formed. Many of these groups,
however, did not consider themselves political, nor even feminist. . . . [T]hese
groups tended to encourage or cajole women to report rapes to the police.

The explicitly political groups have been frustrated—both by the ineffectiveness and unresponsiveness of the criminal justice system and by the steadily increasing rate of reported rapes. While many remain critical of the criminal justice system in theory, most groups, in practice, feel it is important to build or
improve relationships with the police and other criminal justice agencies; they
hope this will lead to increased prosecution and conviction of rapists. In attempting to build these relations, such antirape groups have withheld criticism
of these agencies, as opposed to applying outside pressure through the media,
demonstrations, etc. Consider also that many groups are supported through
government funds. As a result, there is an inevitable push, if not outright obligation, to persuade women to report to the police. . . .

We support the right of an individual rape victim to go through the criminal justice system, if she so chooses, because there aren't many other alternatives. But as antirape groups, we have the responsibility to expose the function
and challenge the process of the criminal justice system. Attempts at "good relations" with the criminal justice system have served to co-opt our movement
and have led to the belief (or hope) that the criminal justice system can solve
the problem of rape. Yet the sexist and racist nature of the criminal justice system only makes the problem worse. . . . [T]he women involved have no power
in the process: it is the police who decide if she was "really raped," the DA who
often decides that it isn't a "good case" so won't prosecute, and the juries who
hesitate to convict a rapist.

It is true that the conviction rate for rapists is very low. This is largely due to
sexism and the sexist myths about rape in our culture. We abhor the reasons for
this low conviction rate, but that doesn't mean we should work for a high conviction rate. Those convicted of rape are most likely to be Third World and/or
poor White men, as is true of convictions of nearly all other crimes. In order for

a DA to "win" a rape case, he (or, rarely, she) must use sexist, racist and classist stereotypes and assumptions, thereby supporting the worst aspects of this society. If the goal of this process is to fight and end rape, it is self-defeating to use racist and classist means to get to that end.

Historically, rape has been a tool used against Third World people. The sexist myth that women "ask for it" and lie about rape is applied many times more to Third World women than to White women. Black women have been particularly subject to rape by White men since slavery, because society has never given them any protection. The myth that most rapists are Black men has had enormous consequences for them. Thousands of Black men have been lynched or legally executed because they "looked at a White woman wrong." Of the 450 legal executions for rape, 408 of these men were Black. In addition, rape has been a primary weapon used against women in the genocidal campaign against Native Americans. It is crucial that antirape groups fight the racist myths, stereotypes, and institutions that are associated with rape. We cannot turn our backs to the racism of the system when a Black man is being prosecuted and expect that same racism not to be used against Joann Little, Yvonne Wanrow, Inez Garcia, and many others. No matter what our intentions are, the system is racist through and through, so the first step in this process is to stop supporting the criminal justice system.

The answer to the problem of rape is not just to get rapists "off the street." Prisons themselves are incapable of changing rapists. The pressures inherent in this society's culture are intensified in prison. Male sex roles, violence, and power relations which lead to rape in the first place are strongly reinforced. Rapists in prison don't stop raping—they simply use their power over men weaker than themselves. . . . Prisons don't deal with the roots of the problem, they only add to the cause. . . .

Those antirape groups who spend time working for reform legislation encounter many of the same problems and obstacles. Sexist attitudes (and actions) cannot be legislated away. . . .

The time and energy that is now used both in developing a working relationship with the criminal justice agencies and on reforming legislation could be much better spent. The antirape movement should work on community education and on developing practical alternatives that deal with both the symptoms and the roots of sexism and violence. . . . Some of our ideas and alternatives are [as follows]:

1. We encourage people to get together to discuss ways to watch out for each other. This includes block watching to make neighborhoods safe, organizing at workplaces to get support to deal with hassles from bosses and fellow workers, and organizing at schools to get self-defense classes, etc.
2. We try to create the consciousness in people that they should respond to a scream or a call for help and that they should go to a woman's aid if it looks like she's being hassled.
3. We print the descriptions of men who rape, hassle, and assault women so

that rape will become a public issue, so that these men will lose their anonymity, and so women can be warned of some particular men.

4. We support confrontations of rapists by women (or women and men). The message we want to present to them is that we know who they are and what they did, that they are responsible for their actions, and that they have the responsibility to change. We try to offer follow-up reeducation by antisexist men. Although we think that each individual confrontation is important, we hope that each one will have the widespread effect of encouraging people to force men to stop violent and sexist behavior. This means that people have to deal with the men close to them— their family, friends, etc., as well as with strangers who hassle women.

A confrontation allows a woman who's been raped or hassled to be active and powerful in a situation in which it is safe for her to be so. She can make the decision about how a confrontation will take place and what she'd like to say. We help her get together a group of women who will be supportive to her during the process. This is very different from reporting a rape to the police where the woman's role is a passive one (as a witness for the state) and where others make decisions about her case for her. . . .

We realize that rape is not going to end by the creation of these few alternatives, that rape will only end with the development of a new system that provides a context for these changes in people's lives. We want to develop a movement that is working toward these changes. It is crucial for antirape groups not to focus on rape as an isolated issue to the exclusion of developing a broader analysis of the society as a whole.

1.A.8.

Daniel Tsang

"Third World Lesbians and Gays Meet" (1980)

The first national Third World Lesbian/Gay Conference was held immediately before the first March on Washington for Gay and Lesbian Rights on October 14, 1979. The conference, which was organized by the National Coalition of Black Lesbians and Gays in collaboration with other groups, drew LGBT people of color from around the United States as well as a small number from outside it. Tsang published this report about the conference in *Gay Insurgent*, a radical gay and lesbian newspaper.

Some five hundred Third World lesbians and gay men converged on the nation's capital the weekend of October 12–15 for the first national Third World Lesbian/Gay conference. The event was almost completely ignored by the corporate media, which missed a historic march October 14 by two hundred of the conferees from the conference site at Howard University to the center of Washington to join the full march on Washington.

The early morning march through the Black neighborhood and through Chinatown was the first time Black and Asian lesbians and gay men had paraded through our own neighborhoods. The mood of the marchers was jubilant, and the reaction from onlookers more surprise than hostility. The dozen or so Asian lesbians and gay men chanted "We're Asian, gay, and proud!" as the street signs turned Chinese at the edge of Chinatown. Many of the Asian marchers faced deportation for so visibly coming out as lesbian or gay, under a reactionary McCarthy period law which bars gay people from abroad from entering this country.

At noon the marchers joined with others forming the main March on Washington and marched as the Third World contingent, right behind the lesbians and handicapped gays who led off. The Third World marchers expressed pride in their gayness and solidarity with national liberation struggles abroad. Chants included "Third World revolution!" When the Latino delegation passed the building of the Organization of American States (OAS) it roared, in Spanish, "These are the people who take away our lands!" Heading the Third World contingent was a small group of Native Americans, holding a sign proclaiming "the first gay Americans."

The march culminated a weekend of intense discussion among Third World lesbians and gay men who attempted to reconcile being both people of color and lesbian or gay in a racist and homophobic society. Participants heard a moving address by keynote speaker Audre Lorde, Black feminist lesbian, and discussed racism and sexism in various workshops. Conferees late Saturday also heard solidarity statements from socialist compañeros from Mexico, who had somehow managed to avoid detection and enter the country.

Thunderous applause greeted a statement by Rodrigo Reyes, from the Gay Alliance of Latin Americans, who read the following statement from Ms. Aura L. Beteta, general counsel of Nicaragua in San Francisco: "To the first national conference of Third World lesbians and gay men, revolutionary Sandinista greetings. May from your conference be born a movement that identifies, that unites and struggles with the liberation movements of all oppressed people."

Conferees appeared moved as Tana Loy, a lesbian member of the newly formed Lesbian and Gay Asian Collective, shared what had happened among the Asian caucus at the conference. She described the tendency for many Asian Americans to avoid each other when they meet—"We run from each other, because of the pain, because of the anguish, because of the deep self hatred of racism in this country. It's a survival response, because for decades of imperialist wars, we have been atomic bombed, we have been napalmed, we have been raped, we have been driven to suicide—and we have built this country from the east to the west, and *we* have been called the barbarian." But at this conference, where many gay Asians met one another for the first time, "We have [. . .] run *toward* each other!"

The late evening sharing of support and solidarity culminated in a disco at the conference ballroom, where many white supporters, including gay poet Allen Ginsberg, joined in dancing with the Third World sisters and brothers present.

The high level of political awareness and militancy among the majority of conference participants suggests that the largely white-dominated gay movement, ten years after the uprising at the Stonewall Inn in New York, now faces a threshold in its history. The next decade may see an autonomous Third World lesbian and gay movement developing, one that seeks to challenge and fight against the racism and reformism in much of the existing gay movement.

1.A.9.

Joseph Beam

"Caring for Each Other" (1986)

In the early years of the AIDS epidemic, US government responses were minimal, alternating between neglect and punitive measures. Activists relied on each other to organize services and advocacy for people with HIV/AIDS. Due to inequities of health care, housing, drug criminalization, and poverty, the epidemic became disproportionately concentrated among Black and Latinx people. Yet most early AIDS organizations were white dominated and failed to organize in communities of color. This essay by Joseph Beam, a prominent Black gay writer and poet, reflects the community ethos and critique of state oppression that have been central to people of color AIDS activism. His essay also suggests the tensions that surround a rhetoric of community and personal responsibility given a context of neoliberal abandonment and neglect.

Some years ago when I was growing up in West Philadelphia there was a brother named Slim who was tall, lanky, and an alcoholic. Most often he could be found at the court on the avenue watching us play basketball. Every so often, no doubt inspired by his drink, he'd demand to play in our game. When refused he'd curse us and start swinging his half-full half-gallon jug. We'd stop the game. Some of us would rest, others would head for the water fountain, but usually two brothers would attempt to console Slim. Almost always, he, happy for the attention, would be escorted home and safely deposited on his front porch. It was never a thought to call the police or an alcohol rehabilitation center, where Slim had been many times. It was a matter of taking care of your own kind. Calling the Man would have introduced another variable, one which too often proved to be a wild card.

I say that to say this: the State (a euphemism for white people) has never been concerned with the welfare of Black people. So it comes as no surprise to me that the Philadelphia AIDS Task Force (PATF) has trouble getting AIDS information to North Philadelphia, that the New York City Gay Men's Health Crisis (GMHC) outreach doesn't quite make it to Harlem, or that the efforts of Washington, D.C.'s, Whitman-Walker Clinic (WWC) fail to extend east of the Anacostia River. It is not a matter of whether their racism is intentional or unintentional. We die "by accident" daily and the State is a witness who documents that demise. Poet Essex Hemphill writes in "For My Own Protection": *We should be able to save each other. / I don't want to wait for the Heritage Foundation to release a study saying / Black people are almost extinct [. . .]*

The current expectation of the Black community that the State would enter and mitigate our problems is a recent one. Thirty years ago we would not have had that expectation. The State, composed of suburbanites and people who have gentrified our neighborhoods, doesn't give a damn about Black gay men and IV drug users and it would be a fatal mistake if we were to relinquish our responsibility for AIDS in the Black community to such an external mechanism.

Our responsibility is twofold: we should continue holding a gun to the heads of PATF, GMHC, and the WWC until minority outreach coordinators are hired and specific programs are implemented. But concurrently we must insure our own safety and administer to our own sick. A Black gay brother, hospitalized in Philadelphia, remains there because he has no place to go. It doesn't require an organizational structure or government funding to provide a home for him. I don't understand he was always quite popular in the bars. In the neighborhood we *know* the brothers who like to freak sometimes. We *know* the brothers who shoot dope. In other words, we *know* who we fuck with our and lives depend upon *us* relaying the necessary information about sexual health concerns. If I can drop at least $10 to get into Catacombs, Paradise Garage, or the Clubhouse, I can spend $2 to buy a condom to save my life and yours. If I can leaf through *Ebony Men* for fashion tips, I can locate information about the methods of safer sex. It's a matter of priorities. For surely while I dress to cavort with my living friends over cocktails, the State is busy taking care of the State and maintaining the current state of affairs. We would be most wise to do likewise or our prospects for survival are slim. Black men loving Black men is the revolutionary act of the 80s. So I say to you: what have you done for us lately?

1.A.10.

AIDS Action Pledge

"AIDS Action Pledge" (1987)

The AIDS Action Pledge formed in San Francisco in the fall of 1986, predating the better-known ACT UP (AIDS Coalition to Unleash Power) by several months. It drew inspiration and structure from the Pledge of Resistance, an antimilitarist organization that mobilized thousands to oppose US intervention in Central America.

We believe that the AIDS crisis calls for a broad movement actively engaged in ending the epidemic. We recognize that AIDS has had a devastating impact on the lesbian and gay community. We further recognize that the AIDS crisis disproportionately affects men and women of color. Any strategies to fight the crisis must incorporate these understandings.

Therefore, we join together to demand:

1. *Massive funding to end the AIDS epidemic,* made available from local, state, and federal governments for research, care, education, anonymous testing programs and any and all treatments.
2. *A federally funded education program* which is comprehensive and sex positive and which promotes safer sex, addiction recovery, and IV hygiene.
3. *Centrally coordinated research* for AIDS treatments, cures and vaccines.
4. *A free, nationalized health care system* guaranteeing equal access, regardless of ability to pay.
5. *Public accountability,* especially to affected communities, regarding any AIDS-related research, funding, and programs, to be controlled by the communities affected by AIDS.
6. *A worldwide, culturally sensitive funding program* focused on ending the AIDS epidemic. The program would be initiated and financed by the United States, in cooperation with international health organizations. The US would encourage the financial participation of other developed nations, with implementation controlled by the recipient nations.

We further join together to oppose:

1. *Quarantine or mandatory testing for HIV exposure* or any coercive, involuntary, or routine measures instituted against any population or individual anywhere.
2. *Discriminatory measures instituted by public or private organizations against any groups or individuals with AIDS or ARC [AIDS-related complex] or who test positive for HIV exposure.* We also oppose any measures against any groups or individuals suspected of HIV-positive status or targeted for discrimination, such as people of color; gay men; women; bisexuals; IV-drug users; prostitutes; prisoners; mental health patients; hemophiliacs; undocumented workers and immigrants; children and youth; or others.
3. *All laws that contribute to the spread of AIDS or discrimination* by invading our right to privacy, such as laws against sodomy and prostitution.
4. *Spending cuts in any social service or health programs* in order to create or increase funding to fight AIDS. Funding must be taken primarily from the military budget.
5. *The use of inflammatory, isolating language* which promotes medical misinformation, fear, and discrimination, such as "AIDS virus," "AIDS test," "AIDS carrier," "AIDS blood," or "AIDS victim."

    I pledge to join with others in fighting for all our lives and liberties during the AIDS crisis. I pledge to participate in forms of protest such as educating, organizing, lobbying, marching, and picketing.

I also pledge to engage, as conscience directs me, in nonviolent direct action, including civil disobedience.

OR: I also pledge to demonstrate, as conscience directs me, my support for those who engage in nonviolent direct action, including civil disobedience.

1.A.11.

Vito Russo

"Why We Fight" (1988)

Vito Russo was a gay and AIDS activist as well as a film historian who examined LGBTQ representation on screen. He gave the following speech at an ACT UP (AIDS Coalition to Unleash Power) demonstration in Albany, New York, on May 9, 1988.

A friend of mine in New York City has a half-fare transit card, which means that you get on buses and subways for half price. And the other day, when he showed his card to the token attendant, the attendant asked what his disability was and he said, I have AIDS. And the attendant said, no you don't, if you had AIDS, you'd be home dying. And so, I wanted to speak out today as a person with AIDS who is not dying.

You know, for the last three years, since I was diagnosed, my family thinks two things about my situation. One, they think I'm going to die, and two, they think that my government is doing absolutely everything in their power to stop that. And they're wrong, on both counts.

So, if I'm dying from anything, I'm dying from homophobia. If I'm dying from anything, I'm dying from racism. If I'm dying from anything, it's from indifference and red tape, because these are the things that are preventing an end to this crisis. If I'm dying from anything, I'm dying from Jesse Helms. If I'm dying from anything, I'm dying from the president of the United States. And, especially, if I'm dying from anything, I'm dying from the sensationalism of newspapers and magazines and television shows, which are interested in me as a human interest story—only as long as I'm willing to be a helpless victim, but not if I'm fighting for my life.

If I'm dying from anything, I'm dying from the fact that not enough rich, white, heterosexual men have gotten AIDS for anybody to give a shit. You know, living with AIDS in this country is like living in the twilight zone. Living with AIDS is like living through a war which is happening only for those people who happen to be in the trenches. Every time a shell explodes, you look around and you discover that you've lost more of your friends, but nobody else notices. It isn't happening to them. They're walking the streets as though we weren't living through some sort of nightmare. And only you can hear the screams of the people who are dying and their cries for help. No one else seems to be noticing.

And it's worse than a war, because during a war people are united in a shared experience. This war has not united us, it's divided us. It's separated those of us with AIDS and those of us who fight for people with AIDS from the rest of the population.

Two and a half years ago, I picked up *Life* magazine, and I read an editorial which said, "It's time to pay attention, because this disease is now beginning to strike the rest of us." It was as if I wasn't the one holding the magazine in my hand. And since then, nothing has changed to alter the perception that AIDS is not happening to the real people in this country.

It's not happening to us in the United States, it's happening to them—to the disposable populations of fags and junkies who deserve what they get. The media tells them that they don't have to care, because the people who really matter are not in danger. Twice, three times, four times, the *New York Times* has published editorials saying, don't panic yet over AIDS—it still hasn't entered the general population, and until it does, we don't have to give a shit.

And the days, and the months, and the years pass by, and they don't spend those days and nights and months and years trying to figure out how to get hold of the latest experimental drug, and which dose to take it at, and in what combination with other drugs, and from what source. And how are you going to pay for it? And where are you going to get it? Because it isn't happening to them, so they don't give a shit.

And they don't sit in television studios, surrounded by technicians who are wearing rubber gloves, who won't put a microphone on you, because it isn't happening to them, so they don't give a shit. And they don't have their houses burned down by bigots and morons. They watch it on the news and they have dinner and they go to bed, because it isn't happening to them, and they don't give a shit.

And they don't spend their waking hours going from hospital room to hospital room and watching the people that they love die slowly of neglect and bigotry, because it isn't happening to them, and they don't have to give a shit. They haven't been to two funerals a week for the last three or four or five years— so they don't give a shit, because it's not happening to them.

And we read on the front page of the *New York Times* last Saturday that Anthony Fauci now says that all sorts of promising drugs for treatment haven't even been tested in the last two years because he can't afford to hire the people to test them. We're supposed to be grateful that this story has appeared in the newspaper after two years. Nobody wonders why some reporter didn't dig up that story and print it eighteen months ago, before Fauci got dragged before a congressional hearing.

How many people are dead in the last two years who might be alive today if those drugs had been tested more quickly? Reporters all over the country are busy printing government press releases. They don't give a shit, it isn't happening to them, meaning that it isn't happening to people like them—the real people, the world-famous general public we all keep hearing about.

Legionnaire's disease was happening to them because it hit people who looked like them, who sounded like them, who were the same color as them. And that fucking story about a couple of dozen people hit the front page of every newspaper and magazine in this country, and it stayed there until that mystery got solved.

All I read in the newspapers tells me that the mainstream, white heterosexual population is not at risk for this disease. All the newspapers I read tell me that IV drug users and homosexuals still account for the overwhelming majority of cases, and a majority of those people at risk.

And can somebody please tell me why every single penny allocated for education and prevention gets spent on ad campaigns that are directed almost exclusively to white, heterosexual teenagers—who they keep telling us are not at risk!

Can somebody tell me why the only television movie ever produced by a major network in this country about the impact of this disease is not about the impact of this disease on the man who has AIDS but of the impact of AIDS on his white, straight, nuclear family? Why, for eight years, every newspaper and magazine in this country has done cover stories on AIDS only when the threat of heterosexual transmission is raised?

Why, for eight years, every single educational film designed for use in high schools has eliminated any gay positive material, before being approved by the board of education? Why, for eight years, every single public information pamphlet and videotape distributed by establishment sources has ignored specific homosexual content?

Why is every bus and subway ad I read and every advertisement and every billboard I see in this country specifically not directed at gay men? Don't believe the lie that the gay community has done its job and done it well and educated its people. The gay community and IV drug users are not all politicized people living in New York and San Francisco. Members of minority populations, including so called sophisticated gay men, are abysmally ignorant about AIDS.

If it is true that gay men and IV drug users are the populations at risk for this disease, then we have a right to demand that education and prevention be targeted specifically to these people. And it is not happening. We are being allowed to die, while low-risk populations are being panicked—not educated, panicked—into believing that we deserve to die.

Why are we here together today? We're here because it is happening to us, and we do give a shit. And if there were more of us AIDS wouldn't be what it is at this moment in history. It's more than just a disease, which ignorant people have turned into an excuse to exercise the bigotry they have always felt.

It is more than a horror story, exploited by the tabloids. AIDS is really a test of us as a people. When future generations ask what we did in this crisis, we're going to have to tell them that we were out here today. And we have to leave the legacy to those generations of people who will come after us.

Someday, the AIDS crisis will be over. Remember that. And when that day comes—when that day has come and gone—there'll be people alive on this earth, gay people and straight people, men and women, black and white, who will hear the story that once there was a terrible disease in this country and all over the world, and that a brave group of people stood up and fought and in some cases gave their lives, so that other people might live and be free.

So, I'm proud to be with my friends today and the people I love, because I think you're all heroes, and I'm glad to be part of this fight. But, to borrow a phrase from Michael Callen's song: all we have is love right now, what we don't have is time.

In a lot of ways, AIDS activists are like those doctors out there—they're so busy putting out fires and taking care of people on respirators that they don't have the time to take care of all the sick people. We're so busy putting out fires right now that we don't have the time to talk to each other and strategize and plan for the next wave, and the next day, and next month, and the next week, and the next year.

And we're going to have to find the time to do that in the next few months. And we have to commit ourselves to doing that. And then, after we kick the shit out of this disease, we're all going to be alive to kick the shit out of this system, so that this never happens again.

Video Activism, AIDS, and New Queer Cinema
Jih-Fei Cheng

In 1992, a group of AIDS video activists called the Testing the Limits Collective created the documentary film *Voices from the Front*. The film demonstrates the protracted struggles of AIDS activists who transformed the initial goal of drug research and treatment into a more radical dream: health care not warfare. The documentary featured footage from the January 23, 1991, "Day of Desperation," an AIDS protest held in New York City during the First Gulf War. Protestors held signs reading "Money for AIDS not War" and "ACT UP, Fight Back, Fight AIDS, Not Iraq." Interviewees discussed the need to address the impact of AIDS on women of color and how the lack of AIDS resources related to the closing of hospitals in communities of color, the rising housing crisis, xenophobia, and the savings and loan scandal. Theirs was a broad vision. Demonstrators could be seen wearing keffiyeh scarves to underscore their solidarity with Palestinians and others living under Israeli occupation.

As Alexandra Juhasz contends, AIDS activists constituted the first US social movement to heavily involve the video camcorder in protests, public debates, and radical organizing. Both institutionally trained artists and community-based collectives participated, with efforts tied to organizations including ACT UP (AIDS Coalition to Unleash Power). Video activists utilized camcorders to gain access to areas designated for the press only, to challenge lies and stigma perpetuated by politicians and mainstream media, to document police brutality, and to physically shield protestors from the words and weapons of hecklers and police. They distributed their VHS tapes by hand, mail, and community-based screenings, sharing the videos in intimate and explicitly politicizing contexts.

The strategies and techniques of AIDS video activism drew from the preceding Third World, feminist, Black, and Native film movements. Video collectives included artist-activists working across mediums and platforms who had postmodern aesthetic and political sensibilities. For instance, the "SILENCE = DEATH" poster became a preeminent logo of the AIDS movement. It was designed by what became the Gran Fury collective. Its political significations were crucial to AIDS art, as performed by Julie Tolentino and Ron Athey. The 1980s and 1990s also saw the pivotal experimental videos of Marlon Riggs, the queer, Black, and HIV-positive filmmaker of titles including *Tongues United* (1989) and *Black Is . . . Black Ain't* (1994). AIDS video activism became fundamental to independent filmmaking, especially to what B. Ruby Rich has dubbed the "new queer cinema."

Video activist collectives were key to the AIDS movement. The feminist and queer Damn Interfering Video Activists, or DIVA TV, was an affinity group of ACT UP that was also fiercely independent and employed what two of its participants called "guerilla video" tactics. Video collectives were involved in everything from direct action to caregiving, as Debra Levine has shown; this included continuing the projects of artist-activists who grew too sick. Today, we can witness such radical activism through footage held in personal and public archives, including the New York Public Library, and adapted into documentary films such as *United In Anger* (2011), about New York ACT UP and its fight against AIDS profiteering, and *How to Survive a Plague* (2012), which focuses on struggles to expand research and treatment. In short, AIDS video activists made possible the varying, sometimes contradictory, audiovisual memories of AIDS activism, including ACT UP.

AIDS activists' early uses of the camcorder helped set the stage for contemporary media activism. Today's handheld smartphone has been a crucial tool for organizing social movements, including #BlackLivesMatter and the Boycott Divestment and Sanctions movement to end Israeli apartheid. When activists record acts of racism and police and military brutality against Black, Brown, Palestinian, and other minoritarian subjects and when they disseminate this evidence through digital platforms, they win greater public witness--even at the risk of desensitizing viewers or causing further trauma. As AIDS video activism shows, video becomes a radical tool when deployed by antiracist, feminist, and queer activists whose approaches are intersectional and coalitional and who have their sights set on revolution rather than piecemeal reform.

ACT UP/Golden Gate

From "Say It!! Women Get AIDS" (1991)

ACT UP (AIDS Coalition to Unleash Power) formed in New York City in March 1987 to seek effective federal and state responses to the AIDS epidemic. ACT UP groups soon proliferated around and even outside the United States. Nationally, one of ACT UP's many campaigns a demand that the Centers for Disease Control, or CDC, expand its definition of AIDS to better recognize and address AIDS in (cis) women, IV drug users, and people in poverty. ACT UP/Golden Gate, which organized in San Francisco, participated in the campaign against the CDC and produced the following document. Activists finally won an expanded CDC definition of AIDS in 1992, and it was put into effect at the start of 1993.

It is estimated that 1.5 million people in the United States are infected with HIV. Because of the long incubation period of the disease, the number of AIDS cases is expected to rise dramatically over the next few years. It is estimated that in 1992, 40 percent of newly reported cases of AIDS will be in women. In New York, AIDS is the leading cause of death for women of childbearing age.

Epidemiologists have been charting the demographic shift of the epidemic toward women, Hispanics, and blacks for several years. Women are among the fastest growing groups of newly infected persons with HIV in the United States. Women are also the most misdiagnosed, underdiagnosed, and underserved population in the AIDS pandemic.

The AIDS Coalition to Unleash Power, ACT UP/Golden Gate's demands to the CDC to improve the lives of women with HIV are:

- that the Center[s] for Disease Control (CDC) redefine AIDS to include diseases which are HIV related and are specific to women,
- that the CDC publish a comprehensive document on the natural history of HIV in women, [and]
- that the CDC revoke guidelines to physicians recommending abortion for HIV+ women and instead establish a standard of care which counsels women on transmission risk but does not advise or coerce abortion.

Of the issues confronting women with HIV, the most serious is the CDC's classifications for AIDS. The Center[s] for Disease Control (CDC) is a clearinghouse of information for diseases and epidemics. It tracks the epidemiology of diseases, manifestation, and demographics and defines diseases based on this information. A case of AIDS is defined as an illness characterized by one or more opportunistic infections depending upon the status of laboratory evidence of HIV infection. The definition of AIDS that the CDC recognizes does not include life-threatening and debilitating illnesses which are specific to women. Pelvic inflammatory disease (PID), chronic candidiasis, chlamydia, and human papillomavirus (HPV) are a few of the manifestations of HIV which are specific to women. Many HIV+ die of complications from these opportunistic infections without ever receiving an AIDS diagnosis, as these illnesses are not classified as AIDS defining. Because the CDC does not recognize women-specific opportunistic infections, women are not accurately represented in national statistics on AIDS. If a woman dies of PID or HPV, even though she is HIV+, her death is not registered as an AIDS death.

50 percent of women infected with the AIDS virus in San Francisco have been HOMELESS at some point during their HIV+ status. An AIDS diagnosis is important to make one eligible for social security benefits and other funding which is available for people with life-threatening illnesses. A diagnosis of PID does not make a woman eligible even for disability insurance, though it is often severe and requires long hospitalizations and frequent surgery when manifested in women with HIV infection. Federal, state, and local governments extend social security and medical benefits, including housing, only to those with CDC-defined AIDS and in some cases AIDS-related complex (ARC). It is apparent that the CDC classification for AIDS plays a direct role in the limited funding currently available to women with HIV. Women with life-threatening and severely debilitating illnesses do not have access to funding due to the lack of a formal AIDS diagnosis. This is wrong. Financial and material assistance must be provided to women with HIV disease.

To improve the lives of women with HIV the CDC must produce a comprehensive document on the natural history of HIV disease. We have known about AIDS for ten years, women have been getting AIDS for ten years, yet still very little is known about the manifestations of HIV in women. A natural history of the epidemic in women would provide a basis for treatment research areas to be established.

The CDC has given guidelines to physicians that pregnant women with HIV should be encouraged to have abortions. If a woman is HIV+ yet asymptomatic, the likelihood of her child being HIV+ is less than 25 percent. If a woman is symptomatic, this vertical infection rate increases. If she is showing positive P24 antigens, an indicator of viral activity, transmission rate increases much higher. Transmission rate from mother to fetus is about 30 percent. There is no substantial evidence that AIDS progresses more rapidly with pregnancy. Still, women are being encouraged and often coerced to abort pregnancy even though chances are quite good that [their] child will not be infected with HIV. *Women should be counseled on the risk of HIV infection to [their] child during pregnancy but [they] should not be advised, coerced, or persuaded in [their] decision on whether or not to carry a pregnancy to term. Proper education must be made available to women.*

Access to health care treatment and education for women is a broad social problem that is not limited to the AIDS pandemic. When these social problems meet the AIDS pandemic, however, the result is fatal. The issues which confront women with HIV infection are broad and varied. There are cultural issues of access to health care which confront women of color, who are the highest population of women

Figure 1.1. ACT UP, "Clean Needles Save Lives/Needle Exchange Now!" / "Una Aguja Limpia Salva Vidas/¡Intercambio de Agujas Ya!" (circa 1990). Image courtesy of ACT UP New York records, Manuscripts and Archives Division, New York Public Library.

currently affected by the AIDS pandemic. There are issues of cultural differences and religious imperatives which hinder access to information to Latina women. There is a profound lack of information on woman-to-woman transmission of the virus, though there are reported cases of lesbian transmission. There are social conceptions that women are vectors of disease, and there is a tendency to treat a fetus rather than a woman. These issues are no less significant than any other issue. The average life span for white men from the day of AIDS diagnosis to death is twenty-four to thirty-six months. The average life span for women from diagnosis to death is fifteen weeks to six months. The average life span for a black woman in New York from diagnosis to death is approximately fifteen days.

The most important issue facing women with HIV infection, however, is the CDC classifications for AIDS. SAY IT!! WOMEN GET AIDS. Unless AIDS in women is recognized and researched more extensively, it is virtually impossible to start to deal with the other issues which confront women with HIV. Women are invisible in the AIDS pandemic. This is wrong. Women get AIDS. Women die from AIDS. Women are being ignored in this pandemic. Effective treatment for women with AIDS cannot be fully established until the CDC acknowledges and reports on how women are being affected by HIV.

1.A.13.

Transgender Nation

Letter to the editor (1992)

Transgender Nation, one of the most important groups in an upsurge of trans activism in the early 1990s, formed in the context of queer antiwar and AIDS organizing. In addition to confronting antitrans hostility in lesbian and gay communities and the broader society, it protested treatment by the psychiatric profession, provided courtroom support to trans sex workers, and joined coalitions against police abuse and for needle exchange. Members of Transgender Nation published their founding statement as a letter to the editor in the *Bay Times*, an LGBT community newspaper in San Francisco.

On October 8, at the first meeting of the newly reorganized Queer Nation, Transgender Nation was formed. By a unanimous vote of the more than sixty-five people present, Queer Nation recognized us as a focus group within Queer Nation. Our purpose is to specifically fight for transgender rights within the general struggle for queer rights.

We felt the need to educate the queer community about transgender issues, as well as the struggle against transgender phobia in the straight community. Transgender people are dying from queer bashing, lack of access to health care, and the medical colonization of the transgender community by nontransgendered people, as well as the lack of human rights for transgendered people.

As a focus group within Queer Nation, we support queer rights in general and specifically promote transgender rights. We are absolutely opposed to homophobia and genderphobia in all manifestations, such as the domination of male-to-female transgender people at the expense of our female-to-male brothers, racism, sexism, and union busting.

We invite anybody interested to join us at the Queer Nation meeting at the Women's Building, 3543 18th St., between Valencia and Guerrero, Wednesday nights at 7:30 p.m.

> Anne Ogborn, Christine Tayleur, Dawn Marie Holland,
> Crystal Erwin, Kevin Horowitz, Susan Stryker

1.A.14.

Call Off Your Old Tired Ethics

Brochure (1993)

The sex workers' organization Call Off Your Old Tired Ethics (COYOTE) advocates for the decriminalization of prostitution. Founded in 1973, it gained renewed energy with projects such as the HIV/AIDS effort CAL-PEP, or California Prostitutes Education Project. COYOTE's influence helped to fuel a broader resurgence of sex worker organizing from the 1990s forward.

COYOTE is a sex workers' rights and education organization, based in San Francisco. Margo St. James founded COYOTE in 1973 to work for the repeal of prostitution laws from the perspective of the women and men who work as prostitutes. Today COYOTE works for the rights of all sex workers: strippers, phone operators, models, porn stars, escorts, etc., of all genders and persuasions.

Other groups developed across America, including: HIRE (Hooking Is Real Employment) started by Dolores French in Atlanta, Georgia, PONY (Prostitutes of New York), [and] COYOTE-Los Angeles, founded by Norma Jean Almodovar (the former LAPD traffic officer turned call girl).

During the founding years of COYOTE, Margo joined with feminist leader Priscilla Alexander and prostitute/activist Gloria Lockett. They formed the National Task Force on Prostitution and later the International Committee on Prostitute's Rights (ICPR), aligning with the prostitute movement in Europe.

In the mid-80s, Margo moved to France. Priscilla and Gloria kept the group alive and started California Prostitutes Education Project (CAL-PEP) in response to the scapegoating of sex workers for the supposed spread of AIDS. Priscilla left COYOTE in 1986 to work for the World Health Organization in Switzerland. Since then Gloria has kept the COYOTE flame alive while developing CAL-PEP into an internationally known AIDS education program. In 1991 Samantha Miller, counselor/sex educator, joined forces with Gloria and infused new life into COYOTE.

Our Goals

COYOTE'S ultimate goal is to decriminalize prostitution. Legalization, as opposed to decriminalization, requires government regulation. Decriminalization means the repeal of all criminal codes regarding voluntary prostitution, removing the existing prohibition against consenting adult activity, and allowing sex workers complete autonomy.

COYOTE believes that no voluntary aspects of sex work should be a crime, including relationships between prostitutes and third-party managers (pimping and pandering), renting a premise for the purposes of sex work, residing in a place where sex work occurs, etc.

COYOTE's primary goal at this time is to provide an educational and support network to raise the overall self-esteem of women and men in the sex industry.

COYOTE seeks to end the stigma surrounding sex work. Prostitution is a time honored and historically valued profession. Sex work in all its variations is a valid occupational choice for women and men.

COYOTE intends to create an open dialogue about the myths and realities of sex work. Accurate and accessible information is needed to address the misconceptions and stereotypes of sex work.

What We're Doing

- We are providing monthly outreach meetings and support groups, safer sex workshops, educational panels, guest speakers, social gatherings, house parties, special events; in settings where sex workers feel safe to attend and actively participate.
- We circulate a monthly publication.
- Our steering committee meets twice a month to plan future strategies and check progress.
- The NOW Task Force on Sex Work and Pornography and COYOTE are working together to present sex-positive educational panels to the public. We provide speakers to community programs, universities, conferences, selected media, etc.
- We maintain a phone line to answer questions from sex workers and the general public. We are a resource for accurate information about sex work.
- COYOTE sponsors fundraising events that are entertaining and educational. We plan to revive the Hooker's Ball.
- COYOTE promotes safer sex education at all of our events.
- We network and share information with other sex workers' organizations throughout the United States and the World.

Gloria Lockett and Samantha Miller share codirectorship of COYOTE.

The Formation of Queers for Economic Justice
Joseph Nicholas DeFilippis

In the mid-1990s, a number of LGBT activists in New York City were working to resist President Clinton's attempts to reform welfare. Many elements of his proposal—abstinence-only sex education, marriage promotion, fatherhood initiatives, and charitable choice programs—had significant implications for LGBT people, especially for those who were low income. Welfare reform, which became law in 1996, harmed the disproportionately large percentage of queer people living in poverty. It also harmed LGBT people of all classes given its overarching concern with ending "illegitimate families." Yet the national LGBT organizations, led predominantly by wealthy white men and focused on a limited set of narrowly defined "gay issues," did not address poverty or speak out against welfare reform. Frustrated with this, in 1999 progressive activists at a number of New York LGBT organizations came together with queer staff members at antipoverty organizations to form the Queer Economic Justice Network (QEJN).

Working together under the umbrella of QEJN, activists started making connections between queer communities and poverty issues.

The network brought together economic justice and LGBT organizations, allowing them to exchange information and to engage in advocacy and public education about how LGBT people were impacted by
welfare reform, homelessness, the Bush administration's war on terror,
the homeless shelter system, and New York's drug laws. Early activities
included community forums, town-hall meetings, and grassroots lobbying in the state capital.

QEJN had an immediate impact. The gay press published several
articles about QEJN's community forums on welfare reform, for example, and the coverage allowed progressive staff to frame poverty and
welfare as "gay" issues among colleagues, clients, and board members. Gradually more mainstream LGBT organizations began to discuss
the issues. For instance, with the help of QEJN, the National Gay and
Lesbian Task Force released a one-hundred-page publication analyzing
the impact of welfare reform on LGBT communities. This in turn generated further press and dialogue.

After three years, members of QEJN decided it was time to build an
organization that could concentrate on these issues full time, with a
mission, resources, and staff centered on the needs of LGBT people in
poverty. In the spring of 2002, after reaching out to more grassroots
organizers and more poor LGBT activists, planning for this new organization began.

A group of multiracial, multigendered, and multiclassed activists
strategized for a year. They identified the organization's priority issues
to be welfare reform, immigration, and homelessness. However, they
also identified the connections between these issues and other social
justice issues, including health care, prison reform, labor and employment, sex work, education, US imperialism, and sexual liberation. They
decided that the new organization would start small and local with
programs focused on welfare and homelessness but that it would keep
broader goals in mind as part of its long-term strategy.

In spring 2003, Queers for Economic Justice (QEJ) was born. Its
board members, staff, and volunteers were multiracial and from all
economic classes, ranging from homeless shelter residents to wealthy
allies. For the next eleven years, QEJ worked with shelter residents,
with people on public assistance, and with immigrants, providing
direct services, public education, and leadership development and
engaging in advocacy and community organizing. Its coalition-based
advocacy work succeeded in overturning several New York policies,
including one that denied transgender people access to homeless shelters. In another victory, QEJ won an expansion in New York City's definition of "domestic partnerships," which enabled many more people to access aid and services. QEJ's organizing built a community of
low-income queer people who worked together for both survival support and structural change. Because of its successful work at the local
level, QEJ became known nationally and began to have an impact on
national LGBT politics. It was invited to offer leadership development

in many cities. It also drew on its coalition origins to form a "Building a Queer Left" alliance of progressive queer organizations across the country.

When funding problems forced QEJ to close its doors in 2014, it left behind a legacy of radical intersectional multi-issue activism. QEJ illustrated the effectiveness of multiracial, multiclassed organizing and challenged assumptions of what constitutes a "gay issue."

1.A.15.

Critical Resistance and INCITE! Women of Color against Violence

From "Gender Violence and the Prison-Industrial Complex" (2001)

By the turn of the twenty-first century, the United States had the world's biggest prison system. Some of the policies that had bolstered support for mass incarceration originated in ostensibly feminist demands, such as the 1994 Violence against Women Act. In response, two high-profile prison abolitionist organizations that formed at the end of the millennium coauthored the following statement, which describes prison as a form of both state and interpersonal violence and demands a noncarceral approach to gender violence.

We call on social justice movements to develop strategies and analysis that address both state and interpersonal violence, particularly violence against women. Currently, activists/movements that address state violence (such as antiprison, anti–police brutality groups) often work in isolation from activists/movements that address domestic and sexual violence. The result is that women of color, who suffer disproportionately from both state and interpersonal violence, have become marginalized within these movements. It is critical that we develop responses to gender violence that do not depend on a sexist, racist, classist, and homophobic criminal justice system. It is also important that we develop strategies that challenge the criminal justice system and that also provide safety for survivors of sexual and domestic violence. To live violence-free lives, we must develop holistic strategies for addressing violence that speak to the intersection of all forms of oppression. The antiviolence movement has been critically important in breaking the silence around violence against women and providing much-needed services to survivors. However, the mainstream antiviolence movement has increasingly relied on the criminal justice system as the frontline approach toward ending violence against women of color. It is important to assess the impact of this strategy.

1. Law enforcement approaches to violence against women may deter some acts of violence in the short term. However, as an overall strategy for ending violence, criminalization has not worked. In fact, the overall impact of mandatory arrests laws for domestic violence has led to decreases in the number of battered women who kill their partners in self-defense, but they have not led to a decrease in the number of batterers who kill their partners. Thus, the law protects batterers more than it protects survivors.

2. The criminalization approach has also brought many women into conflict with the law, particularly women of color, poor women, lesbians, sex workers, immigrant women, women with disabilities, and other marginalized women. For instance, under mandatory arrest laws, there have been numerous incidents where police officers called to domestic incidents have arrested the woman who is being battered. Many undocumented women have reported cases of sexual and domestic violence, only to find themselves deported. A tough law and order agenda also leads to long punitive sentences for women convicted of killing their batterers. Finally, when public funding is channeled into policing and prisons, budget cuts for social programs, including women's shelters, welfare and public housing are the inevitable side effect. These cutbacks leave women less able to escape violent relationships.

3. Prisons don't work. Despite an exponential increase in the number of men in prisons, women are not any safer, and the rates of sexual assault and domestic violence have not decreased. In calling for greater police responses to and harsher sentences for perpetrators of gender violence, the antiviolence movement has fueled the proliferation of prisons which now lock up more people per capita in the US than any other country. During the past fifteen years, the numbers of women, especially women of color, in prison has skyrocketed. Prisons also inflict violence on the growing numbers of women behind bars. Slashing, suicide, the proliferation of HIV, strip searches, medical neglect, and rape of prisoners has largely been ignored by antiviolence activists. The criminal justice system, an institution of violence, domination, and control, has increased the level of violence in society.

4. The reliance on state funding to support antiviolence programs has increased the professionalization of the antiviolence movement and alienated it from its community-organizing, social justice roots. Such reliance has isolated the antiviolence movement from other social justice movements that seek to eradicate state violence, such that it acts in conflict rather than in collaboration with these movements.

5. The reliance on the criminal justice system has taken power away from women's ability to organize collectively to stop violence and has invested this power within the state. The result is that women who seek redress in the criminal justice system feel disempowered and alienated. It has also promoted an individualistic approach toward ending violence such that the only way people think they can intervene in stopping violence is to

call the police. This reliance has shifted our focus from developing ways communities can collectively respond to violence.

. . . Because activists who seek to reverse the tide of mass incarceration and criminalization of poor communities and communities of color have not always centered gender and sexuality in their analysis or organizing, we have not always responded adequately to the needs of survivors of domestic and sexual violence.

1. Prison and police accountability activists have generally organized around and conceptualized men of color as the primary victims of state violence. Women prisoners and victims of police brutality have been made invisible by a focus on the war on our brothers and sons. . . .
2. The antiprison movement has not addressed strategies for addressing the rampant forms of violence women face in their everyday lives, including street harassment, sexual harassment at work, rape, and intimate partner abuse. . . .
3. The antiprison movement has failed to sufficiently organize around the forms of state violence faced by LGBTI communities. LGBTI street youth and trans people in general are particularly vulnerable to police brutality and criminalization. LGBTI prisoners are denied basic human rights such as family visits from same-sex partners, and same-sex consensual relationships in prison are policed and punished.
4. While prison abolitionists have correctly pointed out that rapists and serial murderers comprise a small number of the prison population, we have not answered the question of how these cases should be addressed. The inability to answer the question is interpreted by many antiviolence activists as a lack of concern for the safety of women.
5. The various alternatives to incarceration that have been developed by antiprison activists have generally failed to provide sufficient mechanisms for safety and accountability for survivors of sexual and domestic violence. These alternatives often rely on a romanticized notion of communities, which have yet to demonstrate their commitment and ability to keep women and children safe or seriously address the sexism and homophobia that is deeply embedded within them.

We call on social justice movements concerned with ending violence in all its forms to [do the following]:

1. Develop community-based responses to violence that do not rely on the criminal justice system and which have mechanisms that ensure safety and accountability for survivors of sexual and domestic violence. Transformative practices emerging from local communities should be documented and disseminated to promote collective responses to violence.
2. Critically assess the impact of state funding on social justice organizations and develop alternative fundraising strategies to support these organizations. . . .

3. Make connections between interpersonal violence, the violence inflicted by domestic state institutions (such as prisons, detention centers, mental hospitals, and child protective services), and international violence (such as war, military base prostitution, and nuclear testing).

4. Develop an analysis and strategies to end violence that do not isolate individual acts of violence (either committed by the state or individuals) from their larger contexts. These strategies must address how entire communities of all genders are affected in multiple ways by both state violence and interpersonal gender violence. Battered women prisoners represent an intersection of state and interpersonal violence and as such provide an opportunity for both movements to build coalitions and joint struggles.

5. Put poor/working-class women of color in the center of their analysis, organizing practices, and leadership development. Recognize the role of economic oppression, welfare "reform," and attacks on women workers' rights in increasing women's vulnerability to all forms of violence and locate antiviolence and antiprison activism alongside efforts to transform the capitalist economic system.

6. Center stories of state violence committed against women of color in our organizing efforts.

7. Oppose legislative change that promotes prison expansion, criminalization of poor communities, and [criminalization of] communities of color and thus state violence against women of color, even if these changes also incorporate measures to support victims of interpersonal gender violence.

8. Promote holistic political education at the everyday level within our communities, specifically how sexual violence helps reproduce the colonial, racist, capitalist, heterosexist, and patriarchal society we live in as well as how state violence produces interpersonal violence within communities.

9. Develop strategies for mobilizing against sexism and homophobia within our communities in order to keep women safe.

10. Challenge men of color and all men in social justice movements to take particular responsibility to address and organize around gender violence in their communities as a primary strategy for addressing violence and colonialism. We challenge men to address how their own histories of victimization have hindered their ability to establish gender justice in their communities.

11. Link struggles for personal transformation and healing with struggles for social justice.

We seek to build movements that not only end violence, but that create a society based on radical freedom, mutual accountability, and passionate reciprocity. In this society, safety and security will not be premised on violence or the threat of violence; it will be based on a collective commitment to guaranteeing the survival and care of all peoples.

Fighting the Right

1.B.1.

Ellen Shaffer

From "*Bakke*: Fighting and Winning Together" (1977)

Allan Bakke was a white man who had twice been denied acceptance to medical school at the University of California, Davis. He brought a lawsuit against the University of California, claiming that its affirmative action policies were the reason he had not been admitted. In 1976, the California Supreme Court ruled in favor of Bakke and overturned affirmative action. The case went to the US Supreme Court, which upheld affirmative action in general but struck down quotas (*Regents v. Bakke*, 1978). The *Bakke* case generated significant protest in defense of affirmative action, propelled by coalitions between labor, feminist, and racial justice activists. The following speech was given at a rally to overturn the California *Bakke* decision, held at the University of California San Francisco's School of Medicine, and was then published in the socialist-feminist newspaper *Union WAGE*.

Local 1650 of AFSCME (American Federation of State, County, and Municipal Employees) supports the struggle to defend affirmative action here at the medical school largely because we, as UC [University of California] employees, need affirmative action and we know that the Bakke decision is already affecting programs for employees. . . .

One Way of Winning

The conditions that are making our lives hard affect all poor and working people, white and Third World, women and men, and only by fighting and winning together can we change them. The union is one expression of our collective efforts, fighting and winning grievances. A recent example is the grievance fought by a laundry worker who was transferred from her job of four years, where she could do her work sitting down, to a job where she had to stand although it caused her severe pain. She couldn't get her old job back because her supervisor didn't like the way she talked up about her rights, until she joined with the union, sent around a petition, and got the support of workers all over UC. Then she won back her right to healthy conditions on the job.

United struggles are essential beyond UC as well. Recently, San Francisco General Hospital threatened to close its OB/GYN services, an important source of health care for all working and poor people. Only by united action was the department saved.

But still we find that racism is standing in the way of that unity, that we've allowed the differences among us to be manipulated to keep us apart.

Effect on White Workers

The Bakke case has made affirmative action an issue to talk about.... The response from some white workers has been similar to the response of some white students. Affirmative action, as far as they can see, isn't making life any easier for them but it is—unfairly—making it easier for minorities.

Are minorities taking jobs and scholarships away from whites? No. Unemployment among minorities is many times that for whites. Here at UCSF our local went over the affirmative action statistics for 1975 and found a *drop* in employment for black women, while there was an increase in jobs for white males. When out of fourteen thousand students accepted to medical school only sixteen hundred are minorities, despite the crying need for health care in minority communities, it is clear that the problem is not one of too many minority students. When twenty-seven thousand applicants are rejected, despite the overall need for jobs and services, we have to ask: why so few places in medical school?

Even if we cut the number of minorities admitted to medical school by half, that means only eight hundred white students in the whole country would benefit, compared to over twenty-six thousand still out in the cold. That's the kind of solution we'll get if whites look for ways to get ahead through individual action instead of collective action.

Economy in Trouble

What is going on in this era, after the boom economy of wartime and the peak of militant struggles by Third World people, women, and working people, is recession, unemployment, and cutbacks. The economy may be improving enough for Carter to cancel our $50 tax rebates, but prices aren't going down. There are still too many out of work. It takes an hour to get anywhere on the bus because service has been cut back, and the county hospital is always teetering on the brink of collapse. We're all getting the short end of it—all of us except GM and IT&T. The problem is not enough jobs, not enough health care for people, not enough training program for health workers. It's true that some people have too much, but minorities are clearly not those people.

Still, in these times of scarcity, whites can resort to looking down on Third World people, who are in worse financial shape and are paid less than whites. But to see how we lose when we buy the myth that relative advantage is a real advantage, we only have to look at the South. Sure, whites have more than blacks, but racism has kept workers divided and largely unorganized, so that whites in the South make far less than whites elsewhere. Employers in the North keep costs down by threatening workers that they'll move south if the workers demand higher wages.

We know that white families make more money than Third World families and that most of the wealth is concentrated in the hands of a few. So what happens in situations where Third World families start earning a little more and their income level gets a little closer to that of whites? Does that mean that the incomes of white workers are going down? Studies show that when Third World income goes up—and it goes up as a result of militant struggle—it is the income of the top 1 percent of white families that declines. It cuts into the power of the elite and shores up the position of white workers as well as that of minorities.

Benefits of United Efforts

The civil rights struggles of the 1960s, led by Third World people, were a united effort that included many whites who also benefited as a result. There was a tremendous expansion of social service jobs, vocational training programs, and plans for career advancement through part-time enrollment in college for people of all colors and for women. Children of poor whites who would probably have been shut out of college in the past became entitled to work-study jobs, educational opportunity grants, and other types of financial aid which made higher education a real possibility. Improvements in community services such as new hospitals and schools, low-cost housing, community mental health programs, and free medical clinics oriented toward patient education were obviously gains for whites, who shared these services.

As a hospital worker, I know that only in the last ten years have our wages improved. Working at a hospital no longer means having to supplement your income with welfare because hospital workers, most of them minorities, in New York City, Charleston, South Carolina, and here in Oakland and San Francisco, used the pride and energy they were winning in the civil rights movement to demand decent treatment and decent pay to build unions that would protect those gains. Minorities led in those struggles, but all of us are benefiting.

Women too have advanced. Again, it's important not to exaggerate the improvements—women and minorities still have a long way to go to achieve real material equality, but Third World struggles have given us legal and political precedent for demanding our rights, and Third World and working women have led us in maintaining consciousness around the need to fight for all rather than for advancement of the few.

Figure 1.2. "Break the Silence: Stop Hyde in '79" (1979). Image courtesy of Lincoln Cushing/Docs Populi. Reprinted with permission by Salsedo Press.

What's in It for Us?

These are some of the victories of hard work and unity. The crumbs whites can steal back from minorities are nothing compared to gains we can make together. And we are already suffering losses from a new wave of racist attacks. As the Bakke decision goes to the Supreme Court, the financial elite are desperately trying to cut costs to maintain their profits, and the programs that helped millions of us attend college, find jobs, and live a little easier are rapidly being slashed to the bone. Already Bakke is being used against women in denying pregnancy benefits because they discriminate against men. Workers face [job] speedup and wage raises that don't match inflation. The tide of repression that is hitting Third World people first and hardest is clearly hitting all poor and working people as well.

So let's ask what's in it for us when they try to perpetuate the rip-off of Third World people that this country was built on, when the rich try to tell us that the way for white workers to get ahead is by stealing from black workers, from Chicanos, Native Americans and Asians. When we can see our way clear to answering this question, when we can identify who's really on our side and who's across the line, then we have a fighting chance.

1.B.2.

John Brown Anti-Klan Committee

From "Principles of Unity" and "National Program" in *The Dividing Line of the 80s: Take a Stand against the Klan* (1979)

The John Brown Anti-Klan Committee (JBAKC) formed in 1978 as an outgrowth of the Weather Underground Organization, principally involving white anti-imperialists. The organization had national reach, particularly through its newsletter *Death to the Klan* (later called *No KKK, No Fascist USA*). Its membership was most active in New York, Chicago, and San Francisco. The following sections from the organization's brochure *The Dividing Line of the 80s*, titled "Principles of Unity" and "National Program of the John Brown Anti-Klan Committee," circulated widely beyond the brochure itself.

Principles of Unity—John Brown Anti-Klan Committee

1. Fight White Supremacy in All Its Forms! Death to the Klan!
Support the Struggle of the Black Nation for Self-Determination!
Support the Struggle to Free the Land!

The central task of white people in general, and the John Brown Anti-Klan Committee in particular, is to fight to defeat white supremacy in all its forms. There is no neutral or "third" position for white people; we must either actively fight against white supremacy or support it. We must organize other white people to actively fight white supremacy, to smash the Klan, and to politically and materially support the struggles of Third World peoples for liberation.

The Klan and organized white supremacy are a major way the US has always oppressed Third World people within its borders. White supremacy has been a part of every counterinsurgency terror plan that the US has developed. The struggle to free the land of the Black nation has been a fierce, life-and-death struggle of Black people for four hundred years. The Black nation will win its freedom. The freeing of the land will shake the very foundations of US society; the freeing of the land will defeat white supremacy.

Since its inception in 1868, the Klan has always been the armed militia of white supremacy. Imari Obadele, the former president of the Provisional Government of the Republic of New Afrika, has said, "Our biggest threat comes from the white civilian armies, the Ku Klux Klan and those other semi-official forces who for one hundred years have done the dirty work of military oppression in the South." Today the Klan is re-emerging with that same practice. The Klan, in Tupelo, Mississippi, elsewhere in the South, in northern cities, in prisons and the armed forces, is in open, armed conflict with the Black Liberation Struggle.

The Klan, along with the INS, has become the border patrol of the Mexican/US border; it is one of the major armed forces against Mexicano/Chicano peoples.

We are committed to building a mass movement among white people to smash the Klan and to support materially and politically the struggles of Third World peoples for national liberation and human rights.

2. Follow Black and Other Third World Leadership!

We are committed to following Black and other Third World leadership. The struggle against the Klan is a life-and-death struggle, based on the antagonistic relationship between oppressed nations and US imperialism. Our tasks as white people are defined by and grow out of the strategy and tasks set by the oppressed nations. This leadership is not abstract; it is represented by the militant struggle in Tupelo, Mississippi, by the struggle of Black and Latin prisoners, by the struggle for human rights in New York City. The coming together of these forces of Black liberation within the US and the liberation forces in Southern Africa constitutes the leading strategy to defeat the Klan and white world supremacy. The dominant history and practices of white people in this country have been to reject this leadership. John Brown was a white man who responded to the leadership of the Black Liberation Struggle and actively fought white supremacy. This is why we take the name John Brown Anti-Klan Committee, for it is only under Black and other Third World leadership that we can do our work correctly.

3. Support the Struggle of Third World People for Human Rights!
Oppose White Supremacist Attacks!

The struggle for human rights by oppressed peoples and nations is a struggle against genocide, against mass terror being perpetrated on Black and other Third World communities. Police murder and white vigilante attacks are part of the US government's attempt to destroy the ability of Third World people to fight. All over the US at this time there is a mass struggle for human rights by Third World peoples and a strategy to bring this struggle into the international arena.

We are committed to fighting attacks on Black and other Third World communities and to supporting the struggle to free Prisoners of War, captured freedom fighters, and leaders of the oppressed nations. We are committed to fighting not only the Klan but also police terror, white vigilante attacks by the Jewish Defense League and other zionist forces, white gangs, and all forms of organized white supremacy. . . .

National Program of the John Brown Anti-Klan Committee

Point 1: Death to the Klan!

Until this has been achieved, all chapters of JBAKC have as their central task to educate, agitate, and organize to destroy the Klan and other organized white supremacist forces. We do this on a national basis through distribution of literature, buttons, and posters; speaking tours and forums; and participation in anti-Klan demonstrations. We also do this by exposing and confronting white supremacy wherever it is being organized, under whatever guises, by fighting against the genocidal death penalty; or demanding the removal of Klan prison guards; or exposing the relationship between the Klan and the police; or by opposing the "grass roots" white supremacist organizations that are being built in communities all over the country to defend "white rights" and attack Black and other Third World people. Each chapter of the JBAKC has the responsibility to apply this point of the program to the specific conditions and struggles in their area.

Point 2: Build Support for the Struggles of Black and
Other Third World People for Human Rights.

Every chapter of JBAKC engages in politically and materially aiding the struggles for human rights going on in every community and on a national basis. In the past year (1979), JBAKC worked to build support for the National Black Human Rights Campaign which brought the issue of the denial of Black peoples' human rights to the United Nations. We support the struggle for human rights with the understanding that the most basic and fundamental of all human rights is the right of all oppressed peoples to self-determination. One main focus of this point of the program is the fight against killer cops. JBAKC chapters in many parts of the country are involved in campaigns against police repression because these campaigns strike at key Klan bases and oppose the heightening of racist violence and brutality which infect the US today. The program of support for human rights also means supporting the struggle to free political prisoners and Prisoners of War. Winning the freedom of these freedom fighters and political activists is key to the success of the struggle for human rights and the defeat of white supremacy.

Point 3: Zionism and the Klan Go Hand in Hand.
Fight Zionism and Worldwide White Supremacy.

The fight against white supremacy in the US cannot proceed on a serious and principled basis without struggling against Zionism. This is not a geographic question, and all chapters of JBAKC must confront Zionism in their work. Whether this means opposing the blatant, violent racism of the JDL (Jewish Defense League) or taking on the more "sophisticated" forms of zionist propaganda which attack the struggles of Black people in the US and the liberation movements in Southern Africa as well as the fundamental right of the Palestinian people to live freely in their homeland. The JBAKC opposes white supremacy in all its forms and as a worldwide system.

. . . [M]ore than just a program for the JBAKC, we believe that this is a program that all progressive white people should be involved in. Look at your own city and you will see that the same struggles, the same issues that are addressed by this program, are raging in your area as well. If there is a JBAKC chapter where you live, join it and help implement this program. If there isn't one yet, get together with other people who want to fight white supremacy, contact us and begin a JBAKC chapter. Wherever you are, if you support these principles and this program, you can join us and be a part of building a national movement to defeat the Klan and the system of white supremacy.

1.B.3.

National Anti-Klan Network

"Call for February 2nd Mobilization, Greensboro, North Carolina" (1980)

On November 3, 1979, working with police protection, members of the Klan and American Nazi Party murdered five Communist Workers Party (CWP) members at an anti-Klan march in Greensboro, North Carolina. The CWP had organized the march and was active in organizing mostly Black textile workers in the area. Following the attack, the National Anti-Klan Network penned a document in which it called for a public mobilization in Greensboro.

Conditions in the United States today demand that we call on labor unions, churches, civil rights, human rights, political, and social organizations to take part in a massive peaceful nonviolent mobilization in Greensboro, NC, on February 2, 1980.

We invite all who wish to express their concern for the crisis issues which set the conditions for the recent Greensboro massacre to join us in commemorating the last twenty years of struggle and in launching a new offensive for the 1980s.

The shots that killed five anti-KKK demonstrators in Greensboro November 3 were aimed at all Blacks, working people regardless of class and color, and all who desire justice in America. The police who stood one-half block away, with full knowledge of the KKK's activity, must be held responsible along with those who actually pulled the triggers.

These cold-blooded murders were encouraged by the Bakke and Weber cases, the anti-alien hysteria, proposition 13–type legislation, new attempts at union busting, and the general rise of Klan and Nazi terror.

This nation has not yet shown outrage equal to the acts of murder, intimidation, and attempts to deny our basic humanity perpetrated by the Klan. We refuse to be silenced by KKK terror, government repression, and those who would tell us to close our eyes, hoping that the terror will go away. We must respond with moral outrage commensurate with the magnitude of these atrocities.

The economic crisis has deepened with high inflation, unemployment, and hard times. The powerful and wealthy have tried to create various scapegoats to turn our frustrations toward everything but the real source of our problems. Contrary to what the KKK and others say, unemployment is *not* caused by affirmative action, and Black people are *not* the cause of white suffering and systemic economic problems.

The violence in Greensboro is part of a pattern, and it must be turned around.

Twenty years ago on February 1, 1960, four Greensboro A&T students sat down at the lily-white lunch counter of Woolworth's. Their courage helped accelerate an entire generation of struggle against Jim Crow segregation, the electoral disenfranchisement of Black people, and discrimination. The nation responded, and the people won some meaningful steps toward freedom and justice.

Entering the 1980s, we find ourselves in a situation where even the limited gains achieved during the 60s are under increasing attack. The Klan is a part of that pattern. We will not return to the back of the bus, nor should decent people desire it. Their support, shame, and outrage can create for us a better nation.

Twenty years after the Greensboro sit-ins and the passage of much legislation, the deep yearning for freedom, justice, and liberation of Black people has yet to be satisfied. Increasing poverty, a growing income gap between Black and white, and the lack of real political power necessitates that a new era of struggle for the 1980s be ignited.

Come to Greensboro on February 2, 1980.

1.B.4.

Tede Matthews

"Speech at Anti–Moral Majority Demonstration" (1984)

In July 1984 the Moral Majority, a leading organization of the Christian right, held its annual convention in San Francisco. It was met with fierce protests. Tede Matthews, a member of the gay and lesbian left group Lesbians and Gays Against Intervention, gave this speech at one of the demonstrations against the group.

A plague of bigotry and intolerance has landed in our city. This pestilence, the religious right, has been with us for centuries. The first Europeans invaded with the musket and the bible. Early missionaries wrote that "excessive effeminacy and lewdness" was committed "without a blush" among Indians throughout the Americas. One Jesuit said that because of these Sodomites, "there will be much to do when the Holy Faith is established among them."

Conquistadors killed the gay native king in what is now Chile. They impaled him, up the ass, as an example to his people. In 1973, the CIA led the overthrow of Chile's democratic government. Thousands were killed, including gays. One drag entertainer, Lola Puñales, a favorite of President Allende, was publicly hanged in a red dress. This led SF [San Francisco] gays to form Gay Solidarity with the Chilean Resistance.

Now the God Squad has descended on Sodom with their "divine imperative." Their Family Forum is self-righteously called "I Am My Brother's Keeper." The dictionary definition of "keeper" is someone who guards or maintains [or] a mechanism for holding in place, as a latch. This makes Big Brother Jerry's pearly gates sound like prison bars.

But, don't despair, the definition also says something that resists spoiling, as a fruit. That's where we come in. We're here tonight to resist their narrow vision.

Lesbians and Gays Against Intervention also see the word "American" as covering North, South, and Central America. What are these conservatives doing to save families south of the Rio Grande? These sexist homophobes are also the staunchest supporters of intervention in the region. Senator Jesse Helms is a close buddy of El Salvador's D'Aubbison, head of the notorious death squads and responsible for the death of their Archbishop Romero. Guatemala's recent dictator, Rios Montt, instituted El Verbo Church as his state religion. His Christian soldiers killed Catholic priests, unionists, and whole Indian villages. This same church descends on Castro, Polk, and Mission Streets to save our heathen souls.

The US is the twentieth-century conquistador, and the fundamentalists are their sanctifiers and pacifiers. Our government is already at war in Central America and the Caribbean. How can family life, any life, exist under these conditions? The Moral Majority is outraged by abortion yet blesses the Salvadoran military which bayonets babies in their mothers' wombs.

The BAR [*Bay Area Reporter*] quoted Tom Peretti, president of the gay Republican group, as being "offended at leftist contingents (on Gay Day) that support countries that oppress Gay people." Lesbians and Gays Against Intervention marched to protest our government's backing of death squads that kill "sexual deviates" and who rape and torture women who wear pants or who teach in a religious community or who live in a free-fire zone. We support Nicaragua, whose government has resisted efforts to create antigay laws. What has happened to Grenada's gay group since the US invaded?

Local Salvadoran refugees marched with us on Lesbian/Gay Freedom Day and will be with us at the National Gay Rights March. As they stand with us for our right as lesbians and gay men, we also stand with them for their right to self-determination. We help our gay sisters and brothers of Central America by fighting our government's policies. Gay freedom will never blossom, here or there, under the shadow of the eagle of intervention. We are our brothers' and sisters' keepers. Central America will be free.

1.B.5.

Feminist Anti-Censorship Taskforce

From "Feminism and Censorship: Strange Bedfellows?" (1985)

As pornography became more widely available in the 1970s, many feminists strongly opposed it, seeing it as objectifying and dehumanizing and as provoking rape. By the early 1980s, however, many feminists were identifying themselves as anti-antiporn. These feminists viewed others' efforts to ban pornography as producing dangerous alliances with the New Right. The Feminist Anti-Censorship Taskforce, based in New York, was a leading voice in the anti-antiporn critique.

Does censorship, even if proposed by feminists, benefit women? This question has been raised recently by feminist sponsorship of antipornography legislation. We think there are serious feminist questions about the wisdom and consequences of antipornography legislation.

No group trying to change society can support inroads into free expression. After all, it is new ideas, unpopular ideas, and ideas advanced by those who lack power and seek change that have been the primary targets of censorship. We are concerned that some antipornography feminists are making a dangerous alliance with the right wing, empowering the state in ways that will reduce rather than increase women's control over our personal lives.

The media have portrayed the current debate over antipornography laws as largely one between feminists who support the legislation and civil libertarians who oppose it. The feminist opposition to this legislation has been ignored. The Feminist Anti-Censorship Taskforce (FACT) is a New York–based group of feminist activists, artists, writers and scholars. We believe that the proposed antipornography laws are a misguided, dangerous, and ineffective strategy in the battle against sexism and violence.

1. How has censorship historically affected women? History shows that censorship has not benefited women, even though obscenity laws have been enacted in our names, allegedly to protect America's wives and daughters. The same laws which, it was claimed, were "safeguarding" the right of women not to be shocked or offended by sexually explicit material have been used to oppress many women: those who sought birth control, abortions, or sex information; those who sought to make such information available to others; sexually active women; lesbians (as well as gay men); prostitutes and workers in the sex industry.

2. What is the Minneapolis/Indianapolis antipornography legislation? These laws would allow an individual to sue in civil court for monetary damages and for a court order stopping the distribution of whatever ma-

terials the local court declares to be pornographic under the definition in the law. The legislation defines pornography as "the sexually explicit subordination of women, graphically depicted, whether in pictures or in words." Antipornography bills, developed by Andrea Dworkin and Catherine McKinnon, have been passed and vetoed for the second time in Minneapolis (July 1984), passed and signed into law in Indianapolis (June 1984), and introduced into the Suffolk County, New York, legislature (September 1984).

3. What would the effect of this legislation be? Booksellers, publishers, authors, actors, magazine dealers, art galleries, supermarkets—all could be sued for making or distributing "sexually explicit material which subordinates women." The hallmarks of sexual subordination provided in the bill are sufficiently murky—"women are presented as whores by nature" or "presented in a posture of display"—to allow most sexually explicit images or descriptions to be included, if the viewer disapproves of the sexual act in question and therefore thinks it degrades women.

The bill will have a "chilling effect" on expression. Booksellers, for example, will censor themselves, removing from their shelves material which may or may not be actionable under the law rather than risk a court suit. Hence, the range of material available to the public will shrink. Already in Suffolk County, the right has taken the model of the legislation and revamped it to reflect a "profamily", antigay position while deleting much of the feminist language of the original.

This legislation can become a building block for a larger protectionist document, similar to the proposed Family Protection Act, which could be used as a tool for prosecuting a wide range of unpopular feminist expression on birth control, sex education, abortion, lesbian/gay rights. The law will not empower women. It will empower the state—whose courts, judges, and affirmative action boards will be asked to rule on which sexually explicit images are acceptable.

4. Do all feminists support antipornography legislation? No. While all feminists deplore violence against women, there is a broad range of opinion among feminists on the interrelationship of sexuality, violence, and pornography. Some feminists do not believe that pornography causes violence in any simple and direct way. Many feminists, even those who are critical of pornography, are as disturbed by the idea of putting limitations on First Amendment protection of free speech as they are by the presentation of unsatisfactory images of women in pornography. These laws can be used to attack and limit feminist self-expression, including women's writing about sexuality, abortion, birth control and medical self-help. Once these laws are on the books, feminists have minimal control over their interpretation and enforcement by the courts.

5. Who else supports antipornography legislation? In Indianapolis and Suffolk County, the legislation was introduced by conservative Republicans,

both foes of abortion, lesbian/gay rights, and the ERA. Christian fundamentalists were the primary supporters of these bills. Church groups bused in for public hearings denounced perversion and immorality. . . .

6. But isn't pornography degrading to women? "Pornography" is a body of material diverse in form (for example, nineteenth-century novels, film strips, French postcards, modernist art), and in quality (tasteless, sexist, poorly made;, visionary, rebellious, educational). What is pornographic to one viewer may be erotica to a second and not particularly sexual to a third. Antipornography activists claim that pornography equals violence. But an image of violence is not the same as violence; a description of rape is not rape. And the fact remains that most pornography—however sexist or nonfeminist and however we may wish it were better—does not depict violence.

   Some pornography is insulting to women, but so are ads, situation comedies, and many women's magazines. What distinguishes pornography is its sexual explicitness, an easy target to attack in a conservative political climate. "Degrading to women" is a phrase that has been used consistently to justify limits on women's lives. Within the past century, paid employment, recognition of women's sexuality, and information about birth control have all been called degrading to women. We should be wary of reviving this category as the basis of legislation. However problematic pornography may be for feminists, legislative solutions are not the answer.

7. Does social science research prove that pornography causes violence against women? No. Proponents of antipornography legislation cite a handful of flawed and limited studies to support their claim that pornography causes violence against women. But, in fact, there is no such consensus among social scientists. Even those who argue that violent pornography may harden attitudes in men already angry do not claim a simple cause and effect relationship between image and act.

8. What should we do about violence against women? There is no quick fix to the problem of violence, which has many causes. The current preoccupation with banning pornography diverts money and attention from programs and services that women really need and creates a false sense of security that something important is being done. . . .

   Women do not need the illusory solution of censorship. Women need real equality, real power—strengthened equal rights legislation, affirmative action to achieve economic parity, improved education, access to public office, and better services for victims of violence and abuse. We need to criticize sexism not only in its most graphic manifestations but wherever it appears. We need a more, rather than a less, developed sexual culture where women as well as men freely (and explicitly) express ourselves.

1.B.6.

WHAM!

From *No Choice, No Liberty* (1991)

WHAM!, or the Women's Health Action Mobilization, was founded in New York City in 1989 to defend abortion access and reproductive choice. Sparked by that year's *Webster* ruling, in which the Supreme Court allowed states to ban public funding of abortion services, WHAM! embraced a radical vision and frequently collaborated with ACT UP (AIDS Coalition to Unleash Power). The text here comes from the group's new members' packet, which also included instructions on direct action, clinic defense, and wheatpasting posters.

What Is Reproductive Freedom?

WHAM! does not work solely for absolute access to abortion on demand, although that is one of our important goals. Our aim is to empower all women with control over our reproductive lives by defending our right when and whether to have children. We acknowledge the need for women to make these decisions on the basis of our identities, lifestyles, goals, and aspirations. Therefore, women must be able not only to prevent conception and terminate unwanted pregnancies but also to bear healthy children and to feed, clothe, and educate our families (not to mention ourselves!). We acknowledge and challenge the fact that our access to necessary resources is always [mediated] by our race, economic class, and sexual orientation, among other factors.

Why Is Women's Health Care Political?

Because no birth control is 100 percent effective.

Because in 1971 there were nine companies researching birth control and now there is only one.

Because a woman is raped every six minutes.

Because in 83 percent of counties in this country, there is no abortion provider.

Because before abortion was legal, thousands of women died each year from botched abortions, and 80 percent were Black and Latina.

Because sterilization abuse is still sanctioned by the government, especially for Black and Latina women.

Because 25 percent of Caesarean sections are unnecessary.

Because 20 percent of pregnant women in New York City don't have adequate prenatal care.

Because pregnant women are prosecuted for drug use instead of provided with treatment.

Because the National Institute of Health spends less than 13 percent of its budget on researching diseases specific to women.

Because one in nine women will get breast cancer.

Because women are the fastest growing group of new AIDS cases.

Because 95 percent of women with endometriosis probably don't know [they have] it.

Because women with AIDS die six times faster than men with AIDS, and Black women die nine times faster.

Because some doctors would rather butcher women by performing hysterectomies and mastectomies when simple lump removals are applicable.

Because pap smears are inaccurate.

Because women are dismissed as hypochondriacs when it hurts.

Because women acquire eating disorders to obtain a "perfect" body.

Because women are the caretakers of everyone else before they take care of themselves.

Because homophobia kills women too.

Because childcare is still practically nonexistent.

Because women still make sixty-three cents to a man's $1.

Why Direct Action?

The goal of direct action is to empower individuals. It begins with education. We actively search out and share information about the political issues that affect us. Our anger fuels action for social change—from speak-outs, sit-ins, demonstrations, and acts of civil disobedience to legal action, forums, phone "zaps," tabling, and letter-writing campaigns. Our goals are to pressure officials and institutions at every level to improve their programs and policies (or just to do their jobs) and to raise public awareness of the current crisis in reproductive freedom and women's health.

WHAM! Fights For:

- Access to free, safe, legal abortions with full public funding. No forced abortions.
- No spousal or parental notification or consent for abortions. No limitations on the rights of women under eighteen to full and complete access to abortion on demand.
- Freedom from sterilization abuse. Women should not be coerced into permanently ending their reproductive capacity. Compliance with federal guidelines should be rigorously monitored and enforced, constantly reviewed and strengthened, as necessary.
- Full rights for lesbians and gay men, including custody rights and equal partner benefits.

- Access to complete sex education, beginning at an early age, and to complete information on contraceptive options and use, including side effects and failure rates. Emphasis on safer sex and healthy, reliable contraceptives.
- Development of and access to new, safer, more convenient, affordable methods of birth control for both men and women.
- Access to reproductive technologies that enable lesbians and infertile people to have children.
- No punitive actions against or prosecution of women during pregnancy for so-called fetal abuse. Treatment programs on demand for women who use drugs, alcohol, or any other substances. So-called fetal rights must never take precedence over women's rights.
- Comprehensive and quality pre- and postnatal care.
- Full rights for HIV-positive women, including counseling, no mandatory testing, equal access to experimental drug trials, regardless of age, and freedom from forced abortion or sterilization for women with AIDS/HIV.
- Sexual pleasure for women, independent of reproduction. Sex without punishment.
- A comprehensive national health care plan, which would promote wellness and provide good nutrition as well as cure disease. In particular, this would reduce diseases caused by poverty, such as infant mortality. Increased research into the ways all diseases affect women differently from men.
- Free, quality, twenty-four-hour, community-controlled childcare.
- The right to jobs in all work categories, regardless of reproductive capacity and with full pay equity. The right to unionize; to safe, healthy workplaces; to affirmative action. An end to all forms of discrimination against women in the workplace.
- Decent, affordable housing. End homelessness.
- Free, quality education.

(While every one of us may not completely agree with the emphasis or content of every one of the above principles, we all respect and support the decisions made by WHAM! as a whole to design and execute actions which take them into consideration.)

WHAM! does not condone the use of violence in our struggle to attain these goals.

NC Senate Vote '90

Isabell Moore

In 1990, a broad coalition of LGBTQ, racial justice, and feminist activists formed NC Senate Vote '90 (NCSV90). Though this LGBTQ-led initiative did not succeed in its main goal of defeating Republican senatorial candidate Jesse Helms, it mobilized three hundred volunteers, registered ten thousand new voters, and built an infrastructure for LGBTQ organizing across the state. NCSV90 fused previously disconnected issues and united disparate groups, producing alliances that continue to shape North Carolina politics.

NCSV90 carried on the radical visions of earlier left, gay and lesbian left, and racial justice organizing, adapting these freedom dreams for their own moment. A large-scale initiative focused on electoral politics, NCSV90 developed an intersectional and coalitional approach. Leader Mandy Carter remembered, "We were all upset about Helms's gay record. But as a black lesbian I was also very aware of his horrible record on civil rights." This coalitional, multi-issue strategy was also practical. Carter explained, "Even if we got every gay person to vote we figured it wouldn't be enough. We started to think, who would work with us on this? "Arts, environment, education, people of color, gay and lesbian allies, pro-choice—these were the groups we knew we should be in contact with. It was an alliance that we needed."[1]

NCSV90's history reveals that LGBTQ southerners were much more than scapegoats wielded by conservative politicians. They were key political participants whose savvy strategies and hard-fought coalitions transformed that region. In contrast to what unfolded in urban centers in other regions, LGBTQ North Carolinians' electoral organizing increased the visibility and "clout" of LGBTQ people of color and activists with liberatory politics. In 1993, a group of former NCSV90 leaders founded Southerners on New Ground, which continues to organize a multiracial group of LGBTQ southerners around issues of racial and economic justice today. NCSV90 also laid the groundwork for North Carolina's Moral Monday Movement, now a progressive coalition that relies on many of the alliances built in the 1990 campaign. It has succeeded in countering many of the most egregious moves of the conservative legislature. Starting in the 1990s, several openly gay people were elected to public office in North Carolina. NCSV90's story demonstrates that LGBTQ southerners with left politics have shaped the region, and the group stands as a historical example for those seeking to fuse radical critiques and engagement with electoral politics.

1. Mandy Carter quoted in David Stout, "Helms Created Our Stonewall," *QNotes*, July 26, 2008.

1.B.7.

Washington Area Clinic Defense Task Force

From "Goals and Guidelines" (1990s)

Founded in the 1980s in Washington, DC, the Washington Area Clinic Defense Task Force is one of several grassroots groups that preserve abortion access by providing a physical, supportive presence outside clinics. The organization gathers outside clinics to shield patients and staff from counterprotestors who would harass or threaten them. The following comes from an early handbook of the group.

Because we are fighting to keep abortion safe, legal, and accessible, we have proposed the following goals for the Washington Area Clinic Defense Task Force (WACDTF):

1. To ensure that women have access to all reproductive health care services they desire.
2. To convey the message that women have the right to control their own bodies and lives.
3. To encourage personal empowerment through action.
4. To keep clinics open and functioning at the request of the providers.

To accomplish our goals we propose the following guidelines:

1. In keeping with our nonviolent position for these actions, we will seek to secure the positions required to keep access open, hold our ground, and not be bullied out of position. We will not engage in any physical assault.
2. We will not engage antiwoman activists in debate. We will always attempt to utilize designated spokespersons where the content of our message will reach third parties or the media.
3. Only designated persons should engage in conversations with police or officials. If asked to move by police officers, ask if you will be arrested if you refuse—particularly on private property, if we have permission to be there. Do not applaud the police for reluctantly doing their duty after a long delay.
4. Posters/signs/chants shall be in good taste.
5. We will be cooperative with the leadership of participating organizations, put the purpose of our joint action first, and respect the diversity of participants.

Helpful Hints for the Happy Clinic Defender

These mostly relate to the basics—eating, drinking, peeing. You are not out there to suffer unnecessarily. You should be as comfortable and alert as possible at all times.

- Bring noisemakers.
- *Eat* before you leave. You may be in for a long day.
- While you want to be careful about drinking too much, do not risk dehydration. This can happen even in the coldest weather. Drink something before you leave, preferably something warm in the winter. You *are* allowed, encouraged even, to go to the bathroom during the day, but be advised that facilities may not be readily available.
- Wear your comfortable clothes. In the cold, dress in layers. Hats, gloves, scarves, and warm, thick socks can make an incredible difference. Thick-soled shoes or sneakers will help insulate your feet against the cold ground, too. Don't underestimate March, and even April, cold.
- Bring easy-to-carry, easy-to-dispose of snack food (an apple in a sweatshirt pocket, trail mix, granola bars).
- Bring some form of identification and some extra cash.
- Don't wear jewelry. If you must, at least leave your dangling/expensive jewelry at home. Try not to bring a pocketbook or backpack. A fanny pack is very useful. Your day will be infinitely easier if all you have to carry is you.
- Those with long hair: Pull it back if possible, with something soft (a bandanna, one of those scrunchy elastic things).
- If you have any type of medical condition that could potentially need attention, make sure at least one other person with you knows about it.

Remember: While we have tried to make this training as comprehensive as possible, *nothing* can prepare you for an actual hit. It's cold in the morning. It's chaotic at times on site. Sometimes, it's really boring. While the experience will almost always be somewhat-to-very stressful, it is also supposed to be empowering and sometimes may even be fun. If at any point you feel you've had enough for the day, you are free to take a break or to leave. You are *not* letting anybody down. We appreciate *any* and *all* levels of support.

1.B.8.

Anti-Racist Action

"Points of Unity" (1990s)

Anti-Racist Action was founded in Minneapolis in 1988, with roots in the antiracist skinhead scene. It soon found common cause with antifascist activists up and down the West Coast of the United States and Canada and also drew inspiration from Europe's Anti-Fascist Action. The following principles unite the various chapters of the organization and describe their efforts to confront white supremacist and fascist activity.

The Anti-Racist Action Network consists of people from all different backgrounds, with a lot of different viewpoints. With countless ARA chapters out there, it's not surprising that no two are alike! What we all agree on, however, is the following:

1. *We go where they go.* Whenever fascists are organizing or active in public, we're there. We don't believe in ignoring them or staying away from them. Never let the Nazis have the street!
2. *We don't rely on the cops or courts to do our work for us.* This doesn't mean we never go to court, but the cops uphold white supremacy and the status quo. They attack us and everyone who resists oppression. We must rely on ourselves to protect ourselves and stop the fascists.
3. *Nonsectarian defense of other antifascists.* In ARA, we have a lot of different groups and individuals. We don't agree about everything and we have a right to differ openly. But in this movement an attack on one is an attack on us all. We stand behind each other.

Figure 1.3. "Stop the Fascist Dirtheads" (1994). Image Courtesy of Lincoln Cushing/Docs Populi.

4. *We support abortion rights and reproductive freedom.* ARA intends to do the hard work necessary to build a broad, strong movement against racism, sexism, anti-Semitism, Islamophobia, homophobia, transphobia, discrimination against the disabled, the oldest, the youngest, and the most oppressed people. We want a classless, free society. *We intend to win*!

1.B.9.

"African American Women in Defense of Ourselves" (1991)

On November 17, 1991, sixteen hundred Black women placed the following statement as a full-page ad in several newspapers, including the *New York Times*. The statement, which was published during the same time period as Kimberlé Crenshaw's key texts on intersectional feminism, criticized the confirmation of Supreme Court justice Clarence Thomas, noting the false divisions between the politics of race and gender that characterized the debate over Thomas's fitness to serve on the court.

As women of African descent, we are deeply troubled by the recent nomination, confirmation, and seating of Clarence Thomas as an associate justice of the US Supreme Court. We know that the presence of Clarence Thomas on the court will be continually used to divert attention from historic struggles for social justice through suggestions that the presence of a Black man on the Supreme Court constitutes an assurance that the rights of African Americans will be protected. Clarence Thomas's public record is ample evidence this will not be true. Further, the consolidation of a conservative majority on the Supreme Court seriously endangers the rights of all women, poor and working-class people, and the elderly. The seating of Clarence Thomas is an affront not only to African American women and men but to all people concerned with social justice.

We are particularly outraged by the racist and sexist treatment of Professor Anita Hill, an African American woman who was maligned and castigated for daring to speak publicly of her own experience of sexual abuse. The malicious defamation of Professor Hill insulted all women of African descent and sent a dangerous message to any woman who might contemplate a sexual harassment complaint.

We speak here because we recognize that the media are now portraying the Black community as prepared to tolerate both the dismantling of affirmative action and the evil of sexual harassment in order to have any Black man on the Supreme Court. We want to make clear that the media have ignored or distorted many African American voices. We will not be silenced.

Many have erroneously portrayed the allegations against Clarence Thomas as an issue of either gender or race. As women of African descent, we understand sexual harassment as both. We further understand that Clarence Thomas outrageously manipulated the legacy of lynching in order to shelter himself from Anita Hill's allegations. To deflect attention away from the reality of sexual abuse in African American women's lives, he trivialized and misrepresented this painful part of African American people's history. This country, which has a long legacy of racism and sexism, has never taken the sexual abuse of Black women seriously. Throughout US history Black women have been sexually stereotyped as immoral, insatiable, perverse; the initiators in all sexual contacts— abusive or otherwise. The common assumption in legal proceedings as well as in the larger society has been that Black women cannot be raped or otherwise sexually abused. As Anita Hill's experience demonstrates, Black women who speak of these matters are not likely to be believed.

In 1991, we cannot tolerate this type of dismissal of any one Black woman's experience or this attack upon our collective character without protest, outrage, and resistance.

As women of African descent, we express our vehement opposition to the policies represented by the placement of Clarence Thomas on the Supreme Court. The Bush administration, having obstructed the passage of civil rights legislation, impeded the extension of unemployment compensation, cut student aid and dismantled social welfare programs, has continually demonstrated that it is not operating in our best interests. Nor is this appointee. We pledge ourselves to continue to speak out in defense of one another, in defense of the African American community and against those who are hostile to social justice, no matter what color they are. No one will speak for us but ourselves.

1.B.10.

Marcy Westerling

From "Rallying against the Right: A Case Study in Rural Organizing" (1992)

Marcy Westerling was a community organizer in rural Oregon and a leader of the Coalition for Human Dignity, in whose newsletter this essay was first published. The anti-LGBT measure she mentions, Measure 9, was defeated by Oregon voters thanks in part to the organizing she describes.

Columbia County, in the northwest corner of Oregon, is home to thirty-seven thousand people, the state's only nuclear reactor, and a growing struggle over who will define the community: white supremacists, right-wing Christians, and other organized bigots [. . .] or those who believe in democracy for all. Encompassing seven small rural towns and 620 square miles of surrounding farmland and forests, Columbia County's economy is based on timber, with unemployment now at 13 percent and rising. Like other rural parts of the Northwest, Columbia County seems an ideal haven for white-pride groups and Christian warriors who hope to turn the clock back to a time before the great social justice movements of the twentieth century. Many local residents regularly travel into Portland to act as "foot soldiers" in the fight to shut down access to abortion clinics.

At the same time, many of us in Columbia County have watched the growth of the right wing with alarm from our silent corners of the community. Occasionally we have gathered, such as at the school board meeting in the spring of 1991 where three hundred people debated whether creationism should be taught in our public schools. But even when we found ourselves together in our common concern over what was going on, we were assembled as individuals; we failed to assemble in clear unity. At the end of any given meeting we each went home in despair, feeling as if we were losing control of our community [. . .] and we were.

Naming the Challenge

Back in August of 1991, something hopeful began to happen. A variety of community leaders and everyday citizens (often one and the same) met over a potluck to name what was happening to our community. As elsewhere in the state, the impetus came from the local feminist rape and domestic violence program, the Columbia County Women's Resource Center (CCWRC). With its long history in the community of opposing oppression-based violence, challenging dominant social norms, and organizing among targeted groups, the CCWRC was able to provide a clear analysis of the present danger and the need to develop counterstrategies.

The most immediate cause of alarm which brought people together was the campaign the OCA [Oregon Citizens Alliance] was orchestrating to amend the Oregon constitution to require discrimination on the basis of sexual orientation. Passage of the OCA's initiative would mark the first time a state constitution has been amended to take away the rights of a group of people. People in Columbia County were concerned about the implications: we were not so ready to allow democracy to be weakened.

For the first time we talked about what each of us saw: homophobia, social control, bigotry, Christian authoritarianism, and disinformation. We all shared our clear commitment to reclaim our community as a place that did not tolerate bigotry, as a place that actively protected the minority voice—a community of democracy. The power of this initial meeting where we acknowledged our common concerns gave us tremendous energy to move forward together into action.

Getting Organized

Our immediate strategy was to gather a strong base of support. Our premise was that our strength would come not only from sheer numbers but from the diversity that would truly represent our community. We each took on the task of meeting with neighbors, coworkers, family members, and friends who had a history of leadership and ethics. Such criteria allowed us to approach fundamentalist Christians, loggers, and other individuals not traditionally seen as being aligned with the progressive community. The common ground was concern over the erosion of civil rights and the immediate targeting of the gay and lesbian community. Soon our base of support included people of color, Christians, pagans, Jews, laborers, office workers, a few gays and lesbians, and a lot of committed heterosexuals.

We talked with people about what we were seeing and presented them with the hopeful prospect that a group was organizing to unite our voices. Most people that we approached not only asked for inclusion in the project but also sought out an immediate role for themselves. We found that it became critical to have some tasks that each member could embark on even if the task was as loosely constructed as approaching five others. None of us could remember a time where people were so ready to move into action.

Once we had a base of support of almost fifty people clearly signed on to reclaim our community, we felt we had a credible and safe starting point for formalizing our group. . . .

We drafted a mission statement that clarified why we were gathered together—this was to prove an invaluable tool as we set about to attract additional folks. We struggled to come up with a name that would represent our group perfectly, compromising on a name that offended none in our group. We acquired papers from the county clerk that established the Columbia County Citizens for Human Dignity as an official political action committee (PAC), which enabled us to generate money (we knew that we would need some money). We elected officers. At the close of this two-hour meeting we had dealt with most of the more mundane details of becoming a formal organization. . . .

The Campaign

Selecting an initial strategy for communicating with the community was hard. By then we had had our first (and last) run-in with the OCA. We had peacefully attended a few of their meetings and observed them taking over the only supermarket and post office in one of our towns in an effort to collect signatures. It hurt and almost immobilized us to witness our neighbors advancing bigotry. Our initial response was confusion; for a week we struggled to find a direction for action. Again our high standards slowed us down as we sought the "perfect" strategy. It took a few discussions before we recognized that moving forward with plans that were ethically sound was more realistic than waiting for the perfect campaign plan.

We finally moved forward with some simple steps. We designed a signature waiver form to gather the names of dozens of "friends and neighbors" who would publicly affiliate themselves with us. . . . Another group set about to draft a press release that would announce our formation in our five local papers. A few folks compiled one hundred "organizer's packets." . . . A sequence of small group discussions were set up with potential allies, providing each participant with accurate information and an opportunity to sign on to the campaign. When there have been candidates' forums we have been there to ask clear questions on where each candidate stands on civil rights. We've moved down the roster of churches and community groups and met with them group by group. The local papers have printed editorials, articles, and letters reflecting our views and activities.

Throughout each of these projects we have kept our meetings minimal and fun. Food and casual settings are incorporated whenever possible. We've tried to anticipate possible barriers to participating, finding rides for those without cars. Inclusion of children is standard.

Our campaign, to date, is very much a work in progress. We interweave our strategies into our everyday lives in our community. We have found that our most effective strategies are very simple. Most accomplish the immediate task of breaking down the isolation of rural progressive people and broadening our campaign to provide information to decent, often conservative, people who have rarely needed to challenge their perceptions. Being able to demonstrate to the uncertain the diversity and strength of our numbers inspires many to take one of the first stands they've taken in recent history and, for some, their lives. Again and again we find that a decade of repressive politics has left many people eager to grab hold of the opportunity to belong to a group that stands for human dignity.

Traditionally Democratic but conservative, Columbia County is a community that doesn't seek to be on the front lines of any issue. Our newspapers chronicle the local sports teams and the next citywide cleanup day. People tend to take notice only when their immediate world of job or family is threatened. But Columbia County is like all of our communities in that it is made up of real people struggling with real issues. In 1992, chaos and uncertainty seem to reign. The value of our organizing to date is that we have given a community hope and belief in the power of our collective strength. For now we fight the bigotry being advanced by the OCA, but our real purpose is to assert the vision of inclusion that we have for our community in a time of severe challenge.

The Northwest Coalition against Malicious Harassment/Coalition for Human Dignity

Vernon Damani Johnson

In the 1980s, white nationalism and repressive violence sparked the emergence of the domestic human rights movement in the Pacific Northwest. A key catalyst was Richard Butler's 1970s founding of the Aryan Nations in the Idaho panhandle town of Hayden Lake. Butler advanced the "Northwest territorial imperative," the notion that the states of Washington, Oregon, Idaho, Montana, and Wyoming, already the whitest part of the United States, should—and could—become a separate Aryan republic. The Aryan Nations began to hold an annual World Congress of Aryan Nations in 1979. Hate crimes against racial, religious, and sexual minorities proliferated across the small towns and rural areas of the region.

Residents of Kootenai County in Idaho formed a human relations task force to respond to Aryan Nations violence in 1981. Yet acts of intimidation and violence continued. In 1987, leaders from the five Northwestern states convened in Coeur D'Alene, Idaho, to form the Northwest Coalition against Malicious Harassment (NWCAMH). Two driving forces behind the new organization were North Idaho College professor Tony Stewart and Coeur D'Alene Catholic priest Bill Wassmuth. NWCAMH membership was made up of civil and human rights organizations, religious groups, businesses, labor unions, and law enforcement agencies. The board of directors included five members appointed by the region's governors. NWCAMH thus anchored a broad-based social movement that brought together radicals and activists with more mainstream organizations, state and local governments, and law enforcement. It focused its work on community-based responses to hate groups, such as taking public action against acts of hate and organized bigotry, supporting victims, lobbying community leaders to stand up against hate groups, and teaching acceptance of cultural and identity diversity.

As the regional work evolved, the group became part of a network that included the Coalition for Human Dignity (CHD), which conducted research on the far right, and the Western States Center, which trained progressives for both social movement work and electoral politics. In 1994, faced with a growing threat from the far right there, Colorado activists joined the NWCAMH. For over a decade a unique multi-issue regional movement flourished. By the late 1990s, dozens of local task forces had formed across the six states under the NWCAMH umbrella. Organizers traveled the region training local activists on how to frame community responses to bigotry. NWCAMH's annual conferences attracted hundreds of attendees and featured workshops on the far right as well as on how to build movements in response to it.

In the late 1990s, the CHD began experiencing financial difficulties, and in 1999 it merged with the NWCAMH to form the Northwest Coalition for Human Dignity (NWCHD). However, what had promised to be a fruitful wedding of research to community organizing proved disastrous. The two groups had been allied organizations with similar values and aspirations. But the CHD was primarily made up of leftists, while the NWCAMH—with its government, law enforcement, and religious affiliations—was more mainstream. Tensions immediately surfaced among the merged staffs, and before long, those conflicts rippled into the local task forces across the region. Issues pertaining to political ideology, race, and gender tore the organization apart. The NWCHD closed its doors in 2003.

Although the NWCHD collapsed, it accomplished a lot, including securing the passage of antimalicious harassment laws in five of the six states (all but Wyoming) and the mainstreaming of social inclusion for the identity groups it championed. Further, the network's community organizing led to victory in the $6.3 million lawsuit that terminated the Aryan Nations in 2000. The network underscored the absolute necessity of political work that linked several identity movements in a common vision while also affirming how hard this work is to do in praxis.

1.B.11.

Korean Immigrant Workers Advocates

Editorial (1996)

In the mid-1990s, the issue of affirmative action reemerged in national politics. This time, opponents of affirmative action couched their efforts in civil rights language and sought to win support in communities of color. Korean Immigrant Workers Advocates (now known as Koreatown Immigrant Workers Alliance) was founded to organize Korean and other immigrant workers in Los Angeles. In this editorial to its membership, the organization speaks out for affirmative action.

For a small ethnic community like the Korean community to maintain its health and sustainability, many aspects of it need to be functioning well. There are four main factors or pillars on which our community needs to balance itself. These are: 1) intracommunity relations, 2) interethnic relations, 3) relations with the mainstream, and 4) relations with the homeland. Obviously, these four factors have symbiotic relations which continue to influence each other, creating new conditions and challenges as they evolve with changing policies, issues, and events.

As members of the Korean community, we must always strive for the best possible conditions for all of the factors outlined above. This is by no means an easy task. Right now the Korean community is at a major crossroad. The conservative right has singled us out to play an important role in their broader "scapegoat, divide-and-conquer, or wedge" agenda.

Some of us have been selected to play the "wedge" role at the expense of the rest of the community. Unfortunately, there are those in our community seeking name recognition who would not think twice about coauthoring the misnamed California Civil Rights Initiative [Proposition 209] regardless of the consequences on our community and others. The new, young professional class is economically stable, politically ambitious, [and] upwardly mobile and has the capacity to deliver what the conservative right wants. This class has its support base among the professional and merchant class in the Korean community and is riding on the reactionary analysis of the April 29 [1992] experience [the Los Angeles uprising].

If the efforts of the neoconservative forces are left unchallenged, our community will ultimately face grave consequences. The Korean community will become the "wedge." Imagine Dole and Gingrich saying, "Look at the Korean community. They are a fine example of the reality of the American dream [. . .]" We will forever be labeled as the conservative, reactionary, minority community. Low-wage immigrant workers, seniors who depend on social service programs, children who go to public schools, battered women, the sick, the disabled, and others who are already marginalized will forever be silenced. And we will have Jay Kim and younger carbon copies of him running around representing us.

The monumental task of turning of this conservative tide in our community belongs to each and every one of us. We must wave the red flag and get the community's attention. We must articulate the concerns so that people understand the broader problems. We must propose alternatives so that we are not just criticizing. We must demonstrate that we are not chasing pies in the sky. Through concrete actions, we must improve the lives of those faced with social, political, and economic hardships due to cutbacks and take-away policies of the conservative right. We must organize like never before.

1.B.12.

Kiwi Collective

"Race and Sex: Who's Panicking?" (2000)

In this essay, the queer of color group Kiwi Collective report on Sex Panic!, a group with which they collaborated. Kiwi Collective and Sex Panic! organized in New York City during the late 1990s—a time when Mayor Rudy Giuliani led the way in instituting stop-and-frisk policing as well as a "cleanup" that pushed queer life and sex work out of Times Square and the Chelsea Piers.

The answer to our question [in the title] is reactionary, conservative, or right-wing politics in this country. The following Q&A is meant to help people move a general conversation about scandalized people, places, and practices forward.

What Are Sex Panics?

Noted historian Allan Bérubé has defined a "sex panic" as a "moral crusade that leads to crackdowns on sexual outsiders." Community organizer Eric Rofes has defined a sex panic as distinct from ongoing harassment and vilification of the sexual fringe. He writes, "Among the most effective ways of oppressing a people is through the colonization of their bodies, the stigmatizing of their desires, and the repression of their erotic energies." Continuing work of sexual liberation is crucial to social justice efforts.

Why Is This Group Calling Itself Sex Panic!?

In New York City, only one group has brought sexual freedom of expression to the forefront of the gay community's consciousness by reframing issues of sex, sexuality, and sexual practice in the late '90s. Bars, theaters, and nightclubs had been closed on technicalities and in the name of neighborhood improvement—even in cases where neighbors were not complaining. The homeless, patrons of New York's nightlife, and young queers hanging out in the waterfront had been kicked to the curb in the name of "quality of life"—even though New Yorkers seek diverse qualities of life.

In response, outspoken community organizers, tattooed academics, and pierced activists got together in April '97. The name Sex Panic! was taken ironically, to draw attention to a disturbing history of reactionary politics. The exclamation point was key because it drew attention to the hype and hysteria of antisex forces. The group conducted community forums and seminars, it marched prominently on Lesbian and Gay Pride Day in June, and it generated discussion both in NY and in the national gay press.

In September '97 Sex Panic! hosted a "Take Back the Piers" event that served as both a protest of the restrictions on the historically gay Chelsea piers and a celebration of queer space. The event included a slide show titled "On the Gay Waterfront" by Allan Bérubé and a march of several hundred activists from Sheridan Square to Christopher Street.

Sex Panic! NY allies itself in the fight against sex panics with the following mission statement: "Sex Panic! is a profeminist, antiracist, proqueer direct action group." Their multi-issue agenda aims to defend public sexual culture and safer sex in New York City from police crackdowns, public stigma, and morality crusades.

The group is committed to HIV prevention through safer sex, to sexual self-determination for all people, and to democratic urban space. By November '97 a national Sex Panic! summit had been convened on the West Coast as part of the National Gay and Lesbian Task Force conference, "Creating Change." Because of this national discussion, individuals and organizations from across the country have come together to put sex on the table. The following statement, excerpted from a longer document, was created and endorsed by the November 13, '97 National Sex Panic! Summit in San Diego, California.

A Declaration of Sexual Rights

The LGBT movement, feminism, and AIDS activism all include long histories of advocating the principles of sexual self-determination. These principles are under attack. In the name of "mainstream" acceptance, many are increasingly willing to embrace regulation and stigma for more marginal groups. And in the name of fighting AIDS, many deny that effective HIV prevention must emphasize pleasure and the complexity of sex. Increasingly forgotten are the diverse pleasures, intimacies, meanings, and relations that sex enables. Those with fewer recourses and least access to power—including those marginalized by race, class and gender—suffer disproportionately from denial of sexual rights.

Some people get the need to defend the sexual fringe by protesting the closing of adult business establishments—bookstores, bathhouses, and sex clubs. Some people even understand that these places are unique places in which inventive HIV prevention and sex education can be done. But many just don't understand that wearing your leather, enjoying your fetishes, exploring your fantasies, or relishing your multiple sex partners is political behavior. And this right to be sexual is in danger of being taken away.

Why Should People of Color Be Bothered?

People of color *are* a sex panic in this country. From the lynching of Black men, to the sterilization of Puerto Rican women, to prohibitive immigration laws against the families of Chinese laborers, sex panics have been an integral part of the process—and power—of colonization.

As during so many other American wars, people of color are the worst casualties in the war against AIDS and in the war on poverty. Because of recent panics around sex, we should also be on these front lines defending people living with HIV/AIDS, like AIDS scapegoats for example, and people who are sexually active, like the "welfare queen." The hype surrounding these stories is a call to fight for our right to be sexually active and actively sexual. But the integrity of our choices begins with simple things, like progressive sex education, reproductive rights, access to universal health care, and a deeper understanding of safe, sane, and consensual BDSM.

What Are We Going to Do about the Current Sex Panics?

It is in the politics of speaking that there exists the possibility to make educated, nonjudgmental decisions regarding our sexual practices. It is in the politics of speaking that there exists agency for the long-deferred sexual revolution of people of color.

By sweating sex with race and by cruising race with sex, we might register these politics in the very community networks, neighborhoods, and support groups that already exist. We must talk about sex panics in our discussion groups; we must bring them up in the media when our people and pleasures are demonized; and we must write back with in-your-face editorials. But we must also stand up in town meetings with conviction and act up in the streets with courage. Because race and sex are central to any understanding of the attacks experienced by our people—though talking about them together should not be seen as a problem. They are windows onto the workings of white supremacy and male dominance. And they are places of reflection, where pleasure and fantasy are valued in and beyond themselves.

To ensure that questions of race and gender and sex practices—not just sexuality—are foregrounded and transformed, discussions of explicitly raced bodies and raced pleasures should be nonjudgmental. Since the battle against conservatism occurs on both sexual and racial fronts, why aren't more race activists involving themselves with the New York City–rooted Sex Panic! and more sex activists involving themselves with the Brooklyn-based Audre Lorde Project, center for lesbian, gay, two spirit, bisexual, and transgender people of color communities?

An alliance is needed between those who identify themselves as queers, freaks, whores, and the sexual fringe and those who identify themselves as two spirit, transgendered, bisexual, lesbian, and gay people of color. For when race is rendered invisible and sex is rendered silent—when only half a human is seen and only half the story is told—the complexity of queers of color is lost.

SECTION C

Labors of Survival

1.C.1.

Las Vegas National Welfare Rights Organization

"Attention, Sisters" (1971)

In 1970 the state of Nevada attempted to massively slash welfare benefits, alleging that half its welfare recipients had committed fraud. The National Welfare Rights Organization fought to protect recipients with a combination of legal advocacy and community organizing. The group's campaign, led locally by welfare recipient and activist Ruby Duncan, culminated with a dramatic march on the Las Vegas strip that briefly shut down the casinos in March 1971. The state restored benefits the next month.

> Ain't she sweet
> Makin' profit off her meat—
> She's just America's prime commodity
> Ain't she sweet.

This little tune may refer to Miss Amerika, but welfare mothers want no part of it. When mothers in Las Vegas went to their caseworkers to ask how they were supposed to survive after their [welfare] checks were cut off or reduced, some of them were told that since they had pretty faces and figures, they should know how to make their money. In fact, prostitution and employment as maids are the only two alternatives available to poor women in this female-flesh-oriented city. Prostitution is rampant and glaringly evident as a method of exploiting women to bring more money into a city that makes $600 million a year on "tourism."

It seems no accident that while mothers are being cut off welfare, there is a strong movement in Las Vegas in favor of legalizing prostitution and reforming abortion laws (for the wrong reasons). Someone is watching out for *his* interests, and in fact they are *male* interests. Beyond the essential nature of prostitution—that it exists for the pleasure of men—prostitution in Nevada is controlled basically by two men. In some parts of upstate Nevada, brothels are legal, and one man gets most of the money. In Las Vegas, where prostitution is technically illegal, another male gets fat off kickbacks he gets for insuring "protection." Thus the controversy over legal and illegal prostitution really rages over *which* males will get the money. Women and their bodies are big business in Nevada—and welfare mothers fear being dragged into the mess. These women, already prime victims of a male chauvinistic and patriarchal system, are not ready to cooperate with a mandate that cuts off their right to life and dignity.

Join them on the 13th and 14th of March in Las Vegas for an action on the strip.

1.C.2.

White Lightning

"Drug Plague—a Revolutionary Solution" (1973)

White Lightning organized in the Bronx, New York, bringing working-class white people into coalition with radical Black, Latinx, and multiracial groups. The group confronted poverty, racism, and health inequality, linking these problems by addressing the community effects of drug addiction, the drug economy, and the criminalization of drugs. Among other campaigns, White Lightning opposed the Rockefeller Drug Laws, a set of punitive measures named after the state's governor that imposed mandatory minimum sentences and helped to massively expand the carceral system.

What We Want

1. *We want an end to the conditions that cause people to use narcotics.*

    Unemployment, poor housing, inadequate education, job speedups and oppressive working conditions lead people to use narcotics. These conditions are even worse for Blacks, Latins, Asians, and Indians. The drug plague is a symptom of deteriorating living and working conditions in this country.

2. *We want all narcotics profiteers out of our communities.*

    As difficult as life is for our people, they would not use drugs if they were not available. The addict-pusher doesn't profit from drug sales but suffers from drug abuse. The real profiteers are drug companies who overproduce for the illegal market, doctors and druggists who sell narcotics, and organized crime and their friends in the police, courts, and government.

3. *We want community education about narcotics addiction.*

People must understand why drugs are in our communities and how the government channels us toward using narcotics. Profits are the main reason for widespread narcotics sales. Heroin is a $5 billion a year business, making it the largest import brought into the country. Narcotics also keep people divided and stop them from fighting for better conditions. For both these reasons, narcotics have been used on a large scale since the Civil War. When people fight back, heroin is brought into poor communities, as well as into schools and the armed forces. People are channeled toward drugs by advertising—barbiturates ("downs") for tension and amphetamines ("ups") for overactive children. There are five million alcoholics, one million heroin addicts, and millions of amphetamine and barbiturate users in this country. Big drug and alcohol manufacturers push people to use these chemicals to increase their profit.

4. *We want community-worker-resident control of all narcotics programs.*

Most drug programs are run for profit. Residents, workers, and community people almost never have a say in how the programs function. This is why the programs do not meet the needs of the people. Phoenix House and Synanon each make over $1 million a year in profit. Yet residents in these programs are forced to hustle stores to have food to eat. These programs obviously put profit before people's lives. People in direct contact with drug addiction are most capable of solving the problem. The most effective programs are controlled by community people, workers, and residents. The Lincoln [Hospital] detoxification program is a good example.

5. *We want all drug programs to teach about the real causes of addiction.*

Most programs are based on therapy which has never been shown to help addicts. Therapy starts with the idea that addiction is an individual problem and puts the complete burden for change on the individual person. Thousands of residents in drug programs are told the plague of drug addiction is entirely their fault. When people learn that drugs are a social and not a personal problem, they will be able to do something about it.

6. *We want the elimination of legal addictive drugs such as methadone and heroin maintenance.*

Methadone is more addictive and physically more destructive than heroin. People in methadone maintenance programs are not drug free. They are now controlled by the government, and the money is made by profit-hungry drug manufacturers. Programs using legal addiction as "treatment" should be phased out as drug-free programs replace them. Methadone maintenance programs are used to control people and prevent them from working toward change.

7. *We want the human rights of addicts and ex-addicts to be respected.*

Drug users receive more contempt than pushers, who are responsible for millions of deaths. Widespread prejudice against former addicts denies them schooling and jobs. Instead, people are told, "once a junkie, always a junkie." Ex-addicts are forced into a life of poverty. These brothers and sisters must be respected and seen as victims of the drug plague. People's support can help them make a meaningful contribution to our communities.

8. *We want the release of all prisoners arrested on drug-related charges.*

   The government spends more money building prisons than arresting big dope pushers. 85 percent of the people in New York City prisons are there on drug-related charges. The government usually proposes a police state approach to drug addiction. We need more drug-free programs, job training, and jobs.

9. *We want the government to stop using drugs as an excuse to invade our communities.*

   Undercover agents have used phony searches for drugs as an excuse to occupy communities with horrible living conditions, primarily Black and Puerto Rican communities. Drugs have been planted on activists to stop their struggle to create a decent society. Several laws that decrease our civil rights have been passed under the pretense of fighting the drug plague.

10. *We want working people to control this society.*

    Only a society based on profit makes money off the suffering and death of working people through narcotics sales. When working people control this country, we will be able to end the narcotics problem by eliminating bad living conditions and providing for the needs of the people. This system of people's power is called socialism.

All power to the people!

White Lightning

1.C.3.

Great Lakes Steal

"Women at Great Lakes Steel" (1973)

The early 1970s saw a surge of radical labor activism as well as socialist feminist organizing. These two strands of politics overlapped in many settings, encouraging many men to engage more seriously with feminism, and—together with civil rights legislation—helping women to gain access to industrial jobs. This short essay appeared in *Great Lakes Steal* (misspelling intentional), a radical labor newspaper in Michigan published by Great Lakes Steel (GLS) workers.

Now that Great Lakes Steel has hired a few dozen women for the first time since World War II, there has been a lot of discussion among the men workers. The ones who really know what they're talking about understand that women working here is OK, since many women have to work to support themselves or their families just like men do.

For too many years women have been kept out of the labor force in industry, or at least kept out of certain jobs. They've been forced into lower-paying jobs, and in industries where men and women do work together, the companies usually pay the women much less than the men.

Don't forget that most women, whether or not they can find a worthwhile job, still carry a heavy burden of work as mothers and wives. They are responsible for bringing up and caring for the millions of workers who go out every day and sweat in the factories, mines, hospitals, offices, etc., just to put bread on their families' tables.

For all these reasons, we must respect our sister steelworkers. You know for damned sure that they didn't come to GLS looking for a good time any more than the men did. With prices and taxes going sky high, just one person in a family working isn't enough anymore and hasn't been for years. If the women are single, they need the job to support themselves just as much as a single man. And any woman who wants to work in this plant we think should absolutely have the opportunity to do so.

Our sister steelworkers will sure enough get hip to the struggle that's going on here between workers and the union/management team—but their needs and the workers' cause itself will be seriously hurt if the men at GLS make things miserable for the women. Unfortunately, we see fellow male workers and foremen hassling women workers every day and trying to vamp on them. Most men are definitely cool, but there are still too many whose ideas and actions can do nothing but help the company *conquer* all of us by keeping us *divided*.

The women definitely don't think that the *men* are at GLS just to get picked up, so why should the men think this of the women? If a woman wanted this, she sure wouldn't come to a *steel mill*, and this in fact is not the name of the game for our sister steelworkers. *They are working to earn the money, not to be the object of our psychological frustrations, not to find boyfriends, and definitely not be treated by their fellow workers like a commodity for sale.*

We are also finding out that the company intends to take every advantage it can of its women employees. In the cold mill, for example, women from the labor gang are often ordered to break in on certain lighter jobs, such as weighman. These jobs pay well, and normally a worker must have anywhere from three to fifteen years to hold the job.

We know it's not that the company *needs* weighmen, because they've never ordered *men* to break in on the job. The only reason is to stir up resentment against the women for their being "out of line" so that the company can keep its workers divided. Also, the company hopes to save a few dollars here and there by replacing a vacationing weighman with a young woman instead of paying someone else on the crew time and a half.

In addition, this policy reinforces that stupid and wrong idea that so many males have that women can only do light work.

Male workers who don't understand what's going on will blame the *women* who work these jobs, completely ignoring the fact that *any*one would take a better job if he or she had the chance and completely forgetting that it's not the women's fault but the company's for violating established seniority procedures.

Eventually, we're sure, the women here will see through the company's tactics of using them to stir the workers up against each other. Eventually, too, we hope they will take the special demands they have—such as childcare, maternity pay, and adequate women's lavatories, locker rooms and medical facilities—to the union. Then they will see just how little the union or the company are actually willing to do for them *or any of us.*

Most important, only when *men* realize that management, and not women, is the real problem, will any of us begin to control our lives around this hellhole.

1.C.4.

Women's Brigade of the Weather Underground

From "Message from Sisters Who Bombed HEW for International Women's Day" (1974)

Written at a time of transition in the Weather Underground Organization, this statement is from the final action conducted by the women's unit of the group, targeting the Department of Health, Education, and Welfare (HEW). This action protested both the inadequacy of and the social control enacted through the department's welfare and reproductive health programs. The statement reflects a convergence between the politics of antiracist feminism and revolutionary armed struggle.

This action is for all women who

- *wait* in lines for too few food stamps and brave food distribution lines because our families have to eat.
- *worry* thru degrading forms and humiliating rules and regulations.
- *are kept* out of paying jobs because there are no childcare programs.
- *struggle* to raise our children while we're called "pigs at the trough" and "lazy parasites" by reactionary male politicians.
- *send* our children to schools where illiteracy is taught.
- *fight* to get health care in emergency rooms and county hospitals where our bodies are used for experiments and as practice for doctors.
- *go mad*, go crazy, locked up in prisons and mental institutions.
- *live* in projects.
- *are patronized*, cast away and ignored because we are old.
- *resist!*

And [this action is] especially for Minnie and Mary Alice Relf, blackwomen-children, from Montgomery, Alabama, sterilized by HEW at the ages of fourteen and twelve.

HEW is the Nixon program of counterinsurgency against us.

It shares many things in common with AID [US Agency for International Development]-type programs in Vietnam and Latin America. HEW keeps us below subsistence—not enough food, not health care but health-care-delivery systems, not decent jobs but endless cycles of dependency and anguish.

HEW directly affects the lives of millions of women and their families. HEW decides who eats how much. HEW is the modern faceless tyrant: it is the overseer, the boss, the landlord, the judge, the official rapist. HEW blames women for poverty and then penalizes them. It is a *degrading, violent,* and *aggressive* system of *control over women.*

We attack the Department of Health, Education, and Welfare for International Women's Day, March 8, in solidarity with the rising resistance of women.

HEW Is an Enemy of Women

Hunger is violence. The American Empire creates poverty. Then the Department of Health, Education, and Welfare (HEW) claims to relate to hunger. Its slogan is "People Serving People." In fact, its programs amount to government-enforced malnutrition. Federal food programs offer a half-full, half-empty plate. HEW runs these programs in a patronizing way that tries to create the myth that women are failures—lazy, immoral, and stupid. It is a double standard and a double bind. It is their justification for keeping women as domestic slaves, under the control of men and marriage, poor and without power. . . .

Women are not to blame for the fact that 45 percent of all city families headed by women live in poverty. By government definition, that means they are improperly nourished. In the last year, food costs alone have risen 20 percent. One-third of the world's people go to bed hungry at night. The fat cats are getting fatter.

Food is not a privilege. Food is money to Them. Food is life to Us.

Sterilization is violence. Last year, HEW financed between one hundred and two hundred thousand sterilizations through Medicaid and special family planning clinics. At the same time, US agencies in the Third World have made sterilization and forced birth control programs a requirement for receiving foreign aid money. This is all part of a ruling class plan to prevent the births of more Black, Brown, Yellow, Red and poor babies.

The same men who are responsible for US policy in Vietnam and Africa say that overpopulation creates social unrest and revolution. People are not the problem. Injustice creates revolution. So does the vast inequity of social wealth—the existence of a tiny class of rich men and the great class of poor people. So does the lack of power over our lives and the future of our children.

Women want decent birth control. Women want the choice to control our own reproduction. Instead, Third World women are used as guinea pigs for testing and experimenting. Instead, we all get coils and pills and sterilizations under threat of losing our few crumbs of welfare. Instead, our bodies are made barren because of official medical neglect. This kind of coercion, for economic and racist reasons, constitutes forced sterilization. It is a direct form of genocide against the future, through the bodies of women.

Women and HEW. The size and power of HEW is a measure of the amount of poverty and exploitation in America, not of government generosity. HEW has 250 separate programs and a budget of $80 billion a year. It is the largest domestic arm of the federal government, comparable in size and function only to the Defense Department.

It is a classic institution of male supremacy, built on the oppression of women, children, and old people. It is typical of the male monopoly of power. . . .

The brunt of HEW policies falls on women. Of the fifteen million people on welfare, two-thirds are the women and children of AFDC [Aid to Families with Dependent Children]. Being on welfare is like having a sexist tyrant for an old man. You can't divorce him, but he can cut you off; you give up control of your bodies and most of your dignity as a condition of aid; he controls your money and your privacy. If you are Black or poor or old or a woman-headed household, you are directly affected by HEW programs.

In certain ways, HEW is to poor women like the BIA (Bureau of Indian Affairs) is to all Native American people. It claims to be the giver of life's necessities. But under the guise of providing social services, it functions to control and contain us, after they've ripped us off. It serves as a safety valve against crisis and revolt.

Under imperialism, reforms are turned into weapons against us, especially against Black and Third World women. Demands which were fought for every inch of the way—such as public schools, birth control, social security, trade unions—become their opposite when they remain in the control of the ruling class. HEW is really the Department of Illness, Ignorance, and Wretchedness.

In the United States, women bear the major responsibility for the health, education, and care of families and friends. This is women's work, unpaid at that. Survival questions are treated as personal problems. We're supposed to have it together, but we're deprived of power in any fundamental social institutions. The state sets women against women, forces us into desperate competition, isolates us from sisters in the Third World.

In spite of this situation, women persevere and triumph, struggle and unite, revolt and learn to fight. Our hidden herstory includes great struggles for bread, for schools, for healing, for power—against exploitation, repression, domination and against racism.

We need to remove our struggles from the private sphere where they are fought as individual battles and make them collective—as the tasks of our sex, our class, our people. International sisterhood. The roots of our oppression are connected. We have common enemies. They include specific institutions like HEW, which are fundamentally antagonistic to the emancipation of masses of women.

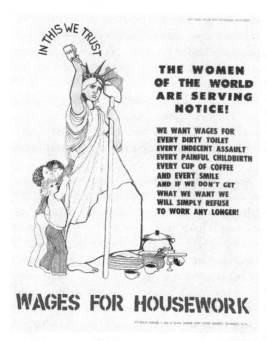

THE WOMEN OF THE WORLD ARE SERVING NOTICE!

WE WANT WAGES FOR
EVERY DIRTY TOILET
EVERY INDECENT ASSAULT
EVERY PAINFUL CHILDBIRTH
EVERY CUP OF COFFEE
AND EVERY SMILE
AND IF WE DON'T GET
WHAT WE WANT WE
WILL SIMPLY REFUSE
TO WORK ANY LONGER!

IN THIS WE TRUST

WAGES FOR HOUSEWORK

Figure 1.4. Jacquie Ursula Caldwell and Judy Quinlan, "The Women of the World Are Serving Notice!" (1974). Image courtesy of Silvia Federici.

Women's liberation is a matter of survival. We need food, decent medical care, good schools, and community-run day care. For this, we need revolution.

■ ■ ■

Four years ago today, our comrades Diana Oughton, Ted Gold, and Terry Robbins died fighting for these same struggles. They are a constant inspiration.

1.C.5.

Coretta Scott King

From Statement to House Subcommittee on Equal Opportunity and Full Employment (1975)

Coretta Scott King was a committed activist, and in the 1970s, she was especially active in the drive for full employment. She gave the statement reproduced here to Congress to advocate for a full employment policy, the Humphrey-Hawkins bill. Corporate and business interests fought hard to limit this policy and to suppress support for it. Although the bill was signed into law in 1978, it has not secured sufficient support to guarantee funding or enforcement. King's statement expresses the original visions behind the full employment goal.

There is no question in my mind that among all the pressing issues and challenges America faces, none is more important to the elimination of human suffering and to the advancement of the nonviolent ideal than the issue of providing jobs for all Americans. . . . Jobs for all the jobless in America would, more than any other social program, move America toward fulfilling its promise of providing justice and a decent life for all its citizens.

It is this belief that led me to accept the task of cochairperson of the newly organized Committee for Full Employment, along with Mr. Murray Finley, president of the Amalgamated Clothing Workers. The statement of purpose of that organization is, I believe, a very clear and cogent statement of the issue we confront. . . . It says:

> We believe the opportunity to work is a fundamental right without which human dignity and equality are diminished or withheld from millions.
>
> The problem which influences all other problems is persisting and increasing unemployment. It stifles hopes for millions, especially the young; it generates insecurity for the unemployed; it is an economic deadweight that results in the loss of billions of dollars in our gross national product.
>
> Full employment is in the interest of employers, because they must depend for their customers on those who are employed; it is in the interest of the employed, because their job security depends on full employment economy; it is in the interest of the nation as a whole, because it is necessary for economic stability, political morality, and social tranquility.
>
> For nearly three decades, the Employment Act of 1946 has promised but never mandated a policy of full employment. . . . The past three decades have also seen the rise of a sophisticated "numbers game" whereby "full employment" is defined as an ever-increasing percentage of unemployment. For us and for the nation, involuntary unemployment at any rate is morally unacceptable. For us full employment means no involuntary unemployment.
>
> Yet another postwar phenomenon is the belief that full employment cannot be achieved without substantial rates of inflation, . . . [but] genuine full employment may help to fight inflation through the increased production of goods and services. . . .

. . . I have no hesitation about asserting that this profoundly pessimistic notion—that full employment is impossible—need not and, in fact, must not be accepted. For if, as the saying goes, war is too important to leave to the generals, then it is equally true that social and economic justice in America is far too important to be left to the economists. There are some things which are self-evident truths, facts which are as much the property of all Americans as the ringing words of the Declaration of Independence.

One is that America is a country rich with resources, wide with land, and heavy with the tools and instruments that build cities and manufacture goods. The goods we produce and the standard of living of most of our citizens make us the envy of the world. It is therefore unacceptable for us to tolerate any argument against full employment that says we simply cannot afford it. If certain European countries, some of which would be no more than states if transferred to America, can employ virtually all their citizens, then so can we.

A second truth is that, for all our wealth, there remains a vast array of tasks that need to be done. It is one of the enduring shames of contemporary history that America, with the highest per capita income in the world, lags behind many countries on health and welfare indices such as infant mortality.

The jobless men in our cities are idle resources which could easily be put to work on needed, valuable projects, enhancing the quality of all our lives through jobs providing better health care, environmental improvement, and the development of new and better systems of transit and housing for urban America. No economic argument, no matter how subtle and complex, can change the reality that there are still vitally needed jobs to be done and idle men and women to do them.

This brings me to the third and final fact which we are all well aware of: that the great wealth and resources of this country are allocated in a profoundly unequal manner. From time to time in the national press, one will encounter some sarcastic mention of the fact that, amid the desperate poverty of India, the Brahma bull is considered sacred, and children will starve while these animals roam the streets unmolested. As often as not, a religious tradition such as this is presented as a foolish waste of resources and offered as a great contrast to our own supposedly enlightened ideas.

But America has its own sacred cows, and our attitude is indeed far less rational than the ethical principles of the Hindu religion. If the people of India forgo their nourishment for the sake of a living creature, what can be said of a country that forgoes the needs of its children and the care of its elderly for gleaming rows of nuclear bombs and other weapons of destruction far in excess of any rational need?

To be frank, I can no longer remember the latest estimate of how many times over our nuclear arsenal can annihilate every living Russian or the relative "superiority" that gives us. But I cannot forget that cutting our military budget by less than 10 percent, it is estimated, would provide the funds for a million new jobs for the jobless. And not only are there stark contrasts between affluence and poverty in America, but our tax system, which purports to be equitable, has allowed millionaires to pay no taxes, while the average American contributes a substantial part of his earnings.

One need only ride through the streets of any city in America to see that, as my husband once noted, we have created miracles of production, but we have achieved only a modicum of justice. . . .

There is simply no question that full employment, a job for every American who needs one, is a real and possible goal if we would choose to make it a national priority.

And there are real and pressing reasons why we should put full employment at the top of our national agenda. It is not only, as I have said, that full employment would be the single most effective cure for the whole host of urban problems that exist but that full employment would certainly create progress in the political and social life of the entire nation. It would bring together in harmony the interests of groups who now face each other across a gulf of mutual distrust and hostility. It would be a program that could win the support of the white construction worker, currently out of work because of the housing slump, and the ghetto youth, who has never had a job. No longer could a Richard Nixon or others of his like pit black workers against whites in order to avoid meeting the needs of either.

The entire cynical politics of racism—the exploitation of white fear of unemployment and black anger at exclusion—would be profoundly weakened, and the serious danger of renewed polarization would be sharply diminished. This, along with the inevitable improvement in the condition of America's ghettos, would usher in a new era in the history of race relations in the USA.

The struggle for full employment is therefore not only vital in its own right but can be the issue that will reunite the powerful forces of dignity and decency, forces which can insure real and meaningful progress in the years ahead.

1.C.6.

Auto Workers United to Fight in '76

"Letter from Rich Off Our Backs July 4 Coalition" (1976)

This letter was written for publication in a radical labor newspaper, *Auto Workers United to Fight in '76*, that worked to mobilize at General Motors plants in Detroit. It promoted radical resistance to the US bicentennial, which received official celebration in July 1976 but also sparked major counter-bicentennial protests in Philadelphia and San Francisco. Members of the coalition behind this letter included Vietnam Veterans against the War, the Unemployed Workers Organizing Committee, the Revolutionary Communist Party, the Revolutionary Student Brigade, NY-NJ United Workers Organization, and the May 1 Workers Organization.

To Auto Workers United to Fight in '76:

From punching in to punching out, every day we're at war with the bosses.

One week we're driven to work faster, the next we're thrown out the door. Forced overtime in the same plants where hundreds, even thousands are laid off. They hold the axe over our heads. Work harder for less, or else. Then who knows where the next check will come from, and how far it will stretch.

For as long as there has been an owning class, we have busted our backs, and they stole it all for their own interests. Two hundred years and things are getting worse.

We are always up against these parasites. Carrying the capitalists is a heavy load, and it is getting heavier. Wage cuts, speedup, layoffs. Discrimination, dirty working conditions. They make us fight to keep from being crushed. The greater their attacks, the greater our determination to hit back.

We are building our strength fighting them on the job, where we work together to produce everything and where we come right up against the capitalists and their mad drive for profits. And we are learning the power of the weapon of organization. We have to get together as workers and stick together and fight for ourselves to get anywhere.

July 4 is a big challenge for us. They are wrapping up their bicentennial blitz with a giant red, white, and blue birthday party.

They are telling the world that this is the way it has to be. National unity they call it. Masters and slaves together, with them on our backs forever after. They will all be there, bankers, politicians, and corporation heads, telling us to tighten our belts and sacrifice. Get ready for more productivity drives and cities crumbling. Get used to millions out of work. And on top of all this, get ready for another war, even a world war. After two hundred years, then say that this is the way it has to be.

Like hell it does. Not for us and especially not for our children. We won't live like this.

What kind of future is it that only offers us a choice between being a strikebreaker and pounding the pavement? Of wage cuts or layoffs, and they try to get us to fight over who gets which?

What kind of system is it that tries to set employed workers against unemployed, and Black against white? That keeps wages down for decades in the South, then shuts northern plants to run South? And tells us to fight among ourselves for the jobs?

What kind of a way of life is it that gears up for another war to send workers here to fight against workers of other lands who have the same problems and aspirations we do?

It's the profit system. It's the bosses' way of life, and their future. And it's not for us.

Thousands of us are going to take up the challenge on July 4. We will give our answer to national unity and belt tightening and all their dirty plans and schemes with a powerful demonstration right in Philadelphia.

We will point the finger straight at the capitalists and their rotten system of rule for every last abuse we face—from being chained to our machines to our children's schools being closed, from their layoffs to their dope pushers and army recruiters competing for a crack at our sons.

We will take the strength and organization that workers have been building and take them on over the whole mess their system has led to. And we will unite with more people and broaden our strength by doing it.

Our July 4 demonstration will show the way we are going. Half our class will not fight the other half. We will use their celebration to tie our forces together even tighter, advancing the real unity that we are building through our struggles.

Workers from auto plants in Detroit will march shoulder to shoulder with miners from West Virginia, garment workers from New York sweatshops, and steelworkers from Alabama. And growing rank and file organizations from across the country will join together to demonstrate.

And all of us will join our unemployed brothers and sisters who are setting up a tent city of the unemployed right in the middle of the bosses' lies of recovery. We will carry the strength of 250,000 of our class on the nationwide Jobs or Income petition. And together with veterans, youth and other fighters, we will march together.

With one voice and the discipline and anger we have learned fighting our common enemy, we will raise loud and clear the call of our class that we won't be ground into the dirt to get the rich out of their mess and keep them in the saddle for another two hundred years. We will fight and we won't ever stop until we have got the whole class of capitalists off our backs.

Fellow workers, July 4 is a big day for all of us. A day to fight back and a day to point to the future. We built this whole country with our brains and muscles, and these brains and muscles, put together and organized, will build a better world. Within our struggles and our movement lies the seed of this.

The powerful demonstration July 4, hitting right at the rich and all their rotten lies and crimes, will be a big step in getting there.

Join us. On to Philadelphia.

The Watsonville Cannery Strike, 1985–1987

Patricia Zavella

The Watsonville Cannery Strike was led by predominantly Mexican and Mexican American women workers. On September 9, 1985, over fifteen hundred cannery workers walked out on the two largest frozen food companies in the United States (Watsonville Canning and Richard A. Shaw Frozen Foods). The strike had been precipitated three years earlier when Watsonville Canning cut wages by forty cents per hour and established a "sweetheart" contract with the Teamsters Union that provided them with an advantage against their other local competitors. In 1985, Shaw Frozen Foods announced a similar cutback, and Watsonville Canning stunned the community by attempting to establish a base pay that was barely half of what it had been in real dollars just three years before. Workers were outraged and staged an immediate walkout.

The strike was somewhat unusual in that rank and file workers initiated the walkout and the Teamsters Union then supported them. Workers demonstrated impressive militancy through daily picket lines—often accompanied by their children—with bilingual signs and visible solidarity from numerous organizations and individuals. Once the canners brought in replacement workers, the strikers rallied around the company doors and screamed, "¡Pinches esquiroles!" ("Damn scabs!"), intimidating many. The strikers galvanized support for their families through food banks and donations to supplement the miserly $55-a-week strike benefits. They also organized frequent mass demonstrations, including a powerful march of women on their knees praying to La Virgen de Guadalupe for her blessing. Finally, after eighteen months—on March 11, 1987—management had conceded to key demands. Though wage cuts remained, workers won medical benefits, seniority rights, and striker amnesty. And by the strike's end, not a single Teamster-unionized cannery worker had crossed the picket line.

Watsonville strikers' militancy challenged the political and economic order. Food processing—canneries, packing sheds, and frozen food plants—had provided highly valued jobs in Watsonville for decades. Starting in the 1960s, growers and processors sent labor recruiters to south Texas to draw women workers, migrants mainly from Mexico, and Mexican Americans, to the Pájaro Valley in California. After a jurisdictional agreement that left the fields to the United Farmworkers, the International Brotherhood of Teamsters unionized the food processing industry so that wages were relatively good and benefits included medical insurance. The availability of off-season unemployment benefits made these jobs particularly attractive to women, who could combine seasonal cannery work with family responsibilities. Women returned to the canneries season after season, some for their entire working lives. By the time of the strike, California was home to 11,500 full-time food processing jobs, and Watsonville offered 5,000 of these at season's peak. Watsonville had eleven food processing plants, and its chamber of commerce promoted it as the "frozen food capital of the world." The power of the food processing industry also shaped local politics. One out of four Watsonville residents were Teamsters, and more Mexicans voted in union elections than in city elections, where it was virtually impossible to elect Latinos to the city council. But in the years leading up to the strike, workers' power was threatened by the global restructuring of agriculture, which prompted local farmers and processors to expand acreage in Mexico, grow new crops locally for the fresh market, and downsize food processing in Watsonville.

The Watsonville cannery strike polarized the city of Watsonville around race, class, and gender. Cannery managers, staff, and the local power structure were offended by the militancy of the predominantly Mexican women strikers, whose leadership made the strike remarkable. Strike supporters critiqued the racialization inherent in police enforcement, challenged court rulings that prevented striking workers from congregating together, and questioned unsympathetic press coverage and the willingness of a local bank to bail out the firm. The strike became a national cause célèbre as labor leaders and political organizers—including César Chávez, Dolores Huerta, and Jesse Jackson—came to Watsonville to voice their support. Solidarity between Mexican American and migrant workers from Mexico and from other racial groups and the support of labor unions, community-based organizations, and individuals from around the country all proved key factors in making the strike successful.

1.C.7.

Victoria Frankovich

From "Frankovich Reflects on Our Past— and the Evolution to Today" (1986)

In 1986 Victoria Frankovich, president of the Independent Federation of Flight Attendants, led her union in a two-month strike of the airline TWA. Her speech, given to the NOW (National Organization for Women) convention in Kansas, was reprinted in the strike newsletter and illustrated flight attendants' labor feminism.

Today, I want to dispel the myth that equality exists and that sex discrimination has been eliminated.

TWA is a microcosm of the failure of our system. Our flight attendants are victims of inequality and sex discrimination by a powerful corporation; they are examples of the bias of the news media (*Newsweek* is an example) and the sexist attitudes prevalent in modern-day corporate, male America. The press perpetuates these stereotypes.

Sex discrimination like race discrimination exists today; many blacks now fare worse today than they did during the 60s. The reason is that the wars were fought in the past. . . . [W]hen the laws changed the internalized discriminatory attitudes have not changed. It is the same with sex discrimination.

Looking back to the 40s and the 50s we all acknowledge that sex discrimination existed in the US. Flight attendants were more victimized than most. . . .

[They] had to resign at age thirty five. They were not allowed to marry, or have children. All the regulations were designed to maintain the image of sexy, young female flight attendants. . . . This era ended in 1964 with a victory in the congress and courts.

In the 60s and 70s we thought discrimination was for history books and it didn't exist now. We should have learned that legal change could not change the corporate conscience. . . . Airlines were drug screaming and crying through the courts. Again we won, or thought we did. Airline marketing continued throughout the 70s with the "coffee, tea, or me" approach. . . . Several years ago a flight attendant was disciplined after refusing a passenger sexual favors. . . .

In the 1980s we find that laws and court orders haven't changed today's mentality. . . .

Progressive victories of the 1970s made possible by the Civil Rights Act were mixed blessings. On the one hand, longer-term careers meant higher salaries. On the other hand with our victories came complacency. . . . Male management still views the job the same old way. They still want females to serve as objects to satisfy male sexual fantasies—the very thing we won in the 60s and 70s. *The very same thing.*

The very thing that made us think we were successful—the opportunity for longer-term careers—is the very thing that put us in jeopardy. I am typical: I've been with TWA seventeen years; I'm thirty-eight years old and no longer fit the nineteen-year-old image. The ivory tower airline corporate executives spurred on by chauvinist macho friends at their clubs expressing views as to what "stews" should be, have decided [. . .][w]e're too old (thirty-five to forty years is too old). We've been here too long; with fifteen to twenty years of service to the company we're at the top of the pay scale, so we're paid too much.

We live in a disposable society—disposable lighters, disposable pens, disposable diapers, disposable bottles—use things once and throw them away. There are strong forces in America that believe women are disposable commodities. Use them for a while and throw them away.

Is the TWA flight attendant situation an aberration, or it is representative of a blatantly discriminatory corporate America fueled by greed and pressured by the forces of competition? People of conscience, working men and women everywhere, need to focus on an answer to that question now.

To put the question in perspective, let me address the most recent sixteen-month history of TWA's efforts to dispose of its senior, experienced flight attendant work force. In May of 1985, notorious corporate raider Carl Icahn . . . began a hostile takeover of TWA. . . . Icahn persisted and gained control of the airline and sought salary and benefit concessions from TWA employees to fund his purchase of the airline. He accepted a 15 percent reduction in salary from management and supervision, . . . nonunion agents, . . . [and the] predominately male mechanics, janitors, and cargo handlers represented by the International Association of Machinists.

We don't minimize these concessions; these represent extraordinary sacrifices. We made the same offer. Mr. Icahn's response to our offer was stewardesses aren't "breadwinners," the "girls" are "second incomes," the girls can afford a larger cut.

Mr. Icahn's demand of flight attendants? A total of 44 percent reduction, 22 percent salary and similar benefit reduction, 22 percent work- rule concessions.

All this translates to fewer people working more hours for less money. The total yearly concessions expected of flight attendants was $110 million.

Let's place this sex-based discrimination into perspective. Nine thousand predominately male employees gave back $49 million, and they were only temporary givebacks. Everything is restored at the end of a three year period. Six thousand predominately female employees were expected to give back $110 million with no snapback. They were expected to settle for a permanent salary, benefit, and work-rule concession of $16,000. This represents a giveback of three times more than [that of] the male employees. *Now, I ask you is this discrimination?*

We offered not only fifteen percent wage cuts . . . but to increase the hours we work each day and each week. And still Icahn rejected it. Not only did Icahn refuse our offer, but he told us he could replace us with nineteen-year-olds, and "replace" is another word for "dispose of."

Is he motivated only by economics or the desire for a nineteen-year-old work force? Carl Icahn, corporate raider, forced us out on strike. He says he has replaced us, another way to say he disposed of us. Five thousand of us. But we're still fighting. Like David fighting Goliath we believe we're going to win, and we'll keep up our fight until we do.

In the larger picture, the issue goes far beyond TWA and our ultimate fate. As Americans we believe it cannot happen here. *But it can and it is.* The most disturbing development, the one fact that can allow this kind of conduct to become the norm is the complacency, insensitivity, and smugness from those very people that in previous decades led the fight to eradicate discrimination. Respected print and electronic media that helped shape the social conscience of America suddenly demonstrates strong signs of deafness and blindness to what is happening. If it seems to make economic sense, it's right regardless of the social consequences. On that same rationale one might argue that black slavery makes sense. Apartheid makes sense. But as free people of conscience we reject these notions. Network television shows and magazines like *Newsweek* have justifiably earned respect for helping to shape public opinion and social awareness. But something has happened. The tone of the questions and the specific questions I've been asked by female reporters: "Why don't you give him what he wants?" and "Why don't you turn this over to a man to negotiate?"

The media is critical of us for resisting. Not only is this offensive, but it ignores our worth. It ignores our contribution, it ignores our equality, and it ignores our years of struggle. Which if forgotten, can only lead to a rampant, discriminatory pre-1960 Civil Rights Act era.

I can only conclude that the media no longer exercises social responsibility but is content to mirror the corporate view of reality. This means that if society disagrees, if men and women of conscience are offended by these trends, we must let it be known.

1.C.8.

September Alliance for Accessible Transit

From "Why Are We Here?" (1987)

The September Alliance for Accessible Transit was a disability rights group in the San Francisco Bay Area that collaborated with American Disabled for Accessible Public Transportation, which had formed in the late 1970s in Denver. This flyer reflects protests, including civil disobedience, that activists engaged in at a meeting of transit lobbyists. The activists demanded that all public transportation be accessible to people with disabilities.

We are fighting to *restore* a national transit policy that gave *all* disabled and elderly people the *right* to ride public transit.

Who Are We?

September Alliance for Accessible Transit (SAAT): a united group of disabled people and their organizations throughout northern California working to *restore* our right by influencing the American Public Transit Association (APTA).

American Disabled for Accessible Public Transportation (ADAPT): a national organization which has been working for access to transportation and other facilities since 1983. ADAPT's strategy of protesting APTA has kept the need for fully accessible transit at the top of the disability rights movement agenda.

We are fighting for our *civil right to public transportation*!

Why Are We Targeting APTA?

The American Public Transit Association [is] the national lobbying arm and trade association of the transit districts of the United States. APTA is *very influential*. APTA used its influence with the federal government which *eliminated* regulations that guaranteed *accessible public transportation*! APTA refuses to vote on or even discuss the issue. . . .

The only way to provide meaningful access to public transportation for disabled and elderly people is through a combination of accessible mass transit systems and paratransit. We have spent years working peaceably to achieve a guarantee of this right, only to lose it again.

We will not stop fighting it until we get it back again, permanently.

The Disability Rights Movement in the 1970s

Paul K. Longmore

On April 5, 1977, disability rights protesters sat in at the headquarters of the US Department of Health, Education, and Welfare (HEW) in Washington, DC, and at regional offices in nine other cities. They demanded that HEW immediately issue the regulations that would make Section 504 of the 1973 Rehabilitation Act an enforceable law. Prohibiting discrimination in federally funded programs against "otherwise qualified handicapped" persons, 504 was the first federal civil rights law protecting Americans with disabilities. In most cities, the HEW protests lasted only hours. In DC, demonstrators stayed overnight and were starved out the following day. But in San Francisco, some 150 protesters stayed overnight, and 120 held on for the next three and a half weeks. Their sit-in was the culminating moment of the US disability rights movement in the 1970s.

Disability activism became more organized, politicized, and militant over the course of the decade. Grassroots and national advocacy groups emerged or expanded among deaf activists, blind people, psychiatric survivors, and people with physical disabilities and intellectual disabilities. All opposed involuntary institutionalization and favored community-based living. Major strategies included litigation, campaigns for accessibility and educational rights, and the establishment of independent living centers. By the 1980s, American Disabled for Accessible Public Transit was employing civil disobedience to achieve accessibility in public transit systems across the country.

Although the disability rights movement as a whole is often framed as being largely white, some advocacy groups such as Fiesta Educativa, which formed in 1978 and represented Latino parents of children with disabilities in Los Angeles, emerged in communities of color. A more extensive change involved cross-disability alliances, as evident through Disabled in Action (DIA), which formed in New York City in 1970 and soon had chapters in other northeastern cities. Taking on a wide range of issues and employing direct action as well as lawsuits, DIA represented a generational shift.

In 1974, the American Coalition of Citizens with Disabilities (ACCD) began to push for the implementation of Section 504. In 1977, after years of delays and rumors of weakened regulations, ACCD issued a deadline: sign 504 implementation by April 4 or face nationwide protests. The deadline went unmet, and sit-ins began.

In San Francisco, organizers planned for a lengthy occupation by building a network of supportive community organizations. Risking arrest, the Black Panthers and the Delancey Street Foundation brought in food donated by unions, churches, stores, and restaurants. These alliances marked a turning point and put local HEW officials on notice to not starve out disabled protesters as they had in other cities. The sit-in got additional support from liberal Democratic congressional representative Phillip Burton and Mayor George Moscone.

Twelve days into the protest, Burton and his colleague George Miller conducted a hearing in the building to take testimony from demonstrators. Protest leaders seized the opportunity to confront a HEW representative on camera. Between that confrontation and the sit-in itself, activists effectively countered HEW's portrayal of Section 504 as a bureaucratic mandate. Instead they framed the situation as disabled Americans battling discrimination while politicians tried "to steal our civil rights." Days later, protest leaders flew to Washington, and a week and half later, regulations were signed. On April 30, 1977, San Francisco protestors triumphantly paraded out of the federal building singing, "We *have* overcome."

Disability rights activism of the 1970s rejected the social prejudice, institutionalized discrimination, domination by professionals, exclusionary design, lack of appropriate support services, absence of accommodations, and bad policies that accompanied the "medical model" of disability. Advocates demanded the means to achieve participation and integration in society through educational opportunities, protection against job discrimination, access and accommodations, and personal assistance services. They claimed these provisions as rights under law rather than as charity that might be withheld. Activists also demanded individual and collective self-determination for disabled people. Though many of their goals were "liberal" reforms, their opposition to the dominant framing of "disability" constituted a radical challenge to society. Through collective action, activists pursued social, economic, and political equity.

1.C.9.

John Mehring

"Union's AIDS Education Committee Helps Health Care Workers, Patients" (1987)

John Mehring was a psychiatric nurse and union activist in SEIU (Service Employees International Union) Local 250. He served as secretary of the union's AIDS Education Committee, whose work he detailed in the essay printed here. AIDS activism in unions advanced quality health care for people with AIDS and built on LGBT-labor coalitions that had grown since the 1970s.

In the summer of 1983 Service Employees Local 250, the largest health care local in the SEIU, established an AIDS education committee. This was two years after the discovery of what came to be known as "acquired immune deficiency syndrome." Local 250 is based in San Francisco and represents over twenty-five-thousand health care workers in northern California.

In a statement to the local's executive board, rank and filers wrote that "a more informed understanding of AIDS and those who are afflicted with it has become necessary in order to combat the fears, apprehensions, prejudices—and even hysteria—of those who feel they may be at risk in contracting the disease."

There was, and is, *no* evidence that human immunodeficiency virus (HIV), commonly called the AIDS virus, is transmitted through casual contact. Though the virus itself was not discovered until 1984, by 1983 medical authorities agreed that AIDS was transmitted by direct, intimate contact with blood and semen.

Still, the San Francisco Bay Area experienced a wave of AIDS hysteria in 1983. For example, some bus drivers refused to handle transfers in gay neighborhoods; street cleaners wore "isolation suits" during their clean-up of Market Street after the annual Lesbian/Gay Freedom Day Parade; and two nurses in San Jose refused to treat a man diagnosed with AIDS.

Fear and Prejudice

To mitigate this fear and prejudice, Local 250 activists proposed that the union conduct an educational campaign for members. Political action was seen as another component of the committee's work: lobbying for increased funds for AIDS services and research and combating AIDS discrimination.

Has the committee's agenda set forth in 1983 been fulfilled? Only in part, given the enormity of the problem. The number of AIDS cases in San Francisco, as elsewhere, has grown relentlessly. In the summer of 1983 the Bay Area had around two hundred AIDS cases. In summer 1987 there are approximately thirty-five hundred cases in San Francisco alone (of whom over two thousand have died).

But the fear and discrimination which accompanied AIDS are under better control among health care workers. San Francisco has one of the outstanding AIDS education programs in the country. The San Francisco AIDS Foundation, a leader in this area, has received financial support from Local 250, including co-sponsorship of a western regional "AIDS and Ethnic Minorities" conference.

But in 1983 there was no brochure directed to health care workers and their specific concerns. Producing the brochure "AIDS and the Health Care Worker" was a high priority for our committee. The first edition was printed in summer 1984.

This brochure is now in its fourth edition, soon to be fifth, and more than one hundred thousand copies have been distributed nationwide by SEIU. SEIU also distributes a comprehensive AIDS handbook, *The AIDS Book: Information for Workers*, which the committee recently helped revise for a second printing.

Not Enough

Important as these materials have been to educate workers about AIDS, experience has shown that reading factual information alone does not address all the continuing questions and feelings health care workers have about AIDS. Periodic work-site education therefore is an important part of effective AIDS education.

Some hospitals—though by no means most—do their own in-services on AIDS, with or (mostly) without union involvement, but [these services are] mainly offered to direct-care providers (nurses and techs) and ignor[e] the needs of other hospital workers. To fill these educational gaps, SEIU conducts its own AIDS education workshops for field representatives, stewards, and interested members. Committee members are an important resource for these sessions.

Many hospitals have AIDS "coordinating committees" or "multidisciplinary resource teams" which review hospital AIDS policies and procedures. The committee includes members who sit on these in-house task forces.

Committee members also serve as advocates for AIDS patients in the hospitals they work in. AIDS health care workers are in increasing agreement that specialized AIDS units in hospitals provide superior care for AIDS patients, for several reasons: workers there have chosen to work with AIDS patients; community support groups can more easily focus their resources in a particular place; and care can be closely monitored and up-to-date information most easily disseminated.

Political Front

On the political front, the committee has put the union on record favoring AIDS antidiscrimination ordinances, and California protects people with AIDS and ARC (AIDS-related conditions) using statutes that ban discrimination against the handicapped.

At the 1984 SEIU quadrennial convention, the committee sponsored a resolution calling for increased government funding for AIDS research and health and social services. At the 1988 convention, the committee will present resolutions relating to AIDS funding, discrimination, and testing.

In San Francisco, 97 percent of all people with AIDS are gay or bisexual men, compared with 74 percent across the country. To get contract protection for members with AIDS, ARC, or HIV-antibody-positive status, the committee has encouraged the union to propose in all its contracts language banning discrimination based on sexual orientation, lifestyle, and handicapped status.

The union is also attempting to negotiate economic benefits for members with domestic (unmarried) partners, extending health insurance and bereavement leave to them.

As the incidence of AIDS rises and encompasses more areas of the country, so will the demand for AIDS education. Unions should consider forming AIDS education committees to coordinate their responses to AIDS or incorporate that response in existing health and safety committees.

1.C.10.

Marian Kramer

From "Remarks on the National Welfare Rights Union" (1993)

Despite being elected with the support of civil rights and feminist organizations, President Bill Clinton led a massive cutback to antipoverty benefits, known as "welfare reform." While the law was enacted in 1996, its threats became apparent a few years earlier, in part because they built on state-level cuts being made around the country. Marian Kramer, a lifelong activist, welfare rights organizer, and Black feminist, described some of these threats and an alternate vision for welfare policy in a speech to the organization she cofounded.

On June 30, 1987, the National Welfare Rights Union was formed in Washington, D.C., on the twenty-first birthday of the national welfare rights movement. From New York to California we are committed to social justice for all members of our society, particularly those who have been excluded from the benefits of this nation. According to our member, the late Annie Smart, the current welfare system destroys families by keeping the husband and father out of the household, penalizing those trying to work themselves out of welfare, and punishing people, especially children, for being poor. Current welfare policies punish all kinds of families by denying the monetary support they need to feed and clothe their children, particularly families headed by women.

All people should have an adequate income, a guaranteed income assuring that no one in this nation will live in poverty. All people should be able to live a life of dignity, with full freedoms and respect for human rights. All low-income people and public assistance recipients should enjoy a fair and open system that guarantees the full protection of the US Constitution. All low-income and public assistance recipients should participate directly in the decisions affecting our lives, but we have been excluded from welfare reform since the day that Clinton came into office. True welfare reform begins with bringing people up and out of poverty. True welfare reform is based on unity and solidarity with the spirit of social justice for all impoverished persons. True welfare reform is supposed to hold families together. It should include at least the following:

1. A minimum wage of $15 an hour;
2. Effective, unified child-support legislation based on the cost of living;
3. Nationalization of welfare recipients—and support for all families, including individuals and couples. The General Assistance program (GA) was eliminated in Detroit, Michigan, in 1991, the results of which have been devastating. We have many seniors who are entering the rolls of the homeless. . . . Michigan, especially Detroit, now looks like a Third World country;

4. Establish uniform standards for eligibility above the poverty line for all public assistance recipients at the state and federal levels;
5. Abolish grant level penalties; and
6. Halt the tax on families for state abuse in the name of fraud. California is one of the leading states in constantly accusing people of fraud and saying the mothers are fraudulent for having food on the table and clothing and shelter for their children. California has sought to justify its practice of compelling people to take lie detector tests, to fingerprint them, and to treat them as if they were criminals because of their poverty.

To us, this government is responsible for condemning people to a life of poverty. It is the worst government in the world because it condemns my children to hopelessness and prevents them from looking forward to a decent education. Those in this government who condemn people to poverty are worse than the savings and loan criminals. It is said that we have freedom of choice and will enjoy it now that the president and his wife are looking into health care. We are saying that we want universal health care, including the right to choice, but that is not part of their health care position. We want dental care, transplants, and the same quality of health care that a person up on Capitol Hill or in Washington now enjoys at our expense.

We want federal support for universally available quality childcare. We want guaranteed, quality affordable housing, and if you don't give us housing, we are going to take it. We will take public housing. We want adequate transitional support so that our children can have a future. All the above should be guaranteed by the Constitution. We believe that the Constitution should guarantee the right to a home. Reality slaps you in the face once you become homeless because there is not a guarantee in the Constitution. We will say to President Clinton, "You might have your working group—we met with them two weeks ago—but when you select someone like David Ellwood, who doesn't even know what it means to be eligible for these programs or what it means to face welfare today, to head your working group, then you have missed the boat."

Not only is the president placing these people in a working group, but they are also talking about eliminating our people from the program after two years. We work every day, we have a job, and there is a difference between working and having a job. Anyone who sits on a working group and talks about work should have the common sense to know that the first thing you must talk about in this country is getting up and out of poverty. We have a mission statement for welfare rights, where we call upon all people to support the principles in the Constitution: adequate income above the poverty level, adequate and affordable housing, employment at prevailing wages, equal and quality health care, and quality childcare. Although slavery was abolished in this country over 120 years ago, mandatory work legislation has in effect restored slavery in this country, regardless of race. Such legislation, and most notably the Family Support Act, which we would never support, restores slavery. We reject all workfare legislation in its current form.

You need to decentralize this conference, to take it down to Watts and talk to the brothers and sisters to find out what they want. They are the true speakers and they know more about their lives than anyone. Take this conference to Atlanta, to where they are knocking down public housing. You need to decentralize this conference and bring it to Detroit. We understand that Clinton's welfare reform is the same kind of reform that New Jersey is pushing, with caps, learnfare, and talk about the social contract, which is outright slavery in Michigan. Programs are being implemented at the state level similar to Clinton's proposals—such as eliminating public assistance after two years. You know, I worked to get the vote out; we got the vote out and the victims in poverty participated in putting this man in the White House. We are also going to participate diligently in getting him out of the White House. People on welfare can manage a budget better than the people in the state capital.

During my ten years on public assistance, it was not the same as it is today. It was not the same public assistance that the vast majority of people face today. We have over seventy-five million people living in poverty. I know that the statistics say thirty-five million, but the figure is higher. When I was on public assistance, it was different from what my daughters are facing today. They are facing homelessness. Programs are being eliminated. People *died* in Michigan when cuts occurred in the General Assistance [program]. A close friend of mine died for lacking the transportation to get to the kidney machine.

We have a tremendous job at this conference. The people here have begun to tie the threads of this discussion together, but you cannot do this unless people in poverty, the victims of poverty, are represented among you. You are the people who can help begin to talk about true welfare reform in this nation. So I hope you rededicate your lives today and understand that you cannot do this unless the victims of poverty are part of the leadership.

. . . We can talk about child support, but many of our men are unemployed. Child support should be the responsibility of the government. We should not penalize our children. Thus, if legislation does not take this as its point of departure, does not stress getting up and out of poverty, then I have problems with it. Our three-pronged attack includes the streets, the legislature, and the courts for helping people out of poverty.

Defending Welfare Rights in the 1990s
Marisa Chappell

In 1992, President Clinton declared an "end of welfare as we knew it," and in 1996 the United States enacted a punitive "welfare reform" law with harsh time limits and deep benefit cuts. In the years leading up to and following the bill, activists and advocates mobilized to advance new ways of framing the struggle for welfare rights and economic justice. Much of the action took place at the local level. Hundreds of local groups organized to block punitive welfare reform. In February 1995, a national day of action to defeat welfare reform generated actions in seventy-seven cities and the National Welfare Rights Union's Survival Summit drew hundreds of women from across the country. Immigrant rights activists, local unions, policy rights lawyers, and feminist policy advocates fought to defend income support programs and advocate for the rights of low-income people.

In the face of strong public support for welfare work requirements, which stipulated that welfare recipients, even mothers of very young children, needed to be employed to receive benefits, some activists adopted an employment approach, demanding "real jobs, not slavery." The Association of Community Organizations for Reform Now (ACORN), for example, organized the growing ranks of workfare participants in several cities. These campaigns organized "unions" of workfare participants to demand labor protections and better employment opportunities. Alliances with local unions, and savvy strategies such as a mock union election that garnered 16,500 votes of support in New York City, won some local and state-level policy concessions, including increased childcare provision, grievance procedures, and job creation legislation. In the 1990s, ACORN and other activists won living wage ordinances in hundreds of cities.

At the same time, feminist-oriented activists questioned the premise of "welfare-to-work" approaches by advocating for "children's right to care" and "carers' right to payment." When Congress passed an initial welfare reform bill, feminist scholars formed the Women's Committee of 100, which held a vigil at the White House and took out a full-page ad in the *New York Times* with the message "a war against poor women is a war against all women." At a welfare mothers' convention before the Democratic National Convention in 2000, the newly organized Every Mother Is a Working Mother network allied with the Los Angeles Coalition to End Hunger and Homelessness to demand "decent wages for caring work." These groups were small but their coalitions won local victories, including the creation of a free after-school childcare program in Los Angeles County. They also achieved minor changes in the federal law, such as a time-limit exemption for victims of domestic violence. However, activists were unable to more generally protect low-income single mothers' entitlement to income support.

Meanwhile, the anti-immigrant provisions of the 1996 welfare law and the growth of the global justice movement in the 1990s encouraged the globalization of the welfare rights movement. In 1998, Cheri Honkala, cofounder of Philadelphia's Kensington Welfare Rights Union, launched the Poor People's Economic Human Rights Campaign, which offered a global framework for the welfare rights movement's long-standing claim of a "right to live." The campaign denounced US welfare policies as violations of human rights, as defined and enshrined in the United Nations' 1948 Universal Declaration of Human Rights. Campaigns to advance the rights of parents, workers, and

immigrants in the United States and beyond saw regulatory and redis-
tributive policies as crucial tools for protecting and advancing human
dignity.

Despite a lack of substantive policy victories, activists continued
to claim economic security as a human right into the twenty-first century. Amid the dramatic growth of income and wealth inequality in the
United States and globally and policies that increasingly criminalized
poverty, movements ranging from Occupy Wall Street to Black Lives
Matter placed economic justice at the center of their campaigns for a
more just society.

1.C.11.

Milwaukee Welfare Warriors

"Apologies Don't Help" (1996)

Written amid the passage of so-called welfare reform, this statement from a
Milwaukee welfare rights organization critiques the public rhetoric surrounding welfare, including as expressed by liberals seeking to achieve compromise in the legislation.

Thank you for your help in publishing facts and myths about those of us who
receive government child support. May we ask you to go one step further in
your support of our families?

Popular lists of "facts" about welfare are defensive: We *only* have two children, *only* stay "on" welfare for two years, *only* receive $370 a month, *only* use up
1 percent of the federal budget, *only* need help temporarily to get us on our feet,
would *"work"* if *only* we could afford childcare/health care or could find a job,
are *mainly* white adults, not teens, and *mainly* children.

These apologetic "facts" present statistical truths about welfare. However,
they omit two profound realities of welfare:

1. AFDC [Aid for Families with Dependent Children] is a public child support program.
2. Most single-mother families on welfare are victims of abuse and/or
   abandonment.

No other moms are called *dependent* or made to feel like parasitical, apologetic
criminals for receiving support for their children. Widowed moms, some divorced moms, married moms all expect and receive support—from both the
government (tax deductions, Social Security) and the biological fathers. Neither they nor their children are accused of being social deviants or mentally de-

fective (low self-esteem, etc.) because they receive economic support. Nor are they labeled "recipients"—an insulting, passive, one-dimensional label of the complex being a single mother on welfare is.

And what about those of us with three, four, or five children or those of us who are teen moms? What about the moms who can't both raise kids alone and work full time? What about the women who aren't white? What about those of us who use the support for far more than two years? Most of all, what about the vast majority of us who will never get our families out of poverty with one woman's salary?

Apologetic statistics are not working to convince Americans that children and mothers have a right to share in our wealth. Apologies are not convincing taxpayers that children need support, even if mom is employed. Apologies are not stopping the violence and terrorism of welfare reform. Apologies are not stopping the government from taking children away from loving homes. Apologies are not stopping the government from giving the majority of our tax money to corporations and the Pentagon. Apologies are not creating living-wage jobs for moms (or dads). Apologies are not helping Americans understand the problem or the solutions. Apologies are not helping single mothers and children retain the strength needed to fight back.

It is time for our allies to do more than apologize for our existence. It is time to stand up for our right to public support for our children and our right to do paid work or get help from a partner without losing that support. It is time for our allies to state loud and clear that they will not tolerate systematic punishing of mothers and children for being victims of abandoning dads and a slave-wage workforce.

It is time for our allies to fight for us, not apologize for our existence.

1.C.12.

Mary Beth Maxwell

From an interview on Jobs with Justice (2013)

Jobs with Justice (JwJ) is a national labor-community coalition that seeks to mobilize public support and moral authority in order to energize worker campaigns and strengthen organizing power despite the diminishing right to organize. This interview with organizer Mary Beth Maxwell, published in 2013, offers insight into Jobs with Justice in the 1990s, particularly in relation to race, gender, and sexuality in the labor movement.

Can you tell us more about how JwJ developed in the first few years you were there, and how its women's retreats and work with Pride at Work fit into everything?

Let me start with a little story. I want to also talk about gender and racial justice in Jobs with Justice. One of my classic JwJ moments was at the Louisville annual meeting [in 1999]. We had this incredible action, classic JwJ action, where people had identified this local struggle of a bunch of UFCW [United Food and Commercial Workers] members who worked in a poultry-processing plant for Tyson. There were getting nowhere with a strike. Tyson was just waiting them out. People did a really good power analysis about what we could do that would really make a difference for these workers and how we could take advantage of hundreds of other activists coming into town. And we planned this incredible action.

It turns out that the world headquarters of Kentucky Fried Chicken are in Louisville. . . . So we came in to do a little tour of the museum about Kentucky Fried Chicken, which is kind of funny, [and] we take over the world headquarters. Hundreds of labor, community, and faith activists take over, until management finally has to come out and hear the demand that, as one of the biggest purchasers from Tyson, *you* can make a difference if you will make a call to Tyson and tell them to sit down at the table and get justice with these workers. It was an incredible event.

As you can imagine, it was a struggle that had been going on for a while in Louisville. There was also in Louisville this amazing LGBT organization called Fairness. It was a group of LGBT activists that really had a race and class analysis of social justice in addition to their vision for justice for people based on sexual orientation and gender identity. We had been building bridges with them over the past year in Louisville. They had come to us and said, "You know, we want to be helpful on these worker campaigns, but we don't know any of these people in the labor movement." These were totally separate movements in this town, and through Jobs with Justice, and over the course of time, relationships started to get built between them. So they were acting in solidarity with each other, which was really amazing and phenomenal. The night of the banquet in Louisville, where everyone was excited because they had done this fantastic action [. . .] we had it lined up that this amazing organizer from Fairness stood up and talked about why all the LGBT activists had stood with the Tyson workers and how important it was that they stand up for them and for their working conditions. So it's like the Jobs with Justice "I'll be there," the "I'll be there for your struggle." And after Carla comes up, this great guy—a good, big, labor guy from the UFCW, a fantastic leader—stood and said, "We are so thankful that Fairness was there for the Tyson workers. But I want to say this. We stood up for Fairness and we supported their campaign, not just because they stood with the Tyson workers. We stood up for Fairness because this is about human rights and this is the right thing for us to do—to insist on human rights for all people whether they're gay or whether they're straight." So as you can imagine, a lot of us are crying at that point. That had never happened before at a JwJ annual meeting.

. . . [T]his notion of solidarity and reciprocity is not a transactional thing. . . [I]n fact, solidarity, as that moment showed, is transformational. Like people's notion of what justice we are fighting for, it grows and expands, and people's notion of who is the "we" grows and expands. That to me is one of the most powerful things about Jobs with Justice. . . .

SOLIDARITY DAY
JOBS · JUSTICE · SOCIAL PROGRESS

TOGETHER
WE SHALL BE HEARD
SEPTEMBER 19, 1981 · WASHINGTON, D.C.
☼ IAM & AW AFL–CIO ☼

Figure 1.5. "Solidarity Day" (1981). Image courtesy of Lincoln Cushing/Docs Populi.

And you asked about gender and women at Jobs with Justice. . . . A lot of our organizers, a fair number of them, were women, and it's not easy to be a woman, to be a young woman, a lot of times as the new organizer helping to build a new labor and community coalition. It's actually pretty hard. "How are we going to sustain folks in this?" we were asking ourselves. It was hard to be the one, and this was also true for people of color who were leaders in JwJ and who often were having to deal with a labor movement or even community organizations that weren't as diverse with regard to race, gender, sexual orientation, or anything like that. For anybody, it's hard to be the only something. So at some point I came to Fred [Azcarate] and said "This is just—you know—we gotta do something, and I think we should organize a women's retreat for Jobs with Justice organizers." . . . Fred right away was like, "Do it. That sounds like a good idea." . . . If you can build a community of people who can build stronger relationships with each other and break the isolation of what they are experiencing, help them share lessons and strengthen each other and build those bonds, that investment in each other—that investment in relationships—is an investment in organizations and in our movements.

There was a similar vision, and I credit Fred Azcarate with this a lot, the notion that we wanted to build JwJ as a place where there was really room for multiracial coalitions and relationships of respect in a multiracial context. For me that actually comes from the United States Student Association, and there's a number of us that come from the USSA. But Fred had been the president [of USSA], and here he was as a young man of color, this new director of JwJ, and building relationships with a ton of amazing people in the labor movement who were totally committed to workers' rights, totally committed to that solidarity and militancy. But that was a pretty white group [laughs], and Fred took this lesson that we had from USSA: if we're going to build real social change in this country, we have got to build relationships across difference and we have to build multiracial organizations. . . . It didn't work if there were one or two people of color who were having to navigate all of the issues of race with a totally majority-white group. And then you had to organize so that those people of color could build support with each other and that we would expect white people to take responsibility for building that multiracial culture as well, but that power had to be shared.

. . . We keep working, we keep learning, every single year, about what other ways we have to stretch ourselves to really make room for every single person who's got to be at that table—whether it's race, gender, class, immigration status, or whatever—you keep investing in that, expanding that, expanding the "we" in Jobs with Justice.

1.C.13.

Tyree Scott

From "Whose Movement Is It Anyway?" (1997)

Tyree Scott was a Seattle labor organizer who worked to open the construction industry to people of color and women, as well as to advance the labor movement toward radical politics grounded in working-class communities of color. This unpublished essay presents his insights into labor organizing both inside and outside unions amid the rise of worker center organizing, labor-community coalitions, and the global justice movement.

That bumper sticker around nowadays [that] says "*The labor movement, the folks who brought you the weekend*" doesn't tell the whole story. This is the movement that brought dignity and hope to the men and women who toil and whose labor has created all the wonderful possibilities that exist in our world.

This movement of the working masses in our own country was compromised by a small group who took control of its most organized part—the trade unions—and called it the labor movement. This mass movement that continues today to break out in different skirmishes all over this country in its many forms was redefined in such a narrow way that it does not recognize itself as a part of "the great labor movement." Working people of color and immigrants fighting for fair wages and equality are not seen as part of the labor movement; women opposing discrimination and demanding equal pay are seen as "feminist activists," not part of the labor movement. And the unorganized sectors of workers are looked upon as people unworthy of certain work and are viewed as the cause of low wages.

When these groups organize into formal organizations, the labor unions are quick to note that these formations do not represent labor. They would be right if they said that these formations do not represent the trade unions. The specter of dual unions continues to be a threat to the labor movement and can never be tolerated under any disguise. However, they are absolutely wrong when they assert that these nongovernmental community-based mass formations do not represent labor. They often represent the labor movement and its ideals far better than many of the trade unions as they are now constituted. These were the very forces that came together in the 1930s and won the compromises that made into law basic human rights such as collective bargaining and freedom from discrimination and harassment by employers.

This redefinition of the labor movement did not take place without a struggle, but in the end the forces that chose the narrow road and called for a separate peace carried the day. The trade unions alone became the labor movement. The leadership replanted the seeds that would divide the labor movement until today. Craft unions adopted membership policies for white male heterosexuals only and limited their numbers. This effort to control the supply of labor and keep wages high was shortsighted and gave rise to an anti–trade union view by those workers who were locked out of those unions. This policy created the conditions for growth of the nonunion sector and has had the effect of holding down wages and working conditions of all workers.

A campaign to buy American-made products was implemented in place of a movement for international solidarity with workers in other countries, creating the notion that US workers have more in common with their local bosses than with foreign workers. . . .

These conditions—which have contributed to the declining power of the trade unions—are able to exist in the absence of recognition of the centrality of the struggle against racism and sexism. They continue to exist in the absence of an international solidarity program and in the absence of a democratic structure in the trade unions themselves. . . .

Resistance to the current attacks on the social safety net that are taking place now in the form of welfare cuts and the anti-immigration laws represent an opportunity for the labor movement to fuse parts and protect its present position as well as hedge its bets for the future. Structural adjustment trends that are taking the form of downsizing and privatization, coupled with the anti–affirmative action trend, are pushing more and more workers into the ranks of the unemployed. They are on a merger course with those who are being driven into the work force by the welfare cuts. The labor community's recognition of itself and this trend would promote the need for all workers to unite in the struggle to resist these attacks. On the other hand, if the movement fails to recognize itself, this merger will turn into a collision with these workers fighting each other over their share of the shrinking pie.

Foreign Policy, Trade, and Immigration

Likewise the union leaders' narrow approach to domestic economic issues has led them to neglect foreign policy and immigration issues that have important trade implications and impact wages and conditions . . . through agreements such as the European Economic Community (EEC), the General Agreement on Tariff and Trade (GATT), [and] the North American Free Trade Agreement (NAFTA) and through organizations such as the World Trade Organization (WTO).

These trade agreements coupled with the unprecedented advancements in communications and transportation in the last two decades have made it possible for the manufacturing sector to join the capital investors abroad. The developing countries who formerly only supplied the raw material now add value into this raw material in the form of processing, refining, assembly, or other methods. This new value-added policy looks like a windfall for the workers in these so-called low-wage countries and a loss for workers in this country. Except that when we look closer we see that these workers are only producing for export. The low wages they receive for their work does not afford them any possibility of consuming what they produce, while the restrictions to their movement assure that they will be available and willing to produce for any wage.

These are the conditions that tie the workers in the developed countries to those in the developing countries. The low wages and exploitation of one will pull down the wages and conditions of the other; any advancement of one is tied to the advancement of the other. It is in this context that makes foreign policy, trade, and immigration central issues to the labor movement. . . .

Workers and the Environment

Finally, protection of the environment, which should be high on the priority list of our movement, is often times viewed as a hostile issue by the rank-and-file worker. Partial blame should be placed at the feet of the leaders of the environmental movement for not making the effects of environmental regulation on workers' lives a central concern in their approach to environmental protection. The trade union leaders must also take responsibility for the view held by workers, since little or no voice has been raised to support or explain the environment issue and its implications on labor. This policy exists in the face of capital's flight to developing countries, where there are few environmental standards that can be enforced effectively. . . . They pass laws that allow the multinationals to operate using standards that are prohibited in the developed countries or they don't enforce their own preexisting standards. In addition to the harm done to local workers and their families, who are forced to produce under these conditions, many of these agricultural products find their way back into our consumer chain.

The movement of working people with all its diverse features does not look like a regular family; one branch [is] mostly white, mostly male, well organized and relatively well off financially, while all other branches are different colors and genders, poor, from different countries, speaking different languages, and organized much more loosely. However, in spite of this diversity, the trade unions, the movements against racism and sexism, the proimmigration movement, and the movement to defend the social safety net programs are all fundamental parts of the labor movement. Some of the participants are fully aware of this while others are not. It is the struggle for economic security that unites all of these working people into the labor movement. It must be from the ranks of these different sectors of the movement that new leadership emerges, from the sectors most in need of change. It will be their recognition of themselves as this great movement with all of its possibilities and a rejection of the narrow definition that will begin the process of its transformation.

PART 2

Walls and Gates

Writing from a jail cell in May 1971, Angela Davis warned that the United States was on the brink of fascism. "Fascism is a process, its growth and development are cancerous in nature," wrote the twenty-eight-year-old Black activist scholar. "While today, the threat of fascism may be primarily restricted to the use of the law-enforcement-judicial-penal apparatus to arrest the overt and latent revolutionary trends among nationally oppressed people, tomorrow it may attack the working class en masse and eventually even moderate Democrats."

A promising instructor of philosophy, Davis was also then a member of the Communist Party and head of the Soledad Brothers Defense Committee, which was advocating for the release of three Black activist prisoners from the Soledad State Prison in California. They were accused of killing a prison guard in retaliation for guards having killed three other Black prisoners. Davis found herself incarcerated and facing conspiracy charges after seventeen-year-old Jonathan Jackson took some of Davis's guns and used them in an ill-fated attempt to free three San Quentin prisoners from a Marin County courthouse. Police killed Jackson and two of the prisoners; a judge who had been taken hostage was also killed, shot both by police and by the assailants. Acquitted in June 1972, Davis remains a prominent public intellectual and an ardent supporter of prison abolition.

The idea that prisons represented the cutting edge of American brutalism was an article of faith among many leftists in the early 1970s. Imprisoned intellectuals and their supporters cast themselves as the canaries in the coal mine of surging racist state violence. They warned that prisoners were increasingly becoming revolutionary and that revolutionaries were increasingly being incarcerated. Subsequent events bore out some of the activists' bleaker fears. When Davis published her essay, there were 250,000 people being held in US prisons and jails. While not low, the country's incarceration rate was not much higher than other Western countries. By the new millennium, however, more than two million people were in prisons, jails, and detention centers in the United States, more people than anywhere else on the planet, both in whole numbers and proportionate to the population. The increase in the *number* of people going to prison was matched by an increase in the *length* of sentences they served, while police enjoyed military weapons and expanded authority with which to use them. The growth in both prison capacity and police power was felt most severely in working-class communities, especially among Black, Latinx, and Indigenous people.

The three decades between Davis's 1971 arrest and the September 11 attacks saw dramatic expansion of the criminal justice system alongside deep cuts to social services and growing divides between rich and poor. Many elites welcomed these changes by appealing to "law and order." In practice, transferring massive resources from social welfare to criminal punishment necessitated a series of domestic wars on crime (first launched in 1965) and drugs (1971), as well as wars on communism, gangs, and ultimately terrorism. Meanwhile, the federal government slashed funds for education and social programs, and cities and states courted increasingly mobile corporations through tax breaks that often worsened fiscal crises. These political-economic transformations left a growing number of people in dire straits. The deepening of poverty and punishment displaced city dwellers, fractured working-class Black and Latinx communities, and repurposed rural space.

Together, these shifts changed not only how people interacted with the government but how they experienced the country's landscape itself. New prisons increasingly filled rural, largely white areas, yet incarcerated urban, largely Black and Latinx people. While many rural areas traded farmland for prisons, the cities that had been the base of insurgent politics became more heavily policed. So too did many suburbs, as wealthy areas developed so-called gated communities to solidify their distance from a feared urban core. These alterations to the US landscape deepened the divides between urban and rural politics, while the growing stigma attached to arrest and incarceration rendered many liberal or progressive organizations unwilling to engage those ensnared in the criminal justice system, even for the millions of people on parole or probation.

This section of *Remaking Radicalism* explores the social movements that arose in opposition to this increasing fortification. It highlights opposition to the punitive state along three axes: political repression, mass incarceration, and the privatization of land and resources.

Section A, "Resisting Repression," explores how activists and their movements analyzed and opposed the expanded punitive turn in American life. It highlights efforts to undermine growing police power. It shows how radicals challenged the use of criminalization to deter political mobilization, a problem apparent through the increasing use and length of prison sentences. As Davis saw in 1971, the government often targeted political activists as a means of both weakening the left and laying the foundation for more extreme forms of punishment. Time and again, radicals warned that what the government did to them would sure enough become generalized, especially in working-class communities of color. In the 1970s and 1980s, this deepening repression pushed some radicals to engage in increasing forms of militancy, such as the bombing of police stations or even attacks on police officers. Such militancy accelerated further repression, leading to the arrest and long-term incarceration of several revolutionaries. Pointing to the political nature of their actions, the disproportionate length of their sentences, and international law that protected even violent actions against racist regimes, these activists described themselves as political prisoners or as prisoners of war.

Many activists saw resisting repression as a matter of movement self-defense—if not from arrest than from imprisonment, and if not imprisonment than from dying in prison. They attempted to defend not only themselves but their movements and communities. As the government utilized new or expanded forms of repression, activists adapted their own techniques. Two of the most significant innovations on the part of the government included an expanded use of long-term solitary confinement and a greater reliance on grand juries to tarnish leftists as engaged in criminal conspiracies. Grand juries cast wide nets and enabled secretive processes that give prosecutors nearly unchecked powers, including to compel testimony from subpoenaed witnesses under threat of imprisonment, to disallow witnesses legal representation, and to force witnesses to answer any question prosecutors asked, no matter how far-fetched. From the 1970s onward, dozens of Black nationalists, Puerto Rican independence activists, white antiracists, radical feminists, and others opted for jail over cooperating with grand juries. Radical environmental and animal rights activists later followed suit.

Prison threatened not just the individuals who were already activists but the often marginalized communities from which many of them came. Section B, "Undermining the Prison State," considers the strategies people used to challenge the deepening centrality of prison to American politics—a phenomenon activists came to label as "mass incarceration" or the "prison industrial complex." Organizing in prison brought together experienced activists with those mobilized by the severity of their conditions. With the widening use of prison as a catch-all response to social problems came the legal or administrative undoing of a number of reform initiatives that incarcerated people had launched, particularly unions and prisoner-led governance. Yet incarcerated people continued to protest, strike, revolt, write, and build other human rights campaigns against physical abuse and medical neglect inside of prisons.

While many Americans supported the "tough on crime" approach, prison conditions did generate fierce opposition outside. Throughout the 1970s and 1980s, clandestine groups targeted department of corrections or police benevolent association offices, while a few incarcerated militants attempted to escape. While opponents of prisons did not employ these tactics as much in the new penal atmosphere of the 1980s, they did continue to support the demands of people inside while protesting the construction of new institutions. Calls for prison moratorium brought faith-based activists together with the secular left. So did many of the campaigns to free political prisoners. By the end of the millennium, these diverse efforts had converged in a new movement for prison abolition.

The final section, "Fight for the City," gathers documents from movements seeking to remake urban space. Beginning in the 1960s, many city elites proposed what they called "urban renewal." Working-class communities of color—Black, Latinx, and Asian American—protested these moves as "urban removal," the transformation of urban space to appeal to white elites fleeing to suburbs. Their efforts confronted twinned changes to capitalism and government. The growing power and mobility of corporations in times of governmental austerity sapped cities of needed tax revenue at the same time as they bolstered the resources and authority of metropolitan police departments to arrest people in response to low-level "quality of life" concerns like homelessness, sex work, drug possession, or graffiti. Activists not only resisted displacement from the city but worked for cities to become more democratic and just. They advocated transformative solutions to political corruption, economic divestment, concentrated poverty, drug addiction, pollution, and police brutality.

Battles over who had a right to the city were intimately connected to the expansion of police power. It was police who enforced the eviction orders when cities used eminent domain to bulldoze poor neighborhoods or landlords tried to displace long-term residents of a building to build luxury high rises. Police were the main government institution poor urban communities encountered, even as public funding for schools, public transportation, and employment declined. The fight for the city was a fight against police brutality. But it was also a fight for an urban infrastructure that provided for people's health, mobility, and well-being. From student strikes to alternative economies, the fight for the city pitted corporate-backed predatory development against universal demands for jobs, housing, schools, and safety.

Resisting Repression

2.A.1.

Lynn Cooper, Elliot Currie, Jon Frappier, Tony Platt, Betty Ryan, Richard Schauffler, Joy Scruggs, and Larry Trujillo

From *The Iron Fist and the Velvet Glove: An Analysis of US Police* (1975)

As the war on crime expanded police militarization and authority in the early 1970s, a group of scholar-activists analyzed some grassroots alternatives. The following excerpt from *The Iron Fist and the Velvet Glove*, a book-length analysis of US policing, evaluates the success of movements for community control of the police forming at the crucible of a new era of control.

Struggles against the police are increasingly taking place throughout the country. Many of them are spontaneous reactions to increased police repression, while others are matters of survival for progressive and revolutionary organizations. These struggles have taken a variety of forms. . . . They have included everything from women organizing against rape, to self-controlled antidrug programs, to new programs of community control of the police. This section will summarize some of these current efforts.

One type of political action around police takes the form of research collectives formed to investigate and disseminate information on the development and use of the police apparatus. . . . Some of these research groups are part of larger organizations (e.g., the National Lawyers Guild Electronic Surveillance Project); others are independently created citizen research groups (Citizen Research and Investigating Committee). Several of these collectives have begun to develop specialized libraries or research files on such topics as wiretaps, police intelligence agencies in the US, police technologies, and so forth, while others have concentrated on supplying community action groups with specific data on police operations in their community, These research collectives are important in that they raise people's consciousness about the dangers of the repressive technologies and strategies being utilized by the police.

Other organizing efforts are taking place in university and youth communities. A recent example of this type of organizing is the Ocean Beach Human Rights Committee. Its program includes the following goals: (1) to effect changes in police practices within the community, and (2) to contribute to the long-run development of community control in Ocean Beach, California, to include all aspects of life. Another example is the Citizens for Police Accountability (CPA) formed in Santa Cruz, California, to prevent the creation of a police-directed communication center. The organizers not only discussed the violations of privacy inherent in centralized communications systems but stressed that the whole criminal justice system was already out of popular control and an instrument of exploitation, racism, and political repression. This analysis, in the era of Watergate, first met with enthusiastic support. But community support has begun to subside and the county administration is attempting to co-opt potential opposition by modifying the existing proposal. And as several organizers have summed up the struggle, "These experiences make clear the need to develop a long-range perspective, to broaden the base of support, and to find ways of injecting radical politics into public issues."

Perhaps the greatest potential for developing effective popular political alliances against the police is in cities with large cross-sections of White working-class and Third World people. There have been several major campaigns of this kind the last few years. Such struggles have primarily taken place in Brown and Black communities (e.g., Newark, San Jose, Detroit, East Los Angeles, etc.) where repression is the most severe. The demands have usually called for the dismissal of "killer cops" (such as the Tyrone Guyton Committee, Oakland; Claude Reeves Jr. and Clifford Glover Committees, New York; etc.) or the abolition of special police units (such as SWAT in Los Angeles and Atlanta, STRESS in Detroit, BOSS in New York City). Some of these campaigns have begun to couple the need to fight particular injustices with the need to transform the whole system. Generally, the problem with those campaigns has *not* been lack of energy of ability but the inability to develop ideology, organizations, and programs that can both win popular community support and link up to broader movements for revolutionary change. . . .

Limits and Possibilities of Community Control

Unlike most other reforms that emerged in the last decade ("community relations," civilian review, community advisory boards, etc.), community control of the police has a strong potential for challenging the racial and sexual bias of police practice. It attacks not only the professional insulation of the police but the political and economic root of their power by asserting the demand for popular control.

The demand for community control opposes the hierarchical nature of police "professionalism" and helps expose the political and economic forces that benefit from the existing police structure. To the extent that it does these things, community control of the police is a potential catalyst for exposing the exploitative nature of society as a whole.

At the same time, however, community control of the police has the opposite potential; it can become an instrument for diverting people's energy, a limited reform which does not change the capitalist system in any fundamental way. This conservative tendency in community control results from (1) the misleading idea of "community," (2) a single-issue orientation, and (3) a vulnerability to co-optation.

First, community control of the police is often based on a narrow conception on a narrow conception of power, limiting struggles to the "local" community and failing to confront the interlocking, national basis of economic power. As Frank Riessman and Alan Gartner have observed, "The danger here is localism and infighting among local cliques of competitive groups for some 'piece of action' and control part of the 'turf.' The attendant danger is participation without power and economic redistribution." Focusing solely on the local community, then, obscures the real nature of power in the United States and thereby creates illusions about how the system can be changed.

Secondly, the focus on a single institution (in this case, the police) can encourage a piecemeal conception of social change (comparable to the approach held by most liberal reformers) and encourage the mistaken belief that a decent police can be created under the conditions of US capitalism. Given the interrelated nature of power and institutions, it is crucial that struggles against the police be linked to similar movements in health care, employment, and other areas.

Thirdly, the idea of community control is vulnerable to government cooptation. In recent years, the Department of Justice, the Ford Foundation, and various government commissions have encouraged *their* version of community control—decentralization of state bureaucracies; creation of community "advisory" boards; "diversion" of juvenile delinquents into "community-based corrections"; and support for "community relations" programs. These ameliorative reforms represent what the sociologist Richard Cloward calls "corporate imperialism in the ghetto," that is, the development of new forms of coercion and integration which attempt to smooth out the rough edges of the system without touching its basic inequities. "Community relations" and "civilian advisory boards" are proposed as alternatives to direct community control; "professionalism" replaces genuine service to the community; and token quotas are advocated as a solution to racist hiring practices instead of requiring the police be hired from the communities in which they work. . . .

The struggle for community control of the police has suffered from a short-range, localistic, and single-issue orientation. So far, it has failed to link up with a broader struggle for "popular, democratic control over all aspects of economic, political, and social life." It has not developed a clear relationship between immediate reforms and protracted struggle, between defensive and offensive strategies. The movement for community control needs to seek out strategies which go beyond the boundaries imposed by the framework of corporate capitalism. . . .

As more enduring forms of organization develop that can unite workers, the unemployed, students, and other progressive forces of all races, the struggles against repression and economic exploitation will be more closely linked. Such organization will give direction and strength to local work and will make it easier for local projects to link up with national campaigns. Ultimately, building a humane and decent society in the United States will depend on our ability to build a movement that can put an end to all forms of exploitation and repression. And effective educational and political campaigns around the police, while they are not ends in themselves, can be a crucial part of that movement.

2.A.2.

Lesbians against Police Violence
Interview with Barbara Lubinski (1979)

In this interview with KPFA reporter Barbara Lubinski, three members of Lesbians against Police Violence in San Francisco (who identify themselves Diane, Mary, and Barbara, respectively) define how police enforce homophobic repression of lesbians and outline a radical queer critique of policing.

[Diane]: The first incident of police violence against lesbians happened outside Amelia's bar in the Mission. What happened was two women, two lesbians, Sue Davis and Shirley Wilson, were confronted by policemen as they were leaving, and they were harassed, attacked, beaten by these two policemen as they were leaving the bar. A whole series of charges were brought against them, criminal charges, that have been dropped, like resisting arrest. They were then brought to the police station, beaten, strip searched, without being given the reason for their arrest or given their right to a phone call. That is the first incident. The second incident happened at Peg's Place, which is another women's bar. Fifty off-duty policemen entered that bar, assaulted women in the bar, one of the women who was assaulted has been in the hospital seventeen days, which is a very long time. The cops were drunk, they were on their way home from Patty Hearst's wedding party. They said things such as, when they were asked what are they doing here, we're cops and we do what we damn well please. To date, one of the officers, Marr, has been charged with battery, but the other officer, Kelly, is still free of any reprisals for this kind of conduct. Mayor Feinstein hasn't made any strong statements condemning the action. She says all she can do is make recommendations to the police chief, but she hasn't made any public statements as of yet. Also, along with the violence against lesbians, there's been a lot of violence against gay men, just held at the police station without proper procedure, beatings and things like that by the police.

[Mary]: We see the police as the force which is responsible to repress protest in this country and to carry out the wishes of those people who are in power. Specifically, they often do that through violence, and police violence has always existed, but we feel that it's on the rise as the economy gets worse. We also feel that the people who are affected most by the crisis in our present economy are, first, Third World people, and then white working-class people, and among white working-class people, especially white women and gay people. And that these groups are therefore often the first ones to protest, and that it's the role of police violence to keep us down, to keep us from protesting. And in recent months in San Francisco, lesbians have been attacked, like Diane was just saying. There's been a lot of brutal beatings, people have hospitalized, strip searched, denied their legal rights. Also, police have been real active in their support of Dan White, and Dan White killed Harvey Milk both because he was gay and progressive, and he was a highly placed public official and was murdered, and the police are being very supportive of his murder, they are going around wearing T-shirts that say "Free Dan White" and are raising money for his defense. We see this murder as part of the overall pattern of police brutality.

[Barbara]: Lesbians against Police Violence began as a meeting called by Lesbian Schoolworkers in early February because of the incident at Amelia's. Over two hundred women came to that meeting. We wanted to give support to Sue and Shirley, and we also wanted to organize ourselves for protection against the police. Out of that meeting, a core group was formed, and now we are an organization, Lesbians against Police Violence, and we've been working since then. In planning all our work against police violence, we wanted [people] to know that there's a move to [the] right in San Francisco and nationwide and that changes in police policy and the actions against women and gay people have escalated especially since the murders of Milk and Moscone. On April 21 we had a picket day and demonstration at the first day of the Dan White trial. We wanted to bring out the connections between Dan White's murder of Milk and Moscone and the police violence against women and gay people and also show that there's preferential treatment for Dan White. Also on May 12 we'll be having a legal rights workshop which is to inform lesbians of their legal rights regarding the police. That will be at the Women's Building, Dovre Hall, 1 o'clock. We urge people to come to the workshop to get information about our group. That meeting is for women only. In the future we plan to do more work making alliances with groups who are working against police violence.

The National Alliance against Racist and Political Repression

Keona K. Ervin

Emerging from the successful "Free Angela" campaign (1970–72), the National Alliance against Racist and Political Repression (NAARPR) sought to turn its success defending University of California, Los Angeles, philosophy professor, communist, and prison abolitionist Angela Yvonne Davis into a mass movement against criminalization. The organization confronted nascent political and economic conditions that compelled the global left to adopt new strategies in defense of its programs.

Those who joined the newly formed, communist-organized NAARPR saw that growing racism and expanding political imprisonment were fast becoming central mechanisms of the repressive state power epitomized by Richard Nixon's—and later, Ronald Reagan's—calls for "law and order" and worked in deep intimacy with transformations in capitalism. NAARPR argued that a broad-based, multinational, multiracial, and coalitional working-class movement organized around the liberation struggles of oppressed people of color was the most effective way to turn back the rising, punitive tide. In the year following Davis's 1972 acquittal on all charges, NAARPR held its founding conference in Chicago, welcoming over five hundred participants from organizations including the Republic of New Afrika, the United Farm Workers of America, the National Conference of Black Lawyers, the American Indian movement, the Puerto Rican Socialist Party, and others. Representatives from political prisoner defense committees were also in attendance.

NAARPR built a broad coalition of leftist movements centered around opposing state repression. Political heavyweights such as Angela Davis, who led in the defense of the Soledad brothers and was a member of the Black communist Che-Lumumba Club, Communist Party leader Charlene Mitchell, Kentucky-based civil rights veterans Anne and Carl Braden, and North Carolinian Ben Chavis, a youth coordinator for the Southern Christian Leadership Conference and a member of Martin Luther King Jr.'s inner circle, formed the group's core leadership and advisors. Organizations at the forefront of US Third World liberation struggles—those formed around Black and Chicano liberation, Puerto Rican independence, and the American Indian Movement—as well as social justice unionism, the defense of political prisoners, and antiwar mobilization drove the NAARPR's efforts to establish a network of local, statewide, and national groups. Hoping to build mass struggle, the NAARPR lent its advocacy through media and educational campaigns, print literature, primarily in the form of its organ, the Organizer, petitions, boycotts, research, films, conferences, speaking tours, and demonstrations.

Transforming the state of North Carolina into a strategic battleground became one of the NAARPR's most important tasks during its early years. Among the organization's notable fights was its defense of Chavis and the nine other members who made up the Wilmington Ten. Wrongfully convicted on arson and conspiracy charges after white racists, supported by the state, engaged in a violent backlash against freedom activists who organized protests in favor of school desegregation and equitable funding, the Wilmington Ten became a cause célèbre for the political prisoners' movement. Members believed that the machinations of power in the Tarheel State, where severe forms of antidemocratic practice, racism, state repression, and labor exploitation formed a crippling nexus of authoritarian power, were emblematic of the overlapping forces working against those who dared to dissent.

The NAARPR understood political repression in expansive terms, seeing it as a malleable and widely applicable technology and a reactionary tool of social control that targeted working-class people, especially people of color. In addition to defending political prisoners, the NAARPR focused on fighting repressive legislation, police brutality, racist and fascist organizations, and the use of behavior modification in prisons, schools, and factories and on promoting worker rights. It shared organized labor's commitment to winning unionization for southern workers and protecting the right of labor to organize without intimidation. Taking a hard stance in opposition to free market capitalism, the organization also supported numerous smaller unionization campaigns and boycotts and helped to defeat a right-to-work bill in Missouri.

Expanding to over forty branches by the late 1970 and representing cities in New York, Hawaii, Florida, Alaska, Kentucky, Illinois, and Missouri, the NAARPR reached its heyday during the 1970s and continued to organize into the 1980s. Today, the organization has active chapters in Chicago and Kentucky. Confronting the crisis of American democracy and exposing the entanglements of state and corporate power that sanction mass political repression, the story of the NAARPR offers an index of carceral expansion in the late twentieth century and shows how disparate strands of the left found common ground in an otherwise politically fractured moment.

2.A.3.

Leonard Peltier

From "Convicted for Being Chippewa and Sioux Blood" (1977)

American Indian Movement member Leonard Peltier participated in many of the organization's dramatic demonstrations in the early 1970s. His leadership in this militant group put him on the FBI's radar. On June 26, 1975, Peltier was on the Pine Ridge reservation in South Dakota, when the corrupt and unpopular tribal chairman Dick Wilson signed away more than 130,000 acres of Oglala land to mining companies. That same day, scores of FBI and police stormed the reservation, resulting in a firefight in which one Native American and two FBI agents were killed. Although hundreds were initially charged, only Peltier was convicted. What follows is an excerpt of the statement Peltier delivered to the judge following a contentious and controversial trial. He remains incarcerated as of 2020, one of the longest-held political prisoners in the world.

You are about to perform an act which will close one more chapter in the history of the failure of the United States courts and the failure of the people of the United States to do justice in the case of a Native American. After centuries of murder of millions of my brothers and sisters by white racist America, could I have been wise in thinking that you would break that tradition and commit an act of justice? . . .

You do not have the ability to see that the government must suppress the fact that there is a growing anger amongst Indian people and that Native Americans will resist any further encroachment by the military forces of the capitalistic Americans, which is evidenced by the large number of Pine Ridge residents who took up arms on June 26, 1975, to defend themselves. Therefore, you do not have the ability to carry out your responsibility towards me in an impartial way and will run my two life terms consecutively.

I stand before you as a proud man; I feel no guilt! I have nothing to feel guilty about! I have no regrets of being a Native American activist—thousands of people in the United States, Canada, and around the world have and will continue to support me to expose the injustices that have occurred in this courtroom. I do feel pity for your people that they must live under such an ugly system. Under your system, you are taught greed, racism and corruption—and most serious of all, the destruction of Mother Earth. Under the Native American system, we are taught all people are brothers and sisters; to share the wealth with the poor and needy. But the most important of all is to respect and preserve the Earth, who we consider our mother. We feed from her breast; our mother gives us life from birth and when it's time to leave this world, she again takes us back into her womb. But the main thing we are taught is to preserve her for our children and our grandchildren, because they are the next who will live upon her.

No, I am not the guilty one here; I'm not the one who should be called a criminal—white racist America is the criminal for the destruction of our lands and my people; to hide your guilt from the decent human beings in America and around the world, you will sentence me to two consecutive life terms without any hesitation. . . .

Finally, I honestly believe that you made up your mind long ago that I was guilty and that you were going to sentence me to the maximum sentence permitted under the law. But this does not surprise me, because you are a high-ranking member of the white racist American establishment which has consistently said "in God we trust" while they went about their business of murdering my people and attempting to destroy our culture.

The only thing I'm guilty of and which I was convicted for was being Chippewa and Sioux blood and for believing in our sacred religion.

2.A.4.

National Coalition for Redress/Reparations

Postconference brochure (1980)

The unjust incarceration of Japanese Americans by the federal government during World War II was taken up a generation later by people who had survived that experience as well as younger Japanese American activists. The Los Angeles–based National Coalition for Redress/Reparations was the most radical of these efforts, demanding not just an apology but reparations to right this historical wrong. Ronald Reagan signed the Civil Liberties Act in 1988, which offered an apology and compensation to survivors.

On July 12, 1980, individuals and organizations from Japanese communities from throughout the nation met and formed the National Coalition for Redress and Reparations (NCRR). The NCRR is an active coalition coordinating a nationwide campaign for justice.

The NCRR has two major aims: (1) to seek restitution for losses and injuries suffered by Nikkei (persons of Japanese ancestry) and others who were unjustly evacuated and incarcerated by the US government during World War II, and (2) to seek preventive steps to insure that similar racist acts and violations of constitutional rights will never occur again.

On November 15, 1980, the NCRR sponsored a conference that presented educational, cultural, and legal workshops. Over four hundred attendees developed strategies for future activities around the campaign for redress and formally adopted principles of unity.

Background to the Redress/Reparations Issue

On February 19, 1942, President Franklin Roosevelt signed Executive Order 9066, authorizing the immediate evacuation and incarceration of 120,000 Nikkei.

The US government used the pretext of "military necessity" to justify the racist imprisonment of the Japanese, the majority being US citizens. No such roundup of Germans and Italians occurred. For the next four years, Japanese lived in barracks under military guard. The ten concentration camps which housed them were located in the most desolate and remote areas of the United States.

Aside from what they carried in by hand, all personal possessions were left behind. Homes, farms, and businesses were lost; bank accounts were frozen; educational and career opportunities were disrupted; and cultural and community ties were destroyed. An estimate by the US Federal Reserve Bank stated that $400 million worth of property losses alone occurred, expressed in 1942 dollars.

In Alaska, the government conducted a similar crime in the evacuation of natives of the Aleutian Islands. Here again, "military necessity" caused the Aleuts to be taken from their homes and interned in abandoned fish canneries and mines which lacked medical and sanitary facilities. When finally released, they found their historic communities destroyed.

The thin excuse given for the Japanese internment was that of security, suspicion of disloyalty and possibly espionage. Yet not one Japanese was ever proven to be engaged in such acts and reparation has never been made for the suffering brought by the incarceration.

Principles of Unity and Goals of the NCRR

The following principles were adopted at the NCRR Conference on November 15, 1980, as guides to action.

1. *Redress/reparations means monetary compensation to all individuals or their heirs who suffered evacuation and/or incarceration.* No sum of money can approach complete compensation for the tremendous social, economic, and psychological trauma or the violation of constitutional rights. But meaningful restitution on the part of the US government is imperative and must include monetary compensation to individuals.

   The exact amount to be sought will be determined on the basis of information and documentation of losses to the Nikkei community by the government and all other relevant documents which may be used in this determination. Compensation must also include persons evacuated from Central and South American countries [and] Hawaii, [as well] Alaskan Aleuts and others forcibly removed from their homes by the US government. The first- generation Issei [first-generation Japanese immigrants to the United States] are to be given immediate priority for direct payments, as most are elderly.

2. *Redress/reparations means restitution to the Japanese American community in the form of a community fund—the exact use of which to be determined by the needs of each respective community.* The purpose of this fund shall be to counteract the effects of the incarceration of the Japanese American communities. This could take the form of funding the development of low-cost housing for the Issei and Nisei (second generation), funding needed social and health services and cultural, and educational projects. This

"Japanese Community Trust Fund" shall be created by appropriations from Congress as well as by unclaimed or donated individual payments.

3. *Redress/reparations means exposing the racism of and overturning the legal basis that has justified the evacuation and the camps.* Overturning the legal basis through congressional or legal action will serve as a deterrent to the reinstitution of the concentration camps in the future. The government should return the FBI and government files on internees since this information has been and can still be used against people. We shall also investigate legal avenues and keep in touch with other groups doing similar suits.

4. *Redress/reparations means supporting others who have or are suffering from unjust actions taken by the US government.* We seek to work with others to insure that they will understand and support our efforts. Likewise, we will support efforts of groups such as Native Americans, Native Hawaiians, Blacks, Chicanos, and others struggling for reparations and justice.

5. *Redress/reparations means that we seek the education of the American public so that future generations may learn from the mistakes of the past and not knowingly allow them to happen again.* It is during times of crisis that extra steps must be taken to guarantee the democratic rights of all individuals. We seek to incorporate the lessons of the camps into the American educational process as a way to insure that similar acts will not be taken in the future against an identifiable group.

2.A.5.

James J. Zogby

"Senate Subcommittee on Security and Terrorism: A Threat to Arab Americans?" (1981)

James J. Zogby cofounded the American-Arab Anti-Discrimination Committee (ADC) after serving as a founding member of the Palestine Human Rights Campaign in the 1970s. In this statement, he highlights how the FBI, the Senate Judiciary Committee, and Zionist organizations leveraged charges of terrorism to stifle the free speech and political associations of Arab Americans.

The American-Arab Anti-Discrimination Committee fears that Arab Americans may face repression at the hands of the newly created Subcommittee on Security and Terrorism of the Senate Judiciary Committee. This new committee, which civil libertarians are warning has inherited the mantle of the McCarthy-era "witch hunt" committees, causes us deep concern. Its creation comes on the heels of a number of disturbing developments which deserve closer scrutiny.

In the past six months, ADC has received reports which point to a campaign of FBI harassment and intimidation of Arab Americans. While not as intense or as frightening as "Operation Boulder" (when in 1972 Arabs and Arab Americans were subjected to a nightmare wave of interrogations, deportations, and other intimidating practices resulting from a Nixonian "Executive Order"), reports and affidavits have been filed noting over one hundred incidents of FBI visitations and/or acts of harassment or intimidation. In each instance reported to us the subject was the political activity, association, or beliefs of members of our community.

Far right-wing and extremist pro-Israeli organizations in the USA have long propagandized that there is an identity between being pro-Palestinian (or pro-Arab) and being "proterrorism." These organizations have frequently applied pressure to the government to have pro-Arab groups or individuals investigated for alleged "links with terrorism." In several specific instances known to us, they have succeeded in suborning government agencies to, in effect, carry out their political program of silencing what they view as their political opposition in the US. While the resultant investigations have never produced any charges of misconduct or criminal activity, the fact of the investigation itself "taints" and often has a "chilling effect" on the activities of the person in question.

In recent weeks there have been developments which accent our concern:

1) A Jewish Telegraphic Agency release (appearing 1/30/81 in the *Cleveland Jewish News*) reports that the American Jewish Congress has filed a "sweeping Freedom of Information request to more than one hundred agencies" calling for the release of an "unclassified documents on the Palestine Liberation Organization and its personnel and *supporters* in this country." The AJC [American Jewish Committee] justifies its unprecedented request on the grounds that the PLO is an "avowed terrorist organization and the nature and extent of *its infiltration into American institutions* are relevant to important issues of domestic and foreign policy."

2) The Reagan administration's announced campaign to "root out" and "eradicate" the "number one menace to humanity"—terrorism—which the administration identifies as being closely linked with the Soviet puppets: the PLO and Libya.

3) And now the creation of the new Senate subcommittee and the naming of the head of the Justice Department's Foreign Agent Registration Unit as the subcommittee's chief counsel. The Foreign Agent Registration Unit has frequently been used to harass and/or smear Arab American political activists and is currently involved in a relentless pursuit of Americans who have had associations with the Libyan government.

It is not the "left" that is the intended target of the new Senate subcommittee and other 1atter-day "witch hunters." In the political demonology of the day, "the foreign threat," "the terrorists," "the corruptors," and "the threat to our society" is perceived of as coming from Palestinians or Arabs in general (read: OPEC, Islamic fanaticism, etc.) and their American supporters.

Evidence of this can be found not only in FBI practices (including ABSCAM [FBI sting operation]) and the propaganda mills of the far right and extremist pro-Israeli organizations, but even Saturday morning on children's television or in the editorial page political cartoons of the daily press.

At this point we ask:

- will the government grant the clearly partisan request of the AJC?
- will the Senate subcommittee, on its own or as a result of outside pressure, go on a witch hunt against Arab "terrorism" and its supporters in the US(how many senators would deny a request for subpoena power, if it is supported by "Friends of Israel" and is, after all, to root out Palestinian terrorists in the US)?

and finally,

- will civil libertarians defend Arab Americans against the continuing (and intensifying) violations of their rights?

2.A.6.

Michael Zinzun

"Zinzun on Police Abuse" (1983)

Michael Zinzun, a former member of the Black Panther Party, gave this interview to the alt-weekly newspaper *LA Catalyst* about his work with the Coalition against Police Abuse (CAPA). Formed in 1971, CAPA continued the radical Black Power and Latinx movements of Los Angeles. An inveterate activist, Zinzun had been arrested while witnessing a police confrontation in a Black neighborhood; the interview took place after charges were dismissed against him.

Catalyst: Congratulations on your victory, Michael.

Michael: Thank you, and I'd like to thank all the individuals and organizations who contributed to this victory.

Catalyst: What do you think was the motivation for the charges being filed against you?

Michael: It was a result of the resistance against police abuse of community people that CAPA has organized in Pasadena and Los Angeles. Our orientation was different from the traditional call for more Black policemen as the solution to the problem. We called for grassroots organizing against police brutality, and we tied this into the overall crisis of the system. This led the entire law enforcement apparatus to see us as a threat.

Catalyst: So, in essence, it's almost like PC [Penal Code] Section 69 [a statute making it illegal to interfere with an officer, which at the time could include photographing police encounters] was used as an experiment and you were the first guinea pig?

Michael: Right, and I believe it's connected to the economic crisis and the current right-wing climate in this country. The whole question of repressive legislation is beginning to reappear. Look at Senate bill 1630, which would prevent exposures like the Pentagon Papers; Executive Order 12333 which further legalizes domestic spying by the FBI and CIA; and the Simpson-Mazzoli bill [which toughened US immigration policy]. The law books are also full of vague, little-used laws. PC Section 69 was one with very little case law, and the district attorney was attempting to set a precedent by using it against me. If they had succeeded they could have arbitrarily arrested and prosecuted anyone who spoke out against incidents of police brutality.

Catalyst: What do you think has been the political significance of your case?

Michael: The most immediate impact was increasing the people's awareness about the danger of PC Section 69 and other repressive laws and the need to organize against them. The police and the DA were also forced to open up their intelligence files, and one significant impact of the case is that the judge did establish some criteria other than the use of words to make PC Section 69 applicable.

Catalyst: What about police abuse in general, is the problem as bad as it was in the past?

Michael: It's as bad as ever. In 1983, there were ninety-two officer-involved shootings. Thirty of those resulted in deaths. The Black community is still the primary victim of police abuse, and the pattern of illegal and unconstitutional stops, searches, and arrests, the senseless beatings and unjustified killing, continues to be just as bad as ten years ago. Public officials still collaborate with the police to cover up their abuses. At this time there are a few organizations but no broad-based active movement with a political platform to effectively struggle against police abuse.

Catalyst: Have the community activists taken a back seat to the more traditional and conservative forces?

Michael: Yes. For example, the demand for a local Freedom of Information Act (FOIA) has been put forward in recent years to combat police intelligence abuses. With the exposure of the Public Disorder and Intelligence Division [PDID] of LAPD, this call for a local Freedom of Information Act has gathered steam. Recently, the city council voted on this issue. The original proposal was worded to uncover past illegal spying and force the police into some accountability for their intelligence operations. But Chief Darryl Gates mobilized right-wing pressure on the city council and got amendments passed which gutted the original proposal. There was no mobilization of grassroots counterpressure and the traditional liberal organizations capitulated to the right and accepted the amended proposal. Our side was just plain weak.

Catalyst: What do you attribute this to?

Michael: That's a tough question. First of all, I think that the state of the movement against police abuse reflects the state of the overall movement for change. The lack of an active mass movement, the rightward drift of many "progressive" groups, the reversals of the '70s, and the current crisis of capitalism all affect the police abuse movement. In particular, though, the sensational nature of police brutality causes many people to get involved, then they drop off when the sensationalism wears off. Also, community groups hate the daily reality of police brutality, but they still feel the need for protection against the ever-present violence and crime in the ghetto. The struggle against police brutality, as a single issue, in many ways hides the real enemy. The police are part of the power structure which maintains capitalism. Because they are so visible and violent, people tend to see them as the enemy, not those behind them that they actually serve.

Catalyst: What do you see is the connection between the movement against police abuse and the other movements for social change?

Michael: The police abuse movement is one current in the overall movement, but anytime you organize resistance on any issue you are going to be met with police abuse and repression. There is a natural thread. But linking the two is very difficult because there is no broad-based political vehicle which could serve as a multi-issue, fight-back organization and tie all those issues and movements together. We need a broad-based coalition effort that sees various social ills as one, or at least as coming from the same source. Once we begin focusing on the real enemy we will see the interconnection between the police and the maintaining of this system.

Catalyst: What are the current issues and battlegrounds of the police abuse movement, and where do you think it is heading?

Michael: Of course the brutalizing and murder of community people is an ongoing issue and battleground for the movement. But in recent years the focus has expanded to include the issue of police intelligence abuses, and the struggle over the Freedom of Information Act is not over. There is also the upcoming major lawsuit, *CAPA vs. the LA Police Commission*, which has 131 plaintiff organizations and individuals. Although a lawsuit is not an ideal form of struggle, it provides exposure and shows the tremendous potential for forming a broad, mass-based coalition effort.

It's up to the activists involved to translate that into political action. This is especially important because the Olympics will be here next year. The police are working now with the FBI and CIA to create a special intelligence apparatus which is sure to continue after the Olympics. During this coming period we have a unique opportunity to integrate the activities of the police abuse movement—around FOIA, the CAPA lawsuit, the PDID's transformation into the Anti-Terrorist Division—into the political struggles of the anti-interventionist movement and other movements. We need to take all these movements to a higher, more effective level.

2.A.7.

Red Guerrilla Resistance

From communiqué on the bombing of the Police Benevolent Association (1985)

This February 1985 statement from the short-lived Red Guerrilla Resistance cell culminated fifteen years of underground left-wing militancy against police violence and other government or corporate abuse, much of it carried out by white antiracists like the Red Guerrilla Resistance. This particular communiqué was issued after Red Guerrilla Resistance bombed the offices of the New York Patrolman's Benevolent Association, a police officer lobbying and public relations outfit that offered public and legal support for any officer accused of brutality while lobbying for even more militarized police power. The bombing occurred after several high-profile killings of Black people by NYPD, as well as support for a white vigilante killer who targeted Black youth on the subway. Several alleged members of Red Guerrilla Resistance were arrested not long after this bombing. They faced several trials, including as part of the Resistance Conspiracy case.

> Remember Malcolm X
> February 21, 1965

Tonight we attacked the Patrolman's Benevolent Association [PBA] to support the demand of Black communities across the country to *stop killer cops.*

Right now in New York City we are experiencing a white supremacist offensive. Bernhard Goetz shoots four Black youths, becomes a white folk hero, lauded by [Mayor Ed] Koch and exonerated by DA [Robert] Morgenthau. Ten thousand armed racists demonstrated their support for the killer of a sixty-six-year-old Black grandmother [Eleanor Bumpurs, killed by NYPD officer Stephen Sullivan in October 1984] and tried to intimidate those who have fought to bring him to justice.

[Patrolman Benevolent Association president] Phil Caruso is right when he says that Stephen Sullivan was just doing his job. His job—their job—is to control oppressed peoples, using violence or the threat of violence. Malcolm X, the Black Panther Party, the Black Liberation Army, named and fought the police for what they are: imperialism's occupying army in the Black community.

Why do cops kill? Why do heavily armed shotgun carrying, bulletproof-vested men shoot down ten-year-old Clifford Glover [in 1973] or sixty-six-year-old Eleanor Bumpurs?

Because they're racist and put no value on Third World people's lives.

Because some of them are outfront fascists and love the sense of power and know they will get away with it.

Because they're afraid. Not fear of Eleanor Bumpurs's knife or Clifford Glover's Afro pick, but the kind of fear that the slaveholders and their overseers had of a slave rebellion. The fear that the oppressor has of the righteous anger of the oppressed. The fear that someday they will be brought to justice.

The cops are the frontline enforcers of a system of colonization of Black, Puerto Rican, Mexicano-Chicano, and Native American peoples. They are backed by that system. The PBA is the organizational and ideological leadership with the NYPD. They provide the funds and the legal defense of killer cops: they work hand in hand with Koch to mobilize racist hysteria and consolidate a base of support among white people. Overwhelmingly they are protected by the DAs and the courts and have been indicted on minor charges only when the pressure by Third World communities is intense and unceasing. The evidence against them is distorted and destroyed by medical examiner Elliot Gross, who was originally brought in by Koch to cover up Arthur Miller's murder [in June 1978].

Police power is part of imperialist violence—violence against Third World people—which will continue to rise as imperialism's crisis deepens. What can we expect from US imperialism in Central America but more violence, when Reagan calls the contras "freedom fighters" and his "brothers"? The months and years of protest by Black people against the South African consulates in the US wouldn't be necessary if the US didn't fully back the violent white colonialist South African government. Within the borders of the US, Black people—on whose labor US imperialism was built—have been completely written off. There is no longer even the pretense that the system will offer Black youth a chance to grow up to an education, a job, even a home. The programs of pacification have ended. In 1985, the US government's main program of "social welfare" is to cut back the minimum wage for Black teenagers. To the imperialist state, Black people's lives are expendable.

The struggle against killer cops and police terror is a struggle against the naked brutality and inhumanity of a system that deprives Third World people of the most basic, fundamental human rights. When "democratic america" systematically denies human rights to Black people, they have the right to fight for human rights, as Malcolm X said, "by any means necessary." When the police, the courts, the politicians don't protect but instead attack Black people, then Black people have the right to organize their communities for self-defense. Black communities organized for self-defense is the only way white supremacist violence like that of the klan and the cops has ever been held in check.

The struggle against killer cops is not a struggle against the excesses of this system but against its fundamental nature. It's a struggle against colonialist domination and national oppression, against imperialism and white supremacy. The only way that will end is through a struggle for power: the struggle of oppressed nations for self-determination and national liberation. Black people have led the struggle for human rights for years—in the courts, in the schools, and in the streets. They have also led by developing the struggle of the New Afrikan/Afro-American nation for land and independence—the only way that killer cops will really be brought to justice, police terror against Black people ended, and the right to survive, grow, and prosper as a nation be won.

Every struggle for human rights and self-determination by New Afrikan/ Afro-American, Native American, Puerto Rican, Mexicano/Chicano peoples— every confrontation with US imperialism—has meant dealing with the police as the frontline of reaction. Before the army, before the National Guard was called out, the cops were there with dogs and cattle prods in Birmingham. Their purpose was to stop the march of Black people for freedom. When the Black Panther Party organized people to defend their homes and their children and to begin waging a struggle for power, police SWAT teams were formed and opened fire on Panther headquarters throughout the US. The imperialist strategy is to terrorize the masses through police brutality and killer cops, to threaten those who protest with imprisonment or physical attack, and to imprison or assassinate the conscious leadership of the national liberation struggle. This is why Martin Luther King, Malcolm X, and Fred Hampton were assassinated. This is why hundreds of Black/New Afrikan prisoners of war and political prisoners— forty combatants of the Black Liberation Army alone—remain imprisoned in US jails. This is why five hundred agents of the NYPD/FBI Joint Terrorist Task Force arrested eight New Afrikan revolutionaries in October 1984. The New York Eight against Fascist Terrorism are a part of the development of a full revolutionary strategy for self-determination and socialism.

Progressive white people have to face the fact that, overwhelmingly, the masses of white people have gladly played their role in this strategy. How else can we explain the massive outpouring of support for Bernhard Goetz—even among supposedly liberal white people? Instead of supporting the Black community's demand to *stop killer cops* and of recognizing the police as our enemy as well, our movements have too often turned to the police for protection— against rape, against the klan, for security at demonstrations and picket lines. We in the oppressor nation have a decision to make about whether to continue to rely on the police or whether to join with Third World people in fighting the police as our enemy.

The struggle against killer cops is one of the main ways that masses of Third World people are fighting and challenging the very nature of the system. When white people take up this struggle, it is a real step towards changing our relationship to the system and becoming a part of the fight for power. Fighting white supremacy is the only basis on which an alliance can be built with the national liberation struggles which are leading and advancing the struggle against imperialism. Supporting the just demands for human rights, self-defense, and self-determination and making these demands our own is the way that we can challenge the degradation and brutality of the system. If our movement will take on this struggle, we can begin to build effective revolutionary resistance.

Fifteen years ago, our movement fought the cops to stop imperialism's war against the Vietnamese people and in support of the civil rights and Black Power movements. Today we are going to have to do the same if we want to help stop imperialism—whether it's in Central America, South Africa, Lebanon, or within its own borders. If we are not willing to fight the police, then we'll be letting the state define what is an acceptable level of protest for our movement.

Figure 2.1. Terry Forman and Fireworks Graphics Collective, "Build a Wall of Resistance—Don't Talk to the FBI" (circa 1980). Copyright © Fireworks Graphics Collective. Image courtesy of Lincoln Cushing/Docs Populi. Reprinted with permission by Scott Braley.

As revolutionaries in the oppressor nation, we choose to struggle for power rather than to beg for change. We hope our action tonight will aid the struggle that is being waged in the Black community against killer cops. We have learned much from this struggle about who the enemy is and what it will take to defeat it. We are glad to be able to do some damage to the white supremacist pigs in the PBS, and we hope our action helps to build an anti-imperialist resistance movement that fights in support of national liberation struggles, upholds the right of self-determination, and organizes itself as an effective force to help to *stop killer cops*.

2.A.8.

Terry Bisson

"RSVP to the FBI" (1985)

Dozens of radicals risked months or years in jail and prison rather than co-operate with federal grand juries investigating left-wing movements in this period. Grand juries are secretive processes controlled by prosecutors. Witnesses are not allowed legal representation and can be jailed for refusing to answer any of the prosecutors questions, no matter how specious. Prosecutors often used grand juries to target activists who had pubicly supported radical underground organizations. Award-winning science fiction writer and member of the John Brown Anti-Klan Committee Terry Bisson penned this poem situating his refusal to cooperate with a federal grand jury as an extension of worldwide struggles against political repression. For his stance, Bisson served three months in jail in 1985.

(On Being Subpoenaed to Give Information
to a Federal Grand Jury
Investigating Revolutionary Movements
inside the USA)

Thank you for handing me this invitation
to talk to you

But I am otherwise engaged.

Thank you for offering me this opportunity
to have a heart to heart
with the murders of Martin Luther King
and Fred Hampton,
not to mention Crazy Horse
Michael Stewart and Eleanor Bumpurs
and nameless millions
who do have and will have names

But I am otherwise engaged.

Thank you for inviting me
to sit down with the brothers
of the somocistas
(as you describe yourselves)
their long knives eager
for the blood of teachers
the blood of nuns
the blood of Sandino
which is right now running
bright like a river in the veins of young
Nicaragua

But I am otherwise engaged.

Thank you for giving me this opportunity
to spit on the graves of Sacco and Vanzetti
to dishonor the memory of the Rosenbergs
or of my ex-father-in-law
who spent ten years not being an actor
rather than ten minutes being a collaborator

But I am otherwise engaged.

Thank you for inviting me to run with the hounds
howling through the ruined cities
trying to hunt down the
FALN, the BLA
the ten or the hundred most wanted
most ready and willing and able
to resist with arms
and heart and ideology
your world
wide crimes

But I am otherwise engaged.

And seriously, thanks
for giving me this chance
to stand fast with the Puerto Ricans
who have gone to jail silent since 1936
rather than drink from your bootprints
To stand fast with the New Afrikans
who like Nat Turner "never said a mumbling word"
To stand fast with the Palestinians
steadfast in Israeli prisons
the Irish deep and defiant in Long Kesh,
the Africans on Robben Island
scorning your offers with songs
To stand fast with the children of Lumumba
and Che and Malcolm X
not to mention my own children and your own as well

Thank you for this chance to stand
not with the defeated but the defiant
who pick up the gun
who pick up the pen
who pick up the baby and the struggle
Thank you for this chance
to stand with humanity against you

Don't mind if I do.

2.A.9.

"Draw the Line" advertisement (1985)

When Philadelphia police dropped a bomb on the West Philadelphia home
of the Black radical MOVE organization, they did so at the orders of the city's

first Black mayor. In response, a diverse group of Black academics (John Bracy, Nathan Hare), activists (Carl Dix, James and Grace Lee Boggs, Chokwe Lumumba, Loretta Ross), attorneys (Conrad Lynn, Flo Kennedy), authors (James Baldwin, Toni Cade Bambara, Audre Lorde, Alice Walker), and others signed on to this advertisement, dubbed "Drawing the Line," condemning the bombing and questioning the significance of electing Black officials to office as a goal in and of itself.

May 13, 1985, we witnessed the Black mayor of Philadelphia take responsibility for the bombing of a house in Philly and the ensuing fire in which eleven people (five of them children) were killed and sixty homes destroyed. Over the past fifteen years, we have witnessed significant increases in the number of Black elected officials. It is often said, and some of us signing this statement do in fact believe, that such increases represent advances in the struggle of Black people. But *all* of us agree on this basic truth: when Black people elected officials use their positions of power to attack Black people, or to cover up for or excuse such attacks, they are no friends of ours and don't speak for or represent the interests of Black people. In the past, lines were clearly drawn on this question. This line must be firmly drawn again. Murder is murder, no matter whether those responsible are Black or white.

2.A.10.

Brian Glick

From *War at Home: Covert Action against US Activists and What We Can Do about It* (1989)

Even though revelation of the FBI's counterintelligence program (COINTELPRO) occasioned much shock and consternation in the early 1970s, police agencies managed to continue to surveil, harass, and arrest diverse social justice activists. In response civil rights attorney Brian Glick penned this short set of guidelines for how activists should respond to repression effected through the legal system (such as grand juries and police investigations), which he included in his book *War at Home*.

Guidelines for Coping with Harassment through the Legal System

1. Don't talk to the FBI, and don't let them in without a warrant. Keep careful records of what they say and do. Tell others that they came.
2. If an activist does talk or makes some other honest error, explain the serious harm that could result. Be firm, but do not ostracize a sincere person

who slips up. Isolation only weakens a person's ability to resist. It can drive someone out of the movement and even into the hands of the police.

3. If FBI or other government agents start to harass people in your area, alert everyone to refuse to cooperate. Warn your friends, neighbors, parents, children, and anyone else who might be contacted. Make sure people know what to do and where to call for help. Get literature, films, and other materials through the organizations listed in the back of this book. Set up community meetings with speakers who have resisted similar harassment elsewhere. Contact sympathetic reporters. Consider "wanted" posters with photos of the agents or guerrilla theater which follows them through the city streets.

4. Organizations listed in the back [of *War at Home*] can also help resist grand jury harassment. Community education is important, along with childcare and legal, financial, and other support for those who protect a movement by refusing to divulge information. If a respected activist is subpoenaed for obviously political reasons, consider trying to arrange for sanctuary in a local church or synagogue.

5. If your group engages in civil disobedience or finds itself under intense police pressure, start a bail fund, train some members to deal with the legal system, and develop an ongoing relationship with sympathetic local lawyers.

6. If you anticipate arrest, do not carry address books or any other materials which could help the FBI and police.

7. While the FBI and police are entirely capable of fabricating criminal charges, your nonpolitical law violations make it easier for them to set you up. Be careful with drugs, tax returns, traffic tickets, and so forth. The point is not to get paranoid but to make a realistic assessment based on your visibility and other relevant circumstances.

8. When an activist has to appear in court, make sure he or she is not alone. The presence of supporters is crucial for morale and can help influence jurors.

9. Don't neglect jailed activists. Organize visits, correspondence, books, food packages, childcare, etc. Keep publicizing their cases.

10. Publicize FBI and police abuses through sympathetic journalists and your own media (posters, leaflets, public access cable television, etc.). Don't let the government and corporate media be the only ones to shape public perceptions of FBI and police attacks on political activists.

If the FBI Drops by, *Just Say No!*

1. You do not have to talk to FBI agents, police, or other investigators. You do not have to talk to them in your house, on the street, if you've been arrested, or even in jail. Only a court or grand jury has legal authority to compel testimony.

2. You don't have to let the FBI or police into your home or office unless they show you an arrest or search warrant which authorizes them to enter that specific place.

3. If they do present a warrant, you do not have to tell them anything other than your name and address. You have a right to observe what they do. Make written notes, including the agents' names, agency, and badge numbers. Try to have other people present as witnesses and have them make written notes too.

4. Anything you say to an FBI agent or other law enforcement officer maybe used against you and other people.

5. Giving the FBI or police information may mean that you will have to testify to the same information at a trial or before a grand jury.

6. Lying to an FBI agent or other federal investigator is a crime.

7. The best advice, if the FBI or police try to question you or to enter your home or office without a warrant, is to *just say no*. FBI agents have a job to do, and they are highly skilled at it. Attempting to outwit them is very risky. You can never tell how a seemingly harmless bit of information can help them hurt you or someone else.

8. The FBI or police may threaten you with a grand jury subpoena if you don't give them information. But you may get one any way, and anything you've already told them will be the basis for more detailed questioning under oath.

9. They may try to threaten or intimidate you by pretending to have information about you: "We know what you have been doing, but if you cooperate it will be all right." If you are concerned about this, tell them you will talk to them with your lawyer present.

10. If you are nervous about simply refusing to talk, you may find it easier to tell them to contact your lawyer. Once a lawyer is involved, the FBI and police usually pull back since they have lost their power to intimidate. (Make arrangements with sympathetic local lawyers and let everyone know that agents who visit them can be referred to these lawyers.) . . .

Not Letting Political Repression Divert Us from Building Strong Movements for Social Justice

Previous attempts to mobilize public opposition, especially on a local level, indicate that a broad coalition, employing a multifaceted approach, may be able to impose some limits on government operations to discredit and disrupt our movements. It is clear, however, that we are not now in a position to eliminate such intervention. While fighting hard to end this hidden war at home, we need to take the time to study the forms it takes and prepare ourselves to cope with it effectively.

Above all, it is essential that we resist the temptation to so preoccupy ourselves with repression that we neglect our main goals. Our ability to resist the government's attacks depends ultimately on the strength of our movements. If we deal openly and well with our differences, covert action will not easily disrupt and divide us. If we show respect for the people we live and work with and help them to fight for their needs, it will be hard for the FBI and police to discredit and isolate us. We will be able, instead, to draw support from our neighbors and coworkers and expose the political police to them. So long as we advocate and organize effectively, no manner of government intervention can stop us.

2.A.11.

Labor/Community Strategy Center

From *A Call to Reject the Federal Weed and Seed Program* (1992)

Los Angeles was a particularly fierce battleground in the war on drugs. The Los Angeles Police Department led the nation in pursuing greater power and authority for police departments, and the city's partnerships with the federal government served as testing grounds for maximizing urban inequality in communities of color. Here, the Los Angeles–based Labor/Community Strategy Center, an urban think tank and organizing project, opposes such criminalization. This opposition was part of a national movement that argued the war on drugs was damaging the urban landscape.

Overview

The Urban Strategies Group of the Labor/Community Strategy Center urges the Los Angeles City Council and Mayor Tom Bradley to withdraw their "in concept" support for the federal Weed and Seed program.

At present, the LA City Council has voted to designate two areas of Los Angeles—one in South Central and one in Pico Union/Koreatown—as pilot projects for the program. Weed and Seed is a program organized, coordinated, and initiated in 1991 by the Department of Justice that links together law enforcement, economic development, and social welfare programs in a supposed effort to "weed" out criminal elements as a precondition to "seeding" local programs with funding. Weed and Seed in reality would:

- preempt the possibility of police reform in Los Angeles.
- use federal laws and agencies to impose a "warfare" approach to urban problems.
- violate the civil rights and civil liberties of low-income communities that are predominantly African American, Latino, and Asian American.
- scapegoat rather than help a lost generation of urban youth.

- impose a two-tiered justice system, with state laws applying to affluent, usually predominantly white communities and federal laws applying to low-income communities of color.
- create an unethical "linkage" between federal social welfare programs and federal military programs and thereby [allowing the federal government to] occupy and dominate the inner cities.
- move US society closer to a police state, especially with regard to urban "policy" targeting low-income, predominantly Black and Latino, communities.

Low-income communities are well aware of how urgently they need expanded social programs and responsible police protection. Funding is needed for public health, education, and income-supplementing programs and for neighborhood and community-based social service agencies. Police protection from violent crime is needed, consistent with ethical police behavior and constitutional safeguards. However, the Weed and Seed program is, by its own definition, not just a *program* but a *strategy*—a right-wing strategy that subverts those legitimate community objectives. It exploits legitimate fear of crime in urban areas in order to position the Department of Justice as the central political force determining urban policy in the United States, with many social agencies subordinated to law enforcement agencies. Its primary approach is not to solve complex urban problems of racism and poverty but rather to suppress the symptoms of urban neglect—drugs, crime, and violence—and in so doing, suppress the youth of the inner city. By "linking" funding for social programs with funding for police repression, it offers what amounts to community blackmail.

There is a need for a multiracial, progressive, citywide social movement in Los Angeles that demands increased social service funding and accountable police behavior. This report is an effort not just to defeat the Weed and Seed program but to play a role in helping to bring into existence that urgently needed social movement. We call on community, labor, civil rights, and civil liberties activists to join with us to persuade the Los Angeles City Council to reject the Weed and Seed program.

Demands

1. We urge the LA City Council and its Ad Hoc Committee on Recovery and Revitalization . . . to hold public hearings on the Weed and Seed program to allow the broadest public input into the process *before* any further votes are taken.
2. We want public information about the Weed and Seed Task Force.
3. We demand that the LA City Council withdraw the city's application to the Weed and Seed program, and withdraw its support for the program in general. We urge that public officials and candidates for office oppose the Weed and Seed program.

4. We urge that public officials and candidates for office oppose the Weed and Seed program.
5. We demand an increase in urgently needed federal social service funding for South Los Angeles, Pico/ Koreatown, and other low-income communities. These funds must be in no way tied to the US Department of Justice or any other federal, state, or local law enforcement agency.

New York City Coalition against Police Brutality, 1996–2000s

Lumumba Akinwole-Bandele and Joo-Hyun Kang

Communities of color have always maintained a vigilant presence in response to police and state violence. The movement in New York City to counter police violence in the 1990s aimed to build on the successes and lessons of prior movement formations—particularly the legacies of Black and Puerto Rican freedom fighters, feminists of color, and LGBT liberationists—by developing grassroots coalitions against police violence as a consistently brutal expression of urban inequality.

Richie Perez, a former member of the Young Lords Party, cofounded the National Congress for Puerto Rican Rights, and in 1996 the New York City Coalition against Police Brutality (CAPB). Fundamental to CAPB's approach in the 1990s through early 2000s was its centering on communities of color, especially those most frequently terrorized by the NYPD: youth, women, immigrants, LGBTQ people, poor/ working-class people, organizers, and activists. Long before the terminology of the "impacted community" was popular in funded movement work, CAPB established the necessity of focusing on those most affected, along with the importance of developing and promoting the leadership and political education of young people. CAPB was intentionally made up of organizations representing the most impacted communities, with predominantly young organizers in their twenties making up the leadership.

CAPB emerged alongside other multi-issue formations confronting institutional violence, including Critical Resistance, INCITE!, immigrant rights, and anti-imperialist organizations, which placed the struggle against police violence in the context of 1990s neoliberalism. Together, these organizations worked to turn the growing but superficial national consensus against racial profiling into concrete alternatives that would provide much-needed relief for communities of color.

CAPB organizations developed a joint analysis of local and global dimensions of state violence. This analysis brought together multiple histories of abusive policing targeting Black and other communities of color, LGBTQ people, youth, immigrants, activists, and low-wage workers, including vendors. The connections linking these communities were not just imagined by activists but evident through police violence. For example, the rise of "broken windows" policing was integrally connected to the displacement of historically low-income communities of color and to citywide budget cuts that accelerated both gentrification and mass incarceration. Young organizers developed an integrated analysis that resulted in CAPB leading broader united front coalitions like Third World Within (TWW). TWW provided political education, carried out actions against immigrant detentions and deportations, and participated in the 2001 UN World Conference against Racism to link New York City struggles with those in the global South. After the 9/11 attacks, TWW converted into an antiwar effort and helped spawn the national Racial Justice 911 network, which opposed the state surveillance and repression of Muslim communities in the early days of the war on terror.

The movement against police and state violence in New York City in the 1990s also saw a resurgence of direct action organizing and civil disobedience tactics. Examples included takeovers of the Bronx and Brooklyn district attorney offices led by Parents against Police Brutality, an organization of families whose loved ones had been murdered by police. Mass protests against the police rape and torture of Abner Louima shook the city. When Rudy Giuliani's mayoral administration proposed placing the NYPD in charge of school safety, thereby increasing the chances that young people would be arrested for what had previously been school disciplinary issues, CAPB led protests. After the officers who murdered Amadou Diallo with forty-one bullets were acquitted, CAPB and the Peoples Justice coalition it created organized a citywide shutdown and forty-one days of action throughout NYC's five boroughs.

Organizations within CAPB engaged in additional proactive and preventative tactics. In 2000, the Malcolm X Grassroots Movement began a copwatch program; drawing inspiration from the Black Panther Party, it monitored police in hopes of reducing its violence. Copwatch activists recorded police encounters and supplied legal information to people stopped by the police. These efforts paralleled similar initiatives nationwide and were later replicated throughout New York City. Following the murder of Amadou Diallo, Richie Perez pushed younger organizers in CAPB to consider combining street action with legal strategy, resulting in a class action lawsuit against the NYPD (*Daniels v. NYC*). This created the legal pathway for *Floyd v. NYC*, the historic 2013 ruling that found stop-and-frisk unconstitutional. The experience and relationships built in the 1990s through CAPB helped develop an analysis of the function of police brutality and a practice for confronting it.

The NYC CAPB consisted, at various points, of the Audre Lorde Project, the Committee against Anti-Asian Violence, the Malcolm X Grassroots Movement, the National Congress for Puerto Rican Rights (now known as the Justice Committee), Sista II Sista, the Student Power Movement (which later became Forever in Struggle Together), and Youth Force.

2.A.12.

Love and Rage Revolutionary Anarchist Federation

"Copwatch: Keeping an Eye on the Cops" (1995)

Many radicals began to monitor police encounters, on the assumption that such public visibility would reduce incidents of police brutality. The most frequent effort, as much a tactic as an organization, was called copwatch. This article, originally published in a special issue of the newspaper of the New York arm of the anarchist organization Love and Rage, outlines the broad theory and action of copwatch programs. While the article focuses on Minneapolis, copwatch efforts could be found in major cities around the country at this time. Armed with cameras, notebooks, and a provisional legal knowledge, activists would noticeably observe police stops.

How can ordinary citizens protect ourselves from the violence of lawless police? What can we do when the police act like just another street gang, one with blue colors? In cities and neighborhoods around the country, people have organized copwatch patrols. They follow police on their beats, as they go about their "business," and record their behavior with cameras or video cameras. They take notes. This is completely legal, so long as the people do not physically "interfere with police business." Even that might be arguably legal, when the police are engaged in criminal behavior. But just by following and watching the cops, people break down the blue wall of secrecy which surrounds the police. It undermines the confidence of the police that they can do whatever they want with impunity. And it gives other people the message that the police need to be watched. It shows people that the cops' authority can be questioned and encourages them to question it themselves.

For example, there is a copwatch project in Minneapolis organized by Anti-Racist Action (ARA). They are inspired by the tradition of the Black Panther Party, which organized people to watch the cops. A group has been going out every other Friday or Saturday evening for almost a year now in downtown Minneapolis. They talk to people and hand out information about ARA and what to do if arrested and, of course, watch the police. During arrests and traffic stops they are witnesses to police conduct and intervene as much as possible. When they are loud enough, the police sometimes let go the person they were arresting and focus on the copwatchers.

The Minneapolis copwatchers are generally perceived as a white group. While people of color also do copwatch, being seen as "white" has some advantages. It gives them the privilege to take things further with the police. They can sometimes get away with things cops rarely tolerate from people of color. They feel that it is important for white folks to take a stand against the cops, to show that they are not all loyal to this oppressive system.

A similar patrol has been organized in Boston. Instead of concentrating on a single area the Boston copwatch uses a car, a police scanner, and a cellular phone to make sure that they are there when the cops are taking action against people in the community.

The police force is one of the most oppressive institutions in many people's lives, especially people of color and working-class people. It is hard to find any African American who has not been harassed, arrested, or assaulted by the police; it is not a question of whether or not it has happened but how many times. Taking a stand against the police is a move against a kind of racism and class oppression that is only slightly more disguised than nazi skinhead violence but is actually more concentrated and real. The police, after all, have the power of the law and the state behind them.

The main way to "fight crime" is to create decent jobs and a just society. On the road to that new world it will be necessary to do away with specialized police (and military) forces over and above the rest of society. The police see themselves as at war with the rest of the population. This makes them perfect tools for the white corporate rich men who rule us. Moving to a free society will require replacing the specialized police with self-policing, with a democratic, popular militia system. Copwatch is a step in that direction.

2.A.13.

Herman Bell et al.

"An Appeal from US Political Prisoners/POWs: Mobilize to Save Mumia Abu-Jamal!" (1999)

The incarceration and looming death sentence of journalist and former Black Panther Mumia Abu-Jamal catalyzed a new wave of activism against the prison system in the mid-1990s. For many, as evident in this letter, written and signed by thirty longtime US political prisoners from a variety of anti-racist and anticolonial movements, Mumia served as a symbol of the problem of the prison system. Not long after this letter circulated, groups of activists staged civil disobedience protest at the Liberty Bell and subsequently at the US Supreme Court in support of Mumia. His death sentence was overturned in 2001, though as of 2020 he remains in prison.

We are prisoners of war and political prisoners (POW/PPs) within the United States. We were variously imprisoned for a range of activities: struggle against white supremacy and colonialism, opposition to the economics of global plunder and class exploitation, efforts against sexism and discrimination, a general unwillingness to abide the multiple ways human beings are demeaned and delimited in this society. We stand for self-determination for all oppressed peoples, for an end to racism, for women's liberation (equality), for economics centered on human need rather than corporate greed.

The reason for this unprecedented collective statement is the urgent situation of fellow political prisoner Mumia Abu-Jamal on death row in Pennsylvania. His legal challenge has now moved to the federal courts, the final area available to him, and these proceedings could be completed within months. While there is overwhelming evidence of his innocence, most of it has been excluded from judicial review. Many of you who have worked hard to save Mumia's life are to be commended. Without your hard work the state probably would have already executed him, but we need to alert you to the urgency of the situation. A measure of the importance of this case can be taken from the recent "big lie" slanders of Mumia by ABC's *20/20* on TV and by *Vanity Fair* magazine. The Fraternal Order of Police, the reactionary criminal justice system, and the corporate media are determined to execute this articulate and courageous brother. It will take a very determined and strong movement to stop the plans for cold-blooded murder.

The urgency is not just because a precious life is at stake but also because of the implications for political and social movements. Mumia has been a singularly eloquent and effective "voice of the voiceless." He has spoken and written powerfully for more than three thousand persons on death row within the US about the fundamental flaws of the criminal justice system, on the foundations of racism and injustice. We want to encourage the range of activist and social justice groups to make Mumia's case their lead project, their key example, in the coming months. Such a focus would not at all mean abandoning broader politics and programs. Mumia's case can powerfully illustrate the general issues of the death penalty, of POW/PPs, of the criminal justice system, and of racism and injustice. He can personify these crucial concerns and help energize each area of work. We call upon all people who care about life and social justice to mobilize for Mumia.

Free Mumia! End the death penalty!

Undermining the Prison State

2.B.1.

The Red Family

From "War behind Walls" (1971)

Prisoners around the country went on strike, protested, or otherwise re-
belled against incarceration in the summer and early fall of 1971. In this excerpt from an article printed in a one-off antiprison newspaper, a group of
San Francisco Bay Area activists analyzes the interlinked rebellions at San
Quentin (California), which culminated in the death of imprisoned intellectual George Jackson, and Attica (New York) prisons as evidence of a new politics of state repression and assess the prospect of success for what was then
called "the prison movement."

The revolt and massacre at Attica State Prison and the slaying of Soledad Brother
George Jackson have made us all aware that something is happening behind
the walls of American prisons. George Jackson called it a "war without terms."

Who is at war and what are the stakes? Why are prisoners risking their lives,
striking, rebelling, taking hostages? Why did authorities sacrifice forty-one lives
to regain control of Attica? Why is George Jackson dead?

Many of us mistakenly think that prisoners live in a closed world, with no
connection to events outside. The history of the last two decades of struggle inside, however, shows that prisoners have kept pace with the political currents.
Prisoners moved beyond traditional food and shelter complaints in the late 50s
and early 60s to demand religious freedoms and civil rights, while the most recent actions have made revolutionary challenges to the prison system itself and
gone beyond to link with a broader movement.

In response, support for the prison movement is growing on the outside.
Groups of legal workers are challenging prison conditions in the courts; support organizations help to secure bail, parole, or transportation for visitors.

At the center of this movement are dedicated men and women inside. Prisoner unions, political education around racism and class exploitation, and militant actions which challenge the unchecked authority of prison officials while drawing national attention are being organized not only by people we all know like George Jackson and Erica Huggins but also by lesser known but equally courageous people like Earl Satcher, Luis Talamantez, Hugo Pinell, Richard Clark, Larry Blyden [Herbert X. Blyden], and Eliot Barklay [Elliot "L.D." Barkley].

The prison movement is growing, but at a high cost. Every gain brings new repression; leaders are persecuted and assassinated. Attica and San Quentin force us to recognize the prison movement as a struggle to the death, which commands our fullest support. . . .

The events of the last year [1971], particularly, have demonstrated a heightened militancy and strength in the movement: the seizure of New York City prisons, the Auburn prison revolt last fall, Attica. In California, the publicity given to the Soledad Brothers, Angela Davis, and Ruchell Magee reached new audiences and generated new support for the movement in general. In the face of these actions the contradictions within the prison administration have intensified to the point that we can begin to see internal disputes among the authorities themselves.

Alongside the "liberal" reformist school of thought, there has always existed a more "hardline," forthrightly fascist approach, held by some guards, lesser officials, and top administrators. There is evidence that as the struggle intensifies, these hardliners are gaining strength. . . .

Actually, this may signal a "closing of the ranks" between liberals and hardliners as much as capitulation. In New York, the assault on Attica's D-Block—a massacre of forty-one people, all by the hands of the police—was accepted by Russell Oswald, commissioner of Corrections, a man who had the reputation of a liberal, almost crusading, reformer. In his previous job as head of Massachusetts Department of Corrections, he came under fire from local papers for "coddling" criminals. And yet that assault took the lives of ten prison employees and thirty-one prisoners. San Quentin is famous for its ironclad law that a guard shoot to kill prisoners taking hostages despite the safety of the hostages. Given the inhuman attitude of the officials, it should be no surprise when some guards start to move on their own. Guards at Attica unfurled a banner sent to them by guards at San Quentin announcing, "We have just begun to fight." . . .

The use of extralegal means such as assassinations may be a last resort, but prison officials are devoting much of their energy to trying to structure the prisons so as to isolate the troublemakers.

Their solution is to isolate this "6 percent" [of the prison population that administrators assumed would always be troublemakers] from the rest of the prison population. Again, California is creating the model in this attempt; for many years, special areas such as the "Adjustment Center" at San Quentin and "0 Wing" at Soledad have kept problem prisoners segregated from the "mainline" prison population. Increasingly, these units have been filled with politically active prisoners. George Jackson spent seven of his eleven years behind bars in these "prisons within prisons."

Other states are following the California model. A de facto "adjustment center" has been set up at the Auburn State Prison in New York since the riots of last November to isolate the prisoners charged with provoking the disturbances. These men, the Auburn Eighty, have been isolated indefinitely: [there is] no indication of when they will be allowed back into the general prison population.

Last May, at a national conference of prison administrators in New Orleans, the question of "the new type of problem prisoner" produced one recommendation for the "establishment of separate institutions for recalcitrant and politically embittered offenders."

A glimpse of the future? The California Correctional Officers Association has submitted a proposal that a new maximum security unit for "the small segment of inmates bent on self-destruction" be added to the facility at Vacaville. Vacaville is the state's medical facility where shock treatment and other "behavior modification" techniques are being used in an effort to insure control over "violence prone" prisoners. Welcome to 1984.

Attica and After

. . . Despite these attempts by the state to suppress the prison rebellion and isolate its leaders, the movement will not be turned back now. Despite any "6 percent" theory, prisons have become not only houses of repression but also cradles of resistance; for those who are murdered or isolated, others will rise to take their places. Even Senator Muskie recognized that "the fact that there are men who are willing to die rather than live another day in prison demonstrated that something is terribly wrong with American prisons."

There is no going back when men reach this point. Either the changes will be made, or there will be more Atticas and San Quentins.

[Black radical prisoner] Jimmy Carr pointed out "the prisons are producing men whom the authorities don't want either on the outside or on the inside." It is producing a group of serious, dedicated revolutionaries. We must all work to support and strengthen their efforts—reform, legal work, militant action are all needed when we are dealing with a war behind the walls.

2.B.2.

off our backs

"How Many Lives?" (1971)

Incarcerated people around the country held memorials and protests after New York State troopers killed forty-one people to end the Attica prison rebellion—including a five-day uprising at Alderson, West Virginia, then the country's only federal prison for women. First published in the radical feminist newspaper *off our backs*, this anonymously authored essay offered a dramatic response to the problem of prison: abolition.

How many years of people's lives must be lost, hidden, and brutalized, before we see that prisons must be abolished?

How many Atticas, San Quentins, and Aldersons will it take till we realize that our society has created these monstrous institutions out of fear—fear of human freedom, cultural differences, loss of capitalist property? The ethics of our society have been distorted by this fear and are then imposed on nonwhite people, poor people, young people, and women to make survival and experimentation crimes. Why should people in Amerika spend years in jail for such "immoral" acts as smoking grass, getting drunk and singing in the streets, making love or printing "obscenity," much less for standing by moral decisions not to kill or work for an immoral government? If prisons were really to protect us from psychopaths, murderers, and thieves, they would contain Nixon, Rockefeller, Mitchell, Reagan, Agnew, owners of motor industries and oil dynasties, slum landlords, church leaders, and Pentagon officials. Prisons are the extreme domestic example of the racism, sexism, militarism, and imperialism that we have been watching for years in Vietnam.

Who needs "rehabilitation" in our society? Not the slaves of ghetto deprivation and drugs pushed by those who wish to dull possible insurgency. Not the men and women who have learned to hustle and survive despite all efforts to destroy them. Not revolutionaries like Angela Davis and George Jackson. The people who need to be "rehabilitated" (if that's even a correct attitude to have toward any human beings) are those whose minds and bodies have been warped by false value systems that convince them that some people must die so they can live, many must starve so they can eat, all must slave so they can enjoy rest.

"Rehabilitation" is the pacification program of liberalism. Even if we did want to "rehabilitate" sick or deviant minds or bodies, prison would be the last place to achieve it. We need to rid ourselves of prisons. They are a danger to society not only because they are schools for "crime" (70 percent of all "crimes" are committed by ex-convicts) but because they try to erase from our consciousness people who could possibly bring about exciting changes in our social order. We need women like Angela Davis, Erica Huggins, and Madame Ngo Ba Thanh among us. We need the Puerto Rican revolutionaries locked inside Alderson.

To abolish prisons we may have to develop "reforms" that carry within them contradictions that will make it hard to achieve them without drastically changing prisons—black prisoners' unions with collective bargaining power, ending detention before conviction, a national prisoner monitoring system, open-door policies, viable alternatives to incarceration. But whatever approaches are used, the goal should be prison abolition. To have no alternative at all would be better than to continue the present reality. And we can't wait for the ending of racism, sexism, and poverty in this country before we begin tearing down the walls. It may be in our own self-interest.

2.B.3.

North Carolina Prisoners' Labor Union

From "Goals of the North Carolina Prisoners' Labor Union" (1974)

Throughout the early 1970s, incarcerated people formed unions to address a wide range of grievances. Perhaps the most determined such initiative took place in North Carolina, where state officials expressed deep hostility to unions in general, much less ones in prison. Nevertheless, eleven prisoners signed on to this document laying out their grievances, demands, and approach. The prisoners ended up taking their case, *Jones v. NCPLU,* to the Supreme Court in 1977, which ruled against them. The ruling essentially squashed the prisoner union movement.

For centuries persons charged and convicted of crimes have been looked upon and treated as less than human beings. This is true today in spite of the fact that current knowledge of society and its patterns of law enforcement teach us that law violations occur among a vastly larger number of persons than those convicted and imprisoned. Moreover, the prisoner, the convict, and ex-convict are treated with extreme hostility and oppression more often because they are poor or members of racial minorities than because they are persons who are actually less deserving of human respect and dignity.

We do not deny that society has a right to punish by imprisonment for law violations, but we submit that this punishment should be imposed by the judicial branch and that prisoners are not sent to prison *for* punishment, but rather, *as* punishment. It is further submitted that this punishment should not be arbitrarily increased or harshened by the prison administration against those few it chooses to separate as "incorrigibles." Moreover, we accept the philosophy of punishment *only* within reasonable periods of time and *only* after conviction of wrongdoing. Beyond this, society should have *no* other rights over the convicted person.

Therefore, we are committed to altering or removing those "correctional" practices which are in conflict with just constitutional and social interests of all persons. The practices which we are primarily concerned at this time fall into the following general categories:

1. *Economic exploitation*: in North Carolina prisoners are forced to supply labor for the state without salary, rights, or other compensation and benefits normally guaranteed workers.

2. *Denial of human and civil rights*: the prisoners imprisoned and incarcerated in the North Carolina Department of Corrections are being mistreated and denied a multitude of basic civil rights. This is completely unnecessary and unjust.
3. *Indeterminate sentencing*: in North Carolina many prisoners are sentenced under an indeterminate sentence system. They are held for indefinite lengths of time, not knowing when they will be released. They have their sentences determined upon irrelevant, arbitrary, or unconstitutional criteria. Furthermore, once determined, their sentences may be again revoked without any new charges being brought against them in due process procedure.
4. *Rehabilitation and return to society*: the present system of rehabilitation of prisoners in the state of North Carolina's Department of Corrections is being applied to only a select few. Thereby, the interests of society as a whole in the rehabilitation process are being neglected insofar as the majority of inmates in prison are only being punished rather than being aided in developing socially beneficial patterns of behavior.

Based upon the foregoing concerns, the North Carolina Prisoners' Union is committed to work towards the following:

1. *An end to employment without reasonable compensation or wage. . . .*
2. *An end to employment without workers' compensation or benefits. . . .*
3. *An end to brutal treatment on the part of prison staffs. . . .*
4. *An end to inferior, insufficient, and inadequate medical treatment and attention. . . .*
5. *An end to the refusal to have an "in-house" law library and legal service. . . .*
6. *An end to the denial of full civil rights upon release. . . .*
7. *An end to arbitrary indeterminate sentences and the mode of their imposition. . . .* In some indeterminate sentence cases prisoners do not receive notification of a release date until they have nearly completed their time. Though a rehabilitative rationale is often used to justify this practice, it is clear that the maximization of conformity and docility is more frequently the basis for such action. This practice results in extreme hardship and mental torture for the prisoner and *must* be halted. The foregoing abuses defeat, we submit, the positive potential within the indeterminate sentencing system, and therefore, such a system must be abolished altogether.
8. *An end to the current practices of the Board of Parole.* Records verify that the Parole Board has not been granting paroles based on assessment of the merits of behavior but rather upon the provisions of what connections an inmate might have. Standards and guidelines as to the granting of paroles and recommendations for commutations should be drawn up and strictly adhered to, without special treatment granted due to political connections. Further, all prisoners must be given due process of law and procedural matters. It is mandatory that a prisoner who has shown

that he/she is entitled to parole consideration be given this consideration without undue delay or excuse.

9. *An end to the denial of gain time without just cause or due process of law.* The North Carolina Department of Corrections for many years has ignored the North Carolina General Stature s/s 14–265 which provides commutation of sentence for Sunday work. This relief, in particular, must be accorded to all imprisoned, as must all other commutations of sentence allowed under existing laws and statutes of the state. Moreover, a commutation of time for extra work performed is a right and cannot be taken away from a prisoner by the prison personnel.

10. *An end to the contract programs due to violations of the agreements.* As it exists now, the prisoner performs the duties and obligations of the contract and rather than receiving his/her merited reward he/she is simply given another contract to be fulfilled. This must be accepted upon penalty of being locked up with all privileges denied. The Department of Corrections is using job contracts and numerous other programs as behavior modification techniques to control the inmate population. The inmates must be made aware of these methods, and the union will expose such practices in the effort to impede or stop such abuses.

11. *An end to the denial of procedural due process of law.* . . .

12. *An end to disciplinary hearings regarding violations which are alleged on the basis of hearsay or suspicion.* . . .

13. *An end to the denial of justified and merited privileges without reason.* . . .

14. *An end to the construction of high-rise maximum security prisons.* . . .

15. *An end to discriminatory sentences based on economic or racial background.* The judicial-prison-parole-industrial complex places unrealistic and harsh prison sentences on persons largely from the poor classes while those with wealth go free. We recognize that this is merely a reflection of society at large and the social and economic prejudices rampant within it. However, we recognize our responsibility to work towards changing this through educational techniques and other appropriate measures.

16. *An end to the disparity in sentencing, by the courts.* . . .

17. *An end to capital punishment.*

Strategies

Through the North Carolina Prisoners' Union there will be a wide variety of strategies pursued to achieve the above-stated goals. At present we will concentrate on the following tactics:

A. Organize a state-wide unified, multiracial prisoners' union at every prison in North Carolina which can work efficiently and dedicatedly towards our goals, with collective strength.

B. Direct outside members of the union and community support groups to appear before the legislature to provide more complete information about prisons and the treatment of prisoners.

C. Educate the public through the news media, union newsletters or publications, and public speaking engagements.

D. Retain attorneys to help gain our objectives through the courts.

E. Use peaceful, lawful, and legal methods to obtain fair treatment and due process of law for all prisoners of the state of North Carolina.

F. Collectively bargain with prison administrations and administrators.

Southern Coalition on Jails and Prisons, 1974–1990

Lydia Pelot-Hobbs

In 1974, as the United States embarked on the political project that would become known as mass incarceration, free-world activists organized the Southern Coalition on Jails and Prisons (SCJP) to resist the growing use of criminalization and imprisonment. The SCJP was formed as a regional organization, and at its height in the early 1980s it had chapters in Alabama, Florida, Georgia, Kentucky, Louisiana, Maryland, Mississippi, North Carolina, South Carolina, and Tennessee. Between 1974 and its demise in 1990, the SCJP focused on four primary issues: reforming prison and jail conditions to ensure the rights of prisoners, halting new prison construction, abolishing capital punishment, and developing alternatives to incarceration.

To meet these goals, the coalition employed a range of tactics. For instance, as part of its activism to reform prison and jail conditions it filed civil action lawsuits along with supporting prisoner strikes and other forms of resistance, such as the North Carolina Prisoners' Union's struggle for official recognition as a union. SCJP understood its constituency to be both friends and family of incarcerated people as well as radicals and progressives without a direct relationship to the penal system but whose politics poised them to be sympathetic to SCJP's aims of countering state punishment with social justice. It established support groups of family and friends of incarcerated people, coordinated carpools for prison visits, and petitioned governors for prison reforms. Through newsletters and conferences, its members strove to inform and mobilize people around the everyday and extraordinary forms of carceral violence, from inadequate health care to solitary confinement to guard beatings. SCJP worked in alliance with legal organizations such as the ACLU and the Southern Prisoners Defense Committee as well as liberal religious groups on lawsuits addressing prison conditions and in advocating for ending the death penalty. The group understood itself to be a regional branch of a national movement against imprisonment and linked itself with organizations such as the National Prison Moratorium Project and Stop the Olympic Prison in Lake Placid, New York.

SCJP organized from the standpoint that the post–civil rights "New South" was not a transformed society—as many southern elites claimed—but was leading the nation in reinforcing racism and class oppression through the expansion of the penal system and the resurgence of the death penalty. In its analysis, the growth of incarceration served to warehouse poor and working-class southerners of color who society had otherwise abandoned. An SCJP flyer described capital punishment as "the ultimate means of disposing of people we no longer know how to deal with."

While self-identified as a penal reform organization, the SCJP's demands often mixed reformist and radical politics in its calls for pretrial release, alternative diversionary programs, and a total cessation of new penal construction. Its campaigns faced the challenge of inadvertently encouraging punitive state building projects. For instance, in the early 1980s, the Louisiana chapter had filed a series of lawsuits against widespread inhumane conditions and premature death in the Louisiana jail system. Yet the state government in alignment with local sheriffs responded to the lawsuits by expanding the jail system rather than expanding release mechanisms. In response, the Louisiana chapter retreated from prison conditions litigation as a decarceration strategy.

As tough-on-crime politics solidified in the 1980s, SCJP campaigns focused less on decarceration and more on ending the death penalty, which was particularly widespread in the South. The coalition opposed the death penalty both at the policy level and by holding protests and vigils; they challenged the state's killing of John Louis Evans of Alabama, executed in 1983, and protested the planned execution of Shabaka Sundiata Waglini of Florida, who was released from death row in 1987 and freed from prison in 1990. While its strategies shifted, the SCJP never abandoned its position that "if the choice were between prisons as they now are and no prisons at all, we would promptly choose the latter."

2.B.4.

National Council on Crime and Delinquency/
Unitarian Universalist Service Committee

From National Moratorium on Prison Construction flyer (1976)

Coalitions of faith-based and secular progressives challenged the federal government's plan to construct additional prisons in the 1970s. The biggest such effort at the time was the National Moratorium on Prison Construction, a joint venture between the Unitarian Universalists and the National Council on Crime and Delinquency.

Why?

- The economic costs of imprisonment and new prison construction are spiraling. Alternatives are cheaper.
- Prisons are cruel and inhumane.
- Because bail means jail for the poor only, jails are unconstitutional. This means a lack of equal protection under the law.
- Prisons do not deter. They seem to produce crime. Prisons do not rehabilitate. They simply isolate.
- The selection of defendants by the criminal justice process is biased. Poorer people and racial minorities are disproportionately chosen.
- The problems of society need examination as well as those of individuals.
- Prisons are a permanent and inflexible "solution." We are stuck with them for generations.
- An experiment that has fumbled for two hundred years deserves unprecedented scrutiny.

. . .

A common argument for the construction of new penal facilities is that the old prisons are horribly overcrowded. Our solution is to cut back the mass of criminal laws and the types of enforcement that send so many people to prisons and to implement various alternatives.

The basic alternative to imprisonment is the achievement of criminal, economic, and social justice. We must therefore be careful to restructure the discretionary decisions which now produce a biased sample of selectees—the poor—for intake into the criminal justice process. Otherwise, programmatic alternatives will but juggle this small selected sample of all those who actually commit crimes from one agency of control to another.

Our Rationale

An Historical Failure

The penitentiary experiment, introduced by the United States to the world in 1790, replaced barbaric physical punishments with yet another horrible punishment—the isolation of the offender from society and the community.

When Charles Dickens visited the United States in 1842, he was appalled at the effects of solitary confinement on men, women, and children. He wrote,

> I believe it in its effects, to be cruel and wrong. In its intention, I am well convinced that it is kind, humane, and meant for reformation, but I am persuaded that those who devised this system of prison discipline do not know what it is that they are doing. I believe that very few men are capable of estimating the immense amount of torture and agony which this dreadful punishment inflicts upon the sufferers. I hold this slow and daily tampering with the mysteries of the brain, to be immeasurably worse than any torture of the body.

Figure 2.2. Michael Kroll and Andy Hall, "STOP the Olympic Prison" (circa 1979). Image courtesy of Lincoln Cushing/ Docs Populi. Reprinted with permission by Michael Kroll.

More recently critics and criminologists have shown that such coercive and involuntary settings as prisons cannot rehabilitate. Further, prisons do not deter criminals or protect society from crime since so many offenders return to crime after prison sentences. . . .

A Sense of Urgency

The United States has the highest crime rate of the industrialized nations of the world. It also has the highest per capita detention rate and metes out the longest criminal sentences in a futile attempt to "crack the crime problem." The United States relies on prisons more than any other developed country, and we are now witnessing a major wave of jail and prison construction.

As of August 1975, our office had identified about 450 cases of new or replacement federal, state, county, or city penal and juvenile facilities that were under serious discussion or actual construction. The cost of a little more than half of these was about $1.7 billion, while the cost of the total number of facilities nationwide (we guesstimated nine hundred) could be $7 billion, a figure that financing costs would more than double.

Thus, we feel it urgent that there be an immediate moratorium on all new penal and juvenile facility construction. Such a moratorium attempts to *provide time and a technique for forcing* an unprecedented analysis and critique of our entire criminal justice flow and the confinement process, as well as time to develop a sensible planning process and to introduce a variety of alternative programs, procedures, policies, and philosophies.

> We must resist the pressure to build new prisons or America will have delayed, and at great cost, the more reasonable solutions which must inevitably be worked out. We can have order without new prisons if we pursue social and economic justice. We will have chaos, even with a thousand new prisons, if we deny it. (William Nagel)

. . .Most importantly, we have begun the work of helping to organize a network of allies to aid this growing movement. Because our research has also identified a critical need for action in the states where per capita detention rates are highest, our organizing and speaking schedules have been heaviest there, and we hope to establish moratorium offices in these target areas.

2.B.5.

George Jackson Brigade

Communiqué on the bombing of the Washington Department of Corrections (1975)

Named after the slain revolutionary prisoner, the George Jackson Brigade was a Seattle-based underground group in the late 1970s composed of formerly incarcerated people and other antiprison activists. This May 31, 1975, communiqué, its first, accompanied the group's bombing of the state Department of Corrections office in solidarity with a prison rebellion at the Washington State Penitentiary.

> Settle your quarrels, come together, understand the reality of our situation, understand that fascism is already here, that people are already dying who could be saved, that generations more will die or live poor butchered half-lives if you fail to act. Do what must be done, discover your humanity and your love in revolution. Pass on the torch. Join us, give up your life for the people.
>
> —George Jackson

There has been an ongoing debate recently over national and local law enforcement policies. On the issue of the criminal sentencing process, for example, there appears to be a conflict of opinion between conservative law and order advocate [Christopher] Bayley (the recently promoted county prosecutor) and liberal [King County Superior Court] Judge [Donald] Horowitz. Bayley adopts a get tough attitude toward crime, the old lock 'em up syndrome, which has proven so ineffective in the past. Horowitz, on the other hand, says warehousing criminals is not only ineffective [but] it is cruel and suggests "treatment" of the offender. Neither Bayley nor Horowitz deals with the type of hypocrisy that allows Nixon and gang to escape justice while the poor and confused are made examples of by the courts.

Crime is not some sort of a disease that suddenly possesses an individual and causes them to act criminally and which requires treatment in order for the offender to be rehabilitated. Nor is crime a problem resolvable by increasing the sentences of the offender. Every day prisoners are released from prison. Give them longer sentences and people would still be leaving the prisons every day; the only difference would be in the degree of anger felt by the released prisoner. The anger gets taken out on the community. The problem has not been solved, simply prolonged and aggravated, like the way [President Gerald] Ford deals with the economy.

Crime is the natural response for those caught between poverty and the Amerikan culture of greed, aggression, sexism, and racism. The increasing level of crime is a measure of the sickness of our society; treating or punishing individuals will have little effect on the rate of crime. Sexual aggression against women, for example, has its roots in the sexist attitudes of men. Rape is the logical extension of the sickness of viewing women as objects to be used or abused like any other possession.

What is going to stop crime is when people get together and drive our criminal ruling class and its fascist government up against the wall. Crime will be eliminated when people create a society based on human need rather than greed; a society in which our children are taught that the object in life is something other than making a buck or being sexy. The Amerikan people support the most notorious criminals in existence: US imperialism. Our high standard of living comes from the outright plunder of the "free" world, especially Third World countries. We share the loot stolen from the mouths of hungry children in Africa, Korea, and even here in Amerika and then wonder why our society is so violent. If people want a better society, they can start by becoming active feminists, antiracists, and anti-imperialists. The ruling class is white, male, and imperialist.

Notwithstanding the rhetoric of the great debaters, the state's actual response to crime is to respond with terrorism. Just as the recapture of the Mayaguez [a US ship seized by the Khmer Rouge government of Cambodia in May 1975, which the US reclaimed after three days] was an international act of terrorism, so too is the shooting of unarmed blacks such as [Seattle resident] Joe Herbert. The national and state governments are so unstable that the only way in which they can maintain "order" is through the selective use of terrorism. Those who maintain rule through the use of terror are fascists. Revolutionary counterterror is the appropriate response to fascist lawlessness.

Maintaining order is not only a problem of the urban and rural governments, it is a growing problem inside the nation's prisons as well. In an attempt to maintain order within the nation's prisons, the government has implemented the practice of behavior modification techniques on prisoners who resist the command to be silent in the face of slavery and mind torture. The effect of behavior modification is to grant freedom to those who are dishonest and deceitful enough to mouth the master's line and to punish with long-term confinement those who are politically or legally active in trying to create a better society.

The "treatment concept" is a euphemism for psychofascism. It consists of electroshock, psychosurgery, massive druggings, averse conditioning, sensory deprivation, and more. Such practices have found their way into the nation's schools, especially in high poverty areas. In fact, it was to stop such abuses that the Symbionese Liberation Army executed [Oakland, California,] school superintendent Marcus Foster [in 1973].

In order to effectively apply the treatment concept, the Adult Corrections Division needs the power to move prisoners from prison to prison (or hospital). The prisoners at Walla Walla realize this fact, and in an attempt to transfer prisoners, they made the following demands central to their struggle: Demand IV (k), "that no member of the population shall ever be transferred to another mental or psychiatric facility out of state unless personally requested by the prisoner in writing." Demand IV (l) goes on to stay "that no member of the population shall ever be transferred to another penal facility in any location unless personally requested by the prisoner in writing." These demands were so important to the prisoners that they followed them up with the only threat of violence in the entire list of demands: VI (m), "that if the foregoing insistence indicated in items (k) and (l) are not honored, the Resident Government Council [a self-governing body of incarcerated people] shall see to the destruction of the Washington State Penitentiary." Prisoners also demanded the removal of the chief doctor, the head nurse, and the associate superintendent of custody. When negotiations failed, prisoners seized 8 wing and the hospital and used hostages in an attempt to push their demands forward.

Today is exactly six months from the final deadline prisoners set for the implementation of their demands. Not a single demand has been met. Today's bombing of the offices of the Washington State Department of Corrections is a measure of our determination to see the implementation of the just demands of the Walla Walla prisoners. We of the George Jackson Brigade hereby demand: (A) that the State give prisoners the power to decide for themselves whether or not they want to be transferred; (B) [that it] stop the use and threatened use of psychofascist techniques on the minds of prisoners and schoolchildren; (C) the removal of three administrators: Dr. August Hovnanian, hospital surgeon, James Harvey, associate superintendent for custody, and Mrs. Eva Nelson, chief nurse; and (D) that the prison administration follow the Resident Government Council's constitution and otherwise follow the law (the RGC must be permitted to exist).

2.B.6.

Sundiata Acoli

"Prison Struggles and Human Rights" (1978)

A NASA engineer who joined the Black Panther Party, Sundiata Acoli went underground after police harassment and a specious two-year conspiracy case against the Panthers' New York chapter functionally shut it down. In 1973 he was arrested along with Assata Shakur on the New Jersey Turnpike in an incident that left fellow Panther Zayd Shakur and a state trooper dead. In this essay, Acoli reviews many of the new forms of isolation to which officials subjected dissident and activist prisoners like himself.

Prisons are the best indicators of human rights policies because it is in the prisons that repression is most blatant. This holds true worldwide, in Latin America, Europe, Afrika, [and] Asia and is no less true in Amerika itself where prison atrocities mount daily.

Recently a busload of federal prisoners being transferred from Atlanta was detoured onto a back highway and pulled over by a swarm of squad cars. Pigs in full riot gear, helmets, face shields, ax handles, and shotguns surrounded the bus. It was no accident that this bus contained a number of political prisoners of war, including Herman Bell, Dixie Picariello, Mark Cook, and many others too numerous to name. These new-styled legalized klansmen satisfied themselves with simply unnerving the prisoners on this occasion, but when the bus reached Lewisburg, Pennsylvania's, federal penitentiary, the other shoe fell. As the prisoners unloaded from the bus, a number of them were brutally set upon with ax handles without any provocation whatsoever while still in shackles and leg chains.

Lewisburg is notorious for its repressive nature and jungle atmosphere and had recently undergone a series of fires of unknown origin and cause. Though still unknown to this day, the officials simply responded with a massive round-up of political POWs, including Michael Ashanti Alston, Marvin Harris, Mark Holder, and others, and herded them off to the infamous Marion Illinois Control Unit and other dispersed kamps.

Prison atrocity is no respecter of sex, as verified by the kidnapping of Assata Shakur and shunting her off to the maximum security unit at Alderson, West Virginia. She is the only black in a unit where a number of white prisoners openly display nazi signs on their doors. Nor is it a respecter of race, for those who seriously attack the state and remain implacably opposed to it also get isolated; e.g., Rita Brown, a political POW of the George Jackson Brigade, is also caged at Alderson. Safiya Bukhari languishes in a maximum security unit in Virginia, still unable to get the necessary surgical operation for an ailment diagnosed over four years ago. Dessie Woods suffers from forced druggings, physical brutality, and attempted murder at the hands of racist pigs in the Georgia prison for women. Joanne Little, under the modern-day fugitive slave law, is forcefully returned to the North Carolina kamp where she fears for her life.

New York State has a maximum security unit on the drawing boards for Auburn prison, which is being specifically designed to cage political POWs. Dhoruba Moore is rounded up at four in the morning and shipped in chains to the dungeons at Dannemora, NY, simply because he had the audacity to say publicly that an explosive Attica-type situation was building up at Green Haven prison. Musa Abdul Mu'Mi was burnt to death in a Green Haven isolation cell under suspicious circumstances after he witnessed a KKK meeting in the prison yard. Albert Nuh Washington is rounded up and given *four months* in the hole at Dannemora for having political literature in his cell.

New York state builds the winter Olympic games site with plans for instant conversion into a new maximum security prison after the games are over. The state of New Jersey, now entering its third year of behavior modification MCUs [management control units], which were copied directly from the similar MCUs at San Quentin, California, has just received $40 million to build similar new maximum security prisons scheduled for completion by 1981. California requested $96 million to build four new prisons, and the Senate gave them $130 million to build *six* "new, more secure" prisons urgently needed in early 1980 accommodate the "expected" rapid rise in the prison population. The list could go on and on [. . .] all over the country there is a massive crash program to build more new maximum security prisons. All over the country, there are moves to lock down political POWs in particular in these superoppressive maximum security cages. So [President] Carter's human rights "talk" notwithstanding, the name of the game is repression, repression, and more repression. The country builds prisons, we must [. . .]

Build to Win!

Trenton State Prison
6/30/78

2.B.7a. and 2.B.7b.

After her arrest on the New Jersey Turnpike in 1973, Assata Shakur became one of the most famous women prisoners in the country. She was subjected to a series of trials and shocking prison conditions—at one point, she was even held in a men's prison—and then escaped from prison in November 1979, days before the Black Solidarity Day rally that was scheduled to be held at the United Nations. Two documents are provided here: the first is a communiqué from the Black Liberation Army on helping her escape, and the second is a statement from Shakur outlining the prospects for social change as a resurgent racism made wider use of incarceration. Both of these statements were read at the Black Solidarity Day rally. Shakur was granted political asylum in Cuba, where she published her autobiography in 1987 and still lives as of 2020.

2.B.7a. Black Liberation Army Coordinating Committee, Special communiqué on the freeing of sister Assata Shakur (1979)

To: The Black Community and the Black Movement Special Communiqué
   (Joanne Chesimard)

From: Coordinating Committee, BLA

Subject: Freeing of Sister Assata Shakur on 2 November 79

The existence of Black political prisoners and scores of BLA prisoners of domestic war in the united states is the result of brutal suppression of Black people's national and human rights. Recent history of the Black movement in the u.s. is cold testimony to this political and social repression carried forward under the auspices of "criminal law enforcement."

Comrade-sister Assata Shakur was freed from racist captivity in anticipation of Black Solidarity Day, November 5, and in order to express to the world the need to Free All Black Political Prisoners in the u.s. The Freedom of Black Political Prisoners is of fundamental importance to the protection of Black human rights in general. The brutal and callous treatment by prison administrators of our captured comrades cannot be allowed to continue unnoticed by the Black Community.

In freeing comrade-sister Assata we have made it clear that such treatment and the "criminal" guilt or innocence of a Black freedom fighter is irrelevant when measured by our people's history of struggle against racist u.s. domination.

Support the struggle for Black human rights!
Free all BLA political prisoners!
Dare to struggle, dare to win!

Coordinating Committee,
BLA

2.B.7b. Assata Shakur, from "Statement from Assata Shakur" (1979)

Uhuru Sisters and Brothers, Revolutionary Greetings,

November 1979 and crosses burn the face of Amerika, November 1979 and hundreds of Klu Klux Klan march all over the country carrying clubs and chains and machine guns. 1979—and Black families are fire bombed. 1979—and over 40 percent of Black youth are unemployed. 1979 and a white policeman shoots a handcuffed Black man in the head and is acquitted. 1979—and five policemen shoot a Puerto Rican man armed only with a pair of scissors twenty-four times. 1979—and Philadelphia, the fourth largest city in the country, is sued by the Justice Department for systematically condoning and encouraging widespread police brutality, especially against Blacks and Puerto Ricans.

We are on the threshold of the 80s entering into a new decade, and we have got to take a look and see what Amerika has in store for us. This country is on the decline. The sun is setting on the Amerikan Empire because of liberation movements around the world. The sources of cheap labor and stolen raw materials are rapidly drying up. Amerika is a vampire, experiencing a blood shortage for the first time. The national trade deficit is about $30 billion a year. The Joint Economic Committee of Congress announced in August that the standard of living of the average Amerikan would be drastically reduced in the 1980s. Blacks and Hispanics, the report said, would be hit the hardest. Now what, I ask you, can be harder than drastic. Unemployment, according to the report, would remain at 7 percent or higher. The committee came to the conclusion that the labor force had to be dramatically reduced in order to minimize the problem. What does that mean—reduce the labor force dramatically? What does that mean? In a country that has had a history of using racism to perpetuate capitalism and oppression, who is going to be the scapegoat? In a country that has historically used Blacks, Hispanics, Orientals, and Native Americans as scapegoats, what do Black and Third World people have to look forward to in the 80s? And what does all this have to do with political prisoners and the prison movement?

Every Black leader in this country with the potential of being a Black messiah has gone to prison, even Black leaders without the potential of being the Black messiah have gone to prison. Marcus Garvey, Martin Luther King, Malcolm X, and countless others who spoke out for human rights went to prison. What does that tell us? Out of the four hundred thousand people in united states prisons, three hundred thousand are Black. 275,000 prison cells are being built or are in the planning stages and every state in this country is trying to implement or reinstate the death penalty. *What does that mean?*

I've been in prison six and a half years, and I can feel what's coming in the air. Prisons are becoming more brutal and repressive. Behavior modification programs are booming. People are receiving longer sentences with fewer chances of being paroled. Thirteen-year-old children are being sentenced to life in prison. The government has stepped up its musical jail policy by shipping prisoners all over the country away from their lawyers, from their families, and from their community. . . .

We already know what we're fighting against, now we've got to determine and decide among ourselves what we are fighting for. How can twenty-five or thirty million Black people in Amerika win our liberation, how can we win? Marcus Garvey—he had a dream, and his dream was that we go back to Afrika. Martin Luther King had his dream, and his dream was that we integrate into Amerikan society, and I don't think that dream was a reality. Amerikan society has told us time and time again that they don't want us. And now looking at Amerikan society, looking at its capitalist, racist system, I don't want to integrate into Amerika. Amerika is a dying country anyway. Malcolm X has his dream, and his dream was *land. Nationhood.* And his dream has become my dream. . . . [O]nce a people start struggling for land, start struggling for *nationhood*—then the whole world can become part of that fight and can take it up—and say look what you're doing, you're killing those people, you're making genocide—those people want a homeland. . . .

We have the natural resources to build a nation. I have come through the struggle, and I've been in the struggle for a little while, and I'm tired of everybody else's dream—I want my own, and nobody's going to tell me which way I have to go to be a free Black woman on this earth. We've got to stop having a minority mentality. White people might be the majority in Amerika, but we're the majority in the world. And when people start talking about, well, this isn't possible, and that it's impossible for us to have a Black nation—well, in that case—was Israel impossible? Was South Vietnam impossible? South Korea? These nations came about as a result of a split, and if it's possible in Israel, it's possible here. And if the Palestine Liberation Organization can go up before the UN and talk about their right to land, then the Black Liberation Organization can go before the UN too. We cannot afford to depend on the white left.

The white left comprises a tiny portion of white Amerika and they're so factionalized to the point where they're just almost totally ineffective. There's an old joke about you put two people on the white left in a room and you sit 'em in front of clock and they'll get into an argument about what time it is. That seems like a joke to a lot of people, but it's true. They are so factionalized 'til they argue about everything. And their arrogance and white supremacist arrogance leads them to believe that *they* are the only ones in the world that have that right answer. *They* are the only ones that can lead the poor and oppressed people to liberation and that's just not true. We couldn't depend on the white left in the 30s, we couldn't depend on the white left in the 50s, what in the world would make us think that we can depend on the white left now? I'm not saying that we couldn't work with white people on whatever level that we want to that fits our interest—but we can't just keep our heads in the sand, and we won't build our movement depending on the white left.

We've got to build our own movement, and our struggle has got to be able to stand if the white left pulls out and the white liberals pull out and whatever—if we have to stand on our own two feet, by ourselves—that's how we've got to build our foundation, that's how we've got to build our movement.

We've got to build a strong human rights movement. We've got to build a strong prison movement. We've got to build a strong Black liberation movement and we've got to struggle for liberation.

Free all political prisoners.

Free Leonard Peltier, Sundiata Acoli, Ruchell Magee, Ben Chavis, George Merritt, Gary Tyler, Geronimo Pratt, Dessie Woods, the RNA [Republic of New Afrika]-11, and the BLA [Black Liberation Army]-25. We must be free.

Assata Shakur
Political prisoner
Clinton, New Jersey

2.B.8.

"Letter from North American Political Prisoners" (1986)

To punish dissidents and prevent the spread of other rebellions, federal officials opened up several new isolation prison cells in the 1980s. Called control units, these new prison wings kept people in their cells for twenty-three or twenty-four hours a day, often under full camera surveillance and removed from human contact. Two of the most extreme were the control units at the men's prison in Marion, Illinois, and at the women's prison in Lexington, Kentucky. Both of them held political prisoners from the Puerto Rican independence, Black liberation, and white antiracist movements. Activists attempted to close both units down; they ultimately succeeded in closing Lexington in 1988. This open letter, published by nineteen political prisoners from different social justice movements, calls for broad left unity to challenge these dangerous isolation units.

April 19, 1986

We, the undersigned, are all North American political prisoners and prisoners of conscience (some of whom have been recently released). We are writing to express our collective condemnation of the building of maxi-maxi units within US prisons, particularly those at Marion and Lexington federal prisons. We endorse the demonstration being called for April 19, 1986, in Marion, Illinois, Lexington, Kentucky, New York City, San Quentin, Tucson, and Puerto Rico.

We condemn these units because we understand that their purpose is to attempt to control and break those prisoners who the US government considers the biggest threat—revolutionaries of all nationalities. We know they are especially directed against the Black/New Afrikan, Puerto Rican, Mexican, and Native American prisoners of war and political prisoners. We have seen the viciousness of these units over the last two and a half years in the complete lockdown at Marion, where every prisoner is kept locked in their cells twenty-three and a half hours a day. We are also aware of the fact that the existence of these units is used to justify increased control of prisoners that administrations consider "behavior" problems—often the most rebellious prisoners who won't accept the prison rules. We, the nineteen of us, represent different aspects of the progressive movement. Some of us are pacifists, jailed because of our actions against nuclear weapons and the war machine. Some of us are grand jury resisters who refuse to collaborate with US government investigations of political movements and clandestine organizations. Some of us are anti-imperialist resistance fighters who are jailed because of our commitment to build armed clandestine organizations, to fight colonialism and war, and to help bring justice to this world. Some of us are imprisoned because we support these efforts. And some of us are jailed because of our outrage at the US government's attacks on the peoples of Central America and our dedication to providing refuge to people thus attacked. Many of us are women, reflecting both the increasing contributions women are making to progressive struggles and our commitment to the liberation of women.

There are many differences among us, and yet we are united in fighting against heightening political repression. Our commitment is to the development of a free and democratic society with an end to war, colonialism, racism and sexism. We believe in justice, and not in laws used to carry out repression and inhumanity. We urge you to do everything you can to expose these units and force their closure.

We unite to protect our movement.

> Signed,
> Liz McAlister, Plowshares prisoner, Alderson FCI
> Shelley Miller, grand jury resister, Alderson FCI
> Anne Montgomery, Plowshares prisoner, Alderson FCI
> Lorry Thomas, sanctuary worker, Alderson FCI
> Helen Woodson, Plowshares prisoner, Alderson FCI
> Ohio 7, anti-imperialist political prisoners, New York MCC
> Marilyn Buck, anti-imperialist political prisoner, New York MCC
> Susan Rosenberg, anti-imperialist political prisoner, Tucson MCC
> Alan Berkman, anti-imperialist political prisoner, Holmesburg Prison, Philadelphia
> Laura Whitehorn, anti-imperialist political prisoner, Montgomery City, Maryland, detention
> Judy Clark, anti-imperialist political prisoner, Bedford Hills, New York, Correctional Center
> David Gilbert, anti-imperialist political prisoner, Auburn, New York, Correctional Facility
> Linda Evans, anti-imperialist political prisoner, New York MCC

2.B.9.

Rafael Cancel Miranda

Speech to stop the Florence Control Unit (1990)

Rafael Cancel Miranda spent almost thirty years in prison for his opposition to US imperialism, especially relative to his native island of Puerto Rico. He served two years in prison for refusing the draft (1949–51) and then twenty-five years, with three others, for shooting inside the US Congress in 1954 to protest US colonial control of Puerto Rico. An international movement led to all of his and his comrades finally being released by 1979. After his release, Cancel Miranda campaigned to free a new generation of Puerto Rican political prisoners and prisoners of war who, like him, were subjected to the most punitive experimental conditions US prisons have. He delivered this speech in 1990 at an annual conference of the Committee to End the Marion Lockdown, focusing on more than a dozen Puerto Rican activists who were then incarcerated. The last of that group, Oscar López Rívera, was freed in 2017.

When I went into prison, they gave me a very big honor. They didn't like me. They sent me straight to Alcatraz, straight from court. I went to Alcatraz [at] twenty-four years old. I came out when I was thirty years old. Then I went to Leavenworth. They put me in isolation in Leavenworth for five months because they said I led a strike. By that time I was already locked up for sixteen years. If after sixteen years I was good enough, strong enough, to still organize a strike, then Alcatraz did nothing to me.

Because of that strike they sent me as a punishment to Marion. They charged me with being the leader of the strike. When I went to Marion they sent me straight to the hole (solitary confinement). They told me they sent me to Marion because I had too many friends. Can you imagine them punishing someone for having too many friends?

At Marion we held another strike, and for some reason they charged me again for being a leader of the strike and put me in solitary. That was the time, right there and then, when they first created the control unit. That happened in 1972. It was just solitary confinement at first, but they transformed it into a control unit, the control unit that we know today but really not as bad as it is today. I spent eighteen months in the control unit. Within that space of time many people killed themselves there. Many also went crazy. They used to give prolixin, thorazine, and valium. Once you get hooked into that, forget it; you're not your own man or woman any more.

I was in the control unit where Oscar [López Rívera] is today. When the prolixin and the thorazine and the valium don't work, they beat you. They use the big stick. It was common for them to beat a prisoner in the control unit and then say he killed himself. Quite a few prisoners killed themselves like that.

It was at that time when I was in the control unit that I met the people in Chicago. Then the battle to free us really started. People from Chicago like Carmen Valentin, Carlos Alberto Torres, Lucy and Alicia Rodriguez, all the brothers and sisters who are in prison now, we owe it all to them. We are enjoying ourselves talking here today thanks to them. They kept moving. They put heart in it. In this type of struggle, you don't go half way. If you don't go all the way, then get the heck out of the way because you are going to be an obstacle. They started moving here in Chicago and from Chicago to New York. And in a few years, that small group of people had the case of the five Puerto Rican nationalists all around the world. It was all across the world, and it all started right here with a group like you. That's why I know the power of a group of people like you. When you really work, you can shake the power of the whole United States system. Five hundred people. Two hundred people even. They underestimate us, but that's good. That means we can make big surprises.

When I was in prison, they were talking about opening a behavior modification prison in Butner, North Carolina, already. Just like they're talking now about Florence. And then a group of people started fighting against Butner, and we won. . . . They never opened Butner.

We can stop control units. We can stop Florence because we have the strength. We have to have the confidence. The only way we can stop nothing is if we do nothing. That is the worst defeat we can have. Doing nothing. Sometimes we get scared. We think they are too overpowering. They are not that strong. Superman and Rambo are fiction. Fiction. *You can do it. I know it.*

If somebody can stop control units, if somebody can stop Florence, if somebody could even change the system in the long run, these are the kinds of people who could do it. This is the type of people. You are the ones who could do it. I know that someday it will depend not on them, but us. How soon it happens will depend on us. We will hear Leonard Peltier from here, from this podium. We will hear Oscar López from here. We will hear Carmen Valentín. We can do it.

All we have to do is have confidence in ourselves. When we are together, we are powerful. They are the weak ones. They are the minority, but they let us believe that they are the powerful ones. If we get organized, we can change the whole system. We have the power. When we get together as one people, George Bush will wind up running away from us. They ask themselves, what the heck makes a man be like Luis Rosa. What makes a woman be like Carmen Valentín. Carmen Valentín is such a little person but with such power, such strength. They cannot understand us. They cannot understand humanity.

When I'm with you, you all are my people. I feel one with you. Thank you very much and keep on.

Out of Control: Lesbian Committee to Support Women Political Prisoners, 1987–2009

Brooke Lober

The organization Out of Control: Lesbian Committee to Support Women Political Prisoners formed in January 1987 in response to the creation of the Lexington control unit (officially known as the Lexington High Security Unit), a sensory deprivation and isolation facility located in the basement of a federal prison in Kentucky where political prisoners Silvia Baraldini, Susan Rosenberg, and Alejandrina Torres were held. Baraldini and Rosenberg were white anti-imperialist militants from New York City; Torres was convicted for her involvement with the Fuerzas Armadas de Liberación Nacional, a clandestine revolutionary Puerto Rican independence group.

Out of Control, a queer women's organization based in the San Francisco Bay Area, brought together leftist politics, lesbian visibility, and antiprison activism with direct action on behalf of women political prisoners and support for anti-imperialist movements around the globe with focus on imprisonment. In collaboration with organizations across the country, Out of Control participated in the National Campaign to Shut Down the Lexington Control Unit, a coalition that was led by the Chicago-based Movimiento de Liberación Nacional and that drew attention to the women prisoners held at Lexington and the revolutionary anti-imperialist, racial and economic justice, and Puerto Rican independence movements in which they participated.

The National Campaign won closure of the Lexington control unit after two years of a vibrant struggle that included public protest, petitions, home meetings, letter writing campaigns, direct support to prisoners, and a lawsuit against the Bureau of Prisons. Throughout this campaign and many others, Out of Control brought leftist militancy and the causes of political prisoners to queer and feminist publics in the San Francisco Bay Area and beyond.

After the victorious closure of the Lexington control unit in 1988, Out of Control continued public advocacy on behalf of women political prisoners and prisoners of war within the United States, educating the public about leftist movements and the politics of incarceration. In a flyer titled "There Are Women Political Prisoners in the usa!!!" the group explained that "womyn are in prison for the following political acts: providing sanctuary for Central American refugees, antinuclear and antimilitary activity, self-defense against sexual abuse, fighting for Black liberation, defending land and treaty rights of Native people, fighting for independence of Puerto Rico from the u.s., defending the rights of lesbians and gay men."

Out of Control signaled potential alliances across movements. While its focus remained on women political prisoners and POWs, it situated these cases in the context of a transnational anti-imperialist movement. Evidencing this broad analysis, the organization promoted the causes of men in anticolonial and anti-imperialist movements who were being held as political prisoners and also raised awareness about women political prisoners outside the United States, from South Africa to Ireland to Palestine. In 1992, Out of Control participated in a tribunal that put the United States on trial "for grave crimes against humanity."

For more than two decades, Out of Control worked in several overlapping spheres. As self-identified dykes, its members promoted lesbian visibility and women's participation in leftist formations, countering homophobia and sexism on the left, but they did not require women activists within the organization to be lesbians, thus challenging separatism and narrow identity politics. They increased the visibility of political prisoners and revolutionary internationalism in lesbian, queer, and women's movements. With a focus on state violence, they exposed the misogyny and homophobia of the punishment system, especially as it affected women political prisoners. Through their newspaper, Out of Time, they communicated with people in prisons and connected them with each other as well as with supporters outside of prisons. Through their presence at the first Critical Resistance conference in 1998 and their participation in related networks, they influenced the movement for prison abolition. In the nascent abolitionist movement, members of Out of Control insisted on the participation and visibility of women, queer people, working-class people, formerly incarcerated people, and political prisoners in the movement.

Out of Control was fiercely independent. The group incorporated communist, socialist, and anarchist ideals but maintained a focus on taking action to support women prisoners rather than on promoting any single political ideology. As white women and lesbians in internationalist and antiracist movements, the members of Out of Control offered powerful examples of solidarity across struggles for freedom and for radical, egalitarian social change. With a focus on the urgency of political prisoner support, their group stayed together, even as other organizations broke on questions of ideology and identity. Their direct action orientation, featuring "dykes out of control" as a visible manifestation of an ethics of freedom, produced a uniquely creative and effective movement discourse that remains salient for antiracist, antisexist, and antihomophobic movements against state violence.

2.B.10.

Laura Whitehorn

"Collectively Asserting Life over Death Creates Power!" (1993)

Starting in the late 1980s, prisoners, with support from activists outside, began developing a series of AIDS projects inside US prisons and jails that provided critical, often life-saving advocacy and peer education. Laura Whitehorn, an anti-imperialist white lesbian who was imprisoned for fourteen years for her part in the Resistance Conspiracy case and became deeply involved in AIDS peer advocacy in prisons, wrote this essay while incarcerated in Florida.

The peer advocacy programs I've worked in over the past four years (Washington, DC, jail, FCI Lexington, FCI Marianna) would not have been possible without the aid and support of AIDS activists on the outside. There are a few things about our work inside that I'd like people outside to know in the interest of furthering the relationship between inside and out. I hope that the more comrades outside understand about HIV/AIDS inside, the more they'll fight for release of all HIV+ prisoners.

To be HIV+ (or to have AIDS) and to fight to live, a person can't be made to feel ashamed of having the disease. It's important to be able to be "out" in at least some part of your life. On the street, you can be "out" as HIV+ to family and friends yet keep it a secret at work or in other circles if necessary. In prison, that's impossible. An HIV+ woman in prison works and lives in the same community. Once one part of her life is aware of her HIV status, it's almost a certainly that all other parts of her life know too. It's very hard to keep secrets in a closed environment—especially one in which boredom and monotony make gossip a major activity. Even if an HIV+ woman creates a small group of supportive friends, she can never relax fully because there's always the danger of disclosure—especially through the staff. There is never a minute's relief from the stress, tension, and fear of exposure—with the danger and cruelty it can bring. This is one part of why HIV in prison is a death sentence and why PWAs [people with AIDS] in prison die faster than those on the street. It's hard for HIV+ women in prison to feel the self-esteem and pride that are basic to the ability to fight for health and life. (That's why a major goal of HIV/AIDS work in prison is to create an atmosphere in which it's safe to be public about being HIV+).

On the street, there are many powerful role models, because AIDS activists have rightly made PWAs the heroines and heroes of the movement. With a few exceptions, that's not yet true in most prisons. This is one reason contact with the outside and the videos and newsletters we get from you (and even more, the HIV+ people who come into the prisons to speak and meet prisoners) are so important to our work; they're the main place HIV+ prisoners can come into contact with a positive view of people with HIV/AIDS.

To fight HIV/AIDS, a support network is essential. In addition to the issues raised above, this is hard inside because we have so little control over association. For instance, at Lexington, the prison administration tried to make it impossible for our support group to meet in a confidential manner. It's common for other prisoners to wonder (and ask) why prisoner X is hanging out with prisoners Y and Z. So unless a support group can meet in a closed, private way, it can't function.

Other obstacles to support networks involve things like lack of control over diet, our inability to accompany another prisoner to see a doctor, lack of access to any alternative treatments, illegality of giving massages, etc.

One thing we've learned from the AIDS resistance movement is the healing role of anger. But this, too, has limited applications inside. HIV+ prisoners can't join others to demonstrate, march, and act against the real enemies. Any effective expression of anger against medical or correctional staff is punished by time in the hole. All of this made the Vacaville resistance movement especially heroic. PWAs on the street take huge risks in exhibiting anger at the medical establishment and the government. But at least on the street if you piss off your doctor you can select another health care provider. In prison, if you get angry at the doctor, there's no one to turn to. And there's no backup readily available to help force the medical department to accede to any demand (such as the demand for more than one Pap smear a year). Our support groups try to provide this backup, and we've often been effective. But it's definitely complex and problematic—for example, when confronted with support for an HIV+ prisoner's demands, prison staff almost always enforce a rule not to discuss one prisoner's case with another prisoner. (But they always seem to overlook that "rule" when it's time to spread rumors or take information from snitches!)

The resources necessary for channeling anger against the prison medical establishment into better self-health care for an HIV+ prisoner are difficult to create. For instance, it helps a lot if an HIV+ prisoner stops smoking and develops an exercise program, cuts out pills and junk food, etc. But that's very hard in an atmosphere where collective wellness programs don't exist—no smokenders class to turn to—and where the self-respect and self-value necessary are under daily bombardment by the entire prison system.

Support from outside helps with all these problems, and expanding contact with local AIDS organizations is very important to our work. One thing that could help a lot would be some adaptation of alternative treatment programs to the horrendous conditions of prison.

Over the past year, we've begun receiving more and more useful information on HIV/AIDS and women. It's clear from the AIDS work inside and out that wherever women with HIV/AIDS is *not* [made] an issue, racism as well as sexism are at work. In addition, for women inside, how to struggle long distance with our children about HIV and AIDS is a major issue our work has to address.

Finally, I guess all of this points to a basic question: how to exert power in a situation doubly geared to produce powerlessness. In our work, as in the work out there, collectively asserting life over death, humanity over prejudice and fear, creates power. Struggling to take responsibility for our own lives and health as women creates power. Over the next period, our work will be most powerful if we can combine forces inside and out to win the demand for compassionate release of prisoners with HIV and AIDS. Between now and that time, it would help a lot if activists outside could put pressure on prison medical departments or monitor the health care available in prisons—federal, state, and county jails—for HIV+ prisoners. Without outside pressure, it's unlikely that even the most minimal standards of care for HIV will be met in the prisons.

2.B.11.

Bill Dunne

From "Crack in the Federal Scheme: The October Rebellion of 1995" (2000)

While prison systems made a number of changes to reduce the outbreak of prison rebellions after the 1970s, uprisings could not be prevented altogether. In 1995, as dissident prisoner Bill Dunne describes here, the federal prison system experienced a wave of protests led by prisoners sentenced as part of the war on drugs.

Between October 19 and October 26, 1995, the US Bureau of Prisons (federal prison system) experienced a series of largely spontaneous but causally related uprisings in its then eighty-four-prison, one- hundred-thousand-prisoner gulag archipelago. Involving a range of demonstrations and direct action, this widespread rebellion ignited by injustices in the imposition and execution of prison sentences was unprecedented in the history of the BOP (Bureau of Prisons). Though its participants caused no deaths, took no hostages, and breached no secure perimeter, their exclamation of discontent resulted in the first nationwide lockdown of federal penitentiaries and correctional institutions and cost $39.7 million.

The BOP's "After Action Report: October 1995 Disturbances" seeks to ascribe the events to external factors beyond BOP control and absolve the prisonocracy of responsibility for the crisis. Officialdom specifically blames congressional refusal to reduce the gross disparity between sentences for crack cocaine and powder cocaine offenses (and media reporting thereon) for causing the revolt. The report claims there was no advance indication that any such action was likely or imminent, and no subsequent indication that internal factors of prison policy, practice, or administration played a significant role. On the basis of this assessment, the report recommends only increasing the repressive capabilities of prison authorities. . . .

The rebellion began at about 6:15 p.m. CDT on October 19, 1995, at FCI (federal correctional institution) Talladega, Alabama. "Several hundred" prisoners assembled in the yard where many armed themselves with bats and other makeshift weapons and donned masks. From there they proceeded to essentially take over the inside of the prison, breaking windows and setting fires throughout. Braving chemical sprays, they refused all orders to stop. Some "indicated" they were motivated by a desire to change the crack laws. The report did not say what other motivations were articulated. A half hour after the "disturbance" began, the warden authorized firearms inside the institution. Guards and local police then confronted the prisoners with pistols, shotguns, and M-16 rifles. Many "warning" shots, gas rounds, and threats forced prisoners back into the units where more of the same forced them into the cells. By 8 p.m. the guards had regained control.

The insurrections at FCI Allenwood and FCI Memphis followed similar trajectories. At about 7 a.m. on October 20, 1995, a large group of prisoners assembled in FCI Allenwood's general compound. From there they moved to food service, housing units, and recreation areas, setting fires, breaking windows, and doing other damage. A 7:15 lockdown announcement was ignored by about one hundred prisoners who continued their activities, battled guards, and encouraged other prisoners to join them. Guards with shotguns and DCTs (disturbance control teams) were then deployed. The housing units were secured and by 9 a.m. the yard was cleared as well.

The FCI Memphis revolt began at noon the same day. Approximately 150 to 200 prisoners gathered on the yard, the only reason given in the report being to protest the congressional vote against rationalizing the crack laws. Another 200 in Unicor (Federal Prison Industries) refused to work, broke windows and equipment, and eventually joined the others on the yard. At about 1 p.m. demands were made, and rejected, for a senator, a congressperson, and media to come to the prison. By 2:45 p.m., fires in at least two units were burning out of control, Unicor had been trashed, and a BOP camera crew had been dissuaded from videotaping prisoners' actions. The command center ordered all staff members to evacuate the prison.

Then DCTs and SORTs (special operations response teams) from several other BOP facilities, plus some two hundred state and local police, as well as FBI SWAT (Federal Bureau of Investigation Special Weapons and Tactics) agents armed with pistols, shotguns, sniper rifles, submachine guns, and M-16 rifles, as well as the usual complement of noxious chemicals, counterattacked. Prisoners were herded into the gym, chapel, and Unicor and bound with plastic restraints. By 8 a.m. on October 21, 1995, all the fires were out and all prisoners were either subdued in locked units or shackled down on BOP busses inside the prison.

In reaction to these events, guards at all federal prisons were placed on a higher state of alert. The BOP director ordered the nationwide lockdown at 3:57 p.m. EDT on October 20, 1995. The abrasive manner in which guards imposed the lockdown, cursing prisoners and demanding they instantly lock in the cells at an unusual time without explanation, caused the FCI Greenville (Illinois) resistance. Verily, the manner in which the lockdown was imposed and conducted was a major contributing if not the causal factor in other incidents as well, a fact the report does not directly admit but implicitly acknowledges.

The variety in extent and character of the many subsequent skirmishes comprising the October rebellion reflected the varying degree of lockdown between institutions. The lockdown prevented any of them from becoming as extensive as those above. Nevertheless, actions ranged from serious resistance that reached multiple parts of the prisons (and included fighting, losses of control, and significant destruction) through group demonstrations (such as refusal to work, refusal to lock up, throwing trash and projectiles, and lighting fires) to isolated and anonymous trash can fires and fixture damage. The report purports there was no retaliation against prisoners for the rebellion. Prisoners, however, tell a far different story. Hundreds did long SHU (special housing unit, aka, "the hole") time, and hundreds more were transferred to more punitive prisons with little regard for what infraction they may have committed, if any. Many were beaten and otherwise abused, while in full restraints and unresisting, in the transfer process. Others were left bound and given no opportunity to wash off the various caustic chemicals with which they'd been doused for long periods. Still others were pushed and hit while bound and forced to run "gauntlets" as they were driven to housing units and SHUs. Some of the get-back came later in the form of pretextual physical abuse, harsh searches, withholding of material like bedding and clothing, food contamination, and destruction of personal property. Medical attention was denied or inadequate in many instances or only enough to protect prison officials from obvious liability. And over fourteen hundred infraction reports were written.

The report's allegation that congressional refusal to reduce crack cocaine sentences to parity with other cocaine sentences was the sine qua non of the whole chain of actions is disingenuous at best. . . .

Among those factors constituting the critical mass for the conflagration was the following: the prison population is increasingly made up of young, black, urban victims of harsh, nonparolable sentences with little opportunity for good time. This population contrasts drastically with the aging, overwhelmingly white, largely rural, conservative prison apparatus. A sharper culture clash couldn't have been deliberately engineered. Further, in 1995, prisoners generally were reaping the results of reactionary politicians opportunistically playing the "tough on crime" card. College programs were eliminated with the abolition of Pell Grants for prisoners. Vocational training opportunities continued their long decline, especially in higher security prisons. Antiprisoner legislation was passed which made prison conditions in federal prisons harsher. That emboldened prisoncrats to treat prisoner protection rules and law as only advisory at best and make grievance resolution generally even more of a joke.

Guard brutality was also an issue. The propensity of guards to manhandle prisoners being segregated was the precipitating factor at USP (US penitentiary) Lewisburg (Pennsylvania), where it had also caused a mutiny in May 1995. Penurious health services increased suffering and insecurity and, thus, tension. Access to weightlifting and other recreational equipment was being reduced and eliminated at many prisons, as was access to cable TV. Overcrowding was another issue: all ten of the places whose revolts were detailed in the report were one-third to two-thirds over capacity, a situation characteristic of the system. Other conditions of confinement were noticeably deteriorating as well.

All such problems are internal management issues, yet the report mentions none of them and claims there were no management issues inculpated in the October events. Though the BOP attributes the worsening conditions to outside politics, in actuality it took opportunistic advantage of the politics to redistribute resources from prisoner to staff purposes.

2.B.12.

Safiya Bukhari

From "Q&A on Jericho 98" (1998)

A former Black Panther who spent more than seven years in prison for her militant activities, Safiya Bukhari took a leading role in launching the Jericho Amnesty Movement to free incarcerated activists. (The organization was first proposed by another former Black Panther, Jalil Muntaqim, who remains incarcerated as of 2020.) This interview, first published in the New Afrikan journal *Crossroad*, outlined Jericho's strategy of building a broad, ecumenical coalition in support of people incarcerated for their militant political actions and associations. Several thousand people attended the initial march outside the White House in the spring of 1998, demanding freedom for US political prisoners.

Q: Why do you say Jericho is more than just a march?

A: . . . Jericho will free up people from various organizations to go back into the community to do the work of organizing our communities for liberation. We feel that we should have done this thirty years ago, so that our political prisoners would have an apparatus and those who were involved in the struggle don't get lost in the shuffle. People would know that if they become involved in political work and activities, they will not be left alone to rot in prison without support networks, without their families being taken care of, without medical care and all those other things that should be accorded to people who get involved in struggle and end up in prison. So this is an attempt to correct a lack of movement within the movement itself, to build structures for people who go to prison—from this point on as well as from the past—so that organizations won't be tied down in it and use all their resources in court proceedings.

The campaign to neutralize our struggles through the use of the criminal justice system was a documented campaign by the federal government, part of COINTELPRO [portmanteau word for the FBI's counterintelligence program]. We can document it and take it back to 1968, in their FBI memorandum talking about imprisoning people even though the evidence is not there to support the crime that they're being charged with. The government made a determination to use the criminal justice system to criminalize the struggles of oppressed people and incarcerate them, to break the backs of organizations financially, and to take away those people who made up the cadre of those organizations. And they did it well, because some of these people fell in the sixties and are still in prison today.

The attack on the movement—the concerted attack by the government on the various movements and the decision to imprison leadership and drain our resources through all the trials—made a lot of us into defendants. A lot of our actions went into keeping courtrooms packed and keeping funds going to make sure that the money is there to pay lawyers. That made it almost impossible for us to continue the organizing around decent housing, quality education, homelessness—all those issues that were part of our struggles in the community, that helped us educate our people to what the situation is. Invariably, the leadership was taken off to prison and building the support mechanisms around these cases kept us from working around the everyday issues affecting our people. Jericho will put together one apparatus around the issue of political prisoners. It will free up the organizations to go back into the communities to do the work of educating and organizing our people. Until now, the organizations either made the decision to organize in the community and therefore neglect the issue of political prisoners or else they made the decision to do the support work around the political prisoners and therefore neglected the work in the community. There has not been a way to fuse both areas of work. . . .

Q: How do you decide which prisoners are on the Jericho list?

A: We need to break the barrier, internationally, on the fact that political prisoners exist in this country. The United States government consistently denies that political prisoners exist. As long as that barrier is not broken, we'll still have our people languishing in prison and not being accorded political prisoner status and treatment under international law as governed by the Universal Declaration of Human Rights. We have to put our strongest foot forward in order to do this. We have strategies and we have tactics. People who went to jail as a result of their work on the street, their involvement in liberation struggles on the street, whose cases from the very beginning started from that point of view and who are still there, are different from those who became political after their arrest. . . .

[W]e know that there are people who became political in prison, but we also know that in order to break that wall of silence we need to begin talking about those other cases, the political ones. We could begin talking about that even if we only had two people on the list. But we have more than sixty people on this list that we can document as being political prisoners. The first tactic is to break down the walls around these people who went to prison as a result of political beliefs and affiliations. Then we have the second phase, where we open the door for those people who became political behind the walls, whose sentences have been lengthened and made harder, who have been tortured and abused because of the political stands they have taken within the prisons. . . .

Q: How have churches responded to Jericho?

A: . . . Part of Jericho is organizing the churches, to educate everybody. We've made a mistake in the past of just talking to those people who were already organized. Now we can't make that mistake again. As organizers we have to talk to everybody.

Q: What is the significance of organizing women in particular for Jericho and for the struggle in general?

A: . . . One thing that's very clear is that much of the work around political prisoners—like much of the rest of the work in our movement—has been done by women. Women are the people who are doing most of the work, but they have been vilified; they've been told that "their place is this" and they have been lacking in the self-esteem necessary to take their real place, their real responsibility, to be able to make the decisions necessary to move our struggle forward. We can't allow anybody to say to us that we can't make decisions, that we're second place in this struggle. No matter what's happening out there in the streets, women are involved. It's our sons and daughters who are being victimized. So

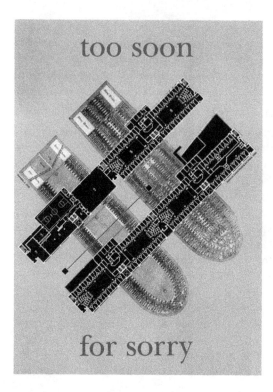

Figure 2.3. David Thorne, "Too Soon for Sorry" (1996). Image courtesy of Interference Archive and reprinted with permission by David Thorne.

we have more at stake than anybody. We can't allow ourselves to be intimidated by the people, especially men, who say this is not our place, or tell us we can't do this, or that we have to listen to the decisions they make. The reality is that some of the bad decisions that have brought us to the place we are at have been made by men, because of ego and everything else. . . . We have taken on, in our movements, the biggest enemy of human beings in the world: the US system of capitalism. Once we take on that system, and we're scared to take on our relationships, or face problems in relationships, or problems in how people deal with each other in an organizational framework, then there really is a problem.

2.B.13.

California Coalition for Women Prisoners

"Critical Resistance: Expanding Our Vision of What Is Possible" (1998)

The 1998 conference Critical Resistance: Beyond the Prison Industrial Complex held in Berkeley brought together more than three thousand activists nationwide from burgeoning movements against policing and mass incarceration. This article by one of the organizations that participated in the conference reflects on what the concept of critical resistance might mean for a growing but often overlooked segment of the prison population: incarcerated women and their loved ones.

For three years now, California Coalition for Women Prisoners has been inspired by the resistance of women inside California state prisons. Through our activities and writings, we try to bring out the voices of women.

Sometimes it is a "simple" story of resisting systematic dehumanization through expression of indignation and anger.

Sometime it's a story of helping other prisoners with their daily life: setting up peer counseling for HIV+ prisoners, helping new women know their rights, helping them fill out a complaint against a particular case of abuse, as well as millions of other ways. Guards consciously play one prisoner against another, heightening racism and all other divisions present in society. Any act of solidarity is precious in that it resists that form of control.

Sometimes this resistance takes the form of an outright challenge to the whole system, such as when Charisse Shumate agreed to become lead plaintiff in a suit charging the whole Department of Corrections, Governor Wilson and the state of California with cruel and unusual punishment of women prisoners through intent or nonexistent health care. She wrote, "Now my concerns are no longer for myself. But my sisters [. . .] who I have seen die."

The courage and vision of the women inside inspire us on the outside to find ways to fight the dehumanization existing in society. The critical connection between the women inside and those on the outside is the way in which the women inside expand our thinking of what is possible. For example, the Department of Corrections claims that the health care given to women inside is comparable to care given on the outside. While that is clearly a lie, Charisse stuck to her position, [namely,] that the quality of care be measured in absolute human terms, not as a comparison to what someone else might or might not be getting.

An important question for the conference on critical resistance is what do we bring to meet the voices and vision from inside? Can we, in solidarity with women on the inside, make it possible to expand what freedom means, so that it does not merely mean releasing prisoners into a society that creates prisons in the first place?

Critical resistance is when:

- Charisse Shumate, who endures constant painful flare-ups of her sickle cell disease, makes the difficult decision to become the lead plaintiff in a suit against the California Department of Corrections for its medical abuse of women prisoners, standing up to a system that is slowly killing her.
- Robin Lucas files a suit against the federal prison in Dublin for systemic rape.

- Theresa Cruz refuses to accept abuse by the injustice system after years of abuse by a former partner and wins a habeas corpus ruling that overturns her conviction in a legal climate where that is nearly impossible.
- Women in the Valley State segregated housing unit blow the whistle on guards who are sexually harassing them even though they know they will face harsh retaliation.
- Mumia Abu-Jamal keeps writing eye-opening, passionate columns from his cell on death row, where he has been kept for sixteen years.
- Women and men in the outside world refuse to cast a blind eye on the horrors that are going on inside prisons all over this country and join with incarcerated people to say we will watch you, expose you, and bang at the gates of the fortresses you try to hide until there is real change!

California Prison Moratorium Project, 1998–2018
Craig Gilmore

The California Prison Moratorium Project (CPMP) was founded in Oakland in 1998, a time when California had built more than one new prison per year over the preceding fifteen years. A small group of activists, most of whom worked with California Prison Focus, saw the need for an organization concentrated on stopping the growth of prisons in the state.

After a summer of planning, the organization announced itself publicly at the Critical Resistance conference in Berkeley in September, sharing a table with the Prison Moratorium Project from New York, whose work had been a major inspiration. Within months, California's new governor proposed building a new prison in Delano. CPMP had its first campaign target.

CPMP's initial approach was to help activists in rural towns targeted for new prisons fight the project at the local level. That strategy drew on the research of scholar and CPMP cofounder Ruth Wilson Gilmore, who showed that most prison towns did not benefit economically from "hosting" a prison. If locals could see that a new prison would hurt the town, might they oppose it? CPMP organizers thought that would-be prison towns were "the points of least resistance" in the chain of ever-growing incarceration. If it became more difficult to build prisons, might the financiers who arranged bond deals of many hundreds of millions of dollars find a new passion for lending money to build hospitals or schools?

CPMP began to work from the assumption that prisons damage almost all people, whether they are inside or out. Asking how they inflict damage became a basic research and organizing question. CPMP found ways that prisons hurt farmworkers and farmers, families and neighborhoods of those incarcerated, rural schools and hospitals, ecosystems and water tables, and rural businesses. All of these became potential allies in the fight. CPMP networked activists from earlier anti-prison fights with others in towns around the state facing the threat of prison construction. It mostly focused its efforts in the state's "prison alley," the south San Joaquin Valley.

In the San Joaquin Valley, the environmental justice movement and the United Farmworkers provided contacts, organizing infrastructure, and models of successful organizing. In 2001, CPMP and Critical Resistance organized a conference in Fresno called Joining Forces at which antiprison and environmental justice activists, urban and rural, came together to find common ground in their work, enabling the campaign to facilitate stronger campaign connections among regions of the state.

After six years of campaigning, the state opened the new prison in Delano, but only after the director of corrections announced it would be the last prison California would build. A relentless publicity campaign on the collateral damages caused by prisons pushed mainstream media first to question whether the state needed more prisons and later to oppose the construction of a second Delano prison.

Despite this opposition, in 2006 California announced a new building project: female rehabilitative community corrections centers. Two statewide coalitions that CPMP helped form during the Delano fight, Californians United for a Responsible Budget and Californians for Effective Public Safety, made up of prison reformers, civil rights, labor, abolitionists and environmental justice groups, opposed these new "miniprisons." Additionally, over three thousand people locked in California's prisons for women signed a clandestinely circulated petition against the proposal. This campaign again put prison expansion on hold in the state. It laid the groundwork for the 2011 Supreme Court decision in *Brown v. Plata* that forced California to reduce the number of people it incarcerated from more than 170,000 in 2008 to fewer than 130,000 in 2018.

CPMP's goal was to halt the growth of the prison system and compel investment bankers, public sector unions, elected officials, and other powerful forces that had benefited from prisons to instead support other uses for state money. The strategy depended on detailed understanding of the system's many sites of vulnerability, an ability to play local governments against the state government, a publicity campaign that drew on an expanding body of research highly critical of the damages prisons do, and the absence of a credible "moderate" center that forced media and politicians to choose between more prisons and a sudden halt. The halt prepared the ground for significant decarceration.

2.B.14.

Brigette Sarabi

"Building the Prison Reform Movement" (2000)

In the late 1990s, after decades of get-tough politics led the United States on an unprecedented prison-building boom, a new prison reform movement began to coalesce. Here, a longtime antiprison activist proposes strategies for mobilizing larger constituencies against mass incarceration in the new millennium. The article first appeared in *Justice Matters*, a newsletter of the Western Prison Project, a grassroots regional initiative covering Idaho, Montana, Nevada, Oregon, Utah, and Washington.

We'd like to discuss the context for changing the current prison crisis, in which the US has launched the largest prison buildup in history and now incarcerated nearly two million men, women, and children. We start from the assumption that all successful efforts for major societal and institutional reform depend on the development of a broad social movement that can mobilize a majority of public opinion and political will. To put it simply: change doesn't happen without the power of the people.

We believe that the prison reform movement at this point in time is characterized by the following:

- the general public is largely oblivious to the need for reform and the problem of overincarceration and indeed is sometimes hostile to our proposals;
- power holders (for example, politicians and the media) continue to whip up the fear of crime, which perpetuates the prison boom;
- legislation and ballot initiatives for policy changes may be introduced but usually fail at this point in time (although they serve an important educational purpose);
- movement organizations, while providing important research and documentation, and offering alternative visions are often perceived as "voices from the wilderness";
- grassroots organizations are springing up to begin educating, organizing, and trying to get the reform point of view into the mainstream media;
- there are increasing efforts in the movement to develop a shared analysis and strategies.

We must look at our work in a broad, long-term context. For many of us, the danger at this stage is despair, burnout, and feelings of hopelessness when some of our individual or local "battles" are lost. And yet there is such exciting potential for creating a powerful movement that can gain widespread public support.

To build public support for this movement, we must be able to appeal to the core values of ordinary citizens—values such as fairness, equality, compassion for one's fellow human beings, and responsibility for one's actions. The primary long-term strategy then is to develop a message that offers a compelling and comprehensive vision for reform that appeals to the core values of most people and realistically addresses concerns about public safety. In addition, our message must include prisoners front and center. We must put a human face on the issue of overincarceration, particularly the disproportionate incarceration of people of color. At this time, prisoners are truly America's disappeared, and once they disappear behind prison walls they are too easily forgotten.

Long term, our strategies must build a movement that effectively harnesses media, public education, legislative advocacy, and electoral organizing to win reforms that have a popular base of support.

It seems to us that in the near term, the strategies that make most sense are

1. to build a larger, better organized and passionate constituency for whom prison/criminal justice reform is a core priority—prisoners' families represent a huge number of people, and we could be very powerful if we organize ourselves;
2. increase public consciousness of the need for reform and the many issues that support reform; and
3. organize aggressively to stop further legislation and policies that expand the prison system (including regressive sentencing legislation, additional prison construction, and prison privatization).

We think there is great potential for building a larger, more organized movement. There are many communities and groups that are affected by the prison crisis or have a good reason to be concerned about it, including prisoners, prisoners' families, human and civil rights activists, students (because more education dollars are being shifted to incarceration), faith-based communities, and low-income advocates. Throughout our region, we have seen growing energy and commitment to take on the issues at the grassroots level.

On the other hand, we face significant challenges in building a strong and effective movement. First of all, people need to be active at the local level (the campus, the congregation, the city, and even state). National organization that focus on policy and research provide important information for activists, but their very nature prevents them from building the popular support the movement needs because they are pretty much inaccessible to the average citizen. And while there are more and more grassroots organizations springing up to work on prison and criminal justice reform, we know that most of our organizations are volunteer based, lack essential resources (staffing, money), often feel isolated, and are stretched thin by current work.

But even though we face challenges, we need to hold the line on the expansion of the prison industry. This will require committed constituencies and effective use of the media, but it also requires intensive community organizing (e.g., turning out local communities to fight prison siting), coalition building, and legislative advocacy and lobbying (e.g., to hold the line on regressive sentencing legislation or to stop the expansion of prison privatization). The tactics of nonviolent protest and direct action can also support this strategy by placing the issues more firmly in the public consciousness and demonstrating a dedicated base of support for reform.

We all know that this is long-term work and that changing the public consensus to focus on deincarceration will not happen immediately. So it is essential that we build a solid and sustainable infrastructure for the movement. We need all kinds of groups and organizations working on prison and criminal justice reform. This is a big issue, and it calls for a big movement—one with a lot of room for all kinds of organizations. We must help each other in every way we can. And we can't lose sight of the fact that literally millions of Americans are suffering the consequences of our mass incarceration policies, and any successful movement must seek to reduce the harm being done while organizing and building for reform.

Fight for the City, Free the Land

2.C.1.

Yellow Seeds

"Unite to Fight for Democratic Rights" (1975)

Amid the economic crisis of the 1970s, low-income urban communities of color suffered increasing rates of displacement due to a variety of redevelopment plans, including highway construction. They were also subjected to higher levels of police brutality. In Philadelphia's Chinatown, members of the Asian American group Yellow Seeds described these phenomena as connected—and requiring a collective, multiracial affirmation of a right to the city.

On June 30, 1975, bulldozers sent by the state tore down more pieces of the Chinese community in Philadelphia for a highway. This was done in spite of the fact that the state had twice "promised" that no more demolition of Chinatown is to be done without the consent of the Chinese community.

That same night on June 30, twenty workers and residents of the Chinese community in New York City were beaten up by the police. The twenty people were among a crowd of two hundred who had gathered to demand an end of police brutality and harassment.

Democratic Rights

Besides taking place on the same day, these two events in Philadelphia and New York City have other things in common. By the use of "laws" and "promises," the government tells us that we have many "rights." But as the above two events show us, in day-to-day living, Asian Americans along with other minorities and working people don't have many of these democratic rights. We cannot trust the state or the police to "guarantee" these rights to us. We have to fight for them.

Economic Crisis and Budget Cuts

At a time when the whole country is in the worst economic crisis since World War II, budget cuts, layoffs, large-scale unemployment, and loss of health care and social services are a daily reality for more and more of us. At the same time, huge profits are a reality to the banks and big businesses, who have the cooperation of the government.

Though our women work long, hard hours in the garment factories and our men work as cooks and waiters, jobs are becoming harder to get. We work long hours for less pay. Our paychecks keep getting smaller, but the price of food and clothing keeps getting higher. Some prices in Chinatown for essential items have risen 100 percent.

Our people work hard so that our children can go to school. Yet budget cuts in the public schools in such areas as bilingual education seriously hurt the education of our children. Though the wealthy areas still have adequate school and hospital budgets, these services in poor areas, especially minority communities, are the first to be cut.

The People Fight Back

As citizens and residents of this country, we are entitled to equal and quality education, decent health care, housing, employment, and equal justice for all.

Figure 2.4. Guy Holman, "Where Will They Go?" (1973).
Image courtesy of Lincoln Cushing/Docs Populi.

These rights are not gifts handed down to us by the government. Working people have worked and fought for them.

Working people all over the country are fighting for our democratic rights. Fearing the strength found in the unity of all groups, the government tries to scare us with harassment and physical violence. They try to keep us quiet by the use of reform, by giving in a little. If this doesn't work, repression is used.

But we are not going to be threatened by this. In Philadelphia, the bulldozers were stopped (we realize only temporarily, the struggle must go on) by a demonstration. In Boston, people raised their voice against police discrimination. In San Francisco, Chinese restaurant workers are organizing unions. In New York City, twenty thousand people demonstrated for democratic rights. We are strong and we will become more united, more organized, and we will fight back even harder.

2.C.2.

Chester Hartman

From "The Struggle for the I-Hotel: What We Won, What We Lost, What We Learned" (1977)

One of the biggest battles against displacement in the 1970s was the almost decade-long struggle to preserve the International Hotel in San Francisco, a residence for elderly people in the Filipino neighborhood known as Manilatown. In 1977, the residents were evicted and the building was razed. Yet the fight to save it was a high point of antigentrification organizing centered in Asian American communities and drawing on the Bay area's multiracial left.

The most significant defeat in the struggle to save the International Hotel is obviously that the tenants have lost the right to stay in their home at least for the present. We were not able to stop the eviction through the courts, political pressure, or militant defense of the building. In the process of the fight, we saw clearly how power works in this country and in whose interest it is wielded. The fundamental issue in the fight to preserve the hotel as low-cost housing in Manilatown-Chinatown was whether these basic human needs are more important than the rights of a large corporation to make profits. The courts, politicians (liberal as well as conservative), and editorials in all the major press from here to New York gave an answer to that question which was loud and clear: when forced to choose, the legal and political system in the US comes down on the side of property.

The Law

We got lots of eviction stays, appeal rights, delays. But in the end, a judge directed the jury to order the tenants evicted; another judge refused to allow the [San Francisco] Housing Authority to use eminent domain to take property from the rich and give it to the poor (even though under urban renewal the Redevelopment Agency is always kicking out the poor via eminent domain, so their property can be given to the rich); and the superior court, appeals court, and supreme court all agreed that the eviction had to be carried out before an appeal on the eminent domain decision could be heard.

Four hundred cops and sheriffs, complete with horses and clubs—costing $250,000 of our tax money—were then sent into action to enforce these decisions. It was a brutal reminder of the armed power of the state—and of its priorities.

Ironically, that quarter of a million dollars spent so unquestioningly to enforce a wealthy man's property rights was about the same amount needed to underwrite the tenants' new plan to save the hotel, but an expenditure of that sort becomes "unrealistic" when it's for low-income housing. . . .

The Movement

One final word about bitter lessons. This one is, perhaps, the most bitter of all because it is a criticism we have to make of ourselves. Despite the fact that thousands of people and many organizations were drawn into the struggle to save the hotel, we failed to build a movement as broad and as unified as we might have. In part this was the result of our own inexperience; in part, the city administration tried to create rifts between community groups and play them off against one another ("if we provide subsidies to buy the hotel, that will take money away from other housing needs"). But, worst of all, our failure stemmed in part from our inability to unify as a movement and to understand the absolute necessity of building that broad base of support.

Nevertheless, despite these heavy lessons, sad mistakes, and the eviction itself, in the nine years of struggle we won important victories. Hopefully, they will be ultimately decisive.

Nine Years' Life for the International Hotel

First, and most concretely, the struggle won nine years for the tenants at the I-Hotel to remain in their homes. The I-Hotel was first scheduled to come down in 1968, so that its owner could build a parking lot. The tenants' successful opposition led to a three-year lease and later to the sale of the hotel to Four Seas. Then the eviction fight against Four Seas began. Altogether, the struggle to save the hotel was probably the longest eviction fight in California's history—and the hotel became a symbol of resistance to redevelopment and the destruction of minority communities.

Thousands Involved in the Struggle

Thousands of San Franciscans were involved in the struggle. Over the nine years, an increasing number of people were drawn into defense of the hotel. For many, it became a deep and central commitment. Some even moved into the hotel. They did everything from community outreach, to medical and legal aid, to external and internal security, to participating in demonstrations—the largest around a local issue in over a decade.

The supporters learned valuable practical skills and political lessons from their involvement. For some, work around the hotel was their first intense political experience, and it will probably change their lives, as the antiwar, civil rights, and labor movements changed lives in the past. For others, it sharpened their understanding of the forces at work in San Francisco and the kind of progressive political movement we must build to force the city to meet the needs of the majority of its people.

The I-Hotel tenants also became more politicized and organized as a result of their struggle. Having experienced racial, national, and class oppression throughout their lives, the taking of their home was part of a familiar pattern to them. Some had been involved in political struggles before—a tenants' fight in Hawaii, organizing in the navy. They, too, grew in political sophistication, individual and collective strength, in the process of the fight to save their home. Their insistence on remaining together as a group is the ultimate expression of that political consciousness.

Widespread Consciousness

Beyond these material gains and our growth as individuals and as a movement, we won citywide and nationwide recognition of the struggle. The fight around the eviction was reported all over the country. Through the efforts of the I-Hotel Tenants Association and its supporters, the struggle was not portrayed merely as a "human interest" story but in terms of its politics. The media coverage by and large recognized and represented the struggle as one of human/ housing rights vs. property/profit rights.

We were creative in how we fought, both tactically and legally. In the process, we introduced the concept of using eminent domain to protect the housing rights of low-income people. This is probably the first time this approach has been used in the US and hopefully will set an important precedent.

Last, we developed a widespread understanding of the forces behind the effort to evict the tenants, the callous bulldozing of low-income, especially minority communities, when they stand in the way of "Wall Street West" . . . and the dozens of other SF land-grab efforts.

We have lost a night's battle. Now is the time, learning from our past mistakes, to build a movement broad enough and unified enough to win the war.

First to save the I-Hotel, then to stop the destruction of low-income, minority neighborhoods throughout San Francisco and to evict from power those who rule our lives by force.

Long Live the International Hotel!

The Puerto Rican Cultural Center and Its Work Fighting Gentrification, 1973–2000s

Michael Rodríguez-Muñiz

Established in 1973, the Puerto Rican Cultural Center of Chicago (PRCC) built a constellation of counterinstitutions in the Humboldt Park/West Town area to address community needs and to build a radical base for Puerto Rican independence. This approach, which would include everything from fighting to free political prisoners to developing a long-standing alternative high school, positioned the group to take on gentrification and displacement.

Although gentrification had not yet begun to impact Humboldt Park/West Town, by the late 1970s the PRCC began to connect local displacement to colonial land theft of the island. Guided by this anticolonial understanding, the PRCC set out to nationalize urban space. Its first effort was an informal housing initiative called Bohio, named after the Taíno (indigenous inhabitants of Puerto Rico) word for dwelling. The initiative aimed to preempt developers and collectively purchase land in the area. Within these collectively owned buildings, the PRCC housed some of its projects, such as Vida/SIDA, its HIV/AIDS prevention program, and the headquarters of the Committee to Free Puerto Rican Political Prisoners and Prisoners of War.

By the early 1990s, the PRCC helped spearhead the founding of the Puerto Rican Agenda to support a broad alliance against gentrification. Composed of community leaders, activists, and elected officials, this group laid out a bold vision for community-led economic and housing development. Its members were instrumental to the establishment of the Humboldt Park Empowerment Partnership (HPEP), a coalition of more than one hundred community organizations, churches, block clubs, and businesses. HPEP generated a holistic revitalization plan that sought to strengthen community ties and build new infrastructures to address long-standing housing, health, employment, and safety needs. Among other outcomes, these efforts increased the community's control over development and cultivated a new generation of activists embedded in community, diasporic, and nationalist struggles.

Preceding and later folded into these efforts was a campaign to place a statue of the iconic Puerto Rican nationalist Pedro Albizu Campos inside of Humboldt Park, located in the neighborhood of the same name. Conservatives, who reviled Albizu Campos as a pro–Puerto Rican independence terrorist, opposed the effort. The campaign became so politically contentious that the then mayor asked for a compromise. Seizing this unplanned opportunity, local politicians and leaders from the Puerto Rican Agenda, including then alderman Billy Ocasio and PRCC executive director José E. López, proposed the Paseo Boricua concept as a preservation strategy against rapidly approaching gentrification. The compromise led to the inauguration of Paseo Boricua in 1995, a half-mile cultural and commercial strip on Division Street, bookended with two fifty-nine-feet high steel Puerto Rican flags.

Paseo Boricua set into motion a new wave of concerted efforts to resist gentrification that continued into the 2000s. These efforts included the building of multiunit affordable housing complexes, the leveraging of aldermanic powers to constrain developers, the launching of organizing campaigns like Humboldt Park No Se Vende (a play on words meaning both "not for sale" and "won't sell out"), and the creation of diverse cultural projects—from murals to youth spaces to cultural festivals—that claimed Humboldt Park as a "pedacito de patria" ("small piece of homeland"). The area would become home to the country's only Puerto Rican museum and boast the city's highest concentration of Puerto Rican businesses. Even now, almost two decades later, Puerto Rican radicals continue to claim space and build parallel institutions against the forces of gentrification. In doing so, they keep alive their old slogan: "Aquí luchamos, aquí nos quedamos" ("Here we struggled, here we shall stay").

2.C.3.

James Yaki Sayles

From "War for the Cities" (1978)

A member of Chicago's Black Arts scene, James Yaki Sayles became a prolific writer and dedicated organizer upon his incarceration in the 1970s. He was a central theorist of a prison-centered Black nationalism that referred to Black people in the United States as "New Afrikans" to honor the particular identity created by the transatlantic slave trade. In his influential essay "War for the Cities," first published in a prison newsletter he edited called the *Fuse* and excerpted here, Sayles locates the growing—and increasingly Black—prison population in the divestment from and displacement of communities of color in Chicago and other major cities. Sayles, who was released in 2004 and died in 2008, would return to these themes often in his prison writings.

Chicago's Afrikan (black), Puerto Rican, and poor white communities are showing much concern over the plans now in progress to remove them from the inner city into outlying areas. Throughout amerikkka the populations of major cities are increasingly poor, and the majority of the poor are Afrikans.

These growing populations have the potential to acquire and use great power. Those who rule amerikkka know instinctively that the cities are politically, economically, and militarily too valuable to them to be allowed to fall under the control of the Afrikan and other oppressed nations. . . .

We think these points have clear connections to the reasons for there being such large numbers of young Afrikan men and women in Illinois and other US prisons. We also think that a better understanding of these and other points will help bring the struggles outside closer to the struggles inside.

We'll start with what should be some of the most evident, easily understood, and accepted points. The first of these is that Afrikan inner city removal is a nationwide strategic objective of those who rule amerikkka. This objective is made necessary in large part by the deepening economic crisis, and the threat of political/social revolution.

The wealth and high standard of living the US prides itself on is based on its history of trickery and robbery. The US is wealthy because it takes the wealth of others, depriving most of the world from using their resources for their own development. When the people in Afrika, Asia, and South America begin to change this state of things, it is reflected in the US by an "energy crisis" and in many other forms.

Also, when amerikkka has less to steal from other countries it has less booty to distribute inside its own borders, [and] jobs grow scarce. So-called affirmative action in employment and school admissions is challenged. School lunch and daycare programs are cut back or halted. Poor women are denied federal funds for abortions, and larger numbers of Afrikan and other oppressed nation women are "intensively encouraged" to adopt birth control and become sterilized. Prison populations increase. And increasing attention is focused on the cities in ways too numerous to list and analyze here.

The next point is that the plans now being carried out to achieve Afrikan inner-city removal are not "new," and certainly not in Chicago. Neither are such plans the only ones being carried out or experimented with to contain and/or manipulate US Third World/oppressed nation populations. . . .

Point three is that the oppressed are not simply being pushed from the inner city to roam and settle wherever we may please. Just as it's being decided where we will move *from*, it's also being decided where we'll be allowed to relocate.

In raising this point many things come to mind. The most immediate is simply the fact that there is no "free choice," no "equal opportunity" for the oppressed in amerikkka to participate in the "democratic process" of city planning. . . .

Point four is that all of the above helps us to see more clearly exactly why our communities have been allowed to deteriorate, why there are increasing cases of arson, why the schools our children attend don't offer them the "quality education" which would allow them to acquire the skills and confidence required of peoples who have the need and desire to govern themselves.

Our communities are filled with abandoned buildings because it's part of the plan to remove the Afrikan and other oppressed peoples from the inner city. Our schools lack qualified teachers in sufficient number, are in poor physical condition, and lack books and other essential equipment because it's part of the plan to relocate us and to keep us ignorant, unskilled, and dependent upon those who rule amerikkka.

Point five is that we are likely to see more "low income housing" going up in suburbs like Arlington Heights. Truly designed with the oppressed in mind.

This low-income housing will likely include innovations which are now being tested in US prisons and in areas such as Cabrini-Green. City, state and federal money has been spent liberally over the past several years on "pilot projects" such as that now operating in Cabrini-Green Housing Project.

The streets and buildings surrounding the housing area have been altered to fit police and military "emergency" needs. The design of the buildings are altered to give only one way of exit and entrance. So-called convenience shops for laundry, dry cleaning, food shopping, and other essential services have been placed in the buildings so that movement outside of them is reduced. Offices are installed for the welfare agent and the security officers. All occupants are issued identity cards to be shown upon entering or leaving the building. The occupants of each apartment are listed in a central register. Electric cameras and other surveillance equipment is installed, allegedly to "provide resident security against crime and criminals."

But cameras operate twenty-four hours a day. They don't turn themselves on automatically by the scent or sound of a "criminal." The cameras watch *everybody*, all the time. Just like they do here in Stateville and other prisons in amerikkka.

Everything described above as part of the "pilot projects" being carried out in Afrikan and other oppressed communities in the US were first pilot projects in the prisons—usually those with the largest number of Afrikan and other oppressed nation prisoners.

The sixth and last point deserves more space than we're able to give it. That is that clear and important connections can be drawn between the plan to remove the oppressed from the inner city and the presence of such a large number of nonwhite youth in illinois and other amerikkkan prisons. In essence, the prisons are filled with Afrikan youth because of the danger they did and do present to the rulers of the US. In the 60s and early 70s, Afrikan people's fight for self-determination was at a high point, and Afrikan youth were playing important roles in many areas of struggle. In the schools, at the job site, on picket lines and demonstrations, and on the street, Afrikan youth were daily becoming a greater threat to the oppressive power. One area where this threat was most clear was among Afrikan youth organizations, where their revolutionary and nationalist potential was evident through their actions in the community. . . .

If black/nonwhite/poor people are to survive and have a future in amerikkka, we must become responsible to and for each other. We must have mutual respect, and we must come to depend on ourselves/each other and break our dependence upon the enemy.

We must accept the fact that those who rule amerikkka are neither willing nor capable of satisfying our needs. It is not in their interest to have us employed, fed, clothed, properly housed, educated, and healthy.

Build to Win!!

2.C.4.

Association of Community Organizations for Reform Now

From "People's Platform" (1978)

Founded in Arkansas in 1970, the Association of Community Organizations for Reform Now, or ACORN, became one of the biggest grassroots membership organizations of poor people in the country. It was, by design, a multi-issue organization that responded to local needs. The group developed this nine-point platform at its first national convention, held in Memphis in December 1978. Some on the left viewed ACORN as taking an instrumentalist approach to organizing. ACORN also became a frequent target of conservatives, and it closed in 2010 following a concerted right-wing effort to defund the organization.

Preamble

We stand for a People's Platform, as old as our country, and as young as our dreams. We come before our nation, not to petition with hat in hand but to rise as one people and demand.

We have waited and watched. We have hoped and helped. We have sweated and suffered.

We have often believed. We have frequently followed.

But we have nothing to show for the work of our hands, the tax of our labor. Our patience has been abused; our experience misused. Our silence has been seen as support. Our struggle has been ignored.

Enough is enough. We will wait no longer for the crumbs at America's door. We will not be meek but mighty. We will not starve on past promises but feast on future dreams.

We are an uncommon common people. We are the majority, forged from all minorities. We are the masses of many, not the forces of few. We will continue our fight until the American way is just one way, until we have shared the wealth, until we have won our freedom.

This is not a simple vision but a detailed plan.

Our plan is to build an American reality from the American rhetoric, to deliver a piece of the present and the fruits of the future to every man, to every woman, to every family.

We demand our birthright: the chance to be rich, the right to be free.

Our riches shall be the blooming of our communities, the bounty of a sure livelihood, the beauty of homes for our families with sickness driven from the door, the benefit of our taxes, not their burden, and the best of our energy, land, and natural resources for all people.

Our freedom shall be based on the equality of the many, not the income of the few. Our freedom is the force of democracy, not the farce of federal fat and personal profit. In our freedom, only the people shall rule.

Corporations shall have their role: producing jobs, providing products, paying taxes. No more. No less. They shall obey our wishes, respond to our needs, serve our communities. Our country shall be the citizens' wealth, and our wealth shall build our country.

Government shall have its role: public servant to our good, fast follower to our sure steps. No more. No less. Our government shall shout with a public voice and no longer jump to a private whisper. In our government, the common concerns shall be the collective cause.

We present a people's platform, not a politician's promise.
We demand the changes outlined in our platform and plan. We will work to win. We will have our birthright. We will live in richness and freedom. We will live in one country as one people.

We will dream of more, but we will not settle for less.

Energy

1. Put people before profits at the utilities. . . .
2. Promote conservation and guarantee safety. . . .
3. Break the grip of the big energy companies. . . .

Health Care

Health care must be

- affordable
- accessible
- of equal quality for all
- controlled by the people of the community, not by doctors, hospitals and insurance companies.

To achieve this, [we must]:

1. introduce a set of immediate reforms in the present health care system. . . .
2. create a new national health care system. . . .

Housing

1. Create more housing for low- and moderate-income people. . . .
2. Prevent the displacement of low- and moderate-income people from their homes. . . .
3. Provide protection for tenants. . . .
4. Clean up public housing. . . .

Jobs and Income

1. Charge private industry with job creation and job training. . . .
2. Charge government and big business with the final responsibility for full employment. . . .
3. Provide an adequate income to every American. . . .
4. Establish the fundamental rights of workers. . . .

Rural Issues

1. Preserve the family farm. . . .
2. Break monopoly control of the food industry. . . .
3. Guarantee a fair share for rural America. . . .

Community Development

1. Clean up the Community Development Block Grant program. . . .
2. Support community-based economic development. . . .
3. Control the effects of private development on the community. . . .
4. Make public services serve the community. . . .

Banking

1. Charter banks to serve the credit needs of the community. . . .
2. Give low- and moderate-income people genuine access to credit and other banking services. . . .
3. Use public money for public benefit. . . .

Taxes

1. Tax the wealth of America. . . .
2. Close the loopholes and simplify the tax system. . . .
3. Remove taxation from the basic necessities of life and from the basic income necessary to live. . . .
4. Base taxes solely on the ability to pay. . . .

Representation

1. More democracy [. . .] in the neighborhood. . . .
2. More democracy [. . .] in elections. . . .
3. More democracy [. . .] in the government. . . .
4. More democracy [. . .] in big business. . . .

2.C.5.

Willie Baptist

From "Five Main Slogans: Lessons from the History of the National Union of the Homeless" (1993)

As automation, globalization, and the defunding of social programs worsened urban poverty in the 1980s and 1990s, the number of people without homes grew rapidly. The National Union of the Homeless analyzed why homelessness was increasingly prevalent, attempted to provide homes and resources for people in need, and sought to organize homeless people to pick up the mantle of the poor people's campaign launched by Martin Luther King in 1968.

The epidemic of homelessness is worsening. The corporate businesses are today compelled by competition to "downsize," employing the labor-replacing devices of electronic technology to cut production costs and maximize profits. Human labor is made increasingly useless and homeless. To eliminate homelessness, this profit-making and people-murdering system cannot be simply bandaided. It must be eliminated. Adequate paying jobs cease to be the source of economic survival for the homeless and millions of the other poverty-stricken as they are hurled permanently outside of the production process.

Homeless Takeovers and the 1992 LA Rebellion

Under these conditions, homeless and poor people have no choice but to take what they need by violating economically unjust laws, confronting directly the governmental apparatuses that uphold them. In the [1992] video, *Takeover*, Ron Casanova—editor of the *Union of the Homeless National News*—spoke to the necessity of these acts of civil disobedience when he stated, "It can be done. It can be done. . . . [F]orget that it's against the law. I'm dying in the streets, I think that should be against the law." This political nature of the problem and solution of homelessness kept asserting itself throughout the National Union of the Homeless Organizing Drive of the late 1980s. . . .

Mission, Organizing Slogans, and Streetheat

The political character of the National Union of the Homeless Organizing Drive revealed itself in every aspect of the drive, from its mission statement and slogans to its militant street actions. In May of 1988 the new homeless executive board members of the union collectively formulated the mission of their organization:

> The heart and soul of the National Union of the Homeless is to commit our lives to ending the oppression of all homeless people and work tirelessly for economic justice, human rights, and full liberation.
>
> We dedicate ourselves to transmitting our awareness of our sisters and brothers, to planning a sustained struggle and to building an organization that can obtain freedom through revolutionary perseverance.
>
> We pledge to deepen our personal commitment to end all forms of exploitation, racism, sexism, and abuse. True solidarity demands that we create not only the new society, but also the *new* human being.

The five main slogans developed and used during the drive were: 1) "Homeless but not helpless!"; 2) "You are but one paycheck away from homelessness!"; 3) "No housing, no peace!"; 4) "You only get what you are organized to take!"; and 5) "Up and out of poverty, now!" They proved to be effective tools for organizing the homeless and their supporters. They also served as tools for political education.

The shrewdly formulated slogan "Homeless but not helpless" initially confused even the most conservative bourgeois foundations into thinking that the homeless organizing drive provided good public relations for their "self-help" theories denying the responsibility and blame of the government and society. So they at first granted some of the drive's efforts much needed financial and media supports. On the other hand, the actual organizing and agitating thrust of the drive made the slogan a declaration of political independence from the poverty-pimp agents of the Powers That Be. . . .

"Homeless but not helpless" meant that the homeless would take the leadership of the struggles against homelessness into their own hands. It provided the homeless organizers a tool for teaching a very strategic lesson of history. . . .

The slogan "You are only one paycheck away from homelessness" served as a weapon to win support from other sectors of public opinion. It also provided a means to expose and explain the class economic causes of homelessness, exploding the myth that the homeless and poor had failed society instead of society failing them.

The slogan "No housing, no peace!" originated out of the [1988] police riots against the homeless takeover of Tompkins Square Park in New York City. The Tompkins Square Park Tent City Homeless Union introduced the slogan to the national union. It later blared forth on to the national scene during the tortuous East Coast "Exodus March to Washington, DC" of some 350 homeless men and women from New England and New York. "No housing, no peace" is a dec-

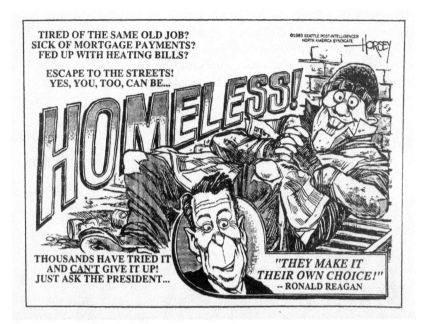

Figure 2.5. David Horsey, "Homeless!" (1989). Image courtesy of Lincoln Cushing/ Docs Populi. Reprinted with permission by David Horsey.

laration of war against the conditions of homelessness and a determination to "stick and stay" the course stopping at nothing short of revolution if necessary to obtain housing for every man, woman, and child.

"You only get what you're organized to take!" was the recognition that take-overs and all efforts must be reinforced by organization, which includes the establishment of "power bases" to sustain operations. The *talk* means nothing without the *walk*. This slogan meant for the poor and homeless fighters, the beginning of the political understanding that the real fruit of any battle or take-over was the consolidation and expansion of their unity and organization. And that indeed and especia1y in America, *political power grows out of organization*.

Obviously this historical and strategic meaning of the slogan "You only get what you're organized to take!" has not been lost on the political police—the FBI and the local "red squads." In the aftermath of the April LA uprising they have concentrated their surveillance and fire on the most organized element of the rebellion, the politicized so called youth gangs.

The National Union of the Homeless took up the slogan "Up and out of poverty, now!" when it joined with the National Welfare Rights Union and the National Anti-Hunger Coalition and convened the National Survival Summit in Philadelphia, PA, in July of 1989. In taking up this call, the homeless union leaders took a gigantic step toward linking up with hundreds of other poverty victim–led organizations and groupings. This slogan is the recognition that only in consciously directed massive numbers do we possess the strength to shake and reshape the economic and political foundations of homelessness and poverty ending these deadly diseases sooner not later.

In the course of its existence, the homeless union has used and will continue to use many slogans to rally, educate, and organize homeless and near homeless people. The five mentioned above are the main ones and have all stood the test of time.

2.C.6.

James Boggs

From "Rebuilding Detroit: An Alternative to Casino Gambling" (1988)

Autoworker James Boggs was one of the most inventive Marxist thinkers of the late twentieth century. He and his wife, philosopher and activist Grace Lee Boggs, developed an influential approach to deindustrialization in Detroit that advocated for people to develop alternatives to capitalism here and now through building local democratic, noncapitalist institutions to transform social relationships. In critiquing the economic development model pursued by the first Black mayor of Detroit, Boggs offers an alternate model of meeting the needs of the city's multiracial working-class communities.

The question which Detroit and other industrial cities are now facing is "What is the purpose of a city?" Up to now, because it has been our historical experience for the last seventy-five years, most Americans have thought of the city as a place to which you go for a job after you have been driven off the land by mechanization. But now we know that the large industrial corporations are not going to provide those jobs in our cities.

What then is going to happen to the one million people who still live in Detroit, half of them on some form of public assistance—not only blacks but Chicanos, Arab Americans, Asians, and poor whites? For most of them, Detroit is the end of the rainbow. They can't go back to the farms from which their parents and grandparents came because these have been wiped out by agribusiness. There are no new industries coming here to employ them. Therefore, if we are to think about a future for Detroiters, if we are going to create hope especially for our young people, we are going to have to break with most of the ideas about cities that we have accepted in the past and start with new basic principles.

To begin with, we have to stop seeing the city as just a place to which you come to get a job or to make a living and start seeing it as the place where the humanity of people is enriched because they have the opportunity to live with people of many different ethnic and social backgrounds. In other words, we have to see that our capital is in people and not see people as existing to make capital for production or dependent on capital to live.

The foundation of our city has to be people living in communities who realize that their human identity or their love and respect for self is based on love and respect for others and who have also learned from experience that they can no longer leave the decisions as to their present and their future to the marketplace, to corporations or to capitalist politicians, regardless of ethnic background. *We, the people*, have to see ourselves as responsible for our city and for each other, and especially for making sure that our children are raised to place more value on social ties than on material wealth.

We have to get rid of the myth that there is something sacred about large-scale production for the national and international market. Actually, our experiences over the last seventy-five years has demonstrated that large-scale production, because it is based on a huge separation between production and consumption, makes both producers and consumers into faceless masses who are alienated from one another and at the mercy of economic forces and the mass media. Instead, we have to begin thinking of creating small enterprises which produce food, goods, and services for the local market, that is, for our communities and for our city. Instead of destroying the skills of workers, which is what large-scale industry does, these small enterprises will combine craftsmanship, or the preservation and enhancement of human skills, with the new technologies which make possible flexible production and constant readjustment to serve the needs of local consumers. . . .

What kids learn from books in schools has little if any relationship to their daily lives. While they are growing up, they are like parasites doing no socially useful work, spending their time playing and watching TV. Then when they become teenagers, we blame them because they have no sense of social responsibility. We have to create schools which are an integral part of the community, in which young people naturally and normally do socially necessary and meaningful work for the community, for example, keeping the school grounds and the neighborhood clean and attractive, taking care of younger children, growing gardens which provide food for the community, etc. etc. Connections should be created between schools and local enterprises so that young people see these as an integral part of their present and future. Our goal should be to make Detroit the first city in the nation to use our schools to support the community rather than as places where young people are upgraded to leave the community.

Because of our declining population many school buildings in Detroit have been abandoned or are about to be abandoned. These schools can be turned into day care centers to care for the children of working mothers and fathers. They can be developed into political and cultural centers for the community— the place for town meetings or for a local museum where the arts and crafts, the workmanship, and the historical achievements of the community are proudly exhibited.

These are only a few examples of the kinds of things we can do to rebuild Detroit once we realize that we can no longer depend upon the corporations or the politicians to save us and begin thinking for ourselves about what we can do and must do. At this point, what we need most to do is to begin discussing how we are going to rebuild our city, in every block club, every church, every school, every organization, and every home—because for the rest of this century and most of the next, the major question in this country is going to be "How will we live in the city?" Up to now we have come to the city expecting somebody else, meaning the corporations, to provide us with a livelihood. Now we are stuck here and we can't run or hide any more. We can't go back to the farm, we can't keep running from city to city. We must put down our roots where we are and put our hearts, imaginations, minds and hands to work, so that we can empower ourselves and one another to create an alternative to casino gambling. [Mayor] Coleman Young's crisis is our opportunity. Let us start the discussion here tonight.

Black-Led Urban Agriculture since the 1960s
Jessi Quizar

At the height of Black Power, many Black radicals called for food security in terms that echoed the Black Panther Party's demand for "land, bread, housing, education, clothing, justice, and peace." From that focus arose a number of Black-led urban agriculture projects between the 1970s and 2000s in cities like Oakland, Los Angeles, Detroit, and Brooklyn. These projects saw control over food production and Black people's greater access to fresh healthy food as issues of Black self-determination.

The Panthers' food programs tended to focus on large-scale giveaways—particularly free food programs and free breakfast for children. As deindustrialization, mass unemployment, and organized abandonment increasingly structured Black communities from the 1970s onward, programs began to focus more on control over production of food rather than just food access. Additionally, throughout the 1980s and 1990s many smaller grocers that had served Black communities closed. Instead, big-box style grocery stores emerged—often sited in suburbs. Urban Black communities increasingly had to rely on liquor stores and convenience stores for most of their food, leading to a dramatic rise in food-related illnesses like diabetes and heart disease. In concrete ways, Black communities' access to healthy foods was a matter of life and death. In providing fresh fruits and vegetables to food-starved neighborhoods, urban agriculture projects emphasized Black economic and bodily self-determination.

Some urban farming projects evolved directly out of the organizing legacy of the Black Panther Party. Community Services Unlimited (CSU) was founded in 1977 as a nonprofit organization administered by the Los Angeles chapter of the Black Panther Party. Initially, CSU ran programs in the tradition of the Black Panther Party's survival programs, which generally provided free items for people's health and community well-being. CSU coordinated a free shoe program, a free food program, and arranged free buses to prisons for residents to visit family members. In the 1990s, however, CSU founder Kwaku Duren began to critique these programs as not promoting community control over production, which meant that ultimately they did not lead to fundamental change in their economic position. By the early 2000s, CSU had shifted its programming to focus almost entirely on urban agriculture and the promotion of food justice in South Los Angeles.

Even those with fewer direct connections with the party still drew on the its lineage. For instance, David Roach, who founded Mo' Better Food in Oakland in 1998 was inspired in large part by his brother's participation in the Black Panther Party's survival programs.

While the political roots of Black-led urban farms were movements for Black autonomy and power, they frequently also drew on skills and legacies of farming cultivated in the Jim Crow South. Detroit became a particular flashpoint for this connection. In the 1980s, a network of elders who had migrated to the city during the Great Migration drew on the agricultural skills that they had gained in their early lives in the South to respond to the organized abandonment of the city. They formed a group called the Gardening Angels to grow food in vacant lots throughout Detroit.

In 1992, longtime Black freedom activists James and Grace Lee Boggs founded Detroit Summer, a program that encouraged young people in partnership with the Gardening Angels to create urban gardens, art, and community spaces. Detroit Summer was inspired largely by the writing of James Boggs, who argued that in the context of deindustrialization and mass unemployment in cities like Detroit, Black communities needed to build their own economies and their own community systems.

The early 2000s saw an explosion of urban agriculture in general, many of which were not focused on social justice. Yet Black-led urban agriculture increased as well, with Black-led farming projects founded in almost every US city with a large Black community. These early foundations in Black radicalism have grounded most Black-led urban agriculture in movements for Black self-determination.

2.C.7.

Crips and Bloods

From "Plan for the Reconstruction of Los Angeles: Give Us the Hammer and the Nails, We Will Rebuild the City" (1992)

When a jury failed to convict four Los Angeles police officers for the on-camera beating of Black motorist Rodney King, Los Angeles erupted in revolt. Even before the uprising, and especially after it, politicians and many journalists blamed the city's problems on gangs—particularly the Crips and the Bloods, two street organizations that formed in the vacuum left by the 1970s urban crisis and the collapse of radical groups like the Black Panther Party. The Crips and Bloods had historically feuded with each other. Yet as the dust settled after the five-day uprising in 1992, members of the Crips and Bloods signed a truce and coauthored this plan to rebuild the city.

Bloods/Crips Proposal for LA's Face-Lift

Burned and abandoned structures: Every burned and abandoned structure shall be gutted. The city will purchase the property if not already owned by the city and build a community center. If the structure is on a corner or vacant lot, the city will build a career counseling center or a recreation area, respectively.

Repavement: All pavements/sidewalks in Los Angeles are in dire need of resurfacing. The Department of Transportation shall pay special attention to the pedestrian walkways and surface streets located in predominantly poor and minority areas. Our organization will assist the city in the identification of all areas of concern.

Lighting: All lighting will be increased in all neighborhoods. Additionally, lighting of city streets, neighborhood blocks, and alleyways will be amended. We want a well-lit neighborhood. All alleys shall be painted white or yellow by the building owners and alley lights will be installed at the cost of the owner.

Landscaping: All trees will be properly trimmed and maintained. We want all weeds/shrubbed areas to be cleaned up and properly nurtured. New trees will be planted to increase the beauty of our neighborhoods.

Sanitation: A special task force shall be assigned to clean up all vacant lots and trashed areas throughout the deprived areas. Proper pest control methods shall be implemented by the city. The city will declare a neighborhood clean-up week wherein all residents will be responsible for their block—a block captain will be assigned to ensure cooperation.

Blood/Crips Educational Proposal

1) *Maximizing education standards* in the low income areas is essential to reduce the possibilities of repeated insurrection. . . .

   a) $300 million will go into the reconstruction and refurbishment of the Los Angeles Unified School District (LAUSD) structures.

   b) $200 million will be donated for computers, supplies, and updated books (each student shall have necessary books).

   c) All teachers' salaries shall be no less than $30,000 a year to give them an incentive to educate in our districts.

d) Re-election shall be held for all Los Angeles Board of Education members.

2) *Reconstruction* shall include repainting, sandblasting, and reconstruction of all LAUSD schools; remodeling of classrooms [and] repainting of hallways and meeting areas; all schools shall have new landscaping and more plants and trees around the schools; completely upgrade the bathrooms, making them more modern; provide a bathroom monitor to each bathroom which will provide fresh-up toiletries at a minimum cost to the students.

3) *A provision for accelerated educational learning programs* shall be implemented for the entire LAUSD to provide aggressive teaching methods and provide a curriculum similar to noneconomically deprived areas. Tutoring for all subjects will be made available to all students after school hours. It will be mandatory for all students with sublevel grades to participate. . . .

4) *The LAUSD will provide up-to-date books to the neglected areas and enough books to ensure that no student has to share a book with another.*

5) *The LAUSD will remove all teachers not planning to further their education along with teachers who have not proven to have a passionate concern for the students.* . . .

6) *All curriculums shall focus on the basics in high school requirements and it shall be inundated with advanced sciences and additional applied math, English, and writing skills.*

7) *Bussing shall become nonexistent in our community if all of the above demands are met.*

Blood/Crips Human Welfare Proposal

Hospitals and health care centers: the federal government shall provide the deprived areas with three new hospitals and forty additional health care centers. Dental clinics shall be made available within ten miles of each community. The services shall be free and supported by federal and state funds.

Welfare: We demand that welfare be removed from our community and welfare programs be replaced by state work and product manufacturing plants that provide the city with certain supplies. State monies shall only be provided for invalids and the elderly. The state of California shall provide a child welfare building to serve as day care centers for single parents.

Parks and recreation: Los Angeles parks shall receive a complete face-lift, and develop activities and programs in the parks throughout the night. Stages, pools and courts shall be reconstructed and resurfaced, and the city shall provide highly visible security twenty-four hours a day for these parks and recreational centers. Programs at the parks shall be in accordance with educational programs and social exchange programs developed by the city for adults and young adults.

Blood/Crips Law Enforcement Program

The Los Angeles communities are demanding that they are policed and patrolled by individuals who live in the community and the commanding officers by ten-year residents of the community in which they serve. Former gang members shall be given a chance to be patrol buddies in assisting the protection of the neighborhoods. These former gang members will be required to go through police training and must comply with all of the laws instituted by our established authorities. Uniforms will be issued to each and every member of the "buddy system"; however, no weapons will be issued. All patrol units must have a buddy patrol notified and present in the event of a police matter. Each buddy patrol will be supplied with a video camera and will tape each event and the officers handling the police matter. The buddy patrol will not interfere with any police matter, unless instructed by a commanding officer. Each buddy patrol will also be supplied with a vehicle.

Blood/Crips Economic Development Proposal

Loans shall be made available by the federal and state governments to provide interested minority entrepreneurs interested in doing business in these deprived areas. The loan requirements shall not be so stringent that it will make it impossible for a businessman to acquire these loans. These loans shall not exceed a 4 percent interest-bearing charge per year. The businessman shall not be required to have security for the loan. However, the businessman must present at least two years of business operations and taxes with a city license before funds will be allocated. The owner must have either an established business [that he or she] desir[es] to expand or a sound business plan. Assistance for business plans shall be made available to these businessmen by the Small Business Administration. Additionally, the Small Business Administration will provide agents to help each business to develop a sound business plan from beginning to end. No one will be neglected in receiving adequate assistance. These business owners shall be required to hire 90 percent of their personnel from within the community and the monies shall not be distributed in a lump sum. Funds will be released in increments outlined by the business plan. Any businessman that doesn't conform to the hiring practices will have funding ceased until they conform.

In return for these demands, the Blood/Crips Organization will

1) *request [that] the drug lords of Los Angeles take their monies and invest them in business and property in Los Angeles.*
2) *encourage these drug lords to stop drug traffic and get them to use the money*

constructively. We will match the funds of the state government appropriations and build building for building.

3) *match funds for an AIDS research and awareness center in South Central* and Long Beach that will only hire minority researchers and physicians in the AIDS epidemic.

Conclusion

Meet these demands and the targeting of police officers will stop! You have seventy-two hours for a response and a commitment, in writing, to support these demands. Additionally, you have thirty days to begin implementation. And, finally, you have four years to complete the projects of construction of the major hospitals and restorations

Give us the hammer and the nails, we will rebuild the city.

2.C.8.

Eric Mann

From *A New Vision for Urban Transportation* (1996)

Through fare hikes and service cuts, public transportation reflected the urban crises of this time period. In Los Angeles, a group called the Bus Riders Union took on "transit racism" by organizing people who rode the bus (overwhelmingly working-class people of color) to demand more, better, and cheaper bus service. And in 1994, the union and its allies won a historic ruling against the city's transportation agency. Bus Riders Union strategist and Labor/Community Strategy Center director Eric Mann reflects on that victory here.

On September 1, 1994, the doors of the federal court building were almost knocked off their hinges. A jubilant crew of Latinos, African Americans, Asians, and whites came running out jumping up and down, screaming and yelling, even shrieking, hugging each other in a rare victory celebration that seemed eerily out of time and place. Even more shocking was the army of photographers, radio reporters, and TV cameras from at least ten local stations, waiting with the fickle embrace saved only for "winners." In English, Spanish, and Korean the urban rebels had to learn almost from scratch how to assume the mature posture of victors without giggling or pinching themselves in public.

Constance Rice of the NAACP Legal Defense Fund, attorney for the plaintiffs, told the press on the courthouse steps,

> Today, federal judge Terry Hatter issued a temporary restraining order, blocking the Metropolitan Transportation Authority (MTA) from rais-

ing the bus fare from $1.10 to $1.35 and also blocked them from eliminating the unlimited use monthly bus pass. The plaintiffs—the Labor/Community Strategy Center, the Bus Riders Union (BRU), the Korean Immigrant Workers Advocates, and the Southern Christian Leadership Conference—argued that the alleged "fiscal crisis" at the MTA is being handled in a racially discriminatory manner in violation of Title VI of the Civil Rights Act of 1964. The judge ruled that the MTA's fiscal problems of their own making cannot be solved on the backs of the city's five hundred thousand poor and overwhelmingly minority bus riders.

Eric Mann, the director of the Strategy Center and a member of the Center's Bus Riders Union, gave a more global spin to the issue and the multiracial grassroots organizing that was driving it:

> This case is not just about reducing bus fares or improving bus service. At stake here is the concept that in the richest nation in the world, transportation is a human right. Government cannot provide and then withhold transportation to determine who can look for a job or get to a job or visit a sick mother or take her kids to childcare or the park based on the ability to pay. This class action suit challenges the corporatization of government—the reactionary notion that public life should be privatized and that the city should run "like a business." It is an effort to revitalize the civil rights movement when it is under attack and to show that a half million low-income bus riders, 81 percent of whom are Latino, African American, Asian/Pacific Islander, and Native American, and 60 percent of whom have family incomes under $15,000, can play a role in making history. . . .

Still, reporters were shocked at the answers they received when they asked "What is it that you people want?" Instead of the perhaps expected "We want the MTA to keep the bus fare at $1.10 and not appeal the judge's reinstatement of the monthly bus pass," they were given the series of interrelated demands that comprise the Billions for Buses campaign.

"We want a fifty cent bus fare with a free transfer."

"We want a $20 unlimited use monthly bus pass."

"We want two thousand new compressed natural gas or other clean fuel buses, until electric and hydrogen fuel cell buses are available—and we want them built in LA in low-income communities."

"We want an end to privatization and a stop to the busting of the bus drivers and mechanics unions."

"We want an end to all rail construction that is stealing funds from the bus system."

"We want an elected MTA board, not the appointed one we have."

"We want an end to transit racism."

One reporter incredulously said, "You don't sound like a protest group.

You sound like you want to *run* the MTA." "You got *that* right," a BRU member responded.

The BRU Story

... The Strategy Center and the Bus Riders Union charged the MTA with setting up a separate and unequal mass transportation system that systematically discriminated against low-income people of color and saw their class action suit, *Labor/Community Strategy Center and Bus Riders Union v. the MTA* as the *Brown v. Board of Education* for transportation. ...

Less than a year later, the morning edition of the [Los Angeles] *Times* announced that the Metropolitan Transportation Authority, claiming fiscal shortfalls which arose under a conservative Republican mayor and governor committed to running government "like a business," would eliminate the free transit pass for students—generating, for the first time, the specter that low-income children could not even get to school. Liberal Democrats issued half-hearted outcries about the new "fiscal and political realities" while simply negotiating the extent of the cuts, and community groups called the decision racist and class-biased, as the new costs per family might be as high as $1,000 a year—denying poor students the chance to attend better schools further away from their homes and reinforcing racial and class segregation. Again, a combination of grassroots organizing and civil rights legal action was planned in response. ...

In Birmingham, Alabama, Washington, DC, and virtually every major urban center in the US the pattern is the same: business-oriented governments are dramatically cutting public services at the same time as they are using valuable public assets, including tax revenues, to bolster private sector profit-driven companies that claim to believe in a free enterprise system but, in fact, are truly addicted to government subsidies. Meanwhile, the urban poor—increasingly Latino, African American, Asian/Pacific Islander, Native American, and female—are too often disorganized and demoralized, as each welfare, health care, and transportation service cut makes the mythical "family" of family values increasingly nonviable, while governmental policies turn to criminalizing those it has assaulted and then abandoned.

The fight for a first-class mass transportation system and the way in which the Strategy Center and Bus Riders Union are theorizing and organizing that fight offer not just an encouraging story but a theoretical and strategic model that challenges much of the existing organizing on transportation and urban issues in the US. It is the effort to put forth an analysis and an organizing model, rooted in a breakthrough social movement and class-action civil rights case, that can generate an urgently needed debate about an alternative vision for mass transportation and urban policy in the age of the bipartisan free market disaster that is destroying US cities. ...

Student Liberation Action Movement, 1995–2004

Suzy Subways

From 1847 to 1976, New York City's public colleges were free, and in 1969, a militant student movement won an open admissions policy that welcomed a majority of people of color as City University of New York (CUNY) students. But by 1995, a series of budget cuts had raised tuition to the point of making CUNY unaffordable for many poor and working-class New Yorkers. The Student Liberation Action Movement (SLAM!) emerged from a tidal wave of youth rage against the ethnic cleansing of the city's public university.

As gentrification pushed Black, Latinx, and poor and working-class people out of the city's neighborhoods, tuition hikes and the repeal of CUNY's open admissions policy began excluding them from higher education. SLAM!'s base, mostly working-class and poor youth of color, used culture as a weapon to unite and resist being pushed out. Hip-hop, slam poetry, R&B and breakdancing flowed as a life force through SLAM!'s protests. Many of SLAM!'s leaders were children of Black and Puerto Rican nationalists or white communists of the 1960s; others were anarchists or leftist immigrants. Black Panther and Young Lords veterans served as mentors.

The mix of hip-hop culture and revolutionary ideas caught fire on March 23, 1995, when roughly twenty-thousand mostly Black and Latinx youth attempted to march from city hall to Wall Street in an unpermitted "Shut the City Down" action. A massive, violent police presence stopped their efforts. Students attempted to push through police lines but were beaten and arrested by the dozens.

It was "Giuliani time." Not only did Mayor Rudolph Giuliani aggressively push the gentrification of CUNY, but his police swept up the city's street life to make room for white middle-class newcomers. Giuliani and police chief Bill Bratton highlighted so-called quality of life concerns as a pretext to arrest people who were homeless or involved in the drug trade or sex work—and even people of color going about their business—and to accelerate the gentrification of the city. Their zeal led to a number of violent police abuses. Among the most jarring incidents were the torturing of Haitian immigrant Abner Louima in 1997 and the killing of Guinean immigrant Amadou Diallo outside his own apartment in 1999.

In March 2000—after the officers who killed Diallo were acquitted, and Patrick Dorismond, like Diallo, was killed by plainclothes cops—over five hundred students from at least nine high schools walked out and marched in protest. SLAM! helped the student organizers coordinate the walkouts, even after other adult organizations pulled their support, uncomfortable with the potential legal risks. For SLAM!, police brutality was an issue faced by young people who would have gone to CUNY if not for the policy changes the group had fought to stop. SLAM! still saw Black and Latinx youth as its base, whether they were students or not.

This organizing allowed SLAM! to build deeper grassroots support for US political prisoners like journalist and former Black Panther Mumia Abu-Jamal. A benefit for Abu-Jamal in June 2000 featured rappers Mos Def and Dead Prez and drew an audience of two thousand. "Amadou's murder and the acquittal of those cops allowed them to look at a situation like Mumia's and really believe that he was framed for killing a cop," SLAM! organizer Rachèl Laforest said in a 2009 interview.[1] As SLAM! became a women of color–led organization in the late 1990s and settled into an eight-year stint running the student government at Hunter College, the group hosted cultural fund-raisers for women political prisoners. SLAM! also pushed for greater attention to the prison industrial complex among the predominantly white sectors of the global justice movement, helping make opposition to the prison industrial complex a plank of the protests in 2000 against the Republican National Convention in Philadelphia.

By passionately fighting for public education and against police brutality and gentrification, SLAM! demanded space in New York City for working-class communities of color to learn, thrive, and develop their revolutionary potential.

1. Suzy Subways et al., "A Culture of Resistance: Lessons Learned from the Student Liberation Action Movement," *Upping the Anti* 8 (2009), https://upping theanti.org/journal/article/08-a-culture-of-resistance1.

2.C.9.

Elizabeth Betita Martinez

From "Be Down with the Brown!" (1996)

In the 1990s, the state government of California moved to cut public education funding, end affirmative action, and curtail the rights of immigrants by restricting social services and bilingual education. These events prompted massive high school student walkouts. In this essay activist and journalist Elizabeth Betita Martinez, a key figure in both the Student Nonviolent Coordinating Committee and the Chicana/o movement of the 1960s, likens the 1996 campaign to 1968 Chicana/o student activism. Like others, she uses the term "raza" to refer not only to Chicanx or Latinx people but also a broader politicized community.

For ten days that shook Los Angeles, in March 1968, Chicano and Chicana high school students walked out of class to protest a racist educational system. The "blowouts," as they were called, began with several thousand students from six barrio schools, then increased every day for a week until more than ten thousand had struck. Shouting "¡Chicano Power!" and "¡Viva la revolución!," they brought the city's school system—the largest in the United States—to a total halt. . . .

Almost thirty years later, Raza high school students from California to Colorado repeated that history with new blowouts demanding more Latino teachers and counselors; Ethnic Studies (not only Latino but also African American, Native American, and Asian/Pacific Islander); bilingual education sensitive to students' cultural needs; and Latino student-retention programs. Other issues were often added; in California, these included combating repressive new anti-crime laws, preventing the reelection of right-wing governor Pete Wilson, and fighting Proposition 187 with its inhumane call to deny educational and health services to anyone suspected of being undocumented.

California's blowouts focused on public schools in the northern part of the state at first, then spread south. The students, mostly of Mexican or Salvadoran background, came from high, junior high, and sometimes elementary schools. Why a walkout during school hours rather than a march or rally on the weekend? Because, as they learned, California's public schools lose $17.20 or more for each unexcused absence per day. This pocketbook damage provided the economic centerpiece of the students' strategy. With it, they made history.

The first wave seemed to burst out of nowhere. On April 1, 1993, more than one thousand mostly Latino junior high and high school students walked out of a dozen Oakland schools. On September 16, celebrated as Mexican Independence Day, more than four thousand blew out in Oakland, Berkeley, San Jose, and the town of Gilroy. Arrests and violence were rare, although in Gilroy police did arrest teenager Rebecca Armendariz and harassed her for months with charges of contributing to the delinquency of a minor, apparently because she signed to rent a bus that students used. In right-wing-dominated Orange County, three hundred students clashed with police while some were beaten and pepper sprayed.

Another wave of student strikes unrolled in November and December in northern California. In Exeter, a small town in California's generally conservative Central Valley, five hundred high school students boycotted classes when a teacher told an embarrassed youth who had declined to lead the Pledge of Allegiance in English: "If you don't want to do it, go back to Mexico." It was the kind of remark that had been heard too many times in this school where 40 percent of the twelve hundred students—but only six of their teachers—are Latino.

At Mission High School in San Francisco, two hundred Latino and other students demonstrated for the same antiracist reasons as elsewhere and also for being stereotyped as gangbangers if they wore certain kinds of clothing. The school board agreed to their main demand for Latino studies, and then offered just one class—to be held before and after the regular school day. The basic message: this concession isn't for real.

On to February 2, 1994, which marked the anniversary of the signing of the 1848 Treaty of Guadalupe Hidalgo confirming the US takeover of half of Mexico—today's Southwest. In Sacramento, the walkout movement spread like wildfire. Some five hundred high school students and supporters from various districts shook up the state capital. "The governor wants more prisons, we want schools. He wants more cops, we want more teachers. We want an education that values and includes our culture. We want all cultures to know about themselves," they said, as reported by the local paper *Because People Matter*.

For Cesar Chavez's birthday in March, nearly 150 Latino students from four city schools marched on district offices in Richmond [in Contra Costa County]. On April 18, half of the elementary school pupils in the town of Pittsburg [in Contra Costa County] boycotted classes, with parental support, because a Spanish-speaking principal had been demoted. They had their tradition: twenty years before, Pittsburg elementary school students had boycotted for lack of a Latino principal.

The spring wave climaxed on April 22 with a big, coordinated blowout involving more than thirty schools in northern California. It was unforgettable. Some eight hundred youth gathered in San Francisco under signs such as "Educate, Don't Incarcerate" and "Our Story, Not His-story" and with beautiful banners of Zapata and armed women of the Mexican Revolution.

Calls for unity across racial and national lines and against gang warfare rang out all day. "Don't let the lies of the United Snakes divide us!" "Latin America doesn't stop with Mexico," said a Peruvian girl. Another shouted, "It's not just about Latinos or Blacks or Asians, this is about the whole world!" Some of the loudest cheers rang out from a sixteen-year-old woman who cried "We've got to forget these [gang] colors!"

In the town of Hayward that day, fifteen hundred high school and junior high students boycotted more than twenty schools. About three hundred of them turned in their red or blue gang rags for brown bandannas—brown for Brown Power and unity. Later some of them set up a meeting to help stop the violence. "You wear the brown rag, be *down*. Be all the way down for every Raza," said Monica Manriquez, age seventeen.

Cinco de Mayo, May 5, brought more blowouts, followed by a June gathering in Los Angeles of nine hundred high school students. The youth themselves were startled by their own success. Sergio Arroyo, sixteen, of Daly City, spoke what others were thinking: "People didn't think it could happen, all that unity, but it did." Lucretia Montez from Hayward High said, "We're making history. Yeah, we're making history."

Why did this new round of blowouts explode in 1993–94? The current generation of Latino teenagers had seen little in their lifetime except the intensified reaction and racism established under Presidents Reagan and Bush [and] unchanged under Clinton. Attempts at multiculturalism, bilingualism, and affirmative action had been repeatedly attacked by staunch advocates of white supremacy. A prolonged recession had further eroded young hopes for a decent life. At the same time, Raza were being fingered as the cause of those economic problems by the campaigns to scapegoat immigrants. . . . Little wonder, then, that the hour of Raza high school students had come.

2.C.10.

CopWatch Atlanta

From "Atlanta '96: No Room at the Inn but Plenty of Room at the Jail" (1996)

Gentrification often went hand in hand with police brutality, as police enforced "quality of life" laws and other policies that made it easier to displace low-income communities—especially by removing homeless people from downtown business districts. Business elites and city officials used the 1996 Olympics as an excuse to redevelop downtown and institute new sweeps of homeless encampments. Activists from CopWatch Atlanta, many of whom came out of an antipoverty group called Empty the Shelters, took the opportunity to challenge the city power structure for promoting both homelessness and police violence.

The 1996 Olympic games are the crown jewel in plans by the Atlanta's business elite to showcase Atlanta as a true international city, past all racial tensions, a veritable capital of the New South worthy of your tourist dollars. For nearly a decade, Atlanta's corporations, working in tandem with government agencies, have pursued a strategy to revitalize the downtown business district into a twenty-four-hour hub of shops, restaurants, and high-income apartments. The idea is to firmly establish Atlanta as a choice location for conventions and high-profile sporting events, as well as to attract suburban exiles (and their tax dollars) back into the fold.

Spearheading this effort is Central Atlanta Progress (CAP), an organization of elite business interests (or, as a former CAP chairman bluntly put it, "white economic power") such as Coca-Cola and Turner Communications. CAP has made it perfectly clear that the poor and homeless have no place in its vision for downtown Atlanta. Its Central Area Study II, a cooperative effort between CAP and the city of Atlanta, ranks homelessness a "high priority concern" and recommends a number of measures to assist the police in safeguarding the image of downtown, including the creation of a new police zone solely for the central area, the employment of "undercover methods of surveillance," and the construction of the new zone headquarters in CNN Center, as well as a minizone headquarters in Underground Atlanta, a theme shopping mall. . . .

The Olympics have presented downtown planners with the golden opportunity to do just that, all in the name of international hospitality. One of their tactics, used successfully in many cities around the nation, was to make it easier to arrest homeless people by passing laws that criminalize behaviors necessitated by the status of living on the street or which are vague enough to be selectively enforced against undesirables. In 1991, shortly after the International Olympic Committee awarded the games to Atlanta, the city council enacted three ordinances that effectively constitute a de facto vagrancy-free zone. The new laws outlaw soliciting alms by "forcing oneself upon the company of another," entering vacant buildings, and walking across a parking lot without owning a vehicle that is parked there. The three ordinances also come in addition to an arsenal of other laws, one of which is the decades-old and absurd DC-6 violation, which makes it illegal to be in a "known drug area." The laws are clearly ambiguous and duplicate existing laws. For example, the begging ordinance is supposedly designed to protect the lives of pedestrians, but threatening behavior was already a crime in Atlanta. It's called assault.

Adding to the horror, the city council also voted to increase the maximum sentence for a municipal ordinance violation from two to six years. And, last year, the city completed construction of a new $56 million, one-thousand-bed jail. At a recent public safely task force meeting, Tom Pocock, director of Atlanta's Pretrial Detention Center, declared the jail to be "the first Olympic project completed on time." . . .

Atlanta's poor and homeless are beginning to fight back. In the month preceding the 1994 Super Bowl, a small group of homeless people, anticipating the inevitable police sweeps that would occur during the much-hyped event, demanded a meeting with Mayor Bill Campbell to address the problem. After several tries, Campbell finally consented to a public hearing with the homeless, at which he stated publicly that the police sweeps will stop.

Not surprisingly, in the week before the Super Bowl, sweeps occurred as usual, but nobody could predict the sheer intensity of the police presence. Atlanta's elite drug squad, the Red Dogs, was deployed on every street corner. CopWatch received reports of massive numbers of arrests. Typically, the Red Dogs would order any man or woman who looked homeless and had less than $10 off their beats. Homeless activists, enraged that Campbell had not held to his promise, organized a march during the Super Bowl. Although it received no media coverage, shortly afterward Robert Ferrell, one of the marchers, started the Atlanta Union of the Homeless.

The idea of the homeless organizing for themselves is a potentially powerful one here in Atlanta. The thought of all the poor people made homeless from Olympic development uniting with thousands of sisters and brothers on the street into one united organization may be distant, but it is the ultimate nightmare for the business and political establishment, and it is, we feel, the only way homelessness and the problems associated with it will ever cease. It is the homeless themselves, not advocates or students, who have felt firsthand the unwarranted blow of a police officer's baton or the humiliation of being jailed for sleeping in a public park. Those of us who are not homeless have an important role to play, but we must always bear in mind who ultimately owns the struggle to end the criminalization of poverty.

Working in a rare partnership, Empty the Shelters, the student organization that founded CopWatch Atlanta (hats off to the folks in Berkeley), has begun to unite with the Union of the Homeless around issues of police accountability. Although CopWatch's base is still predominantly young people, during the times when union members have gone out on street patrols, we have witnessed a remarkable change in the attitudes of many members of the homeless community. Imagine the difference between college students passing out know-your-rights pamphlets and actually homeless or formerly homeless people doing the same. In the latter instance, the action becomes not just a service but an organizing tool as well!

Realizing, however, that street patrols alone are not enough to solve the problem of police harassment, CopWatch has begun work with a legal team to repeal the antihomeless ordinances. Empty the Shelters has also inaugurated an innovative media campaign named SpoilSport. SpoilSport is the mythical half sister of official Olympic mascot Izzy. She's much smarter than her half-wit brother, though, and is on a quest to publicize Olympic-related human rights abuses. SpoilSport has already received enthusiastic media coverage around the world, everywhere from Chicago to Tokyo. She hopes to come soon to newspaper or television near you.

Whether or not we get prime-time coverage during July of 1996, CopWatch knows that even when the Olympics end, our work will have only just begun. The number of homeless in Atlanta continues to grow, and CAP recently announced plans to implement a business improvement district, which would finance a private security force downtown. Even more ominous, the four hundred security cameras that Olympic planners are going to install at various points around the city are staying—permanently! CopWatch will continue a strategy of direct street patrols, legal pressure, media zaps, and grassroots homeless organizing, and we will not stop until Atlanta's war on the poor ceases once and for all.

2.C.11.

Queer to the Left

"Housing Is a Queer Issue" (2002)

While increased lesbian and gay visibility resulted in corporate sponsorship for annual Pride events, poor people in LGBTQ communities suffered the effects of gentrification. The Chicago group Queer to the Left, which described itself as "a multiracial group of lesbian, gay, bisexual, transgender and queer people who fight for racial, economic, gender and sexual justice" and are "committed to forming coalitions with others to stop gentrification, police brutality, the death penalty, and the racism and growing conservatism of the mainstream lesbian and gay movement," distributed this flyer, featuring characters from the *Wizard of Oz*, at the 2002 Pride Parade.

For low-income lesbian, gay, bisexual, and transgender (LGBT) people being displaced by gentrification and cutbacks in public housing, housing is an issue.

For LGBT youth tormented by their parents and neighbors, with nowhere to go, housing is an issue.

For LGBT youth on the streets, with nowhere to go, housing is an issue.

For people living with AIDS living on a fixed income watching rental units disappear and prices rising as Chicago neighborhoods gentrify, housing is an issue.

For people living with AIDS and other disabilities who have special needs that neither the market nor public housing address, housing is an issue.

For LGBT victims of domestic abuse needing a safe space, housing is an issue.

For lesbian or bisexual women trapped in a heterosexual relationship because they cannot afford to leave and live on their own, housing is an issue.

For LGBT seniors living on fixed incomes in neighborhoods where they have built community for themselves over many years now facing skyrocketing taxes and rents as Chicago neighborhoods gentrify, housing is an issue.

For LGBT people of color who face racial discrimination from landlords, neighbors, lenders, and real estate agents, housing is an issue.

For transgendered people facing transphobic discrimination from landlords, neighbors, lenders, and real estate agents, housing is an issue.

For LGBT people who face homophobic discrimination from landlords, neighbors, lenders, and real estate agents, housing is an issue.

For LGBT people who believe that the struggle for sexual freedom requires building coalitions with others fighting for social justice, housing is an issue.

There Is No Place like Home (If You Can Afford One)

In the last decade the population of metropolitan Chicago grew by more than half a million people, but the number of rental units actually decreased by fifty-two thousand. Rents are rising by more than twice the overall rate of inflation. Nearly 40 percent of all renters now pay more than a third of their income on rent, with nearly two hundred thousand people paying more than 50 percent of their income on rent. Many people would be surprised to know that only about one in five people living in poverty receives any type of housing subsidies and that at the same time, nationwide, homeowners, who are overwhelmingly middle or upper class, are subsidized to the tune of $100 billion a year through federal income tax deductions for their mortgage payments. Here in Chicago, the number of Section 8 rental units is shrinking because landlords are choosing to take advantage of the overall housing shortage in the city to rent their units on the open market to higher-income people. Over the next five years, about ten thousand Section 8 units in Chicago are set to convert to private market rates. In this context, landlords have been given an incentive to discriminate against people of color, poor people, and people with large families. How many more units will be lost to "condo conversions?" Already over the last five years, the North Side of Chicago has lost nearly eight thousand rental units to "condo conversions." This gentrification process also includes large national retail chains coming into neighborhoods and threatening small independent LGBT-owned businesses. Meanwhile, the needs of low-income people with disabilities who have special housing needs go completely unaddressed. One-half of Chicago's PWAs [people with AIDs] live below the federal government's poverty level. One-third have been homeless at some point. (Statistics come from a recent study carried out by the AIDS Foundation of Chicago). Queer to the Left recently has been working in coalition with other organizations to address housing issues in Uptown, and there is more work to be done in various other Chicago neighborhoods.

LGBT folks live in various Chicago neighborhoods. We find ourselves in widely varying housing situations, based on our income, household size, race, nationality, gender, age, physical and mental abilities and our health. Historically, many of us have tried to build "community" within particular urban neighborhoods. Some LGBT people have lived in a specific community for a long time (e.g., Lakeview, South Shore, Uptown, Ravenswood, Logan's Square). Others are relatively new, some pushed out of, or excluded from, more established "gay neighborhoods" because of rampant gentrification there. Vibrant "gay residential neighborhoods" cannot survive gentrification—Lakeview is proof of that. Most LGBT folk cannot afford to live within walking distance of the Pride Parade route.

We all have a stake in maintaining the economic, racial and ethnic diversity of our neighborhoods, whether we simply need affordable and accessible apartments or if we want a vibrant queer culture we all have access to.

PART 3

Borders and Maps

From the late 1970s to the early 1990s, the Central American solidarity movement organized to stop US intervention and to support national liberation and social justice movements in Nicaragua, El Salvador, and Guatemala. The movement came into conflict with the US government, and the FBI and CIA pursued a sustained campaign to disrupt this solidarity activism. Between 1981 and 1987, the FBI investigated over one hundred thousand people and three thousand organizations across the United States. The FBI focused its harshest efforts on the Committee in Solidarity with the People of El Salvador (CISPES), classifying the group's support of leftist national liberation movements as "terrorism." Federal agents infiltrated the Dallas chapter of CISPES and coordinated dozens of break-ins at activist offices and homes nationwide. In addition, as an informant who infiltrated Dallas CISPES revealed, the FBI and CIA provided the Salvadoran National Guard with the names of Salvadoran leftists deported from the United States. The National Guard's death squads assassinated many of these activists in El Salvador and even extended their reach to California: in 1987, members of the National Guard kidnapped a Salvadoran refugee outside a Los Angeles CISPES office and then raped and tortured her.

As these attacks demonstrate, both repressive violence and radical resistance circulated transnationally. "Borders and Maps" illustrates how activists contested the ideological, political, and economic dominance that the United States exerted in the world from the 1970s through the immediate aftermath of September 11, 2001. Three frameworks guided the US state over these years: the Cold War, global capitalism, and antiterrorism. While overlapping, each framework produced distinct maps of danger and erected new borders. Radicals responded with their own maps of the world, rewriting US state logics through principles of national liberation, global justice, and solidarity against white supremacy, settler colonialism, and neocolonial regimes.

In responding to dominant cartographies and in crafting their own, activists fueled varying causes. For example, they supported liberation movements in Central America and Palestine, opposed the brutal apartheid regime in South Africa, and worked to end predatory national debts and abuse of workers supported by US corporations and US-backed financial entities in the Global South. Radicalism moved—imaginatively and organizationally—across geographies.

Immigration profoundly shaped radical activism. The Immigration and Nationality Act of 1965 enabled a more multiethnic and multilingual United States by removing some of the decades-old restrictions against migration to the US by people from Latin America, Asia, Africa, and the Middle East. Many migrants fled wars and inequality directly backed by the United States; they also brought critical knowledge into oppositional movements. Although the US government, especially under President Reagan (1980–88), worked to close the doors to leftist refugees in these years, immigrant communities became home to diasporic radicalisms. Immigrants' knowledge of the effects of neoliberalism, their experiences as workers in the US service economy, and their status as frequent targets of state repression made them key players in international solidarity, global justice, and labor organizing.

"Borders and Maps" starts with the transition from the anti–Vietnam War movement to other modes of international solidarity. The United States withdrew troops from Vietnam in 1973, and in 1975 communist forces in Vietnam, Cambodia, and Laos declared victory. Millions of people, primarily Southeast Asian civilians, died in US-backed wars in the region, and millions more were made refugees. Though the anti–Vietnam War movement did not end US aggression in Southeast Asia, it did help curtail bombings, stop the US draft, reveal lies by the military and political elites, and foster transnational activism. It also radicalized millions of Americans. As US wars in Cambodia, Laos, and Vietnam came to a close, large numbers of radicals continued to embrace anti-imperialism and international solidarity, particularly with socialist and communist struggles.

Section A, "Anti-Imperialism beyond Vietnam," tracks these reverberations. It focuses especially on Central America solidarity but also includes sources from Puerto Rican independence, opposition to US military occupation in South Korea, Indigenous internationalism, and a growing Arab American left. Jimmy Carter's presidency (1976–80) marked a reprieve from strident Cold War rhetoric, as he expressed support for the United Nations and extended amnesty to Vietnam War draft resisters. Reagan embraced anticommunism fervently and placed the locus of Cold War containment in Central America. During Reagan's presidency and that of his successor, former CIA director George H. W. Bush (1988–92), the United States backed the right-wing Salvadoran government against leftist rebels. In Nicaragua the United States covertly funded a proxy army, known as the contras, that sought to overthrow the socialist Sandinista revolution. Bush aimed to implement what he called a "new world order" of US hegemony over global diplomacy following the Cold War. He pursued, and largely won, United Nations approval of the US-led Gulf War (1991).

Anti-imperialists contested Reagan and Bush by arguing for the right to self-determination and by revealing the US sponsorship of Third World violence. They also drew comparisons to recent memory, as through the ubiquitous bumper sticker, "El Salvador is Spanish for Vietnam." Activists embraced multiple tactics, including nonviolent direct action, direct aid and travel brigades, and refugee sanctuary—the last especially through churches. The movement contained many differences of ideology and demographics. One strand limited itself to opposing US intervention, drawing in liberals as well as radicals and gaining considerable mobilizing power. Another strand went farther, supporting left-wing movements in El Salvador, Nicaragua, Palestine, and Puerto Rico. Nonintervention presented the whitest face of the movement, while refugees and immigrants participated in greater numbers in backing radical groups of the Global South.

Section B, "From Anti-Imperialism to Global Justice," demonstrates how radicals responded to corporate globalization with a globalization of their own—what was variously termed the antiglobalization, alterglobalization, or the global justice movement. While capitalism could move more freely after the dissolution of the Soviet Union in 1991, everyday people faced militarized borders. In US electoral politics, Democrats and Republicans coalesced around deregulation and privatization. Meanwhile, new cohorts of activists sought a radicalism that did not reproduce ethnic, linguistic, religious, or sexual exclusions, problems that had marked many leftist governments worldwide. A growing number of radicals reframed the idea of the global, organizing at scales both smaller and larger than the nation-state. They pursued anticapitalist "globalization from below" and built ties with nonstate organizations and communities in the global South. Often embracing anarchism or other "horizontalist" politics, many worked toward more radical conceptions of affinity than encompassed by either "national liberation" or "human rights."

Left critiques of corporate globalization also presented a referendum on US domestic politics, challenging anti-immigrant vitriol amid a weakened labor movement. Given how NAFTA and other policies undermined union power, the acceleration of globalization posed a fork in the road for organized labor, pitting labor's history of racial exclusion against its internationalist legacy. But several hopeful directions for worker organizing emerged, including immigrant labor organizing, independent worker centers, and the campus-based antisweatshop movement that targeted major universities whose collegiate sport apparel was produced in countries where exploitative labor practices were widespread.

Section B tracks these trends. It begins with the anti-apartheid movement, which mobilized in radical union locals, built student-labor coalitions, and popularized the economic tactics of boycott, divestment, and sanctions. These tactics carried influence in the 1990s. Illustrating these ties, section B places anti-apartheid materials alongside sources from the global justice and immigrant worker movements. It includes items on the use of large-scale direct action, which reached its height in 1999 when fifty thousand people shut down the World Trade Organization meeting in Seattle. It further demonstrates how immigrant worker organizing intersected with antiracism and by what tactics immigrant workers won power.

Section C, "Not in Our Name," uses an oft-repeated activist slogan to highlight how US radicals opposed wars of occupation in the Middle East. As the US security state shifted its declared enemy from (Soviet) communism to (Muslim) terrorism, US military intervention assumed a civilizing mission. Against such a rationale, radicals worked to reveal the economic and political interests—as well as the racist and sexist ideologies—driving US approaches to the Middle East. Arab American, Muslim, and Jewish activists played key roles in bringing critiques of Zionism into antiwar politics and in building feminist and queer Palestinian solidarity. Activists' opposition to wars in "our name" gained even greater importance after the attacks of September

11, when the US invaded Afghanistan and Iraq, instituted widespread domestic surveillance and detention under the USA PATRIOT Act, and employed systematic torture in the military prisons at Guantánamo Bay and Abu Ghraib.

"Not in Our Name" tracks sources from the 1970s through the initial aftermath of September 11. Materials from the early period include Iranian American radicalism, Palestinian solidarity, and radical critiques of Zionism. While often tentative in the early 1980s, these politics gained greater energy after the first intifada—the Palestinian uprising against Israeli occupation of the West Bank and Gaza that took place from December 1987 until 1993, when the Oslo Accords were signed. Feminist and queer challenges to occupation, orientalism, and Zionism played pivotal roles in challenging Islamophobia and thereby in strengthening antiwar activism. Activism against the 1991 Gulf War was brief but prompted many radicals to pursue more purposefully antiracist and people of color-led organizing. In the aftermath of September 11, activists of color and immigrant radicals—especially Arab American, South Asian, and Muslim people—moved toward centerstage in confronting the repression targeting their communities. As much as 9/11 was a world-altering event, both radical and state responses reflected the ideological, social, and tactical maps each side had drawn over the preceding decades.

Anti-Imperialism beyond Vietnam

3.A.1.

Association of Arab-American University Graduates

"Statement Adopted at the AAUG Sixth Annual Convention" (1973)

The Association of Arab-American University Graduates (AAUG) was founded in 1967, catalyzed by the June 1967 (Arab-Israeli) War and a spike in anti-Arab racism across the United States. For the next forty years, it served as a forum in which activist-scholars could discuss and speak out about the Arab world and Palestinian solidarity. The AAUG's conferences, publications, and network of speakers built understanding of Arab and Palestinian politics in the broader US left.

The Association of Arab-American University Graduates, at its Sixth Annual Convention, in Washington, DC, on October 19, 20, and 21, conducted an in-depth investigation of the various aspects of settler colonialism in the Middle East and Africa. Having had the benefit of listening and responding to the numerous scholarly presentations submitted by the distinguished participants and having conducted this investigation and the business of the Association against the background of the resumption of full-scale armed hostilities in the Middle East between the settler colonial regime of Israel and the Arab peoples, the association adopted the following statement:

The association reaffirms all previous pronouncements and resolutions expressing its active opposition to the continued presence of settler colonialism, in all of its manifestations and effects, in all parts of the Third World. This opposition to settler colonialism, whatever the impetus for that colonialism, stems from colonialism's essentially chauvinist and racialist character, its alliance with and dependence on the imperialism of great powers for its implementation and security, and its continued opposition to and thwarting of the legal, social, economic, and political rights and aspirations of the indigenous peoples.

The association greatly appreciates the successes which have been realized in various parts of Africa and Asia against settler colonialism, particularly in the national liberation of a major part of Guinea-Bissau, and pledges continued support for and solidarity with the movements for liberation from the yoke of settler colonialism in other parts of Africa and Asia.

The association notes with appreciation the recognition accorded by significant sectors of the international community of the anticolonial and anti-imperial nature of the Palestinians' armed struggle for the national liberation of their homeland.

The association resolves that the present, continuing sacrifices of the Arab peoples in the current phase of their struggle against imperialist and colonial domination, and against the local surrogates of that domination, demand the broadest possible mobilization of the human, material, and political resources of the Arab peoples in the service of that struggle. In this connection the association comprehends the necessity for a correct understanding and analysis of current developments and condemns any attempt to manipulate the heroic sacrifices that the Arab peoples have made in the cause of liberation. Any acceptance of a cease-fire agreement that does not fully restore the national rights of the Palestinian and Arab peoples, which rights are accepted and secured in international law and accepted by a majority of the population of the world, will constitute a reversal and betrayal of the Arab peoples' sacrifices and struggle.

Accordingly the association further resolves that under no circumstances shall any Arab government negotiate away lands or rights of the Palestinians or of any other Arab people.

The association, as on numerous occasions in the past, reiterates its resolute support for the just and universalist demands of the people of Palestine for a return to their homeland and for the dismantling of the international Zionist infrastructure, which is aided and abetted by imperial powers, principally the United States and the settler-colonialist state of South Africa.

The association reaffirms the right of the Arab peoples, and of all peoples, to self-determination, security, and social and economic emancipation and justice. The association voices its continued support for and solidarity with those sectors of Arab society which continue to challenge feudalism, reaction, and all forms of inequality.

The association affirms its support for the just struggle of the United Farm Workers for union representation of farm workers and views this as an important part of Chicano and immigrant Arab labor efforts to achieve a decent life.

The association rejects political manipulation as a means of realizing Arab and Palestinian rights. Rather, the association calls for, promotes, and encourages the broadest possible participation by the Arab peoples and a widening of the role of the Arab-American community in seeking the support of more Americans to combat the increase in anti-Arab and pro-Zionist sentiments in the American media and other American institutions.

The association seizes this opportunity to reiterate its condemnation of the US government's politically inspired harassment of Arab-Americans in the United States.

The association views with increasing alarm and apprehension the increasing moves toward greater US intervention in the Middle East and issues a call to all peace-loving sections of the American public, and particularly to those persons who have been active in opposition to American military intervention and involvement in Southeast Asia, to vigorously organize in opposition to American interventionism in the Middle East. This involves a process of education for the American public, informing them that the American involvement in Vietnam had far more modest beginnings than those currently existing in the Middle East and that the threat of great-power nuclear confrontation is much graver in the Middle East than it was in Southeast Asia. Moreover, only when this effort is conducted in a coordinated and organized fashion will it be able to secure the desired impact on those American policy makers who have been and continue to be unresponsive to the concerns and wishes of the American people relative to US involvement in the Middle East.

3.A.2.

Fuerzas Armadas de Liberación Nacional

"Communiqué No. 1" (1974)

The FALN, or Fuerzas Armadas de Liberación Nacional (Armed Forces of National Liberation), formed in 1974 to press for the independence of Puerto Rico from the United States. The following communiqué explains the FALN's first action, when it exploded five large bombs in Manhattan on October 26, 1974 (on Wall Street, at Rockefeller Center, and on Park Avenue, causing property damage, though no injuries). Numerous FALN members were imprisoned in the 1980s, fourteen of whom were granted clemency in 1999.

Today commando units of FALN attacked major Yanki corporations in New York City. These actions have been taken in commemoration of the October 30, 1950, uprising in Puerto Rico against Yanki colonial domination. These bombings are also to accent the seriousness of our demands for the release of the five Puerto Rican political prisoners, the longest-held political prisoners in the hemisphere, Oscar Collazo, Lolita Lebron, Rafael Cancel Miranda, Andres Figueroa Cordero, and Irvin Flores, and for the immediate and unconditional independence of Puerto Rico.

The corporations that we bombed are an integral part of Yanki monopoly capitalism and are responsible for the murderous policies of the Yanki government in Puerto Rico [and] Latin America and against workers, peasants, and Indios throughout the world. It is these corporations which are responsible for the robbery and exploitation of Third World countries in order to make greater profits and increase their capital. They are the ones which often decide who shall govern countries, who shall live, and who shall die.

For these reasons these corporations and the criminals who run them are the enemies of all freedom-loving people who are struggling for self-determination and the right to decide their own destinies.

We, the *guerrilleros* of the FALN, have undertaken these bombings not only against the presence of the Yanki corporations in Puerto Rico but as part of the international workers' revolution and all people fighting for national liberation.

These actions, along with the bombings of major department stores for three consecutive days in late spring and the dynamite blasts at Newark police headquarters and city hall, demonstrate what we have said since 1969: that the Puerto Rican people are organizing and arming in order to form a People's Revolutionary Army which will rid Puerto Rico of Yanki colonialism. We have opened two fronts, one in Puerto Rico, the other in the United States, both nourished by the Puerto Rican people and allies within Northamerica.

We are not pure militarists. Therefore we do not oppose those parties or people who believe in mass organization. However, to be truly revolutionary, a party must educate and organize the masses for the seizure of power by way of an organized and disciplined vehicle, a People's Revolutionary Army. A party

Figure 3.1. Ricardo Levins Morales, "Chile: 11 de Septiembre 73." Image courtesy of Lincoln Cushing/ Docs Populi. Reprinted with permission by Ricardo Levins Morales.

which fails to do this falls into reformism and becomes an agent of the bourgeoisie for the continued exploitation and oppression of the people.

The importance of a People's Revolutionary Army is that it arms the masses, produces cadres to lead the masses to victory and the development of a Marxist-Leninist party, tried and tested under fire, which will educate and organize the people for the construction of a socialist society.

Finally, the FALN supports the demonstration at Madison Square Garden on October 27 in support of the independence of Puerto Rico. We view this as a significant step in the formation of an anti-imperialist front in the United States, which will support and fight for the national liberation of Puerto Rico and educate the American people to the murderous and genocidal policies of the Yanki capitalists throughout the world.

Long Live Free Puerto Rico
Long Live the Unity of All People in Struggle against Imperialism
FALN Central Command

3.A.3.

US Out of Korea Committee

"When People Here Are Hungry, Should Your Dollars Go for War and Dictatorship in South Korea?" (1977)

The US Out of Korea Committee was a project of Youth Against War and Fascism, affiliated with the Workers World Party. Its work reflected a continuation of anti-interventionist politics in the aftermath of the US war in Vietnam. Later anti-intervention efforts tied to the Workers World Party include the International Action Center, founded in 1992, and ANSWER (Act Now to Stop War and End Racism), founded in 2001. The following is a flyer promoting a rally to end US intervention in Korea that was held on March 19, 1977, in New York City.

$189,000,000,000!

US government figures show that from 1946 to 1976 $189 billion of our taxes was spent on south Korea!

With this kind of money, the run-down, poverty-stricken cities of this country could be made livable again.

Two million people could be put to work for nine years building day care centers, hospitals, and decent housing at an annual salary of $10,000 each— and there'd still be $9 billion left over! This could wipe out unemployment in the oppressed Black and Latin communities, where it has been at depression levels for years.

War

Instead, Washington spent the money on a devastating war (1950–53) and on aid to military dictatorships in south Korea that would serve US big business. Ever since the war (which has never officially ended) the US has kept over forty thousand troops armed with nuclear weapons right on the demilitarized zone dividing Korea in half.

Dictatorship

Has this brought "freedom and democracy" to south Korea? *No!* It has brought Emergency Decree No. 9. Under this decree by President-for-life Pak Chung Hee, any kind of opposition or dissent is prohibited. Even former president Yun Po Sun and Pak's opponent in the last "election," Kim Dae Jung, are in jail. So is national poet Kim Chi Ha.

Torture

Amnesty International has documented the hideous tortures inflicted by the Pak regime on its opponents: electric shock, water tortures, beatings, deprivations of sleep, and others.

Bribery

It has now come to light that at least ninety members of the US Congress have received bribes to pass legislation continuing massive aid to the Pak military dictatorship.

These criminals in Congress are spending your money for dictatorship abroad—but they cry that there isn't enough to keep open schools, hospitals, libraries, and fire stations in New York City!

What Can We Do about It?

- Demand the withdrawal of US troops and weapons from Korea. With the opposition to Pak increasing, let's prevent Washington from unleashing another Vietnam War!
- Demand the US government end the state of war with the Democratic People's Republic of Korea (north Korea) and sign a peace treaty!
- Demand an end to all US aid to the Pak regime!
- Call for an end to political repression in south Korea! Freedom for all political prisoners!

3.A.4.

International Indian Treaty Council

From "Decolonization, Liberation, and the International Community" (1977)

Founded in a 1974 gathering at the Standing Rock Reservation, the International Indigenous Treaty Council formed to provide a platform for Indigenous people to advocate for themselves within the United Nations. This article, first published in the *Treaty Council News*, identifies the significance of international work for the daily life of Indigenous people.

When the Treaty Council was founded at Standing Rock in June 1974 by five thousand Indian people from all over the continent, we did not know exactly what we were getting into or where it might lead us. Many of us thought that seeking recognition by the United Nations was our goal, but not knowing what that would [be] or even it was possible. Some have become disillusioned that we have not moved faster than we have. Most are just confused about what the process is and what it means to our day-to-day struggles and lives.

Decolonization, or a better term, liberation, is a slow, painstaking process. What the colonialists accomplished over the past four centuries cannot be overcome easily. We, the native peoples of the Americas, are in the weakest position, as the first colonized. We live, as Russell Means said at the Geneva Conference, in the belly of the monster. The tools of US colonialism toward Indians in the US are subtle and difficult to resist. The most advanced methods are used to pacify Indian people, at the same time that genocide continues.

The US uses newspapers, TV, and the educational system to convince people in America that the US is the most humane country in the world.

How then do we proceed? The main purpose of the Treaty Council organization and its work is to organize international support. To do this, it is of primary importance that we be unified, that we work through the organization, that we take the initiative to relate our work to the organization's work. A large part of the process is one of learning—and teaching: learning the steps other liberation movements have taken and teaching the international community about our own situation, so that they may know how best to give us support and publicize our struggles.

When we began this work we saw it as a first stage of development to gain recognition of our sovereign nations in the world community. Perhaps we have underestimated the importance and value of our present work in overemphasizing the larger goal. As an NGO, an international organization, we relate to hundreds of other international organizations.

It is more important that we organize world opinion now than that we get recognition by the United Nations. The former colonies which have been able to achieve liberation and get UN recognition have done so only after decades of all-out war. Some, like the Puerto Rican [independence] movement, are in about the same position as ourselves, though they began to approach the international community nearly twenty years ago.

These comments are not meant to discourage people in the continuing work to be done. Rather it is to bring a sober and serious recognition of the difficulties. We are face to face with the most powerful and organized colonial power that has ever existed and which still dominates the world economically. Though the US is losing power politically, it still has tremendous resources at its command to control much of the world. We must take great care in our work. We will make mistakes, but we can learn not to fall into the traps that the US sets or respond to the propaganda it creates to divide and destroy our movement. The US tries to use everything to its advantage. It has political and social scientists, biologists, ethnologists, legal experts, and every imaginable kind of technological data and equipment at its fingertips to inform it of the moves to take. We must, like other liberation movements, outsmart that mechanical brainpower, and we can. But we must think and plan very carefully and cautiously, and we must be organized, build the organization to carry on a consistent and unified mission in the world community.

We must make our position very clear to the world community, and we must inform ourselves of the international situation and the way in which the colonialists work if we are to resist, grow, and eventually triumph in the liberation of Indian people from bondage. Internally, among ourselves, in our own communities there are many issues to be discussed—our worldview, religions, social systems, how we relate outside our communities to other Indian people and to non-Indian people. In the international community we must speak with one voice, clearly, and not bring our internal differences to the world to resolve. Only we can do that. We must find those common grounds, and they are many, to present to the world as *Indian* people—one people. When we go to the world community we must speak for all Indian people, not for any one tribe or even many, but as one people with a common oppression. Only then will we be heard and will our support grow, so we may be freer to carry on our many and varied struggles throughout the hemisphere.

3.A.5.

National Resistance Committee

From "Resistance Statements" (1980)

In 1979, President Jimmy Carter renewed Selective Service registration for young men eighteen and over, and draft resistance gained renewed importance. Large numbers of people protested or refused to register, with reasons for opposition ranging from committed pacifism to critiques of US imperialism. The statements were compiled by the antidraft group the National Resistance Committee and published in its newsletter *Resistance News*.

I will not register for the draft. Nor will I cooperate in any way with the Selective Service system or the US military. I realize the possible consequences of my action.

My noncompliance with registration stems from reasons of personal conscience. I believe in nonviolent solutions to international problems, and I refuse to support any system designed for the destruction of human life. Registration for the draft is the equivalent to such support, and is the first step toward killing another human being.

I am a pacifist. But I recognize the existence of an almost infinite variety of reasons to say "no" to registration, and I encourage everyone to resist, no matter what his reason.

I don't like what is happening to my country, to my government, and to my world, and I think that resistance against registration and the draft is a straightforward and effective way to voice my intense dissatisfaction. With enough collective support, I believe that I and other young people like myself can overturn the draft and change the course of foreign and domestic policy.

We must work against the military system and refuse to play games with the government. Such so-called options as medical deferments and legal conscientious objector status are really not options at all, since they inherently favor white, educated, middle-class persons like myself and tacitly support the very system we are trying to abolish. We cannot escape the choice at hand, which is cooperation or noncooperation with registration.

Don't be intimidated by the federal government. It's plain to see, by its bungling of such national and international crises as Three Mile Island and the Iranian situation, that the US government is an overburdened instrument with little power to enforce its policies. I don't think I need fear prosecution by this piece of clay. But I would take my stand no matter what the personal consequences and encourage everyone to do the same.

The draft affects us all. Don't register.

—David Wayte, Santa Cruz, CA

To my fellow citizens:

In just one week I will be asked to register my cooperation with the draft. In a year or two I will be asked to take up a gun or computer terminal to kill men, women, and children fighting or suspected of fighting for food, independence, and freedom. I will refuse.

Registration is so simple; walk down to the local post office and fill out a postcard. So easy to forget what you are really doing. Your registration says to the government, "Come and get me when you want me, I'll be your slave, I'll kill without question." When you register not only do you register away your life, but also your conscience.

Do not be taken in. War for oil is a good battle cry in an election year. That's what Iran and Afghanistan are all about. Politicians who ask for sacrifice to save oil to protect national security are driven from office. The politicians who threaten war, tempting a nuclear holocaust, for that same oil, are reelected by landslides. Ask yourself for whose interests you will be fighting for in the third world? Are your interests the same as those of the multinational conglomerates that exploit cheap labor and resources overseas? When those companies move their factories it is Americans who become unemployed.

Because registration is not in our interests, nonregistration has been made hard and registration simple. Nonregistrants face possible years of imprisonment and gain nothing except peace of mind. But refusal to register interrupts the entire military machine, lessening the chance of draft or war. Do not wait until it is too late; if a draft is wrong, resistance must begin now.

—David Drager, Courtland, NY

I refuse to register for the draft on the grounds that all outward war or registration for war (particularly that which is based on economics, energy or politics) is a statement that human life has no value beyond the significance of death, or that someone else's life is worth less than my own. I refuse to make that statement and I accept the consequences for this action.

—Nathanial James, Minneapolis, MN

Draft Resistance, 1979–1985

Matt Meyer

In 1973, activists had succeeded in ending the draft: widespread opposition and resistance, including mass rallies centered around draft card burnings, won a suspension of military conscription. But in 1979, President Jimmy Carter called for reinstitution of registration—the first and essential name-and-address-collecting phase of the draft process. Beginning in June 1980, all eighteen-year-old men were required to register for the draft. Resurrecting a slogan popularized in the 1960s, many thousands declared, "Hell no, we *still* won't go!"

An unlikely coalition organized the Mobilization against the Draft in Washington, DC, on March 22, 1980. More than thirty thousand people participated in the march. The event brought together major leaders of the anti–Vietnam war movement, including Kwame Ture (formerly Stokely Carmichael), Dave Dellinger, Pete Seeger, and Women's Strike for Peace. The coalition also included democratic socialists, religious leaders, Students for a Libertarian Society, the American Civil Liberties Union, and the newly formed Committee against Registration and the Draft (CARD). That summer, the coalition succeeded in scheduling a speaker at the Democratic National Convention give an antireg-istration speech on the floor of the convention.

After Ronald Reagan was elected president, the tide of antidraft attention largely turned to the small but vocal group of young men who decided to publicly refuse to register and who faced up to five years in prison and $10,000 fines for their refusal. After just a few months of mounting opposition the draft resisters received national media attention in early 1981. Only twenty indictments were ever issued, mostly targeting resisters from largely military towns; Ben Sasway of San Diego was the first. Nine of the twenty indictees were incarcerated, most for six months or less.

Groups like CARD, Black Veterans for Social Justice, the United States Student Association, the Progressive Student Network, and especially the National Resistance Committee became centers of revitalized organizing. Building on historic opposition to the draft, the intense, ideologically diverse grassroots organizing between 1979 and 1985 rendered a significant militaristic policy largely moot.

3.A.6.

Women's Pentagon Action

"Unity Statement" (1980)

Women's Pentagon Action formed in 1980 through a nonviolent direct action in which women marched from Arlington Cemetery to the Pentagon, encircling that building and carrying out symbolic act of mourning and protest. It continued for several years as a feminist antinuclear organization and contributed significantly to the development of ecofeminism.

We are gathering at the Pentagon on November 16 because we fear for our lives. We fear for the life of this planet, our Earth, and the life of the children who are our human future.

We are mostly women who come from the northeastern region of our United States. We are city women who know the wreckage and fear of city streets; we are country women who grieve the loss of the small farm and have lived on the poisoned earth. We are young and older, we are married, single, lesbian. We live in different kinds of households: in groups, families, alone, or as single parents.

We work at a variety of jobs. We are students, teachers, factory workers, office workers, lawyers, farmers, doctors, builders, waitresses, weavers, poets, engineers, home workers, electricians, artists, and blacksmiths. We are all daughters and sisters.

We have come here to mourn and rage and defy the Pentagon because it is the workplace of the imperial power that threatens us all. Every day while we work, study, and love, the colonels and generals who are planning our annihilation walk calmly in and out of the doors of its five sides. They have accumulated over thirty thousand nuclear bombs, at the rate of three to six bombs every day. They are determined to produce the billion-dollar MX missile. They are creating a technology called Stealth—the invisible, unperceivable arsenal. They have revised the cruel old killer, nerve gas. They have proclaimed Directive 59, which asks for "small nuclear wars, prolonged but limited." The Soviet Union has worked hard to keep up with US initiatives. We can destroy each other's cities, towns, schools, and children many times over. The United States has sent "advisors," money, and arms to El Salvador and Guatemala to enable those juntas to massacre their own people.

The very same men, the same legislative committees that offer trillions of dollars to the Pentagon have brutally cut day care, children's lunches, and battered women's shelters. The same men have concocted the Family Protection Act, which will mandate the strictly patriarchal family and thrust federal authority into our home life. They have prevented passage of the Equal Rights Amendment's simple statement and supported the Human Life Amendment, which will deprive all women of choice and many women of life itself.

We are in the hands of men whose power and wealth have separated them from the reality of daily life and from the imagination. We are right to be afraid.

At the same time, our cities are in ruins, bankrupt; they suffer the devastation of war. Hospitals are closed, our schools deprived of books and teachers. Our Black and Latino youth are without decent work. They will be forced, drafted to become the cannon fodder for the very power that oppresses them. Whatever help the poor receive is cut or withdrawn to feed the Pentagon, which needs about $500 million a day for its murderous health. It extracted $157 billion last year from our own tax money, $1800 from a family of four.

With this wealth our scientists are corrupted; over 40 percent work in government and corporate laboratories that refine the methods for destroying or deforming life. The lands of the Native American people have been turned to radioactive rubble in order to enlarge the nuclear warehouse. The uranium of South Africa, necessary to the nuclear enterprise, enriches the white minority and encourages the vicious system of racist oppression and war.

The US president has decided to produce the neutron bomb, which kills people but leaves property (buildings like this one) intact. There is fear among the people, and that fear, created by the industrial militarists, is used as an excuse to accelerate the arms race. "We will protect you," they say, but we have never been so endangered, so close to the end of human time.

We women are gathering because life on the precipice is intolerable. We want to know what anger in these men, what fear, which can only be satisfied by destruction, what coldness of heart and ambition drives their days. We want to know because we do not want that dominance, which is exploitative and murderous in international relations, and so dangerous to women and children at home—and we do not want that sickness transferred by the violent society through the fathers to the sons.

What is it that we women need for our ordinary lives, that we want for ourselves and also for our sisters in new nations and old colonies who suffer the white man's exploitation and too often the oppression of their own countrymen?

We want enough good food, decent housing, communities with clean air and water, and good care for our children while we work. We want work that is useful to a sensible society. There is a modest technology to minimize drudgery and restore joy to labor. We are determined to use skills and knowledge from which we have been excluded—like plumbing or engineering or physics or composing. We intend to form women's groups or unions that will demand safe workplaces that are free of sexual harassment and equal pay for work of comparable value. We respect the work women have done in caring for the young, their own and others, in maintaining a physical and spiritual shelter against the greedy and militaristic society. In our old age we expect our experience, our skills, to be honored and used.

We want health care that respects and understands our bodies. Physically challenged sisters must have access to gatherings, actions, happy events, and work. For this, ramps must be added to stairs and we must become readers, signers, and supporting arms. So close, so many, why have we allowed ourselves not to know them?

We want an education for children that tells the true story of our women's lives, which describes the earth as our home to be cherished, to be fed as well as harvested.

We want to be free from violence in our streets and in our houses. One in every three of us will be raped in her lifetime. The pervasive social power of the masculine ideal and the greed of the pornographer have come together to steal our freedom, so that whole neighborhoods and the life of the evening and night have been taken from us. For too many women, the dark country road and the city alley have concealed the rapist. We want the night returned: the light of the moon, special in the cycle of our female lives, the stars, and the gaiety of the city streets.

We want the right to have or not to have children—we do not want gangs of politicians and medical men to say we must be sterilized for the country's good. We know that this technique is the racists' method for controlling populations. Nor do we want to be prevented from having an abortion when we need one. We think this freedom should be available to poor women as it always has been to the rich. We want to be free to love whomever we choose. We will live with women or with men or we will live alone. We will not allow the oppression of lesbians. One sex or one sexual preference must not dominate another.

We do not want to be drafted into the army. We do not want our young brothers drafted. We want *them* to be equal with us.

We want to see the pathology of racism ended in our time. It has been the imperial arrogance of white male power that has separated us from the suffering and wisdom of our sisters in Asia, Africa, South America, and in our own country. Many North American women look down on the minority nearest them: the Black, the Hispanic, the Jew, the Native American, the Asian, and the immigrant. Racism has offered them privilege and convenience; they often fail to see that they themselves have bent to the unnatural authority and violence of men in government, at work, at home. Privilege does not increase knowledge or spirit or understanding. There can be no peace while one race dominates another, one people, one nation, or where one sex despises another.

We must not forget the tens of thousands of American women who live much of their lives in cages, away from family, lovers, all the growing-up years of their children. Most of them were born at the intersection of oppressions: people of color, female, poor. Women on the outside have been taught to fear those sisters. We refuse that separation. We need each other's knowledge and anger in our common struggle against the builders of jails and bombs.

We want the uranium to be left in the earth and the earth to be given back to the people who tilled it. We want a system of energy that is renewable, that does not take resources out of the earth without returning them. We want those systems to belong to the people and their communities, not to the giant corporations that invariably turn knowledge into weaponry. We want the sham of Atoms for Peace to end, all nuclear plants to be decommissioned, and the construction of new plants stopped. That is another war against the people and the child to be born in fifty years.

We want an end to the arms race. No more bombs. No more amazing inventions for death.

Figure 3.2. Terry Forman and Fireworks Graphics Collective, "¡Si Nicaragua Venció, El Salvador Vencerá!" Copyright © Fireworks Graphics Collective. Image courtesy of Lincoln Cushing/Docs Populi. Reprinted with permission by Scott Braley.

We understand all is connected. We know the life and work of animals and plants in seeding, reseeding, and simply inhabiting this planet. Their exploitation and the organized destruction of species never to be seen again threaten and bring us sorrow. The earth nourishes us as we with our bodies will eventually feed it. Through us, our mothers connected the human past to the human future.

With that sense, that ecological right, we oppose the financial connections between the Pentagon and the multinational corporations and banks that the Pentagon serves. Those connections are made of gold and oil. We are made of blood and bone; we are made of the sweet and finite resource, water. We will not allow these violent games to continue. If we are here in our stubborn thousands today, we will certainly return in the hundreds of thousands in the months and years to come.

We know there is a healthy, sensible, loving way to live, and we intend to live that way in our neighborhoods and on our farms in these United States and among our sisters and brothers in all the countries of the world.

3.A.7.

Armed Resistance Unit

"Communiqué from the Armed Resistance Unit, April 26, 1983" (1983)

The Armed Resistance Unit was formed by anti-imperialist white revolutionaries with histories in the May 19 Communist Organization, Prairie Fire Organizing Committee, and Weather Underground. From 1983 to 1985, the group carried out several bombings of US government and military sites, providing taped warnings to ensure only property damage would be committed. The group's members were arrested in 1985 and later charged in the Resistance Conspiracy case.

Solidarity with the peoples of Central America! Fight US imperialism!

> inside the belly of the beast [. . .] we must build an active resistance to the US war machine

Tonight we attacked Fort Lesley McNair Military Base in Washington, DC. Fort McNair houses one branch of the US War College, the National Defense University, and the Inter-American Defense College (IADC). This action was taken in solidarity with the growing liberation movements in El Salvador, in Guatemala, and throughout Central America and with the socialist government of Nicaragua. This region today is the center of world revolution and the front line in the defeat of US imperialism. For this reason, it is currently the target of the most vicious US counterrevolutionary attacks.

At the IADC, the US government trains high-ranking military officers from Latin America in its program of counterinsurgency warfare. Trained in torture and terror, tied to the US military and the CIA, its graduates are responsible for the overthrow of progressive and democratic governments throughout Latin America and for the establishment of fascist military regimes that oppress the masses of people. They are responsible for the murder of over thirty thousand El Salvadorans. The IADC serves to keep Latin America as the backyard of Yankee imperialism and the graveyard of millions.

The people of El Salvador, under the leadership of the FMLN/FDR [Farabundo Martí National Liberation Front/Revolutionary Democratic Front] are fighting to end the oppression. Their righteous struggle for peace, self-determination, economic and social justice is a beacon for the peoples of Latin America and the world who have seen their lives, labor, and resources sacrificed for the enrichment of US imperialism and its multinational corporations.

The US response is to use all the techniques of counterinsurgency taught at the IADC. Green Berets fight directly in El Salvador while thousands of El Salvadoran government troops train at Ft. Bragg and Ft. Benning, hundreds of millions of dollars of military aid is given to the junta, and massive "war games" are conducted by US troops throughout the region. The CIA has hundreds of agents in Central America and is training and supplying thousands of mercenaries and ex-members of Somoza's National Guard, who are currently invading Nicaragua. The US is openly transforming Honduras into a garrison state to implement US military strategy in the region. Facing military defeat in El Salvador, the US is implementing "rural pacification" programs that will result in the deaths of tens of thousands, the forced displacement of hundreds of thousands of campesinos into barbed-wire-enclosed strategic hamlets, and the destruction of the land. Faced with a people's war, the US attempts to kill the people. This is full-scale counterinsurgency war, and we must actively oppose it.

This is not the policy of just one bad administration. It is the reality of US imperialist control in the Third World. It is the result of a system based on maximizing profit for relatively few through the oppression and exploitation of hundreds of millions throughout the world and within its own borders. Caught in a political and economic crisis of its own making, faced with the growing struggles of people throughout the world for national liberation and socialism, the response of the US is war, fascism, and genocide.

The courage, sacrifice, and determination of the people of El Salvador is an inspiration to oppressed people throughout the world. Our action is part of the growing worldwide solidarity with that struggle.

We in the US are inside the belly of the beast. Solidarity is growing, but alongside our protest we must build an active resistance to the US war machine. The growing militarization of our society means that the military is everywhere—and vulnerable to our action. Recruiting stations dot neighborhoods, ROTC functions on campuses, factories produce the weapons, military bases train the men. Resistance is not only an act of solidarity—it is the basis for our own revolutionary movement.

El Salvador will win, Guatemala will win, the people of Latin America and the Caribbean will be free, US imperialism will be defeated.

Comandante Ana Maria (Melinda Anaya Montes) esta presente
Victory to the FMLN/FDR!
Solidarity with the peoples of Central America!
Build a revolutionary resistance movement!
Fight US imperialism!
Defend the Nicaraguan revolution!

3.A.8.

Palestine Human Rights Campaign

From "No Vietnams in Central America or the Middle East" (1984)

Formed in 1977 and backed by a broad array of prominent radicals, the Palestine Human Rights Campaign (PHRC) sought to expose abuses of Palestinian activists in Israeli prisons and to galvanize the US left to oppose Israeli policy and its US support. This flyer shows that the PHRC hoped to build a broader radical consensus on Israel by comparing US efforts there to those in Vietnam and Central America.

Israel and Central America

The Reagan administration's support for right-wing dictatorships in Central America is well known. But how many Americans are aware that Israel is a key supplier of arms and advisors to these repressive regimes? According to the Stockholm Peace Research Institute, Israel supplied 80 percent of the Salvadoran military's arms from 1972 to 1980, including Uzi submachine guns, Galil assault rifles, fighter and transportation aircraft, rocket launchers, patrol boats, and spare parts. Similar equipment, along with hundreds of Israeli military advisors, have been provided to the genocidal regime in Guatemala. Before the victory of the Sandinistas in 1978, Israel supplied nearly all of the arms used by the Somoza dictatorship.

Israel is also playing a key role in the regionalization of the Central American conflict. General Alvarez of Honduras visited Israel in July 1982 to arrange the purchase of Kfir planes for use against Nicaragua, and Israeli advisors have been seen at Honduran airbases. Israel has already furnished the Honduran air force with Dassault bombers, Arava transport planes, and Westwind reconnaissance planes, making it the most powerful air force in the region. Patrol boats and armored cars have also been sold to Honduras by Israel. . . .

Supporters of Israel argue that such arms sales are made out of purely financial considerations, because of Israel's economic isolation within an over-whelmingly hostile Third World. But Third World solidarity against Israel is a response to Israel's very nature as a settler colonial state, based on the expulsion and/or subjugation of the indigenous Palestinians. The creation and maintenance of Israel as a close ally of the United States owes much to its strategic value as a military strike force for Western interests in the Middle East. But Israel also serves as a convenient proxy for US dealings with repressive regimes in Africa, Asia, and Latin America.

As we have recently seen, the spheres of US military intervention are becoming more closely interrelated. In Lebanon, for example, the US and Israel have intervened to prop up the authoritarian minority regime of Amin Gemayal and the Phalangists against the Lebanese progressive forces and their allies. This direct US military intervention—the first since the Vietnam war—went largely unchallenged by the American peace movement. When more than 230 American marines were killed in Beirut, the Reagan administration was able to use both the precedent of the Lebanon intervention as well as the patriotic hysteria in the US to carry out the preplanned and criminal invasion of the tiny Caribbean nation of Grenada.

The US intervention in Lebanon, the invasion of Grenada, the CIA-sponsored attacks against Nicaragua, the massing of US troops in Honduras, and the positioning of a US taskforce off the Persian Gulf are all part of a Reagan plan for more Vietnam-style interventions around the world. These moves also risk a world nuclear confrontation—a holocaust that could destroy all of humanity.

The Palestine Human Rights Campaign

Established in 1977, the Palestine Human Rights Campaign is a coalition of concerned individuals from peace, academic, civil rights, and religious organizations who are united in support of the national and human rights of the Palestinian people, including

- the right of the Palestinians to full self-determination, including establishment of an independent state in their own homeland.
- the right of Palestinian refugees to return to their homes or, if they choose, to receive full compensation for properties seized by Israel in 1948, 1967, or since.
- full civil rights for Palestinians who are Israeli citizens.
- the right of the Palestinians to be represented by their own leadership, the Palestine Liberation Organization, in any negotiations.

. . . The peace movement can no longer afford to ignore US military intervention in the Middle East, or such issues as the regional and global role of Israel or the plight of the Palestinians. We urge you to join with us in demanding no Vietnams in Central America and the Middle East! US forces out of Lebanon, the Caribbean, and Central America!

We believe that there can be no just peace in the Middle East without recognition of these basic Palestinian rights. But we also work on a day-to-day basis to publicize and protest specific violations of Palestinian human rights, through our national Action Alert Network. We invite you to join us in this vital effort.

The Chilean Solidarity Movement

Tamara Lea Spira

On September 11, 1973, the US-backed Augusto Pinochet military regime overturned Salvador Allende's democratically elected Unidad Popular (UP) revolution in Chile, installing a military dictatorship that would remain in power for seventeen years. The world watched aghast as fighter jets stormed the presidential palace and people were rounded up en masse and tortured in broad daylight. This image clashed violently with the symbolic promise of the Chilean revolution, which had advocated for a peaceful path to socialism through the ballot box. Consequentially, opposition to the dictatorship was diverse and far ranging, encompassing fledgling human rights organizations, anti-imperialist activists, radical cultural workers, and Chilean exiles that organized into transnational networks.

Two main organizations that anchored the ideological poles of the Chilean solidarity movement in the United States were Nonintervention in Chile (NICH) and the National Coordinating Committee in Solidarity with Chile (NCCSC). Founded in 1971, NICH often aligned ideologically with the Chilean armed revolutionary left organization Movimiento de la Izquierda Revolucionaria (MIR). Understanding the Chilean case as one node in a larger war, NICH prioritized the linking of grassroots anti-imperialist movements across contexts through campaigns organized around the CIA's role in supporting imperialist regimes from Vietnam to Chile and, later, Central America. To this effect, it led a boycott of the International Telephone and Telegraph Company (ITT), which symbolized corporate control over Third World peoples and was directly implicated in the overthrow of Allende through its demonstrated ties with CIA efforts to create "economic chaos" to undermine Allende's success. NCCSC, by contrast, centered on questions of human rights and antifascism. Their strategy was to isolate the junta, lobby US Congress, defend high-profile political prisoners by exerting international pressure for their release, and boycott Chilean goods in coordination with organized labor.

The solidarity movement also featured radical cultural workers who organized poetry readings, concerts, and *peñas*, or political and cultural community centers. Homages to Víctor Jara and Pablo Neruda were one catalyst for important events. For example, in October 1973 the Third World Communications Collective, based in San Francisco, organized a poetry reading that was the first public event opposing the coup. Additionally, in their publications and public demonstrations, feminist organizations put forward an intersectional analysis of the dictatorship as bringing together interlocking systems of racism, patriarchy, imperialism, and homophobia.

Throughout the 1980s and 1990s, a core of committed activists sustained efforts to take down the regime from abroad. Journalists exposed the CIA's role in Operation Condor, which was responsible for disappearances, political assassinations, and terror throughout South America. Another sustained hub of solidarity activism was the North American Congress on Latin America (NACLA), a media outlet formed by several North Americans who had been in Chile during the coup and who remained committed to providing analysis of Chile and the culpability of the US state. By the 1980s, however, many activists from the Chilean solidarity movement were shifting their focus to Central America, especially the Sandinista struggle in Nicaragua.

After a long and bitter battle, Pinochet was ousted from power in March 1990 through an electoral referendum energized by massive protest. To critics' chagrin, the transition left intact an enduring system of neoliberalism—or what some referred to as "el Pinochetismo sin Pinochet" ("Pinochetism without Pinochet"). Nonetheless, the practical and symbolic importance of the regime's end cannot be understated, particularly among survivors of the dictatorship. Pinochet's defeat sent a clear message that the international community would not tolerate authoritarian regimes. Further, it set the stage for redemocratization across the region. The solidarity movement was instrumental in bringing this victory; as scholars and activists have argued, it forged a new vocabulary of human rights and, in particular, offered a model for solidarity movements on an international scale.

3.A.9.

Lesbians and Gays Against Intervention

"Principles of Unity" (1983)

LGBTQ people have been active leaders of antiwar, anti-imperialist, and other radical organizing for decades. However, queer activists have sometimes faced hostility from other leftists, especially those asserting that sexual and gender diversity are inherently bourgeois, Western, white, or capitalist. In the 1980s, the Central American solidarity movement became an important place to reject those notions. Lesbians and Gays Against Intervention (LAGAI) was a key organization of LGBTQ radicalism in this era. The group remains active today as LAGAI-Queer Insurrection and through its offshoot Queers Undermining Israeli Terrorism, or QUIT.

Lesbians and Gays Against Intervention was formed in December 1983 by the membership of the Lesbian/Gay Taskforce of the El Salvador Initiative Campaign in San Francisco, California, USA. The initiative called for an end to all military aid to El Salvador. After the victory of the initiative and our effective work as a taskforce, we saw the necessity of continuing our work. We wanted to remain an autonomous gay group in opposition to the role of the US government and corporations in Central America and the Caribbean. US corporations profit handsomely from the control they exercise over the economies in this region. The US government acts hand in hand with these aims as the military/political force which keeps this system of economic slavery institutionalized. This results in the dissolution of local autonomy and a blatant disregard for human rights. As residents and citizens of the US, we elect to support and join in the struggle for freedom and self-determination in Latin America.

Points of Focus

1. *Stopping US intervention in Central America and the Caribbean*: LAGAI's main purpose and major focus is combatting the US government's aggressive role in the internal affairs of Latin America. As residents of the US, we think we have an important role to play in halting the expansion of imperialism. It is imperative that we actively support the popular peoples' struggles in Central America and the Caribbean for self-determination.
2. *Creating gay visibility in the solidarity movement*: The effectiveness of the US solidarity movement will be measured by its ability to mobilize the many sectors of the US population. "Mass" organizations have generally failed to activate a representative percentage of ethnic, racial, and sexual minorities into anti-intervention work. We support the formation of groups whose aim is to organize these various sectors. In light of this, we think the lesbians' and gay men's communities can be more effectively mobilized by a gay group at this time. Many gay people are involved at all levels of solidarity work, but our contributions can be downplayed because of homophobia and our own internalized oppression. LAGAI will fight homophobia in the solidarity movement by creating a visible presence of progressive lesbians and gay men, working in coalition with other solidarity groups.
3. *Working with progressive Caribbean and Central American groups*: LAGAI will contact the various Central American and Caribbean organizations in the San Francisco Bay Area which are working against US intervention. We will work toward building mutually supportive relationships. We support their just struggles for self-determination and human rights. We aim to raise consciousness about the lesbians' and gay men's communities in order to further a better understanding of gay liberation in the US and Latin America.
4. *Solidarity with Latin American lesbians and gay men*: Gay people in Latin America suffer the overall economic and national oppression inflicted by

imperialism. They must also face the daily realities of homophobia in a patriarchal culture. Lesbians also confront sexism in their lives. Gays in some countries throughout the region have organized in various gay and feminist groups. We will contact the existing groups and outspoken individuals to aid the formation of an inter-American progressive lesbian/gay movement/network. There is very little information available in North America about the lives of Latin American gays. Throughout our outreach and through contacts with the media, we will disseminate information that we receive from gays in the region. We will work in various creative ways to support the struggles of our southern sisters and brothers.

5. *Outreach to Third World gay individuals and groups*: Most lesbian and gay male groups are mostly white and fail to address the issues and needs of people of color. LAGAI will be most effective in its work by being a multiracial, multinational organization. Our literature will be printed in both Spanish and English.

6. *Supporting antiracist work in the lesbian/gay men's communities*: Racism must be fought in order to address existing inequalities, prejudices and stereotypes. This struggle is of major importance. In order to create a representative movement, people of color must be empowered. National chauvinism is also a detriment to progress and is rampant in the US. Peoples of other lands are scapegoated for the failure of the US system to meet the needs of its citizens. For instance, undocumented workers are blamed for the job shortage. In reality, the overbloated defense budget robs resources from human services. These cutbacks hit minorities the hardest. Racism and national chauvinism create the smokescreen on which the myth of US superiority is projected. Fighting racism and national chauvinism will enrich the humanity of all people. International solidarity demands an end to these forms of bigotry. It is important that we, as a progressive force in the lesbians' and gay men's communities, be outspoken in support of the struggles of people of color and members of national minorities.

Points of Clarification

1. LAGAI is an *anti-imperialist* group and we fight US expansionism at its source.

2. LAGAI is a *gay liberation* group. We actively fight homophobia. We support our sisters and brothers worldwide, especially those most disenfranchised.

3. LAGAI is a *feminist* group. We support women's struggles and realize the centrality of feminist issues in the general fight against oppression.

4. LAGAI is *internationalist*. Our freedom as lesbians and gay men in the US is integrally linked to the worldwide fight against all forms of oppression.

5. LAGAI is a *left* group. We will fight all forms of red baiting as detriments to the realization of freedom and independence. We are an autonomous

group and are not tied to any existing party or mass organization. We welcome gay people of various progressive politics to join us as individuals.

US out of Latin America and the Caribbean now!

3.A.10.

Marisa Pruitt

"Victoria Mercado Brigade" (1985)

Solidarity brigades served as an important tactic in the Central American solidarity movement. Activists, especially those from the global North and from across Latin America, traveled to Nicaragua under the invitation of the Sandinista government, and to El Salvador and Guatemala in solidarity with leftist and Indigenous groups. The Victoria Mercado Brigade, which traveled to Nicaragua in 1985, was the first such project to be specifically and openly lesbian and gay. This article was published in *Voices*, the newsletter of the Redwood Records Cultural and Educational Fund.

The Victoria Mercado Brigade is a group of lesbians and gay men doing solidarity work against US intervention in Central America and support of people around the world struggling for self-determination.

We see our responsibility as political people to mobilize and educate our communities on the issues of nonintervention and on the importance of the links between our struggle for self-determination and the self-determination of all people. We went to Nicaragua Libre as an open lesbian and gay brigade to make our continuing solidarity with the Sandinista revolution and the people of Nicaragua visible through our concrete work, helping to rebuild the new Nicaragua and to make our work inside the solidarity movement as proud lesbians and gays struggling for a better world visible also.

For years we have worked in organizations in the US solidarity movement. Some of us, foreigners like me, have worked in liberation organizations in our own countries, hiding our lesbian and gay identities. Homophobia in our political groups kept us silent. Often we were made to feel that our issues and concerns, our "lifestyles," were inconsequential private matters. Yet, at the same time, lesbians and gay men were raising issues of sexism, interpersonal power relations, the politics of sexuality, and a critique of the nuclear family and patriarchal culture, all within the context of revolutionary change.

In the seventies and eighties we began to come out of the closet in our work. In response to the assassination of President Salvador Allende in Chile and the murder of hundreds of gays and thousands of civilians in Chile, gay solidarity with the Chilean Revolution [Gays in Solidarity with the Chilean Resistance] was formed in 1973 in San Francisco. BAGL (Bay Area Gay Liberation) was also active in the left, and in 1979 GALA (Gay Latino Alliance) was formed, providing an outlet for Latin gays and lesbians. GALA produced many benefits for El Salvador and Nicaragua and was actively involved with Cesar Chavez and the farm workers. More recently in 1983 a lesbian and gay task force played an effective role in the successful El Salvador Initiative campaign in San Francisco. And in December of last year Lesbians and Gays Against Intervention (LAGAI) was created as a direct outgrowth of this lesbian and gay task force.

In September 1984, after making contact with some Nicaraguan gays and lesbians, the project of a gay brigade to Nicaragua was on its way. The initial organizing and outreach was done by LAGAI. The first meeting was attended by over sixty people with a noticeable lack of people of color. In December 1984 a small group of us formed a Third World Caucus and did our own outreach, achieving more than 50 percent representation in the brigade membership. From this time on the brigade took on another dimension. We, the people of color, held our own separate caucus and prioritized the work. Internal study groups were set, workshops on racism were held, Nicaraguan history and Spanish lessons were mandatory for all brigadistas, discussions of class and culture differences were always taking place. This process was necessary in order to make our group a comprehensive. Today this group of progressive whites and Third World/people of color can say that it was not easy but it worked.

We raised our money through dances, benefits, raffles, and a grant from the Vanguard Foundation. We set scholarships for those who otherwise could not afford to go. We bought the tools for the project in Nicaragua and brought cash to buy materials to do our work. The brigade went to Nicaragua on May 8, 1985, and worked for a month, doing construction work in the very militant barrio, Selim Shible, in Managua. Some of the *brigadistas* went to a resettlement village outside Somoto, which is fifteen kilometers from the Honduran border. Some went to the beautiful mountains of Matagalpa. Dialogue was initiated with the women of AMNLAE, the women's association of Nicaragua. The work situation was under the supervision of the CNSP, Nicaragua Committee in Solidarity with the People. Religious people were contacted, the AMES childcare center was visited, and we took material aid there. And throughout all of our travels and interactions we met lesbians and gays of Nicaragua.

A principle of the Victoria Mercado Brigade is support for the Sandinistas and respect for the Nicaraguan culture. We see Nicaragua as a unique example of a free people demonstrating what tremendous advances are possible when a US-sponsored dictatorship is overthrown. Nevertheless we all know that Nicaragua is still in a state of war and we, as part of the solidarity movement and as oppressed people in struggle, have the responsibility to oppose Reagan's classist and racist policies in the Americas and to work tirelessly to end US involvement in Central America and in the rest of the world. United we will win. *Que viva Nicaragua Libre!*

3.A.11.

Committee in Solidarity with the People of El Salvador

From "Convention Decisions" (1985)

Committee in Solidarity with the People of El Salvador (CISPES) was one of the largest, most influential organizations in the Central American solidarity movement. Defining itself as "the North American front of the Salvadoran revolution," it worked in support of El Salvador's Frente Farabundo Martí para la Liberación Nacional, or Farabundo Martí National Liberation Front (FMLN), and the Frente Democrático Revolucionario, or Revolutionary Democratic Front (FDR).

CISPES'S Purpose and Goals

The convention strongly affirmed that the main purpose of CISPES is solidarity with the Salvadoran people's struggles for liberation and that our strategy and program should be designed to best meet the needs of the Salvadoran struggle, as opposed to CISPES declaring itself an overall Central America solidarity organization. CISPES's new points of unity now read as follows: "Our central purpose as CISPES is to support the Salvadoran people in their struggle for self-determination. We work to:

1) End all US intervention in El Salvador and all of Central America and the Caribbean.
2) Provide direct support for the Salvadoran people and their struggle through:
    a) material support;
    b) political support for the FMLN-FDR.

Recognizing the regional nature of US intervention in Central America, we further:

3) Support the people of Nicaragua and defend the Sandinista revolution;
4) Support the people and revolutionary movement of Guatemala, the URNG."

While not endorsing a merger with the other two national networks, NISGUA and the Nicaragua Network, the convention delegates voted to increase coordination between the three organizations at all levels. This coordination would be geared towards joint anti-intervention projects and improving the support given the local committees, the vast majority of which do solidarity work for all of Central America.

Strategy and Program

The convention set CISPES's national strategy nearly unanimously [as follows]:

1) CISPES will expose what has become invisible, the step-by-step escalation of US military involvement in Central America and build strong, broad responses to each and every step with a variety of tactics from letter writing to civil disobedience.

2) CISPES will strive to dispel the myth that Salvadoran President Jose Napoleon Duarte is a moderate reformer and clarify to the US public that social, economic, and political conditions have worsened in El Salvador: repression continues, but the Salvadoran people are *still* struggling for peace and social justice. CISPES will bring the reality of El Salvador closer to the people of the US with delegations to El Salvador, tours of Salvadorans here, and aggressive media campaigns.

3) CISPES will dramatically increase its support for the Salvadoran popular movement—the trade unions, teachers, students, human rights groups, and others—through the presence and work of US delegations in El Salvador, stepping up our humanitarian aid to both projects in the cities and the zones of popular control and intensifying our human rights campaigns for political prisoners and the "disappeared."

4) CISPES will conduct intensive grassroots organizing programs based on the house-meeting drive model. Through them we will significantly expand CISPES's base and that of the anti-intervention movement. National CISPES was mandated to make development and training for such organizing drives a priority.

We reaffirmed that CISPES needs to emphasize the connections between social conditions and Reaganomic spending cuts here and social oppression and US military aid in El Salvador in order to build strong people-to-people ties. We agreed that in national campaigns, CISPES should highlight the shared desires of the peoples of the United States and Central America for peace and social justice.

In line with this overall strategy, the convention passed the following programs:

- To expose the terrible reality of the counterinsurgency war in El Salvador, CISPES's *campaign to stop the bombing in El Salvador* will be extended and broadened, with an emphasis on massive public education, congressional pressure, and timely actions.
- We will begin work on a major national anti-intervention campaign for 1986, *Cities for Peace in Central America*, which [will] involve a range of local coalitions and organizations in citywide ballot initiatives and related efforts across the United States, timed to coincide with the 1986 congressional elections.
- Our *congressional pressure* campaign will focus on the administration's attempt to secure almost a half a billion dollars in aid to the Duarte regime

in the fiscal year 1986 budget to be voted on this fall. We will oppose this aid, and all future aid, by combining pragmatic lobbying with escalating protest, including September '85 national days of action.

- An exciting package of new *people-to-people* programs was passed, including greatly expanded support to the developing popular movement in El Salvador. For our work in the US, an overall goal of $300,000 in humanitarian aid was set to be raised by CISPES committees in the coming year, in particular for new medical aid projects in El Salvador. The convention strongly endorsed as many solidarity activists as possible traveling to El Salvador to meet and work with the various opposition organizations in the urban areas.
- Proposals for a *national media coordinator* and production of resources dealing with the true record of President Jose Napoleon Duarte and the situation in his government in El Salvador passed easily. With an increased commitment to CISPES's student organizing, developing *student-to-student* ties and material support for the University of El Salvador and the Salvadoran Students Association, AGEUS, was unanimously voted as the number one priority for our student work, and a proposal to support *campus sanctuary* work was also passed.
- Finally, in the crucial area of building our capacity to respond to the constant, incremental US escalation in Central America and El Salvador, we agreed to both expand CISPES's participation in the pledge of resistance and to develop our own *CISPES emergency response network*.

Movement Building and Alliances

The convention adopted a movement-building strategy that concentrates CISPES' efforts on building a "sharply-focused anti-intervention movement." Specifically, CISPES will initiate and deepen joint work with those organizations that will develop a broad national movement whose primary purpose is to halt US intervention in Central America. This includes:

the religious community, and working to support the Sanctuary movement and to help build the pledge of resistance;

the peace and disarmament groups that are already opposing war and interventionism in different parts of the world;

the anti-apartheid movement, a strong new current of solidarity with which we have a natural kinship and many common interests;

Black and Latino political leaders, many of whom have taken the strongest public stands against US intervention;

expansion of our grassroots organizing work in the Chicano/Latino communities;

the reviving student movement, a key sector for solidarity organizing;

the anti-intervention wing of the labor movement.

Organizational Issues

Interim bylaws were adopted which established principles of democratic functioning for CISPES, including decision making by majority vote, when consensus cannot be reached. The national convention was defined as the highest decision-making body of CISPES, with the National Administrative Committee (NAC) continuing to be the main decision-making body between conventions. A three-member executive committee was created as the day-to-day decision-making body between quarterly NAC meetings, responsible for implementing the strategy, program, and other policy decisions of the convention and the NAC.

The convention also unanimously approved an affirmative action hiring policy for regional and national staff.

By acclamation, the convention agreed to form the Chicano/Latino Caucus of CISPES, a body that will plan and implement organizing in the Chicano and Latino communities and will represent the perspective of Chicanos and Latinos within CISPES and on the NAC.

Recognizing the growth of student activism, the convention authorized a student commission to further develop CISPES's student work and form a student caucus.

An internal bulletin was agreed to, written by and for local committee members, to extend the productive and lively debate and sharing of experiences at the convention into an ongoing process.

3.A.12.

Witness for Peace

Brochure (1985)

Witness for Peace was founded in 1983 in opposition to the United States' funding and training of the contras, a network of right-wing paramilitaries seeking to unseat the socialist government of Nicaragua. The participants of Witness for Peace, typically working through Christian faith-based groups, traveled to Nicaragua to observe and report contra activity, including human rights violations.

Purpose of Witness for Peace

To develop an ever-broadening, prayerful, biblically based community of United States citizens who stand with the Nicaraguan people by acting in continuous nonviolent resistance to US covert or overt intervention in their country. To mobilize public opinion and help change US foreign policy to one which fosters justice, peace, and friendship.

Although most of us in Witness for Peace are Christians, we welcome others who vary in spiritual approach but are one with us in this effort.

Together, we make the following covenant:

1. We commit ourselves to a prayerful, biblical approach and unity with one another as the foundations for this project.
2. We commit ourselves to nonviolence in word and deed as the essential operating principle for Witness for Peace.
3. We commit ourselves to honesty and openness in our relationships with one another.
4. We commit ourselves to maintaining the political independence of Witness for Peace.
5. We commit ourselves to act in solidarity and community with the Nicaraguan people, respecting their lives, their culture, and their decisions. We will respect the guidelines worked out with the Nicaraguan government in regard to our presence and mobility in the war zones.
6. We commit significant time and financial resources on a regular basis to Witness for Peace.

Witness for Peace is a grassroots, nonviolent, faith-based movement committed to changing US policy on Nicaragua. Central to US policy is the funding of a war against the people of Nicaragua. CIA-backed counterrevolutionaries, or contras, are making repeated incursions into Nicaraguan territory.

In April and July of 1983, US Christians traveled to the border area between Nicaragua and Honduras and witnessed the terrible suffering of the Nicaraguan people as a result of the contra terror. More than one thousand Nicaraguans have been killed, and thousands more have been displaced from their homes.

While the US citizens were on the border, contra violence in that area ceased. Nicaraguans believed that the presence of the North Americans helped to stop the contra attacks. They asked that more North Americans come to Nicaragua. Soon the idea was born of maintaining a continuous, prayerful US presence in the Nicaraguan war zones as an offering of friendship and a witness to the possibility of peace for the Nicaraguan people.

In cooperation with Nicaraguan Christians, Witness for Peace places dozens of North Americans each month in the war zones of Nicaragua. Members of the long-term witness make commitments of six months or more to maintain the continuous presence in Nicaragua. Every two weeks they receive short-term teams of approximately 18 members from different parts of the United States, representing a broad spectrum of church and other religious groups. While in Nicaragua, they hold prayerful vigils, document contra activity, and do constructive work. Upon return to the United States, they engage in press work, public education, and political action.

Witness for Peace is made possible by thousands of other people in the United States who participate in local support work, funding, and public education. They work at the vital task of mobilizing US public opinion to change misdirected US policy. Witness for Peace has participants in every state and is broadly ecumenical.

Because the US government is carrying out a violent and destructive policy against Nicaragua, US citizens have a right and a responsibility to be there to offer a different kind of US presence. Our hope is that Witness for Peace will help save lives; urge the US government to reexamine and change its policy toward Nicaragua; provide a continuous flow of eyewitness reports on the consequences of US policy in the area; and show the Nicaraguans that the policies of the US government do not represent all North Americans.

Witness for Peace is a growing venture in faith. It requires the resources and commitment of many people. We invite you to join us in prayer, in financial support, and in active participation.

The 1980s Sanctuary Movement
Norma Stoltz Chinchilla

Between 1980 and 1991, nearly one million Central Americans, particularly from El Salvador and Guatemala, crossed the US border seeking asylum. The US government, arguing that these were economic migrants fleeing poverty rather than refugees fleeing governmental repression, responded by making the migrants subject to deportation, with their claims to protection summarily denied. Visa approval rates for Guatemalans and Salvadorans, who were fleeing US-backed regimes, fell to under 3 percent in 1984. This stood in contrast to high rates of approval for those coming from communist countries.

The 1980s US sanctuary movement was a religious political movement with two central goals. One was to protect refugees from deportation back to the conditions from which they came. The second was to confront the Reagan administration's policies of material and political support to the de facto military governments that caused the refugees to flee. The United States aided such governments under the guise of combatting communism and Soviet intervention into "our" hemisphere. The sanctuary movement was both a response to a humanitarian crisis and an attempt to address the roots of that crisis, which included the "social sins" of persecution, repression, inequality, and lack of respect for human rights.

The concept of sanctuary has religious roots dating back to ancient times; it is in evidence in the Old Testament account of Moses setting aside cities and places of refuge in Canaan where the persecuted could seek asylum. It is also reflected in the Judeo-Christian tradition of providing protection to persons fleeing the law until their cases can be adjudicated, as well as in the Underground Railroad of the nineteenth century, the hiding of Jews during World War II, the protection of deserters and draft resisters during the Vietnam War, and the safeguarding of women seeking abortions before *Roe v. Wade*.

The 1980s sanctuary movement began in Tucson, Arizona, after Jim Corbett, a Quaker, and John Fife, a Presbyterian minister, along with other residents, were threatened by the Immigration and Naturalization Service (INS, precursor to ICE) for illegally escorting undocumented Central American refugees across the US-Mexico border and providing them shelter in churches and homes. Fife and his congregants publicly declared Tucson's Southside Presbyterian Church a sanctuary on March 24, 1982. Between 1980 and the mid-1990s, more than five hundred churches and temples from a wide range of denominations across the United States joined in the act of civil disobedience of "declaring sanctuary."

Throughout the 1980s, the sanctuary movement was part of a larger movement of organizing around Central America, which opposed US intervention, embraced solidarity with the Nicaraguan revolution, and supported groups seeking change in Guatemala, El Salvador, and Honduras. In cities such as Los Angeles, San Francisco, and Chicago, there was often close coordination among secular and faith-based groups, and membership often overlapped.

The sanctuary movement included both clandestine and public acts of defiance and civil disobedience. Publicly declaring churches, temples, and later university campuses and cities as sanctuaries allowed refugees to tell their stories directly to the US public, which had the effect of challenging the Reagan administration's frame of the Central American conflict as a war of communism versus anticommunism. The social networks of religious institutions reached across categories, such as conservative versus liberal and rural versus urban, in ways that more secular campaigns could not. Furthermore, sanctuary held a moral authority and legitimacy that other groups challenging US policy lacked. The focus on core values and spiritual teachings, together with the powerful stories of refugees, in the context of extraordinary organizing by Central American and other dedicated activists won changes in US foreign and asylum policies.

The situation for immigrant justice activists in the US today is more complex than in the 1980s, requiring a rethinking of the concept of physical sanctuary, especially for people facing deportation who are rooted in local communities and lack remedies for legalizing their status. Storytelling by those directly affected will continue to be a powerful tool for changing hearts and minds, and justice movements that emphasize core values and reach across traditional divides will undoubtedly go farther than those that do not. But in the face of long-term stagnation around immigration reform and a prison industrial complex that incentivizes detentions and streamlines deportations, direct action in the form of disruption will be more important in the effort to dismantle an unjust and inhumane system.

3.A.13.

"The Pledge of Resistance: A Growing, Nonviolent Movement for Peace in Central America" (1986)

The Pledge of Resistance was a national network of individuals and organizations committed to opposing US intervention in Central America through nonviolent direct action, including civil disobedience. It formed in late 1983 in response to the US invasion of Grenada, and by fall 1984 had established a growing national organization.

What Is the Pledge of Resistance?

The Pledge of Resistance is a commitment to join with others in nonviolent opposition to the US war in Central America. All across the United States, people of conscience, including people of faith, have signaled their dissent from this policy by publicly taking this pledge of action.

The Pledge community includes the more than eighty thousand people who have taken this bold step. As the war has widened, many have honored their commitment by participating in nonviolent direct action in their city or town—and by preparing to respond if necessary to a US invasion or other major escalations.

What Are the Pledge's Goals?

The Pledge of Resistance seeks to promote genuine peace with justice in Central America. We work to prevent or halt direct US intervention or other major escalations in Central America; end all support for the war in El Salvador; end all funding for the contras, halt the destabilization of Nicaragua, and lift the trade embargo against Nicaragua; end US intervention in Guatemala and Honduras; and promote a peaceful solution to the conflicts in the region.

How Does the Pledge Resist?

The Pledge opposes the US war in Central America by mobilizing nonviolent grassroots resistance to this conflict. Nationally, the pledge has responded to every major escalation of the war since 1984. Nonviolent direct action takes many forms in over three hundred local pledge groups across the United States. Pledge actions include vigils, leafletting, interfaith services, and demonstrations. In addition, over eighty-five hundred people have been led by conscience to engage in nonviolent civil disobedience.

By publicly protesting this policy, the Pledge has played an important role in stopping military aid to the contras and preventing an outright US invasion. Now, the Pledge is facing the new challenge of halting an ongoing war which puts tens of thousands of people at risk.

The Pledge: Nonviolent Direct Action

Historically, the principles of nonviolent direct action have been used in key American struggles for social change: the women's suffrage movement, the civil rights movement, and the anti-Vietnam War movement. In following this tradition, all who sign this pledge are asked to abide by the following guidelines of nonviolence:

- Our attitude will be one of openness, friendliness, and respect toward all whom we encounter as we engage in our witness against the US war in Central America.
- We will use no violence, verbal or physical, toward any person.
- We will not damage property.
- We will not bring or use any drugs or alcohol other than for medicinal purposes.
- We will not run—it creates panic.
- We will carry no weapons.

Sign the pledge—and help stop the war!

The Pledge of Resistance

I pledge to resist the ongoing US war in Central America! This intervention takes many forms, including:

- financing and directing a costly and bloody war in El Salvador, ranging from aerial bombing of civilians to death-squad killings,
- contra terrorism and political and economic destabilization in Nicaragua,
- support for repression in Guatemala,
- war maneuvers by US Army and National Guard troops throughout Central America,
- the expanding US military presence in Honduras,
- and the persistent, real threat of direct US invasion.

Nonviolent Civil Disobedience Pledge: I pledge to resist this ongoing war by joining with others in acts of nonviolent civil disobedience as conscience leads me! *Nonviolent Legal Protest Pledge*: I pledge to resist this ongoing war by joining with others in acts of legal protest as conscience leads me—and by demonstrating my support for those engaging in nonviolent civil disobedience!

3.A.14.

Rio Grande Defense Committee

From statement regarding US policy in Central America and description of the Border Witness Program (1991)

Since the late 1970s, wars and other conflicts in Central America have spurred large-scale migration of Central American refugees to the United States. In the 1980s and 1990s, the US government set up stiff barriers to those fleeing from right-wing regimes in El Salvador, Guatemala, and Honduras. The Rio Grande Defense Committee of Harlingen, Texas, was one among many efforts to protect these refugees. This document includes excerpts from the organization's newsletter that outline the its concerns about US policy and describe the organization's Border Witness Program for prospective volunteers.

The Rio Grande Defense Committee wishes to express its concern that the Immigration and Naturalization Service [INS] in the Harlingen [Texas] District may be gearing up for another campaign of massive detention of Central American refugees. The erection of the circus tents at PISPC [Port Isabel Service Processing Center] once again is an ominous sign. Last year, these tents became a symbol of injustice, of summary asylum denials and coercive, illegal conditions of confinement. The deportation of several thousand Salvadoran, Guatemalan, and Honduran asylum seekers was carried out at enormous expense and constituted an abuse of asylum rights guaranteed under the 1980 Refugee Act. The INS was found to have violated federal court guidelines in carrying out their campaign of mass deportations.

Refugee legal and social workers in the Rio Grande valley are virtually unanimous in ascribing the current influx of Salvadoran refugees to the high level of repression and political violence in El Salvador since the November 11, 1989, FMLN [Farabundo Martí National Liberation Front] offensive. The US-supported Cristiani government has closed the little political space that remained for nonviolent, open opposition. Refugee workers report that the current group of Salvadoran refugees include persons with very strong asylum claims. *The connection between political violence in Central America and the refugee flow into south Texas has never been more direct and clear.* . . .

We ask that Central American asylum seekers not be crammed into circus tents to coerce them to abandon asylum claims.

We ask that the Immigration and Naturalization Service continue to allow Central American asylum applicants to be released and to travel to their destinations, where friends or families await them.

We ask that the INS and State Department end the policy of attempting to use Mexican authorities to keep refugees out of the US at the cost of the violation of the rights of refugees, who are subject to abuse and extortion in Mexico.

We ask the INS and the State Department to be honest with the American people and to admit that many if not most of the current wave of Salvadorans are bona fide refugees deserving of humanitarian protection.

We ask those who are concerned, or who claim to be concerned with the presence of Central Americans in south Texas, to work to end military aid to the death squads and torturers who murder priests and peasants in El Salvador. Only pressure on the Salvadoran generals through restrictions on military aid will force the Salvadoran government to the negotiating table.

The presence of Salvadoran, Guatemalan, and other refugees in south Texas is the direct consequence of the policy of military intervention being carried out by our government in Central America.

The Rio Grande Border Witness Program

> Shame on you! You who make unjust laws, and publish burdensome decrees, depriving the poor of justice, robbing the weakest of my people of their rights, despoiling the widow and plundering the orphan. What will you do when called to account, when ruin from afar confronts you? (Isaiah 10:2–3)

South Texas, the closest US border to Central America, is a land of torment and fear for refugees seeking safety further north. To reach any northern point, they must first endure the risk of apprehension by the US Border Patrol and subsequent deportation by the Immigration and Naturalization Service. Dozens for whom the way through inhospitable ranch country was too dangerous are buried in paupers' cemeteries. Some who cross the river drown. Most often, refugees who are unaccompanied or in the hands of commercial smugglers face dangers no matter what course of travel they choose: bus, plane, freight train, highway, boat, or walking. Some refugees stand out and are easily identifiable. Their timidity, unsureness of gait, facial features, out of mode dress, nonlocal accent in Spanish, eyes filled with fear and anxiety, make them easy prey for the Border Patrol.

The Program

The Border Witness Program, sponsored by the Rio Grande Defense Committee, exists to create an informed testimony against the current administration's continued denial of Central American refugee rights as they enter the United States at the Texas-Mexico border. This program intends to have informed adults from various parts of the country monitor and record activities of government representatives which violate the rights of refugees and of their defenders. Witnesses are then expected to incorporate this information into presentations and actions in their home communities.

Expectations

Refugees are all around us here. Hundreds of men, women, and children from Central America are detained in INS camps in the valley at any given time. The daily routine is continual, fraught with pressure, and occasionally tense. Much traveling is required. Flexibility, independent thinking, alertness, and a sense of humor are absolutely necessary for everyone. Those with an overriding need for order or with fixed expectations will be frustrated.

Activities

Witnesses will receive guidance, support, evaluation, and instruction from the Border Witness coordinators and other workers. The basic schedule of activities within an eight- to ten-day period (shorter periods arranged by request) includes:

- *orientation*: visits with some of the many providers of social, legal, shelter, and spiritual support services offered here in the valley. Interviews with officials of the detention/deportation system. Detailed written materials are also available.
- *days of witness*: visits to public areas and gathering of information illustrating the persecution of refugees.
- *evaluation*: an opportunity to assimilate what has been learned and decide how best to apply that knowledge to education for action in the witness's home community.

Witnesses will be offered choices in assigned activities. However, all witnesses will be accountable to the coordinators and always expected to function within the program guidelines. Witnesses will not be asked to engage in any activities currently defined by the Justice Department as illegal, and the program will assume no responsibility for anyone who does so.

From Anti-Imperialism to Global Justice

3.B.1.

African Liberation Day Coalition

"Fight Imperialism and National Oppression from the USA to the USA" (1977)

The anti-apartheid movement in the United States held deep roots in Black radicalism. This flyer from the African Liberation Day Coalition draws links between US and South African policies, not least through the countries' shared acronym USA. It further marked an upsurge of organizing across southern Africa.

Fight Imperialism and National Oppression from the USA (Union of South Africa) to the USA (United States of America)!

Today the flames of freedom flash across the African continent and everywhere the people are in rebellion. The great armed struggles against Portuguese colonialism are matched now by the growing struggles against white minority rule in southern Africa and neocolonial rule in countries such as Ethiopia.

In South Africa young people have taken to the streets to demonstrate against the segregation of the apartheid system. Black workers by the tens of thousands are refusing to go to work in the foreign-owned mines and factories. In Zimbabwe (Rhodesia) there is increasing unity between the liberation forces; and the unity of ZAPU-ZANU [Zimbabwe African People's Union-Zimbabwe African National Union] has brought the people of Zimbabwe closer to victory. The ruling whites, who are outnumbered twenty-three to one, can only delay the arrival of democratic majority rule, not stop it. In Namibia (South West Africa), SWAPO [South West Africa People's Organisation] continues to make important gains against the South Africans, while in the north, the Eritrean people advance in their struggle against the Ethiopian military junta. The heroic fight of the African people against oppression has rallied the support of people around the world. As part of this worldwide support movement, the African Liberation Day Coalition, a broad coalition that seeks to unite with others, is calling a demonstration at the White House at 1 p.m. on African Liberation Day, May 28.

On this day thousands of people of all nationalities will be marching on the White House to demand the US out of southern Africa. Why? The struggle in southern Africa is a just one—the struggle against the hated system of apartheid, the African people breaking the chains of white minority rule. People of these countries are saying the end is coming for colonial rule where British and American companies are free to rob the riches of their country, particularly the labor of the people. The African struggle for liberation and independence is a struggle for all who want to see freedom replace tyranny and equality replace discrimination.

In particular, for those who have felt the lash of racial discrimination, the struggle against apartheid and white minority rule is a clarion call. Four hundred years of national oppression prove the rulers of this country will not end discrimination in Africa. Blacks who have been turned away at the hiring halls for the crime of being Black and who have faced the humiliation of systematic inequality know well the US is not serious in reaching a settlement in the interest of the African people, only in its interests—profits ($).

People of all nationalities should stand up for freedom in Africa. We are victimized by the same rulers as the people of Africa, and together we must fight them. These are the same financial magnates like IBM, GM and Polaroid who profiteer from apartheid, drag us into wars we never asked for, force us into unemployment, cut back our social services. We can influence history by supporting the African people as we have in the past in the fight against slavery, the Black liberation struggles of the 60s, and the Vietnam protests. A victory for the African people is a victory for ourselves. It's the African people themselves who are making the change. They are building the struggle for their independence. The African people are not content to let a few Black puppets replace the white settler regime; they are fighting for freedom and independence. *Victory to the people of southern Africa*!! It's a struggle against the white settler states who impose apartheid, concentrate millions into segregated areas, and demand passbooks for Blacks to travel in the country. *Down with white minority rule!*

Backing these settler states has been US imperialism. The US has blocked every move for freedom diplomatically and militarily. Without US support the settler states of southern Africa would quickly collapse. However, the US has demonstrated that it will do everything it can to protect its $1.6 billion investment in southern Africa. Jimmy Carter and Andy Young and the rich men they represent are now trying to trick the American people and divide the African people with their phony scheme of "peaceful transition to majority rule." Imagine that! Right when the African people are on the verge of winning, they want them to lay down their guns and negotiate for their freedom. The African people have said no to that. The American people have said no to that. Let the ruling classes of southern Africa and the US tremble at the onslaught of African revolution!

Waiting in the wings, pretending to be socialists, is the other superpower, the Soviet Union. Using empty promises and wallets full of rubles ($), they hope to use the African peoples' aspirations as a sword against their US rival, so that they can take over. The Soviet Union not only tries to prevent unity among the liberation groups, but it also pits one against the other. While they supported the military junta in Ethiopia, they branded the Eritrean freedom fighters (in Ethiopia) and PAC [Pan Africanist Congress] (Azania) as CIA agents and fronts. This clearly unmasks the great power imperialist policies of the USSR. The people of Africa and the world are increasingly aware of the contention and collusion between the US and the USSR for the resources of Africa. They are determined to enjoy complete freedom and will not exchange one master for another. *US out of southern Africa; superpowers hands off*!!

The African Liberation Day Coalition is calling on all who want to organize and reach out to the millions of potential fighters for freedom to join us. Join our campaign to isolate the white settler states and force the US out of the area.

Educate and mobilize the American people to understand Africa and to reject Carter's phony pretensions of favoring majority rule.

Collect all the necessary material aid that will enable the freedom fighters in Africa to pursue their just cause.

Oppose the US support for the settler states. Demand that banks stop selling the coin that pays for apartheid—the Kruggerand. Stop the arms sales and mercenaries that prop up illegal regimes in Africa. End university investment in corporations that do business in southern Africa.

A crucial part of the support campaign is African Liberation Day. Historically thousands have marched on this day to support the people of Africa. This year we will be making clear that the American people are part of the international movement going for the liberation of Africa. We'll be militant, we'll be loud and serious, we'll be disciplined and we'll be going right up to the doorstep of Jimmy Carter. Thousands of us will be bringing the determination and understanding gained in Selma, the Watts rebellion, the Vietnam mobilizations, the Black Panther movement, and other struggles to reaffirm our desire to see freedom in Africa and an end to the oppression of minority nationalities here in the United States.

The vast majority of working people have nothing in common with the rich rulers of this country or their buddies in South Africa and stand opposed to them. We must unite our ranks. *Now is the time* to stand up. *Now is the time* to bring our forces together. On May 28 we will be out, thousands strong, showing our support for the freedom fighters in Africa. On that day we will yell loud and clear: *US out of southern Africa, superpowers hands off! Fight imperialism and national oppression from the USA to the USA!*

3.B.2.

Bay Area Free South Africa Movement

"Statement of Purpose" (1985)

Overlapping with its base among Black radicals, the anti-apartheid movement held an important foundation among radical labor activists, who
worked to undermine the apartheid regime through targeted strikes and
boycotts. This history is evident in the Bay Area Free South Africa Movement
(BAFSAM), which linked labor, student, and many other activists.

The Bay Area Free South Africa Movement is a local, broad-based grouping of
men and women—members of community, labor, religious, political, peace,
youth, and student movements—who are determined to change the United
States' government policies supportive of the racist apartheid regime in South
Africa.

We are a multiracial group seeking to be firmly based in the Black community and strongly allied with the organized trade union movement, especially
the rank and file. We view our work on economic links between the United
States and South Africa as an important contribution to the momentum of the
growing national Free South Africa Movement. We fully support the liberation movements and the trade union movement of South Africa, and recognize
that these movements are part of the international peoples' struggle for world
peace and justice. We fully support the South African struggle as an extension
of our own struggle in the United States for political and economic equality,
and against racism, sexism, and Reaganism.

History

On November 23, 1984, the longshoremen of the ILWU Local 10 refused to un-
load South African cargo in the port of San Francisco. The Bay Area Free South
Africa Movement was originally launched to give public support to the actions
of those longshoremen. Since that time, BAFSAM has been working with the
community to organize events and channel the growing public outrage over
the racist policies of the South African government and the Reagan policies of
"constructive engagement" that encourage it. Those activities have included:

1. Maintaining an active picket line every week day at the Pacific Maritime
   Association in Oakland, since the original longshoremen refusal to un-
   load cargo,
2. Participating in the civil disobedience which led to the arrests of twenty-
   eight people on this picket line, including twenty-two members of the
   clergy,

3. Originating the Red Ribbon Campaign to encourage members of the community to wear the red ribbon as a visible symbol of their opposition to apartheid,
4. With the Oakland–Berkeley Rainbow Coalition, manning informational tables at shopping centers throughout the Oakland Black community,
5. Holding a successful International Women's Day rally in Oakland, where hundreds of women participated in symbolically burning the hated passbooks all South African Blacks are forced to carry,
6. Holding a children's demonstration on March 15 at the offices of IBM in Oakland to call attention to the role of this corporation in providing the technology the South African government needs to maintain its racist practices,
7. Organizing a BAFSAM student network at East Bay community colleges that has generated various anti-apartheid activities at various campuses; supporting/consulting with student activist leaders at UC Berkeley, San Francisco State, Cal-State Hayward,
8. Contributing to the success of the April 20 mobilizations by participation in the planning/execution of same,
9. Planning and executing a cultural observation of South African Women's Day on August 9 at the Church of All Faiths that was *excellent*—standing room only, with a crowd of 250–300,
10. Implementing a planned BAFSAM/Peace Navy boat blockade of the ship carrying South African goods at San Francisco, Pier 80, August 1985; blockades are planned for each "visit" of such cargo in the future,
11. Writing and lobbying for the divestment legislation passed by the city of Oakland in July 1985; this legislation is considered the most comprehensive and powerful legislation within the nation for a major US city,
12. Initiating, organizing, and cosponsoring the West Coast Campaign to Stop South African Trade, August 17, 1985, [a] meeting of trade unionists, church, community, and progressive organizations to launch coastwide boycott of South African cargo,
13. Initiating "prayer rallies," presentations at First Universe, Allen Temple, and other East Bay churches.

The present focus of BAFSAM includes working with the Oakland Port Commission to encourage them to refuse to accept cargo of South African origin and initiation of boycotts against banks and businesses supportive of the South African regime.

Chair: John George
Coordinators: Lorenzo Carlisle, Franklin Alexander, Willia Gray

Student Activism against Apartheid in the United States

Amanda Joyce Hall

US student resistance to South African apartheid was one of the longest continuous youth movements of the twentieth century, spanning nearly the duration of apartheid itself from 1948 to 1994. It found early roots in African American anticolonial activism and among law students inspired by human rights discourses. In the 1960s and 1970s, migrant and exiled South African students at US universities built on these initiatives, echoing South African liberation groups' call for international sanctions. They advocated the boycotting of South African goods and personal disinvestment from South African finance. In the aftermath of the 1976 Soweto Uprising, in which South African police opened fire on unarmed youth protesting the teaching of Afrikaans in township schools, American students began to target corporations and high-profile institutional investors in the apartheid regime. This shift challenged both corporate America and higher education. Students argued that universities were complicit in apartheid because endowments and staff pension funds reaped dividends from companies conducting business in South Africa; such stock holdings amounted to hundreds of millions of dollars.

The divestment campaign reached its climax in the mid-1980s, with students demanding that higher education be made "South Africa free." Protests sprang up at more than two hundred colleges and universities across the country. From Columbia to Berkeley, the University of Illinois to Spelman, a diverse coalition of students pressured their trustees to divest from all South Africa–related companies. The students, many of whom were women and people of color, built a multipronged movement that reverberated across national borders. Locally, the movement targeted university complicity. Nationally, it challenged the Reagan administration's policy of "constructive engagement," which discouraged apartheid policies while maintaining diplomatic relations, thus circumventing United Nations mandates and global pressure to isolate the regime. Student activism varied from campus to campus, often shaped by geography, demographics, the size of university endowments, and administrative approaches to student protest.

Student leaders employed a variety of tactics. They began by raising consciousness through teach-ins, conferences, symposiums, concerts, film screenings, and meetings. Faced with intransigent administrations, they escalated their demands for divestment through direct action. They picketed trustee meetings, occupied buildings, renamed popular campus spaces, and engaged in guerrilla theater. The most visible tactic was to erect makeshift wooden structures, called shantytowns, on campus quads. The shanties symbolized solidarity with Black South Africans who lived in poverty under apartheid. In daytime, they functioned as the administrative headquarters for student protesters, while at night, students slept in them for months as evidence of their dedication and to ensure that they would not be torn down. Shanty-town protests spread to more than one hundred universities between 1986 and 1987. They stood as the hallmark of student anti-apartheid activism and the culmination of years of campus divestment activities. While direct actions generally led to mass arrests, shantytowns espe-cially attracted harsh, even violent, responses from conservative stu-dents and groups. At Yale and Dartmouth, the shanties were the target of arson, defacement, or demolition on multiple occasions. Campus anti-apartheid groups also faced controversy on the left, as students struggled to navigate interracial organizing. Black student groups pushed activists to focus on racism in the United States and on cam-pus, and some saw shanties as a dilettante white performance of Black subjectivity.

Nonetheless, the student divestment campaign captured public attention and won material change. By the end of the 1980s, approx-imately 150 colleges and universities had divested completely from South Africa. Student activism resulted in some of the first ethical investing policies in universities and the corporate world. The student anti-apartheid movement was the largest youth mobilization since the antiwar protests of 1968, and the young people who participated con-tinued to serve social justice causes for decades, applying their campus experience to union organizing, protecting civil liberties, and speaking out against police brutality. They forged ties across racial and class bar-riers, creating a broad-based coalition that drove the issue of apartheid directly to the heart of American intellectual life.

3.B.3.

Africa Fund

From "National Weeks of Anti-Apartheid Action Spark Spring Campus Upsurge" (1986)

The Africa Fund, associated with the American Committee on Africa, coor-dinated a national network of campus anti-apartheid activism that helped students share information, tactics, and news. This newsletter reveals the scale of campus activism at this time, the popularity of shantytown protests, and student activists' familiarity with South African, Namibian, and global politics.

Protests against US support for apartheid swept across the nation during weeks of anti-apartheid action from March 21—the anniversary of the 1960 Sharpe-ville Massacre in South Africa—through April 6—the anniversary of the execu-tion of African National Congress freedom fighter Solomon Mahlangu.

On fifteen campuses the dramatic construction of shantytowns—symbolizing the living conditions of South African Blacks—provided a major focal point for action as did the April 4 National Divestment Protest Day commemorating Martin Luther King during which many groups tied anti-apartheid action to struggles against racism in this country. In addition, around the March 21 Sharpeville anniversary there were successful efforts to link opposition to US funding for UNITA in Angola and for the contras in Nicaragua. In all anti-apartheid activities occurred on over one hundred campuses in thirty-five states, and more than three hundred protestors were arrested during the weeks of action.

. . . [W]e have seen the campus anti-apartheid movement develop in important ways:

First, there have been serious efforts to link the anti-apartheid movement to struggles against domestic racism. Second, there has also been greater stress placed on providing material and political support for the liberation movements of Namibia and South Africa. This political development has underscored that divestment is a means to assist the liberation struggle and not an end in itself. Third, direct action involving blockades, sit-ins, and building occupations in addition to shanties has become an integral component of campus anti-apartheid organizing. Student organizers feel that the publicity from escalated actions directly discourages US investment in South Africa—in the last year twenty-eight companies announced plans to withdraw—while broadening the student network.

Historic Protests at University of California Berkeley

The University of California system has investments of $2.4 billion in thirty-three US companies involved in South Africa, by far the largest such holdings of any US university. The size of the holdings and intransigent position of the university have led to building blockades at UC Berkeley in December 1984, April 1985, December 1985, and intense protests during the weeks of action.

On March 31 the three main campus anti-apartheid groups—the UC Berkeley Campaign against Apartheid, United People of Color, and the UC Divestment Committee—held a rally of twenty-five hundred people culminating in a march to California Hall, the main administration building. There, protesters constructed fifteen shanties and blockaded the building's entrances, demanding full divestment as well as an end to institutionalized racism as reflected in admissions policies, curricula, and faculty hiring. At 2:00 a.m. on April 1 over one hundred policemen arrested sixty-one protestors defending the shanties while other supporters built barricades preventing police vans from leaving campus for several hours. Next day five hundred people marched back to California Hall and reconstructed twenty shanties. . . . At 2:45 a.m. two hundred policemen in riot gear began an assault on the shanties by arresting all legal observers and clubbing a press photographer, who was hospitalized. Two hundred protestors defended the shanties by linking arms while a crowd twice that size built barricades. . . . Outraged by police brutality, demonstrators fought back with bare hands, bottles, and stones and prevented the buses filled with arrested activists from leaving campus till 7:30 a.m. Over 120 people were arrested and two dozen protesters hurt, many seriously.

The day after the police assault on April 4 eight hundred people rallied on campus, and on April 8 several hundred blockaders shut down California Hall for seven hours, resulting in twelve arrests. Another rally was held on April 29 in which fifteen shanties were brought back onto the campus.

Western States

At UCLA students . . . have maintained a shanty [for six weeks]. . . . Long Beach campus students have also constructed a shanty, and protests occurred at UC-San Diego. At Stanford University students have built several shanties this April.

At the University of Utah in Salt Lake City, students erected their third shanty. . . . At the University of Wyoming in Laramie students . . . forced the school to totally divest . . . of $1.45 million. . . . [A]n anti-apartheid protest was held at the University of Hawaii. . . . [A]t the University of Washington in Seattle, students held a divestment protest involving the symbolic burning of passbooks and constructed a shanty. . . .

Student Actions against IBM

In Portland, Oregon, on April 4 twelve students from Portland State, Reed, and Lewis and Clark Colleges were arrested after a four sit-in at the offices of IBM, a supplier of computers to the South African regime. . . . [F]ourteen students from Brown University and the University of Rhode Island in Providence . . . [and] twelve students from Marist, Dutchess Community, and Vassar Colleges were also arrested for sitting in at IBM offices. . . .

Midwestern States

In Madison students from the University of Wisconsin marched to the capitol green in support of state divestment and built a shanty on April 4, which was then razed by police, . . . reconstructed three shanties the next day before seventy policemen tore them down with protesters still inside, . . . [and] reconstructed ten shanties which were demolished at 5:00 a.m. next morning. . . . [S]tudents at the University of Illinois in Champaign constructed a sprawling shantytown complex, and sixty students were then arrested during a building occupation two days later. In Ann Arbor at the University of Michigan a shanty was built on the center of campus March 20 and was put up again after a fire attack by right-wingers on April 5. Five hundred Michigan students also held a march against racism and apartheid on April 4 which ended in the Black community of Ann Arbor. Western Michigan University students also marched . . . in opposition to the Reagan administration's southern African,

Central American, and domestic policies. . . . [T]here were also protests at University of Chicago, Northwestern, Kansas University, . . . Grinnell College, University of Iowa, University of Minnesota, [and] Macalester College and rallies for state and university divestment in Cleveland and Denver.

Southern States

Following anti-UNITA and divestment rallies during the weeks of action, forty-two activists at the University of Texas in Austin were arrested defending a shanty. . . . At the University of North Carolina in Chapel Hill shanties stood for over four weeks. . . . [I]n Atlanta a large commemoration of Sharpeville was held and on April 4 a picket of Coca-Cola headquarters. Other actions occurred in Houston (with daily pickets of Shell Oil) and at Vanderbilt University (site of a shanty), University of Virginia (sit-in), University of Florida, University of Arizona, Alabama A&M, and a speaking tour [was] organized by the Africa Fund and CISPES which linked US policy in southern Africa and Central America and traveled to Alabama, South Carolina, North Carolina, Texas, and Kentucky. At Duke University seven students were arrested defending a shanty on April 26.

Northeastern States

On April 4 at Yale University students erected shanties on the main campus green, and after several threats the administration had the police demolish the shanties and arrest seventy-eight students on April 14. Since then the Yale coalition has organized blockades of administrative offices resulting in over one hundred more arrests, and on April 22 a community and union civil disobedience of 109 people supported total divestment. . . .

In Washington, DC, the DC Student Coalition against Apartheid and Racism kicked off the weeks of action on March 21 by erecting a shanty outside the State Department to protest US funding for UNITA. At the University of Maryland in College Park students set up a shanty. . . . Georgetown University students staged a reverse apartheid simulation. . . . At Johns Hopkins . . . and American University shanties have also been constructed, and George Washington University students disrupted a trustee meeting. . . .

At Boston University twenty-one students fasted during the weeks of action, and the university attempted to evict one faster for hanging an anti-apartheid banner outside his dorm window. On April 4 three hundred BU students rallied . . . and then joined a rally of five hundred students from thirty-five schools on the Boston Common. Among the participants were Wellesley College activists who had occupied their administration building . . . [and] students from MIT, where eight were arrested. . . . At Harvard students have set up several shanties and a fifteen-foot high "ivory tower" where supportive professors are holding classes. In New Hampshire at Plymouth State College five students were arrested for sitting in. . . . [A]t Keene State College activists staged a "die-in" out-

Figure 3.3. Lincoln Cushing, "End Apartheid" (1985). Image courtesy of Lincoln Cushing/Docs Populi. Reprinted with permission by Lincoln Cushing.

side a trustee meeting before marching in. Smith College was the site of an April 4 rally involving five local schools.

In New York City 350 people marched in the pouring rain on April 4 against CITIBANK, Shell Oil, and Mobil Oil for their South African investments. Participating in the march were students from City University and Columbia University. . . . The same day Dartmouth College students and the United Steel Workers of America cosponsored a rally of 250 people outside Phelps Dodge headquarters on Park Avenue. The Dartmouth coalition brought down their shanty (which had been vandalized by right-wing students) and demanded that Phelps Dodge chairman George Munroe resign from the Dartmouth Trustee Board because of his company's South African operations and hardline anti-unionism.

. . . [A]t Hamilton College in upstate New York two hundred students rallied and occupied the campus business office. . . . [A]t Cornell University twenty students occupied the president's office. . . . Shanties have been up now for over six weeks at Penn State University, where sixty-five faculty members fasted for a week. . . . [S]everal hundred students from Carnegie Mellon University and the University of Pittsburgh held a joint anti-apartheid march. . . . [S]tudents at the University of Pennsylvania held a mock funeral procession. . . . Recently full divestment was achieved at Northwestern ($14 million) and the University of Connecticut ($200,000).

Justice for Janitors

"What Is Justice for Janitors?" (1990)

Catalyzed by sharp cuts to wages and benefits, Justice for Janitors formed as a militant campaign of largely immigrant workers. After two small campaigns in Pittsburgh and Denver, Justice for Janitors gained significant power through organizing in Los Angeles, winning strikes there in 1990 and 2000. The flyer below reflects community outreach during the 1990s strike. Today Justice for Janitors (often referred to as JforJ) organizes with the Service Employees International Union (SEIU) across the United States and Canada.

In the last few years, by underbidding each other, cleaning contractors have slashed the standard of living of their workers. Now, the janitors are fighting back.

While architects such as I. M. Pei, Michael Graves, [and] Cesar Pelli resculpt the image of downtown Los Angeles, cleaning companies such as ISS have turned its buildings into vertical sweatshops. These contractors, in conjunction with the downtown real estate players, have quietly driven janitorial wages to poverty levels. Janitors are easily exploited because they work late at night, isolated and out of public view. By 1988, the minimum wage, without health insurance, had become the norm.

The Justice for Janitors campaign is our response. Earlier this year we negotiated with downtown union contractors a starting rate of $5.00 per hour. By the end of the three-year contract all of us will enjoy health insurance and wages of at least $5.50 per hour.

Justice for Janitors is committed to decent wages and health benefits for all janitors, and one contract that sets the standard for all janitors in all buildings. Until then, cleaning companies will continue to underbid each other by underpaying their janitors. The result will be a struggle that affects all building owners and managers.

The majority of buildings in downtown Los Angeles now use contractors who will provide benefits, pay better wages, and treat us with respect. However, our fight is far from over. At $5.00 per hour, we still earn less than the poverty level. Contractors such as ISS threaten to replace union companies by paying the minimum wage and no benefits.

We are fighting back on several fronts. The majority of janitors in downtown's nonunion buildings have joined the union and take part in demonstrations and other actions. We are in court to compel ISS to arbitrate its refusal to abide by the union contract. Inevitably, building owners and managers are drawn into these lengthy, expensive proceedings. Although our current efforts are to unionize downtown, any building that uses contractors that pay substandard wages will be held accountable. We have also carried out actions at private country clubs, fancy restaurants, and in exclusive neighborhoods of contractors and building owners who exploit us.

Billions of dollars are being invested and earned in the development of downtown, while we suffer with no health coverage and starvation wages. Developers who participate in and profit from the creation of LA's new downtown must meet the basic levels in our current contract. And multinational cleaning companies such as ISS should not be able to cash in on the downtown real-estate boom by exploiting their workers.

3.B.5.

Lillian Galedo

"No One Is 'Illegal'" (1994)

Anti-immigrant racism won a growing voice at the ballot box in the 1990s. One example was California's Proposition 187, which sought to bar undocumented immigrants from publicly funded schools, health care, and other services. Organizers in communities of color fought back, protesting criminalizing rhetoric and reframing histories of immigration. This essay, published in the newsletter of Filipinos for Affirmative Action and written by the organization's director, provides an example.

"No one is illegal" is a slogan promoted by the Coalition for Immigrant and Refugee Rights and Services (CIRRS) which represents the sentiments of many immigrant and civil rights organizations. In the face of reckless anti-immigrant hysteria that is sweeping California, it would be prudent to remember this slogan.

With Proposition 187 on the November ballot and attacks on immigrants as the centerpiece of Governor Pete Wilson's reelection campaign, we will be bombarded with more anti-immigrant scapegoating. Even liberal political figures have convinced themselves that some concession to this hysteria is necessary to insure their political survival. Their response has been to say, "We're not against immigrants. We're just against illegal immigrants." This has led to proposals to exclude undocumented immigrants from coverage under the single-payer health proposal, to send the National Guard to the Mexican border, to support sanctions for employers who hire the undocumented, and more and more legislation against the undocumented themselves.

It is not uncommon to hear Filipino voices in the debate also saying that penalizing the undocumented, even children, is only just because they are here illegally. Others argue that the undocumented are Mexicans and Central Americans, not Filipinos. We need only worry when attacks are made against "legal" immigrants.

We deny the fact that undocumented immigrants exist in our own community in significant numbers [and maintain] that advocating policies against the undocumented divides us against ourselves.

Filipinos (or Chinese) may rank fifth among the nation's undocumented after Mexicans, Central Americans, Canadians, and Italians. (Filipino undocumented are thought to number less than twenty thousand nationally.) In California, Filipinos are possibly the third largest undocumented population. These people are not strangers—they are our mothers and fathers, grandparents, aunts and uncles, brothers and sisters and yes, they are children, too.

Why do they come here if they know it's against the law, when others had to wait years to get precious visas? The truth is that they leave the Philippines without documents for the same reasons that people leave with documents. The economy of the Philippines cannot support its populace. They come to the US for the same reasons that many of the rest of us did, to be with immediate family members. Their reasons are compelling, not frivolous, and cannot be denied: survival itself, hope for a future for their children.

US presence in the Philippines contributed to the problems of economic dependence and political repression which increases the pressure to immigrate. This can be said of El Salvador, Haiti, Mexico, the list goes on. Our government has a responsibility to the fate of the people of countries where our foreign policy has contributed to economic and political instability.

Today there are one hundred million people in migration across the globe. Never before in the history of this planet have so many people been uprooted. Their movements reflect the continuing globalization of economic and social forces that have displaced millions of people. The governments of the world, including our own, must turn their attention to finding global solutions if we want to curb world migration.

Filipinos are part of this enormous diaspora that is caused by war, ravaged economies, environmental degradation, and political and social instability.

Proposals such as Prop 187 are just another smoke screen for the real problems that our leaders are not addressing. Immigrants did not close California's defense plants, cut taxes and social services, pass NAFTA, loot savings and loans, or formulate the economic policies which throw people out of work. We will not solve these problems by making scapegoats of undocumented.

Asian Immigrant Women Advocates' Garment Workers Justice Campaign

Stacy Kono

In 1992, a group of twelve Chinese immigrant garment workers from Lucky Sewing Company in Oakland, California, approached the offices of the community-based organization Asian Immigrant Women Advocates (AIWA). In an experience common to many workers in the industry, this group of workers' paychecks had bounced, and their boss closed the doors to the business. As a subcontracting industry in which immigrant-owned garment factories compete for jobs from multimillion-dollar manufacturers and retailers, factories would bid the lowest amount to win contracts—leaving immigrant garment workers with sweatshop working conditions and low wages, if they were paid at all. Workers who confronted their bosses were often fired and blacklisted from the industry.

AIWA had opened its doors in 1983 with the mission of improving the living and working conditions of immigrant women, providing literacy classes, workers' rights workshops, and leadership training. AIWA conducted research with the workers from Lucky Sewing Company and found that they had been sewing the Jessica McClintock (JM) label—a San Francisco company known for fancy wedding and prom dresses and owned by the eponymous business owner. Understanding that manufacturers held the power to change their workplace dynamic, the workers courageously decided to approach McClintock herself, asking her to meet with them and to take responsibility for their unpaid wages. When she declined to meet with the workers, they launched a national direct action campaign and boycott, one of the first corporate responsibility and antisweatshop campaigns of the 1990s.

Chanting "Boycott McClintock," workers and supporters conducted creative direct actions outside McClintock's mansion in a wealthy San Francisco neighborhood. They picketed in front of her boutiques in New York, Beverly Hills, Minneapolis, and Chicago and in front of her flagship store in San Francisco—which closed in 1995 due to the pressure from the campaign. A wide array of supporters joined the campaign, from labor and women's rights leaders to Asian American activists, who defied the model minority stereotype of quiet obedience. High school students publicized the boycott to their peers at prom time, and activists interrupted wedding shows where JM dresses were being modeled.

In 1996, McClintock finally buckled under the national grassroots pressure and sat down with Lucky Sewing Company workers to reach a significant settlement. Workers received monetary contributions, and McClintock pledged to establish an education fund for garment workers and their families and to set up bilingual hotlines for workers to report violations to the McClintock company directly. Several other Bay Area manufacturers followed suit in establishing corporate responsibility programs to monitor the conditions in their contractor factories, a significant win for garment workers.

The most important accomplishment of the campaign, however, was the visible and powerful leadership of immigrant women. At the first direct action at McClintock's San Francisco headquarters, the women had been so intimidated that they wore masks. But over the course of the campaign, immigrant women spoke out publicly at rallies, testified at hearings, and trained other workers to take collective action. As a result, AIWA leaders have expanded their campaigns to include working for health and safety on the job and on issues of language access in the workplace. At the heart of these fights, AIWA continues to foster the leadership and collective power of immigrant women workers.

3.B.6.

Nora Rosenberg

"The Sweat-Free Campus Campaign" (1998)

College campuses witnessed thriving new forms of labor organizing in the late 1990s. United Students Against Sweatshops—a federation of affiliated student groups—coordinated local campaigns around the country in support of service, clerical, and other workers at colleges and universities, as well as in solidarity with workers who produced collegiate apparel, often in sweatshops. The following article was first published in the newsletter of the Center for Campus Organizing, a national organization that trained and networked student activists.

At BJ&B, a Korean-owned sweatshop in the Dominican Republic, more than two thousand workers, mostly teenage girls and young women, spend fifty-six hours a week stitching Champion baseball caps. One factory worker told the US garment union UNITE that "when you get in trouble, the managers will grab your face and smack you on the head. There is one that goes around with a stick and will hit you on the head with it."

The women worry that their managers will touch them inappropriately. No one dares to drink the "drinking" water; it is contaminated. The prospect of ever purchasing one of the baseball caps they sew is nonexistent. With an income of $40 per week, they are unable to cover basic living expenses for themselves, let alone for their families. When workers tried organizing to demand better conditions, BJ&B management retaliated with mass firings of suspected union sympathizers.

Several thousand miles away, the baseball cap sits on a shelf in a university bookstore, with a $19.99 price tag dangling from it. It is embroidered with an emblem of school pride: a university's logo or insignia. Ultimately, it is purchased and lands upon a head that will never stop to think about that hat's history. The consumer has no way of knowing that of the $19.99 they paid, the worker receives a meager eight cents.

Juxtaposing the lives of the producers and consumers of our college gear reveals the striking discrepancy between poverty and privilege. Unfortunately, the sweatshop conditions uncovered at BJ&B are not the exception; they typify the garment industry.

Over the last year, a grassroots movement has been sprouting up on campuses across the country in an effort to reform industry practices and create space and respect for union organizing in these factories. Student activists are working on an effort known as the Sweat-Free Campus Campaign. We are pressuring our universities to adopt codes of conduct, business and labor standards that companies must adhere to in order to maintain and renew their licensing agreements.

Duke University and Brown University passed codes of conduct last spring. These codes require companies that the universities license with to comply with basic labor standards. For example, the codes require companies to limit weekly hours to avoid forced overtime, eliminate or refrain from using forced or child labor, pay a minimum wage, maintain a safe and healthy work environment, and respect the right to freedom of association and collective bargaining.

In response to a decade of companies adopting codes of conduct that serve as public relations tools, not reform instruments, students are pushing their universities to adopt independent monitoring. Working as an enforcement system, independent monitoring is a process of external groups regulating factory compliance through worker interviews, as well as both scheduled and unannounced factory inspections. Ideally, this work will be done by credible labor, human rights, and religious groups that already have the trust of the local workers.

In July, activists from about thirty colleges and universities met at a conference in New York to discuss strategy and structure for the Sweat-Free Campus campaign. We organized into a national coalition, United Students against Sweatshops (USAS). Through an e-mail listserv, USAS maintains an ongoing dialogue of code-related issues and coordinates unified campus actions. We also seek to expand to new campuses.

Currently, USAS is directing its energy toward two issues that companies, and subsequently school administrations, find unfriendly: full public disclosure and living wages. Public disclosure would require companies to provide the university community with basic information—names, addresses, and contact information—of contracting and subcontracting factories. It allows students or local nongovernmental organizations to investigate these factories, ensuring that companies are abiding by the principles of the code and that monitors are fulfilling their functions. Public disclosure is a check on the entire system, providing workers with an added tier of protection and companies with an added level of pressure.

USAS activists are committed to including a living wage provision in all new codes and adding them to all existing codes. A living wage is enough purchasing power to at least cover basic costs of living for the average size family, plus a small discretionary amount. A small sum out of the company's pocket can make a huge difference in the hands of a worker, twenty-four cents instead of eight cents for the $19.99 Champion hat would be sufficient to account for this. Surely Champion could cough up sixteen extra pennies.

Both the Duke and the Brown Codes currently lack living wage clauses; they only require companies to pay the minimum wage. However, in most countries, from the developing world to the United States, minimum wages are insufficient for meeting basic needs. In order to attract industry to their countries, governments compete in a race to the bottom in terms of wages. We, as university consumers, can break this trend by pressuring companies.

In recent months, a great deal of effort has centered on getting student representation on the Collegiate Licensing Company (CLC), a middleman between hundreds of licensing companies and 160 universities. Licensing directors and CLC lawyers are currently in the process of finalizing a CLC code which has thus far ignored USAS pressure for student representation. USAS fears that without a USAS voice, the CLC will come out with a weak code which lacks the necessary provisions, especially a living wage and full public disclosure. A code of conduct that, for example, does not require a living wage is a stamp of approval on worker poverty. In December and January, the CLC code will be distributed to all 160 schools for comment and adoption. USAS is planning actions to pressure our administrations to pressure the CLC to adopt meaningful standards.

Expanding the number of campuses with sweat-free campaigns, and ultimately with strong codes, is crucial. Without this strong base of solidarity, companies may abandon their contracts with individual schools, rather than changing their labor practices.

We can be influential if we exercise our collective power as market consumers to demand corporate responsibility in employment and workplace practices. Almost every material object we encounter is an artifact with a history of human labor. We must question the nature of this history and then demand that these goods come from workplaces that respect human, civil, and labor rights.

It is ironic that allegedly enlightened universities, many of which have mission statements that value community stewardship, engage in behaviors that promote exploitation. For our school logos to truly represent excellence they must be stitched under sweat-free circumstances. The only sweat involved in a sweatshirt should be the proud sweat of the athlete who wears it, not the suffered sweat of the workers who produce it.

3.B.7.

Jessica Roach

"Strawberry Workers Fight to Organize" (1998)

In addition to organizing on campus, student labor activists in the 1990s also worked in solidarity with agricultural, manufacturing, and service workers seeking union power, better wages, and dignity on the job. Many campaigns were bolstered by students training with formal unions, such as the AFL-CIO Organizing Institute, or by formations such as the Student Labor Action Coalition. These efforts, as seen through the strawberry worker campaign on the West Coast, emerged at the nexus of labor, immigrant, radical people of color, and global justice activism.

Last April, a few UW [University of Washington] students trekked down to Watsonville, CA, and rallied with forty thousand other people in support of a campaign by the United Farm Workers (UFW) to organize California's strawberry industry.

The campaign came to campus last quarter with the founding of the Strawberry Worker Solidarity Coalition (SWSC). Members of the SWSC include the Student Labor Action Coalition [SLAC], CSA/925-SEIU (the union representing many UW clerical workers), the International Socialist Organization (ISO), the Chicano/Latino student group MEChA, the Young Socialists, the YW@UW and the Women's Action Coalition.

The SWSC is supporting the strawberry workers' efforts to improve their working conditions. The UFW is working to unionize twenty thousand strawberry workers who, according to union research, work eight- to twelve-hour days, earning about $8,500 a year. While this wage has remained stagnant for decades and has actually fallen in real terms, the profits of the strawberry industry have continued to double every ten years.

Due to the intense stoop work involved in harvesting strawberries, many workers sustain back injuries on the job but have no health insurance. Many have to leave the industry by age thirty. In some fields, there are no bathrooms or drinking water, and many workers complain of harassment or unjust firings.

According to Anne Atkeson, a UFW community organizer, "The overall mission of the UFW with strawberry workers is to create economic independence with collective bargaining agreements, which are union contracts."

This is no simple task. Workers at three strawberry farms voted in recent years for union representation, only to see growers plow under their fields or permanently shut them down. The UFW has now focused their efforts on pressuring the cooling and distribution plants, where industry power is concentrated. Eight of these cooler-shippers control the production of 270 growers along the central coast of California, who produce 80 percent of US strawberries.

The UFW is currently using a campaign to get grocery stores and food-service agencies to sign the Food-Service Pledge for Strawberry Workers' Rights. The pledge asks an agency to sign a simple statement: "We recognize that farm workers are an essential part of the nation's food-production system. We endorse the following rights for strawberry workers: a living wage, proper field sanitation, job security, health insurance, and a voice to end sexual harassment and other abuses. We encourage the strawberry industry to recognize these basic rights."

These pledges will be used to show the strawberry industry nationwide support for the workers, and the UFW hopes that this economic leverage will bring shippers of strawberries to the bargaining table. Atkeson says forty-six thousand grocery stores across the country, including major chains such as Safeway, have signed the pledge. Locally, the Puget Consumers Co-op also signed.

Last December the SWSC approached Paul Brown, director of UW Housing and Food Services, and asked him to sign the pledge as well. He responded, "I can't make a political statement for the University of Washington and the state of Washington."

As a result, the SWSC has decided to build student support for the pledge to pressure UW's administration to sign.

The SWSC is not the only group on campus presently focusing on farm worker issues. MEChA, the ISO and SLAC, all part of the coalition, are also supporting farm worker groups in other ways.

SWSC has worked closely with MEChA's campaign to boycott Gardenburgers and other products made by NORPAC, a major food distributor. The boycott is a national effort in support of PCUN, a farm workers' union in Oregon whose workers face similar conditions to those in the strawberry industry.

The ISO and SLAC have also been working with the UFW and with the teamsters in their joint effort to organize apple workers in eastern Washington. (Last month, workers at major distribution plants Washington Fruit and Stemilt voted against union representation. Campaign organizers and workers who support the union promised to challenge the outcome of this vote, alleging unfair election practices.)

This is not the first time members of the university community have organized around farm workers' issues. Erasmo Gamboa, professor of history and American ethnic studies, recently spoke to the coalition about the UFW grape boycott of the 1960s and the University of Washington Boycott Committee (UWBC), which organized a boycott of grapes at the UW in support of the UFW. This assemblage of students worked to educate the campus community about farm workers' issues and eventually convinced the UW, through a massive show of support from students and faculty, to boycott nonunion grapes. Similar to the UWBC, SWSC hopes to support farm workers in their organizing efforts through education and mobilization of the UW community.

3.B.8a. and 3.B.8b.

The Direct Action Network (DAN) was a key leader in organizing the protests that shut down the meeting of the World Trade Organization (WTO) in Seattle in 1999. Guilloud's statement and the text that follows it were circulated through the DAN broadsheet, or newspaper-sized flyer, typically printed on both sides of a large, folded piece of newsprint paper.

3.B.8a. Stephanie Guilloud, "Why Come to Seattle?" (1999)

- *We eat food.* The WTO regulates the standards by which our food is grown, processed, and sold to us. The WTO determines the labor and environmental practices that determine how our food is grown.
- *We work.* The WTO sets the standards by which employers determine who to hire, how much to pay, what kind of benefits we receive, and the safety conditions of our workplace.
- *We breathe.* The WTO has already ruled that breathing clean air is not a priority. Higher profits for oil companies is far more important to the benefit of the world.
- *We go to school.* The WTO wants to create educational standards that limit public sector educational services to the standards that businesspeople and corporations decide. Math programs designed by M&M Candies (what's the chance of a green one?) have already entered our school systems.
- *We live* in an industrialized country that exploits other nations and other peoples for the sake of comfortable living conditions in the US. We have a responsibility to understand the reality of the global economy beyond our own lives and speak out against these policies. Seattle offers an amazing opportunity to stand together as human beings and declare our sovereignty. Making these connections is the necessary step in creating institutions for our own communities, our needs, our children, and ourselves.

3.B.8b. Direct Action Network, "Globalize Liberation, Not Corporate Power: A Call to Action" (1999)

Resist the World Trade Organization
Come to Seattle Nov. 29–Dec. 3, 1999
Festival of Resistance * Nonviolent Direct Action * Street Theater

Increasing poverty and cuts to social services while the rich get richer; low wages, sweatshops, meaningless jobs, and more prisons; deforestation, gridlocked cities, and global warming; genetic engineering, gentrification, and war: despite the apparent diversity of these social and ecological troubles, their roots are the same—a global economic system based on the exploitation of people and the planet.

From Nov. 29 to Dec. 3 in Seattle, WA, thousands of leaders of transnational corporations, government officials and an army of bureaucrats will come to the World Trade Organization's summit to further their drive for profits and their control over our political, economic, and cultural life, along with the environment. Their new strategy to concentrate power and wealth, while neutralizing people's resistance, is called "economic globalization" and "free trade." But these words just disguise the poverty, misery, and ecological destruction of this system.

Tens of thousands of people will converge on Seattle and transform it into a festival of resistance: mass nonviolent direct action; reclaim the streets with giant street theater, puppets, celebration, music, street parties, and pleasure; vibrant sounds of community, creativity, and resistance and glimpses of life as it could be in the face of hundreds of deadening businessmen, bureaucrats, and politicians. A new world is possible and a global movement of resistance is rising to make it happen. Imagine replacing the existing social order with a just, free, and ecological order based on mutual aid and voluntary cooperation. Join us. Come to Seattle.

Nov. 30 Shut Down the WTO
Mass Nonviolent Direct Action Info

We are planning a large-scale, well-organized, high visibility action to *shut down* the World Trade Organization on Tuesday, November 30. The World Trade Organization has no right to make undemocratic, unaccountable destructive decisions about our lives, our communities, and the earth. We will nonviolently and creatively block them from meeting. Hundreds of people will risk arrest, reflecting the diversity of groups and communities impacted by the WTO and corporate globalization. We envision colorful and festive actions with large-scale street theater as a major element. We will make space and encourage mutual respect for a variety of nonviolent action styles reflecting our different groups and communities. The WTO summit offers a historic opportunity to halt corporate globalization and to help catalyze a widespread mass movement in North America.

Why Nonviolent Direct Action and Street Theater?

It is time to raise the social and political cost to those who aim to increase the destruction and misery caused by corporate globalization, as movements in other parts of the world have. Nonviolent direct action can force corporate globalization onto the front burner of public discussion and, coupled with high visibility street theater, will get national and international alternative and mainstream media coverage. The time is ripe for massive nonviolent direct action against the World Trade Organization (WTO) and the corporate globalization it serves. Demonstrations and protest have been an essential part of every successful social change movement in North American history, but they are too often marginalized by corporate media, too easily dismissed by those we want to engage, and bore participants. Street theater used as a tool for making social change can break into people's consciousness, communicate powerfully, and capture the imagination of participants and observers. Well-planned nonviolent direct action can intervene into a process that we have been left out of, showing the depth of our opposition and forcing the issues onto the public agenda. There is an incredible opportunity to use street theater—art, dance, music, giant puppets, graffiti art, and theater—and nonviolent direct action to simplify and dramatize the issues of corporate globalization and to develop and spread new and creative forms [of] resistance. This will help catalyze desperately needed mass movements in the US and Canada capable of challenging global capital and making radical change and social revolution.

Direct Action Network (against Corporate Globalization)

The Direct Action Network is a network of local grassroots groups and street theater groups across the western United States and Canada who are mobilizing our communities to creatively resist the World Trade Organization and corporate globalization.

WTO Radical Cheerlead

They're trying to take control to do as they please
Globalizing power for their corporate sleaze
WTO, your plan has got to go
Your scheming system we are gonna overthrow
(everyone shout:) Take back the power! End corporate greed!

Well there's poverty and misery all over the land
The situation's gotten out of hand
When so few own so much it's time to take a stand
(everyone shout:) Take back the power! End corporate greed!

The Road to Seattle: Global Justice in the 1990s

Chris Dixon

When an estimated fifty thousand protestors shut down the World Trade Organization (WTO) Ministerial Conference in Seattle in 1999, the mainstream media pronounced the birth of an "antiglobalization movement." However, as experienced activists emphasized, Seattle was not the beginning. A worldwide revolt against neoliberalism had been in swing since the 1970s, and US activists had targeted international financial institutions and trade agreements since the early 1990s. The road to Seattle was paved with years of organizing, confrontational struggle, and cross-border movement building.

Starting in the mid-1980s, activists in the global South—especially Africa and Latin America—organized large-scale protests against austerity measures mandated by the International Monetary Fund (IMF). Building on anticolonial and anti-imperialist movements, these popular mobilizations fought IMF-imposed price hikes and cuts to social spending. By the early 1990s, the World Bank and WTO faced massive protests from Bangalore to Berlin and beyond.

Simultaneously, several movements converged in the United States. During the early 1990s, many activists found common cause in the fight against the North American Free Trade Agreement (NAFTA). Although ultimately unsuccessful, that struggle forged important cross-movement relationships. Organized labor, international solidarity groups, Indigenous activists, environmentalists, consumer advocates, and human rights organizations all took aim at free trade, arguing that it strengthened corporate power, slashed protections for workers and the environment, and degraded standards of living.

On January 1, 1994, the day that NAFTA went into effect, the Zapatista Army of National Liberation stepped onto the world stage by seizing seven cities in Chiapas, Mexico. They said "Ya basta!" ("Enough!") to the Mexican government and neoliberalism. Bringing together leftist and Indigenous Mayan traditions, the Zapatistas offered an autonomous anticapitalist politics that captivated movements across the globe. They also facilitated transnational movement links. Starting in 1996, the Zapatistas sponsored face-to-face global Encuentros (Encounters) that served as key meeting points for the global justice or alterglobalization movement.

In 1998 the Encuentros led to the formation of Peoples' Global Action (PGA), which brought activists in the global North together with massive movements in the global South, such as the Landless Workers' Movement in Brazil and the Karnataka State Farmer's Movement in India. Core PGA principles included a rejection of "all forms and systems of domination and discrimination," "a confrontational attitude," "a call to direct action," and "an organizational philosophy based on decentralization and autonomy." Through the PGA, an anticapitalist current engaged in discussion and planning emerged.

By the late 1990s, actions and campaigns against corporate globalization could be found across the United States. Activists targeted the IMF and World Bank, and engaged in a sustained fight against the Multilateral Agreement on Investment. Antisweatshop campaigns blossomed on university campuses, and environmental and labor groups built coalitions to challenge corporate dominance. All of this activity bolstered a spirit of confrontational collective action. A direct antecedent for Seattle was the mobilization in Vancouver in 1997 that attempted to disrupt the summit of the Asia-Pacific Economic Cooperation, a regional trade agreement among a number of Pacific Rim economies.

Anarchism centrally animated the anticapitalist current. This was an anarchism that combined a far-reaching critique of domination with a commitment to direct action and direct democracy. Throughout the 1980s and 1990s, anarchists had participated in a succession of direct action movements and forged a set of protest tactics and nonhierarchical organizing practices, which became widely influential in the global justice movement. Anarchists were also deeply inspired by the Zapatistas and had been some of the first to work with the PGA. Following the example of their European counterparts, many US activists began to respond to the PGA's "global days of action," involving coordinated international protests against institutions of neoliberalism.

When Seattle was announced as the choice for the WTO's Millennium Round in early 1999, activists nationwide began planning protests. A movement was in motion.

3.B.9.

D2KLA

"Direct Action: Challenge the Republican and Democratic Parties This Summer in Philadelphia and Los Angeles" (2000)

Riding on the energy of the global justice movement, in summer 2000, activists convened on the Republican and Democratic national conventions to demand economic, social, and racial justice and to protest corporate influence over politics. Riffing on the term "Y2K," referring to a feared computer bug at the turn of the millennium, the protests were named "R2K" (held outside the Republican convention in Philadelphia) and "D2KLA" (held outside the Democratic convention in Los Angeles). These following statements come from the D2KLA broadsheet.

Take Action for Global and National Justice!
Abolish the Prison Industrial Complex

The Democratic and Republican parties will be convening this summer to "select" their candidates. These conventions are nothing but a dog and pony show created to divert our attention away from the fundamentally undemocratic nature of the US political system. This system is bought and paid for by a rich and powerful few, pushing policies that further enrich the corporations they own at the expense of the vast majority of the people. Join us in taking nonviolent direct action to challenge the policies of the Democratic and Republican parties at their conventions this summer July 31–Aug 3 in Philadelphia [Republican] and August 14–17 in Los Angeles [Democratic].

The Evil of Two Lessers

It is no secret that both the Republicans and the Democrats are in the pockets of major corporations. These corporations not only control our economy and media, but they have also tightened their hold over our political system and culture. Any minor differences between the two parties are steadily disappearing as they compete to pocket the most corporate cash.

Domestically, both parties have been pushing an agenda that puts profits over people, benefiting the wealthy few at the expense of the many, especially people of color, the poor, and women. Corporations receive billions in welfare payments while education and social programs are slashed. Republicans and Democrats alike race to imprison and execute record numbers in a racist appeal to fear while the actual crime rate plummets. And they pretend to be environmentalists while the planet continues to burn.

Internationally, the US government promotes "free trade" policies designed to strengthen the control of the multinational corporations over all the people of the world. This rogue superpower stands on the necks of the people of Vieques, Iraq, Colombia, Yugoslavia, and any other people who get in the way of the US goal of ruling the world.

Power to the People!

At the same time, from Soweto to Seattle, from Delhi to DC, people around the world are standing up to demand a fairer world. We must say: Enough! No more business as usual! It is time for domestic and global justice! It is time to directly act to intervene and challenge the legitimacy of both these dominant US political parties and their complicity with corporate interests.

During the conventions we will be taking to the streets for racial, economic and environmental justice and for equality for people of all sexual and gender orientations. We will demand an end to police brutality, an end to the growing prison industrial complex, and an end to the death penalty. We will be calling for freedom for Mumia Abu-Jamal and all political prisoners and for immigrant and workers' rights. And we will be continuing our call for an end to global corporate domination.

We want a real democracy that gives everyone meaningful power over the decisions and resources that matter in our neighborhoods, towns, schools, and workplaces. We can and will create this real, direct democracy in the streets, in our communities, in our workplaces, and in our political systems.

Join us! Nonviolent direct action has been an essential part of every successful social change movement in US history. It is used by people all over the world to take the power back from corporations and governments. Democrats and Republicans, your party's over!

3.B.10.

Catalyst Project

"Tools for Antiracist Organizing" (2002)

Soon after the shutdown of the WTO, lifelong activist Elizabeth (Betita) Martínez wrote an article on race in the global justice movement, "Where Was the Color in Seattle?" Her essay resonated with many and helped to accelerate efforts towards multiracial and people of color organizing. One such effort was spearheaded by the Catalyst Project, which trains white activists in antiracist organizing.

Develop Analysis

1. Study the historical development of white supremacy and how white supremacy connects with capitalism, patriarchy, heterosexism, the gender binary system, and the state.
2. Develop analysis of how white supremacy impacts the issues you work on. Prioritize analysis by left/radical people of color in your study.
3. Study social movements led by people of color past and present.
4. Learn about the struggles of people of color where you live.
5. Study white antiracist history, find other white antiracists to talk with and get support.
6. Study women of color feminism and develop analysis of intersections of oppression and privilege.
7. Form study groups and do political education in your organization.

Build Organization and Deepen your Antiracist Practice

8. Join existing organizations working from an antiracist politics and/or support the process of moving your existing organization towards antiracist politics. Organizations are often difficult because in them we practice the real-world application of our principles and we are accountable to other people. Organizations are key to transforming relationships of power towards equality in society. Challenging times should be expected.
9. Find other people to work and talk with to support one another in your development as an antiracist and as a revolutionary. Develop a process of praxis: putting analysis into practice, reflecting on that practice to develop your theory, and so on.
10. Find ways to support people-of-color-led organizations you share political affinity with. This could include you and your friends volunteering to do childcare, getting your organization to participate in campaigns led by people of color, [and] developing longer-term political alliances.
11. Challenge privileged/oppressive behavior in yourself and in others. Strug-

gle to do this from a place of love. Remember that in doing this work, you will make mistakes and so will other people. The mistakes are inevitable; the process of learning from those mistakes requires humble and honest reflection. The more work you do, the more mistakes you will make.

12. Struggle against individualism and competition that distort the goals of this work to becoming "the perfect antiracist". Remember that we are engaged in a struggle to make history, not escape it.

13. Find a mentor, someone who has more experience than you who will not only share lessons from their history but who helps you learn from your own experiences and who encourages you to think through the challenges you face.

14. Develop your skills, analysis, and confidence to struggle for social justice. Become as effective, dynamic, strategic, and healthy as you can be in our work for a free society.

Build Movement

15. Build relationships with the people you are working with and build relationships with people in the broader community you work in.

16. If you are in a multiracial organization find ways to openly and honestly talk with activists of color you work with about white supremacy and race with a focus on how to work together to build power for justice.

17. In mostly or all-white organizations, work to build relationships of trust and accountability with organizations and communities in struggles for racial justice. See if there are ways to do solidarity work and eventually, if there are ways to collaborate. Develop your organization's work with goals of challenging white supremacy in society and building antiracist principles in white communities.

18. Commit to developing a practice of solidarity with oppressed peoples for collective liberation and a practice of accountability to the people you work with in your organization and in particular accountability to oppressed people you work with and have relationships with. Such a practice is nuanced, complex, and develops over time through practice, [so] be patient.

19. Know that your liberation is tied to the liberation of all. While people with privilege are often less affected, find your self-interest in a free society and work to build it.

20. Remember that we are in this together and you are not alone.

Catalyst Project is a center for political education and movement building.
We thank our mentors and allies for help developing this list.

3.B.11.

Farm Labor Organizing Committee

"Campaign for Legalization of Undocumented Immigrants Winning Support" (2001)

Issues of labor and global justice converged in the late 1990s through organizing for immigration reform, especially amnesty for undocumented immigrants. This essay speaks to the optimism surrounding immigration reform in early 2001, hopes that were quickly dashed by policies implemented in response to the September 11 attacks.

In April of 1999 the Farm Labor Organizing Committee (FLOC) and other immigrant-based unions and community and faith-based organizations established the National Coalition for Dignity and Amnesty for Undocumented Immigrants. Our purpose: to build a strong movement for immigrant labor and human rights led and organized by immigrants.

For FLOC members, the fight for legalization of their immigration status is pivotal. Without documentation, our people have extremely limited legal recourse to address their problems, and they are unable to bargain collectively for improvements because of fear of deportation. Immigrant workers face a multitude of problems, including low wages, nonpayment of wages, sexual and physical abuse, inhumane working conditions, lack of benefits, and constant fear of deportation.

Our fight emphasizes the human right to move and live where we can provide a decent life for our families. The new corporate-dominated global era is challenging us to find new and just systems that allow for the free and dignified movement of people, as capital is free to move. Our first campaign calls for a general unconditional amnesty for all undocumented immigrants and for a redefinition of immigration policies so the US government can manage migration flows in a more realistic and humanitarian manner.

Our coalition launched the campaign with a national march held in Washington, DC, on October 16, 1999. It was *the first popular mobilization for a general amnesty in the country*. We mobilized over fifteen thousand immigrants and supporters and over 150 organizations protesting the situations suffered by immigrant workers and demanding a new amnesty. The impact of this massive mobilization was felt even before the march. Several legislators endorsed the call to a general amnesty including Luis Gutierrez (D-IL), Sheila Jackson Lee (D-TX), and Carrie Meek (D-FL). We won the endorsement of prominent national organizations and labor unions, such as LCLAA [Labor Council for Latin American Advancement], the National Council of La Raza, LULAC [League of United Latin American Citizens], the Laborers International Union (LIUNA), UE [United Electrical, Radio, and Machine Workers of America], . . . several of the Carpenters Unions], UNITE [Union of Needletrades, Industrial, and Textile Employees] and SEIU [Service Employees International Union] locals.

Since then, we have been building our base by establishing local organizing committees, and from them, local and statewide coalitions. Our campaign combines grassroots organizing and legislative advocacy with popular mobilizations. Marches and rallies continued on May Day 2000 (and again in 2001), [in] July 2000, and October 14–15, 2000, with nationally coordinated regional marches in six major US cities. The mobilizations in New York, Chicago, Miami, Seattle, Austin, and Portland drew over one hundred thousand immigrants and supporters. These events were followed by local ecumenical services and vigils in front of congressional district offices on November 2, "the Day of the Death," to call attention to the hundreds of migrants who die every year at the border. In addition, we moved and helped pass city council resolutions in support of amnesty in Chicago, Cleveland, Toledo, and New York. We disseminated press releases and organized media events all over the country, significantly increasing exposure of the situation of undocumented immigrants.

Our work for the last two years was very successful in exposing the existence and situation of undocumented immigrants in the country. As a direct result of the work of the coalition, the legalization of the over six million undocumented workers in the USA is no longer perceived as a taboo subject but rather as a pressing social issue that needs to be debated in the US Congress and in communities around the US. The scenario has radically changed. Our popular mobilizations helped propel the issue into the national labor agenda and

Figure 3.4. Lalo Alcaraz, "FRaid Anti-Immigrant Border Spray" (1994). Image courtesy of Lincoln Cushing/Docs Populi. Reprinted with permission by Lalo Alcaraz.

contributed to other organizations now recognizing the justice of our demand, most prominently, the Catholic Church and the AFL-CIO. Our public actions revealed the existence of a growing immigrant rights movement that is organized and ready to take to the streets with its demands.

Furthermore, in February 2001 Congressman Gutierrez (D-IL) introduced the first bill for a general legalization of undocumented immigrants. This bill is a very important first step towards the solution of the problems faced by immigrants and their families.

While we keep building our base, this coming year we will prioritize the work of building broader coalitions with all other organizations fighting for a new legalization program. At the same time, it is also crucial to build alliances with other social justice movements outside the immigrant communities. This broader base of support will put us in a better position to educate our congressional representatives and the public about the justice of our demands and how this ultimately will help build a better society for all.

New immigrants can and will reenergize the labor movement, but only if the labor movement responds to the needs and demands of immigrant workers. Both the AFL-CIO and LCLAA have taken important first steps to respond to these demands. We encourage both to continue on in this direction. Hasta la victoria!

3.B.12.

Coalition of Immokalee Workers

From "Consciousness + Commitment = Change" (2003)

The Coalition of Immokalee Workers (CIW) is a community-based worker organization based in Florida, with members who include Latinx, Haitian, and Mayan Indian immigrants. It takes its name from Immokalee, FL, where the state's tomato and citrus industries are based. The following excerpt details the CIW's powerful organizing at the intersection of immigrant organizing, labor, and the global justice movement, even in the absence of labor protections.

. . . As the CIW motto goes: "Consciousness + Commitment = Change," and popular education, in many forms, is the way CIW members build consciousness among their fellow workers.

Popular education is a method of education and organization born in the countryside of Brazil and developed in struggles throughout Latin America and the Caribbean. Several of the CIW's original founders not only had experience with popular education but were trained practitioners of the approach through their community organizations at home. At its heart is the use of "codes"—drawings, theater, song, video, stories, and so forth—designed to capture a piece of community reality and to present that reality for reflection in a group. . . .

The objective of popular education is to oblige workers to confront the problems in their community in a form that allows, and in fact actively encourages, even the most reticent workers to participate. . . . By making political analysis understandable and facilitating the group reflection in a way that brings peripheral members to the center of the process, it challenges workers to abandon their apathy and isolation, to actively analyze their reality, and to redefine their relationship to the forces that shape their lives. It is education for action, and as such its effectiveness must ultimately be measured by the degree to which it moves the community to take action, fight for change, and win a degree of control over its collective destiny.

Leadership development as practiced in the CIW's work also draws its inspiration from the Latin American and Caribbean organizing experience. In Immokalee, farmworkers interested in sharpening their leadership skills and learning new tools for working with the community can participate in intensive workshops, lasting from two to seven days, where workers study and practice everything from techniques of popular education to the history of the labor movement, labor, and human rights, how to plan and run community meetings, the practice of popular theater, economic and political analysis, and even techniques of video production. Participation in the CIW leadership development process is self-selected and is open to any and all members, from the longest-term veterans to the most recently arrived workers, as one of its primary goals is to constantly broaden the leadership base of the organization. In that way, the CIW is best able to counter the erosion of that base caused by the movement of even the most dedicated leaders out of Immokalee toward better, more stable employment.

CIW staff is composed of workers elected by their fellow workers at the annual general assembly. . . . Staff members get hands-on training in important new skills and gain insight into the world of organizing in the United States, including the use of computer technology (through email and the CIW website), the ins and outs of the US political system, press outreach, and fundraising. To guarantee that those elected to the staff remain rooted in farmworker reality, however, CIW members established several key organizational bylaws. Staff salaries are commensurate with farmworker wages, the staff structure is nonhierarchical, and staff members are required to spend a significant amount of time every year working in the fields. . . .

In a certain sense, it can be said that the CIW has made a virtue of necessity in two important ways, both of which are made necessary by the high turnover of the Immokalee community. Because every season—every month, even—brings a significant percentage of new workers to Immokalee, the CIW can never abandon the basic political education process (popular education) that informs [workers] and motivates them to become active CIW members. And because even the most committed leaders inevitably move on to better work in distant states or back home to their families in Mexico, Guatemala, and Haiti, the CIW must maintain a constant process of leadership development to grow and replenish its leadership base.

From this base, the CIW has organized various high-profile, aggressive, successful actions since 1995. The first major, community-wide action came as a response to the beatings and abuse of workers in the field, which in the early nineties was a widespread practice by many local contractors. When a worker who had been beaten for drinking water without permission came to the coalition with his ripped and bloodied shirt, we responded with a five-hundred-person March to End Violence to the home of the contractor who had perpetrated such a heinous act. Since that time the reports of such intolerable abuses in the Immokalee area have come to an end. Actions since 1995 have included three community-wide general strikes, a thirty-day hunger strike by six CIW members ended by the intervention of former president Jimmy Carter, a two-week, 240-mile march across south and central Florida, and now a national boycott of Taco Bell, a major buyer of tomatoes picked in Immokalee.

The centerpiece of the boycott to date has been the Taco Bell Truth Tour, a cross-country bus and van tour from Florida to California by seventy workers and thirty students, with stops for rallies and protests in major cities across the way in March 2002. The fifteen-city, seventeen-day tour culminated in massive protests—bringing together allies from across the spectrum, including students, anarchists, labor, community, and religious organizations—in Los Angeles and Irvine, California, home of Taco Bell's corporate headquarters. It was the first major "convergence style" action directed at an individual corporation, resulting in a historic first-time meeting between executives of a multinational fast-food corporation and the farmworkers who produce the raw materials for their products.

Because farm workers are exempted from the NLRA, the CIW has had to carry on the tradition of high-profile actions that have become typical of farmworker organizing since the fasts and marches of Cesar Chavez and the UFW [United Farm Workers] in the 1960s and 1970s. Without access to NLRB [National Labor Relations Board] mediation and the more rational, democratic means of an election/appeals process to compel employers to the table, farmworkers have little choice but to use spectacular protests to bring public pressure to bear on the industry for the right to negotiate for better wages and working conditions.

But the CIW also looks at these actions as opportunities for further conscientization and leadership development and thus strives to shape its actions so as to maximize those opportunities. . . .

The hunger strike of 1997–98, for example, was a historic, month-long political statement by six tomato pickers, supported by a committee of several other members that watched over the strikers twenty-four hours a day. . . . Similarly, CIW strikes have not been specific to one grower but have involved the entire community and have taken on the industry as a whole. This is in part due to the community labor pool structure of the labor market in Immokalee but also to the CIW's casting of grievances in political as well as economic terms. Because CIW members generally understand and define strikes within the broader framework of human rights, strike actions tend to become events that galvanize the entire community and challenge the basic assumptions of agriculture's oppressive power structure. CIW marches also follow this pattern, with the routes covering several days or even weeks of ten- to twenty-mile stretches by day, followed by public meetings and internal reflections by night. The marches, like most CIW actions, have been radicalizing experiences that cement bonds between members and do much to counteract the forces that atomize the Immokalee community and contribute to its unequaled transience. . . .

The Taco Bell Truth Tour is an example of the emphasis on long-duration, participatory tactics. Furthermore, the decision to explicitly link the boycott to the broader movement for global justice, through the focus on building strong ties to the youth and radical sectors that have been at the forefront of that movement and through the "convergence style" actions in front of Taco Bell headquarters, reflects the conscious effort on the part of the CIW to place the farmworkers' struggle firmly within the growing debate over globalization, corporate responsibility, and human and economic rights. . . .

For workers forced from their countries by economic and political conditions linked, in large part, to World Bank and IMF [International Monetary Fund] policies, workers who find themselves now in the United States exploited by a major multinational corporation that profits directly from their poverty, the leap from general strikes in the tomato fields to global mobilizations for economic justice like those in Seattle, Washington, and Genoa, is not a difficult one.

Not in Our Name

3.C.1.

Confederation of Iranian Students

"Condemn Shah's US Visit; Free One Hundred Thousand Political Prisoners in Iran" (1977)

In the late 1970s, Iran saw a populist revolution against the shah, or monarch, Mohammed Reza Pahlavi. Opposition came from both secular and religious quarters and included leftist as well as Islamist groups. This resistance was echoed by many Iranians abroad, including in the United States. This flyer is dated November 1977, one month after protests began in Iran, and calls for demonstrations to be held in the United States.

Once again the fascist shah of Iran is making a trip to the United States. Why is he making such a trip? What is the purpose behind Carter's calling of this servant of monopolies and big business interests to the United States?

This trip has vital significance for the fascist regime of the shah and the so-called defender of human rights, the Carter administration. The fascist nature of the shah's regime as manifested in the one-party system, "Rastakhiz," the total suppression of basic democratic rights and all political resistance, and the worldwide infamy of SAVAK [Iranian secret police] and its practices of torture, do not fit in well with the Carter administration's false propaganda about "human rights." Faced with this problem they are trying to construct a democratic mask for the shah in order to continue justifying the US support for this fascist dictatorship. The shah's regime, in order to give an image of enjoying popular support is

1) bringing several planeloads of SAVAK agents from Iran to participate in pro-shah demonstrations and attack the progressive and anti-shah demonstrations,

2) bringing all Iranian military personnel training in this country to these same demonstrations, and,

3) offering round trip tickets, hotel accommodations, and a bribe of $300–400 to any Iranians within the US who will go to Washington to demonstrate in favor of the shah.

This is a desperate conspiracy on the part of both the United States and Iranian governments to mislead the public about the realities of the shah's regime, and we condemn it strongly.

The shah of Iran, who regained power in August 1953 through a CIA-engineered coup d'état, has been thoroughly serving the interests of big monopolies, such as oil and arms conglomerates. For years he has let the foreign powers plunder our country and ruthlessly exploit it. Due to this enormous oppression and exploitation, our country has become totally dependent on foreign domination and imperialism, and our national interests have been undermined.

- Once a self-sufficient agricultural society, Iran today cannot produce more than 7 percent of its internal needs. Last year alone more than $4 billion was spent on food imports.
- Under the rule of the fascist shah, all the wealth and natural resources of Iran are used to serve the interests and needs of the imperialists and the people's needs at most receive token consideration. For example: in the fiscal year 1975–76 more than 40 percent of the total national budget, or $12 billion, was allocated for the military and internal security expenses, while the total allocation for education was a mere $232 million (less than 2 percent of the military budget). The total health, medical, and nutritional allocation was a negligible $900 million (less than 8 percent of the military budget). These figures have to be viewed within the context of a nation with a population of over thirty million, 60–70 percent of whom are illiterate, and with a 60 percent infant mortality rate and an average life span of thirty-eight years.
- All opposition movements are suppressed to the fullest extent. The one hundred thousand political prisoners, who have heroically resisted the shah's regime, continue to struggle inside the medieval-type prisons in Iran. Hundreds of the best sons and daughters of the Iranian people have been murdered under torture or executed by firing squads, over three hundred in the last two years alone.
- It is well known that human rights under the rule of the fascist shah are totally denied, but in a report to Congress which was prepared by the State Department and signed by Secretary of State Cyrus Vance, the administration stated in regard to "human rights" [that] "disassociation, however does not necessarily promote human rights, and a number of countries with deplorable records of human rights observance are also countries where we have important security and foreign policy interests" (*SF Chronicle*, 7/12/77).

However, the people of Iran have a long history of valiant and heroic struggle against the fascist reign of the regime of the shah and against foreign domination, especially domination by US imperialism. Faced with unbearable living and working conditions the militant Iranian workers have organized many strikes despite the fact that they are illegal and met with great violence. The students in Iran's universities have held massive demonstrations, the existence of which the regime was forced to admit publicly and condemn in its newspapers. This combined with the increasing activities of the revolutionary organizations is testimony to the universal truth that "wherever there is repression there is struggle and wherever there is struggle there are victories and defeats, but the final victory belongs to the people." In the not too distant future the Iranian people will surely destroy the fascist regime of the shah and kick out all imperialists. The shah has been called to the US at this time to receive further instructions on how to better safeguard the interests of US imperialism. This is the purpose of his trip; to further conspire against the national interests of the Iranian people and to maintain the dominance of US imperialism in Iran.

The Iranian Students Association in the United States (member of the Confederation of Iranian Students—CIS) is holding a series of demonstrations to oppose this trip by the shah of Iran. We call on all democratic-minded and freedom-loving people to join us in opposition to this trip, in opposition to the fascist dictatorship of the shah of Iran, and in opposition to imperialist intervention in Iran. These demonstrations will be held in Washington, DC, and San Francisco.

Down with the US-backed regime of fascist shah!
All imperialists out of Iran!

3.C.2.

Palestine Solidarity Committee

Letter to supporters (1980)

In this April 9, 1980, letter to supporters, the Palestine Solidarity Committee situates Israel as a primary recipient of US military resources, and emphasizes a Cold War context for US policy regarding Israel-Palestine. The piece offers insight into the relatively small scale of Palestinian solidarity activism at this time, as well as the importance of reaching media and presenting new narratives in order to grow the movement.

Dear friends,

As you know, we have organized a mass protest against the Salute to Israel parade annually for the past four years. There are many reasons why the demonstration against this year's parade—scheduled for Sunday, June 1 [in New York City]—should be bigger than ever before.

Israeli settlement of the West Bank and Gaza Strip has intensified; not only has the US government failed to make any effective protest against it, but the Carter administration has even increased the subsidies and weapons which facilitate the Israeli seizure of Palestinian land. The US remains committed to preventing Palestinian self-determination; Carter reiterates his opposition to an independent Palestinian state and to dealing with the Palestine Liberation Organization as the representative of the Palestinian people.

And, very alarmingly, Carter has taken a sharp turn toward militarization of US policy toward the Mideast. His new Cold War is being waged in the name of saving the Middle East from the Soviet Union. Meanwhile his preparations for a rapid deployment force for invasion of the area, the increase in the US naval and air presence in the Gulf and Indian Ocean, the search for US bases in the area, and the escalation in arms shipments to unpopular regimes show that the real threat to self-determination in the Mideast is in the White House, not the Kremlin.

Of course, this regional militarization of US policy has a great impact on the Palestinian issue. Zionist lobbyists, depicting Israel as a potential "refueling station" and "unsinkable aircraft carrier" for the US in the region urge the Carter administration to send ever more sophisticated weapons to the Begin government; Carter willingly accedes. The first victims of these new aircraft given by the US will be the Palestinians and Lebanese civilians in southern Lebanon.

But now it is not only the Mideast which will suffer from Carter's policies. People in this country will be affected too: certainly by the diversion of tax funds to destructive military purposes in the Mideast rather than expenditures for human needs here [and] possibly by reintroduction of the draft or even direct US involvement in a new war in the Mideast.

Let's use the occasion of the Salute to Israel parade to make these points forcefully and publicly. We've always been able to get rather extensive media coverage for the protest itself. Even before the demonstration, let's plaster the city with stickers and posters to publicize the message. *We really need your help* [. . .] a hand in the office with mailings and the myriad of other behind the scenes tasks [. . .] posting stickers and posters [. . .] a contribution for printing. Please let us know how you will participate in building this demonstration by filling out the coupon below.

Sincerely,
Sheila Ryan

No More Witch Hunts

"No More Witch Hunts: A Day of Resistance" (1981)

Early in his presidency, by means of an executive order, Ronald Reagan loosened restrictions on the FBI and CIA. Activists soon faced a noticeable uptick in government surveillance and harassment. By 1983, many leftist and progressive groups were reporting mysterious break-ins at their offices. The "No more witch hunts" protests, held on June 19, 1981, sought to inform activists about these threats and to mobilize support against them.

Our civil liberties are endangered. Together we must resist Congressional Investigative Committees and any attempt to label dissent as terrorist. We must stand up for the right to address public issues. *You have a right to voice your opinion. You have a right to work for change.*

If you have actively supported any of these issues, you may become a target of the committees:

- racial and economic justice
- solidarity with international liberation struggles
- make human needs a budget priority
- slash the military budget
- stop nuclear terror
- no draft
- worker's rights
- women's rights
- end racism
- lesbian and gay rights
- honor Native American treaties
- defend the Freedom of Information Act
- support First Amendment liberties

  Say no to the Senate Subcommittee on Security and Terrorism
  Say no to the House Internal Security Committee
  Say no to spies in our homes
  We resist

  Witch hunt: A searching out of victims professedly for exposure on charges of subversion, disloyalty, or the like, but ulteriorly for harassing proponents of an incompatible political philosophy (Webster's New Collegiate Dictionary, 1961).

- The Senate has just established a Judiciary Subcommittee on Security and Terrorism (SST). Hearings have been scheduled for April 24 on Terrorism: Its Origins, Directions, and Support.

- There is a drive in the House to revive the Internal Security Committee.
- The president has proposed an executive order which will unleash the CIA and FBI in "legitimate" domestic surveillance.
- Hearings have been called to exempt the FBI and CIA from the Freedom of Information Act.

The government sees the need to rally its supporters by creating the notion of a domestic "terrorist" threat which is linked to "international terrorism." Only in this way can it get the people to support an increasingly bellicose foreign policy and the curtailment of our civil liberties at home. The SST may be used as the propaganda vehicle geared to this task.

The SST has the power to require people to appear before it and give testimony. The first hearing, called for April 21 and 22 in Washington, DC, will focus on terrorism, its origins, direction, and support. Witnesses are expected to be friendly—the hearing's goal will be to garner public support for the subcommittee's work.

The Witch Hunt Has Begun

It is essential to unify and oppose these committees. It is not a question of whom they will investigate—they shouldn't investigate anyone. A revival of McCarthyism, with its consequent intimidation tactics and potentially stepped-up domestic spying, harassment, and threats to the FOIA, must be resisted *now* before it has time to mushroom.

Join us in an evening of resistance: information fair, slide shows, dramatic presentations, political overview, declaration of resistance, and more; or, *plan a resistance activity in your city or town*. Call . . . for more information.

> *Initial sponsors*: Center for Constitutional Rights, Coalition for a People's Alternative, the Chrystic Institute, Covert Action Information Bulletin, Fund for Open Information and Accountability, Inc., Government Accountability Project, Grand Jury Project, Harlem Fight Back, Institute for Labor Education and Research, Interreligious Foundation for Community Organization, National Alliance Against Racist and Political Repression, National Committee Against Repressive Legislation, National Emergency Civil Liberties Committee, National Lawyers Guild, North American Congress on Latin America, Viet Nam Trial Support Committee, Women Strike for Peace

3.C.4.

New Jewish Agenda

From "New Jewish Agenda National Platform" (1982)

New Jewish Agenda, active in the United States from 1980 to 1992, played a major role in advancing progressive politics among American Jews. The national platform excerpts provided here center on discussion of Israel and Palestinian solidarity. The platform also address issues of feminism and reproductive rights, lesbian and gay inclusion, people with disabilities, antiracism, civil liberties, the environment, economic justice and labor, nuclear weapons, ties between Israel and apartheid South Africa, and the situation of Jews in the USSR, Argentina, and Ethiopia.

Statement of Purpose

We are Jews from a variety of backgrounds and affiliations committed to progressive human values and the building of a shared vision of Jewish life.

Our history and tradition inspire us. Jewish experience and teachings can address the social, economic, and political issues of our time. Many of us find our inspiration in our people's historical resistance to oppression and from the Jewish presence at the forefront of movements for social change. Many of us base our convictions on the Jewish religious concept of *tikun olam* (the just ordering of society and the world) and the prophetic traditions of social justice.

We are dedicated to insuring the survival and flourishing of the Jewish people. Jews must have the rights to which all people are entitled. But survival is only a precondition of Jewish life, not its purpose. Our agenda must be determined by our ethics, not our enemies. We need creative and vital Jewish institutions and practices that affirm the best of our traditions and involve members of our community who have historically been excluded.

We call on all Jews who share our vision to join us in working to achieve our goals in the Jewish and wider communities. To those whose visions differ from ours—let us discuss those differences. Authentic Jewish unity grows from respect for and understanding of diversity.

Society can be changed and human cooperation can be achieved. Working for social progress not only reflects Jewish ideals but enhances Jewish security. New Jewish Agenda's national platform upholds progressive Jewish values and affirms that the goals of peace and justice are attainable. . . .

Relations between Israel and North American Jewry

New Jewish Agenda upholds the tradition that *kol yisrael areivim zeh b'zeh*, all Jews are responsible one for another. Our histories, traditions, values, and sentiments have created a connection between us and the Jewish state of Israel. We believe that the fate of the Jewish people in one part of the world is linked to the fate of the Jewish people in other parts of the world.

Israeli and North American Jews share a concern for each other's secure future and ethical character. Decisions about Israel's life and policy must be made by the Israelis, just as we must make decisions affecting North American Jewish life. Nonetheless, we recognize our relations as one of mutual responsibility, including the obligation to address each other's weaknesses as well as strengths. To fail to speak in candor is to decline this responsibility and to imply that we do not care.

We affirm the right and necessity of Jews everywhere to engage in democratic debate and open discussion regarding Israeli policies. As progressive Jews, we in New Jewish agenda identify with the Jewish historical emphasis on peace and social justice and support those in Israel who are working toward these goals. . . .

Israel, the Palestinians, and Arab Neighbors

After decades of hatred and bloodshed, it is clear that there can be no peace in the Middle East without a political resolution of the conflict among Israelis, Palestinians, and the Arab states. For many Jews, Israel represents the fulfillment of a dream of an independent homeland and a refuge from centuries of persecution in many lands. The Palestinians have also been exiled, dispersed, denied their rights, and have been kept from establishing political sovereignty in a land of their own. Regardless of how either side views the "historical legitimacy" of the other, both Israeli Jews and Palestinian Arabs are in the Middle East to stay.

Our Concern as Jews

As Jews committed to the existence of Israel, we recognize that peace between Israel and its Arab neighbors is essential to Israel's survival. The continuing state of war and military rule over another people diminishes the prospects for Israel's long-term viability. We believe that Israel cannot rule over the Palestinians as an occupying force without degrading the Jewish and human ideals which served as a basis for Israel's creation. A key to the solution of the Arab-Israeli conflict is compromise between Israeli and Palestinian nationalisms. It is not possible to solve this conflict through military means.

Principles of Peace

We believe that to be successful and lasting, a comprehensive settlement must embody the following principles:

1. The Jewish people's right to national self-determination in the state of Israel.
2. National self-determination for the Palestinian people.

3. Mutual recognition and peaceful relations among Israel, the Arab states, and the Palestinians.
4. Withdrawal by Israel from territories occupied since June 5, 1967.

Guarantees for Israeli security with recognized borders and mutually agreed-upon provisions responding to the fears and real security needs of all concerned parties.

Toward these ends, we join with Israelis and others in calling for:

1. Renunciation by all parties of all violence, including terrorism, as means to achieve their aims.
2. Recognition by the Arab states and the Palestine Liberation Organization (PLO) of the right of the state of Israel to exist within secure and recognized borders.
3. Recognition by the state of Israel of the right of Palestinians to national self-determination, including the right to the establishment, if they so choose, of an independent and viable Palestinian state in the West Bank and Gaza, and an end to the repression of Palestinians.
4. Direct negotiations between Israel and legitimate representatives of the Palestinian people, including the PLO, on the basis of mutual recognition and a commitment to peaceful coexistence.

Arab American Queer Activism

Umayyah Cable

Motivated by political events in Arab homelands and their effects on the diaspora, namely the first Palestinian intifada (1987–89) and the first Iraq War (1990–91), lesbian and gay Arab Americans started mobilizing into groups in major US cities in the late 1980s and early 1990s. Groups such as the Arab Lesbian Network (ALN) in San Francisco, the Lesbian Arab Network (LAN) in New York City, and the Gay and Lesbian Arabic Society (GLAS) in Washington, DC, and Los Angeles provided social support for lesbian and gay Arab Americans who felt alienated by anti-Arab racism within lesbian and gay social circles on the one hand and homophobia within the Arab American community on the other.

First among these groups was ALN, which was founded by Palestinian American Huda Jadallah in the San Francisco Bay Area in the late 1980s. (It later became the Arab Lesbian and Bisexual Women's Network, at which time a second group, the Arab Lesbian and Gay Network, was also established.) In addition to holding regular social gatherings, the ALN also served as a wellspring of Arab American lesbian political activism. ALN members collaborated with other leftist groups, such as Lesbians and Gays Against Intervention (LAGAI), to help make lesbian and gay Arab existence visible and to educate their communities about how and why Arab American issues were relevant to lesbian and gay politics. One of ALN's first public events was held on June 8, 1989, where approximately eighty women gathered at the Women's Building in San Francisco's Mission District to attend "The Palestinian Uprising and the Lesbian Community: An Evening for Lesbians about Palestine." Organized by ALN and the LAGAI-affiliated group Lesbians in Solidarity with the Palestinian People (LISPP), the forum was hosted by the ALN's Dina Jarrah and Huda Jadallah. The evening covered four interrelated issues: the roots of the intifada, the role of women in the intifada, anti-Arab racism in the lesbian community, and homophobia in the Palestinian community.

In her speech that evening, Jadallah outlined several reasons why Arab lesbians were socially and politically isolated in the United States. She explained that Palestinian lesbians were "invisible lesbians of color," referring to the ways that Arab racial formation in the United States functions to legally subsume Arab ethnicity into the white racial category, while at the same time, American support for Zionism and ignorance about the Israeli occupation produces what scholar Helen Samhan has referred to as "political racism." The speech was printed in several outlets of the leftist lesbian and gay press, including in LAGAI's monthly newspaper *OUT!*, the Boston-based *Gay Community News*, and the GLAS newsletter.

Through press releases and letters to the editors, ALN continued to challenge anti-Arab racism and Zionist biases in the lesbian and gay press. For example, in December 1989 ALN and LISPP coauthored a letter to the editor in the *San Francisco Bay Times* in response to an article titled "Building Lesbian/Gay Pride in Israel." The letter critiqued the omission of information about the Israeli occupation and oppression of the Palestinian people—including gay and lesbian Palestinians.

ALN and LISPP activities in 1989 exemplify some of the earliest resistance to Zionist "pinkwashing," or the promotion of Israel as a gay-friendly liberal democracy as a way to distract from, downplay, and even justify Israel's apartheid regime and violation of Palestinians' human rights. Anti-pinkwashing activism intensified throughout the 1990s and 2000s. Today, activist groups such as Queers Undermining Israeli Terrorism! and Bay Area Art Queers Unleashing Power continue the work started through the ALN-LISPP collaboration in the late 1980s.

3.C.5.

Joseph Gerson

From introduction to *The Deadly Connection* (1986)

Joseph Gerson's *The Deadly Connection* offered an important and influential explanation of the ties between nuclear weapons and US intervention against national liberation movements. Due in significant part to debates regarding Middle East policy, nuclear and anti-intervention activism were frequently distanced from one another. Gerson's introduction explains the political stakes of this division and lays out major lessons gained from examining the problem.

In recent years the term "deadly connection" has become something of a slogan or cliché for the peace movement. . . . [T]he "deadly connection" is the extraordinarily close relationship between US nuclear war policy and US foreign intervention. Its four principle components are the historical use of nuclear blackmail, a first strike nuclear war policy which serves as a shield to protect US intervention in the Third World, the erosion of the "firebreak" between nuclear and conventional war, and intervention in industrialized and Third World nations to build and to maintain US bases and installations necessary for fighting nuclear war. Like all other aspects of militarism and the arms race, the deadly connection has demanded a heavy price from our civil society and from our economy. . . .

The concept of the deadly connection grew directly from the US-approved Israeli invasion of Lebanon in June 1982 and from the massive March for Disarmament and Human Needs held in New York City that same month. . . . On June 12, when we marched through New York's concrete canyons into Central Park, it was not yet clear that the Syrians and Soviets would stand aside as the Israelis drove on and into Beirut. We faced the possibility that the superpowers would find themselves forced to support their Middle East clients, just as they had done during the 1973 Middle East war. In the final days of that war, President Nixon placed US forces on a DEFCON 3 alert to prevent the Soviets from coming to aid of the defeated, encircled, and starving Egyptian Army, which was trapped in the Sinai Desert.

On June 12 in Central Park only one woman had the insight and courage to say anything from the podium about the war then raging in Lebanon. No one was moved to say that the Israeli-Syrian confrontation could trigger the nuclear holocaust we had come to prevent. While people left encouraged by our numbers and thrilled by the demonstration, some of us were not as excited. We knew people on all sides of the war in Lebanon, and we could not ignore the war's human and possibly nuclear dimensions. The June 12 march, which was one of the American peace movement's greatest achievements, also revealed serious shortcomings. Our silence spoke all too loudly.

I spent much of the summer following the June 12 march trying to understand what had and had not happened in New York and learning about the relationship between nuclear war and foreign intervention. The information was sparse. . . .

In September 1982 representatives from a number of Boston-based organizations responded enthusiastically to an AFSC [American Friends Service Committee] invitation to consider and plan what became the first "deadly connection conference." These organizations included the Massachusetts Council for a Nuclear Weapons Freeze, the Central America Solidarity Association, Catholic Connection, Mobilization for Survival, and Oxfam. With their help we secured commitments from an impressive array of speakers and assembled three hundred representatives from more than one hundred local, regional, and national peace organizations. . . .

Five of the basic lessons we have learned . . . [are the following.] To begin with, Nagasaki was not the last time the United States "used" its nuclear arsenal. . . Our commanders in chief have repeatedly threatened to use nuclear weapons against the Soviet Union and Third World nations to retain US control over "the Grand Area", the sphere of influence won as a result of World War II which extends from our shores to the borders of the Soviet Union and China.

Second, we have learned that although the nuclear arms race is suicidal, it has not been as unthinking as many of us first believed. It has been fueled by the United States' effort to obtain a first strike capability, the ability to destroy, or threaten to destroy, the Soviet Union without fear of retaliation. In Randall Forsberg's words: "The arms race has nothing to do with defense, little to do with deterrence, and everything to do with a monopoly of US intervention in other countries." Euromissiles, MX, and other first strike weapons have been deployed to create a shield allowing the United States to intervene in Third World nations with reduced fear of Soviet retaliation. The Soviet Union, with its inferior but all too powerful nuclear arsenal, has done its best to raise a nuclear umbrella, based apparently more on deterrence rather than a first strike capability, over Eastern Europe as well as the Soviet Union itself.

Thirdly, the "firebreak" between conventional and nuclear war is rapidly disappearing. . . . The incentive and ability to keep a conflict "conventional" is thus being reduced. . . .

Fourth, we have also learned that the protests in Japan against the deployment of Tomahawk cruise missiles, New Zealand's ban on visits by nuclear-powered or nuclear-armed vessels, and European resistance to the deployment of Pershing II and cruise missiles are struggles for national sovereignty *and* survival. They result from US intervention in industrialized and Third World nations to build and to maintain the technological infrastructure for fighting nuclear, as well as conventional, wars. The nuclear arms race itself has thus become another driving force for intervention.

Finally, we have recognized that in the post-Vietnam War era the US peace movement allowed itself to become divided into two wings, one focusing on disarmament and the other on intervention in the Third World. They rarely communicated, cooperated, or learned from one another. The lesson is being learned that focusing individual or organizational efforts on only the nuclear arms race, or on only one manifestation of intervention, often fragments and weakens the struggle for peace, justice and survival. . . .

What can we do? We can begin to learn about and to understand better the threats to our, and to others', survival. We can teach, organize, write to and meet with our Congressional representatives, declare nuclear-free zones, go to jail, demand an end to the war in Central America, assist people in need of sanctuary, and learn and speak about the Middle East. What will it take to survive? Being stubborn enough to pursue the meaning of things, being brave enough to speak to our neighbors and friends, being patient enough to walk in endless marches, being bold enough to think and act as if our lives and those of our children were more important than reasons of state or corporate dividends.

3.C.6.

Rachelle Marshall

"From Israel to America: The Women in Black" (1990)

Founded in Israel, Women in Black now organizes around the world. This report explains the group's formation in Israel and its early replication in the United States. In both places, Women in Black has held a strong base among Jewish feminists. The author of this essay, Rachelle Marshall, was a longtime activist and journalist who published this report in the widely circulated *Washington Report on Middle East Affairs*.

Just as the intifada has changed forever the relationship between Israel and the Palestinians under occupation, it has also brought about deep and lasting changes in the role of women on both sides of the conflict. With thousands of Palestinian men in Israeli prisons, in hiding, or seriously injured, women in the West Bank and Gaza have of necessity come out of their homes to take on vital jobs in community organizations and in active support of the uprising. Many have themselves gone to prison. Virtually all of them have seen a father, husband, son, or brother suffer arrest, injury, or death.

In Israel, women experience the reverse side of the intifada. It is their husbands, sons, and brothers who must carry out the government's policy of crushing the uprising with bullets and clubs. As a result, Rachel Ostrowitz writes in *New Outlook*, there is increasing violence in Israel itself, and particularly against women.

"The use of violence in the West Bank and Gaza acted as a boomerang," she claims. "It brought the intifada into our homes." According to Ms. Ostrowitz, a number of Israeli women came to regard Israel's oppression of the Palestinians as linked to the oppression of all marginal groups, including themselves. As the intifada continued, hundreds of them lost patience with established peace groups in Israel and launched a protest movement of their own, which frequently works closely with Palestinian women.

The Women's Peace Movement, a coalition organized in Jerusalem in early 1989, now includes an Arab women's group, the Democratic Women's Movement, which has worked for equal rights for Israeli Arabs since 1948. Women in Support of Women Political Prisoners publicizes cases of brutality against Palestinian women prisoners and provides material support for them and their families. The Jerusalem-based Women Against the Occupation sponsors lectures by Palestinians as well as Israeli women activists as part of a broad educational and political program. Bridge to Peace and the Women's International League for Peace and Freedom include both Israeli and Arab women, who go on regular "solidarity visits" to the occupied territories.

Although the number of Israeli women involved in the peace movement is still relatively small, one peace group, the Women in Black, is able to reach an estimated twenty thousand people each week. For nearly two years they have conducted vigils every Friday at noon at busy intersections in Tel Aviv, Haifa, Jerusalem, and other cities, holding signs that read "End the Occupation" and "Talk to the PLO." Despite verbal harassment, physical abuse, and occasional teargassing, the organization continues to gain new members, so that now at least twenty-four vigils are held every week throughout Israel. In early October, three hundred members of Women in Black gathered together with Palestinian women from the West Bank to hold workshops and share experiences. The group sent a telegram to the Israeli government protesting the tearing apart of Palestinian families because of deportations from the West Bank of women who lack residence permits.

The example of a women's protest movement based on the unassailable principle that it is wrong for one group of human beings to dominate another by force touched a sympathetic nerve among American women who had been shocked by reports of Israeli army brutality. The Women in Black vigils in Israel began in February 1988. Just two months later, the Brooklyn-based Jewish Women's Committee to End the Occupation (JWCEO) began weekly vigils in New York. During the following months, Women in Black vigils spread across the continent, with groups forming in Massachusetts, Michigan, Missouri, Washington, Oregon, California, and Canada. Since last spring, the JWCEO has acted as a coordinating committee for Women in Black and other women's peace groups, but there is actually no formal organization—no membership lists, no dues, and few, if any, meetings.

Ruth Michaels of the Berkeley, California, Women in Black, which just celebrated its one-year anniversary, says that members of her group "feel they've gone to enough meetings in their lives." They have found that vigiling on a regular basis has promoted cohesiveness and dedication they have seldom experienced before and a greater feeling of satisfaction. Ms. Michaels, like one or two others in her group, is a Holocaust survivor.

Women in Black groups in the United States appear to spring up spontaneously, when two or three women agree to put on black outfits, paint a sign, and take to a street corner. Dr. Lilliam Moed, a founder of the Israeli group Women Against the Occupation, tours the United States once a year, speaking to women's peace groups. She believes the close contacts that exist between Israeli and American Jewish women are largely responsible for the spread of Women in Black. American women traveling in Israel often take part in vigils in Tel Aviv or Jerusalem and bring back word of Women in Black to peace groups at home.

Dr. Moed, a professional psychologist who holds dual US-Israeli citizenship, believes that American Women in Black are of crucial importance to the Israeli peace movement. Because of Israel's dependent relationship with the United States and the close sympathy between the two countries, "the more support we get from Americans the more likely we are to influence our own government," she says. In line with this reasoning, many Women in Black groups across the United States call for pressure on Washington to in turn pressure Israel to negotiate a just peace with the Palestinians.

In Palo Alto, California, for instance, Women in Black distribute leaflets urging that letters be sent to the State Department and to congressional representatives asking that they "support national independence for both Israelis and Palestinians, end support for Israel's occupation, and press Israel to negotiate with the Palestinians' chosen representatives, including the PLO." Other groups appeal directly to the Israeli government by distributing petitions calling for an end to administrative detention, collective punishment, and the mistreatment of prisoners. All of the Women in Black give weekly evidence that they endorse Rachel Ostrowitz's declaration that "we will not allow our senses to be numbed by the daily killings. We will not accept oppression, discrimination, or exploitation as part of our political system. We won't give up or shut up or put up with the current version of reality."

3.C.7.

Out Now

From *War Watch* special report (1991)

Based in Salinas, California, Out Now organized against the Gulf War in 1990–91. The following is excerpted from its newsletter published soon after the formal conclusion of the military conflict. It illustrates both the mainstream political rhetoric surrounding the Gulf War and how grassroots activists sought to contest US militarism over the long term, including the "new world order" proclaimed by President George H. W. Bush.

Who's Next?

Just days after the fighting stopped a euphoric president declared: "By God, we've kicked this Vietnam Syndrome." The very name suggested for twenty years that the American public's opposition to US wars in the Third World was a sickness. The president saw it as an addiction that was kicked, cold turkey. A measure of the power of Vietnam was shown in prewar polls. In October 90 percent opposed the US starting a war. By March 90 percent were cheering the slaughter.

. . . Who will be next? There is a long list of possibilities. . . . There is no way of knowing what country will next experience the New World Order. Perhaps none will dare cross the path of the world's only superpower. Perhaps Bush's New World Order will be like Pax Romana (the Roman Peace)—decades of peace through superior firepower.

Perhaps the Vietnam "syndrome" is like a chronic disease—you are never really "cured." Perhaps this wave of victory euphoria will begin to ebb. Perhaps the American people will realize that the price of the New World Order is war and the endless preparation for war—and the responsibility for death on a grand scale. Perhaps we will say no.

What Can We Do?

First, we must demand that the United States make a major contribution to UN efforts to provide *immediate* medical relief to Iraq. After World War II, the US led efforts to rebuild Europe's (including Germany's) economy. President Bush has pledged *not* to provide a single cent of US aid to rebuild Iraq but has said he might allow some humanitarian aid. The first task is to demand massive and immediate US medical aid through the UN. We should also demand that Congress immediately hold hearings on reconstruction aid to Iraq.

Second, we must speak out against this slaughter. Now, when the polls demonstrate such overwhelming support, *every* voice of opposition is critical. You can write letters to the editor, call radio talk shows, wear buttons that say, "Not all of us are proud of this." Such actions are not simply acts of defiance—they are the first step in the long process of *changing public opinion*.

The overwhelming support for this war is built upon the image that it was a cheap and easy victory. Our immediate task is to expose the full cost of this war—because war is never cheap. This report focuses on the staggering loss of Iraqi life. But the full cost of the war includes the suffering of hundreds of thousands in Kuwait and Jordan. It includes all those in this country who would benefit from the peace dividend we rightfully expected a year ago. It includes the cost of a permanent US military force in the Gulf and a new generation of weapons for the next war. They are already talking about tanks we can air lift, faster ships, better missiles.

Much of our task now is to struggle for the hearts and minds of the American people. We do it one on one, we help pay for ads, we organize forums, we go to demonstrations. We do it by finding ways to stay informed and keep our perspective despite the waves of White House and military- generated propaganda. We are a small, discouraged, angry minority right now—and that makes every vote critical.

We are also the hope of millions of people throughout the Third World, people without our free speech rights, people who face not discouragement and isolation but the deadly onslaught of the world's only superpower. Our inaction is a luxury they cannot afford.

As we act to expose the truth about this war—and stop the next one—we should also take time to learn from our mistakes during the past six months.

- We focused too much attention on the possible loss of US lives—on avoiding another Vietnam. The Gulf War makes clear that the US military is capable of inflicting massive destruction with minimal loss of US life.
- It is too easy to send a standing (volunteer) army to war. Unlike Vietnam, the only people who had something personally at stake this time were those who had loved ones in the Gulf. And those people tend to be from the working class and poor—those with less power and influence in this country.
- The movement was too slow to respond to the initial US deployment in August—falling for the line that this was to defend Saudi Arabia. We need to see *each* US action in the context of a worldwide pattern of intervention. We need to remember the central lesson of Vietnam: they lie to us. And we need to learn how to read the hints broadly dropped in the media. In *August* US officials were saying on "background" that there would be a war and the goal was to destroy the Iraqi military.
- We were too timid to push Congress to act sooner. The dance with our "allies" in Congress is an old one. We say you have to act, they say we don't have the votes, give us time. By the time they're ready the president has created a crisis and manipulated the situation. This time the crisis was the eve of the UN deadline. We should do what the right wing does: pressure those closest to you—because they are the ones you have the most power over.
- We are too dependent on the mass media which will inevitably march to the White House drummer during a crisis. There are alternative sources of information, and the mainstream media does provide some critical information. *But* the dominant images in the mainstream press will be those fed to it by the White House and the military.

Ultimately, our actions must be built upon an alternative vision to the New World Order so dramatically begun in the Gulf. We must question the right of the United States to consume the lion's share of the world's resources—and to use its overwhelming military power to get them. Our actions will often place us in the minority here, but we will stand with the great majority of the world's poor—all of them potential victims of the world's only great empire.

3.C.8.

Roots Against War

"Queers Get RAW!" (1991)

Activism against the Gulf War was strongly tied to preceding antiwar activism and to AIDS, LGBTQ, and racial justice organizing. These strands converged in events such as ACT UP's Day of Desperation, held on January 22,

1991, in which activists protested against the Gulf War with slogans including "fight AIDS, not Arabs" and "money for AIDS, not war." Similar connections are evident in the following document, written by queer-identified members of the people of color organization Roots Against War (RAW). A predecessor of the influential group STORM (Standing Together to Organize a Revolutionary Movement), RAW was active in the San Francisco Bay Area.

We lesbian/gay queer members of RAW do not support Bush's Gulf War. We cannot condone the spending of trillions of dollars for cheap oil, the destruction of Arab land, and genocidal acts against Arab people or the disproportionate amount of US troops of color. Yet Bush still cuts welfare programs, housing, education, and the US government has yet to adequately fund AIDS research and care. In fact, in the first weeks of this war the US has spent more on funding its military machines of death than it has in a decade of AIDS research, treatment, and care!

This is in a time when, if our lives continue to be declared expendable here and abroad, AIDS will soon be the number one killer of women and men of color. African Americans and Latinos make up 45 percent of people living with AIDS. Currently Chicanos/Latinos make up 8 percent of the US, yet they are 14 percent of the HIV population. AIDS is the number one killer of African American women in New York City and, nationwide, 50 percent of all women with AIDS are African Americans. Eighty percent of children born HIV-infected are African American. Ten percent of the Native American population is HIV positive, which is the size of many whole tribes. Pilipinos are soon becoming San Francisco's largest HIV-positive group. And, on an international level, the presence of US military in the "Third World" has usually coincided with a high rate of HIV infection for indigenous populations.

We refuse to die for oil overseas and we will not allow this government to neglect our lives within this country!

Our people need education regarding safe sex and all forms of health care rather than becoming pawns in Bush's oil war game. Queers of color cannot stand by and remain silent—we need to get on the streets with our love and our rage because, this being wartime, we are all at high risk.

Roots Against War is an alliance of people of color dedicated to fighting this current war [and] the racist and sexist assaults on our communities, as well as [to] struggling with our people with regards to heterosexism and homophobia.

3.C.9.

Angela Davis

"Keynote Speech Delivered at CAAAV's Fifteenth Anniversary Fundraiser in New York City" (2001)

In this speech, given just over two weeks after the attacks of September 11, Angela Davis addressed the importance of distinguishing grief from national-ism. She spoke at a gathering celebrating the fifteenth anniversary of CAAAV: Organizing Asian Communities, an event that had been planned before Sep-tember 11 and now took place in an altered political context. Founded in 1986 as Communities against Anti-Asian Violence, CAAAV organizes low-income Asian immigrant communities in New York City on issues ranging from police brutality to housing to street vendors' rights.

As the US flags wave against the backdrop of such evocative phrases as "we as a nation" and "we as Americans" (when what is really meant is "we as US cit-izens"), CAAAV compels us to respond in a way that moves beyond the easy and dangerous frame of US nationalism with its bellicose anthems and its hate-ful exclusion of those who are or appear to be noncitizens. This is a national-ism that requires leaders on which to displace the responsibility of national salvation.

So a major question for the people of this country—those who a few weeks ago were not so quick to accept George W. Bush as their leader (or New York-ers not so quick to accept Giuliani as their leader)—is how to maintain a criti-cal posture toward the current leadership. This requires us to maintain a criti-cal historical memory. We have heard the media indicate many times that after September 11, things will never be the same. Yes, this is true—never again can we assume that the United States is invulnerable. But we cannot assume that ev-erything has changed. The attack on the World Trade Center and on the Pen-tagon does not annul the history of US militarism. It does not cover up the fact that people of Japanese ancestry were held in internment camps during World War II. It does not diminish the meaning of war against Vietnam. And it should not camouflage the fact that the US significantly helped to create the condi-tions that led to the violence of September 11. It should not blind us to the fact that—if Osama bin Laden is indeed the culprit and that if the Taliban is sup-porting him and his organization—that the US supported both bin Laden and the Taliban against the former Soviet Union. It should not blind us to the fact that the US has refused to listen to the impassioned pleas of Afghan women who try to resist the patriarchal policies of the Taliban.

Why has George W. Bush suddenly emerged as a heroic figure, when not long ago, the results of the election were severely questioned all over the coun-try and throughout the world? Thousands of innocent people were killed on

September 11—and many of us have personal experience of this loss. Those of us who have no direct personal loss feel that we or our families could just as easily been among those who died. But this is a time to distinguish between the people of this country and the government and institutions that control the country. It is right to claim the innocence of those who died, but when we look at the governing institutions and leaders, we do not discover the same innocence.

The attack on September 11 has been represented as an attack against global capitalism and the US flag as its symbol. But we must consider that many of those who died were already targets of the daily violence of global capitalism. This is not a time to wave the US flag, to claim the superiority of America and American citizens. This is not a time to claim the preeminence of Western civilization as Italian prime minister Silvio Berlusconi did on Wednesday. In his words, according to the *New York Times*, "We should be confident of the superiority of our civilization, which consists of a value system that has given people widespread prosperity in those countries that embrace it and guarantees respect for human rights and religion." He went on to say that the West "is bound to occidentalize and conquer new people." Berlusconi also implicated the antiglobalization protestors in Genoa in a terrorist project linked to the violence of September 11. What is important about Berlusconi's remarks is that he gave voice to the civilizational thinking that lurks about official discourse today. As the attack is described repeatedly as not just an attack against "America" but against "civilization," Bush makes reference to "smoking the terrorists out of holes" and "tracking them down in their caves."

This is why [Senator] Dianne Feinstein feels justified in calling for a six-month moratorium on student visas. But let us not forget that the so-called superiority of American freedom means oppression for the people of the southern region, and when convenient, it also excludes workers, citizens, and noncitizens alike. The government is willing to bail out the airlines, but the airlines invoke their emergency clauses to avoid giving severance pay to laid-off workers.

I want to suggest that we need to take our emotional responses seriously, that is, we should understand them as emotional and not as the basis for foreign policy, not as the basis for new ways of thinking about entire populations, cultures, and religions. Some of you may remember the initial responses to the bombing of the Oklahoma City Federal Building. In a recent interview in *Z* magazine Noam Chomsky pointed out:

> When a federal building was blown up in Oklahoma City, there were immediate cries to bomb the Middle East. These terminated when it was discovered that the perpetrator was from the US ultra-right militia movement. The reaction was not to destroy Montana and Idaho, where the movements are based, but to seek and capture the perpetrator, bring him to trial, and—crucially—explore the grievances that lie behind such crimes and to address the problems. Just about every crime—whether a robbery in the streets or colossal atrocities—has reasons, and commonly

we find that some of them are serious and should be addressed. Matters are no different in this case—at least, for those who are concerned to reduce the threat of terrorist violence rather than to escalate it.

Although there have been many official pleas against racial profiling, there have also been innumerable attacks on people and institutions perceived to be associated with the individuals and organizations that may be responsible for the terrorist attacks in New York and Washington. Muslims, Arabs, [and] South Asians have borne the brunt of this racial profiling. Mosques have been attacked. South Asians have been murdered. People perceived to be of Middle Eastern descent have been removed from airplanes for no other reason than their physical appearance. This means that we will have to think more deeply about ways in which racism stimulates militarism and vice versa, how militarism promotes racism.

I must tell you that of the many thousands of candidates for whom I have ever voted in my life, there is one person who will always stand head and shoulders above all the rest. I voted for Barbara Lee to represent the congressional district in which I reside and I want to publicly congratulate her for having had the courage to stand up against militarism.

The use-of-force resolution passed 98–0 in the Senate and 420–1 in the House. Lee was the only person who voted against giving Bush a blank check for war. John Lewis said that "several other members wanted to be there also but at the same time, like me, they didn't want to be seen as soft on terrorism."

Barbara Lee has reminded us that it is precisely in times of crisis like this that we must hold on to our principles, that we should treasure our political memory. In this moment of intense communal mourning, we should be aware of the ease with which collective emotions can be politically manipulated toward ends that promote more violence and racism. Violence, as CAAAV points out, that will also be intensified by the INS [Immigration and Naturalization Service]—the federal agency that has more armed agents than any other, the FBI included. There are countless numbers of people of Middle Eastern descent who are currently being held by the INS, who have joined the thousands of others who languish in detention centers or jails and prisons. As the INS is a significant component of the prison industrial complex with evident links to the military industrial complex, it should be clearer than ever that prison activists need to join activists who work against racist immigration policy and practices.

In this context, I must mention the recent appointment of Tom Ridge to head the newly created Office of Homeland Security. Imagine now that Condoleezza Rice and Tom Ridge are in charge of the security of the country. Ridge has signed more than two hundred execution warrants since becoming governor of Pennsylvania in 1995, including two warrants for Mumia Abu-Jamal. The fascist resonances of this notion of "homeland security" should not be ignored, nor the fact that this is throwback to the internment camps for people of Japanese descent and a throwback to the McCarthy era.

The invocation of freedom as what the announced war against terrorism is designed to defend is the kind of ideology that has led historically to attacks on countless number of people—on their bodies and on their rights. When I hear the word "freedom" emanating from the mouth of Bush, from the mouths of Bushes, I ask—whose freedom and freedom toward what end? The market's freedom? Freedom to hire Filipina women at subminimum wage to provide domestic service for the affluent? Freedom to refuse to send a top-level delegation to the World Conference against Racism? Freedom for the delegation to walk out of the conference and thus to refuse to help chart a global course to eradicate racism, including racism against Palestinians perpetrated by the Israeli government? Including reparations for the historical and current damage created by slavery and by genocidal colonialist practices against indigenous peoples throughout the world?

This is not the kind of freedom most of us would want to support. If we wish today to look toward a world in which we can engage in the practice of freedom, the major question confronting us today is how to rebuild a strong antiwar movement with an equally strong antiracist consciousness. In South Africa, at the World Conference against Racism, many people learned that instead of looking toward the US government, they should look elsewhere in the US for leadership—to organizations like Third World Within, like the Women of Color Resource Center from the Bay Area (my own delegation) and, of course, to CAAAV: Organizing Asian Immigrant Communities.

3.C.10.

Purvi Shah, Sakhi for South Asian Women

"The Rain of Sorrows" (2001)

Founded in 1989, Sakhi for South Asian Women works to address domestic violence in New York City's South Asian communities. In the following excerpt, Purvi Shah (then a board member of Sakhi, later its executive director) speaks to the experiences of South Asian communities targeted in the aftermath of the September 11 attacks.

September 11 is a day that changed all of us. As a board member at Sakhi for South Asian Women, an anti–domestic violence organization based in New York City, I grieve for a longtime friend and fellow volunteer who worked on the ninety-fourth floor of 2 World Trade. Swarna Chalasani is still "missing": for me the world has taken on a haunting quality and signifies not the possibility of return but that I miss Swarna's presence in my life and will do so for the rest of my life.

Swarna gave so much love and attention to the Sakhi survivors she supported. She provided women who wanted to break free of violence a chance to do so, not only by offering emotional support but also by giving women facing violence financial assistance from her own pockets. By donating money to buy sewing machines or other resources, Swarna helped women strive for their dreams. The world will never know what it lost—what dreams never had a chance to become reality—as a result of the terrorist attacks on September 11.

I want to thank the firefighters, police officers, and rescue workers who struggled to save so many individual lives—and in the process may have lost their own. Yet the people who are lost to the rubble of the World Trade Center, the Pentagon, or the crashed airplanes are not the only victims of the September 11 terrorist attacks. After the second round of American bombing, four Afghan UN aid workers were killed when their building was destroyed. As the United States drops bombs over Afghanistan, the victims are also innocent Afghans who have been trying to escape a country torn by war and instability for more than two decades. How do we mourn the four Afghan demining workers lost in the ruins of their bombed building? How do we prevent further misdirected American attacks on humanitarian agencies such as the International Red Cross Center? How do we demonstrate the same value for individual lives that the rescue workers showed in New York City for people who live outside America?

We should start by safeguarding and respecting the people in our own communities inside the United States who are facing a racist backlash in the wake of the attacks. One Sakhi survivor braved verbal attacks from fellow residents of a mainstream shelter, women who asked, "How could your country do this? How can you support terrorists?" This survivor, a Muslim Pakistani, did not know how to confront the ignorance or racism or need to proclaim her innocence. Even more troubling is that no caseworker or shelter staff person jumped in to aid her. Many women we work with—Muslim women, women who wear traditional South Asian dress, and undocumented immigrants—have so much more to fear now (as do other American Muslims, Arab Americans, Sikhs, and South Asian Americans).

Since September 11 Sakhi and sister organization Women for Afghan Women have been busy planning peace rallies and memorials in New York City. By some accounts, more than 300 Indians, 150 Pakistanis, and 50 Bangladeshis were killed in the World Trade Center: these numbers do not even count the undocumented workers. At Sakhi and Women for Afghan Women, we have felt the need to create a community forum for families to grieve and come together in the hopes for creating peace. We sought to carve a space that condemned the violence of the terrorist attacks and advocated against further violence [. . .]

We Americans of South Asian origin also have to be afraid of the enemy from within. In the early wake of the attacks in America, Balbir Singh Sodhi, a Sikh gas station worker in Mesa, Arizona, and Waqar Hasan, a Pakistani grocery store owner in Dallas, Texas were shot by men who saw themselves as American patriots. Those working-class members of our community, those who work in public spaces such as grocery stores, gas stations, or taxis, are especially vulnerable to random violence—racism justified as patriotism. In a nation founded on the idea of innocent until proven guilty, how is it possible that so-called patriots can justify taking another life or hurting another person in the name of America? These American vigilantes who are targeting their Muslim, Arab American, Sikh, and South Asian American neighbors and community residents are the ones guilty—guilty of committing hate crimes against innocent members of American society. This racism cannot be tolerated. No person deserves to be abused based on their physical appearance, ethnicity, national origin, or creed. Domestic terrorism must be stopped because all of us deserve equal protection under the law—these are the ideals we Americans cherish [. . .]

In the four weeks since the tragedy, more than 645 incidents of racial abuse against Muslims, South Asians, and Sikhs have been reported. Will justice be brought to those who have suffered racism unjustly? Those who are victims of hate crimes should report the violence in order to document the abuse and provide impetus for policy and educational actions. We must remember that after the bombing of Pearl Harbor in World War II, more than 120,000 Japanese Americans were dispossessed of their homes and belongings and rounded up into internment camps—simply because they looked like the enemy. While no such overt government action has been taken against those of us who look the current enemy, the Mobilization against Terrorism Act includes provisions which would expand search and seizure and wiretapping laws as well as say it is legitimate to indefinitely detain legal immigrants suspected of terrorism. After the September 11 attacks, the FBI received more than one hundred thousand tips of terrorist activity: you do the math. Most of these tips were probably given by people who "suspected" their innocent Muslim or South Asian neighbors. In a time when South Asians are being removed from certain flights due to racist fear, are we willing to let our civil liberties be curtailed—perhaps forever? As America fights in the name of democracy and freedom, we cannot let the structures of democracy and freedom crumble here at home.

Desis Rising Up and Moving, 2000–Present
Simmy Makhijani

Founded in 2000, Desis Rising Up and Moving (DRUM) is a multi-generational membership-based organization made up of South Asian and Indo-Caribbean low-wage immigrant workers, youth, and families in New York City, who are organizing for economic and racial justice. DRUM's primary commitment is to mobilize and build its members' capacity for strategic social and policy change, with emphases on immigrant rights, education reform, civil rights, gender justice, worker rights, and global justice.

DRUM initially formed through the forty-one days of action, a series of community responses to the acquittal of four undercover police officers who killed unarmed immigrant Amadou Diallo, shooting him forty-one times on February 4, 1999. The officers were acquitted one year later. Kazi Fouzia, longtime DRUM member and current director of organizing, reports that through the forty-one days of action, working-class South Asians found each other on the streets, bound by a shared struggle against police brutality and racial profiling.

Founded at the grassroots through living room discussions, DRUM was initially composed predominantly of working-class South Asian youth. In the aftermath of the devastating attacks of September 11, 2001, DRUM sharpened its focus, spearheading a coordinated response to the spike in hate violence and racial and religious profiling against South Asians. DRUM quickly became a critical organizing and legal resource for New York's Muslim, Arab, and South Asian families who were targeted through unlawful arrests, surveillance, detention, and threats of deportation. DRUM established a twenty-four-hour hotline, organized rallies, marches, vigils, political education workshops, and offered vital legal support. The organization's communities were heavily impacted by the INS Special Registration program, a post-9/11 policy that required boys and men from twenty-five predominantly Muslim countries to register with US immigration authorities. Under the program, some eighty-three thousand Muslims in the United States were rounded up and questioned, approximately fourteen thousand were placed in deportation proceedings, and several thousand were deported; none were prosecuted on terrorism charges. DRUM built a database to track community members that were vanishing into deportation centers and prisons.

Through its work, DRUM drew large numbers of South Asians into an organizing framework that developed an increasingly growing membership base. It prioritized member governance over decisions and the day-to-day running of the organization. This ensured members could exercise their leadership by taking charge of policy campaigns and by engaging in public speaking, testifying, strategizing, coalition building, research, mobilizing, and direct action.

Since the Ferguson uprising of 2014, DRUM has continued to work hard to build solidarity across unevenly impacted communities while also challenging the ways in which anti-Black racism is perpetuated in non-Black communities of color. DRUM has also been crucial in post-Trump organizing through its creation of a community defense network called the Hate Free Zone. Its core commitments revolve around base building, leadership development, public policy change, and institution building. DRUM claims over four thousand workers as members and coordinates its work with a robust staff, core set of leaders, and board.

"Desi" is the colloquial word used to loosely reference peoples from South Asia. For DRUM this includes Afghanistan, Bangladesh, Bhutan, Guyana, India, Nepal, Pakistan, Sri Lanka, Suriname, Trinidad and Tobago, and beyond. See DRUM's mission statement at www.drumnyc.org/about-us.

Not in Our Name

"Pledge of Resistance" (2002)

Written by longtime activist Starhawk and poet and musician Saul Williams, this pledge of resistance is one of two major statements issued by Not in Our Name, a national antiwar organization founded in March 2002 to protest US responses to the September 11 attacks. Not in Our Name won a broad set of endorsers, and its poster became a common sight in communities where antiwar organizing was strong.

We believe that as people living
in the United States it is our
responsibility to resist the injustices
done by our government, in our names

Not in our name
will you wage endless war
there can be no more deaths
no more transfusions of blood for oil

Not in our name
will you invade countries
bomb civilians, kill more children
letting history take its course
over the graves of the nameless

Not in our name
will you erode the very freedoms
you have claimed to fight for

Not by our hands
will we supply weapons and funding
for the annihilation of families
on foreign soil

Not by our mouths
will we let fear silence us

Not by our hearts
will we allow whole peoples
or countries to be deemed
evil

Not by our will
and not in our name

We pledge resistance
We pledge alliance with those
who have come under attack
for voicing opposition to the war
or for their religion or ethnicity

We pledge to make common cause
with the people of the world
to bring about justice freedom and peace
Another world is possible
and we pledge to make it real

Figure 3.5. "Fight My War/Follow the Leader/Finance My Debt" (2001). Image courtesy of Interference Archive.

Retort

"Neither Their War nor Their Peace" (2003)

This essay, written by a collective of writers, artists, and activists, was produced as a broadsheet and distributed at demonstrations against the US invasion of Iraq. Held on February 15, 2003, these protests drew millions of people in over six hundred cities worldwide.

Last week, at American insistence, the copy of Picasso's *Guernica* in the anteroom to the UN Security Council chamber was curtained over—not "an appropriate backdrop," it was explained, for official statements to the world media.

We have no words for the horror to come, for the screams and carnage of the first days of battle, the fear and brutality of the long night of occupation that will follow, the truck bombs and slit throats and unstoppable cycle of revenge, the puppets in the palaces chattering about "democracy," the exultation of the anti-Crusaders, Baghdad descending into the shambles of a new, more dreadful Beirut, and the inevitable retreat (thousands of body bags later) from the failed McJerusalem.

We have no Olympian predictions. We do not know what happens next. We shall not ape the ludicrous certainty of the CIA hacks on the news, trotting out tonight's "analysis" (tonight's excuses for a half million dead and wounded in a single laser-guided week).

The best we can offer is negative wisdom, addressed to comrades in a dark and confusing time.

- The answer to war is not peace. "War is the health of the state," as Randolph Bourne indelibly put it, but so is the so-called peace that the state stage-manages for us the peace of cemeteries, the peace of "sanctions" and "containment," the peace of the "peace process" (photo opportunities on the White House lawn plus gunships and bulldozers in Jenin), the decade of Iraqi deaths unseen on your TV screens. "Neither their war nor their peace" should be our slogan.
- It is time to make war on the warmongers. Which means a struggle waged across long years, a campaign of attrition and demoralization. It matters greatly that already, before the war begins, millions of people are in the streets. But marching is no substitute for Mario Savio's call to "put your bodies upon the gears, and upon the wheels, upon the levers, upon all the apparatus." Don't mistake the elation of the stroll down Market Street for the painful, dangerous, month-by-month business of sapping the will of the political-military machine. We know that its will can be broken. We know that a time can come when the customary ignoring of the ruled by the rulers becomes dysfunctional and leads the state to catastrophe.

"Vietnam" is the word for that twilight of the gods. Cheney and Rumsfeld blurt it out every night in the small hours and wake with their pacemakers knocking.

- Terror too is the health of the state. Underneath the absurdity of the duct tape and plastic sheeting advisories lies a serious policy, which our present leaders seem poised to pursue to the bitter end—the fomenting of a permanent culture of terror, sealing each of us into a pod of fear and isolation and feeding our every movement into the Total Information Awareness databank. We are already in a spiral, where terror and the state embrace more tightly each day. And the target is us, our freedoms, our common resources, our possibilities of invention and ease.

- Don't put your faith in the blood-stained "international community." Remember the UN's record through the years as the hand-wringing front man for any and every initiative of power. Remember Kofi Annan's role as chief blind eye to the Rwandan genocide. Don't think that Swiss banker Blix will fail to do his masters bidding in the end. Don't mistake the German government, which happily goes on hosting one hundred thousand American troops, for a real opponent of the US Reich. The dogs will all want their share of the spoils. And even if, at the last minute, a nauseous "diplomatic solution" is cobbled together, have we any doubt who will go on paying the costs? The curtain could be rolled back again to reveal Guernica, the suits could make speeches congratulating themselves on the triumphs of military humanism, and still the shit-smeared three-year-olds in the hospital beds in Baghdad would be writhing in agony under Blix's well-fed gaze. For such is the price of containment.

- Look through the mind-numbing speeches in the Security Council to the real pressure, the mass disaffection, that is making the present prewar scenario unlike any other. This is the real ground for optimism, we believe— limited optimism in an otherwise nightmarish situation. The dreary ghost of "public opinion," which the states of the world are normally so adept at conjuring and pretending to obey, has suddenly become a destabilizing factor in the final arrangements for war. Schroeder thought he could call the pacifist beast into the streets strictly in order to take the Reichstag and then retreat gracefully to the usual politics of "meeting our international obligations." Blair thought the eternal British love affair with "their finest hour" would steer him past the familiar shoals of anti-Americanism. It has all turned out to be more difficult than Straw and Chirac ever dreamt. Let us keep up the crude pressure of refusal. Let us keep on setting the diplomatic lapdogs at each other's throats.

- This is a war for global capitalism, not for oil alone. The annals of oil are an uninterrupted chronicle of violence, genocide, and the cynical lawlessness of the corporate frontier. Iraq itself was born from this vile trinity. Now oil men parade the corridors of the White House. All five permanent members of the UN Security Council speak obediently for oil companies that have proved themselves specialists over the years in "regime change," whenever it suits their interests. Nobody, not even Bush, contests the fact that the US industrial-military machine is a hopeless oil junkie. War is inevitable, it is said, not because of American imperialism but because of its addiction to the automobile. Dirty mobility is what America means by freedom. All of which is true. Petroleum is global capitalism's great lubricant, its key means of production. But the case is not proven that Iraqi oil, specifically, is a necessary part of the world picture. In hard cash terms, the Iraqi embargo matters little for corporate profits. Pay heed to the yearly reports and "position papers" churned out by Halliburton and Shell. What they truly covet is not sabotaged wells in the desert but the deep-water fields beneath the warm seas of the Bight of Benin, the Gulf of Mexico, and coastal Brazil. So let us not see in the slaughter of Iraqi civilians only the murderous logic of the SUV. It is not oil capital but capital in general that we must confront. Look around as you march up the Boulevard of Shame, at the bland headquarters of Bechtel, Esprit, and Chevron. Which of the three has the cleaner hands worldwide? To fixate on a single commodity and its detritus obscures the full horror and ruthlessness hidden by the word "globalization": primitive accumulation, predatory and profligate, careering forward on a planetary scale.

- In the destruction of Baghdad resides the logic of empire. Oil is a metaphor for something more lethal, more destructive. What is at stake is the true madness of the world market, the hubris of an imperial "grand design" intended to make the world safe, once and for all, for capital. The map of the oil-rich Middle East will be redrawn, but that will be only the beginning. "American internationalism reflects [. . .] our national interests [. . .] a single sustainable model for national success": such is the breathtaking monism of the new National Security Strategy. Is it any wonder that the costs of empire mount? More than half of all federal funds flow to the military. American "bases" metastasize across the planet in 130 countries by the last count and rising steadily. The homeland economy is bloated and debt ridden.

- As for the miserable fantasy of the war as a blow struck in the name of the Iraqi people against their oppressor—the "mercy by any means necessary" thesis—the best we can do in the face of such looking-glass politics is go back to Edmund Burke. Long ago he had this to say about the sudden discovery of human wickedness that regularly precedes an invasion: "It is not with much credulity I listen to any, when they speak evil of those whom they are going to plunder. I rather suspect that vices are feigned or exaggerated, when profit is looked for in their punishment. An enemy is a bad witness: a robber is a worse." These are words for the times. The earth is crammed full of atrocities, and tyrants are always the true humanitarians.

- What matters on a march is speech, not speeches, the centrifuge of voices, rhythms, and banners, not the hectoring of stale celebrities. Least of all does it matter what CNN makes of the occasion. We recognize that, whether we like it or not, part of what's happening here is a numbers game, a counting of heads. But don't expect the stenographers of power to do anything else than traduce what you see.

- Trust your senses. A march, among other things, materializes the dead percentages in the polls and takes life for a moment off the flickering screen. It is a reminder, a fleeting and artificial one but nonetheless welcome of what the public realm could be.

PART 4

Utopias and Dystopias

In July 1980, more than eleven thousand people braved the summer heat as they converged on a ranch outside of Rapid City, South Dakota. In the shadow of the Black Hills, the assembled crowds gathered over nine days with a major goal in mind: stopping the end of the world.

The Black Hills International Survival Gathering was a stunning example of the unexpected coalitions that had been developing in the Great Plains: Native Americans linking with white ranchers to protest resource extraction and treaty violations carried out by major corporations and their government backers. The gathering was organized by the Black Hills Alliance (BHA), which brought Lakota activists connected with the American Indian Movement and the International Indian Treaty Council together with local ranchers and environmentalists. Dedicated to protecting the nearby Black Hills from uranium mining and toxic dumping, the gathering was further fortified by activists from the growing antinuclear and environmental movements. Camping on the land of a white farmer and BHA member, activists participated in workshops, listened to speeches, and voiced their support for Indigenous sovereignty, ecological sustainability, and energy alternatives.

Taken by the novelty of their approach, activists would later dub their coalition the Cowboy-Indian Alliance. The levity of the name notwithstanding, activists' purpose was serious: it was increasingly apparent that planetary survival itself was imperiled by the trifecta of environmental devastation, corporate greed, and US militarism. This trifecta was on full display in South Dakota: the Survival Gathering took place next to the Ellsworth Air Force base, and uranium mining on the land would enrich nuclear weapons as well as nuclear energy.

With its bold and broad appeal, the Black Hills International Survival Gathering suggested that many activists saw that the fate of the world was at stake. If communist and capitalist states had all failed to prevent the environmental and nuclear precipice, perhaps other forms of protest were needed to make possible a better world. With a shared emphasis on industrial development, both capitalist and communist states take the natural world for granted. Both frameworks also assume that nation-states are a necessary and desirable form of political organization. Indigenous cosmologies—which emphasize nonstate nationalism and see as primary the interconnections between the earth, animals, and people—reject capitalism and exceed Marxism.

For many radicals, the crises of the time period also provided an opportunity to renew and revive alternate approaches. Such efforts at renewal were undoubtedly varied, in both attempt and execution. Some activists revised what had been done before, whereas others sought to chart paths well outside the conventions of American protest politics. Across this spectrum, activists adapted their approach in relation to the changing conditions. Their alertness took many forms: it included a greater appreciation of the natural world as the foundation of all things, as well as stronger emphasis on Indigenous sovereignty as a more harmonious and just approach than either a capitalist status quo or Soviet-style Marxism. For others, the political climate fostered renewed interest in anarchist and other decentralized forms of organization.

Section A, "Stopping the End of the World," illustrates the blend of critique and practicality that defined the movements themselves. Activists honed the techniques of nonviolent direct action through mobilizations against nuclear war, environmental destruction, and bipartisan budgetary priorities that enabled such crises. Drawing on multiple political traditions, they generalized their knowledge of civil disobedience and affinity group organizing into training manuals, a number of which we excerpt in this section. Protests at nuclear or military sites spawned long-term encampments, which, in turn, generated intense debates about leadership, decision making, and how activists should respond to the racist impacts of environmental devastation.

Pollution, deforestation, and other ecological ruin wrought the most damage on working-class communities of color and Indigenous communities, sparking the rise of a movement calling for environmental *justice*. While the conservationist movement focused on rural lands, environmental justice activists brought the fight to urban areas. The idea of environmental justice came into being when longtime community organizations began identifying the environmental impact of structural inequality. They also challenged the funding priorities, action strategies, and overwhelming whiteness of both large and grassroots environmental organizations. Their framework for justice was a challenge to both major corporations and the mainstream environmental movement.

The challenge that environmental justice activists posed to mainline environmentalism was a particularly powerful example of how radicals applied their core principles to a changing landscape. Political ideologies are always in transit, perhaps especially so in moments of upheaval. Section B, "Left Visions in Transition," assembles a series of attempts to articulate a political framework appropriate to the shifting ground of the time period. In particular, radicals grappled with two major tectonic developments. First, the waning of the Cold War dissolved a conflict that had defined the country for more than half a century. For decades, the positions of many American radicals had been refracted through the country's conflict with the Soviet Union and to a lesser extent China. Leftists, liberals, and conservatives each understood US interventions in the global South as proxy wars against presumed Soviet or Chinese allies throughout the Third World. Yet especially after 1989, the year German citizens tore down the Berlin Wall and Chinese democracy activists squared off against government tanks, the specter of foreign communist influence no longer dominated US politics. The end of the Cold War bolstered a conservative triumphalism for unbridled capitalism, popular among both political parties.

Activists labored to articulate a world vision outside of traditional US political frameworks. While some organizations could not survive the change brought about by the challenge to communism, others were energized by it. Some radicals viewed this moment as an opportunity to articulate a new kind of politics that could attend to the failures of existing socialist states. Theirs was a vision of a small-s socialism that was antiracist, antisexist, anti-imperialist, and antihomophobic, as well as committed to grassroots democracy and transnational solidarity. Anarchism also saw growing popularity, as evident in the growth of civil disobedience and direct action as well as of groups pursuing autonomous political culture, aided by the increasing ubiquity of new media. The spread of these politics raised a series of questions. What role should electoral politics play in social change? How should progressives and leftists respond to the growing power of the right? What is the relationship between organization building and mobilization, and how can activists sustain momentum beyond moments of uprising? How should activists relate to the growing power of technology?

Asking these and other critical questions led many radicals to confront the origin stories and accepted political strategies of the United States. In particular, as the documents in the final section show, activists worked to transcend the individualism and isolation that grow out of settler colonialism. Section C, "Land, Decolonization, Interdependence," foregrounds Indigenous and other decolonial activism, which has often been distanced from even other aspects of left politics. The documents here highlight fundamental questions of sovereignty: who has the power to rule and what does that power look like? Reworking antiwar catchphrases such as "US out of Vietnam!," some Indigenous activists championed sovereignty by calling for the US to get out of North America. This effort was more than witty sloganeering. Indigenous groups pursued their own forms of sovereignty against the theft of Native land, language, and life. As the documents here suggest, Indigenous people continually asserted their sovereignty in the face of US militarism and corporate resource extraction. Black nationalists and Black farmers saw access to cooperatively owned land as an essential metric of racial justice. Meanwhile, the austerity economics that wreaked such havoc on urban communities of color also blighted many (largely white) rural areas—particularly farm areas in the Midwest and Plains states.

The Indigenous and Black nationalist emphasis on decolonizing land shifted the political center of gravity away from the country's conventional institutions. Seeking to extend such moves, some non-Native radicals proposed other alternatives to US sovereignty. Here, the influence of Indigenous politics joined with anarchist, feminist, surrealist, and ecological critiques of the US state, allowing activists to imagine other forms of social and political organization. Radicals developed theories, built coalitions, and crafted campaigns outside of traditional institutions. An example of the fruits of their labors could be found in what inveterate organizer Judi Bari described as the growing "feminization" of a radical ecology movement that had been dominated by white men who romanticized a preindustrial past. Another iteration could be seen in feminist and queer activists' rejection of the use of the US criminal justice system as a solution to gendered violence or to homophobic and racist attacks. Here and elsewhere, US radicals confronted the entrenched power of settler colonialism and state violence, instead seeking to create forms of mutuality.

Demanding resolution to deep injustices at home and abroad, social movements responded to the changing context by asking different questions about the source of peril. Wedged between dystopian fears and utopian hopes, a variety of social movements sought to break through the stalemate of how protest was supposed to happen. Activists approached the social and environmental problems of the era with a resolve born of the belief that they were fighting to preserve the conditions of existence. The prospects of this activism were uncertain, with no guarantee of success. Yet there was hope too, for in its struggles lay the possibility for a brighter future.

Stopping the End of the World

4.A.1a., 4.A.1b., 4.A.1c., and 4.A.1d.

Across the period covered in this book, activists utilized mass civil disobedience actions to shut down everything from nuclear power facilities and
weapons manufacturers to Wall Street and political party conventions. Most
mass actions circulated handbooks outlining how to engage in nonviolent
direct action and what might happen as a result. The following are representative excerpts of such handbooks reflecting the information they routinely
conveyed. (We do not include text describing "action scenarios," which identify such details as the location of a civil disobedience or the local jail, or advice on dealing with media, medical needs, or police repression, as media
ecosystems, crowd control techniques, and possible dangers have evolved
over time.) Of these documents, 4.A.1a concerns the philosophy of nonviolent direct action; 4.A.1b describes the affinity group structure and consensus
decision-making process used during protests; 4.A.1c attends to interrupting
sexist practices in organizing, as well as to what activists can expect in jail;
and 4.A.1d explains the philosophy of "jail solidarity" for detained activists.

4.A.1a. Coalition for Direct Action at Seabrook/ Clamshell Alliance, from *Occupation/Blockade Handbook* (1980)

Collective Nonviolent Direct Action

We have chosen to act directly and nonviolently to end the violence of nuclear
power and the system that fosters it. Our commitment to nonviolence in this
action means that we carry no weapons and that we refrain from all threats and
acts of violence despite provocation. Nonviolence does not exclude tactical and
logistical planning; this is an integral part of the collective process of preparing

ourselves. Nonviolence does mean that, though we do not seek to be hurt, we are willing to take risks in order to achieve our goal. . . .

The decision to take nonviolent direct action is more than a decision to simply refrain from violence. We have chosen to act collectively, relying on our commitment to our goals and to each other, rather than on military strength and leaders. Our nonviolence is not a passive thing, nor is it a sign of weakness. It is a way of action both powerful and empowering.

All of us see nonviolence as tactically powerful. Many hold nonviolence as a moral principle. Though our reasons may differ, we tend to agree on the following.

To the greatest extent possible, we want the methods of our struggle to embody the world we are trying to create, a world of reverence for all life and respect for the individual. *Whatever our political backgrounds, we agree that at this time, nonviolent direct action is the best means [of action].* . . .

Following are some reasons people have chosen nonviolence:

- We live in a violent society—not only open political violence and the threat of violence on which the system is based but also the violence in the media, street, and home, which we are trained to accept and even applaud—and in resisting that system, we must resist violence;
- We choose to take the risk of violence on ourselves rather than attempt to do violence to others;
- The power of the state is based on brute force and economic coercion, while our power is based on the internal strength of individuals acting collectively for something we know to be right—nonviolent direct action is on *our* terms rather than those of the police/state;
- It makes no sense to attack when the state's forces are so much stronger;
- Nonviolent tactics, coupled with thorough preparation and trust in each other, can help prevent panic and hysteria in the face of police repression, furthering our chances for success;
- Our desire for a world without nuclear power, exploitation, and all forms of oppression leads us to act in a way that is powerful yet does not harm people.

For many, nonviolent direct action also includes attempting to communicate with those opposing us. While we recognize and condemn the role played by police and others defending the [nuclear] plant, it is important that we continue to respect them as human beings. This does not mean the police are our friends or that we are relying on our ability to convince the authorities to cease their attacks. It does mean that we try to take our message to all individuals. (This is *not* negotiating with authorities. It might include such things as leafleting National Guard barracks.) . . .

We value human life over private property. It is consistent with our goals and nonviolent tactics to remove a fence protecting a piece of property whose very existence threatens all life. . . .

We recognize the possibility that our peaceful actions may be met with violence. But we reject the notion that we are responsible whenever police act violently. Historically, police violence has seldom been a spontaneous response to protestors; rather it has been the result of orders from above, given when the interests the police were protecting were seriously threatened by popular resistance. . . .

There will always be those who tell us that we are weak or cowards for choosing nonviolence, and those who call us violent and blame us for any violence which may occur. It is important to remember that we have made a positive choice to act in the way we see as best and to maintain faith in ourselves, each other and our nonviolent actions.

4.A.1b. Blockade the Bombmakers, from *Civil Disobedience Campaign Handbook* (1982)

Affinity Groups and Support

Affinity groups [AGs] are self-sufficient support systems of about five to fifteen people who work together towards a common goal. If you are planning to do civil disobedience it is important to either form an affinity group or join an already existing one. Affinity groups serve as a source of support and solidarity for their members. Feelings of being isolated or alienated from the movement, the crowd, or the world in general can be alleviated through the familiarity and trust which develops when an affinity group works and acts together. By generating this familiarity the affinity group structure reduces the possibility of infiltration by outside provocateurs. However, participants should be prepared to be separated from the AGs.

Affinity groups will form the basic decision-making bodies of the action. As long as they remain within the nonviolent guidelines and nonviolence trainings, affinity groups are encouraged to develop any form of participation they choose. (If you do not plan to adhere to the Guidelines, please do not come.) Every affinity group must decide within itself how it will make decisions and what it wants to do. This process starts when the affinity group forms. The group will decide what role it wants to play in the action and what legal stance it will take. If a new person asks to join an affinity group, they should find out what the group believes in and what they plan to do and decide if they can share it. Some groups ask that all members share a commitment to feminism, for example, or to nonviolence as a way of life. Others, which have specifically formed to do a particular action, might have less sweeping agreements.

A group cannot hope to reach consensus decisions without having some base of agreement. Once a base is agreed upon, working out the details of specific issues and actions is not as difficult as one might expect, providing that there is a willingness to go along with a good idea, even if it is someone else's. If you find that you cannot work effectively with your group, it might be better to try to find another one.

Affinity groups are usually formed during the nonviolence training sessions. It is a good idea to meet with your affinity group a few times before the action to get to know them if you are not already friends and to discuss the action and the role your affinity group will play. After the action, it is also good to meet with your group to evaluate and share experiences. . . .

Roles within the Affinity Group

- facilitator(s), vibes-watchers (see consensus section).
- spokesperson to convey AG decisions to core support and other AGs.
- media spokesperson represents your AG to the media. Be sure to tell reporters you are speaking for your AG only.

It is a good idea to rotate the above functions so no one gets bored or left out. Other functions, which are difficult to rotate, are:

- contact person [who] receives information for the group.
- medic
- support person(s): once you take on this responsibility, you should see it through.

Support

It can be hard for you to decide whether to do the civil disobedience or do support. It is important to emphasize that both roles are crucial to the success of the action and either choice will be encouraged. We strongly encourage those considering being support to go through nonviolence training. In making the decision, you could consider how each role will affect your family, job, and other commitments, as well as one's legal status (i.e. being on probation, a non-US citizen, etc.).

Support responsibilities include:

BEFORE AN ACTION

Help the affinity group decide upon and initiate their action, provide physical and moral support, and share in the excitement and sense of determination.

- Know the people in your group by name and by description.
- Make sure the group fills out the affinity group check-in sheet.
- Make a confidential list with the following information:
  - name of arrestee,
  - name used for arrest,
  - whether or not individual wants to bail out,
  - who arrestee would like contacted and under what circumstances, [and]
  - special medical information.

- Hold money for emergencies, use in jail (if allowed) and bail if desired.
- Hold IDs for J. Does in case they decide to give their names.
- Take care of arrestees' cars, personal belongings, etc.

DURING THE ACTION

- Keep in touch with protesters for as long as possible, knowing their arrest strategies (noncooperation, no bail, etc.).
- Be ready to follow police wagons or buses to police stations or jails (see legal section).
- If members of your affinity group are arrested . . .
  - write down the individual's name and the time and nature of the arrest.
  - note the activity of the person being arrested and their treatment by the arresting officer—if possible, get the badge number.
  - keep track of who is noncooperating and relay that information to the action headquarters.
  - be there to greet folks when they are released.

AFTER ACTION—DURING JAIL TIME

Based on past NYC actions, it is unlikely that people will be kept in jail for any length of time, unless they are noncooperating. However, while there are people in jail it is important for their supporters to be on hand.

- Try to arrange for someone to be near the phone most of the time so that calls from jail may be received.
- Be present during arraignments and be sure to keep accurate notes regarding future court dates and charges.
- You will probably be the go between for your AG members who are not jailed together.

AND BEYOND—COURT TIME

- Help with rides to court appearances.
- Help gather legal information for pro se defendants when asked.
- Attend court appearances.

Working with other affinity group support people will ease the load on you. . . .

Consensus Decision Making

What Is Consensus?

Consensus is a process for group decision making. It is a method by which an entire group of people can come to an agreement. The input and ideas of all participants are gathered and synthesized to arrive at a final decision acceptable to all. Through consensus, we are not only working to achieve better solutions, but also to promote the growth of community and trust.

Consensus vs. Voting

Voting is a means by which we choose one alternative from several. Consensus, on the other hand, is a process of synthesizing many diverse elements together.

Voting is a win or lose model, in which people are more often concerned with the numbers it takes to "win" than with the issue itself. Voting does not take into account individual feelings or needs. In essence, it is a quantitative, rather than qualitative, method of decision making.

With consensus, people can and should work through differences together and synthesize seemingly contradictory ideas. We believe that people are able to talk peacefully about their differences and reach a mutually satisfactory position. It is possible for one person's insights or strongly held beliefs to sway the whole group. No ideas are lost, each member's input is valued as part of the solution. . . .

What Does Consensus Mean?

Consensus does not mean that everyone thinks that the decision made is necessarily the best one possible or even that they are sure it will work. What it does mean is that in coming to that decision, no one felt that his/her position on the matter was misunderstood or that it wasn't given a proper hearing. It also means that the final decision doesn't violate someone's fundamental moral values, for if it did they would be obligated to block consensus. Hopefully, everyone will think it's the best decision: this often happens because, when it works, collective intelligence does come up with better solutions than could individuals. . . .

Difficulties in Reaching Consensus

If a decision has been reached, or is on the verge of being reached, that you cannot support, there are several ways to express your objections:

- nonsupport ("I don't see the need for this, but I'll go along.")
- reservations ("I think this may be a mistake, but I can live with it.")
- standing aside ("I personally can't do this, but I won't stop others from doing it.")
- blocking ("I cannot support this or allow the group to support this. It is immoral.")
- withdrawing from the group.

Obviously, if many people express nonsupport or reservations, stand aside or leave the group, it may not be a viable decision even if no one directly blocks it. This is what is known as a "lukewarm" consensus, and it is just as desirable as a lukewarm beer or a lukewarm bath.

Attitudes and Behaviors Which Help a Group Reach Consensus

- responsibility: participants are responsible for voicing their opinions, participating in the discussion, and actively implementing the agreement.
- self-discipline: blocking consensus should only be done for principled objections. Object clearly, to the point, and without put-downs or excessive speeches. Participate in finding an alternative solution.
- respect: respect others and trust them to make responsible input.
- cooperation: look for areas of agreement and common ground, and build on them. Avoid competitive, right/wrong, win/lose thinking.
- struggle: use clear means of disagreement—no put-downs. Use disagreements and arguments to learn, grow, and change. Work hard to build unity in the group, but not at the expense of the individuals who are its members. . . .

Dealing with Racism and Classism during an Action, Arrest, and Jail

- Be aware of how police are dealing with Third World, gay, lesbian, and known movement people during arrest situations. Be prepared to come to the aid of anyone who has been singled out by the police and may be receiving harsher treatment than others.
- Realize that during the booking process questions that are being asked to determine whether or not people can be released on their own recognizance, are particularly discriminatory. These questions concentrate on your economic, social, sexual, and prior arrest standing.
- Realiz[e] that bail is the most blatant example of classism. Those who have money get out of jail—those who don't stay in.

4.A.1c. Livermore Action Group, from *Livermore Weapons Lab Blockade/Demonstration Handbook* (1982)

Overcoming Male Oppression

. . . Here are some specific ways we can be responsible to ourselves and others in groups:

- *not interrupting people who are speaking.* We can even leave space after each speaker, counting to five seconds before speaking.
- *becoming a good listener.* Good listening is as important as good speaking. It's important not to withdraw when not speaking; good listening is active participation.
- *getting and giving support.* We can help each other be aware of and interrupt patterns of domination, as well as affirm each other as we move away from those ways. It is important that men support and challenge each

other rather than asking women to do so. This will also allow women more space to break out of their own conditioned role of looking after men's needs while ignoring their own.

- *not giving answers and solutions.* We can give our opinion in a manner which says we believe our ideas to be valuable, but no more important than others' ideas.
- *relaxing.* The group will do fine without our anxiety attacks.
- *not speaking on every subject.* We need not share every idea we have, at least not with the whole group.
- *not putting others down.* We need to check ourselves when we're about to attack or "one-up" another. We can ask ourselves, "Why am I doing this? What am I feeling? What do I need?"
- *interrupting others' oppressive behavior.* We should take responsibility for interrupting a brother who is exhibiting behavior which is oppressive to others and prohibits his own growth. It is no act of friendship to allow friends to continue dominating those around them. We need to learn caring and forthright ways of doing this. . . .

Doing Your Time in Solidarity

. . . Just as we are able to influence the behavior of the police by how we demonstrate and exercise civil disobedience, so we are able to influence our guards and judges. The key is to 1) follow through with the affinity group process, 2) adhere to the nonviolence guidelines, and 3) exercise jail solidarity. Jail will not be a picnic, but it has been for most [activists] an enriching and empowering experience.

Even though you will probably be in jail with your friends [from the action], the experience will be difficult and emotionally painful. As a temporary resident [of the jail], you can expect:

1. You may be denied bathing privileges for several days.
2. You may be detained outdoors for many long hours in excessively hot or rainy weather.
3. Telephones may not be easily accessible.
4. Visitors may have great difficulty getting in to see you.
5. You may be strip-searched.
6. You will be constantly "jacked around."
7. It will be difficult for support persons to get books and other items to you.
8. You will not be entitled to keep personal property in the jail. Items brought to you there will not leave with you.
9. You may not be popular with other inmates, particularly if you accept preferential treatment from the authorities.
10. You will finally appreciate the play Waiting for Godot.

Do not expect the guards to be sympathetic to your political concerns, although some of them probably are. They will not understand the consensus process or the spirit of solidarity. To some extent, they are intimidated by both, so you may use them effectively to "short-circuit" their dehumanizing methods. Long exposure to jail, whether as a prisoner or a guard, tends to have a corrosive effect on one's confidence in human nature and goodness, and the guards are victims of this as well, although at least they get paid. They expect the worst of people, and not surprisingly, they are not often disappointed. Their principal concern is to preserve order, which demands an atmosphere of unquestioning respect (fear) for authority. Keep expecting that they should act with respect and compassion, and you may be surprised by the results. Perhaps you will surprise them in remembering that they and the prisoners in their charge share a common humanity. At least you may establish a basis for dialogue. But at the same time that you recall the humanity of your guards, don't forget that, in the end, you and they have different jobs to perform. Let them be responsible for keeping order; you are responsible for keeping your conscience.

4.A.1d.

Unconventional Action, from *Unconventional Action Guidebook* (1996)

Jail Solidarity

Through jail solidarity we take power in a situation designed to make us powerless. We do this by making our decisions as a group, by acting in harmony with each other, and by committing ourselves to safeguard each other's well-being. Jail solidarity has been used very effectively in the civil rights, antinuclear power, and disarmament movements.

The power of solidarity lies in three basic facts. 1) In a mass arrest situation the authorities need our cooperation to process us—from booking to jail to court. 2) It is very expensive to keep us in jail. 3) There is little room for us in an already overcrowded prison system; thus we have great collective bargaining power. Additionally, public support and pressure to release us can place even more pressure on authorities.

Why Jail Solidarity?

- to insure that all who participate in our action are protected from discriminatory treatment.
- to get our court appearances and sentencing over with quickly, freeing us for work or other actions.
- to make it possible for those from other areas to participate in civil disobedience without having to return for future court dates.
- to serve our time in jail and face court together with the strength of a group, rather than as separate individuals.

- to extend the action, keeping the attention of the public and the media, and demonstrating a strong commitment to affecting change.

For these reasons and more, jail solidarity strengthens our movement and gives us a greater sense of community.

Solidarity Demands

Here are some goals for which solidarity has been used, but they are not the only ones that can be considered:

- equal and fair treatment for everyone in jail and in sentencing. No one should be singled out and subjected to harsher treatment, even those with previous arrests, publicly known organizers, and noncooperators. Everyone should receive the same sentence for similar acts.
- no isolation of individuals or parts of the group.
- communication with the legal team and through them, between women and men and any other separated groups.
- no sentences of fines and probation or at least the option of serving our own sentence in jail.
- mass arraignment in the largest groups possible. This way we know for sure that our sentence demands are being met and thus can respond appropriately.
- people with medical or other needs must be given treatment or medication for whatever their condition requires.

Solidarity Tactics

If we resolve to noncooperate peacefully or to stay in jail we have great bargaining power. Here are some of the ways we can nonviolently use our solidarity to achieve our demands:

- refusing "cite outs," also called citation releases. In most actions individuals are offered a chance to sign a citation release, which is a promise to appear at a later date for arraignment. We have usually recommended refusing this privilege, because the presence of our physical bodies in jail is the greatest leverage we have on the system. If we cite out and come back for arraignments separately, we have no way of assuring that all of us will receive equal sentences.
- refusing to give identifying information (name, address, etc.).
- refusing food.
- refusing to participate in the jail routine.
- refusing to walk.
- singing, dancing, or praying.
- refusing arraignment. We can refuse to move to the court until assured by our own legal team that our demands have been met. We can remain silent or refuse to enter a plea at the arraignment if our demands are not being met.

- pleading not guilty, demanding an individual jury trial, and not waiving our right to a speedy trial. This powerful bargaining tactic pressures the court into granting our sentencing demands.

4.A.2a. and 4.A.2b.

The Clamshell Alliance, so named because clams were among those most immediately threatened by the construction of the Seabrook nuclear power plant in New Hampshire, accelerated the power of the antinuclear movement through its commitment to nonviolent civil disobedience. Its pledge to shut down the Seabrook Power Plant and subsequent "Declaration of Nuclear Resistance" marked a new, more militant phase of the campaign against nuclear power in the United States.

4.A.2a. Clamshell Alliance, "We Can Stop the Seabrook Power Plant" (1977)

On April 30 the Clamshell Alliance will undertake the first mass citizen occupation of a nuclear power plant site in the US. The occupation will be an organized nonviolent statement of active opposition to nuclear power. . . .

The Clamshell Alliance was formed in July 1976 to stop construction of the Seabrook, New Hampshire, nuclear power project and to oppose construction of other nuclear plants in New England. It includes groups and individuals of all ages and backgrounds from New England and has sponsored two smaller "citizen occupations" of the project site in Seabrook. On August 1, over 600 people rallied as 18 New Hampshire residents went on the site and were arrested. On August 22, over 1200 people rallied as 180 New England demonstrators, organized in small affinity groups, went on the site, sat down, and were removed by police and arrested. These arrests, the first in protest of the nuclear plant proliferation that threatens our lives and communities, attracted attention and support from people all over the country.

The Clamshell believes that direct, nonviolent action is necessary at this point to halt the expansion of dangerous, expensive, and unnecessary nuclear plants. We also encourage widespread public education and the continuation of the many legal battles against nuclear power. The Clamshell, through its affiliated groups, has helped organize college teach-ins, collected signatures on petitions, held public meetings throughout New England, and encouraged hundreds of people to take an active role in opposing nuclear power.

Every action and demonstration that we have sponsored has been the largest ever to take place against nuclear power plants in this country! And the public pressure against the Seabrook nuke is having results. Spiraling costs, local nuclear opposition, and legal challenges backed up by direct action have brought the project close to cancelation several times already. The initiative is ours.

Our plans to occupy will only be changed if construction of the plant is completely and permanently stopped. We offer this handbook as preparation for our action and as a guide to other groups who want to organize direct action campaigns against proposed plants in their area.

No Nukes in Seabrook and Nowhere Else!

4.A.2b. Clamshell Alliance, "Declaration of Nuclear Resistance" (1977)

We, the members of the Clamshell Alliance, demand an immediate and permanent halt to the construction and export of nuclear power plants and facilities and nuclear weapons and supporting technology.

Nuclear power is dangerous to all living creatures and to their natural environment. The nuclear industry is designed to concentrate profits and the control of energy resources in the hands of a powerful few, undermining basic principles of human liberty.

A nuclear power plant at Seabrook, New Hampshire, could lock our region into a suicidal path. As an affiliation of a wide range of groups and individuals, the Clamshell Alliance is unalterably opposed to the construction of this, and any other, nuclear power plant.

We recognize

- that the present direction in energy research and development is based on corporate efforts to maximize profits and recoup past investments rather than on meeting our real energy needs;
- that there is a direct relationship between nuclear power plants and nuclear weapons. The arms industry has used the "peaceful atom" to legitimize its technology. The export of nuclear reactors makes possible the spread of nuclear bombs to nations all over the world. The possibility of nuclear thievery and sabotage of nuclear facilities poses further danger to our civil liberties and our lives;
- that the centralized nature of nuclear power takes control of energy from local communities and strengthens the monopoly of the utilities;
- that a political and economic environment committed to the nuclear age is not conducive to the development of, and implementation of, renewable energy sources. With changes in the regulatory and political climate, renewable sources of energy—such as solar technologies—would become competitive, conservation would flourish, and the alleged "need" for nuclear energy would vanish. Awareness of the fact that we live within a balanced, natural ecosystem necessitates changes in "traditional" economic and social values;
- that nuclear power plants have proved to be an economic catastrophe. Expensive, inefficient, and unreliable, they require immense investments of capital and create fewer jobs than comparable investments in conservation and solar energy;

- that the dangers of nuclear power plants are intolerable. They include release of "low-level" radiation—a cause of cancer and genetic disorders; the creation of deadly radioactive waste which must be completely isolated from the environment for 250,000 years; the destruction of our lakes, rivers, and oceans by thermal pollution; and the possibility of a catastrophic meltdown. No material gain, real or imagined, is worth the assault on life itself that atomic energy represents.

We therefore demand

- that not one more cent be spent on nuclear power reactors or nuclear weapons, except to dispose of those wastes already created and to decommission those plants and weapons now in existence;
- that our energy policy be focused on developing and implementing clean and renewable sources of energy in concert with an efficient system of recycling and conservation;
- that all people who lose jobs through the cancelation of nuclear construction, operation, or weapons production be offered retraining and jobs in the natural energy field at decent, union-level wages;
- that the supply of energy should, in all cases, be controlled by the people. Private monopoly must give way to public control. In concert with public ownership, power supply should be decentralized so that environmental damage is further minimized and so that control can revert to the local community.

We have full confidence that when the dangers and expense of nuclear energy are made known to the people, they will reject this tragic experiment which has already cost us so much in health, environmental quality, material resources, labor, and control over our own lives.

The Clamshell Alliance will continue its uncompromising opposition to any and all nuclear construction in New England and elsewhere.

Our stand is in defense of the health, safety, and general well-being of ourselves and of future generations of all life on this planet.

We therefore announce that, should construction continue at Seabrook, we will mobilize the citizenry and return to the site to blockade or occupy it until construction has ceased and the project is totally and irrevocably canceled.

4.A.3.

Clams for Democracy

From flyer (1978)

Like other movements that began out of popular insurgency, the antinuclear movement faced pressures to professionalize and become more moderate as it grew. Written by Clams for Democracy (CFD), a group of dissident members of the Clamshell Alliance, this flyer insists that the antinuclear movement should retain its emphasis on direct action and direct democracy as essential ingredients for tackling the severity of nuclear power and other threats to planetary survival.

A large number of people have expressed dissatisfaction with the shallowness of political debate and development within Clamshell. The leadership's private dealings with the state in recent weeks has aggravated the situation, creating doubts about the alliance's ability or desire to stop nuclear power through democratic direct action.

For too long, those of us who are critical of Clam's politics, actions, and procedures have been isolated by the organization's bureaucracy. We need time to get together with people who feel Clam is constraining and most importantly people who sense a new direction is necessary if the antinuclear movement is to stop nuclear power at is roots.

To these ends we propose a series of workshops examining the relationship of the state, private property, direct action, and democracy to the future of the antinuclear movement. Specifically we want to discuss the following points:

1. *The state* (that is, all governmental authority) *is a major component of nuclear development.*

    To fight nuclear plants, it is necessary to oppose the state and its allies. Clam has tied many decisions to electoral campaigns and has viewed the state as an "honorable" adversary and at times even as a partner. How can we mobilize ourselves in solidarity *against* the state?

2. *Property relations,* corporate (as well as state)

    Capitalism is a major component of nuclear power. Beyond the abstract, what strategy is best in breaking the propertied classes' control of social resources? Nuclear power comes from private property. How do we end both?

3. *Direct action*

    Within Clam, ill-defined words like "CD" [civil disobedience] and "occupation" have shut off debate and have been used to deliberately mislead people into believing that they are going to take part in a direct action. Occupation means collectively taking possession of property to halt continued corporate and governmental violence against ourselves and the earth. This is clearly different from symbolic action. What is the relationship between nonviolence, civil disobedience, and direct action?

4. *Decentralized democracy*

    Tough decisions get made by central Clam groups. Too often we (the membership) find out what "we" decided in the media. Why doesn't consensus work? Why are Clam debates coercive? How can we develop our collectivity? It's more important to develop respect with each other than to develop respect with the media.

5. Ultimately the big problem is *what happens next?*

    What will be the future of the antinuclear movement? What structures should we create within, or outside, of Clam that can stop the nuclear state? Is there commitment to and desire for new directions or organizations? How can we best realize our goals?

. . . September–October '78: Clams for Democracy found itself shrinking, like much of the alliance. Let's face it, for all of us, inside the organization and outside of it, the level of energy rises when we plan for an occupation because people think *that* is something worth working for. The remaining coherent CFD affinity groups expressed the following view of activity, which we feel provides compost for a renewed occupation effort:

Our priority is to stop nuclear power and weapons and to transform society through education and collective direct action. This can only be done by acting for ourselves without appealing to or recognizing the legitimacy of state or corporate authority. We also feel that direct action does not depend on media coverage for its effectiveness because it accomplishes undeniable and concrete change.

Direct action, to us, then becomes distinct from civil disobedience, which we feel has been useful but has inherent limitations in that it legitimizes the stuctures of authority and control which direct action intends to supplant.

4.A.4.

Bruce Kokopeli and George Lakey

From *Leadership for Change: Toward a Feminist Model* (1978)

As activists turned toward large-scale nonviolent civil disobedient demonstrations, they also debated how to practice more democratic forms of leadership within their organizations. In this excerpt from the booklet *Leadership for Change*, two members of the Philadelphia-based ecofeminist Movement for a New Society outline a theory and structure of shared leadership, which they locate in the feminist movement's rejection of patriarchal approaches to leadership.

Shared Leadership

If authoritarian and paternalist patriarchal leadership forms are inadequate for a liberation movement, and the antileadership reaction prevents dynamic and effective action, where shall we turn? We need a vision of what leadership could be. . . .

"Democratic decision making" is not enough. Decision making is an inflexible exercise of power after the terms are set; the structure designates who can make what decisions under what circumstances. Leadership, on the other hand, is a flexible use of power to influence other group members, thereby formulating the terms in which the decision is made. In addition to democratic *decision making*, therefore, we need democratic—or shared—*leadership*. . . .

Shared leadership can only persist in a cooperative *structure*. When people grow tired of depending on the supermarket and decide on an alternative, they don't simply buy food from a farmer and dump it on someone's lawn, leaving it there for the taking. They create a structure for cooperation, with attention to sharing responsibility as well as benefits. Without a structure, a food co-op could not do its job . . . .

In addition to knowledge and skills related to the group's task (peace action, tenant organizing, strike support, etc.), group members also need the knowledge and skills of *group process*. Fortunately, the knowledge and skill of good process isn't hard to learn, except for people deeply entrenched in patriarchal leadership styles. Once learned, the knowledge enables the functional shifting around which the feminist perspective points to, for no one or few any longer hold a monopoly of knowledge of what makes a group go.

Shared leadership liberates leaders! It frees people who have been worn down by years of extra responsibility to water their gardens and nurture their souls. It enables them to share their experienced wisdom at one moment and follow through with manual tasks the next. It frees them to take risks, the risks which inevitably accompany personal growth, for they now know that others are accepting responsibility. They can also say goodbye to loneliness as they "move in a common rhythm," to quote from Marge Piercy's poem. . . .

Most important, shared leadership puts the members of the group in charge. It demystifies leadership by getting everything into the open and clarifies each individual's opportunities for maintaining and changing the direction of the group. It reduces irresponsible withdrawal because everyone can see clearly that the functions are shared; blame cannot be dumped on "the leader." It inhibits power seekers still under the influence of patriarchal styles. Because everyone performs some leadership functions at some time, it builds appreciation for the work of leadership—not the old appreciation born of indebtedness to the leader who does so much for us, but an appreciation rooted in our own experience of power and responsibility. . . .

4.A.5.

C. T. Butler and Keith McHenry

"Why Food Not Bombs?" (1992)

From its origins in the 1980 antinuclear movement, Food Not Bombs grew from a street theater group providing food to protestors to a grassroots franchise that combined direct service to hungry and homeless people with a critique of the country's bloated military budget. Food Not Bombs chapters sprang up across the country, implicitly challenging US waste and militarism while directly providing food to people in need. True to the organization's direct action origins, its members often risked arrest in sharing food with people city elites wanted to keep out of the parks and off other public property where it distributed its food.

Food

The world produces enough food to feed everyone, if distributed equally. There is an abundance of food. In fact, in this country, every day in every city, far more edible food is discarded than is needed to feed those who do not have enough to eat.

Consider this: before food reaches your table, it is produced and handled by farmers, co-ops, manufacturers, distributors, wholesalers, and retailers. Some perfectly edible food is discarded for a variety of business reasons at every step. In the average city, approximately 10 percent of all solid waste is food. This is an incredible total of forty-six billion pounds nationally per year, or just under two hundred pounds per person per year. Estimates indicate that only four billion pounds of food per year would be required to completely end hunger in America. Clearly there is an abundance of edible, recoverable food being thrown away.

To recover this edible food and use it to feed people, three key elements must be combined. First, the food must be collected. Second, it must be prepared in a form appropriate for consumption. Third, the food must be made easily accessible to those who are hungry.

The reason this is not already happening is no accident. We do not have a democratic say in how food is produced or distributed. People would certainly elect to eat, but in hierarchical economies, the threat of job loss allows owners to keep wages low. An underclass results from such policies that encourage domination and violence. In our society, it is acceptable to profit from other's suffering and misery. . . .

Clearly, the majority of people going hungry today are not the stereotyped street person as the media would have you believe. Hungry people are children and single parents (mostly women), the working poor, the unemployed, the elderly, the chronically ill, and those on a fixed income (such as veterans and people with physical and mental challenges/differences/disabilities). All of these people find themselves in the clutches of oppressive poverty even while trying to improve their condition. In addition to the collection and distribution of surplus food to help solve this problem, Food Not Bombs encourages vegetarianism. If more people were vegetarian and demanded organically grown, locally produced foods, this would encourage organic farming practices and support smaller farms. This in turn would make it easier to decentralize the means of food production and to create democratic control over the quality of the food produced and the stewardship of the land. More people can be fed from one acre of land on a vegetarian than meat-based diet. Our society's current meat-based diet allows for huge "agribusinesses" and dependency on chemical fertilizers and pesticides, resulting in the declining nutritional value of the food produced and also destruction of the environment. All mass-produced meats in this country are full of chemicals, drugs, enhancers, and preservatives and all milk is contaminated with radioactive fallout. Vegetarianism would be better for the environment, consume less resources, and be healthier for us. While we encourage awareness of vegetarianism for political and economic reasons, this policy also has several more immediate benefits. The potential for problems with food spoilage are greatly reduced when dealing strictly with vegetables, and members of the group tend to eat a more healthy diet as they learn more about vegetarianism. Also, teaching people about the health benefits of a vegetarian diet actually creates a healthy, caring attitude towards ourselves, others, and the planet as a whole. Therefore, all of the food we prepare is strictly from vegetable sources, that is, no meat, dairy, or eggs. People know and trust this standard for Food Not Bombs food whenever they come to our table.

Not Bombs

It will take imagination and work to create a world without bombs. Food Not Bombs recognizes our part as providing sustenance for people at demonstrations and events so that they can continue participating in the long-term struggle against militarism. We also make bringing our message to other progressive movements part of our mission. We attend other organizations' events and support coalition building whenever possible. We work against the perspective of scarcity which causes many people to fear cooperation among groups. They believe that they must keep apart to preserve their resources, so we try to encourage the feelings of abundance and the recognition that if we cooperate together, all become stronger.

Being at the center of the action with our food is part of our vision. Sometimes we organize the event; sometimes we provide food at other organizations' events. Providing food for more than one day is more than just a good idea, it is a necessity. Either the movement can seek food services from the outside and be dependent upon businesses which may not be progressive or we can provide for ourselves. Clearly, it is Food Not Bombs' position that providing for our own basic needs, in ways that comprehensively support the movement, is far more empowering. We have provided food at long- term direct actions such as the annual peace encampment sponsored by the American Peace Test at the Nevada Nuclear Weapons Test Site; tent cities which highlight homelessness and hunger in San Francisco, Boston, New York, and Washington, DC; and for the regular feeding of the homeless in highly visible locations in many cities throughout the country.

How Food Not Bombs Got Its Name

During 1980, a group of friends who were active in the protests against the Seabrook nuclear power project were searching for a way to make the connection between the issues of nuclear power and militarism. One of our many activities was to spray paint antinuclear and antiwar slogans on public buildings and sidewalks using stencils. One of our favorites was to spray paint the words "Money for food not for bombs" on the sidewalk at the exits to grocery stores in our neighborhood. One night, after an outing of spray painting, we had the inspiration to use the slogan "Food not bombs" as our name. By having a slogan, the message of our group would be clear, and by repeating our name over and over again even the media would be getting the political concept of food, and not bombs, to the public. We would not have to proselytize because our name would say it all. As we arrived with the food, people would say, "Hey, here comes Food Not Bombs."

The Rebellious Possibility of the MOVE Organization

ethan ucker

MOVE, a revolutionary religious organization with a predominately Black membership, coalesced in Philadelphia in the early 1970s. In 1973, a few years after a charismatic autodidact named John Africa (née Vincent Leaphart) founded the organization, a handful of its members and their children moved into a house, which doubled as MOVE's headquarters, in the West Philadelphia neighborhood of Powelton Village. The organization grew steadily, from about twenty-five members in its early days to around sixty active members and a slightly larger network of supporters in the late 1970s and early 1980s.

MOVE's religion was oriented around respect for and protection of all forms of life; members believed humans to be inescapably enmeshed in and responsible to an interwoven network of relations that included animal, plant, and land-based kin. Though not biologically linked, members considered themselves part of the same extended family. With its rubrics of kinship and interdependence and its attunement to the natural world, MOVE's religion is more closely akin to an Indigenous metaphysics of relationality than to Judeo-Christian theological traditions.

According to Ramona Africa, MOVE's minister of information, the organization was opposed to anything "that imposes on any, *any* form of life." They believed that repertoires of separation, individualism, domination, and containment violate the essential, all-inclusive unity of life. Early on, their opposition was directed primarily against the confinement of animals: they picketed outside zoos, pet stores, circuses, and veterinary clinics. These disruptive public protests made MOVE the target of a brutal counterrevolutionary campaign by Philadelphia mayor Frank Rizzo: MOVE members were demonized in the media and routinely beaten and arrested by the city's white, working-class police force. Racial antagonisms deepened and violent clashes escalated, culminating in two confrontations. On August 8, 1978, police laid siege to the organization's Powelton Village headquarters and forcibly evicted MOVE; nine members (dubbed "the MOVE Nine" by supporters) were convicted of killing a police officer and sentenced to thirty to one hundred years in prison. MOVE regrouped and in 1981 established a new headquarters in the community of Cobbs Creek. There, on May 13, 1985, the police dropped a FBI-supplied firebomb onto the roof of MOVE's property and let the subsequent fire burn until it destroyed sixty-one surrounding homes. Two MOVE members escaped the burning house alive; eleven others— six adults and five children—were trapped inside and incinerated.

Studying MOVE's sophisticated abolitionist praxis, their insistent coupling of opposition with invention, provides the beginning of an answer as to why the state attacked them so viciously.

MOVE members were urban separatists. They recognized that abuses of life were constitutive of modern society and concretized in postindustrial US cities and that abdicating to the country would be, as one MOVE member explained, "to divert from the problem and not to correct it." So, throughout the mid-1970s and early 1980s, MOVE used outlays of capital from legal and extralegal economic enterprises to acquire almost twenty disparate properties, a small fleet of trucks and vans, and a robust bail fund. They built out an autonomous infrastructure though which to move, order, and organize themselves, clearing ground in the heart of the city for the insurgent culture on which they would raise their children.

MOVE children grew up in communal homes, heated by wood and lit by candles, which they shared with dozens of stray dogs and cats and hundreds of rats and insects; all forms of life were welcomed and fed. The children ate only raw and unprocessed foods (primarily fruits, vegetables, and nuts), exercised daily, and wore minimal clothing. They were not allowed to attend schools because MOVE believed that the systems of meaning conveyed there—reading, writing, arithmetic—engendered possibilities of partitioning, differentiation, measurement, and hierarchy. They did not learn to count, and they could not read clocks.

MOVE members saw their progeny as a revolutionary vanguard. They weaned their children off of the corrosive influences of modern society by cultivating a lifestyle structured around practices of relationality, accountability, care, communalism, and nondisposability and around epistemological, ontological, and temporal frameworks that were incommensurable with statist and capitalist logics, institutions, and technologies. At the end of the 1978 confrontation, the police stood down while MOVE adults, after surrendering, walked eleven children out of their Powelton Village house. But the police would not make the same mistake twice. In the 1985 confrontation, of the six children trapped in the basement of MOVE's bombed Cobb Creek headquarters, only one made it out alive. The other five who tried to escape the raging inferno were driven back inside by police gunfire. MOVE children modeled a refusal to be governed by the US nation-state, sited within and yet wholly dissociated from it. They posed a comprehensive challenge to the state's legitimacy; their futurity was a rebellious possibility that the state could not abide.

4.A.6.

Black Hills Alliance

Black Hills Alliance position paper (1980)

In organizing the International Survival Gathering in 1980, the Black Hills Alliance identified its vision of an environmentally sustainable, anticolonial approach to land use that joined Indigenous claims with those of settlers opposed to the pollution of extractive industries. The position paper is a call for democratic and relational self-government.

1. Creating a "National Sacrifice Area" from the northern Great Plains is unnecessary to meet our country's energy needs and is incompatible with the principles of democracy, environmental preservation, and self-determination.
2. Uranium mining and milling, called the most dangerous part of the nuclear chain by the Nuclear Regulatory Commission, threaten:
   - our home with contaminated water, air, and land;
   - our people with cancer, birth defects, and shortened lives;
   - and those who eat our area's products with unfit meat, grains, and vegetables.

These things have happened in other uranium districts, and we can't assume "it won't happen here."

1. The Bureau of Reclamation states that energy development will result in the "disappearance or loss of tribal cultural heritage" among Indian people. Events in Wyoming show the loss of rural cultural heritage in energy-impacted areas. We value our quality of life and our ways of life and will not sell them for corporate profits or short-term gains.
2. Under international law, the Black Hills belong to the Lakota (Sioux) people. The illegality of treaty-breaking land grabs in the 1800s has been admitted by the United States Court of Claims. Recent corporate and government actions should be recognized as a continuation of these practices, not only in the Black Hills but for all native peoples threatened by energy resource exploitation.
3. Agricultural families are the keepers of the American way of life. Government actions that encourage loss of land to large corporations and banking interests remove the guardians of the land, encourage exploitation of the land, and lead to further concentration of employment opportunities and power in the hands of the few.
4. Current energy policies are destructive because they concentrate decision making in the hands of a few people who are concerned only with profits. These people, including the oil companies and the members of the

Trilateral Commission, have shown their lack of concern with the will of the people, future generations, wildlife, people's health, a life-supporting earth, local values, and laws and regulations.

5. Alternatives to centralized energy have been proved safe, viable, less expensive, and a boost to employment. We advocate a community-based appropriate technology, the end of government blocks to that technology, and a national program to provide permanent ways that will provide our energy needs without destroying the land and people.

4.A.7.

Southwest Organizing Project and others

Open letter to the National Wildlife Federation (1990)

As an ever-growing number of communities confronted the social and health problems that accompany environmental destruction, gaps grew between community organizations and large conservation NGOs such as the Sierra Club and the Audubon Society. This letter, addressed to the National Wildlife Federation and taking on a set of environmental NGOs known as the "big ten," highlighted the environmental concerns of working-class communities of color and Indigenous people that such large nonprofits were ignoring or disrespecting. The letter was initiated by the Albuquerque-based Southwest Organizing Project and signed by one hundred organizers from across the southwest. Reflecting the growing environmental justice movement, it brought attention to the race, class, and geographic disparities of environmental collapse.

Dear Mr. Hare:

We are writing this letter in the belief that through dialogue and mutual strategizing we can create a global environmental movement that protects us all. We are artists, writers, academics, students, activists, representatives of churches, unions, and community organizations writing you to express our concerns about the role of your organization and other national environmental groups in communities of people of color in the Southwest.

For centuries, people of color in our region have been subjected to racist and genocidal practices including the theft of lands and water, the murder of innocent people, and the degradation of our environment. Mining companies extract minerals leaving economically depressed communities and poisoned soil and water. The US military takes lands for weapons production, testing, and storage, contaminating surrounding communities and placing minority workers in the most highly radioactive and toxic worksites. Industrial and municipal dumps are intentionally placed in communities of color, disrupting our cultural lifestyle and threatening our communities' futures. Workers in the fields are dying, and babies are born disfigured as a result of pesticide spraying.

Although environmental organizations calling themselves the "Group of Ten" often claim to represent our interests, in observing your activities it has become clear to us that your organizations play an equal role in the disruption of our communities. There is a clear lack of accountability by the Group of Ten environmental organizations towards Third World communities in the Southwest, in the United States as a whole, and internationally.

Your organizations continue to support and promote policies which emphasize the cleanup and preservation of the environment on the backs of working people in general and people of color in particular. In the name of eliminating environmental hazards at any cost, across the country industrial and other economic activities which employ us are being shut down, curtailed, or prevented while our survival needs and cultures are ignored. We suffer from the end results of these actions but are never full participants in the decision making which leads to them.

These are a few examples which we have witnessed of the lack of accountability by the Group of Ten:

- Legislation was passed in December 1987 to annex lands to form El Malpais National Monument in New Mexico. Thirteen thousand acres were considered to be the ancestral holdings of the pueblo of Acoma. "Conservation" groups such as the Sierra Club and the Wilderness Society supported the bill in complete disregard for the cultural heritage of the Acoma people. . . .
- The Nature Conservancy, National Audubon Society, and others are opposing the grazing of sheep on the Humphries and Sargent Wildlife areas by a local, highly successful economic development project run by Chicanos in northern New Mexico, one of the most economically depressed areas in the United States, . . . [by] those who have lived in the region for hundreds of years.
- Organizations such as the National Wildlife Federation have been involved in exchanges where Third World countries will sign over lands (debt-for-nature swaps) to conservation groups in exchange for creditors agreeing to erase a portion of that country's debt. In other cases the debt is purchased at reduced rates; the creditors can then write it off. This not only raises the specter of conservation groups now being "creditors" to Third World countries but legitimizes the debt itself through the further expropriation of Third World resources. . . .
- The lack of people of color in decision-making positions in your organizations such as executive staff and board positions is also reflective of your histories of racist and exclusionary practices. Racism is a root cause of your inaction around addressing environmental problems in our communities.
- Group of Ten organizations are being supported by corporations . . .

[that] are known polluters [and] whose disregard for the safety and well-being of workers has resulted in the deaths of many people of color. It is impossible for you to represent us in issues of our own survival when you are accountable to these interests. . . .

Comments have been made by representatives of major national environmental organizations to the effect that only in the recent past have people of color begun to realize the impacts of environmental contamination. We have been involved in environmental struggles for many years and we have not needed the Group of Ten environmental organizations to tell us that these problems have existed.

We again call upon you to cease operations in communities of color within sixty days, until you have hired leaders from those communities to the extent that they make up between 35–40 percent of your entire staff. We are asking that Third World leaders be hired at all levels of your operations.

Although some Group of Ten organizations have sent general information on the people of color within their staffs and boards of directors, the information has been insufficient. Again we request a comprehensive and specific listing of your staff of non-European descent, their tenure, salary ranges, and

Figure 4.1. "This Is Where the 90s Begin: Redwood Summer" (1990). Image courtesy of Lincoln Cushing/ Docs Populi.

classification (clerical, administrative, professional, etc.). Also provide a list of communities of color with whom you provide services or Third World communities in which you have organizing drives or campaigns and contacts in those communities.

Finally, we call upon your organization to cease fund-raising operations in communities of color within sixty days until a meeting is held with you including representatives of our choice. Once your organization responds to these requests you will be invited to confer with other national leaders on the poisoning of United States Third World communities. . . .

It is our sincere hope that we be able to have a frank and open dialogue with your organization and other national environmental organizations. It is our opinion that people of color in the United States and throughout the world are clearly endangered species. Issues of environmental destruction are issues of our immediate and long-term survival. We hope that we can soon work with your organization in helping to assure the safety and well-being of all peoples.

4.A.8.

First National People of Color Environmental Leadership Summit

Principles of Environmental Justice (1991)

Delegates to the First National People of Color Environmental Leadership Summit held on October 24–27, 1991, in Washington, DC, drafted and adopted these seventeen principles of environmental justice. Since then, the principles have served as a defining document for an intersectional approach to ecology, sustainability, and a just transition. Grounded in Indigenous communities and communities of color, environmental justice emphasizes the ecological politics of everyday life.

We, the people of color, gathered together at this multinational People of Color Environmental Leadership Summit, to begin to build a national and international movement of all peoples of color to fight the destruction and taking of our lands and communities, do hereby reestablish our spiritual interdependence to the sacredness of our Mother Earth; to respect and celebrate each of our cultures, languages, and beliefs about the natural world and our roles in healing ourselves; to ensure environmental justice; to promote economic alternatives which would contribute to the development of environmentally safe livelihoods; and, to secure our political, economic, and cultural liberation that has been denied for over five hundred years of colonization and oppression, resulting in the poisoning of our communities and land and the genocide of our peoples, do affirm and adopt these principles of environmental justice:

The Principles of Environmental Justice (EJ)

1) *Environmental justice* affirms the sacredness of Mother Earth, ecological unity and the interdependence of all species, and the right to be free from ecological destruction.

2) *Environmental justice* demands that public policy be based on mutual respect and justice for all peoples, free from any form of discrimination or bias.

3) *Environmental justice* mandates the right to ethical, balanced, and responsible uses of land and renewable resources in the interest of a sustainable planet for humans and other living things.

4) *Environmental justice* calls for universal protection from nuclear testing, extraction, production, and disposal of toxic/hazardous wastes and poisons and nuclear testing that threaten the fundamental right to clean air, land, water, and food.

5) *Environmental justice* affirms the fundamental right to political, economic, cultural, and environmental self-determination of all peoples.

6) *Environmental justice* demands the cessation of the production of all toxins, hazardous wastes, and radioactive materials and that all past and current producers be held strictly accountable to the people for detoxification and the containment at the point of production.

7) *Environmental justice* demands the right to participate as equal partners at every level of decision making, including needs assessment, planning, implementation, enforcement, and evaluation.

8) *Environmental justice* affirms the right of all workers to a safe and healthy work environment without being forced to choose between an unsafe livelihood and unemployment. It also affirms the right of those who work at home to be free from environmental hazards.

9) *Environmental justice* protects the right of victims of environmental injustice to receive full compensation and reparations for damages as well as quality health care.

10) *Environmental justice* considers governmental acts of environmental injustice a violation of international law, the Universal Declaration of Human Rights, and the United Nations Convention on Genocide.

11) *Environmental justice* must recognize a special legal and natural relationship of Native peoples to the US government through treaties, agreements, compacts, and covenants affirming sovereignty and self-determination.

12) *Environmental justice* affirms the need for urban and rural ecological policies to clean up and rebuild our cities and rural areas in balance with nature, honoring the cultural integrity of all our communities, and to provide fair access for all to the full range of resources.

13) *Environmental justice* calls for the strict enforcement of principles of informed consent and a halt to the testing of experimental reproductive and medical procedures and vaccinations on people of color.

14) *Environmental justice* opposes the destructive operations of multinational corporations.
15) *Environmental justice* opposes military occupation [and] repression and exploitation of lands, peoples and cultures, and other life forms.
16) *Environmental justice* calls for the education of present and future generations which emphasizes social and environmental issues, based on our experience and an appreciation of our diverse cultural perspectives.
17) *Environmental justice* requires that we, as individuals, make personal and consumer choices to consume as little of Mother Earth's resources and to produce as little waste as possible and make the conscious decision to challenge and reprioritize our lifestyles to ensure the health of the natural world for present and future generations.

Nevada Test Site Resistance

Bob Fulkerson

Since its establishment in 1951 on treaty lands of the Western Shoshone Nation, the Nevada Test Site (NTS) has been ground zero for the US antinuclear weapons protest movement. Five hundred protests occurred over the following fifty years, which were attended by anywhere from a handful of participants to many thousands and that resulted in over fifteen thousand arrests for nonviolent civil disobedience. Beginning in the 1970s, NTS became a convergence site for indigenous people, faith-based groups, peace activists, and environmentalists. These activists worked in coalition, using direct action to resist environmental destruction and militarism.

Activism at the NTS produced many watchdog groups. Nevada's Sagebrush Alliance drew its name from the Clamshell Alliance, which organized the largest antinuclear power protests in US history at the Seabrook nuclear power plant in New Hampshire, and worked with the Franciscan Center in Las Vegas to organize local people against nuclear testing. It was an uphill battle because the test site was critical in the southern Nevada economy.

In 1975, the predecessor of today's Department of Energy announced plans to dump high level radioactive waste at the NTS. This prompted long-time Nevada philanthropist and activist Maya Miller and other women to form Citizen Alert, which hired the first paid community organizers in Nevada outside of labor unions and created a statewide movement against the dump and the proposed MX missile system. Citizen Alert helped win passage of the Radiation Exposure Compensation Act, which provided remuneration to atomic veterans, uranium miners, and civilians downwind of NTS.

Actions at the NTS inspired other efforts, both domestically and around the world. In 1985, members of the National Freeze Campaign founded the American Peace Test to coordinate nonviolent action at the NTS. In 1987, activists from eastern Tennessee participated in mass civil disobedience at NTS, then returned home to form the Oak Ridge Peace and Environmental Alliance, which focused attention on the nuclear bomb factory there. That same year, fifty-five young people from Denmark came to southern Nevada to meet with fellow students in Las Vegas and to hold a concert at the NTS. They raised funds to tour the United States on a trip called Next Stop Nevada. In 1989 the youth led Next Stop Soviet, which catalyzed antinuclear activism in the Soviet Union and led to the closure of the nuclear test site at Semipalatinsk in 1991.

Mass protests wound down following the last nuclear weapon test explosion in September 1992. Activism at the NTS had won a halt to nuclear weapons testing and a US government fund to compensate radiation victims. In addition, NTS actions helped to elevate Western Shoshone treaty rights and to delay plans for nuclear waste disposal at Yucca Mountain.

In 1994, Western Shoshone spiritual leader Corbin Harney, who led numerous protests at the NTS, Yucca Mountain, and other Western Shoshone treaty lands, formed the Shundahai Network to bring non-Native people into his work. Other legacies from NTS demonstrations include the No MX Alliance, which successfully defeated the proposed MX missile system, and the Lenten Desert Experience, out of which grew Pace Bene, a Las Vegas faith-based organization promoting nonviolence. Today, the Franciscan Center of Las Vegas and Western Shoshone leader Jonnie Bobb continue to lead demonstrations against simulated nuclear tests and waste storage and to protest the premature deaths and health crises caused by nuclear radiation.

The history of resistance at the NTS gives a lie to the notion that the United States won the Cold War without firing a shot. Ordinary people rose up, created lasting organizations and coalitions, and put an end to nuclear weapons testing. They remain a source of inspiration for what people power and direct action can accomplish.

4.A.9.

Indigenous Antinuclear Summit

Declaration (1996)

While the civil disobedience campaigns against nuclear power subsided by the late 1980s, opposition to nuclear energy, nuclear waste, and nuclear war continued. The fight against nuclear power was especially prevalent in Indigenous communities, whose lands were often targeted for uranium mining and whose cosmology held protection of the earth and all things on it as sacred.

We, the Indigenous peoples gathered here for this summit, standing in defense and protection of our Mother Earth and all our relations, do hereby unanimously express our total opposition to the nuclear power and weapons chain and its devastating impacts and deadly effects on our communities.

The Indigenous Antinuclear Summit brought together a network of Indigenous peoples from different areas of Mother Earth that are negatively impacted by the nuclear chain. These impacted areas of the nuclear chain include: uranium mining in the Grants Mineral Belt that has had devastating health and environmental impacts on Navajo and Pueblo peoples in New Mexico; the uranium mining industry has actively targeted northern Saskatchewan where the mining exploration process has already had negative implications on the culture of Chipewyan, Metis, Dene, Blood, and other Indigenous peoples in the region; conversion fuel fabrication, and enrichment have impacted Indigenous peoples in Oklahoma who live near the Sequoyah Fuels Uranium Processing Plant, and among Indigenous people whose way of life depends upon the Columbia River where the Hanford Nuclear Reservation is located (Washington/Oregon); the power plant operation at the Prairie Island Power Plant has manufactured deadly waste impacting the Mdewankanton Dakota; and storage has been a tool of divide and conquer among Indigenous nations targeted for the United States Department of Energy's monitored retrievable storage proposals.

Although we are varied in language and beliefs, we have the common ground of being Indigenous peoples who have no desire to give up the traditional laws that the Creator gave us and accept the deadly, unsustainable ways the colonists have tried to force upon us. We are not asking anyone else to accept our ways; however, we are exercising our right to live our sustainable lifestyles in our own lands.

The nuclear industry which has waged an undeclared war has poisoned our communities worldwide. For more than fifty years, the legacy of the nuclear chain from exploration to waste has been proven, through documentation, to be genocidal and ethnocidal and a most deadly enemy of Indigenous peoples.

United States federal law and nuclear policy has not protected Indigenous peoples and in fact has been created to allow the nuclear industry to continue operations at the expense of our land, territory, health and traditional ways of life. This system of genocidal and ethnocidal policies and practices has brought our people to the brink of extinction and amongst some Indigenous peoples it is believed that if they die, all life on Earth will stop. Therefore, we demand an immediate stop to these crimes against our peoples, communities, and future generations by the nuclear industry, their stockholders, and nuclear governments including the United States, Japan, France, Canada, and China.

We demand all levels of governments, including tribal, state, national and international, do whatever possible to stop all uranium exploration, mining, milling, conversion, testing, research, weapons, and other military production, use, and waste disposals onto and into Mother Earth.

We further demand increased research and development, funding allocations and utilization of sustainable energy such as solar, wind, and appropriate technologies that are consistent with our natural laws and respect for the natural world (environment).

We particularly call upon tribal governments to measure their responsibilities to our peoples, not in terms of dollars but in terms of maintaining our spiritual traditions and assuring our physical, mental, spiritual well-being. It is our responsibility to assure the survival of all future generations.

We invite you to join us by:

1. At the summit, October 13 (Unplug America—Give Mother Earth a Rest Day) and July 25 (anniversary of the Rio Puerro nuclear accident and nuclear testing by the French in the Pacific at Bikini Atoll) were designated as national days of acknowledging the devastating impacts of the nuclear industry against Indigenous peoples. We encourage you to create an event in your community that brings awareness and attention to these issues.

2. Recognizing that the proposed transportation of nuclear waste will affect numerous communities throughout the United States, we encourage you to contact your local representatives and let them know that you place health and safety as a priority and that you believe it is their job to protect human rights and opposed transportation through your region.

3. If you live in a state that currently depends upon nuclear power plant(s) for energy we encourage you to contact your representative to phase out nuclear power plants and implement sustainable energy production methods (i.e. solar energy, wind energy, etc.).

4. You are invited to join as a cosigner of this declaration. . . .

5. Please circulate this declaration through newsletters, mailings, tables at events, etc.

UPROSE and Environmental Justice in New York City

Julie Sze and Elizabeth Yeampierre

In environmental justice campaigns, community leaders both draw attention to the toxic effects of crucial municipal services such as garbage, power, sewage, and sludge on poor communities of color (effects that are typically invisible to people outside of those communities) and challenge the public perception of these neighborhoods as sites of blight, pollution, and decay, a perception that depends on the identification of these neighborhoods as areas where marginalized racial populations live. As low-income communities of color faced this contradiction of invisible impacts and visible disdain in the 1990s, they fought several significant siting and pollution battles in response to accelerating trends of deregulation and privatization in New York City.

From the North River Sewage Treatment Plant in West Harlem to incinerator battles in Williamsburg and the South Bronx, these battles were pitched and furious. Polluters, with the support from government, sought to make decisions that would negatively impact communities. Environmental justice activists and organizations fought back, insisting on more expansive decision-making power on the grounds that community organizations ought to be "at the table." Local organizations such as West Harlem Environmental, UPROSE in Sunset Park, El Puente in Williamsburg, and the South Bronx Clean Air Coalition—with leaders including Peggy Shepard and Cecil Corbin-Mark in Harlem and Luis Garden Acosta in Williamsburg—fought on many fronts against environmental racism and inequality. They also organized in coalitions such as the Organization of Waterfront Neighborhoods and the New York City Environmental Justice Alliance. City-wide organizers like Eddie Bautista adopted a strategy to prevent sewage treatment plants, incinerators, and waste transfer stations from being moved to less powerful neighborhoods. Coalitions ensured that local groups could connect their issues and share resources and strategy. Many important leaders of these fights became influential in the city's later sustainability efforts. As a result of their work, community participation and environmental justice gained traction in the policy realm.

Sunset Park, a historically Puerto Rican community with growing populations of Asian, Arab, and Latino neighbors, faced particular land use and environmental threats. Its activists became skilled in working at multiple scales, including at citywide, national, and international levels. They faced off with questions of how community organizations could respond to geographically expanding threats. UPROSE, Brooklyn's oldest Latino community-based organization, came to understand local threats expansively and through a radical lens, exemplifying a shift in environmental justice politics. Under Mayor Giuliani, the organization had lost its public funding and was on the verge of shutting down. In 1996, civil rights lawyer Elizabeth Yeampierre became executive director, and the organization's focus shifted from social services to organizing, advocacy, and the development of intergenerational leadership. UPROSE also came to embrace a multiethnic model of community development and base building.

UPROSE's leadership proved central to 1990s campaigns against garbage privatization and energy deregulation. Today, its work encompasses popular education, youth training, advocacy and direct actions, and community-based planning. The group has emerged as a national leader on issues of climate justice, a just transition from fossil fuels, and community-engaged economic development. It played a major leadership role in the 2014 People's Climate March that brought over four hundred thousand people to the streets of New York City.

While UPROSE is now a multiethnic institution, it honors its historical roots. The Puerto Rican community is one that celebrates difference, practices solidarity with others, and exists at the intersection of colonization and self-determination. UPROSE has also broadened its range, reached across ethnic boundaries, and redefined struggle at the crossroads of social, economic, environmental, and climate justice. This continuing evolution is a testament to the ideals of the civil rights movement, the legacy of the organization's founders, the power of solidarity, and the resilience of the grassroots.

4.A.10.

Laotian Organizing Project

From *Fighting Fire with Fire: Lessons from the Laotian Organizing Project's First Campaign* (2001)

The Laotian Organizing Project (LOP) began in 1995 to organize the heavily refugee community in Contra Costa County, an industrial and heavily toxic area in California's East Bay. After a 1999 chemical explosion and subsequent leaks at the Chevron oil refinery in the county, the LOP organized to improve the county's emergency response system and prevent future catastrophes. This excerpt from a report analyzing the successful campaign highlights the group's approach.

Advancing Systemic Social Change

LOP believes deeply that none should be exposed to environmental degradation from industrial production. In order to truly change the rules of the game, our campaigns need to add up to more than reforming a system that maintains the rights of polluting industries. People have a right to a clean and healthy environment in which they can live, work, learn, play, and thrive.

Defining the long-term social change goals of an organization is essential to building a plan to achieve that vision. LOP would like to see systemic social change where fundamental rules of the game are altered and root causes of the problems are addressed.

Systemic social change can take the form of policies that shift large-scale public resources towards eliminating inequities and injustices and laws that guarantee human rights and the protection of mother earth. Systemic social change promotes the right of every person to a decent, safe, affordable quality of life, the right of every person to participate in collectively made decisions that affect our lives, and prioritizes public good over profit. Systemic social change seeks not only to change policies but also to transform worldview and to equalize power relations. Some examples of advancing systemic social change relevant to LOP's work are a moratorium on new polluting facilities, public-directed planning and development of toxic sites, phasing out of the production of polluting compounds and transitioning facilities to clean production, and production that is locally owned and run where workers and residents are protected and valued first.

LOP sees direct organizing as a key strategy that emphasizes developing the skills, abilities, and political consciousness of a growing mass base in order to exercise power to achieve systemic social change. Direct organizing also embodies the principle of shared power to create a process where our communities can speak for ourselves.

Building Politically Conscious Organized Power

LOP's campaign experience confirms a lesson some groups already know: developing a politically conscious mass base committed to developing and exercising the power of the organization is essential to both winning our immediate campaigns and to building infrastructure for a social movement. People who enter our organizations do not automatically come with all the necessary skills, abilities, or experience to formulate an informed opinion or develop an action plan on an issue. It is our responsibility as organizing institutions to develop methods and processes that both value the experiences members bring [and] also engage them in critical thinking, analysis, and planning.

Leadership activities do not happen in a vacuum but in the context of our campaigns. Through campaigns we push proactive solutions to institutional problems and challenge the dominant worldview that exists in our own communities that promotes individualism, competition, racism, classism, sexism, patriarchy, ageism, homophobia, and corporate power and government privatization. The development of mass-based democratic leadership requires systematic and ongoing recruitment and programs because there are no shortcuts in the daily, direct work with people to build grassroots power.

Building a Movement for Environmental Justice

During this campaign it became clear to us that the only way LOP can build the scope and scale necessary to achieve systematic social change is through building alliances with other grassroots organizations and progressive institutions. The movement as a whole needs both strong organizations and strong multiracial and multi-issue alliances because alliances are only as strong as the grassroots organizations that comprise them. LOP believes that multiracial and multi-issue alliances, led by people of color, poor people, women, and young people, can achieve systemic social change goals, and we organize and develop the leadership of low-income APIs [Asian Pacific Islanders] within this framework.

LOP recognizes that no one organization can bring about the possibility of large-scale structural change. While this campaign victory represents an important shift in the power relations between local government and the Laotian community, if LOP were able to organize every man, woman, and child in the

Laotian community of West County, we still would not be able to win the level of systemic social change that would significantly improve the day-to-day quality of life of the community. To achieve systemic social change we need a movement with infrastructure. We need permanent organizations and networks of organizations that build strong, organized, and politicized power bases in all poor, working-class, people of color, and Native communities. The environmental justice movement is one vital social movement in the United States that has effectively brought together these sectors.

4.A.11.

Dave Foreman

From *Ecodefense: A Field Guide to Monkeywrenching* (1985)

Frustrated by what he saw as the limited scope of the dominant environmental movement of the 1970s, Dave Foreman quit his job at the Wilderness Society and, in 1980, cofounded a more radical alternative. Earth First! took as its tagline "No compromise in defense of Mother Earth." Contra to environmental justice organizations, Earth First! was predominantly white, non-urban, and engaged in dramatic forms of protest over grassroots community organizing. Among the most controversial tactics used at the time was a form of sabotage proponents called "monkeywrenching." Foreman—a registered Republican—describes the tactic in this excerpt from his book *Ecodefense: A Field Guide to Monkeywrenching*.

It is costly for the Forest Service, the BLM [Bureau of Land Management], timber companies, oil companies, mining companies, and others to scratch out the "resources" in these last wild areas. It is expensive to maintain the necessary infrastructure of roads for the exploitation of wildlands. The cost of repairs, the hassle, the delay, and the downtime may just be too much for the bureaucrats and exploiters to accept if a widely dispersed, unorganized, strategic movement of resistance spreads across the land.

It is time for women and men, individually and in small groups, to act heroically in defense of the wild, to put a monkey wrench into the gears of the machine that is destroying natural diversity. Though illegal, this strategic monkeywrenching can be safe, easy, fun, and—most important—effective in stopping timber cutting, road building, overgrazing, oil and gas exploration, mining, dam building, powerline construction, off-road-vehicle use, trapping, ski area development, and other forms of destruction of the wilderness, as well as cancerous suburban sprawl.

But it must be strategic, it must be thoughtful, it must be deliberate in order to succeed. Such a campaign of resistance would adhere to the following principles.

Monkeywrenching Is Nonviolent

Monkeywrenching is nonviolent resistance to the destruction of natural diversity and wilderness. It is never directed against human beings or other forms of life. It is aimed at inanimate machines and tools that are destroying life. Care is always taken to minimize any possible threat to people, including the monkeywrenchers themselves.

Monkeywrenching Is Not Organized

There should be no central direction or organization to monkeywrenching. Any type of network would invite infiltration, agents provocateurs, and repression. It is truly individual action. . . .

Monkeywrenching Is Individual

Monkeywrenching is done by individuals or very small groups of people who have known each other for years. Trust and a good working relationship are essential in such groups. The more people involved, the greater the dangers of infiltration or a loose mouth. Monkeywrenchers avoid working with people they haven't known for a long time, those who can't keep their mouths closed, and those with grandiose or violent ideas (they may be police agents or dangerous crackpots).

Monkeywrenching Is Targeted

Ecodefenders pick their targets. Mindless, erratic vandalism is counterproductive as well as unethical. . . . Senseless vandalism leads to loss of popular sympathy.

Monkeywrenching Is Timely

There are proper times and places for monkeywrenching. There are also times when monkeywrenching may be counterproductive. Monkeywrenchers generally should not act when there is a nonviolent civil disobedience action e.g., a blockade taking place against the opposed project. . . . Monkeywrenching may also not be appropriate when delicate political negotiations are taking place for the protection of a certain area. There are, of course, exceptions to this rule. The Earth warrior always asks, Will monkeywrenching help or hinder the protection of this place?

Monkeywrenching Is Dispersed

Monkeywrenching is a widespread movement across the United States. Government agencies and wilderness despoilers from Maine to Hawaii know that their destruction of natural diversity may be resisted. Nationwide monkeywrenching will hasten overall industrial retreat from wild areas.

Monkeywrenching Is Diverse

All kinds of people, in all kinds of situations, can be monkeywrenchers. Some pick a large area of wild country, declare it wilderness in their own minds, and resist any intrusion into it. . . . Even Republicans monkeywrench.

Monkeywrenching Is Fun

Although it is serious and potentially dangerous, monkeywrenching is also fun. There is a rush of excitement, a sense of accomplishment, and unparalleled camaraderie from creeping about in the night resisting those "alien forces from Houston, Tokyo, Washington, DC, and the Pentagon." As Ed Abbey said, "Enjoy, shipmates, enjoy."

Monkeywrenching Is Not Revolutionary

Monkeywrenchers do not aim to overthrow any social, political, or economic system. Monkeywrenching is merely nonviolent self-defense of the wild. It is aimed at keeping industrial civilization out of natural areas and causing industry's retreat from areas that should be wild. . . .

Monkeywrenching Is Simple

. . . The most effective means for stopping the destruction of the wild are often the simplest. There are times when more detailed and complicated operations are necessary. But the monkeywrencher asks, What is the simplest way to do this?

Monkeywrenching Is Deliberate and Ethical

Monkeywrenchers are very conscious of the gravity of what they do. They are deliberate about taking such a serious step. They are thoughtful, not cavalier. Monkeywrenchers—although nonviolent—are warriors. They are exposing themselves to possible arrest or injury. It is not a casual or flippant affair. They keep a pure heart and mind about it. They remember that they are engaged in the most moral of all actions: protecting life, defending Earth.

A movement based on the above principles could protect millions of acres of wilderness more stringently than could any congressional act, could insure the propagation of the grizzly and other threatened life forms better than could an army of game wardens, and could lead to the retreat of industrial civilization from large areas of forest, mountain, desert, prairie, seashore, swamp, tundra, and woodland that are better suited to the maintenance of native diversity than to the production of raw materials for overconsumptive technological human society.

If logging firms know that a timber sale is spiked, they won't bid on the timber. If a forest supervisor knows that a road will be continually destroyed, he won't try to build it. If seismographers know that they will be constantly harassed in an area, they won't go there. If ORVers [off-road vehicle drivers] know that they'll get flat tires miles from nowhere, they won't drive in such areas.

John Muir said that if it ever came to a war between the races, he would side with the bears. That day has arrived.

4.A.12.

Judi Bari

From "The Feminization of Earth First!" (1992)

The radical environmentalist group Earth First! was founded by five white men whose concern for the environment did not necessarily translate into organizing for universal progressive social change; indeed, many in early years of Earth First! distanced themselves from workers rights, antiracism, and the left. Feminist, musician, and labor activist Judi Bari shifted the tenor of Earth First! by developing common cause between environmentalists and timber workers. She reflects on her efforts here, including FBI and timber industry attempts to silence her. Bari was targeted in a bomb attack while organizing Redwood Summer, a campaign to save California's redwood trees from logging that was inspired by the civil rights movement's 1964 Mississippi Freedom Summer.

It is not surprising that I, a lifetime activist, would become an environmentalist. What is surprising is that I, a feminist, single mother and blue-collar worker, would end up in Earth First!, a "no compromise" direct action group with the reputation of being macho, beer-drinking ecodudes. Little did I know that by combining the more feminine elements of collectivism and nonviolence with the spunk and outrageousness of Earth First!, we would spark a mass movement. And little did I know that I would pay for our success by being bombed and nearly killed and subjected to a campaign of hatred and misogyny.

I was attracted to Earth First! because they were the only ones willing to put their bodies in front of the bulldozers and chainsaws to save the trees. They were also funny, irreverent, and they played music. But it was the philosophy of Earth First! that ultimately won me over. This philosophy, known as biocentrism or deep ecology, states that the Earth is not just here for human consumption. All species have a right to exist for their own sake, and humans must learn to live in balance with the needs of nature, instead of trying to mold nature to fit the wants of humans. . . .

For years the strategy of Earth First!, under male leadership, had been based on individual acts of daring. "Nomadic action teams" of maybe ten people would travel to remote areas and bury themselves in logging roads, chain themselves to heavy equipment, or sit in trees. There were certainly brave and principled women who engaged in these actions. And a few of the actions, notably the Sapphire Six blockade in Oregon, even had a majority of women participants. But by and large, most of the people who had the freedom for that kind of travel and risk taking were men.

I never consciously tried to change Earth First!, I just applied my own values and experiences to my work. I have nothing against individual acts of daring. But the flaw in this strategy is the failure to engage in long-term community-based organizing. There is no way that a few isolated individuals, no matter how brave, can bring about the massive social change necessary to save the planet. So we began to organize with local people, planning our logging blockades around issues that had local community support. We also began to build alliances with progressive timber workers based on our common interests against the big corporations. As our successes grew, more women and more people with families and roots in the community began calling themselves Earth First!ers in our area. . . .

Earth First! had never initiated any violence. But neither did we publicly associate our movement with an overt nonviolence code. After all, that would contradict the he-man image that Earth First! was founded upon. Yet I did not see how we could face the increasingly volatile situation on the front lines without declaring and enforcing our nonviolence. And considering the rate at which the trees were falling and the overwhelming power of the timber corporations, I did not see how we could save the forest with just our small rural population and the small group of Earth First!

So, drawing on the lessons of the civil rights movement, we put out a nationwide call for Freedom Riders for the Forest to come to northern California and engage in nonviolent mass actions to stop the slaughter of the redwoods. We called the campaign Redwood Summer, and, as it became clear that we were successfully drawing national interest and building the infrastructure to handle the influx, the level of repression escalated again.

As Redwood Summer approached, I began to receive a series of increasingly frightening written death threats, obviously written in the interest of Big Timber. The most frightening of these was a photo of me playing music at a demonstration, with a rifle scope and cross-hairs superimposed on my face and a yellow ribbon (the timber industry's symbol) attached. When I asked the local police for help they said: "We don't have the manpower to investigate. If you turn up dead, then we'll investigate." When I complained to the county board of supervisors they replied, "You brought it on yourself, Judi." Finally, on May 24, 1990, as I was driving through Oakland on a concert tour to promote Redwood Summer, a bomb exploded under my car seat. I remember my thoughts as it ripped through me. I thought "This is what men do to each other in wars."

The bomb was meant to kill me, and it nearly did. It shattered my pelvis and left me crippled for life. My organizing companion, Darryl Cherney, who was riding with me in the car, was also injured, although not as seriously. Then, adding to the outrage, police and FBI moved in within minutes and arrested me and Darryl, saying that it was our bomb and we were knowingly carrying it. For eight weeks, they slandered us in the press, attempting to portray us as violent and discredit Redwood Summer, until they were finally forced to drop the charges for lack of evidence. But to this day, no serious investigation of the bombing has been conducted, and the bomber remains at large.

There were indications in advance that the attack on me was misogynist as well as political. For example. one of the death threats described us as "whores, lesbians, and members of NOW." But soon after the bombing, a letter was received that left no doubt. It was signed by someone calling himself the Lord's Avenger, and it took credit for the bombing. It described the bomb in exact detail and explained in chilling prose why the Lord's Avenger wanted me dead.

It was not just my "paganism" and defense of the forest that outraged him. The Lord's Avenger also recalled an abortion clinic defense that I had led years ago. . . .

Meanwhile, out in the forest, Redwood Summer went on without me. Before the bombing I was one of a very few women who had taken a prominent leadership role in Earth First! But after the bombing, it was the women who rose to take my place. Redwood Summer was the feminization of Earth First!, with three-quarters of the leadership made up of women. Our past actions in the redwood region had drawn no more than 150 participants. But 3,000 people came to Redwood Summer, blocking logging operations and marching through timber towns in demonstrations reminiscent of those against racism in the South. . . .

Being the first women-led action [within Earth First!], Redwood Summer has never gotten the respect it deserves from the old guard of Earth First! But it has profoundly affected the movement in the redwood region. It brought national and international attention to the slaughter of the redwoods. The two-thousand-year-old trees of Headwaters Forest, identified, named and made an issue of by Earth First!, are now being preserved largely due to our actions. The legacy of our principled and nonviolent stand in Redwood Summer has gained us respect in our communities and allowed us to continue and build our local movement. And our Earth First! group here, recently renamed Ecotopia Earth First!, is probably the only truly gender-balanced group I have ever worked in, now equally led by strong women and feminist men.

I believe that the reason I was subjected to such excessive violence was not just what I was saying, but the fact that a woman was saying it. I recently attended a workshop in Tennessee on violence and harassment in the environmental movement. There were thirty-two people in the circle, drawn from all over the country. As we each told our tale, I was struck by the fact that the most serious acts of violence had all been done to women. And of course this is no surprise. Because it is the hatred of feminine, which is the hatred of life, that has helped bring about the destruction of the planet. And it is the strength of women that can restore the balance we need to survive.

4.A.13.

George Katsiaficas and Paul Messersmith-Glavin

From *Why Wall Street? The Case for Green Direct Action* (1990)

To counter individual and consumerist solutions to ecological ruin, some fifteen hundred radicals organized into affinity groups to shut down Wall Street on the twentieth anniversary of Earth Day with a combination of civil disobedience, nonviolent protest, and black bloc militancy. The action, whose coalition principles were collectively authored and endorsed by more than fifty groups, was also intended to persuade the nascent Green movement to disengage from national electoral politics and embrace a social movement direct-action approach. It fused ecology and anarchism in massive direct action campaigns. The following excerpt from an essay that appears in the handbook activists developed in building for the action highlights the ecological problem of capitalism and militarized nation-states and calls for solidarity across struggles.

At their best, direct action movements are *antisystemic* movements representing the potential for a direct democratic future, working for the transformation of society. Direct action is an expression of people's desires for a new way of life, embodied in the communities we create—with a decentralized participatory emphasis in fundamental opposition to the current antidemocratic control by entrenched elites.

The ecological crisis is an outgrowth of the crisis in society, a society marked by race, sex, and class divisions. By taking direct action at Wall Street we are pointing at the root of the social and ecological crisis in capitalist and statist systems, systems which have developed out of, and are interconnected with, other forms of hierarchy and domination, such as racism, sexism, homophobia, ageism, and the attempt to dominate nature. Wall Street is specifically a symbol of capitalism: with its endless need to expand, its exploitation of human labor, and its putting of profit ahead of all else, capitalism is inherently antidemocratic and antiecological—the future of life depends upon capitalism's abolition. . . .

The politics of confrontation are difficult to actualize in the US: middle-class lifestyles, heavier police tactics than in Europe, and the near hegemony of a particularly dogmatic pacifism in many movements make the emergence of an extraelectoral direct action movement problematic. Yet if we dare[d] to make our actions militant and creative, nonviolent and confrontational, spontaneous and coordinated, a social ecological alternative would be powerfully voiced and our commitment to such an alternative would be conveyed to millions of Americans. Direct action would draw attention to the ideas of those of us advancing the antiauthoritarian left tradition through an ecological critique, making people aware that a new political alternative is emerging. Direct actions also provide a clear indication of the urgency of the present crisis, integrating fragmented single-issue energies while facilitating dialogue between otherwise isolated activists. . . .

We have waited too long for a revitalized popular movement to bring about fundamental change. A new social movement, combined with a decentralized, yet continentally coordinated political organization is urgently needed. As part of this movement we need to engage in an ongoing educational process, as well as develop a democratic-decentralist organization which would be controlled by its members, able to weather the inevitable ups and downs of a popular movement. We need to better communicate with those presently active around single-issue concerns to begin drawing out the connections between issues. We need to better explain our perspective, engaging in a genuine dialogue with those experienced in organizing and direct action. And perhaps most importantly, we need to think through our relationship to the most oppressed in the United States. We need to consider ways of coloring in the green in the rainbow, of bringing to the Rainbow Coalition's constituency a sense of the need for a whole new system, not simply new laws and different candidates for the same offices. If we are to participate in a movement directed at achieving global peace and justice, it is critical that we link our vision to the needs of the most oppressed in the United States—a "rainbow from below" is one way to think of this. . . .

Coalition Principles

The following points serve as a basis of agreement for groups who join the coordinating council to help shape the action. These points serve as broad policy guidelines, condensed for publicity materials and expanded upon in this handbook. Local activists are, of course, free to prepare organizing materials oriented toward their particular constituencies:

1. The military-industrial systems of both the East and the West are the root cause of social and ecological destruction. Both systems demand growth for the sake of growth and thrive on the centralization of power, competition for resources, and a relentless militarism. Growth-oriented economics, whether explicitly capitalist or claiming to be socialist, is incompatible with ecological stability.
2. Genuine grassroots political and economic democracy are necessary for the realization of both human and broader ecological needs in a mutu-

ally harmonious manner. This includes 1) decentralization of political and economic power under direct face-to-face community control; 2) cooperative organization and community ownership of productive resources, with community control of distribution and consumption patterns; and 3) workers' control of the immediate labor process. Fully participatory confederations of democratic community assemblies should make decisions about common needs and questions of distribution and sharing of resources.

3. We demand a sweeping program for social and ecological reconstruction, beginning with the thorough demilitarization of our economy and culture. Some elements of such a program include

   a. cutting military expenditures on the order of 95 percent via a non-nuclear, noninterventionist, home-based defense policy
   b. providing decent housing, fulfilling work and adequate means of support for everyone
   c. free public health care and child care
   d. canceling Third World debts
   e. solar-based renewable energy to replace nuclear power and fossil fuels
   f. organic family farms and community agriculture in place of toxic agribusiness
   g. full recycling of wastes [and] a ban on incineration and on the production of toxic chemicals
   h. community control and ownership to end land speculation
   i. rebuilding and expanding public rail transportation and bicycle use
   j. vastly expanding public parks, wilderness areas, and wildlife habitat; ban clearcutting, herbicide and pesticide use, and other abusive practices on the land.

4. We take a principled stand against all forms of domination, oppression, and hierarchical social structures. Our vision of an ecological society requires an end to racism, sexism, ageism, homophobia, and all forms of coercive human relationships.

5. A political movement to articulate the Green alternative needs to be independent, outside of and basically opposed to the establishment political parties. We are evolving a new politics based on locally rooted grassroots groups that are engaged in a mix of extraelectoral and electoral activities and coordinated on a regional, national, and international basis.

6. We seek to build a broad-based ecological movement that opposes capitalism because it is destroying the planet. Our perspectives should be expressed to the public through our slogans and our imagery with an unmistakably Green identity, substantially expanding upon the opposition to capitalism that we inherit from the more traditional left.

4.A.14.

Rod Coronado

"'Spread Your Love through Action': An Open Letter from Rod Coronado" (1995)

One of the few Native Americans in the animal rights movement, Rod Coronado had been involved in a series of militant efforts to stop animal abuse: as part of the Sea Shepherd Conservation Society, he participated in sinking two Icelandic whaling ships in 1986. As he outlines here, Coronado later went after the US fur industry, committing several acts of arson and vandalism in the early 1990s as part of a decentralized clandestine group called the Animal Liberation Front. Though he was eventually arrested and incarcerated, Coronado's efforts inspired a radical wave of animal rights activity throughout the decade.

On March 3, 1995, I pled guilty to aiding and abetting a fire at Michigan State University (MSU) that destroyed thirty-two years of research intended to benefit the fur farm industry. The Animal Liberation Front (ALF) claimed responsibility for the raid, the seventh in a series of actions dubbed "Operation Bite Back" which targeted fur farms and universities engaged in taxpayer supported research jointly funded by the fur trade. I also pled guilty to one count of theft of US government property; in particular, a journal belonging to a Seventh Cavalry Officer killed at the Little Bighorn near Crow Agency, Montana, in 1876. This negotiated plea agreement is the result of a seven-year investigation by the FBI into my activities and the federal government's continued targeting of indigenous activists who assert their sovereignty and continue their fight for cultural survival. It is also the culmination of nine federal grand juries that have lasted over three years, subpoenaed over sixty political activists, jailed four for six months each, and harassed and intimidated countless others in the hunt for members of the ALF.

In return for the guilty pleas, the US government promises not to seek further prosecution of me in the remaining districts investigating the ALF, nor subpoena me to testify against others suspected of ALF activity. The price I pay for not testifying against my compatriots is a three- to four- year prison sentence . . . .

This is only the latest attempt by the US government to make an example of those who break free from the confines of legitimate protest. At a time when ecological and cultural destruction is commonplace and within the perimeter of the law, it sometimes becomes necessary to adhere to the higher laws of nature and morality rather than stand mute witness to the destruction of our lands and people. I believe it to be the obligation of the earth warrior to never be ashamed of one's own actions to honor the sacred tradition of indigenous resistance. Therefore, I accept full responsibility for my actions and remain grateful to have had the honor of serving as a member of the ALF as their spokesperson and supporter.

With a record of over three hundred animal liberation actions and rescues in the US without injury or loss of life, yet thousands of lives spared from the horrors of vivisection and fur farming, the women and men of the ALF remain to me some of the most respected of nonviolent warriors in the struggle to save our planet. My role in the raid at MSU was as a nonparticipant, acting as a conduit for the truth hidden behind the locked laboratory door. While in Ann Arbor, Michigan, awaiting instructions, I received a phone call from an anonymous ALF member detailing the raid for inclusion into a press release. Later, I received research materials and evidence seized during the raid. These documents would have exposed taxpayer-sponsored research benefiting the fur farm industry and experiments where mink and otters are force-fed toxins and other contaminants until they convulse and bleed to death. Accompanying these documents was a videotape of the cramped and unsanitary conditions mink and otter endure at MSU's research laboratories. My desire to release this information to the public was much greater than my desire to protect myself from rabid investigations by the FBI and the ATF. Seventeen months later, I was indicted by the Michigan grand jury based on this evidence.

Earlier in the month of February 1992, I was at the Little Bighorn River in Montana. I went to the sight of the infamous battle and was shocked at this, the only monument I know of that glorifies the loser. In further disgrace to the warriors who lost their lives defending their families and homelands, the monument paints a one-sided story of the conquest of the indigenous peoples of the Great Plains by the US military. The truth remains that George Armstrong Custer and his Seventh Cavalry were an illegal occupational force trespassing in clear violation of the Fort Laramie Treaty of 1868 to attack peaceful encampments of noncombatants in the heart of the Lakota Nation. The theft of the cavalryman's journal is a reminder of indigenous discontent with the treatment of our heritage and culture by the US government.

Over the last ten years I have placed myself between the hunter and the hunted, the vivisector and the victim, the furrier and the furbearer, and the whaler and the whale. These are my people, my constituency. It is to them that I owe my life. I have chosen to continue the time-honored tradition of resistance to the invading forces that are ravaging our homes and people. Many people have been tortured, murdered, and imprisoned on this warrior's path, yet we must continue to stand tall against the tyranny that has befallen this continent in the last 503 years. As warriors we must accept that prison awaits those who are unwilling to compromise the earth and her people when we choose to remain allegiant to fellow warriors whose identity remains unknown. We are all Subcomandante Marcos, Crazy Horse, and the ALF. Never, ever, should we forget that in order to achieve the peace and liberation we strive for some sacrifice is necessary. This will not be the first time an indigenous person has gone to prison while upholding the obligation to protect our culture, homelands, and people, and it most definitely will not be the last. It is with total love that I say goodbye to my earth mother for a little while to enter the concrete and steel prisons the US government reserves for its discontented citizens. Such rewards await those who must give their lives and freedom to prevent the destruction of the most beautiful planet in the universe, our life-support system, our beloved mother earth.

To those who have fought beside me, you will always be my friends and families, and for you I will give up that which I love the most, my freedom. I will face prison rather than speak one word against those on the frontlines of the battle to protect earth. Our relationship is a sacred one, and in your own freedom I pray that you spread your love through action that continues to rescue all that remains wild. Never surrender!

4.A.15a. and 4.A.15b.

From its inception in 1997, the Earth Liberation Front (ELF) used sabotage, vandalism, and arson to target corporate or government buildings that members saw as threatening the planet. Their targets included everything from SUVs and power lines to the Bureau of Land Management and a horse slaughter house. Its biggest action was the arson of a fancy ski resort in Vail, Colorado. ELF actions caused millions of dollars in damage. Since 2002, more than twenty people have been prosecuted for having carried out a string of attacks in the Pacific Northwest in the late 1990s. What follows are excerpts from a document describing the organization and from a 1997 communiqué.

4.A.15a. Earth Liberation Front, "Frequently Asked Questions" (1990s)

About the ELF

The Earth Liberation Front is an international underground movement consisting of autonomous groups of people who carry out direct action according to the ELF guidelines. . . . Modeled after the Animal Liberation Front, the ELF is structured in such a way as to maximize effectiveness. By operating in cells (small groups that consist of one to several people), the security of group members is maintained. Each cell is anonymous not only to the public but also to one another. This decentralized structure helps keep activists out of jail and free to continue conducting actions.

As the ELF structure is nonhierarchical, individuals involved control their own activities. There is no centralized organization or leadership tying the anonymous cells together. Likewise, there is no official "membership." Individuals who choose to do actions under the banner of the ELF are driven only by their personal conscience or decisions taken by their cell while adhering to the stated guidelines.

Who are the people carrying out these activities? Because involved individuals are anonymous, they could be anyone from any community. Parents, teachers, church volunteers, your neighbor, or even your partner could be involved. The exploitation and destruction of the environment affects all of us—some people enough to take direct action in defense of the earth.

Any direct action to halt the destruction of the environment and adhering to the strict nonviolence guidelines, listed below, can be considered an ELF action. Economic sabotage and property destruction fall within these guidelines.

Earth Liberation Front Guidelines

> to inflict economic damage on those profiting from the destruction and exploitation of the natural environment.
> to reveal and educate the public on the atrocities committed against the earth and all species that populate it.
> to take all necessary precautions against harming any animal, human and nonhuman.

There is no way to contact the ELF in your area. It is up to each committed person to take responsibility for stopping the exploitation of the natural world. No longer can it be assumed that someone else is going to do it. If not you who, if not now when?

Earth Liberation Front FAQ

. . .

Q: Are you terrorists?

A: No, we condemn all forms of terrorism. A common definition of terrorism is "to reduce to a state of fear or terror." We are costing them money. If change falls out of your pocket, you are not in a state of fear or terror. If you give money to the homeless, you are losing money, but you are not being terrorized. Even if your house is robbed, you are not being terrorized. We are nonviolent. Houses were checked for all forms of life, and we even moved a propane tank out of the house all the way across the street just because—in a worst-case scenario—the firefighters could get hurt. We show solidarity with our firefighters, and we are sorry to wake you up in the middle of the night. Don't be mad at us, be mad at urban sprawl. We encourage all citizens to donate generous contributions this year to your local volunteer firefighters. . . .

Q: Why don't you use legal methods?

A: They don't work as well. Mahatma Gandhi disobeyed the law to free his people. Harriet Tubman used illegal methods to free slaves on the Underground

Railroad. Nelson Mandela even used violent methods to end apartheid. John Brown killed slaveowners and raided a federal arsenal to try to start a slave revolt. How many successful movements in history can you think of off the top of your head that came about only by education? How do you "protest" against slavery? Holding signs and handing out flyers on southern plantations? Today, these "unlawful" people are all seen as martyrs, and someday we will too. Try to realize this *now*. Not all laws are just. Malcolm X says "by any means necessary" in order to obtain freedom. But we do not hurt people, we never have in our long history, and we never will. We respect all life, even our worst enemies that give us cancerous drinking water. . . .

The earth isn't dying, it's being killed, and those who are killing it have names and addresses. What are *you* doing for the earth tonight? *No compromise in defense of our earth! Stop urban sprawl or we will.*

4.A.15b. Earth Liberation Front, "Beltane, 1997" (1997)

Welcome to the struggle of all species to be free.

We are the burning rage of this dying planet. The war of greed ravages the earth and species die out every day. ELF works to speed up the collapse of industry, to scare the rich, and to undermine the foundations of the state. We embrace social and deep ecology as a practical resistance movement. We have to show the enemy that we are serious about defending what is sacred. Together we have teeth and claws to match our dreams. Our greatest weapons are imagination and the ability to strike when least expected.

Since 1992 a series of earth nights and Halloween smashes has mushroomed around the world. Thousands of bulldozers, power lines, computer systems, buildings and valuable equipment have been composted. Many ELF actions have been censored to prevent our bravery from inciting others to take action.

We take inspiration from luddites, levelers, diggers, the autonome squatter movement, the ALF, the Zapatistas, and the little people—those mischievous elves of lore. Authorities can't see us because they don't believe in elves. We are practically invisible. We have no command structure, no spokespersons, no office, just many small groups working separately, seeking vulnerable targets and practicing our craft.

Many elves are moving to the Pacific Northwest and other sacred areas. Some elves will leave surprises as they go. Find your family! And let's dance as we make ruins of the corporate money system.

Form "stormy night" action groups, encourage friends you trust. A tight community of love is a powerful force.

Recon

check out targets that fit your plan and go over what you will do

Attack

> power lines: cut supporting cables, unbolt towers, and base supports, saw wooden poles.
> transformers: shoot out, bonfires, throw metal chains on top, or blow them up.
> computers: smash, burn, or flood buildings.

Please copy and improve for local use.

Left Visions in Transition

4.B.1.

John Trudell

From "We Are Power" (1980)

Delivered at the opening session of the Black Hills International Survival
Gathering on July 18, 1980, this speech by the American Indian Movement
cofounder John Trudell (Santee Sioux) outlined an Indigenous framework for
earth-based liberation movements as the necessary foundation for building
the coalition needed to save the world and all creatures on it.

This is a survival gathering and one of the things I hope you all learn while
you're here is [. . .] to appreciate the energy and power that the elements are,
that of the sun, the rain, and the wind. I hope you go away from here understanding that this is power, the only real, true power. This is the only real, true
connection we will ever have to power, our relationship to Mother Earth.

We must not become confused. We must not become confused and deceived
by their illusions. There is no such thing as military power. There is only military terrorism. There is no such thing as economic power. There is only the economic within these illusions so we will believe they hold power in their hands.
But they do not. All they know how to do is act in a repressive, brutal way.

We are a natural part of the earth. We are an extension of the earth; we are
not separate from it. We are part of it. The earth is our mother. The earth is a
spirit, and we are an extension of that spirit. We are spirit. We are power. They
want us to believe that we have to believe in them, that we have to assume these
consumer identities and these political identities, these religious identities and
these racial identities. They want to separate us from our power. They want to
separate us from who we are. Genocide. . . .

And they have limited our ability to see the necessity for our survival because
they want us to believe that genocide just means physical extinction. We must

consider the *spiritual* genocide that they commit against us: the spiritual genocide that white people have been victimized for thousands of years, the spiritual genocide that told them not to respect the earth—the spiritual genocide that told them not to respect the life that is the earth—but to pay all their tribute through the churches to god and heaven, that heaven would take care of them in the afterlife. They tried to take and suppress our natural identity, our natural spiritual connection to the earth.

We must move to the time when we truly understand our connection to real power because these people who deal with illusions and imitations, these men who have attempted to "improve upon" nature, they want to keep us confused. They want to keep us confused with sexism and ageism, racism and class. They want to keep us in confusion so that we will continue to believe in one lie after another as they program them into our minds and into our society.

There is no hope for the American political system. The ruling class, the exploitative 1 percent who control world economics today, are not going to change under the existing political rules. . . .

When I go around America and I see the bulk of the white people, they do not feel oppressed. They feel powerless. When I go amongst my own people, we do not feel powerless. We feel oppressed. We do not want to make the trade. We see the physical genocide they are attempting to inflict upon our lives, and we understand the psychological genocide they have already inflicted upon their own people, . . . that this is the trade-off they want us to make for survival, that we become subservient to them, that we no longer understand our real connection to power, our real connection to the earth. . . .

We must be willing in our lifetime to deal with reality. It's not revolution we're after; it's liberation. We want to be free of a value system that's being imposed upon us. We do not want to participate in that value system. We don't want to change that value system. We want to remove it from our lives forever. Liberation. We want to be free. But, in order for us to be free, we have to assume our responsibilities as power, as individuals, as spirit, as people. We are going to have to work at it. We are going to have to be committed to it. We must never underestimate our enemy. Our enemy is committed against us twenty-four hours a day. They use 100 percent of their efforts to maintain their materialistic status quo. 100 percent of their effort goes into deceiving us and manipulating us against each other. We have to devote our lives. We have to make our commitment. We have to follow a way of life that means we are going to resist forever.

In the 1980s, we have to start working more realistically with a resistance consciousness. A resistance, something we can pass on as strength to coming generations. A resistance where organizational egos do not get in the way, a resistance where the infiltrators and the provocateurs and the liars and the betrayers and the traitors do not get in the way. We will not get our liberation if we do not seriously analyze the experiences of our own lifetimes. The other side, the enemy, has studied. They understand what we were up to in the 1960s. They understand what we wanted in the early '70s. They have studied us. . . .

We must go beyond the arrogance of human rights. We must go beyond the ignorance of civil rights. We must step into the reality of *natural* rights because *all* the natural world has a right to existence. We are only a small part of it. There can be no trade-off. . . .

They have every intention that they are going to use the nuclearization of the world to colonize you all. There is a new Indian this time. The new Indian is white. They don't need you anymore because they've got an entire potential world market with millions and millions of consumers. So, all the lies they've dangled in front of your faces, well, they're going to start pulling back on these lies a bit, and they're going to start slapping you all with a bit of reality: the reality that there are not political freedoms in America; the reality that there is not religious freedom in America. You all are going to have to deal with reality and stop making excuses for America.

We Indians are going to have to act as runners and messengers. We are going to have to run and act as teachers. We are going to have to talk to all the people who will listen to us about what we believe, what it is that we know to be right. . . .

It doesn't matter how many jail cells they build. It doesn't matter how many racist judges, sexist judges, ageist judges, and class judges they have. It doesn't matter how many of their side they put into illusory positions of "respectability." It doesn't matter what they throw at us because *we* make the difference. *We* make the decision. *We* are power. . . .

We always had to struggle, so let's not fool ourselves and try to make ourselves quit what we believe just because it's going to be hard. Let's struggle for a purpose. Let's struggle for the freeing of the earth because only by freeing the earth, and those who would attack the earth, can we be free ourselves. It is the only way we can do it.

There have been many social revolutions in America. There have been many social organizations. There have been women's rights movements; there have been equal rights movements; there have been union movements. And look who's still controlling our lives. We've got to deal with that reality. The people have risen before. The people have spoken before. The people have tried before. But somewhere they did not put it all together, the reason being that they always attempted to change the social conditions of America without addressing the issue of our relationship to the land. [Yet] they cannot create a repressive military regime without the land. They cannot exploit economics without the land. . . .

They have been attacking indigenous people, and they have been misusing white people, and they want to push us all into a position where all we think about is ourselves. They want us to forget the earth, just like they used early Christianity to make the Christians forget the earth. They want to do it to all of us again, in this generation. They want to isolate us and call us names like "communist" and "anarchist" and "terrorist" and "criminal." They want to attack us. They want to use terrorism to intimidate us. We must build a resistance in our hearts that says we will not accept it, we will *never* accept it. . . .

No matter what they do to us, no matter how they strike at us, every time they do it, we must continue. But we must never become reactionary. The one thing that has always bothered me about revolution is that every time I have met the revolutionaries they have acted simply out of hatred for the oppressor. What we must do is act out of love for our people. No matter what they ever do to us, we must always act out of love for the people and for the earth. We must *never* react out of hatred for those who have no sense.

4.B.2.

Center for Third World Organizing

From "Voter Registration: Will It Build the Power of Low-Income People, or Deliver Them to the Democratic Party?" (1983)

The early 1980s brought renewed attention to what the Democratic Party had to offer working-class communities of color—most notably through Jesse Jackson's insurgent although ultimately unsuccessful campaign for the Democratic Party presidential nomination in 1984. Similar dynamics played out in mayoral elections for progressive Black candidates in Chicago, Boston, and elsewhere. Left organizations debated whether and how to relate to electoral politics. In this essay from its newsletter, the San Francisco Bay Area's Center for Third World Organizing suggests that grassroots organizers ought to recognize voter registration as a necessary but insufficient way to build political power.

All over the country, low-income people generally, and people of color in particular, are being accosted by the advocates of the New Movement Strategy. We are organized on the food stamp lines, agitated as we try to get our unemployment checks, and hustled as we trek down to the welfare department to try to qualify for emergency assistance and processed cheese. The strategy? Assault the White House? Rip off the big chain supermarket? Eat the rich? No—register to vote!

Noting that huge numbers of unregistered voters could make a significant difference in the '84 presidential election, literally hundreds of student groups and community organizations, as well as the whole social welfare establishment, have taken up the banner of voter registration as a major progressive counterthrust to the New Right's control over the fiscal and political levers of federal and state government.

Certainly the notion of registering voters to ensure accountability from the state is not new. . . .

So why the big splash in 1983 over voter registration?

First, the right has done what no progressive organization or charismatic leader of the left has been able to do: provide a unifying focus for those of us on the other side. The massive redistribution (read cutbacks) of the budget from human needs to the military budget, failure to initiate a jobs program, intervention in Latin America coupled with continued support for repressive regimes around the world (e.g., South Africa, the Philippines, Guatemala), and the escalated possibility of nuclear war has forged a broad-based anti-Reagan constituency whose common basis of action is the ousting of Reagan. . . .

So what could be wrong with a voter registration campaign focusing on low-income third world people?

First, there is the question of options—for whom or what will people be able to vote? A choice between [Walter] Mondale and [John] Glenn is not particularly exciting. Nor do these candidates represent political positions that are in concert with the interest of low-income people of color. On the contrary, one could argue that they represent corporate interests that demand increased tax breaks, lower labor costs, and decreased regulation of plant mobility, occupational health and safety, and environmental safety.

Then there is the question of realignment. In looking at the rule changes within the Democratic Party, one might note that the party has already been realigned—*towards the party regular*. While the Democratic Party opposed Reagan on some issues, there has been no significant Democratic opposition to workfare *or* free enterprise zones *or* Simpson-Mazzoli [restrictive immigration bill] *or* subminimum wage. So as we embrace the "strategic opportunity" afforded us by our friends in the Democratic Party, we ought not be surprised if they act like they knew we had no place else to go and they don't have to make *us* any concessions.

If there *are* concessions, who'll cut the deal for low-income people of color? Aside from the Democratic Party heavies like [Detroit's first Black mayor] Coleman Young, the most likely person to be in a position to cut deals will be Jesse Jackson. Yet no other aspect of the issue of running a Black presidential candidate has caused such an uproar and split in the Black leadership as the prospect of Jesse Jackson being that candidate.

Voter registration experts note that Jackson's candidacy will spur Black voter registration and that the support generated for Jackson's candidacy will certainly give him some deal-making ability after the primaries. But questions arise concerning whom and what Jackson represents. As Brasher points out in the *New Republic*, "[Although] praised for his dynamics and his electricity, Jackson is chided for being arrogant, shallow and a one-man show whose programs are long on style and short on content and execution. Jackson is no revolutionary; he seldom takes a position that might alienate his supporters. His beliefs are still basically Baptist and fundamentalist, including his (now-muted) anti-abortion stand." So the question remains whether registering to vote gives low-income people of color any real choice.

While it is true that registering low-income people to vote may be an important *tactic* in pressuring the Democratic Party (the spigots of social spending

the WHY CHEAP ART? manifesto

PEOPLE have been THINKING too long that
ART is a PRIVILEGE of the MUSEUMS & the
RICH. ART IS NOT BUSINESS !
It does not belong to banks & fancy investors
ART IS FOOD . You cant EAT it BUT it FEEDS
you . ART has to be CHEAP & available to
EVERYBODY . It needs to be EVERYWHERE
because it is the INSIDE of the
WORLD .

ART SOOTHES PAIN !
Art wakes up sleepers !
ART FIGHTS AGAINST WAR & STUPIDITY !
ART SINGS HALLELUJA !
ART IS FOR KITCHENS !
ART IS LIKE GOOD BREAD!
Art is like green trees!
Art is like white clouds in blue sky !
ART IS CHEAP !
HURRAH
Bread & Puppet Glover, Vermont, 1984

Figure 4.2. Bread and Puppets, "The Why Cheap Art Manifesto" (1984). Image courtesy of and reprinted with permission by Josh Krugman for Bread and Puppet Theater.

will definitely open wider), it is without question not a *strategy* for party realignment, let alone for fundamental change.

In order to move a disenfranchised low-income constituency into a position where we can effectively manipulate the State, it is necessary to demonstrate electoral clout. Voter registration alone, however, does not constitute a strategy, for a strategy would include a process of organization which would develop grassroots analysis and action on issues; a tactical repertoire of direct action as well as electoral activity; and the development of an alternative social and economic program so that, regardless of the personalities involved, we could understand not only what we are against but what we are *for*.

While voter registration does have tactical importance, it is clear that the current campaign may not reach the strategic level of projected political significance unless political education, direct action, and policy development become an integral part of the organizing thrust.

4.B.3.

Youth Greens

From "Summary of Youth Green May Gathering" (1989)

The Youth Greens started as a Youth Caucus in the Green Committees of Correspondence, a network of Green locals from around the US that would eventually become the Green Party. At a gathering in 1989 in Ohio, the Youth Caucus decided to become an autonomous organization focused on building grassroots social movements. The organization argued against getting involved in national electoral politics and reform and instead embraced revolutionary politics. A mix of anarchists, feminists, socialists, and other young radicals, the Youth Greens were inspired in part by the anarchist movement, social ecologist Murray Bookchin, queer identity and theory, and the German autonomen. The group played a major role in the 1990 Earth Day mass civil disobedience on Wall Street, which also featured one of the first uses of black bloc tactics in the United States. This excerpt on pursuing a strategy of "oppositional politics" comes from its founding statement of principles.

Oppositional Politics

The Youth Greens support an explicitly oppositional politics, as only an oppositional politics can pave the way for the revolutionary changes which we seek. The crises we are faced with require fundamental structural change. Existing institutions and elites are unwilling and incapable of initiating the required changes, as their power and privilege rest upon the status quo. Mere appeals to their conscience and goodwill have repeatedly been proven ineffectual.

We thus have no choice but to look to other times and places where similar deep-ranging social change has been won. The farmer, labor, women's, Black Power, and Native American movements are examples of insurgencies which achieved hard-won victories in the face of elite intransigence. At their peak, the politics of all these movements was fundamentally oppositional; they demonstrate conclusively that social change is made through struggle.

The Youth Greens therefore reject the idea that social change only requires individual transformation. Changes in individual attitudes are indeed necessary. However, overemphasis on this has led to the view that all individuals are equally responsible for the world's problems. This is misleading; we are faced with entrenched power structures which benefit some at the expense of others and can only be challenged through large-scale confrontation. Additionally, participation in collective social practice is essential to the radical transformation of individual attitudes necessary to the creation of an ecologically sustainable society. Preoccupation with the individual must therefore be expanded to encompass an understanding of the dialectical relationship between social and personal transformation.

An oppositional politics requires political coherence, accountability, direct democracy, and commitment. Furthermore, we need to develop a general theory of struggle which will guide us between the twin dangers of liberal-democratic co-optation and isolated adventurist posturing. We reject the Weather Underground's macho glorification of violence as well as the sellout and corruption eventually suffered by many insurgent movements. Avoiding both of these errors is essential; we must creatively balance the tension between broadening the base and moving forward.

The Green philosophy of democratic decentralization is an essential component to building an oppositional politics. There is an infinite variety of sociopolitical contexts in the United States; this variety requires local autonomy in determining appropriate strategies and tactics. Generally, we call for creative, tactically flexible direct actions which effectively express our opposition to entrenched power. We prefer nonviolence to violence as more conducive to democratic process and green politics. But we do not wish to restrict our future choices to dogmatic pacifism; in particular, we affirm the right of self-defense.

Resisting co-optation is crucial. It can occur both internally, through bureaucratization, and externally, through manipulation and sellout. One manifestation of co-optation in political movements today has been the increasing dominance of a narrowly defined view of "nonviolence." Permissible strategies for protest have increasingly been limited to tame, choreographed spectacles preapproved by the forces of repression. The Youth Greens reject this as inauthentic opposition. It robs protest of possibility, and protest without possibility is not oppositional.

Revolutionary Dual Power and Radical Municipalism

In our struggle for a fundamental restructuring of society, it is imperative that we create a movement outside of the capitalist power structure. We take a principled stand and are against state and national electoral politics. This system, controlled by corporate interests, is inherently undemocratic. The "representative" system creates government that is not accountable to the citizenry.

We see fundamental societal changes as especially desirable from the local level. A citizenry which is informed and self-organized, acting at the grassroots level, can begin actualizing direct democratic ideals. Such a strategy can begin with working in our communities to create neighborhood assemblies or other local groupings. Communities working together and confederated across the continent can create a popular counterpower to the existing corporate and military power structure. This is revolutionary dual power.

Towards this end, Greens work in ways which are both electoral and non-electoral. Greens work outside of the electoral system to create counterinstitutions in this dual power effort. For example, food co-ops, free schools, collective gardens, alternative energy projects, squatted homes, and other alternative institutions can nurture the development of a revolutionary culture outside the one-dimensional sphere of domination. Through municipal elections Greens can also run directly accountable candidates who seek to create a counter-power. These two types of politics are not mutually exclusive. Greens should understand and respect both means of social change.

Local groups should use tactics they feel are appropriate in their situation. Creativity and communication with other local groups are essential in the creation of dual power. Youth Greens recognize that radical municipalism and dual power constitute an organic, growing theory of social change. We realize however, that these theories will be improved through experimentation and practice.

Democratic Decentralism

The Youth Greens are democratic decentralists. Our organizational forms demand strict accountability of delegates, spokespeople, and members to policies set by the membership. Democratic decentralism affirms the right of minorities to dissent. These minorities have the right and responsibility to publicly dissent and organize so long as they clearly distinguish their position from the official two-thirds vote of the Youth Greens. Majorities should be accorded the right to make decisions in the name of the organization. It is because we value diversity and pluralism that we embrace democratic decentralism.

Anarchist Gatherings, 1986–1998

Lesley Wood

Gatherings or conferences can be critical for connecting activists from different locations, tendencies, and generations. Such events were especially crucial to the growth of anarchist politics in the 1980s and 1990s. In 1986, anarchists began to gather in a new way, combining free school activities, trading of materials, meetings, performance, music, art, and socializing. These types of interaction helped to create continent-wide networks and shared identities. Chicago anarchists organized the first large, multitendency, non-decision-making anarchist gathering in the United States or Canada in 1986. Between three hundred to five hundred anarchists converged for workshops on everything from child rearing to technology, attended concerts and performances, and participated in a rowdy march. The event built ties between anarchists in different cities, led to the launch of a shared newsletter, and built relationships that would form the backbone of subsequent gatherings. About 250 people attended a 1987 event in Minneapolis, 800 came to Toronto in 1988, and 1,500 to San Francisco in 1989. The San Francisco "Without Borders" conference featured 113 workshops, 16 network meetings, 9 event planning sessions, plus opportunities for "spontaneous events."

After this massive event, organizers shifted their attention away from mass events and toward protest campaigns instead. Direct action protest activity was on the rise and anarchist activists increasingly engaged in street demonstrations on a range of issues. The Love and Rage Network (which produced the continental anarchist *Love and Rage* newspaper between 1989 and 1998), Anti-Racist Action, and the Food Not Bombs Network provided sites for experimentation in organizing and movement strategy. These formations, alongside the nascent internet, helped to create a decentralized US-Canadian network of activists who were explicitly engaged in movement building. The set of strategies promoted in this network included community organizing, alternative economics, the building of revolutionary movements, and creative direct action. These four themes became the core of the next two anarchist gatherings, both of which were known as Active Resistance (Chicago 1996; Toronto 1998). Each one attracted around eight hundred people, and at each, attendees built networks and participated in rowdy street protests. The relationships formed and the politics articulated at these events subsequently influenced the emergence of the global justice movement at the dawn of the new millennium.

4.B.4.

Prairie Fire Organizing Committee

"Crisis in Socialism: The Discreet Charm of the Bourgeoisie" (1990)

In this editorial from its journal *Breakthrough*, the Prairie Fire Organizing Committee reflects on the challenges socialists faced after the collapse of the Soviet Union. In addition to outlining some of the problems of Stalinist regimes, Prairie Fire highlights a crucial element of its internationalist and anti-imperialist worldview: the most exciting examples of socialism were not European but African, Asian, and Latin American. Prairie Fire urges readers to keep focus on those regions of the world and on the disparate global power and influence of the United States.

Communist leaders and parties are being thrown in the dustbin of history. Statues of Lenin are crashing down. Can socialism survive and, if so, what will it look like and what will it mean to us? Socialism through Red Army fiat is certainly dead. The speed with which the Eastern European CPs [communist parties] have unraveled indicates just how little they understood or represented their own people and just how much they depended on Soviet power. In the process, fundamental failings of the system of socialism, as constituted in Eastern Europe and the Soviet Union since Stalin, have been revealed:

- Central planning had failed either to generate growth competitive with capitalism or to meet the demands and expectations of consumers. Internal and external debt has slowed growth to a crawl.
- The "dictatorship of the proletariat" had become the dictatorship of a party elite, using its position to secure privileges and wealth at the expense of the people.
- Basic democratic freedoms and self-determination of nations were trampled on in the name of state security.

In Eastern Europe, Poland and Hungary are racing to embrace Western investment and capitalism, in the process reducing themselves to the status of developing countries. Responding to International Monetary Fund austerity recommendations (the conditions for $3.5 billion in new loans), the Solidarity government of Poland has announced plans to cut state subsidies by approximately 50 percent, allow price increases from 25 percent to 50 percent per month, and lay off four hundred thousand workers. How well this capitalist medicine will go down with the workers who brought Solidarity into power is an open question.

Socialist movements in East Germany and Czechoslovakia have a longer history and stronger base among the people. But the stultification of Stalinist regimes, excesses and corruption by party leadership, and decades of repression by state security police and the Soviet military have destroyed most of the credibility communists ever claimed. Reformers in the ranks are trying to reestablish an organic connection between party and people. But even if these efforts succeed, fashioning an economy incorporating market features with some of the social values we associate with socialism is a daunting task.

The best chance for revitalizing socialism lies within the Soviet Union itself, where glasnost and perestroika unleashed the current upsurge in popular democracy. Unlike Eastern Europe, where Stalin's tanks imposed his particular brand of socialism, the Soviet Union did undergo a revolution, and the efforts to revitalize socialism are led by a party which, for the moment at least, is basically intact. Working against Gorbachev, though, are major obstacles: an intractable economy and a multinational empire coming apart at the seams.

Gorbachev's efforts are taking place in a perilous international environment. Western Europe and the US hover like hungry birds of prey, waiting to descend on the carcass of an impoverished and dismembered Soviet Union. "Z" (the anonymous author of a recent article entitled "To The Stalin Mausoleum") probably reflects a significant sector of the Bush administration Cold Warriors when he asserts the inability of socialism to reform itself and advocates continuing a containment strategy against the Soviet Union.

All this, of course, is creating a heyday for anticommunists and consternation among liberal critics of capitalism. But we can't just limit the discussion to a comparison of advanced industrial nations like West Germany or the US on the one hand and Eastern Europe and the Soviet Union on the other.

Imperialism is a global system. The social cost of the relative prosperity of the West is the impoverishment of Asia, Africa, and Latin America, where half the world's population still wonders where its next meal is coming from. US, German, and Japanese banks and corporations (and economies) benefit from a massive transfer of capital in the form of interest payments on huge debts and unfair terms of trade. If Mexico or Mozambique wants aid, the terms are IMF austerity measures like those faced by Poland. Socialist economics may not work yet, but capitalism sure continues to kill.

Acknowledging the failings of socialism is disconcerting. Fundamental principles—the rationality of central planning, the leading role of the party, democratic centralism, the dictatorship of the proletariat, the belief in moral incentives—are now up for grabs. And the retrenchment of Soviet economic and political priorities threatens support for national liberation struggles. The new rubric of "peaceful resolution of regional conflicts" seems to dictate withdrawal of Soviet support for revolutionary movements and countries—from Nicaragua and Cuba to the ANC—without any reciprocal lessening of US support for repressive dictatorships.

At the same time, if we are honest, we would have to admit that most of us did not look to either the Soviet Union or Eastern Europe for examples of what we thought of as socialism. Although we can't overestimate the importance of support by socialist countries for national liberation movements, we've always had to question the kinds of societies many of the Soviet bloc nations had at home. And our idealism about China was dashed long ago, by the exposure of the excesses of the Cultural Revolution and Chinese support for counterrevolution in the Third World.

In fact, one strength of anti-imperialists has been the understanding of the role of national liberation struggles in creating a more humane world. Although victorious national liberation movements certainly haven't brought about the end of global capitalism, in the face of a deadly counterassault and tremendously complex economic and political conditions, revolutionaries in El Salvador, Nicaragua, Palestine, and the Philippines are still trying in different ways to grapple with these realities and fight for a new life for their people. In this context, we need to look closely at the critiques of perestroika, glasnost, and the events in Eastern Europe coming from Cuba and other socialists in the developing world.

If Gorbachev and other reformers are able to achieve the revitalization they seek, the possibilities are immense. Democracy under capitalism, while an advance in human thought at its historic moment, has always been at the cost of colonialism and human misery. But the possibility of combining the economic ideals of socialism with true democracy is very exciting to imagine. Will this happen, and, if so, will it happen within the next twenty years? Like everyone else in the world, we have to wait and see and hope for the best.

It's easy to become cynical, to look at the world and say "nothing can ever change." But it's not as though life in the US is so great either. For while the left debates the future of socialism in Europe, conditions here are deteriorating. We might not know how to rebuild socialism, but we do know that homeless people are on the streets; that racism is rampant; that violence against women is at an all-time high; and that gay and lesbian liberation is certainly not around the corner. Our job has to be developing strategies and movements that address these and a myriad of other issues, such as health care, education, and the environment, that are on the agenda.

It ought to be an interesting decade!

4.B.5.

Joel Olson

From "Why the Masses Ain't Asses" (1993)

Originally published in the Minneapolis-based punk zine *Profane Existence*, "Why the Masses Ain't Asses" outlines a theory of mass politics for punk rockers. In this excerpt from the article, Joel Olson, a punk activist who later became a political science professor, argues against a cynical rejection of everyday people in favor of a structural analysis of power, privilege, and political action.

Weapons of the Weak

. . . [I]f the masses aren't asses, how can we explain the fact that there hasn't been a revolution that freed us all yet, despite the thousands of zines, demonstrations, and political organizations telling folks what's up? If folks are so smart, why don't they revolt against this fucked-up world? I think there are three reasons for this:

1) People, especially extremely poor people, do what they have to do to survive, and immediate personal and family concerns take precedent over more broader political concerns. These folks aren't stupid, they're just too busy trying to survive in this system to try to change it as well. This description fits some people but it leaves a lot of folks out (especially the middle class).

2) People don't passively accept this fucked-up system; they *do* resist it every day and in many ways. However, due to physical or political limitations (anything from death squad terror in Central America to lack of experience in democratic processes in the US), a lot of people aren't able to organize effectively and resist collectively. People *don't* blindly obey; they resist in any ways they can. Sometimes they don't even see it as blatant resistance: timecard padding, loafing on the job, lying to your boss, cheating the landlord, cheating on your taxes, stealing stuff from work, sabo-

taging capital. Sure, people do these things for self-interested reasons, but don't ignore the important fact that these actions make the powers that be *mad*. . . .

3) I think some people genuinely enjoy this sick system because they benefit from it. George Bush and Bill Clinton aren't brainwashed fools; they are men who have used the privilege and power accorded to their race and sex and class position to mold the world in their favor and in the favor of people like them. (Of course, I'm a white male too, but I like to think that I'm using my privileged status in this society to *undermine* society and the privilege it grants me. It's my responsibility to use my power to support others so that one day we will all have equal social and political power.)

People like Bill Clinton and Al Gore and [Chrysler executive] Lee Iacocca aren't brainwashed; they are our *enemies*, plain and simple. People who like this system because they profit off of it are those we must struggle against. I know that because this is *Profane Existence* you think I mean we need to run out and bash all their heads, but I don't. I mean that we have to devise tactics and strategies that confront people like them and hold them responsible for their actions while celebrating all people struggling against the New World Order at the same time.

As soon as I start talking about politics as a struggle of the powerful against the powerless (to put it very crudely), someone always gets upset and blubbers something about how people can change, so don't drive them away from your cause by declaring them your enemy. Well, of course people change, but social classes *don't* change. The rich will always abuse and exploit the poor even if Donald Trump gives all his millions to the New Jersey anarchist collectives. Some people may change but most won't because to do so would mean they have to give up too much of their wealth, and the system of injustices certainly won't change unless we challenge it. . . . In resisting this world, radicals need to realize that not everyone is going to join us, and while that's sad these people also do it for a reason: they benefit from the status quo and won't surrender their privilege without a fight.

What's Wrong with the Masses?

But if the masses aren't asses, how can we explain why so many people are elitist, racist, sexist, homophobic, and generally intolerant of others? . . . People everywhere do what they feel is necessary to survive, and in doing so, they usually fill a role according to the needs of social institutions. For example, capitalism needs a large pool of unemployed workers to keep wages down, so some people become unemployed and blame immigrants for it. A patriarchal society needs rapists to physically intimidate women to maintain power over them, so it creates a rape culture in which any male can rape a woman and (usually) get away with it. This fucked-up world creates fucked-up roles for people to play, and, sadly, people play them. . . .

If you put a person in a different world, s/he'll be a different person. Would you think and act the same if you were from another country, a different class background, a different race, and/or a different gender? Not likely. Would you have been a Nazi supporter if you were a poor white Gentile German worker in 1937? Quite possibly. The key, then, is to hold people responsible for their actions but to also work to change the social conditions that make it advantageous to them for being racist, misogynist, homophobic, elitist, and/or a cop.

Changing these social conditions means struggling against the dominant powers that be, not harping on people for their stupidity. Taunting and guilt-tripping people into revolutionary movements obviously isn't working for the obvious reason that it insults people's intelligence. If we're trying to create a revolution in this society we have to give people good reasons to exchange what privileges they have now for the chance to recreate the world.

So do me a favor: stop saying the masses are asses and start looking for little ways people resist hierarchy and authority. Appreciate those efforts and look for ways to turn those individual acts of resistance into collective forms of defiance and self-determination. Show people that their little acts of sabotage are also forms of political resistance and explain how they can get a lot more than an extralong lunch break if we resist together. Know your enemy. Stop believing that everyone can be changed and that someday we'll all be one big happy family. Take what people say at face value instead of calling them brainwashed. If we stop assuming the masses are asses and concentrate on the political and social conditions that make people "asses," the anarchist movement might just become threatening again.

4.B.6.

Mab Segrest

From "A Bridge, Not a Wedge" (1993)

Mab Segrest is a longtime antiracist, feminist, queer organizer and scholar. Segrest worked for North Carolinians against Racist and Religious Violence (NCARRV) from 1983 to 1990, doing intersectional grassroots organizing against a variety of far-right groups. She originally delivered the excerpt that appears here as a keynote at the National Gay and Lesbian Task Force's Creating Change Conference in Durham, North Carolina, in November 1993. She outlined the need for queer socialist politics. It appears in her book *Memoir of a Race Traitor*, first published by South End Press.

When we don't get race, it kills us. When we don't understand capitalism, not only are we more confused about race, not only do we confuse power with money, not only do we deny our clearest voices—we also fail to understand the forces driving the history of our times. . . .

While the New Right's "family values" campaigns of the 1970s and 1980s pumped up hostility against gay men and lesbians, the forces that eventually brought Reagan and Bush to the White House stole this country. . . . In the 1960s and '70s, the men who run the multinationals responded with mergers and hostile takeovers to try for fast profits, rather than using the money to re-tool basic industries and maintain our infrastructure. They did not improve our products—how many of you began driving Volkswagens or Hondas rather than American cars in the 1970s and 1980s? Rather, they cut labor costs—by attacking unions and by sending our basic industries to Third World countries, where people work for one-tenth the wages (maquila workers make $4 a day). . . .

How does this economic stuff affect us as gay people? Pitiful funding for AIDS and breast cancer is an obvious answer, but let's look deeper. . . .

As the South goes, so goes the nation. As North Carolina (the most industrialized state in the country, losing jobs to automation and "economic integration") goes, so goes your state. And the real problem, with this region and this country, is that slavery was never really abolished. It just got reinstituted in other forms: Jim Crow, sharecropping, subsistence-wage labor jobs for people of color that often amount to involuntary servitude. Today's proposals for "free enterprise zones" in blighted and abandoned cities and even "don't ask, don't tell" are descended from the heinous logic of biological and social superiority and an economic system that requires a dehumanized category of workers to reap its profits. We gay men and lesbians should not be surprised when this country does not treat us well.

We can meet till the cows come home and discuss how to "fight the right" without recognizing that in some cases we are the right. Lance Hill, who directed the Louisiana campaigns against neo-Nazi David Duke's candidacies, told me that Duke's campaign for governor in 1990 was active in the gay bars of the French Quarter in New Orleans. Neo-Nazis could have access there because those bars are largely segregated. I offer this example not to say that Louisiana is an anomaly but to say that the Duke campaign brought out a weakness of gay movements in most cities. We gay people look with justified concern at the way the religious right uses homophobia to divide, for example, the African American community, to persuade some of its church people to organize against us to their own detriment and destruction. We need to look with equal concern at the practices of our movement, our community, which are also the dry wood on which fascism burns. For many gay and lesbian people of color, it is every bit as much an expense of spirit to be in a room with us radical queer white activists as with the most hair-raising fundamentalist minister, just as exhausting and insulting. We can no longer take for granted the presence of our brothers and sisters of color among us, their talents and their resources. The arsonists of the Christian Coalition have lit their fires, and the hot winds are rising.

. . . [N]o movement or person in this country can escape the repression and dehumanization that was required for the genocide of Native peoples and the enslavement of Africans. That's what we fight when we "fight the right." Let our presence in the South this weekend remind us of that. The only "special right" that the United States gives to minorities is the right to be the target of geno-cidal policies. We have only to look at AIDS policy to confirm this truth. Just as we do not want people of color buying the right's homophobic argument that we are after "special rights," not civil rights, it is also vital that our movement does not buy the racist backlash to affirmative action propagated over the last two decades by the same Republican forces. When we put both parts of their strategy together, it's clear that, to them, *all* civil rights are "special rights" that victimize privileged white men. When any "minority," whether racial, ethnic, gendered, or sexual, buys into these wedge strategies, we play ourselves for fools and disrupt the possibility of a transformative political majority in the next century.

It's my belief that racism shapes all political movements in the United States, for better and for worse, but because white people so seldom talk about how we are affected by racism, we don't understand how to counter it. We just act it out. In the lesbian and gay movement, much of our analysis has flowed from an un-derstanding of gender, leaving race and class at two removes from our analy-sis. But approaches to racism have shaped the debates within our own commu-nity on issues such as passing and assimilation, radical transformation versus reform, [and] legal strategies for empowerment of the grassroots. . . .

We don't need a queer nationalism—as powerful as the militancy and anti-assimilationist stances of Queer Nation have been. We need a queer socialism that is by necessity antiracist, feminist, and democratic; a politics that does not cut us off from other people but that unites us with them in the broadest possi-ble movement. . . .

This queer socialism of a "newer left" would recognize the damage done by five hundred years of colonial rule. People of color have suffered for five hun-dred years from the European/Christian war between mind and body, soul and body, projected onto all women and onto cultures that often had more holis-tic worldviews and darker skins. The mind/body split allows the hundred white men owning poultry plants in Mississippi to tell the Black women workers, "We only want your bodies, not your minds," as those men lock the women into plants where twenty-seven out of thirty in one factory acquired carpal-tunnel syndrome. It generates rape and devastating physical and psychological vio-lence against women. It also defines gay men and lesbians in this period as only perverse bodies engaged in sinful/sick/illegal physical acts, as "abominations." And it discards the old and the disabled. When we lesbians and gay men see that Black women in Mississippi poultry plants and Mexican women in maqui-las are also defined as only bodies, to be used and discarded, machines without feelings and souls, we can understand more fully how our fates are implicated in theirs. When we don't respond to others being hurt by similar forces, how can we expect them to respond to our crises and pains? As Rabbi Hillel taught two thousand years ago, "If we are not for ourselves, who will be for us? [But] if we are not for others, who are we?"

As queer socialists we would bring our insights and strengths to a range of progressive struggles. A queer socialism would be inevitably inflected for gender, would have our anger and our militancy, our humor and our flair, and would shape a movement that includes gay and lesbian homeless people, many of them cross-dressers and many [of them] people of color. . . . A queer socialism would clarify our roles as workers, as "means of production." But we gay people also bring the knowledge that humans are not only "means of production," however much capitalism seeks to define us that way. We know and insist that our needs include not only the survival needs of food, shelter, health care, and clothing but also dignity, pleasure, intimacy, and love. . . .

A queer socialism would not be provincially urban. It would recognize that the most crucial battles for gay/lesbian politics in the next decade will not be in the cities . . . [but] in areas that are more rural and historically more conservative. In those areas, we will develop new models not dependent on a critical gay mass and gay infrastructure. We will create broad-based movements against homophobia and all forms of social injustice rather than movements only for gay and lesbian rights. These movements will hold heterosexuals accountable for heterosexism, generating heterosexual allies, then trusting them to do their jobs. The trust we will gain through this process is one of the opportunities within the crisis. Heterosexuals will increasingly learn how their fates are implicated in ours, how homophobia erodes their most intimate relationships and corrupts their institutions, building repression into our military, fear into our schools' quest for understanding and knowledge, and mean-spiritedness into proclamations of love from churches, mosques, and synagogues. If the religious right has its way, they will use homophobia as an ax against the very taproot of this country's democratic potential, the revolutionary concept of human dignity and equality. . . .

This reenergized movement will be, in Suzanne Pharr's eloquent terms, "not a wedge, but a bridge"; not a point of division but of expansion and connection. To those who insist on denying us our full humanity, we will insist on the sacred humanity of all people. *A bridge, not a wedge. A bridge, not a wedge.* It has a nice *ring* to it. We can say it like a mantra when we feel the right getting too hot. Folks from San Francisco can help us in this imaging—all those bays, all that steel hanging up in the air and people got the nerve to drive across it. How does it stay up there, anyway, across the blue expanse?

Yes, the fires are burning. But think of all that water.

And, even in a hot wind, bridges will sing.

South End Press, 1977–2014
Alexander Dwinell

In 1978, a new collective named South End Press published its first book. The press had been established the prior year by eight organizers coming out of the antiwar New Left who set out to form a nonhierarchical, feminist publishing house whose books would, as the press's mission statement declared, "encourage critical thinking and constructive action on the key political, cultural, social, economic, and ecological issues shaping life in the United States and in the world."

South End was a mission-driven publishing house for the activist left, seeing in book publishing a way for movements to both produce new ideas and establish links across struggles. South End continually brought new voices and viewpoints to wider audiences with the goal of pushing for radical social and economic change while resisting being aligned with any one ideology or faction. The press published hundreds of books on a diverse range of topics from the New Right to queer politics, from Native American struggles to the environmental justice movement, from labor struggles in North, South, and Central America to resisting imperialism in Palestine and the Middle East, from NAFTA to Black liberation struggles, and from COINTELPRO (the FBI's counterintelligence program) to the nonprofit industrial complex. Throughout its years of existence, the press found a home in the academy and the movement by publishing books that were recognized and used in both contexts without being beholden to either.

South End published new and established authors. Feminist scholar bell hooks was just starting to make a name for herself when South End published her first book *Ain't I a Woman* in 1981. The author's *Feminist Theory: From Margin to Center* followed, helping to build the foundation of intersectional feminist theory that to this day still challenges existing practices at both the center and on the left. At this time, even authors that had wider name recognition, such as Noam Chomsky and Ed Herman, were being ostracized and suppressed by the corporate media.

From its beginnings, members of the press worked to share power and confront workplace hierarchies, formal and informal. Initially, no one in the collective was paid but rather received room and board and lived together in a five-story townhouse in Boston's South End (hence the press's name). Work responsibilities were similarly equal. As the years went on, early ideals carried forward while strategies to realize them evolved. The collective moved on to a system of equal pay for all, strove to reduce the workday, and eventually ended a practice of paid sabbaticals so the work week could be reduced to thirty-two hours (though often everyone worked more than that when book or project deadlines approached). To reduce the barriers to continuing to work at the press once a collective member became a parent, the collective implemented a three-month paid parental leave and a dependent salary adjustment.

The makeup of the collective and the distribution of tasks also aimed for a more equal sharing of power. Collective members worked to diversify the collective itself; from its origins as a majority white-male collective, it had by the mid-1980s become majority women, and, by the mid-1990s, it was majority people of color. This effort overlapped with South End's focus on collectivizing its work. Each collective member had both editorial and administrative tasks. They also took turns answering the phone and cleaning the bathroom. Collective members rotated jobs in order to combat informal power hierarchies stemming from one person being an "expert" in knowing how to do something that other people did not. This approach to labor sought to enable the sharing of knowledge, prevent burnout from overspecialization, and utilize peer mentoring.

South End Press supported radical social movements not only through publishing but also through direct participation. The press was a place where ideas were worked through and then made their way out into the world as books as well as a space where collective members sought to put equality into action in the work place. Until its demise in 2014, the press continued to publish texts documenting the critical debates of the social movements of its time while also being transformed by them.

4.B.7.

Blue Mountain Working Group

From "A Call to Defend Democracy and Pluralism" (1994)

The Blue Mountain Working Group's influential "A Call to Defend Democracy and Pluralism" identified a shared progressive agenda in defending democracy and the gains of progressive movements against racism, sexism, homophobia, and class oppression. The statement, born of a national coalitional effort to make sense of the growing power of the far right within and outside the electoral realm, was signed by twenty-one activists, academics, journalists, and others representing a wide cross-section of progressive action.

We are a group of individuals interested in joining with others to rebuild a multi-issue movement for progressive social change that can assist in forming and organizing broad coalitions to reverse the ominous right-wing backlash currently sleeping the United States. In May 1993, we came from across the nation to a conference center in Blue Mountain, New York, to share our concerns about the growing prejudice and scapegoating being provoked by intolerant and antidemocratic religious and secular movements of the hard right.... We see the current general right-wing backlash is one of the most significant political developments of the decade, combining well-funded national institutions with highly motivated grassroots activists. To effectively conquer this movement, we believe it is essential to understand the specific and complicated component of the political right wing across its many forms and the often conflicting and competing aspects of right-wing theory and practice. . . .

We feel the phrase that best describes the essence of the contemporary activist right-wing movement is "antidemocratic right." The main goal of the antidemocratic right is to craft a reactionary backlash movement to co-opt and reverse the gains of the progressive social movements of the 1960s and 1970s which sparked the ongoing civil rights, student rights, antiwar, feminist, ecology, and gay rights movement. . . .

The antidemocratic right seeks to control what we read, the music we hear, the images we see, how we learn, what happens to our bodies, how we worship, and whom we love. . . .

It may seem a remote possibility, but it can happen here. We know from history that authoritarianism, theocracy, demagoguery, and scapegoating are building blocks for fascist political movements, and that people mobilized by the cynical, regressive, populous-sounding sentiments sewn by a Ross Perot can be harvested by the angry, divisive, racial nationalist rhetoric of a David Duke or Pat Buchanan. We also know the paradox of fascism is that when most people finally are asking whether or not it is too late to stop it—it is. Better that resistance be early and preventative rather than late and unsuccessful.

Because we believe the antidemocratic right is a growing social movement, we see three immediate tasks to protect democratic values: 1) defending diversity within the pluralistic society, 2) maintaining the separation of church and state, 3) protecting the right to privacy for all people.

We share a sense of urgency. Time is of the essence. We must stop the hard right antidemocratic backlash movement before it inflicts more damage in our society. In defending democracy and pluralism we must refrain from using the same polarizing techniques of scapegoating, demonization, and demagoguery that have been so successful for the antidemocratic rights. As we fight intolerance we will consciously strive to resist using the same intolerant tactics we oppose. We will respect diversity while defending democracy. We recognize that many of the individual grassroots activists being mobilized by the leadership of the antidemocratic right are sincere and honest people with real fears concerning jobs, family, schools, and personal safety. They are not our enemies, they are our neighbors—and potentially our allies.

We defend the rights of all persons to hold religious beliefs and moral codes without government restriction or interference. We insist that in a constitutional democracy the arguments for legislation and regulation be based on rational debate and factual evidence that demonstrate a useful purpose and a compelling government interest.

The leaders of the antidemocratic right wave the flag, wrap themselves in the cloak of religion, and claim they speak for God and country. We are not attacking God when we confront those who pridefully presume to speak for God. We are not attacking religion when we challenge those who imply that only persons who share their specific narrow theological viewpoint can claim religious or moral values. We are not attacking our country when we rebuke those who peddle a message of fear, prejudice, and division.

To stop the right-wing backlash we must help to build broad popular coalitions that include at the core all the communities under attack by the antidemocratic right and its many incarnations, and we must also include in these coalitions all persons of good conscience willing to defend democratic pluralism. Our allies are all persons who oppose theocracy and control by an authoritarian elite and all persons who are willing to stand up for a real, dynamic, and vibrant democracy.

As progressives we believe there're many values we must uphold in building any principled coalition. Our method of work as a progressive coalition must reflect diverse styles, perspectives, and goals. We must speak with many different voices representing the many different threads that weave the social fabric of our nation. We see progressive social change as an ongoing process involving persons from many constituencies and issues working together whenever possible in alliance for democracy and pluralism. . . .

We see a synergistic interactive relationship among activists, organizers, researchers, journalists, and academics from these various movements and constituencies as resulting in the most informed and useful analyses, strategies, and tactics to bring about effective action for social change. We believe there must be two-way interaction between the national and local levels. The needs and specific issues of local partners must inform and shape national strategies, and at the same time, the resources developed by national groups must be made available to grassroots organizers to stimulate informed discussion of various strategies and tactics. At the leadership level, there has not yet been sufficient cooperation of potential progressive allies, and many people in the national organizations still need to be educated about the serious nature of the threat posed by the antidemocratic right.

Hard experiences have taught us that short-term tactics that divide community for the sake of individual electoral victories are short-sighted, frequently backfire, and, even when successful, weaken the type of long-term coalition building that is necessary for eventual victory. It is essential to develop an analysis that bridges issues, helps communities understand the threats to them, and pulls together diverse constituencies and issues. The antidemocratic right has been successful in reframing the public debate over key issues such as family, morality, and children. We must participate in and reclaim this debate.

We believe in full equality for everyone—nothing more, but nothing less.

Ours is a vision of democracy where all have an equal voice. Of a democracy where progressive populism encourages active participation by all residents in open, full, and honest debates over legislation and government policies. Where we elect our government representatives on the basis of ideas, not images. Where the consent of the governed is informed consent, not manipulated consent. Where the wealth of wisdom possessed by a political candidate is more important than the reach of their wallet. Where elections offer real choices rather than rotating elites. Where the majority sets policies while consciously respecting the rights of the minority, and both the majority and minority have their grievances carefully considered and have access to representation. Our goal is twofold: we must stop the hard right, and we must pursue the unfulfilled promises of a healthy pluralistic democracy: justice, equality, security, and fairness—the real American dream. . . .

The antidemocratic right has a multi-issue strategic agenda, but its tactic is to focus its attacks on one high-visibility target constituency at a time. No single segment of our society has demonstrated an ability to resist these attacks alone. We must learn to work together. We urge everyone who desires to defend and extend democracy to join together in forming broad and diverse locally based coalitions to resist the rollback of rights, to block the backlash, to fight the right.

The leaders of antidemocratic right say their movement is waging a battle for the soul of America. They call it a culture war. We believe the soul of America should not be a battleground but a birthright and that culture should be celebrated not censored. We believe America is defined by ideas and values, but not those limited by religious police, biology, bloodline, or birthplace of ancestors.

The time has come to stand up and vigorously defend democracy and pluralism against the attacks orchestrated by cynical leaders of antidemocratic right. History teaches us that there can be no freedom without liberty, no liberty without justice, and no justice without equality, and we look forward to success because we know it is through the never-ending struggle for equality, justice, liberty, and freedom that democracy is nourished.

4.B.8.

Love and Rage Revolutionary Anarchist Federation

"What Kind of Revolutionary Organization Is Useful Today?" (1995)

The Love and Rage Revolutionary Anarchist Federation was the most developed anarchist formation in North America in the 1990s. Through its national newspaper and local chapters, the organization took on issues such as police brutality, educational equity, antifascism, and solidarity with the Zapatista insurgency in Mexico. This article, first published in the *Love and Rage* newspaper, identified an approach of "revolutionary pluralism" as a way to organize against oppression in a broad-based, democratic fashion.

The multiple problems facing the world today require a revolutionary response. The troubles faced by the oppressed—especially people of color—exist not because the promise of liberal democracy is yet unfulfilled throughout the globe but because of inherent contradictions within liberalism and capitalism itself.

Because capitalism requires the many to work for the profits of the few, modern society cannot provide full freedom for all. Further, because capital will not surrender its privileged position without a fight, the struggle for a truly free society requires a revolutionary struggle against capitalism and all forms of oppression.

Given this, the revolutionary question is: What kind of revolutionary organization is effective at this time? Historically, there have been two answers to this question. The most common is the Marxist-Leninist vanguard party. The vanguard strategy, from the Russian Revolution to the present, is to build an organization of an elite cadre of militants who will guide the masses through a revolution and lead them to a socialist society. This strategy has proven to be an utter failure because it has failed to fulfill the promise of freedom. By creating a highly centralized and undemocratic organization, vanguard approaches have reproduced these same power structures in society, with the party as the new ruling class.

The second strategy is less well known but is currently popular in many North American anarchist circles. This strategy, which could be called the storefront approach to social change, advocates creating "temporary autonomous zones" (TAZ) of collectives, infoshops, community centers, and other countercultural outposts throughout the land. These storefronts, the argument goes, will inspire thousands of other TAZs to organically sprout up in the rest of society, transforming the world without a center of power or a hierarchical chain of command. This strategy is admirable for its critique of authoritarianism and for its commitment to decentralized forms of organization. However, it is unrealistic because it does not present a plan to directly challenge and defeat the fundamental structures of state power. Nor does it suggest a way to democratically bring these multiple TAZs and storefronts together to collectively craft a vision of a free society.

The ineffectiveness of these two strategies requires a different response. This third view, which could be called revolutionary pluralism, is the position Love and Rage has arrived at after six years of debate and struggle. It is based on our perception of what a twenty-first-century mass movement against oppression will look like. While movements aimed at organizing factory workers may have been appropriate in the late nineteenth and early twentieth centuries, the ever-changing landscape of capital and imperialism has grown much more complex today. The mass movements against them will inevitably reflect this diversity and complexity. The struggles of women, people of color, and oppressed nationalities throughout the world are no longer secondary to the struggle of "the proletariat" (in reality, were they ever?) but constitute the potential, in their plurality, to be the foundations for a new mass movement. What will bring these diverse struggles and peoples together? Only a deliberate effort to unite them into a radically democratic and plural movement that will maintain their autonomy and challenge the existing power structure. This is revolutionary pluralism.

If the mass movements of the twenty-first century are going to be plural, diverse, and emanate from a variety of locations, what is the role of a revolutionary organization? Clearly, such an organization should not attempt to make itself the "vanguard" and force the entire movement to conform to its ideology and be subordinate to its own organs of power. However, this does not mean there is no role at all for revolutionary organization, as advocates of the storefront strategy claim. The role of a revolutionary organization like Love and Rage in a mass movement is not to lead the movement but to participate in it as equals with other organizations and people. Through such participation we seek to do two things: 1) to argue for the most democratic mass movement possible, one that gives every person the ability to participate in it fully; and 2) to argue for our antiauthoritarian politics within this plural movement in order to influence it into struggling against all forms of oppression.

Of course, a plural and diverse mass movement does not exist in North America. At present, groups like Love and Rage are organizations without a movement. We do not pretend to be able to be this movement nor to be able to create it ourselves. That is the work of millions of the downtrodden and oppressed. However, we can and do participate in small movements right now, with the eye toward not only winning these smaller struggles but also toward bringing them together into a larger movement. We do this through active participation and by arguing for our politics in a free and open manner.

With this in mind, Love and Rage sees three current struggles that are not yet mass movements but that hold great potential. The struggle against white supremacy—not only against the far right but also against the principal institutions of this society (cops, courts, capital)—will be key to any revolutionary

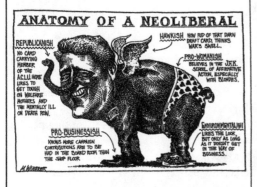

Figure 4.3. Matt Wuerker, "Anatomy of a Neoliberal" (1992). Image courtesy of and reprinted with permission by Matt Wuerker.

movement. Secondly, the Zapatista uprising indicates that México will be a central point of resistance to the global order in the upcoming century, and so we work to support our comrades in México and to open up a "northern front" in the US and Canada. And finally, we focus attention on prisons and the criminal justice system, not only to support our imprisoned revolutionary comrades but also to reveal prisons as the lynchpin of social control under capitalism and as a key weapon of Black genocide. Coupled with revolutionary pluralism, these three struggles offer a guide to building a new world within the complex and confusing shell of the terrible one we live in now.

4.B.9.

Labor Party

From "A Call to Economic Justice" (1996)

In an effort to challenge bipartisan support for expanded corporate power and a constricted social safety net, more than one thousand delegates founded the Labor Party in 1996. Its platform, titled "Call to Economic Justice," identified what the party elsewhere described as an "organizing approach to politics": rather than focus on running or defeating candidates, the party developed initiatives—particularly for universal health care—that would serve to improve the lives of working-class people.

Preamble

We are the people who build and maintain the nation but rarely enjoy the fruits of our labor.

We are the employed and the unemployed.

We are the people who make the country run but have little say in running the country.

We come together to create this Labor Party to defend our interests and aspirations from the greed of multinational corporate interests. Decades of concessions to corporations by both political parties have not produced the full employment economy we have been promised. Instead income and wealth disparities have widened to shameful extents.

We offer an alternative vision of a just society that values working people, their families, and communities.

We, the members of this Labor Party, see ourselves as keepers of the American Dream of opportunity, fairness, and justice. In our American Dream, we all have the right

- to a decent paying job and a decent place to live
- to join a union freely without fear of being fired or other retribution

- to strike without fear of losing our job
- not to be discriminated against because of our race, gender, ethnicity, disability, national origin, or sexual orientation, at work or in our communities
- to free, quality public education for ourselves and our children
- to universal access to publicly funded, comprehensive, quality health care for all residents
- to retire at a decent standard of living after a lifetime of work
- to quality of life in our communities enhanced by a fully funded public sector.

The Democratic and Republican parties serve the corporate interests that finance them. We oppose corporate power that undermines democratic institutions and governments. We oppose corporate politicians and parties that provide billions in corporate tax breaks and subsidies to the rich, selling themselves to the highest bidder. We reject the false choice of jobs versus environmental responsibility. We will not be held hostage by corporate polluters who poison our workplaces and our communities. We reject the redistribution of billions of dollars of wealth from poor and working people to the rich. And we reject every opportunist who plays the race, gender, or immigrant card to keep us from addressing our real needs and the needs of our families and communities.

Our Labor Party understands that our struggle for democracy pits us against a corporate elite that will fight hard to retain its powers and privileges. This is the struggle of our generation. The future of our children and their children hangs in the balance. It is a struggle we cannot afford to lose.

Amend the Constitution to Guarantee Everyone a Job at a Living Wage

... First and foremost everyone, both in the private and public sectors, needs a guarantee of a right to a job at a living wage—one that pays above poverty-level wages and is indexed to inflation. And in today's world that comes to a minimum of about $10 an hour. We want this right written directly into the US Constitution. . . .

Pay Laid-Off Workers Two Months Severance for Every Year of Service

... We ... propose a job destruction penalty act modeled after the one proposed by the New Jersey Industrial Union Council, AFL-CIO (which covers all workers except those in hiring hall types of employment). Under the act corporations with one hundred or more employees globally will be required to pay each eligible laid-off worker two months severance pay for every year of service. And they will be required to pay $25,000 per eligible laid-off worker to the local community to offset rising social costs. . . .

Restore Workers Rights to Organize, Bargain, and Strike

... Today, nearly one out of ten workers involved in union organizing drives is illegally fired by employers who wage a campaign of fear, threats and slick propaganda to keep workers from exercising a genuinely free choice. That is why union membership is declining. And as union membership falls so do the wages of all working people, union and nonunion alike. . . . As a labor party, we will support the courageous efforts of our brothers and sisters out in the streets and in the fields all over this nation to overcome these legal handicaps, especially in the South and Southwest where the laws are most hostile. . . .

End Bigotry: An Injury to One Is an Injury to All

... We can curb corporate power only if we unite around a commission of economic justice and fairness. Real democracy includes all of us. . . . From the shop floor to the executive suite, we believe the workforce should reflect the wonderfully diverse face of our nation. We stand for justice and the end to discrimination.

Guarantee Universal Access to Quality Health Care

... We call for universal entitlement for all residents to comprehensive health care benefits including preventive, curative, rehabilitative and long-term care. . . .

More Time for Family and Community

a thirty-two-hour, four-day work week
Double-time minimum for all overtime
An hour off with pay for every two hours of overtime
Twenty Mandatory Paid Vacation Days for All
One year paid leave for every seven years of work . . .

... Taken together these proposals will create millions of new jobs and allow us free time we need to care for our families and to participate in our communities. More family time and more community participation should be the fruit of increased labor productivity.

Protect Our Families

paid family leave
flexible working schedules
affordable child and elder care for all
mandatory minimum pensions for all
guaranteed adequate annual income for all

... While politicians babble about family values, this Labor Party intends to do something real to protect our families. We call for a basic benefit package that covers all working people—full-time and part-time workers, employed and unemployed.

Ensure Everyone Access to Quality Public Education

... We call for a renewed commitment to high quality public education for all, not voucher systems and other privatization schemes that further reduce resources for our public schools.

Stop Corporate Abuse of Trade

... Our Labor Party will actively promote a strategy of international solidarity and cooperation with labor movements and labor parties in other nations through the exchange of information, worker organizing, collective bargaining, and other actions and strategies that demonstrate our commitment to work together to confront the global attacks on our environment and living and working conditions. ...

End Corporate Welfare as We Know It

... This Labor Party opposes all forms of welfare for corporations and the rich. We support a total end to corporate tax breaks and subsidies. We call for an end to the war between the states. To stop the tax concession competition among states and communities, all corporations should pay a standard community investment tax wherever they go. ...

Make the Wealthy Pay their Fair Share of Taxes

... From 1983 to 1989 alone the top one percent of all families increased their wealth by over $1.45 trillion. During the same period the national debt increased by $1.49 trillion. We need a just and simplified tax system to reclaim what is rightfully ours.

Revitalize the Public Sector

... A government that works for us would provide critical goods and services that cannot, and should not, be run for profit.

End Corporate Domination of Elections

The current system of privately financed elections essentially takes away our right to vote. Today Corporate America and the rich use their vast wealth to dominate the election process. As a result, politicians put the vested interests of the rich and powerful ahead of the needs and concerns of their constituents and the nation as a whole. It is virtually impossible to pass legislation that protects and empowers working people. Instead we are forced to watch elected politicians of both parties routinely rob the public treasury of billions of dollars, giving their rich and powerful donors tax breaks, subsidies, bailouts, and regulatory exemptions. We demand an end to this robbery.

Build a Just Transition Movement to Protect Jobs and the Environment

This Labor Party affirms its commitment to a clean and safe environment. We all need clean workplaces, clean air, and clean water. But we also need our jobs. We reject the false choice of jobs or the environment. We will not be held hostage by corporate polluters who poison our workplaces and our communities. . . .

Enforce Safety and Health Regulations with Worker Inspectors

. . . We call for national legislation to train and deputize workers to be on the job inspectors in each and every workplace. . . .

Reclaiming the Workplace: Job Design, Technology, and Skill

. . . . Corporations implement technologies and designs that make it profitable to replace full-time workers with an army of temporaries. To fight back we call for the creation of a labor-based, publicly funded Technology Democratization Commission, which will work to ensure that labor plays an important role shaping the development and implementation of technology.

4.B.10.

Black Radical Congress

"A Black Freedom Agenda for the Twenty-First Century" (1998)

Mass incarceration, police brutality, and attacks on affirmative action, welfare rights, and other gains of the civil rights movement had weakened the Black left as a national force. Bringing together diverse segments of Black progressive activists from around the country—including veterans of earlier attempts to build independent Black political organizations—the Black Radical Congress was founded as a national network in 1997. Its freedom agenda self-consciously blended the Black Panther Party's ten-point program, the

Freedom Charter of the African National Congress, and the feminist vision of the Combahee River Collective statement.

The realization of genuine democracy in the United States requires radical solutions. To be "radical" means to get at the root of real problems, seeking effective solutions. What we want is an end to the exploitation of capitalism, white racism and every manifestation of human oppression, a revolutionary transformation of the state and society, and the realization of humanistic values. What can unite us in struggle is a common vision and agenda for the twenty-first century, reflecting our aspirations and ideals, for the construction of a new society and a new humankind.

1. *We want an end to the exploitation of corporate capitalism.*

   We fight for the abolition of white supremacy and capitalist domination over our people and oppressed peoples and nations throughout the globe. Capitalism is the root cause of the major forms of social misery, hunger, and exploitation in the United States and the world.

2. *We want freedom, self-determination, and full human rights.*

   We want an end to all forms of human oppression—racism, homophobia, sexism, discrimination against disabled people, anti-immigrant discrimination, class exploitation, and imperialism. We assert our right to self-determination.

3. *We want a social policy agenda which invests in human beings.*

   We believe in a society in which all people have the resources to develop to their fullest potential. This can only occur when the basic needs of all people are met. At minimum, this includes free and universal health care, free child care, quality public education, lifelong access to retraining and vocational learning, and low-cost public housing.

4. *We want a comprehensive national economic policy which places the interests of people above profits.*

   We believe that US corporate capitalism is structurally incapable of addressing the basic economic needs of African Americans, as well as the overwhelming majority of US working-class and poor people. Therefore, we support aggressive measures to restrict and regulate the power and resources of corporations. Government must halt the transfer of capital and jobs out of the country. Plant- and business-closing legislation should be passed which requires public hearings and direct compensation to workers who lose their jobs. Tax the rich. Zero taxes for all earning under $30,000 a year. Replace the minimum wage with mandated "living wage" for all Americans.

5. *We want a society which allows for the healthy and positive development of our children.*

   Children are society's most precious resource. But in a racist and capitalist society, black children are frequently the first casualties. We demand quality education, health care, housing, and safety for every child.

6. *We want justice in the legal system.*

One-third of all young African American men are currently in jail and prison, on probation, parole, or awaiting trial. The US prison industrial complex has become a vast warehouse for millions of unemployed and low-wage laborers. In the past ten years, the number of black women in prison has more than doubled. Any black person is four times more likely to receive the death penalty than any white person convicted of the same crime. For these reasons, we call for the abolition of the death penalty, the twentieth century's version of lynching. We denounce the recent "three strikes" criminal justice provisions as inherently racist and discriminatory to black and poor people. We demand the release of all black prisoners convicted of nonviolent crimes. We call for full voting rights for people convicted of felonies, both in prison and after their release, and amnesty for all political prisoners, including those forced into political exile outside the United States. We demand the right of all African Americans to be tried by a jury of their peers.

7. *We want an end to police brutality and state terrorism in our communities.*

There are six hundred thousand police officers in the US, most of whom function like an occupying army in our communities. We call for the strict civilian control of our neighborhoods and citizen review boards which are empowered to discipline police misconduct. We denounce the deliberate trafficking of drugs and the proliferation of weapons in our communities by organized crime, the CIA, and other institutions of the state. We condemn the deliberate criminalization, incarceration, and execution of black youth as a clear violation of human rights.

8. *We want a clean and healthy environment for our people.*

We oppose the policy of environmental racism—the fact that three out of every five African Americans live near dangerous toxic waste sites. US industries today are pumping 2.4 billion pounds of toxic chemicals into our air and billions more into our drinking water. Thousands of black people have died prematurely and needlessly, because of corporate greed in the environment.

9. *We want full employment and a guaranteed income for all those unable to work.*

We know that twenty million US residents today are either unemployed or work part time and want full-time employment. We need a constitutional, legal right to a job, as much as a right to vote. We need governmental investment in community-based and cooperative institutions which generate jobs. We demand emergency action by the government, especially in areas of concentrated high employment, to create real jobs at living wages. We strongly support the struggles of black working women and men inside the trade union movement, fighting for economic justice.

10. *We want civil rights, affirmative action, and compensation for centuries of institutional racism.*

We defend the policies of affirmative action, race-based scholarships, and all equal opportunity legislation as absolutely essential in attacking racial inequality. We demand just compensation and reparations for the systematic brutality and exploitation our people have suffered historically and continue to experience today. We claim the legal and moral right to demand and receive just compensation for oppression which was responsible for the destruction of millions of black people's lives.

11. *We want liberation for all oppressed people throughout the world.*

The struggles of peoples of African descent are inextricably linked to the many diverse struggles of oppressed people and nations across the globe. Black liberation cannot be achieved inside the United States outside of the larger, pan-Africanist and internationalist struggle which is being waged between the haves [and] the have-nots. Our vision of black freedom in the twenty-first century must be internationalist.

12. *We want a real democracy in the United States.*

The real majority in this country consists of African Americans, Latinos, women, lesbians and gay men, workers, unemployed and low- income people, and other oppressed people. We favor the abolition of the winner-take-all electoral system and the creation of proportional representation government. We call for an end to the two-party system that functions essentially as one party of capitalism and racism. We support the creation of a new mass political party representing the interests of the overwhelming majority of US people.

Without justice there can be no peace. We are committed to the fight for the realization of a truly democratic and socially just society. We dedicate ourselves to the abolition of racism and all other forms of human oppression and the cultural integrity and political liberation of our people.

Black Student and Youth Activism in the 1990s and 2000s

Sekou M. Franklin

Throughout the 1990s and 2000s, young Black activists were instrumental in jump-starting social movements that targeted racial, economic, and social injustices. Taking on everything from voter education and police brutality to worker rights, gun violence, and the school-to-prison pipeline, these young activists advanced a new paradigm of justice beyond the civil rights movement.

One important organization that emerged in this period was the Black Student Leadership Network (BSLN). The BSLN was launched in 1991 in partnership with the Children's Defense Fund and the Black Community Crusade for Children. For six years (1991–96), the BSLN linked a national advocacy campaign with local political and community initiatives in an effort to combat child poverty, political apathy, and public health epidemics.

Through its Ella Baker Child Policy Training Institute and advanced service and advocacy workshops, the BSLN trained over six hundred young Blacks from colleges, universities, and youth development agencies in direct action organizing, voter education, child advocacy, and teaching methodology. The organization developed freedom schools in dozens of urban and rural cities and teamed with child advocacy groups to spearhead anti–childhood hunger initiatives. It also organized national day of action against violence activities, which reached forty cities in 1994 and dozens more in 1995 and 1996. The activities, which included youth speak-outs, parent and community meetings, letter writing campaigns, and lobbying against the Violent *Crime* Control and *Law* Enforcement Act of *1994*, highlighted community-based strategies for reducing gun violence and police misconduct.

Among the more interesting set of youth and intergenerational initiatives of the era was the Juvenile Justice Reform Movement (JJRM). JJRM campaigns in Louisiana, Maryland, California, and New York set out to reverse zero-tolerance measures that criminalized young people for minor misbehavior at school, to shut down youth prisons that were known for human rights abuses, and to end the disproportionate confinement of Black and Latino youth in the juvenile justice system. These initiatives were led by youth advocacy and community organizations such as Youth Force of the South Bronx and New York's Justice 4 Youth Coalition, adult-led groups such as Project South in Atlanta, Prison Moratorium Project in New York, and Baltimore's Reclaiming Our Children and Community Projects, Inc., and grassroots organizing and advocacy coalitions such as the Juvenile Justice Project of Louisiana, Families and Friends of Louisiana's Incarcerated Children, Maryland Juvenile Justice Coalition, and Critical Resistance, a national prison abolition coalition. At the height of the JJRM, the Annie E. Casey Foundation's Juvenile Detention Alternatives Initiative (JDAI) supported and funded local activities. Led by Bart Lubow, JDAI worked in seventy-five jurisdictions in nineteen states.

Moreover, the labor movement, represented by the AFL-CIO, made a concerted attempt to mobilize young people, especially Black students, from 1989 to 2005. In 1996, it created Union Summer, which placed young people as frontline organizers on local campaigns. Nearly a thousand interns participated in the program in its first year. Modeled after the 1964 Freedom Summer, Union Summer intentionally recruited Black students, reaching out especially to historically Black colleges and universities. Students and youth of color, including Black activists, made up the majority of Union Summer organizers.

Collectively, these initiatives underscore how young Blacks can propel grassroots mobilization initiatives. They exemplify that progressive and radical movement infrastructures can generate opportunities for young Blacks to participate in movement campaigns and intentionally position young Blacks at the forefront of critical policy debates.

Gary Delgado

From "The Last Stop Sign" (1998)

Gary Delgado got his start as a community organizer in the welfare rights movement in 1970 and went on to work for a variety of antiracist organizing projects, including the Center for Third World Organizing. By the end of the century, Delgado was one of many to notice that a reliance on foundation funds and a focus on service provision had severed many community organizations from movements for broader progressive change. To bridge that chasm, Delgado argues here, community organizations need to address entrenched structures of power.

From the Small to the Significant

Even thirty years ago, the simplest way to get a stop sign on a neighborhood corner was to dig a hole, set in a wooden post, and power staple on a readily available plastic replica. For time and effort exerted, this method beats talking to 125 community residents to get a group of 50 or 60 people to go down to the city's Office of Public Safety and demand one. The stop sign itself, however, was not the point. The point was that ordinary people were contesting for power around small "winnable" things and, if they were successful, eventually we could all vie for power around larger, more significant political issues.

Right-wing grassroots efforts—to close abortion clinics, kill affirmative action, and put gays and lesbians back into the closet—have never bothered with stop signs at all. Perhaps they know something that we forgot. Good organizing issues are deeply felt, controversial. Our problem is that the gap from the "small and winnable" to the large and significant is often unbridgeable.

As community organizers what are we really trying to do? Are we trying to change the size of the negotiating table, add a chair or two, or saw it up and see that everyone gets a fair piece? Or, are we saying, "Wait a minute, the table is in a room, the room is in a house, and the house occupies a particular space in relation to the city, country, planet, and universe?"

Heady stuff, community organizing [CO].

CO's Contributions

I don't mean to suggest that traditional community organizations have not made some significant strides. Our process of finding and developing grassroots leaders is an important contrast to the notion that the only people that can solve problems are anointed experts. We have helped people understand that their opinions count, that there is power in numbers, and that, even though there may be conflict within an organization, democratic decisions are possible. We have also contested for and won power—to reverse discriminatory loan policies, force the development of low-income housing, influence school curricula, stop illegal dumping, enforce first-source hiring, and reassess corporate taxes.

We also won a hell of a lot of stop signs.

But let's be clear: the world of traditional community organizing is almost completely separate from the parallel world of progressive activism. It was that activism which, during the 1970s, '80s, and '90s, built the women's and gay and lesbian movements, protested apartheid in South Africa and US intervention in Central America, fostered an immigrant rights movement, and responded to "benign neglect" and institutional racism in communities of color by building independent racial justice organizations. If traditional CO is to become a force for change in the millennium and beyond, it must proactively address issues of race, class, gender, corporate concentration, and the complexities of a transnational economy. . . .

Community Organizing and the Politics of Power

In truth, organizing people for power raises the question: power for whom and to do what? Our confusion too often begins with questionable politics, gets reflected in poor methods and misconceived notions of "wins," and ends by blurring our vision of power.

Let's start with the right's favorite wedge—race. Killing multiculturalism is the wet dream of choice for white privilege apologists. Whether the grand wizard of the Idaho Aryan Nation or liberal academics like Todd Gitlin and Arthur Schlesinger, these people would like us not to talk about race.

But the conversation about welfare reform, even though most recipients are white, is about race. The expression "urban core," where most community organizations work, is a reference to race. Three strikes is about race, and bilingual education is about race, language, and assimilation. Yet how many community organizations, even those in communities of color, have had explicit discussions about race relations and the racial impact of particular policies? Very few.

Yet we cannot organize a multiracial movement without an explicit racial politics. . . .

As these situations illustrate, organizing people for power begs the question: power for whom and to do what? How is it that some community organizations support more police and greater penalties while others support increased prevention programs and alternatives to incarceration? Where do community organizers and community organizations stand on the issues that "wedge" our people apart—abortion, gay rights, affirmative action, crime, the death penalty, vouchers? How do the religious-based organizations come down on school vouchers? School prayer? Can we really afford the claim that if it doesn't come up in the one-on-ones, informational door knocks, or issue development sessions, it's not an issue that our group should work on? I don't think so.

These portentous political questions are reflected in the internal workings of our organizations. For instance, what does it say about community organizations when many gay and lesbian people feel that they have to stay in the closet because the organization is not "queer positive"? Again, power for whom and to do what? . . .

Developing a Political Vision

In order to really address the changing political environment, even the more authentic community organizations will have to change. We must not be afraid to use analytical and ideological tools to develop political vision. By political vision, I mean a vision that takes us past the strategies of a campaign, a power analysis of key players, or the tactics of a good accountability session. In order to be a critical element in future change efforts, we must work with our constituents to develop our vision of a future society. . . .

How do we arrive at a vision that takes into account and combines our own political beliefs, values, aspirations, and experiences with those of our constituents? Very slowly. But we will only arrive if we allocate the resources, create the organizational space, and make a commitment to read, study, and discuss wedge issues and political vision as part of the culture of our organizations. In finding ways to build our vision, we don't have to agree on everything. However, if we have any hope of affecting larger societal issues and continuing to be relevant to our own constituents, we have to create space for discussing and developing a collective vision. . . . Remember, the grassroots movement of the right does not begin, or end, with stop signs.

When many of us began organizing, we believed that the organizations we built would form the base for a movement. Somewhere along the line, many of us got stuck in our own brand of organizing. Instead of believing that all of our organizations might have a shot at building a movement, we began to believe that our network was the movement and that everybody else should join, die, or get out of the way.

Given our current political situation, we may just want to rethink that position.

4.B.12.

Andrew Boyd

From "Truth Is a Virus: Meme Warfare and the Billionaires for Bush (or Gore)" (2002)

Longtime creative campaigner Andrew Boyd reflects on how economic justice activists combined irony, satire, media savvy, and a DIY ethos to challenge the neoliberal consensus among Democrats and Republicans in the 2000 election.

"Truth is a virus." When I first saw this phrase, defiantly spray-painted on the walls of a suburban high-school, it thrilled me. . . . I soon came to see, however, that lies are also viruses. Lies and myth and kitsch and advertising jingles and corporate logos and mood rings and the idea that free trade is free—all of these are viruses. I came to think of the matrix of hearts and minds and media as a vast theater of viral warfare. . . .

I was interested in viruses of political ideas and action. For several years, as "minister of culture" for the social justice group United for a Fair Economy, I experimented with various media viruses, taking on issues of taxation, sweat-shops, wage inequality, and corporate welfare. In the spring of 2000 we developed a very virulent strain: Billionaires for Bush (or Gore).

The Billionaires campaign was devised to educate the public about the twin evils of campaign finance corruption and economic inequality. With the pay gap between CEOs and workers at 475 to 1, both Democrats and Republicans renting themselves out to big money donors, and 97 percent of incumbents running for reelection being returned to Congress, these problems had reached crisis proportions by the 2000 presidential election. Our idea was to create a humorous, ironic media campaign that would spread like a virus via grassroots activists and the mainstream media.

In early May, in New York City I pulled together a team of talented volunteer designers, media producers, and veteran street theater activists[,] . . . [and] we began to put the pieces of the campaign in place. We created a stylish logo by splicing together a donkey and elephant, and a "candidate" by digitally morphing photos of presidential candidates George W. Bush and Al Gore into a single eerie image. Riffing off of slogans like "Free the Forbes 400," "Corporations are people too," "We're paying for America's free elections so you don't have to," and "We don't care who you vote for, we've already bought them," we created bumper stickers, buttons, a series of posters, and a kick-ass website that eventually won more than a few awards. We also created a set of more content-rich materials, including a political platform, a full campaign speech, a candidate product comparison chart, as well as a campaign-contribution-return-on-your-investment-analysis. We even made mock radio ads, pressed them onto CD and sent one hundred out to stations across the country. The satire was compact, funny, and politically on target. The look was slick, and the message was unified across a whole range of media. It was quite a package. And we launched it all with a "Million Billionaire March" at the Republican and Democratic national conventions.

We designed the campaign to be participatory: a simple concept that was easy to execute yet allowed for rich elaboration. Through the website, activists could download all the materials they needed to do actions in their own communities. By June, wildcat chapters were springing up. In Denver a Billionaires squad barged into the Green Party convention and tried to buy off Ralph Nader, much to the delight of delegates and the media.

By the time we arrived in Philadelphia for the Republican convention in late July, we were already a minor sensation. Advance articles in *Time* magazine and major dailies, radio coverage, and internet buzz had put us on the map. Our website was getting one hundred thousand hits a day (twenty thousand unique page views). Everybody was asking for our buttons and stickers and posters. Nearly a hundred Billionaires in full dress joined us in the streets, chanting, singing, burning money, smoking cigars. We also staged a "vigil for corporate welfare" and auctioned off merchandising rights to the Liberty Bell (would it become the Taco Bell Liberty Bell or the Ma Bell Liberty Bell . . . ?) The media were all over us. FOX, MSNBC, CBS, CNN, BBC, radio, print, corporate, independent—it was a feeding frenzy. An informal poll of photojournalists voted us "favorite protest." We were certainly one of the more focused and cohesive. . . . My Billionaire character, Phil T. Rich, and Jenny's, Millie O'Naire, became hits on the radio interview circuit and web site traffic shot up to two hundred thousand hits per day.

As the campaign picked up, . . . [United for a Fair Economy] became the organizational hub of an ad hoc network of do-it-yourself movement grouplets. . . . "Cheney is flying into town next week," a young student in Ashland, OR, told me in a typical call. "I've gotten a bunch of folks together and we're going to meet him at the airport. The local thrift store has already donated ten tuxedos." This student had first seen the Billionaires on a late-night mainstream news program. He then went to the "Be a Billionaire" section of our website, downloaded the slogans, posters, and sample press releases. The group chose satirical names for themselves, called to give us a heads-up, and went into action. While other participants first heard about the campaign through activist email networks or via word of mouth, penetration of corporate mass media was key to the Billionaires' success.

It took ingenious "viral design" to get our message through the corporate media's editorial filters and out into the datasphere at large. We built our virus by embedding a threatening idea inside a nonthreatening form. The "protein shell" of our virus: "Billionaires for Bush (or Gore)." Our meme, or hidden ideological code: Big Money owns both candidates/parties; both candidates/parties are roughly the same. Elegantly encapsulating the core ideas of the campaign into a funny five-word concept made for a sleek and potent virus. This concision also served as an "inoculation" against distortion. . . . If they also got our tag line, "Because inequality is not growing fast enough," then the message deepened. . . . When they invited us on the air for lengthy radio interviews, we could eventually drop character and proceed with a straight-up critique. The campaign had layers of code—concentric rings of more and more elaborate messaging. . . .

The Billionaires used irony's double edge—its capacity to simultaneously pose both a straight literal meaning and a subversive implied meaning—to neatly flip between the virus's outer shell and its inner code. In this way we could reach our two disparate audiences—corporate media and grass-roots activists—at the same time. Activists immediately picked up on the various layers of irony. While the mainstream media could be seduced to "play along" with the literal, tongue-in-cheek meaning, letting the public decode the implied and subversive meanings for themselves.

Some of the most powerful media viruses—virtual reality, smart drugs, compassionate conservatism—are actually oxymorons. Activist viruses are no exception. Groups working to rein in excessive government subsidies, handouts, and tax breaks to corporations hit on the phrase "corporate welfare." By meshing two seemingly incompatible notions into a new concept, such a phrase demands thought: "Huh, corporations get welfare?" It creates its own unique conceptual slot in the minds of people who hear it. The phrase demands conscious attention, providing an opportunity for the virus to attach itself and inject its meme code into the public mind. The Billionaires virus made a similar demand: "Huh, billionaires are protesting? Huh, Bush *or* Gore?"

To be successful, a media virus need not be ironic or oxymoronic. It must, however, be mobile, easily replicable, and well suited to the particular vectors of the media ecosystem that it has to travel. The Billionaires virus was virulent partly because it was a carrier on the megavirus of the presidential campaign itself. It was designed to appeal to the media: it was timely, visual, funny, and accessible. It was familiar yet different: a new and provocative way to say what everybody already secretly thought. The virus attached easily to a range of physical and semantic "carriers"—logo, posters, slogans, fake radio ads, street actions, email, buzz, laughter, media story, etc.—and we introduced it into the media stream in a manner calculated to maximize its propagation. Content and humor were tightly meshed. Not only did the humor help carry the content (in the way that laughter makes it easier to bear the truth), but if the media wanted the humor (and they did), they had to take the content too. The materials were catchy and accessible, and the action model was easy to DIY. Thus the meme "spread, replicated, and mutated." . . .

Social movements cannot live by meme alone. Yet memes are clearly powerful—both analytically and operationally. A vital movement requires a hot and happening meme. The Declaration of Independence, the *Communist Manifesto*, sit-down strikes in the 30s, campus building takeovers in the 60s—arguably, these were all memes—no more or less, maybe, than the militant street carnival of the past decade. What is different in each case is the shape and flow of the specific media pathways these memes must travel and the culture with which they must connect. The contemporary movements profiled here and the techniques they have pioneered will hopefully be of service to those of us who believe that truth is a virus and whose aim is to subvert the corporate meme machine with a sly guerrilla war of signs.

West Palm Beach Radical Cheerleaders

"Rebel" (1998)

Bored by the typical protest chanting, a group of sisters in south Florida began what they called "radical cheerleading," incorporating witty call-and-response rhymes and accompanying dances. The effort spread, as radical cheerleading squads formed in different cities and created their own chants to inject some participatory levity into demonstrations.

> Sound off
> I don't wanna work anymore!
> What did you say?
> I said the system doesn't work no more!
> What did you say?
> I said *stomp*, smash the state
> Let's liberate
> Acknowledge me or go to hell
> Another womyn to rebel
> *Stomp*, smash the state
> Let's liberate
> Acknowledge me or go to hell
> Another womyn to rebel!
> I said *stomp*, smash the state
> Let's liberate

Land, Decolonization, and Interdependence

4.C.1.

Akwesasne Notes

From *Voices from Wounded Knee* (1973)

After years of dramatic, largely urban, protests against US settler colonialism, members of the American Indian Movement (AIM) joined with Oglala Sioux people on the Pine Ridge reservation in South Dakota to seize the town of Wounded Knee in protest of corruption and brutality by tribal chairman Richard Wilson, his paramilitary mercenaries, the Bureau of Indian Affairs [BIA], and the police. FBI and US marshals surrounded the town, which had also been the site of a massacre of Lakotas by US troops in 1890. The seventy-one-day standoff marked a new phase in how Indigenous people proclaimed and practiced their sovereignty, as different AIM leaders testified to anonymously in the pages of the Indigenous newspaper *Akwesasne Notes*.

Independent Oglala Nation Declaration

Let it be known this day, March 11, 1973, that the Oglala Sioux people will revive the Treaty of 1868 and that it will be the basis for all negotiations.

Let the declaration be made that we are a sovereign nation by the Treaty of 1868. . . . [We want] to abolish the tribal government under the Indian Reorganization Act [of 1934]. Wounded Knee will be a corporate state under the independent Oglala Nation.

In proclaiming the Independent Oglala Nation, the first nation to be called for support and recognition is the [Iroquois] Six Nation Confederacy. [We] request the confederacy send emissaries to this newly proclaimed nation immediately to receive firsthand all the facts pertaining to this act. . . .

The American Indian Movement

... The real violence in America is committed by the government against our people. The real violence is the fact that on a reservation our women are taken and raped in the back seat of these police cars. The real violence is the fact that our children are never able to learn to live in a society that is completely alien to them, and so they suffer tremendous disorientation in their own lives which many times leads to suicide, or drunkenness—which is another form of suicide—or drugs. The real violence is when the Bureau of Indian Affairs, who is supposedly holding our lands in trust for us—because they say we are incompetent to handle our own affairs—reduces our land base by 160 thousand acres or so every year. And it's violence against our people when they build dams and flood our ancestral lands and disturb the graves of our past generations.

We first started taking direct action on the Sioux reservation around 1969 when some of our people tried to force the BIA to deal with the issue of Indian problems. We were trying to change the educational system. They taught our Indian children that wearing their hair in the traditional manner was bad for them, that Indian people were savages, and that our religion was paganism. We tried to get them to start teaching our children that religion is the very basis of Indian life, and the way we wear our hair or the way we dress in no way interferes with the way we can learn. ...

The American Indian Movement and the Oglala Sioux people here have what every race in America dreams of having. We have a land base, we have a government here, we have the support of the mass of Indian people on the Pine Ridge Reservation. And what is at stake here at Wounded Knee is not just the lives of a few hundred Indian people. It is a way of life that we believe could lead to the complete salvation of the United States and Western civilization. We're trying to make everyone realize that from here, a true revolution in the way people live can start.

Looking Ahead

... Our prophecies predicted when the white people would come here and start destroying our mother earth. But they also talk about how Indian people, after being conquered and subjected to the degradation that we have been subjected to, would eventually come back and show everybody in the whole world the way that they could live on this earth. One of our prophecies says that there's going to be someone coming from the east who will have a face like death. It will be all white and he will be all powerful. He can make things disappear before your very eyes, and he'll come here and do much harm to Indian people—and if Indian people don't hold tight to their religion and tight to their circle of life, he will completely destroy them. It goes on to say that in the seventh generation after the second coming of the white people, our young will begin to rise up against this type of oppression and they will start waging a war that will eventually free the people.

Of course, you can't go back to the old Indian way of life at this point. We have to deal with the mother earth in its present conditions, which is pretty bad. Right now the United States has to be constantly building— they call [it] building, we call [it] destroying—or else it begins to degenerate. We would allow that physical and economic degeneration to begin taking place. It would be a transition where we didn't explore the new modes of destroying our mother earth or increasing our technology, but at the same time we wouldn't take it all away and stop industry. But we wouldn't pave over the whole United States the way they're doing now. We'd stop that. You know, just to stop building roads would slowly bring about the cessation of industrialization. Because as roads over the years degenerated, things would have to slow down, and by slowing things down America could begin to get a grip on itself.

. . . This land has the ability to sustain all the people here, and it's not necessary for us to build great industries to do that—I think the very basic thing that you have to realize is that Indian people, Indian religion, and Indian society are readily adaptable. Our society and our peoples have changed with various things that have come into our lives over ten thousand years. But we never lost sight or focus of one thing—that we don't have to take away from other earth. . . .

The American Indian revolution is right now pointed towards showing the people that they can struggle against the US government, and that they can win. That's why it's important the leadership of the American Indian Movement not be sent to prison—not because any of us are vital to the movement, but because we're symbolic of resistance. As long as we are out, going around and talking to our people, they can see that "this man led the people against the US government in a fight, and he's still here and he's going to fight some more pretty quick and maybe I should join him." They see that they have a chance to win, where before there was despair.

Wounded Knee was an educational process for all Indians. Right there you had Indians from Los Angeles and San Francisco, New York and Chicago, Minneapolis and Oklahoma City—big cities where Indians live and become urbanized. They went into Wounded Knee and met there Indians who had never been off the reservations, who live the traditional way. The two of them met together and found out that they were still one people, still one race, and that they can be together again.

4.C.2.

"We Will Remember" Survival School

From pamphlet (1974)

By 1974, many of the men leaders in the American Indian Movement were facing lengthy prison terms for their involvement in the Wounded Knee occupation or other contentious standoffs with the government. That year, women in AIM opened the "We Will Remember" Survival School in South Dakota to emphasize sustainable, long-term community building. A similar effort was undertaken in Minneapolis as well, along with the Black Panther– run Oakland Community School.

The "We Will Remember" Survival Group

The "We Will Remember" Survival Group is a group of Indian people living to- gether for the purpose of educating each other in all areas of study. Our cur- riculum is based on the truth. We chose not to call our group a school because we are more than just a school. A school is an institution were young people are forced to conform to the ways, ideas, and values of present day civilization. Those who don't conform are then labeled slow learners or dropouts. When, in reality, these young people are forced out. These are the young people we are trying to reach. We feel it's necessary to work with these students on a full-time basis in order for them to better deal with the constant inadequacies placed upon them by the American system. Our young people have to deal also with the daily barrage of half-truths and lies sent out by TV, newspapers, and all es- tablished media. The institutions and media of this country have uneducated the American people to the point where they can't show concern for anything that doesn't affect their daily comfort and existence.

Now we are at a point in time where the natural resources that exist aren't going to be here forever. The people of America haven't learned to survive on this continent. If there is going to be a future for the children, the American people must stop and learn from the natural people of this world. They must take the necessary steps to assure the survival of the Earth. If there is no water, there is no life.

We don't expect any government funds of any kind. If we are to learn the truth about the history of the Lakota since the start of colonization and its re- sults called genocide [and] the facts about treaty rights violations, as well as [re- tain] the right to teach and practice the traditional ways of life of Native peo- ples, we must maintain our independence. To learn the true meaning of Native American sovereignty, we must have full control of what our young people are taught. The brainwashing and pacification programs of the United States of America must be stopped. The leaders of tomorrow must be told the truth about the rip-offs of lives and lands of Indigenous peoples of the entire world.

Our students are not confined to classroom work. We are a group involved in educating ourselves. One of the many ways we've found to best educate our- selves is to actually experience the things we are studying.

This involves a lot of travel, which is something we enjoy already. Instead of just making a round trip to some way-off place, we go to actual events as they happen; for instance: judicial proceedings involving Native Americans—our rights, natural resources, legislative issues, treaty issues, etc.

We also enjoy the company of many of our brothers and sisters of Indian na- tions throughout this country. We have gone on many field trips to demonstrate our plight, attended Native conferences, and have involved ourselves in the present issues facing Native Americans.

We have also found that our students are more apt to learn when they are confronted with the actual situation, rather than through forced learning in a confined area. They are also able to see both sides of the story, instead of the one-sided effect most books present today. This has caused an immense improvement in attitude, behavior, ambition, and potential.

Spiritual Involvement

The most important part of our daily lives is our relationship to the religion of our grandfathers. We have recognized the power of the Sacred Pipe, for without it we would not have survived as a People. At every opportunity, we encourage our young people to participate in spiritual ceremonies. Not only have we traveled many miles to attend certain spiritual gatherings, but our Sacred Pipe is ever present in our home and the Sacred Sweat Lodge in our backyard is utilized often to cleanse our mind and body. We realize that if young people can maintain their spiritual development, then, and only then, can they develop their own personal learning processes. . . .

Communications

Our major procedure for communications is to establish a direct line to the people who want information concerning various issues dealing with treaty rights, natural resources, prisoners' rights, prisoners of war, water rights, etc. Thus it enables us to speak freely to the Native people who want to know all about the facts involved in the various struggles across the land.

Communication and organization are priority problems that have slowed down the people and the struggle. It is mandatory that we set up information stations throughout our communities to provide information about the problems of the people, the world around us, and what we're doing to correct them. We must make other Indian people aware!

With the use of communications, the people will know what's happening and begin to organize more effectively.

With organization, we can deal with our oppressors more effectively and firmly.

It is up to the youth to carry on the struggle and educate the people. . . .

Hopes for the Future

We have a set a goal for ourselves. In the near future, we intend to be totally self-sufficient. We have developed a cattle project that, hopefully, will be implemented this year. We have chosen this endeavor because the land that we have available to us is best suited for this type of project.

Not only will this provide a learning experience, but it will also serve as an example to other Indian people. If we hope to achieve freedom as a people, then we must break the colonial yoke that has made us dependent.

4.C.3.

Native American Rights Fund/National Indian Law Library

From "The Declaration of Indian Independence" (1975)

Indigenous struggles concerned not just "land" in the abstract but battles over natural resources and whether they would be privatized or stewarded for the collective good. Riffing on the US founding narrative, the Native American Rights Fund penned this declaration of Indigenous environmental ethics.

On December 18, 1973, more than one hundred Northern Great Plains Indian people met on the Fort Berthold Reservation in North Dakota. They had assembled that day to discuss their *Winters* [case] doctrine water rights to the rivers flowing through and the groundwater underneath their reservations. The atmosphere was full of tension and concern due to the fact that federal agencies, the states, and private interests were rapidly making plans to use more water than there was on the northern Great Plains.

Because of their endemic poverty these tribes had not been able to develop their reservations and make use of the water which was rightfully theirs. Now there was a recognition that they had marketable mineral resources which could, if they so chose, bring them the income they needed to develop their reservations and for which they would also then need their own water. From the beginning of the meeting, it was clear that a mutual line of defense was about to be formed of these tribes, some of whom had only one hundred years before been at war with each other. This time, however, they were going to make one last stand on the northern Great Plains together. . . .

The Second Continental Congress

On March 27, 1974, almost a year after the Northern Cheyenne had started the revolution, the northern Great Plains Indian delegates met again in Billings, Montana, to adopt a constitution and bylaws for what that day was named the Native American Natural Resources Development Federation (NANRDF). Most importantly, like the original Second Continental Congress, the Indian delegates also voted on and unanimously passed [the] Declaration of Indian Rights to the Natural Resources in the Northern Great Plains:

> The Indian tribes and people of the northern Great Plains, being confronted with an all-pervasive crisis threatening the present and future

uses of their natural resources, including but not limited to their land, right to use of water, and their coal, do hereby declare as follows:

The northern Great Plains area of the United States is presently attracting international attention due to the energy crisis which makes the vast coal resources of this area very appealing for immediate development. The development of this coal and the concomitant use of water, air, and other natural resources threatens the viability of our environment and the continued existence of the twenty-six tribes which occupy the northern Great Plains within the states of Montana, Wyoming, North Dakota, South Dakota, and Nebraska. . . .

The tribes have been asked to participate in numerous work group statements on this matter, but it is readily apparent that the major impact upon the survival of these Indian tribes will be foisted upon the erosion of their water rights and the depletion of water resources due to the need for massive quantities of water to develop the coal. The Indian water rights here involved, then, are like the Indian fishing rights considered by the United States Supreme Court. . . . [T]hey are "not much less necessary to the existence of the Indians than the atmosphere they breathe."

The Indian tribes of the five states do hereby give notice to the world that they will maintain their ownership to the priceless natural resources which are geographically and legally related to their reservations. . . .

In view of the tribes' prior and paramount rights to all the waters to which they are geographically related, it is self-evident that any major diversion of said waters for any purpose would constitute an encroachment upon Indian water rights. All federal agents or agencies . . . are, therefore, put on notice that any diversion or use of such tribal waters shall be at their own risk. . . .

Project Independence vs.
the Declaration of Indian Independence

. . . [T]he Declaration of Indian Rights to the Natural Resources in the Northern Great Plains was the first formal notice given to the US government, the states, and individual corporate interests that the Indian tribes of the Great Plains intended to fight to protect, preserve, and conserve the resources which their forefathers gave their lives to retain.

The declaration put all parties on notice that any further abuse of Indian rights would not be tolerated and set out for federal officials, the states, and the rest of the country a summary of the legal basis for the prior and paramount water rights of twenty-six tribes. It also stated Indian principles for planning and development of this water, the minerals, and the other natural resources on their land.

The conflict was readily apparent. A large portion of the natural resources essential to the US government's ability to meet the goals of [Richard Nixon's proposed] project independence were located on Indian reservations. In fact, the billions of tons of low sulfur Indian coal were considered to be the key to the whole effort. That coal had the potential of making the northern Great Plains into the boiler room of the nation—or as some called it, "a national sacrifice area."

4.C.4.

Michael Figures

From "Opening Address—Minority Landowners Conference" (1976)

In the wake of both the civil rights movement and the Great Migration, Black people in the South confronted a new landscape in the 1970s. Central to their concerns was land itself. Automation and privatization had weakened Black family farms and, with it, Black economic and political power. As highlighted in this 1976 talk delivered in Tuskegee, Alabama, the preservation of Black land ownership was critical to provide much-needed economic sustenance, political power, and personal resources.

. . . Black land ownership continues to decline at an alarming rate, from its peak of about 15 million acres in 1910 to less than 5.7 million acres now and going steadily—and tragically, most of the decline has occurred since 1950 when Black folks owned 12 million acres. Of the remaining 3 million or so Black-owned acres the vast majority is located in the eleven southern states and most of that is located in states represented at this conference.

If we know now the importance of land ownership—if we know the reasons (some of which I will allude to throughout this presentation) why Black land is lost—if the Emergency Land Fund [ELF] continues to spread the word—then why does the loss continue almost unabated? The reasons are several and not the least of which is the fact that there is presently no organization at all existing on more than a very local level, if even there, that is composed of Black landowners. There is *no Black landowners association* to address any of the problems faced by Black landowners in terms of retention, acquisition, utilization, etc.

To be sure, the Emergency Land Fund and others have sought to address problems connected to Black land ownership—but we *do not own any land!* We cannot exert the kind of pressure on the powers that be to force them to service the needs of present Black landowners and potential Black landowners. But we, the Alabama Center for Higher Education [ACHE] and Tuskegee's Human Resources Development Center, can try to bring you together and assist you in understanding the needs and in organizing yourselves so that you, as Black landowners, can have a positive voice in determining the destiny of our people.

It is you who must utilize the land, make it productive, put the idle acres into use, who must teach our children the value of land—you must take the lead, you are the landowners. I do not mean to suggest that the job is all yours—that ELF's and ACHE's jobs end here. By no means—we must all continue to work together—we must continue our educational effort, and your association must help us and in turn help the Black land situation. . . .

Just think what it would be like if Black landowners throughout the South would come together into an association. Its implications blow the mind—the impact of such an organization could be devastating. The collective voice it would provide through strong leadership could not under any circumstances be ignored by the political establishment. It could begin to change the face of the economy in the South and *right that* it should, for it was on the backs of your forefathers and mine that this region was built into all it's ever been. A *King Cotton economy*—and you have the power within your grasp.

And why not form an association? Is there any logical reason not to? Does not your presence here indicate that you recognize the need? Can any Black landowner fail to heed the call or his own destiny? Are not your problems similar? And don't you get similar responses to your problems from local institutional creditors (lenders), [the] government (FHA [Federal Housing Administration]), and private banks? Don't you need an information bank, technical assistance? . . .

It is historically appropriate that Black landowners should organize now, in 1976, against any further rip-offs of Black-owned land, to advance and bring attention to the needs of Black landowners. . . . For it was about one hundred years ago, during this . . . country's "centennial celebration" to be exact, that the federal government, pursuant to the Rutherford B. Hayes sellout of Black folks to the South in exchange for the presidency, began to finally dismantle those reconstruction programs which had been established to assist Black folk in land acquisition and utilization, such as the Freedmen's Bureau. Hayes made sure that the promised forty acres and mule would never be delivered to Black folks. Yes, it is very significant that we, one hundred years later, direct, in Tuskegee, Alabama, the nation's attention to these same problems existing in 1976, the bicentennial year, that existed in 1876, the centennial year.

But it is imperative that we organize, for unless we do, this nation will do the same thing in 1976 that it did in 1876. It has already started. . . . We are at the height of political power again, but we must not lose it this time. A Black landowner's association could help prevent such a loss. . . .

But let us also learn from the teachings of history—let us ring this nation's Liberty Bell to the tune of no more retreats on the rights of Black folks—to the tune that we will own land in this country, that we will develop that land and put our idle acres into production—that we will not be deterred. That we will become a bigger force than ever before. *Organize!* We have Black state legislators—let's make sure that they understand their own problems and direct their energies toward eliminating them. . . .

We must keep what we got, and in the words of James Brown, soul brother no. 1, "We must use what we got to get what we want." . . . The time is right—it is now—we must speak to the problem now or forever hold our peace. It is our destiny. It may well determine the manner of this country's celebration of the tricentennial—it may well determine if there is one! God bless you and keep you and remember that land is the essence of us all.

4.C.5.

Governing Board of the National Council of the Churches of Christ

From *Rural Crisis: A Call for Justice and Action* (1983)

The upward distribution of wealth decimated rural America—including many white farmers and others in Midwestern and Plains states. In 1983, an ecumenical gathering in Des Moines tried to provide a progressive faith-based solution for farmers at risk of losing their land to political economic crises and who were being recruited by right-wing movements in response.

We warn that America is teetering on the slopes of a dark precipice: we are dangerously close to abandoning the egalitarian and communitarian goals of our religious and social heritage. We are well on the way to becoming a landless and fragmented people subject to the whims of those few holding disproportionate wealth and power.

Like our ancestors of the Farmers Alliance of one hundred years ago, our cry seems to be lost in the void. Then, as now, family farmers were being driven off the land due to a mixture of high interest rates, low prices for farm produce, and a stagnant economy. Now, as then, the people of the land are told that this is the result of the inevitable march of history, that this disenfranchisement of the people from the land marks a steady onrush of the tide of progress. One hundred years ago the people of the land looked in vain to their elected representatives for assistance. Now, as then, our Congress has favored the proponents of the "trickle-down" theory of economics, allowing the wealthy to pile riches upon riches while the people of the land diminish in number.

Our present period of crisis is unparalleled since the days of the Great Depression. An economic crisis in agriculture—one result of decades of public policy aimed at displacing people from the land—hastens the demise of our family-owned and operated farms. Ownership and control of our rich land base is being consolidated at an alarming rate, and the loss of farms and people from the countryside is causing serious economic problems in our rural communities. Our cities are experiencing high unemployment rates among workers associated with agriculture-related industries. The economy of our states and of the nation itself is deteriorating because the foundation of that economy—agriculture—is suffering extraordinary losses.

This course of tragedy, which can be charted by statistics, masks an ever deeper and widespread suffering in the countryside. Economic stress results in personal and family stress; many farm families facing financial difficulties are being personally blamed for their plight, even though it is due to circumstances well beyond their control. There are signs of increasing family tensions and even family violence, and the outright discussion of larger acts of violence against people and institutions indifferent to the rural crisis is heard more and more often. . . .

It is into this ethical vacuum that members of the faith community, and their organizational leadership, must plunge. It is true that over the past fifteen years individuals, churches, and representative bodies of the Christian faith have spoken often and eloquently in support of family farm agriculture and of the principle of widespread ownership of land. Yet, the larger society's pursuit of unbridled individualism and of the accumulation of wealth without limit has continued without interruption. . . .

The people of the land demand that we be loyal to our faith and, in so doing, come to their assistance.

The Call to Justice

God still calls us to give our all to the creation of a just world and, even now, summons us to action and justice with and on behalf of the suffering people of the land, regardless of color, race, or creed.

We pledged ourselves to heed that call!

We call upon our brothers and sisters of good will:

to realize a conversion of heart, to recognize that the values of individual enrichment and material accumulation are false gods, designed not only to lead one from God's Covenant but to destroy community and harmony in our land.

to remember the teachings of Francis of Assisi, who counseled the need to live in harmony with nature and to utilize tenderness in our dealings with others and not to follow the path of competition or hostility; who spoke of the need to live minimally and not to pursue the accumulation of surplus goods; and who said that we must live as an integral part of nature, not as one sundered from our roots: from the land and each other.

to stand side by side with their neighbors who suffer personal loss as a result of the economic crisis on the land, and to bring to a halt once and for all the demise of family farm agriculture by supporting actions and public policies that will bring about peaceful change in rural America.

We call upon our church leaders to make the continuing tragedy of rural America—the erosion of our fields and small communities, the demise of family farming and the forced liquidation of family farm operations, the growing concentration of land ownership—an urgent part of each church's national agenda for action.

We call upon our church leaders and members alike to press for enlightened public policy that will end existing favoritism towards speculators in land owner-ship and to create, in turn, public policy that has as its aim the preservation of diverse ownership of land and the continuation of the family farm system with its attendant values of stewardship, family, and community responsibility.

This we do as a people of God, struggling to be honest to the call to disciple-ship in rural America and all the world and believing that future generations will judge us harshly if we fail in this time of grave urgency.

4.C.6.

Akinyele Umoja

"Why We Say 'Free the Land'" (1984)

An outgrowth of the Republic of New Afrika, the New Afrikan People's Orga-nization (NAPO) was a revolutionary Black nationalist organization inspired by Malcolm X and headquartered in Mississippi. This essay by the organiza-tion's national secretary was published in its newspaper, *By Any Means Nec-essary*. In it, Umoja identifies land as a source of political power and collec-tive survival for both Black and Indigenous people.

"Free the Land" is the battle cry of the New Afrikan Independence Movement. The NAIM is part of the Black Liberation Movement in North America that wants an independent Black nation on land in North America. The land identi-fied by the New Afrikan Independence Movement is primarily known as South Carolina, Georgia, Alabama, Mississippi, Louisiana and other areas of what is now called the Black-belt South (the southeastern part of the North American continent where Afrikan people are in the majority or have a historical/eco-nomical/sociocultural relationship to). When We say "free the land," this is the land We are talking about freeing.

Malcolm X once stated:

> Revolutions are fought to get control of land, to remove the absentee landlord and gain control of the land and institutions that flow from that land. The Black man has been in a very low condition because he has no control whatsoever over any land.

He later stated:

> A true Negro revolt might entail, for instance, fighting for separate Black states within this country.

All nations and people wanting liberation from alien domination and seek-ing self-determination are fighting for land. When Angola, Mozambique, [and] Guinea-Bissau were fighting Portuguese colonialization they were fighting for land. When Zimbabwe was fighting for independence it was fighting for control of its land. Azania (south afrika), Palestine, Northern Ireland today all struggle for land and independence. New Afrikans—Black people—in North America need land and independence.

Land is essential for a people's development. In order to grow food and obtain natural resources (oil, gold, uranium, timber, etc.) land is necessary. A landless people is a dependent people. A nation with land can utilize its labor and technology to develop in its own best interest.

Land is also important for national identity—a nation's sense of peoplehood. People develop a material and spiritual relationship to land. Land they tilled; land they built upon; developed families and communities on. The land becomes tied to a people's national consciousness as a consequence of their social and national development.

A nation for people means control over specific national territory with specific geopolitical boundaries. Boundaries determine where the nation's political jurisdiction begins and ends.

NAPO sees that We must "free the land" of New Afrika because land and independence can best guarantee self-determination and liberation for our people. Without independent nationhood the amerikkkan empire will always control the affairs of New Afrikans. They will control our economy; our education, security, and all aspects of development. Only when We control the land and the institution on the land can we be the masters of our own destiny.

New Afrika—South Carolina, Georgia, Alabama, Mississippi, Louisiana and other areas of the "Black-belt South"—must be free. Afrika is the homeland of all Afrikan people, but We have no realistic plan to transport thirty million captive New Afrikans back to Afrika. While in North America, New Afrikans have developed historical, economic, social-cultural and spiritual ties to the New Afrikan national territory in North America. This is the land We became a unique New Afrikan nation on. This is the land We tilled without pay as bondspersons (slaves) and as sharecroppers. This is the land our people demanded after the Civil War and even attempted to establish New Afrikan governments on, only to be subjugated by the united states army and the ku klux klan. This is the land We have fought to stay on even though millions of us were forced to flee to become refugees in northern and western ghetto reservations through white terrorism and economic pressure. This is the land We must have to be free.

We recognize the claims of Native American Indians to this land and will struggle side by side to help them to regain their land. At the same time since our captivity in the Western Hemisphere progressive Native Americans have recognized We had no choice in coming to North America and the majority of us have no realistic way to get back to Afrika.

We say "free the Land" because We wish that our children live in dignity and prosperity. We wish to build a new society with new values and relationships. We say "free the land" because We want independence so We can insure our human rights are protected and that our land will be a zone and base for all who seek liberation and freedom.

Free the land!

International Tribunals for Self-Determination, 1990–1993

Luis Alejandro Molina

Thanks to the vision and organizing focus of Puerto Rican sociologist, lawyer, and activist Luis Nieves Falcón, a coalition of Black, Native American, Mexican, and Puerto Rican organizations developed three international tribunals in the early 1990s. These tribunals aimed to strengthen solidarity among antiracist and anticolonial organizations in the US, and to place them within the framework of international human rights.

The initial effort was the Special International Tribunal on the Human Rights Violations of Political Prisoners and Prisoners of War in the United States, held at Hunter College in December 1990. More than eighty-eight organizations across the US dissident spectrum, from pacifist Catholics to groups that explicitly defined themselves as national liberation movements, worked together for over a year to produce an internationally recognized public forum. Organizers modeled the event on two tribunals earlier organized by British philosopher and activist Bertrand Russell, the first of which brought to light US war crimes against the people of Vietnam. The 1990 tribunal highlighted the human rights abuses visited on more than one hundred "political prisoners and prisoners of war" in the United States. These people, all members of movements that had been targeted and repressed by the FBI's counterintelligence program, faced unduly harsh sentences even as the US government denied the political nature of their incarceration and many progressive activists gave them little support. The following two tribunals, in 1992 and 1993, addressed issues of settler colonialism and Hawaiian sovereignty.

Each of the tribunals worked with renowned human rights attorneys and presented a bill of charges against the US government. Yet the success of the tribunal strategy was not juridical. Rather, success was found through the collective decision to make the tribunal organizing process a struggle against the isolation and criminalization of movements, and by extension, of political prisoners. To this end, international jurists from over twenty-seven countries listened to dozens of expert witnesses—activists, academics, family members, clergy, movement leaders—testify about their experiences of state repression.

The tribunals were anchored by volunteers from different movements with a history of organizing and defense of political prisoners. Prisoner defense campaigns, attorneys, and prisoners stood at the center of these tribunals: the first tribunal focused on political repression while the subsequent ones used the existence of political prisoners as one example of US internal colonialism. Crucial leadership was also extended by national liberation movement organizations such as the American Indian Movement, New Afrikan Peoples Organization, Movimiento de Liberación Nacional Mexicano, and Movimiento de Liberación Nacional Puertorriqueño and by solidarity organizations such as the National Committee to Free Puerto Rican Political Prisoners and Prisoners of War, the Prairie Fire Organizing Committee, the May 19 Communist Organization, and the John Brown Anti-Klan Organizing Committee. The support of antiwar and Christian left organizations, ranging from the National Council of Churches to the War Resisters League, expanded the tribunals' base of support.

Each of the three tribunals built on the success of the previous one. Activist and historian Richard Kekuni Blaisdell testified at the San Francisco Tribunal in 1992, and the organization he led, the Pro-Kanaka Maoli Sovereignty Working Group, then helped convene the Ka Ho'okolokolonui Kānaka Maoli Tribunal in 1993 to elevate the issue of Hawaiian sovereignty. The 1992 tribunal used the occasion of the Columbian quincentennial, and the 1993 effort marked the one hundredth anniversary of the overthrow of Hawai'i's Queen Liliuokalani. The nine-day Hawai'i tribunal visited each of the islands taken between the United States' so-called annexation of Hawai'i on August 12, 1898, and the proclamation of Hawaiian statehood on August 21, 1959, to center an indigenous claim for sovereignty against the United States on an international stage.

The 1990–93 tribunals contributed to a heightened consciousness about US political prisoners, both within the communities they came from and broader US civil society. They helped to build the capacity and reach of their organizational members and to build toward gains such as the 1998 National Jericho March to Free All Political Prisoners, which gave birth to the ongoing Jericho Amnesty Movement. The tribunals were particularly meaningful for the Puerto Rican independence movement, which built on their work to achieve several gains, including the release of eleven Puerto Rican political prisoners in 1999, the ouster of the US Navy from Vieques in 2003 (following another tribunal in 2001), freedom for Puerto Rican political prisoner Carlos Alberto Torres in 2010, and the 2017 commutation of the sentence of Oscar López Rivera, long considered the "Mandela of the Americas."

4.C.7.

Hawai'i Ecumenical Coalition on Tourism

From "The 1989 Hawai'i Declaration of the Hawai'i Ecumenical Coalition on Tourism" (1989)

The reinvigoration of the Hawaiian sovereignty movement in the 1980s took on several aspects of colonial land use—including, as identified in this declaration delivered at a 1989 conference at St. Stephen's Diocesan Center on O'ahu tourism. Nearly half of participants were Native Hawaiians and represented a diverse range of denominations.

The plight of Native Hawaiian people is but one example of the destructive impact that tourism is having on indigenous people in communities around the world. All is not well in "paradise." Indeed, a state of emergency exists in regard to the survival, the well-being, and the status of the native Hawaiian people on the one hand and the near extinction of the precious and fragile natural environment on the other.

Call to the Churches

The churches have a moral obligation and responsibility to raise awareness in their congregations and in the state of Hawai'i about tourism's negative impacts and consequences on Native Hawaiians. The churches are called upon to "wrestle against the principalities and powers" that exploit people.

Furthermore, the churches must examine their history of involvement in Hawai'i's past and recognize their role in the loss of Native Hawaiian control over their land and destiny and in the overthrow of the Hawaiian monarchy. Such a recognition should lead to concrete actions on the part of the churches to rectify the wrongs which have been done.

Given these harsh and continuing realities, we, the participants of the conference, call upon the churches and religions institutions of Hawai'i, in consultation with Native Hawaiians, to initiate a process of reconciliation and reparations as follows:

- Acknowledge the anger expressed by Native Hawaiian people for the past actions of the missionaries, their descendants, and the churches and institutions they established;
- Recognize that this anger is an expression of the suffering of the Native Hawaiian people; and
- Publicly apologize to the Native Hawaiians within their own congregations and the larger Native Hawaiian community for the churches' involvements and participation in the destruction and erosion of Hawaiian culture, religious practices, land base, and the overthrow of Queen Lili'uokalani and the Hawaiian monarchy.

Priority Rectifying Actions

We call upon the churches and religious institutions of Hawai'i to redress these injustices by advocating the following:

- A. The return of public and private trust lands to the control of the Native Hawaiian people;
- B. An immediate ban on all resort and related developments in those areas designated as sanctuaries by Native Hawaiians and in rural Hawaiian communities. . . .
- C. Technical, financial, and other support from the state of Hawai'i to Native Hawaiian projects which encourage economic self-sufficiency.

Furthermore, we call upon the churches and religious institutions of Hawai'i to support the political claims of Native Hawaiians to establish a sovereign entity, separate from the existing state and federal governments, in order that they may achieve self-determination.

Public Witness

We call upon the churches and religious institutions of Hawai'i to take a stand for social justice and engage in political action, as follows:

A. Make public an inventory of the holdings and use of all church lands;
B. Return those church lands that justly belong to the Native Hawaiian people;
C. Reexamine the church lands and divest church funds currently being used for tourism purposes that negatively impact Native Hawaiians;
D. Refuse to participate in the public blessing of those projects that adversely impact Native Hawaiians or the environment;
E. Support worker demands for higher wages, a full-time work week with benefits, and better working conditions in the tourist industry;
F. Hold the tourist industry and government accountable for the social problems associated with tourism: increased crime, racism, sexual and domestic violence and disruption, substance abuse, housing costs, and land taxes; and
G. Support policies to reverse current trends of tourist industry growth. The human and natural resources cannot withstand the near doubling of total annual tourists to Hawai'i from its current 6.5 to 11 million over the next two decades, projected by the Hawai'i Visitors Bureau.

Education

We call upon the churches and religious institutions of Hawai'i to utilize and distribute educational materials and programs for both clergy and congregations in order to reevaluate misconceptions and dependency on tourism. These materials should:

A. Focus on Native Hawaiian culture;
B. Detail the negative effects of tourism on Native Hawaiian land and water rights, economy, and social lifestyle;
C. Promote Native Hawaiian self-sufficiency, sanctuaries, and sovereignty; and
D. Present a truthful view of Hawaiian history, including the involvement of the church and the US government in the loss of Native Hawaiian land and power and the overthrow of the Hawaiian monarchy.

We call upon the churches and religious institutions of Hawai'i to acknowledge and respect Native Hawaiian rights to:

A. Practice and participate in traditional ceremonies and rituals with the same protection offered all religions;
B. Determine access to and protection of sacred sites and burial grounds and public lands for ceremonial purposes; and
C. Utilize and access religious symbols for traditional ceremonies and rituals.

4.C.8.

Winona LaDuke

From "We Are Still Here: The Five Hundred Years Celebration" (1991)

An environmental and feminist activist, Winona LaDuke (Ojibwe White Earth) highlighted Indigenous efforts to mark the quincentennial anniversary of Columbus's arrival in the Americas with renewed attention to the ongoing struggles of Native people across the hemisphere.

To "discover" implies that something is lost. Something was lost, and it was Columbus. Unfortunately, he did not discover himself in the process of his lostness. He went on to destroy peoples, land, and ecosystems in his search for material wealth and riches. . . .

Columbus was a perpetrator of genocide, responsible for setting in motion the most horrendous holocaust to have occurred in the history of the world. Columbus was a slave trader, a thief, a pirate, and most certainly not a hero. To celebrate Columbus is to congratulate the process and history of the invasion. . . .

Although Columbus himself later returned to Europe in disgrace, his methods were subsequently used in Mexico, Peru, the Black Hills of South Dakota, and at Wounded Knee and Sand Creek. They are still being used in Guatemala and El Salvador, and in Indian territory from Amazonia to Pine Ridge in South Dakota. The invasion set into motion a process, thus far unabated. This has been a struggle over values, religions, resources, and, most important, land.

The "Age of Discovery" marked the age of colonialism, a time when our land suddenly came to be viewed as "your land." While military repression is not in North American vogue (at least with the exception of the Oka-Mohawk uprising of the summer of 1990), today legal doctrines uphold that our land is your land, based ostensibly on the so-called doctrine of discovery. This justifies in the white legal system the same dispossession of people from their land that is caused by outright military conquest. But in a "kinder, gentler world," it all appears more legal. . . .

The devastation of the ecosystems and the people is relentless. In short, the problem or challenge posed by 1992 is the invasion, and the reality is that it continues.

We understand that "to get to the rain forest, you must first kill the people," and that is why since 1900 one-third of all indigenous nations in the Amazon have been decimated, while during the same time one-quarter of the forest has disappeared. There is a direct relationship between how industrial society consumes land and resources and how it consumes peoples. . . .

Most disgraceful of all is the self-congratulatory hoopla under way in most colonial and neocolonial states. In 1992, the governments of Spain, Italy, the United States, and thirty-one other countries are hosting the largest public celebration of this century to mark the five hundredth anniversary of the arrival of "Western civilization" in the hemisphere. . . .

It is in the face of this celebration of genocide that thousands of indigenous peoples are organizing to commemorate their resistance and to bring to a close the five-hundred-year-long chapter of the invasion. indigenous organizations such as CONAIE (Confederation of indigenous Nationalities of Ecuador), SAIIC (South and Central American Indian Information Center), the indigenous Women's Network, Seventh Generation Fund, the International Indian Treaty Council, UNI [Union of Indigenous Nations, in Portuguese] (from the Brazilian Amazon), and other groups have worked to bring forth the indigenous perspective on the past five hundred years.

For several years, indigenous people appealed to the United Nations to designate 1992 as the "year of indigenous peoples." They faced stiff political opposition from Spain, the United States, and other "pro-Columbus" nations. 1993, instead, has been designated as such. However, a number of indigenous nations are actively working on the United Nations Environment Program Conference in 1992 in Brazil and demanding, among other things, full participation of indigenous peoples in the "nation-state" agenda.

CONAIE and other groups hosted an intercontinental meeting of indigenous peoples in Quito, Ecuador, in July 1990. The meeting brought together hundreds of people from throughout the Americas to share common histories and strategies to mark 1992 and to plan for the next five hundred years. It was hailed by the Native people in attendance as a fulfillment to a traditional prophecy of the Runa people of Mexico.

The prophecy reports that many years ago the indigenous people of the Americas were divided into two groups, the people of the Eagle (those from the North) and the people of the Condor (those from the South). According to the prophecy, when the tears of the Eagle and the Condor are joined, a new era of life and spirit will begin for Native people. As the delegates joined together in work, prayer, and ceremony, they felt a joining of the vision and the people. According to CONAIE, "The basic objective of the mobilization is to recover the dignity of our peoples and reject all forms of submission, colonial practices, and neocolonialism."

A number of other meetings have been held, including a huge First Peoples gathering in June in Winnipeg, Manitoba, which was attended by more than five hundred representatives from the Americas. Other work continues among indigenous nations, internal in the communities, and in coalition with other groups. A series of tribunals on colonialism have been proposed in several locations in North America, as well as educational and cultural events. A number of Native writers, including Gerald Vizenor, M. Scott Momaday, Louise Erdrich, and Joy Harjo, are completing books and anthologies on the five hundred years. And a great number of indigenous peoples are calling on other groups—nationally and internationally—to mobilize around 1992 as a year to protect the Earth and the people of the Earth.

Indeed, the ecological agenda is what many indigenous people believe can, and must, unite all peoples in 1992. That agenda calls for everyone to take aggressive action to stop the destruction of the Earth, essentially to end the biological, technological, and ecological invasion/conquest that began with Columbus' ill-fated voyage five hundred years ago.

Through it all, indigenous people will continue to struggle. It is this legacy of resistance that, perhaps more than any other single activity, denotes the essence of 1992. After all the hoopla and celebration by the colonial governments are over, the Native voice will prevail. It is like a constant rumble of distant thunder, and it says through the wind, "We are alive. We are still here."

Figure 4.4. Glenn Morris, "Abolish Columbus Day" (1992). Image courtesy of and reprinted with permission by Glenn Morris.

4.C.9.

League of Indigenous Sovereign Nations of the Western Hemisphere

"Draft Declaration of Principles" (1991)

Against the backdrop of the quincentennial, Indigenous communities forged new coalitions in the 1990s. Founded in 1991, the League of Indigenous Sovereign Nations attempted to forge a confederation that could bring together veterans of the 1970s-era Indigenous sovereignty movements with younger generation Indians.

Between May 24 and 27, 1991, Indigenous people came from across North America to discuss the formation of the League of Indigenous Sovereign Nations of the Western Hemisphere. As a result, the following declaration of principles was drafted.

Considering that Indigenous sovereignty, self-determination, land rights, and human rights present nonnegotiable conflicts which stand in the way of meaningful growth in life and will not be resolved until the demands, needs, and natural rights of Indigenous peoples are recognized, addressed, and implemented,

Affirming the Universal Declaration of Human Rights, and related covenants, as well as the Declaration of Principles for the Defense of the Indigenous Nations and Peoples of the Western Hemisphere, and the Declaration of Quito, Recognizing that no proper channels now exist to address the issues of concern to Indigenous peoples, and that most of the world has absolutely no knowledge of the forces of genocide we still confront each day,

Acknowledging that the Indigenous peoples of the Western Hemisphere have reached a united consciousness in recognition of the need for a concerted course of action to achieve our rights,

Be it affirmed that,

1. The League of Indigenous Sovereign Nations of the Western Hemisphere shall be a representational body of Indigenous peoples, groups, and individuals in the Western Hemisphere to be recognized by the following definitions:
    a) Nations shall have a permanent population, a defined territory, a traditional government, and the ability to enter into relations with other states.
    b) Groups will be identifiable by having bonds of language, heritage, tradition, or other common identity.
    c) Individuals will demonstrate verifiable ties to such nations or groups or will present evidence of Indigenous identity acceptable to the league.

2. No Indigenous nation or group shall be deemed to have fewer rights or lesser status for the sole reason that the nation or group has not entered into recorded treaties or agreements with any states.
3. The league will strive to work in cooperation with other Indigenous organizations in order to strengthen the struggle for our rights.
4. The league will work toward the following goals:
    a) Begin the process of uniting all Indigenous peoples of the Western Hemisphere together into one great league.
    b) Establish world recognition of the league as an instrument that will effect the political empowerment of our nations as one people.
    c) Represent our people to the international community.
5. The league will implement the following modified goals put forth by the Declaration of Quito:
    a) Ratify our resolute political project of self-determination and our autonomy in the framework of nation-states, under a new popular order with respect for whatever forms of organization each nation determines appropriate for their situation.
    b) Affirm our decision to defend our culture, education, and spirituality as fundamental to our identity as peoples, reclaiming and maintaining our own forms of spiritual life, communal coexistence, and governance, in an intimate relationship with our Mother Earth.
    c) Defend and conserve our land and natural resources, which now are being attacked. Environmental damage inflicted upon any land of the Western Hemisphere may affect the livelihood and personal integrity of Indigenous peoples. We are convinced that effective defense will be realized when it is Indigenous peoples who administer and control the territories where we live according to our own principles of organization and communal life.
    d) Oppose national judicial structures which are the result of the process of colonization and neocolonization. We seek a new social order that embraces our traditional exercise of common law and expression of our culture and forms of organization.
    e) Assert ourselves as separate and distinct peoples under international law and that this recognition be incorporated into the respective nation-states.
    f) Work for the elimination of the victimization of Indigenous peoples through physical, spiritual, emotional, and intellectual violence and persecution, which constitutes a flagrant violation of human rights. We assert respect for our right to life, to land, to free organization, and expression of our culture. We will work for the release of our people who are held as political prisoners, a return of our children and the bones of our ancestors, an end to repression, and restitution for the harms done to us.
6. Participants in the league will conduct themselves in an ethical manner described in a consensually agreed upon code.

4.C.10.

Bernice Lalo

"Sovereignty: A Western Shoshone Perspective" (1994)

Stretching across the Shoshone ancestral lands in what now includes parts of California, Idaho, Nevada, and Utah, the Western Shoshone Defense Project [WSDP] was formed in 1992 to uphold the treaty rights established in the 1863 Treaty of Ruby Valley. Throughout the 1990s, the WSDP resisted the imposition of mining, nuclear power, and other threats to their sovereignty.

On April 29, 1994, President Clinton reaffirmed the federal Indian policy according the tribal governments in matters affecting "tribal lands" and reiterating two themes: 1) that the federal government work directly with governments on a "government to government" relationship, [and] 2) that the federal government pursue the principal of Indian self-determination.

Many people are appalled that the federal government has been neglecting the Native people. It has neither honored their rights [or] our treaties nor provided avenues for equal justice within their realm. It is from this stance that they challenge our sovereignty; yet it is this sovereignty which allows us to deal and negotiate with the federal government regarding land issues. Most often it is their negligence recognizing this issue. They have various departments that try to incorporate the "Indian" issues. They do not follow through with their concepts. These footnotes are written into their quarterly reports. These are just words on paper. They renege on their words. They write us saying that they will consult with us on mining issues and on nuclear issues, but it is just a thought which is erased by the wind.

We are sovereign within ourselves. It is as inherent as the air we breathe. We did not ask for this. We are who we are and did not ask for this sovereignty, yet it is as close to us as the blood that runs through our veins.

When the Treaty of Ruby Valley was signed in 1863, we were already a nation. Just because it was written on paper, it does not negate our claims to the lands. They have failed to live up to and honor their words written on so many pieces of white paper. We were a sovereign nation then and we dealt with each other on those terms. We defined our lands in agreements with the Palutes, Washoes, and Utes who interfaced Western Shoshone country. They recognized us and we recognized ourselves.

We are who we are because our nation survived here. It is written on our earth. We have arrowheads, burial grounds, sacred sites, and all other prehistoric evidence which tells us that we are a sovereign people. We tell our stories in which we incorporate our mountains, valleys, campsites, foods, and lifestyle. Due to our inherited sovereignty, we as Shoshone people, who still speak the language and have not given up tradition, are obligated to continue it. These traditions are kept alive through storytelling about creation [and] our ancestors' activities such as basketry and many others, along with our other relatives, the rabbits, coyotes, and all other animals that are part of the desert. Our only interdependence was the reciprocal agreements that were made with our relatives, the animals, who gave up their lives so we could live.

We are a sovereign nation. We have not given this up to anyone. We are sovereign in all ways. We acknowledge that changes have been made in our world but we are still sovereign. We acknowledge that when the tumble weed blows to another place, it has changed the environment, but the land is still there. We acknowledge when the energy of the wind funnel lifts up and touches the earth in some other place, it has changed the environment, but the land is still there. We acknowledge changes, but we still live in a sovereign Shoshone country. We will never allow the government to conquer our minds. As a nation, we Shoshone have continued to process certain information which is recognized by us as sovereign citizens of the Shoshone Nation. We are as sovereign as our language and culture, which are tied to the landmarks of the Shoshone landscape.

We challenge the federal government concerning our land issues, environmental change, nuclear issues, and mining issues because of our sovereign status. We are a nation with sovereign rights which are inherent in our beings and our souls. Our beliefs are connected to the earth and even to the spirits who are not visible. We recognize the interdependence on this earth only and our relatives who gave us this land on which we live on and are sovereign in our beliefs and our minds.

Even though the government tries to deny us these rights—why do they come to us then? Is it because they recognize this relationship? They know that throughout history, they have never consulted with the Indigenous people. Now, through their history books, they deny us our rights. We cannot cease to be sovereign until the day we die because this is who we are and until our breath is our last, and our relatives cut their hair in grief, we will remain sovereign because they have not conquered our spirit.

Even in their history, their people came to use recognizing our stewardship of the land to have their military people come to the Shoshones with their thundersticks to coerce the old people to sign their Xs.

The Ruby Valley Treaty recognizes our sovereignty. We have learned how to use the piece of wood to scratch marks on a piece of material. We have learned how their words have meaning to them. We have Shoshone people who have learned how to use these new sounds which articulate our thought in their way. But we also have our own language, lifelines, and relationship with this land. This is something thy cannot fathom. Our sovereignty state is only limited in our interdependence on our relatives of the earth. Until we allow them to sever these relationships with the earth, we will remain a sovereign nation.

Taku Wakan Tipi/Minnehaha Free State, 1998–2001

Grace Handy

The Minnesota Department of Transportation released plans in 1996 to extend Highway 55 through public land that ran through Camp Cold-water Spring, sacred to American Indian groups. In addition, the high-way plans cut through the four oaks, a sacred site and possibly a Men-dota Mdewakanton Dakota burial ground. After failed attempts to prevent the reroute in the courts, on August 10, 1998, a Native-led occupation formed the Minnehaha Free State (its Dakota name was Taku Wakan Tipi, meaning "dwelling place of the gods").

The Minnehaha Free State marked the latest example of Indige-nous nations partnering with majority white groups to protect rural lands. Such coalitions popped up throughout the 1990s in the Mid-west and Plains states, as well as the Pacific Northwest. While many of these efforts, like the Cowboys and Indian Alliance that formed in the Dakotas, used traditional forms of protest, Taku Wakan Tipi developed a more militant posture that combined the spirit of American Indian Movement (AIM) occupations of the 1970s with the growing environ-mentalist opposition to clear-cutting and road construction.

On August 10, 1998, these group began occupying the highway route on Riverview Road. They lived in tree houses, tents, and homes that the Minnesota Department of Transportation had been buying up to demolish as part of the highway construction plan. Residents included Mendota Mdewakanton Dakota tribal members, AIM activ-ists, historians, religious leaders, Earth First! activists, and more. Res-idents handed out informational pamphlets, held strategy meetings, did security patrols, constructed tree sits, and gave tours to visitors. After the Free Staters refused to vacate the site, Governor Arne Carlson launched the largest law enforcement operation in Minnesota history at 4:30 am on December 20, 1998, when six hundred officers stormed the encampment. Officers used pepper spray and bolt cutters, arrested thirty-three of the activists, and evicted the rest.

The homes were demolished, but protestors soon returned to build another encampment in the path of the highway near the four oaks. The new site was still known as "free state" but also as the Four Oaks Spiritual Encampment. The activists asserted that the four oaks was a sacred site for the local Mendota Mdewakanton Dakota, but the state denied these claims in court. On December 11, 1999, the police raided the encampment for the last time, and the four oaks came down.

In 2001 a law was passed to preserve Coldwater Spring, and the highway plan was adjusted. The Minnehaha encampment represented the alliance of many activists from a variety of backgrounds to pre-vent a construction project and led to solidarity and strategy sharing between different communities. The encampment and legal battles involved in protecting the area also serve as one example in a long history of the US settler state commandeering the ability to assess Indigenous peoples' claims of sacred land.

4.C.11.

Ashanti Alston

From "Beyond Nationalism but Not without It" (2001)

Ashanti Alston joined the Black Panther Party as a teenager in New Jersey, later going underground with the Black Liberation Army and serving more than ten years in prison as a result. His studies in prison led him to both postmodernism and anarchism. In this essay, first published in his zine *Anarchist Panther*, Alston outlines the relevance of Black nationalism to the new social movements of the twenty-first century.

. . . There are all kinds of nationalisms and there are all kinds of reactions to nationalism. Personally, I have moved through and grown within some of the black nationalisms specific to the black community.

Black nationalism saved my life, in a sense, as a teenager in the 1960s. It "jarred" my unconscious acceptance of amerikkanism dogging my peoples and helped me see the larger picture. I am a 60s child. There was Malcolm, there was H. Rap Brown and Stokely Carmichael of the Black Power movement, and then there was the Black Panther Party. All were nationalists, all represent an evolution of nationalism within the black community. . . . It was about our survival as a people, not as that mythical "working class" or that equally mythical "citizen." For me, as this teenager who had just witnessed the 60s rebellions in my own thoroughly racist hometown, nationalism was a lifesaver: "*We must love each other.*" "*Black is beautiful.*" "*We must control our own communities.*" . . .

Nationalism and statism are different because nationalism can be antistate. But they can have commonalities in that nationalism may only be against a particular kind of state, such as a racist state, or a fascist state. Anarchism and nationalism are similar in that they are both antistatist, but what does it mean when the specific anarchist movements within a specific country are racist and dismissive of any and all nationalism, be it reactionary or revolutionary? For me, even the nationalism of a Louis Farrakhan is about saving my people, though it is also thoroughly sexist, capitalist, homophobic and potentially fascist. Yet it has played an important part in keeping a certain black pride and resistance going. Their "on the ground" work is very important in keeping an antiracist mentality going. As a black anarchist, that's *my* issue to deal with cuz they'se *my folks*. But it points to where anarchism and nationalism have differences: most anarchists in the US have *no* understanding of what it means to be *black* in this fucked-up society. We do not have the luxury of being so intellectual about this excruciating boot on our collective neck, this modern-day middle passage into the prison industrial complex and other forms of neoslavery.

As a postmodernist anarchist, identity politics is important to me. Every time I hear someone talk about my people as if we are just some "working class" or "proletariat" I wanna get as far away from that person or group as possible, anarchist, Marxist, whatever. . . . My nationalism gave me that kind of pride because it was such a rejection of white thinking or at least a decentering of the primacy of white thought, capitalist, socialist, whatever. Folks outside of our experience need to respect that they ain't got no monopoly on revolutionary thinking and damn sure ain't got none on revolutionary practice. It is easy to sit back and intellectualize about our nationalism from the modernist, eurocentric framework of rational, scientific, materialist models. While one does that, it is our nationalism that constantly rallies our people to come together, remember our history, love ourselves, dream on and fight back. Black anarchists and antiauthoritarian revolutionaries understand the limitations of nationalism in terms of its historical sexism, hierarchy, or its modernist trappings in general. But we also recognize anarchism's modernist trappings in the form of American racist/class privilege when it comes to people of color. . . .

White folks need to deal with being *antiracist allies* to folks of color communities and activists. Activists in particular because we are usually whites' entry point into any possible relationship with our communities. Anarchist theory and practice cannot take the form of a mere adherence to the founding fathers and canonical practices, such as Kropotkin, Bakunin, and the Spanish Civil War. Tired of hearing it! Anarchism *here* in Babylon must reflect our unique problems and possibilities for struggle. Our struggles are not just against capitalism. Too simple. Our struggles are not just against racism. That's also too simple. There are all kinds of negative "isms" we are fighting against and, just as important, all kinds of worlds we are fighting for. That's why the whole idea and practice of "convergences" and "spokescouncils" are so important to activists in general to learn from and enhance because they are about making space for all "voices" to be heard and factored into the decision making so that whatever activities come forth from it prefigures the kind of new worlds we truly want.

I end this by advising: *white anarchists: deal with being the best antiracist allies you can. We need you—and you need us—but we will do this shit without you.*

To my folks of color: *come envision*: envision a world of worlds within our world where there's principled coexistence within the wonderful diversity of the black community.

Figure 4.5. Patricia Valencia, Aida Salazar, and Shawn Mortensen, "Third World Is Your World" (1996). Image courtesy of and reprinted with permission by David Thorne.

Harlems / Spanish Harlems / Watts / hip-hop communities / villages of the Carolina coast / college communities / gay-lesbian-bisexual-transgender communities / zulu nation / New Afrikan / religious communities that come together mainly on Saturday or Sunday / squatter communities / outlaw communities / kemetic communities / Ibo-Ghanaian-Sierra Leonean-Ethiopian-rasta neighborhoods / nomadic poet-artist tribes / and then those of us who just be plain ignant and harmless and crazy when we have to be and fun loving and like to journey through and between communities and sometimes just create new mixed ones [. . .] *what if?* [. . .] and *how?*

Ella Baker said we can do it if we can trust ourselves and get away from leadership-led revolution; Kwesi Balagoon said we can do it if we willing to create a chaos that will shut this mutha down; Audre Lorde said we can do it if we *learn to love and respect our beautiful diversity* and reject the tools of our oppressors; Harriet Tubman said, ain't a better way to live *than at war for a righteous cause*; and Frantz Fanon said if we smack that mutha across the face, drive that pig outta our territory at the point of a gun, it *is liberating for the soul.*

Through the imagination, all is possible.

4.C.12.

Kay Whitlock

From *In the Time of Broken Bones* (2001)

By the new millennium, mainstream civil rights, feminist, and gay rights organizations often found themselves supporting tougher state punishments in the form of legislation against "hate crimes." In this excerpt from a section titled "Creating Just, Beloved, and Generous Community" in a report published by the American Friends Service Committee, longtime activist Kay Whitlock wrote that state punishment was a form of violence and therefore could not be an effective strategy against violence. Instead, Whitlock argues, the work of social justice is to foster greater interdependence.

In the end, the culture of domination has nothing more to offer us than a world consumed by policing: a world in which the semblance of security rests on exclusion. In such a world, while we do not even know our neighbors, we are deeply suspicious and resentful of them nonetheless. We will permit anything in exchange for the promise of protection: for ourselves, our value systems, and our possessions. We will willingly sacrifice the human rights and even the lives of others, if we are led to believe that is what it takes.

AFSC [American Friends Service Committee] believes that we must reject this constricted vision, not piecemeal, but altogether. Through our words and deeds, we seek to base our lives in a larger, more generous, and ultimately more joyous vision of wholeness. We believe that wholeness comes, in part, from understanding—and living—the interrelatedness of all struggles for peace and for social and economic justice.

We cannot reach for wholeness alone; nor can we pretend that we do so only for the sake of poor, suffering others. Our own struggles are part of what we must affirm. "The illusion of inclusion," in which we create token representations of diversity without changing the distribution of power and access, will not take us forward.

Within our various communities, many activists have responded to exclusion and injustice by creating spaces and strategies for survival within the dominant culture: freedom schools, antiviolence projects, advocacy networks, crisis centers and shelters, health centers, mentoring programs, restoration of sacred ceremonies and spiritual traditions, prison-based programs, legal education and defense funds, human rights watchdog organizations, social services, and more.

No matter who we are—people of color, women, queers, people with disabilities—when the dominant culture told us our lives did not matter, we resisted erasure and responded by loving ourselves enough to try to save our own lives. Sometimes we succeeded; sometimes we did not. We must never forget, however, that we know how to build sanctuary upon a foundation of love, a love that is expressed in part as our relentless determination to survive. Within these sanctuaries we have shared stories, laughter, rage, and tears; held each other through dark nights; bound one another's wounds; drawn on one another's creativity; gathered strength; and emerged together to mount even more powerful public challenges to injustice and the violence directed against us.

We have not always known, however, how to create sanctuary for one another. We have often failed to appreciate and address the intertwining effects of class, race, gender, culture, and sexuality within our own communities, much less in the larger society. If we are honest about our own weaknesses and our own fears, however, we can create intentional ways of learning from one another through cross-constituency dialogue.

We see evidence in many settings of a hopeful and inspiring insistence on wholeness. Prophetic voices, many of them from young people, call us to a new understanding. Single-issue approaches to organizing are giving way to a more integrated vision that refuses to shortchange the complex realities of human lives. . . .

Community building and coalition efforts designed to withstand turbulent storms of adversity must be rooted in mutually supportive, engaged, consistent, and trustworthy relationships that extend into the spiritual, cultural, social, political, and economic realms. Only from such relationships can just, beloved, generous, and inclusive community truly emerge. In AFSC's experience, relationships among people who are racially, ethnically, culturally, sexually, and spiritually diverse must be built on a foundation of respect, understanding, and integrity. They must be supported by consistent, visible efforts to shoulder one another's burdens of injustice. Such relationships across constituencies and movements must be rooted in something far deeper than a political marriage of convenience forged in crisis, in reaction to the initiatives of the secular and religious right.

After decades of fragmentation in progressive movements, we believe the moment has arrived to explore the relationship between hate violence and structural violence. We believe it is necessary to connect our discussions and our work across constituencies. Community capacity does not yet exist in most places to begin experimenting with new justice practices, and we must not be naïve about how challenging creating such a capacity will be. Even so, we can begin to establish a foundation for the work that is yet to come.

The leadership for such efforts must come from those most affected by every form of violence. Regardless of who we are, however, we can encourage, support, and sustain one another along the way. In doing so, it is essential that we begin to formulate and lift up a coherent moral, social, and economic vision that reflects the values of love and healing justice.

We cannot cease to lift up our voices against injustice wherever we find it. At the same time, to work in ways that are simply reactive to the injustices around us is dispiriting and exhausting and will lead us ultimately into fanaticism. Intolerance, whether from the right or the left, is a strange glue, binding the hater to that which is hated. When we fail to keep the values of love, justice, and interdependence at the center of our work, we risk becoming a mirror image of that which we oppose.

With the values of love and justice at the center of our work, all things are possible. Imagine, for example, community organizing around funding for public education that links the struggles of LGBT and questioning youth, people of color communities, criminal justice activists, and others. Imagine linking the work of many different antiviolence and criminal justice activists together at the community level, in ways that finally dissolve the distinction between "public" and "private" violence, that link hate violence to the violence of the state, and that pay close attention to the interaction of gender, sexuality, race, and class. Imagine community-based organizing around the theme of creating just, safe, caring, and sustainable community. Imagine the prophetic voice that religious and spiritual communities could bring to work carried forward within this framework of interdependence. Imagine the vision of justice that could arise when we refuse to cast anyone, including one another, aside.

Claiming the value of interdependence permits us to tear down the citadel of privilege, establishing in its place a life-giving foundation of love and healing justice. This is how we are called in our own day to follow the ancient practice, found in every major spiritual and ethical tradition, of transforming adversity into compassion, compassion into love, and love into justice.

BIBLIOGRAPHY

There is a vast and growing body of literature about—and from—the time period covered in this book. Here we provide a list of some of the key texts that we used or that informed the snapshots and that can provide further context to the documents gathered in this anthology. We have emphasized books over journal articles, though both appear.

ACE Program of the Bedford Hills Correctional Facility. *Breaking the Walls of Silence: AIDS and Women in a New York State Maximum-Security Prison*. New York: Overlook Press, 1998.

Ahmed, Sara. *On Being Included: Racism and Diversity in Institutional Life*. Durham, NC: Duke University Press, 2012.

Akwesasne Notes, ed. *Voices from Wounded Knee, 1973, in the Words of the Participants*. Rooseveltown, NY: Akwesasne Notes, 1974.

Anderson, John, and Hilary Hevenor. *Burning Down the House: MOVE and the Tragedy of Philadelphia*. New York: Norton, 1987.

Anzáldua, Gloria, and Cherríe Moraga, eds. *This Bridge Called My Back: Writings by Radical Women of Color*. Latham, NY: Kitchen Table Press, 1981.

Bacevich, Andrew J. *American Empire: The Realities and Consequences of US Diplomacy*. Cambridge: Harvard University Press, 2002.

Bailey, Beth L., and David R. Farber. *America in the Seventies*. Lawrence: University Press of Kansas, 2004.

Baldwin, James, and Frank Shatz. "John Brown's Body." *Transition* 81/82 (2000): 250–66.

Barrett, Dawson. *The Defiant: Protest Movements in Post-Liberal America*. New York: New York University Press, 2018.

Beal, Frances M. "Double Jeopardy: To Be Black and Female." *Meridians* 8, no. 2 (2008): 166–76.

Beam, Myrl. *Gay, Inc.: The Nonprofitization of Queer Politics*. Minneapolis: University of Minnesota Press, 2018.

Belew, Kathleen. *Bringing the War Home: The White Power Movement and Paramilitary America*. Cambridge, MA: Harvard University Press, 2018.

Berger, Dan. *Captive Nation: Black Prison Organizing in the Civil Rights Era*. Chapel Hill: University of North Carolina Press, 2014.

———, ed. *The Hidden 1970s: Histories of Radicalism*. New Brunswick, NJ: Rutgers University Press, 2010.

———. *Outlaws of America: The Weather Underground and the Politics of Solidarity*. Oakland, CA: AK Press, 2006.

Berlet, Chip, and Matthew N. Lyons. *Right-Wing Populism in America: Too Close for Comfort*. New York: Guilford Press, 2000.

Berry, Mary Frances. *History Teaches Us to Resist: How Progressive Movements Have Succeeded in Challenging Times*. Boston: Beacon Press, 2018.

Best, Steven, and Anthony J. Nocella II. *Igniting a Revolution: Voices in Defense of the Earth*. Oakland, CA: AK Press, 2006.

Blackwell, Maylei. *¡Chicana Power! Contested Histories of Feminism in the Chicano Movement*. Austin: University of Texas Press, 2011.

Bobo, Kimberley A., Jackie Kendall, and Steve Max. *Organizing for Social Change: A Manual for Activists in the 1990s*. Washington, DC: Seven Locks Press, 1991.

Boggs, Grace Lee. *Living for Change: An Autobiography*. Minneapolis: University of Minnesota Press, 1998.

Boggs, James. *Conversations in Maine: Exploring Our Nation's Future*. Boston: South End Press, 1978.

Boggs, James, and Grace Lee Boggs. *Revolution and Evolution in the Twentieth Century*. New York: Monthly Review Press, 1974.

Bookchin, Murray. *Anarchism, Marxism, and the Future of the Left*. San Francisco: AK Press, 1999.

Bost, Darius. *Evidence of Being: The Black Gay Cultural Renaissance and the Politics of Violence*. Chicago: University of Chicago Press, 2019.

Boyd, Andrew, and Dave Oswald Mitchell, eds. *Beautiful Trouble: A Toolbox for Revolution*. New York: OR Books, 2012.

Boyette, Michael, and Randi Boyette. *Let It Burn: MOVE, the Philadelphia Police Department, and the Confrontation that Changed a City*. San Diego, CA: Endpapers Press, 1989.

Brenner, Aaron, Robert Brenner, and Cal Winslow, eds. *Rebel Rank and File: Labor Militancy and Revolt from Below during the Long 1970s*. New York: Verso, 2010.

Brick, Howard, and Christopher Phelps. *Radicals in America: The US Left since the Second World War*. New York: Cambridge University Press, 2015.

Brier, Jennifer. *Infectious Ideas: US Political Responses to the AIDS Crisis*. Chapel Hill: University of North Carolina Press, 2009.

Briggs, Laura. *How All Politics Became Reproductive Politics*. Oakland: University of California Press, 2017.

Bronfenbrenner, Kate. *Organizing to Win: New Research on Union Strategies*. Ithaca, NY: ILR Press, 1998.

Brown, Wendy. *Undoing the Demos: Neoliberalism's Stealth Revolution*. Brooklyn, NY: Zone Books, 2015.

Bulkin, Elly, Minnie Bruce Pratt, and Barbara Smith. *Yours in Struggle: Three Feminist Perspectives on Anti-Semitism and Racism*. New York: Long Haul Press, 1984.

Bullard, Robert, and Glenn Johnson. "Environmental Justice: Grassroots Activism and Its Impact of Public Policy Decision Making." *Journal of Social Issues* 56, no. 3 (2000): 555–78.

Burbach, Roger, and Jim Tarbell. *Imperial Overstretch: George W. Bush and the Hubris of Empire*. London: Zed Books, 2004.

Burke, Kyle. *Revolutionaries for the Right: Anticommunist Internationalism and Paramilitary Warfare in the Cold War*. Chapel Hill: University of North Carolina Press, 2018.

Burton-Rose, Daniel. *Creating a Movement with Teeth: A Documentary History of the George Jackson Brigade*. Oakland, CA: PM Press, 2010.

———. *Guerrilla USA: The George Jackson Brigade and the Anticapitalist Underground of the 1970s*. Berkeley: University of California Press, 2010.

Burton-Rose, Daniel, George Katsiaficas, and Eddie Yuen. *Confronting Capitalism: Dispatches from a Global Movement*. New York: Soft Skull Press, 2004.

Cacho, Lisa Marie. *Social Death: Racialized Rightlessness and the Criminalization of the Unprotected*. New York: New York University Press, 2012.

Carroll, Tamar. *Mobilizing New York: AIDS, Antipoverty, and Feminist Activism*. Chapel Hill: University of North Carolina Press, 2015.

Carter, Mandy. "The Emperor's New Clothes, or How Not to Run a Movement." In *This Is What Lesbian Looks Like: Dyke Activists Take on the Twenty-First Century*, ed. Kris Kleindienst, 62–69. Ithaca, NY: Firebrand Books, 1999.

Cebul, Brent, Lily Geismer, and Mason B. Williams, eds. *Shaped by the State: Toward a New Political History of the Twentieth Century*. Chicago: University of Chicago Press, 2019.

Chang, Jeff. *Can't Stop Won't Stop: A History of the Hip-Hop Generation*. New York: Picador, 2005.

———. *Who We Be: The Colorization of America*. New York: St. Martin's Press, 2014.

Chappell, Marisa. *The War on Welfare Family: Poverty, and Politics in Modern America*. Philadelphia: University of Pennsylvania Press, 2010.

Clawson, Dan. *The Next Upsurge: Labor and the New Social Movements*. Ithaca, NY: ILR Press, 2003.

Cobb, Daniel M. *Say We Are Nations: Documents of Politics and Protest in Indigenous America Since 1887*. Chapel Hill: University of North Carolina Press, 2015.

Cohen, Cathy J. "Punks, Bulldaggers, and Welfare Queens: The Radical Potential of Queer Politics?" *GLQ: A Journal of Lesbian and Gay Studies* 3, no. 4 (1997): 437–65.

———. "What Is This Movement Doing to My Politics?" *Social Text* 61 (1999): 111–18.

Cornell, Andrew. *Oppose and Propose: Lessons from Movement for a New Society*. Oakland, CA: AK Press, 2011.

Collins, Patricia Hill, and Sirma Bilge. *Intersectionality*. Cambridge, UK: Polity, 2016.

Cowie, Jefferson. *Stayin' Alive: The 1970s and the Last Days of the Working Class*. New York: New Press, 2010.

———. "'Vigorously Left, Right, and Center': The Crosscurrents of Working-Class America in the 1970s." In *America in the Seventies*, ed. Beth L. Bailey and Dave Farber, 75–106. Lawrence: University Press of Kansas, 2004.

Crenshaw, Kimberlé. "Demarginalizing the Intersection of Race and Sex: A Black Feminist Critique of Antidiscrimination Doctrine, Feminist Theory, and Antiracist Politics." *University of Chicago Legal Forum* 1 (1989): 139–67.

———. "Mapping the Margins: Intersectionality, Identity Politics, and Violence against Women of Color." *Stanford Law Review* 43, no. 6 (1991): 1241–299.

Crimp, Douglas. *Melancholia and Moralism: Essays on AIDS and Queer Politics*. Cambridge, MA: MIT Press, 2004.

Cvetkovich, Ann. *An Archive of Feelings: Trauma, Sexuality, and Lesbian Public Cultures*. Durham, NC: Duke University Press, 2003.

The Damned. *Lessons from the Damned: Class Struggle in the Black Community*. New York: Monthly Review Press, 1979.

Danaher, Kevin. *Corporations Are Gonna Get Your Mama: Globalization and the Downsizing of the American Dream*. Monroe, ME: Common Courage Press, 1996.

Davis, John, ed. *The Earth First! Reader: Ten Years of Radical Environmentalism*. Salt Lake City, UT: Peregrine Smith Books, 1991.

Davis, Julie L. *Survival Schools: The American Indian Movement and Community Education in the Twin Cities*. Minneapolis: University of Minnesota Press, 2013.

Davis, Mike. *City of Quartz: Excavating the Future in Los Angeles*. London: Verso, 1990.

de Jong, Greta. *You Can't Eat Freedom: Southerners and Social Justice after the Civil Rights Movement*. Chapel Hill: University of North Carolina Press, 2016.

Dellinger, Dave. *More Power Than We Know: The People's Movement toward Democracy*. New York: Anchor Books, 1975.

Deming, Barbara. *Remembering Who We Are*. Tallahassee, FL: Pagoda Press, 1981.

Deming, Barbara, and Jane Meyerding. *We Are All Part of One Another: A Barbara Deming Reader*. Philadelphia: New Society Publishers, 1984.

Diaz-Cotto, Juanita. *Gender, Ethnicity, and the State: Latina and Latino Prison Politics*. Binghamton: State University of New York Press, 1996.

Dinges, John. *The Condor Years: How Pinochet and His Allies Brought Terrorism to Three Continents*. New York: New Press, 2005.

Dixon, Chris. *Another Politics: Talking across Today's Transformative Movements*. Berkeley: University of California Press, 2014.

Duggan, Lisa. *The Twilight of Equality? Neoliberalism, Cultural Politics, and the Attack on Democracy*. Boston: Beacon Press, 2004.

Dujon, Diane, and Ann Withorn, eds. *For Crying Out Loud: Women's Poverty in the United States*. Boston: South End Press, 1999.

Duncombe, Stephen, ed. *The Cultural Resistance Reader*. London: Verso, 2002.

Dunbar-Ortiz, Roxanne. *Blood on the Border: A Memoir of the Contra War*. Boston: South End Press, 2005.

Earth First! *Direct Action Manual: Uncompromising Nonviolent Resistance in Defense of Mother Earth*. Eugene, OR: Feral Press, 1997.

Elbaum, Max. *Revolution in the Air: Sixties Radicals Turn to Lenin, Che, and Mao*. London: Verso, 2002.

Encke, Anne. *Finding the Movement: Sexuality, Contested Space, and Feminist Activism*. Durham, NC: Duke University Press, 2007.

Engler, Mark, and Paul Engler. *This Is an Uprising: How Nonviolent Resistance Is Shaping the Twenty-First Century*. New York: Nation Books, 2016.

Epstein, Barbara. *Political Protest and Cultural Revolution: Nonviolent Direct Action in the 1970s and 1980s*. Berkeley: University of California Press, 1991.

Estes, Nick. *Our History Is the Future: Standing Rock versus the Dakota Access Pipeline and the Long Tradition of Indigenous Resistance*. New York: Verso, 2019.

Fadda-Conrey, Carol. *Contemporary Arab American Literature: Transnational Reconfigurations of Citizenship and Belonging*. New York: New York University Press, 2014.

Farmer, Ashley. *Remaking Black Power: How Black Women Transformed an Era*. Chapel Hill: University of North Carolina Press, 2017.

Fawaz, Ramzi. *The New Mutants: Superheroes and the Radical Imagination of American Comics*. New York: New York University Press, 2016.

Featherstone, Liza, and United Students against Sweatshops. *Students against Sweatshops: The Making of a Movement*. London: Verso, 2002.

Felker-Kantor, Max. *Policing Los Angeles: Race, Resistance, and the Rise of the LAPD*. Chapel Hill: University of North Carolina Press, 2018.

Ferguson, Roderick A. *We Demand: the University and Student Protests*. Oakland: University of California Press, 2017.

Fernandez, Ronald. *Prisoners of Colonialism: The Struggle for Justice in Puerto Rico*. Monroe, ME: Common Courage Press, 1994.

Finlay, Barbara. *George W. Bush and the War on Women: Turning Back the Clock on Progress*. London: Zed Books, 2006.

Fithian, Lisa. *Shut it Down: Stories from a Fierce, Loving Resistance*. White River Junction, VT: Chelsea Green Publishing, 2019.

Foley, Michael Stewart. *Front-Porch Politics: The Forgotten Heyday of American Activism in the 1970s and 1980s*. New York: Hill and Wang, 2013.

Franklin, Sekou M. *After the Rebellion: Black Youth, Social Movement Activism, and the Post–Civil Rights Generation*. New York: New York University Press, 2014.

Fraser, Nancy. *Fortunes of Feminism: From State-Managed Capitalism to Neoliberal Crisis.* New York: Verso, 2013.

Freeman, Joshua. *American Empire: The Rise of a Global Power, the Democratic Revolution at Home.* New York: Penguin, 2013.

Gaard, Greta Claire. *Ecological Politics: Ecofeminists and the Greens.* Philadelphia: Temple University Press, 1998.

Gilmore, Ruth Wilson. *Golden Gulag: Prisons, Surplus, Crisis, and Opposition in Globalizing California.* Berkeley: University of California Press, 2007.

Gitlin, Todd. *Twilight of Common Dreams: Why America Is Wracked by Culture Wars.* New York: Holt, 1996.

Goodyear-Ka'ōpua, Noelani, Ikaika Hussey, and Erin Kahunawaika'ala Wright, eds. *A Nation Rising: Hawaiian Movements for Life, Land, and Sovereignty.* Durham, NC: Duke University Press, 2014.

Gould, Deborah. *Moving Politics: Emotion and ACT UP's Fight against AIDS.* Chicago: University of Chicago, 2009.

Grandin, Greg. *Empire's Workshop: Latin America, the United States, and the Rise of the New Imperialism.* New York: Holt, 2007.

Greenwald, Dara, Josh MacPhee, and Exit Art. *Signs of Change: Social Movement Cultures, 1960s to Now.* Oakland, CA: AK Press, 2010.

Grossman, Zoltán. *Unlikely Alliances: Native Nations and White Communities Join to Defend Rural Lands.* Seattle: University of Washington Press, 2017.

Haider, Asad. *Mistaken Identity: Race and Class in the Age of Trump.* New York: Verso, 2018.

Hall, Jacqueline Dowd. "The Long Civil Rights Movement and the Political Uses of the Past." *Journal of American History* 91, no. 4 (2005): 1233–63.

Hall, Stuart. "The Problem of Ideology: Marxism without Guarantees," *Journal of Communication Inquiry* 10, no. 2 (1986): 28–44.

Hancock, Ange-Marie. *Intersectionality: An Intellectual History.* Oxford: Oxford University Press, 2016.

Hanhardt, Christina. *Safe Space: Gay Neighborhood History and the Politics of Violence.* Durham, NC: Duke University Press, 2013.

Hardt, Michael, and Antonio Negri. *Empire.* Cambridge, MA: Harvard University Press, 2000.

Harvey, David. *A Brief History of Neoliberalism.* Oxford: Oxford University Press, 2007.

———. *The Condition of Postmodernity: An Enquiry into the Origin of Cultural Change.* Malden, MA: Blackwell, 1991.

Hewitt, Nancy. *No Permanent Waves Recasting Histories of US Feminism.* New Brunswick, NJ: Rutgers University Press, 2010.

Hickmott, Alec. "Black Land, Black Capital: Rural Development in the Shadows of the Sunbelt South, 1969–1976," *Journal of African American History* 101, no. 4 (2016): 504–34.

Hinton, Elizabeth. *From the War on Poverty to the War on Crime.* Cambridge, MA: Harvard University Press, 2016.

Hobson, Emily K. *Lavender and Red: Liberation and Solidarity in the Gay and Lesbian Left.* Oakland: University of California Press, 2016.

Hobson, Maurice J. *The Legend of the Black Mecca: Politics and Class in the Making of Modern Atlanta.* Chapel Hill: University of North Carolina Press, 2017.

HoSang, Daniel Martinez. *Racial Propositions: Ballot Initiatives and the Making of Postwar California.* Berkeley: University of California Press, 2010.

How to Survive a Plague. Directed by David France, 2011.

Hudson, Michael. *Super Imperialism: The Origin and Fundamentals of US World Dominance*. London: Pluto Press, 2003.

INCITE! *The Revolution Will Not Be Funded: Beyond the Non-Profit Industrial Complex*. Durham, NC: Duke University Press, 2017.

Jaimes, M. Annette, ed. *The State of Native America: Genocide, Colonization, and Resistance*. Boston: South End Press, 1992.

James, Joy, ed. *The Angela Y. Davis Reader*. Malden, MA: Blackwell, 1997.

———. *Imprisoned Intellectuals America's Political Prisoners Write on Life, Liberation, and Rebellion*. Lanham, MD: Rowman and Littlefield, 2004.

———. *The New Abolitionists: (Neo)slave Narratives and Contemporary Prison Writings*. Albany: State University of New York Press, 2005.

———. *States of Confinement: Policing, Detention, and Prisons*. New York: St. Martin's Press, 2000.

———. *Warfare in the American Homeland: Policing and Prison in a Penal Democracy*. Durham, NC: Duke University Press, 2008.

Janken, Kenneth Robert. *The Wilmington Ten: Violence, Injustice, and the Rise of Black Politics in the 1970s*. Chapel Hill: University of North Carolina Press, 2015.

Johnson, Cedric. *Revolutionaries to Race Leaders: Black Power and the Making of African American Politics*. Minneapolis: University of Minnesota Press, 2007.

Juhasz, Alexandra. *AIDS TV: Identity, Community, and Alternative Video*. Durham, NC: Duke University Press, 1995.

Katz, Michael B. *Why Don't American Cities Burn?* Philadelphia: University of Pennsylvania Press, 2012.

Kauffman, L. A. *Direct Action: Protest and the Reinvention of American Radicalism*. New York: Verso, 2017.

———. *How to Read a Protest: The Art of Organizing and Resistance*. Oakland: University of California Press, 2018.

Kazis, Richard, and Richard L. Grossman. *Fear at Work: Job Blackmail, Labor, and the Environment*. New York: Pilgrim Press, 1982.

Khasnabish, Alex. *Zapatistas: Rebellion from the Grassroots to the Global*. London: Zed Books, 2013.

Kelley, Robin D. G. *Freedom Dreams: The Black Radical Imagination*. Boston: Beacon, 2002.

Killen, Andreas. *1973 Nervous Breakdown: Watergate, Warhol, and the Birth of Post-Sixties America*. New York: Bloomsbury, 2006.

Kleindienst, Kris, ed. *This Is What Lesbian Looks Like: Dyke Activists Take on the Twenty-First Century*. Ithaca, NY: Firebrand Books, 1999.

Kohler-Hausmann, Julilly. *Getting Tough: Welfare and Imprisonment in 1970s America*. Princeton, NJ: Princeton University Press, 2017.

Kornbluh, Felicia, and Gwendolyn Mink, eds. *Ensuring Poverty: Welfare Reform in Feminist Perspective*. Philadelphia: University of Pennsylvania Press, 2018.

Kruse, Kevin M., and Julian E. Zelizer. *Fault Lines: A History of the United States since 1974*. New York: Norton, 2019.

Kuipers, Dean. *Operation Biteback: Rod Coronado's War to Save American Wilderness*. New York: Bloomsbury, 2009.

Kurshan, Nancy. *Out of Control: A Fifteen-Year Battle against Control Unit Prisons*. San Francisco: Freedom Archives, 2013.

LaDuke, Winona. *All Our Relations: Native Struggles for Land and Life*. Boston: South End Press, 1999.

Laffin, Arthur J., and Anne Montgomery, eds. *Swords into Plowshares: Nonviolent Direct Action for Disarmament*. New York: Harper and Row, 1987.

Larson, Eric, ed. *Jobs with Justice: 25 Years, 25 Voices*. Oakland, CA: PM Press, 2013.

Latner, Teishan. *Cuban Revolution in America: Havana and the Making of a United States Left, 1968–1992*. Chapel Hill: University of North Carolina Press, 2018.

Law, Victoria. *Resistance behind Bars: The Struggles of Incarcerated Women*. Oakland, CA: PM Press, 2012.

Levine, Debra. "Another Kind of Love: A Performance of Prosthetic Politics." *E-mísferica*, 2, no. 2 (2005). hemisphericinstitute.org/journal/2_2/levine_pg3.html.

Lockman, Zachary, and Joel Beinin, eds. *Intifada: The Palestinian Uprising against Israeli Occupation*. Boston: South End Press, 1999.

Longmore, Paul K. *Why I Burned My Book and Other Essays on Disability*. Philadelphia: Temple University Press, 2003.

Losure, Mary. *Our Way or the Highway: Inside the Minnehaha Free State*. Minneapolis: University of Minnesota Press, 2002.

Louie, Miriam Ching Yoon. *Sweatshop Warriors: Immigrant Women Workers Take on the Global Factory*. Boston: South End Press, 2001.

MacLean, Nancy. *Democracy in Chains: The Deep History of the Radical Right's Stealth Plan for America*. New York: Viking, 2017.

———. *Freedom Is Not Enough: The Opening of the American Workplace*. New York: Russell Sage Foundation, 2006.

Mahler, Anne Garland. *From the Tricontinental to the Global South: Race, Radicalism, and Transnational Solidarity*. Durham, NC: Duke University Press, 2018.

Maira, Sunaina Marr. *The 9/11 Generation: Youth, Rights, and Solidarity in the War on Terror*. New York: New York University Press, 2016.

Mann, Eric., and Labor/Community Strategy Center. *LA's Lethal Air: New Strategies for Policy, Organizing, and Action*. Los Angeles: Labor/Community Strategy Center, 1991.

Markowitz, Gerald E., and David Rosner. *Deceit and Denial: The Deadly Politics of Industrial Pollution*. Berkeley: University of California Press, 2002.

Martin, Bradford. *The Other Eighties: A Secret History of America in the Age of Reagan*. New York: Hill and Wang, 2011.

Martinez, Elizabeth Betita. *De Colores Means All of Us: Latina Views for a Multicolored Century*. Boston: South End Press, 1999.

———. "Where Was the Color in Seattle?" *Colorlines*, March 10, 2000.

McAlevy, Jane, with Bob Ostertag. *Raising Expectations (and Raising Hell): My Decade Fighting For the Labor Movement*. London: Verso, 2012.

McCartin, Joseph A. *Collision Course: Ronald Reagan, the Air Traffic Controllers, and the Strike That Changed America*. New York: Oxford University Press, 2011.

Means, Russell, and Marvin J Wolf. *Where White Men Fear to Tread: The Autobiography of Russell Means*. New York: St. Martin's Press, 1995.

Medsger, Betty. *The Burglary: The Discovery of J. Edgar Hoover's Secret FBI*. New York: Vintage, 2014.

Melamed, Jodi. *Represent and Destroy: Rationalizing Violence in the New Racial Capitalism*. Minneapolis: University of Minnesota Press, 2011.

Minchin, Timothy J. *Labor under Fire: A History of the AFL-CIO since 1979*. Chapel Hill: University of North Carolina Press, 2017.

Mittelstadt, Jennifer. *The Rise of the Military Welfare State*. Cambridge, MA: Harvard University Press, 2015.

Mohanty, Chandra Talpade. *Feminism without Borders: Decolonizing Theory, Practicing Solidarity*. Durham, NC: Duke University Press, 2003.

Mohawk, John, and José Barreiro. *Thinking in Indian: A John Mohawk Reader*. Golden, CO: Fulcrum, 2010.

Molina, Alejandro Luis, ed. *USA on Trial: The International Tribunal on Indigenous Peoples and Oppressed Nations in the United States.* Chicago: El Coquí, 1996.

Morris, Glenn T. "Coalitions and Alliances: The Case of Indigenous Resistance to the Columbian Quincentenary." In *The Politics of Minority Coalitions: Race, Ethnicity, and Shared Uncertainties,* ed. Wilbur C. Rich, 215–31. Westport, CT: Praeger, 1996.

Moughrabi, Fouad. "Remembering the AAUG." *Arab Studies Quarterly* 29, nos. 3/4 (2007): 97–103.

Murakawa, Naomi. *The First Civil Right: How Liberals Built Prison America.* Oxford: Oxford University Press, 2014.

Murphy, Ryan Patrick. *Deregulating Desire: Flight Attendant Activism, Family Politics, and Workplace Justice.* Philadelphia: Temple University Press, 2017.

Muzio, Rose. *Radical Imagination, Radical Humanity: Puerto Rican Political Activism in New York.* Albany: State University of New York Press, 2017.

Nadasen, Premilla. *Welfare Warriors: The Welfare Rights Movement in the United States.* New York: Routledge, 2005.

Notes from Nowhere. *We Are Everywhere: The Irresistible Rise of Global Anticapitalism.* London: Verso, 2003.

Ostendorf, David, and Daniel Levitas. "Education for Empowerment and Social Action in Rural America." *Mid-American Review of Sociology* 12, no. 1 (1987): 55–64.

Parham, Vera. *Pantribal Activism in the Pacific Northwest: The Power of Indigenous Protest and the Birth of Daybreak Star Cultural Center.* Lanham, MD: Lexington Books, 2018.

Pellow, David N. *Garbage Wars: The Struggle for Environmental Justice in Chicago.* Cambridge, MA: MIT Press, 2002.

———. *Total Liberation: The Power and Promise of Animal Rights and the Radical Earth Movement.* Minneapolis: University of Minnesota Press, 2014.

Pennock, Pamela E. *The Rise of the Arab American Left: Activists, Allies, and Their Fight against Imperialism and Racism, 1960s–1980s.* Chapel Hill: University of North Carolina Press, 2017.

Pharr, Suzanne. *Homophobia: A Weapon of Sexism.* Inverness, CA: Chardon Press, 1988.

Pickering, Leslie James. *The Earth Liberation Front, 1997–2002.* 2nd ed. Portland, OR: Arissa Media Group, 2007.

Piven, Francis Fox, and Richard A. Cloward. *Poor People's Movements: Why They Succeed, How They Fail.* New York: Vintage, 1979.

———. "Toward Class-Based Realignment of American Politics: A Movement Strategy." *Social Policy* 13, no. 3 (1983): 3–14.

Ponce de León, Juana, ed. *Our Word Is Our Weapon: Selected Writings of fInsurgente Marcos.* New York: Seven Stories Press, 2002.

Potter, Claire Bond, and Renee Christine Romano, eds. *Doing Recent History on Privacy, Copyright, Video Games, Institutional Review Boards, Activist Scholarship, and History That Talks Back.* Athens: University of Georgia Press, 2012.

Power, Margaret. "The US Movement in Solidarity with Chile in the 1970s." *Latin American Perspectives* 36, no. 6 (2009): 46–66.

Pratt, William C. "Using History to Make History? Progressive Farm Organizing during the Farm Revolt of the 1980s." *Annals of Iowa* 55, no. 1 (1996): 24–45.

Prison Research Education Action Project and Critical Resistance. *Instead of Prisons: A Handbook for Abolitionists.* Oakland, CA: Critical Resistance, 2005.

Pulido, Laura. *Black, Brown, Yellow, and Left Radical Activism in Southern California.* Berkeley: University of California Press, 2006.

Pulido, Laura, Laura R. Barraclough, and Wendy Cheng. *A People's Guide to Los Angeles.* Berkeley: University of California Press, 2012.

Randolph, Sherie M. *Florynce "Flo" Kennedy: The Life of a Black Feminist Radical*. Chapel Hill: University of North Carolina Press, 2015.

Ransby, Barbara. *Ella Baker and the Black Freedom Movement a Radical Democratic Vision*. Chapel Hill: University of North Carolina Press, 2003.

———. *Making All Black Lives Matter: Reimagining Freedom in the Twenty-First Century*. Oakland: University of California Press, 2018.

Reddy, Chandan. *Freedom with Violence: Race, Sexuality, and the US State*. Durham, NC: Duke University Press, 2011.

Reed, Adolph Jr., ed. *Without Justice for All: The New Liberalism and Our Retreat from Racial Equality*. New York: Routledge, 1999.

Rich, B. Ruby. "New Queer Cinema." *Sight and Sound* 2, no. 5 (1992): 30–34.

Robinson, Cedric J. *Black Movements in America*. New York: Routledge, 1997.

Robinson, Nathan J. *Superpredator: Bill Clinton's Use and Abuse of Black America* Somerville, MA: Current Affairs Press, 2016.

Rodgers, Daniel T. *Age of Fracture*. Cambridge, MA: Harvard University Press, 2011.

Rorty, Richard. *Achieving Our Country: Leftist Thought in Twentieth-Century America*. Cambridge, MA: Harvard University Press, 1999.

Rosen, Ruth. *The World Split Open: How the Modern Women's Movement Changed America*. New York: Penguin, 2000.

Rosenblatt, Elihu, ed. *Criminal Injustice: Confronting the Prison Crisis*. Boston: South End Press, 1996.

Ross, Loretta, Lynn Roberts, Erika Derkas, Whitney Peoples, and Pamela Bridgewater, eds. *Radical Reproductive Justice: Foundation, Theory, Practice, Critique*. New York: Feminist Press at CUNY, 2017.

Rossinow, Doug. *The Reagan Era: A History of the 1980s*. New York: Columbia University Press, 2016.

Roth, Benita. *The Life and Death of ACT UP/LA: Anti-AIDS Activism in Los Angeles from the 1980s to the 2000s*. Cambridge: Cambridge University Press, 2017.

———. *Separate Roads to Feminism: Black, Chicana, and White Feminist Movements in America's Second Wave*. Cambridge: Cambridge University Press, 2003.

Saalfield, Catherine, and Ray Navarro. "Shocking Pink Praxis: Race and Gender on the ACT UP Frontlines." In *Inside/Out: Lesbian Theories, Gay Theories*, ed. Diana Fuss, 341–69. New York Routledge, 1991.

San Filippo, Roy, ed. *A New World in Our Hearts: Eight Years of Writings from the Love and Rage Revolutionary Anarchist Federation*. Oakland, CA: AK Press, 2003.

Sayles, James Yaki. *Meditations on Franz Fanon's "Wretched of the Earth": New Afrikan Revolutionary Writings*. Montreal: Kersplebedeb, 2010.

Scarce, Rik. *Eco-Warriors: Understanding the Radical Environmental Movement*. Walnut Creek, CA: Left Coast Press, 2006.

Schmalzer, Sigrid, Daniel S. Chard, and Alyssa Botelho, eds. *Science for the People: Documents from America's Movement of Radical Scientists*. Amherst: University of Massachusetts Press, 2018.

Schrader, Stuart. *Badges Without Borders: How Global Counterinsurgency Transformed American Policing*. Oakland: University of California Press, 2019.

Schweik, Susan. "Lomax's Matrix: Disability, Solidarity, and the Black Power of 504." In *Foundations of Disability Studies*, ed. Matthew Wappett and Katrina Arndt, 105–23. New York: Palgrave, 2013.

Segrest, Mab. *Memoir of a Race Traitor*. Boston, MA: South End Press, 1994.

Self, Robert O. *All in the Family: The Realignment of American Democracy Since the 1960s*. New York: Hill and Wang, 2013.

Sen, Rinku. *Stir It Up: Lessons in Community Organizing and Advocacy*. San Francisco: Jossey-Bass, 2003.

Shakur, Assata. *Assata: An Autobiography*. London: Zed Books, 1987.

Shepard, Benjamin, and Ronald Hayduk, eds. *From ACT UP to the WTO: Urban Protest and Community Building in an Age of Globalization*. New York: Verso, 2002.

Shinnick, Phillip. "Natural Sport, the Olympic Prison, and the Fight for Sovereignty Rights of the Mohawks." *Journal of Ethnic Studies* 9, no. 1 (1981): 43–52.

Singh, Nikhil Pal. *Race and America's Long War*. Oakland: University of California, 2017.

Smith, Neil. "Contours of a Spatialized Politics: Homeless Vehicles and the Production of Geographical Scale." *Social Text* 33 (1992): 55–81.

———. *The New Urban Frontier: Gentrification and the Revanchist City*. London: Routledge, 1996.

Smith, Paul Chaat, and Robert Allen Warrior. *Like a Hurricane: The Indian Movement from Alcatraz to Wounded Knee*. New York: New Press, 1996.

Solnit, David, ed. *Globalize Liberation: How to Uproot the System and Build a Better World*. San Francisco: City Lights Books, 2004.

Solnit, David, and Rebecca Solnit, eds. *The Battle of the Story of the Battle of Seattle*. Oakland, CA: AK Press 2009.

Solnit, Rebecca. *Savage Dreams: A Journey into the Hidden Wars of the American West*. San Francisco: Sierra Club Books, 1994.

Sonnie, Amy, and James Tracy. *Hillbilly Nationalists, Urban Race Rebels, and Black Power: Community Organizing in Radical Times*. New York: Melville House, 2011.

Spira, Tamara Lea. "Intimate Internationalisms: 1970s and 'Third World' Feminist and Queer Solidarity with the Chilean Revolution." *Feminist Theory* 15, no. 2 (2014): 119–36.

Springer, Kimberly. *Living for the Revolution: Black Feminist Organizations, 1968–1980*. Durham, NC: Duke University Press, 2005.

Starhawk. *Webs of Power: Notes from the Global Uprising*. Gabriola Island, BC: New Society Publishers, 2002.

Staudenmaier, Michael. *Truth and Revolution: A History of the Sojourner Truth Organization, 1969–1986*. Oakland, CA: AK Press, 2012.

Strub, Whitney. *Perversion for Profit: The Politics of Pornography and the Rise of the New Right*. New York: Columbia University Press, 2013.

Sze, Julie. *Noxious New York: The Racial Politics of Urban Health and Environmental Justice*. Cambridge, MA: MIT Press, 2007.

Taylor, Keeanga-Yamahtta. *From #BlackLivesMatter to Black Liberation*. Chicago: Haymarket Books, 2016.

———. *How We Get Free: Black Feminism and the Combahee River Collective*. Chicago: Haymarket Books, 2017.

Thompson, Becky. "Multiracial Feminism: Recasting the Chronology of Second Wave Feminism." *Feminist Studies* 28, no. 2 (2002): 337–60.

———. *A Promise and a Way of Life: White Antiracist Activism*. Minneapolis: University of Minnesota Press, 2001.

Thompson, Heather Ann. *Blood in the Water: The Attica Prison Uprising of 1971 and Its Legacy*. New York: Pantheon, 2016.

Thuma, Emily. "Against the 'Prison/Psychiatric State': Anti-Violence Feminisms and the Politics of Confinement in the 1970s." *Feminist Formations* 26, no. 2 (2014): 26–51.

———. *All Our Trials: Prisons, Policing, and the Feminist Fight to End Violence*. Champaign: University of Illinois Press, 2019.

———. "Lessons in Self-Defense: Gender Violence, Racial Criminalization, and Anti-carceral Feminism." *Women's Studies Quarterly* 43, nos. 3/4 (2015): 52–71.

Torres, Andrés, and José E. Velázquez, eds. *The Puerto Rican Movement: Voices from the Diaspora*. Philadelphia: Temple University Press, 1998.

United in Anger: A History of ACT UP. Directed by Jim Hubbard and Sarah Schulman, 2012.

Vaid, Urvashi. *Virtual Equality: The Mainstreaming of Gay and Lesbian Liberation*. New York: Anchor, 1996.

Vigil, Ernesto B. *The Crusade for Justice: Chicano Militancy and the Government's War on Dissent*. Madison: University of Wisconsin Press, 1999.

Vitale, Alex. *The End of Policing*. New York: Verso, 2017.

Voices from the Front. Directed by Testing the Limits Collective, 1992.

Wacquant, Loïc. "Three Steps to a Historical Anthropology of Actually Existing Neoliberalism." *Social Anthropology* 20, no. 1 (2012): 66–79.

Wainwright, Joel, and Morgan Robertson. "Territorialization, Science, and the Colonial State: The Case of Highway 55 in Minnesota." *Cultural Geographies* 10, no. 2 (2003): 196–217.

Wall, Derek. *Earth First! and the Anti-Roads Movement: Radical Environmentalism and Comparative Social Movements*. London: Routledge, 1999.

Ward, Stephen M., ed. *Pages from a Black Radical's Notebook: A James Boggs Reader*. Detroit, MI: Wayne State University Press, 2011.

Weather Underground. *Prairie Fire: The Politics of Revolutionary Anti-Imperialism*. San Francisco: Communications Co., 1974.

Whitebear, Bernie. "Taking Back Fort Lawton: Meeting the Needs of Seattle's Native American Community Through Conversion." *Race, Poverty and the Environment* 4/5, no. 1 (1994): 3–6.

Whitlock, Kay, and Michael Bronski. *Considering Hate: Violence, Goodness, and Justice in American Culture and Politics*. Boston: Beacon Press, 2015.

Wiegman, Robyn. *Object Lessons*. Durham, NC: Duke University Press, 2012.

Wilkinson, Charles F. *Messages from Frank's Landing: A Story of Salmon, Treaties, and the Indian Way*. Seattle: University of Washington Press, 2000.

Windham, Lane. *Knocking on Labor's Door: Union Organizing in the 1970s and the Roots of a New Economic Divide*. Chapel Hill: University of North Carolina Press, 2017.

Witham, Nick. *The Cultural Left and the Reagan Era: US Protest and the Central American Revolution*. London: I.B. Tauris, 2015.

Wojnarowicz, David. *Close to the Knives: A Memoir of Disintegration*. New York: Vintage, 1991.

Woodhouse, Keith Makato. *The Ecocentrists: A History of Radical Environmentalism*. New York: Columbia University Press, 2018.

Zaretsky, Natasha. *No Direction Home: The American Family and the Fear of National Decline, 1968–1980*. Chapel Hill: University of North Carolina Press, 2007.

———. *Radiation Nation: Three Mile Island and the Political Transformation of the 1970s*. New York: Columbia University Press, 2018.

Zinn, Howard. *A People's History of the United States*. New York: Harper Perennial, 2003.

DOCUMENT SOURCES AND PERMISSIONS

Part 1. Bodies and Lives

Section A. Feminist and Queer Flashpoints

1.A.1.   Combahee River Collective, "A Black Feminist Statement," in *This Bridge Called My Back*, ed. Cherríe Moraga and Gloria Anzaldúa (Latham, NY: Kitchen Table, 1981), 210, 212–14, 217–18. Reprinted with permission by Zillah Eisenstein and Barbara Smith.

1.A.2.   Iris Morales, "Sterilized Puerto Ricans," in *The Young Lords: A Reader*, ed. Darrel Enck-Wanzer (New York: New York University Press, 2010), 165–66. Reprinted with permission by Iris Morales.

1.A.3.   United Front, "Forward Macho," *Hansen Free Press* 2, no. 1 (1973): 4–5.

1.A.4a.   "Racist Sexism in the Trial," *The Feminist* (November 1974): 2, 12. Reprinted with permission by Gale/Cengage.

1.A.4b.   "We Need the Power to Defend Ourselves!," *The Feminist* (April 1975): 2. Reprinted with permission by Gale/Cengage.

1.A.5.   Yvonne Swan, witness statement, in *Crimes against Women: Proceedings of the International Tribunal*, ed. Diana E. H. Russell and Nicole Van de Ven (Berkeley, CA: Russell Publications, 1990), 70–72. Reprinted with permission by Yvonne Swan.

1.A.6.   Lavender and Red Union, "Gay Liberation/Socialist Revolution," in *The Lavender and Red Book: A Gay Liberation/Socialist Anthology* (Los Angeles: Lavender and Red Union/Peace Press, 1976), 51–52. Document courtesy of ONE Archives at the USC Libraries.

1.A.7.   Robin McDuff, Deanne Pernell, and Karen Saunders, "An Open Letter to the Antirape Movement," *Second Wave: A Magazine of the New Feminism* 5, no. 1 (1977): 11–13. Reprinted with permission by *Second Wave*.

1.A.8.   Daniel Tsang, "Third World Lesbians and Gays Meet," *Gay Insurgent* 6 (Summer 1980): 11. Reprinted with permission by Daniel Tsang.

1.A.9.   Joseph Beam, "Caring for Each Other," *Black/Out: The Magazine of the National Coalition of Black Lesbians and Gays* 1, no. 1 (1986): 9. Reprinted with permission by the estate of Joseph Beam.

1.A.10.   AIDS Action Pledge, "AIDS Action Pledge," *Call* (Autumn/Winter 1987). Ephemera Collection (AIDS Action Pledge Folder), Gay, Lesbian, Bisexual, Transgender Historical Society. Document courtesy of Gay, Lesbian, Bisexual, Transgender Historical Society.

1.A.11.   Vito Russo, "Why We Fight," ACT UP demonstration, Albany, New York, May 9, 1988. Reprinted with permission by Arnie Kantrowitz.

1.A.12.   ACT UP/Golden Gate, "Say It!! Women Get AIDS," press release, 1991. Queer Nation Records, Gay, Lesbian, Bisexual, Transgender Historical Society. Document courtesy of Gay, Lesbian, Bisexual, Transgender Historical Society.

Reprinted with permission by Michael Lauro for Survive AIDS (formerly ACT UP/Golden Gate).

1.A.13a. Transgender Nation, letter to editor, *San Francisco Bay Times*, November 5, 1992, 14. Reprinted with permission by Susan Stryker.

1.A.14. Call Off Your Old Tired Ethics, brochure, 1993. Document courtesy of Archives and Special Collections, University of California San Francisco Library. Reprinted with permission by Norma Jean Almodovar, COYOTE-LA.

1.A.15. Critical Resistance and INCITE! Women of Color against Violence, "Gender Violence and the Prison-Industrial Complex," in *Color of Violence: The INCITE! Anthology*, ed. INCITE! Women of Color against Violence (Durham: Duke University Press, 2016), 223–26. Reprinted with permission by Duke University Press.

Section B. Fighting the Right

1.B.1. Ellen Shaffer, "*Bakke*: Fighting and Winning Together," *Union WAGE*, July-August 1977, 2, 11. Reprinted with permission by San Francisco State University Labor Archives and Research Center.

1.B.2. John Brown Anti-Klan Committee, *The Dividing Line of the 80s: Take a Stand against the Klan* (1979): 2–3, 30–31. Document courtesy of Freedom Archives.

1.B.3. National Anti-Klan Network, "Call for February 2nd Mobilization, Greensboro, North Carolina," letter, December 19, 1979.

1.B.4. Tede Matthews, "Speech at Anti–Moral Majority Demonstration," San Francisco, July 12, 1984. Printed with permission by Charles Barragan for the Tede Matthews Archive, San Francisco.

1.B.5. Feminist Anti-Censorship Taskforce, "Feminism and Censorship: Strange Bedfellows?," flyer, 1985. Reprinted with permission by Ann Snitow.

1.B.6. WHAM! (Women's Health Action Mobilization), *No Choice, No Liberty* (New York: WHAM!, 1991), 3–4. Reprinted with permission by Elizabeth Meixell.

1.B.7. Washington Area Clinic Defense Task Force, "Goals and Guidelines," 1990s. Reprinted with permission by Washington Area Clinic Defense Task Force.

1.B.8. Anti-Racist Action, "Points of Unity," 1990s. https://antiracistaction.org/points-of-unity.

1.B.9. "African American Women in Defense of Ourselves," *Black Scholar* 22, nos. 1/2 (1991–92): 155. Reprinted with permission by Taylor and Francis on behalf of the Black World Foundation.

1.B.10. Marcy Westerling, "Rallying against the Right: A Case Study in Rural Organizing," *Oregon Witness: The Journal of the Coalition for Human Dignity* 2, no. 1 (1992): 20.

1.B.11. Korean Immigrant Workers Advocates, editorial, *KIWA News* (Summer 1996): 2. Document courtesy of University of California, Berkeley, Ethnic Studies Library, Asian American Organizations and Newsletters. Reprinted with permission by Koreatown Immigrant Workers Alliance (formerly Korean Immigrant Workers Alliance).

1.B.12. Kiwi Collective, "Race and Sex: Who's Panicking?," *Black Leather in Color* 8 (Fall/Winter 2000): 25–26. Reprinted with permission by Lidell Jackson.

Section C. Labors of Survival

1.C.1. Las Vegas National Welfare Rights Organization, "Attention, Sisters," in *Welfare: A Documentary History of US Policy and Politics*, ed. Gwendolyn Mink and Rickie Solinger (New York: New York University Press, 2003), 357. Reprinted with permission by Ruby Duncan.

1.C.2.   White Lightning, "Drug Plague—a Revolutionary Solution," *White Lightning* 15 (April 1973): 11. Document courtesy of Freedom Archives.

1.C.3.   Great Lakes Steal, "Women at Great Lakes Steel," *Great Lakes Steal* 3, no. 1 (1973): 1.

1.C.4.   Women's Brigade of the Weather Underground, "Message from Sisters Who Bombed HEW for International Women's Day," 1974. Document courtesy of Interference Archive.

1.C.5.   Coretta Scott King, statement of Coretta Scott King, in *Hearings on Equal Opportunity and Full Employment, HR 50, April 4, 1975*, 94th Cong. 1st sess. (Washington, DC: GPO, 1975), 253–56.

1.C.6.   Auto Workers United to Fight in '76, "Letter from Rich Off Our Backs July 4 Coalition," *'76 Contracts—A Time to Fight!* 2 (June–July 1976): 6.

1.C.7.   Victoria Frankovich, "Frankovich Reflects on Our Past—and the Evolution to Today," *Off the Line: The Newsletter of Un-Flight Services* (Fall 1986): 1–2, 10.

1.C.8.   September Alliance for Accessible Transit, "Why Are We Here?," flyer, 1987. Disability Rights and Education Defense Fund Collection, carton 27, folder 64, Bancroft Library Special Collections, UC Berkeley.

1.C.9.   John Mehring, "Union's AIDS Education Committee Helps Health Care Workers, Patients," *Labor Notes* (August 1987): 5. Reprinted with permission by *Labor Notes*.

1.C.10. Marian Kramer, "Remarks on the National Welfare Rights Union," *Social Justice* 21, no. 1 (55) (1994): 9–11. Reprinted with permission by *Social Justice*.

1.C.11. Milwaukee Welfare Warriors, "Apologies Don't Help," in *For Crying Out Loud: Women's Poverty in the United States*, ed. Diane Dujon and Ann Withorn (Boston: South End Press, 1996), 367–68. Reprinted with permission by Ann Withorn.

1.C.12. Mary Beth Maxwell, interview on Jobs with Justice, in *Jobs with Justice: 25 Years, 25 Voices*, ed. Eric Larson (Oakland, CA: PM Press, 2013), 95–105. Reprinted with permission by PM Press.

1.C.13. Tyree Scott, "Whose Movement Is It Anyway?," 1997, unpublished essay. Printed with permission by Cindy Domingo.

Part 2. Walls and Gates

Section A. Resisting Repression

2.A.1.   Lynn Cooper, Elliot Currie, Jon Frappier, Tony Platt, Betty Ryan, Richard Schauffler, Joy Scruggs, and Larry Trujillo, *The Iron Fist and the Velvet Glove: An Analysis of US Police* (Berkeley, CA: Center for Research on Criminal Justice, 1975), 153–58. Reprinted with permission by *Social Justice*.

2.A.2.   Lesbians against Police Violence, interview with Barbara Lubinski, 1979. KP 289: General Materials, Freedom Archives. Document courtesy of Freedom Archives.

2.A.3.   Leonard Peltier, "Convicted for Being Chippewa and Sioux Blood," in *The Indigenous Voice*, ed. Roger Moody (Utrecht: International Books, 1993), 330–33. Reprinted with permission by Leonard Peltier.

2.A.4.   National Coalition for Redress/Reparations, postconference brochure, 1980. Reprinted with permission by National Coalition for Redress/Reparations.

2.A.5.   James J. Zogby, "Senate Subcommittee on Security and Terrorism: A Threat to Arab Americans?," 1981. Nabeel Abraham Papers, box 1, folder ADC, Bentley Historical Library, University of Michigan. Reprinted with permission by Bentley Historical Library, University of Michigan.

2.A.6.   Michael Zinzun, "Zinzun on Police Abuse," *CAPA Report* (July 1983): 8. Document courtesy of Southern California Library.

2.A.7.   Red Guerrilla Resistance, communiqué on the bombing of the Police Benevolent Association, 1985.

2.A.8.   Terry Bisson, "RSVP to the FBI," in *Hauling Up the Morning*, ed. Tim Blunk, Raymond Luc Levasseur, and Terry Bisson (Trenton, NJ: Red Sea Press, 1990), 241–43. Reprinted with permission by Terry Bisson.

2.A.9.   "Draw the Line" advertisement, 1985.

2.A.10.   Brian Glick, *War at Home: Covert Action against US Activists and What We Can Do about It* (Boston: South End Press, 1989), 53–59. Reprinted with permission by Brian Glick.

2.A.11.   Labor/Community Strategy Center, *A Call to Reject the Federal Weed and Seed Program* (Los Angeles: Labor/Community Strategy Center, 1992), 2. Reprinted with permission by Eric Mann.

2.A.12.   Love and Rage Revolutionary Anarchist Federation, "Copwatch: Keeping an Eye on the Cops," *Love and Rage*, special anti-cop issue (1995): 2. Reprinted with permission by Audrey Creed.

2.A.13.   Herman Bell et. al., "An Appeal from US Political Prisoners/POWs: Mobilize to Save Mumia Abu-Jamal!," in *Let Freedom Ring*, ed. Matt Meyer (Oakland, CA: PM Press, 2008), 429–30. Reprinted with permission by PM Press.

Section B. Undermining the Prison State

2.B.1.   Red Family, "War behind Walls," *War behind Walls* (September 1971): 1, 6–7, 16. Document courtesy of Tony Platt.

2.B.2.   "How Many Lives?" *off our backs* 2, no. 1 (1971): 1. Reprinted with permission by Karla Mantilla.

2.B.3.   North Carolina Prisoners' Labor Union, "Goals of the North Carolina Prisoners' Labor Union" (1974). T. J. Reddy Collections, Special Collections, University of North Carolina Charlotte. Reprinted with permission by Chuck Eppinette.

2.B.4.   National Council on Crime and Delinquency/Unitarian Universalist Service Committee, National Moratorium on Prison Construction flyer, 1976. Reprinted with permission by Rachel Gore Freed, Unitarian Universalist Service Committee.

2.B.5.   George Jackson Brigade, communiqué on the bombing of the Washington Department of Corrections, in *Creating a Movement with Teeth: A Documentary History of the George Jackson Brigade*, ed. Daniel Burton-Rose (Oakland, CA: PM Press, 2010), 77–79. Reprinted with permission by PM Press.

2.B.6.   Sundiata Acoli, "Prison Struggles and Human Rights," in *Sunviews* (Newark, NJ: Creative Images, 1983), 29–31. Reprinted with permission by Sundiata Acoli.

2.B.7a.   Black Liberation Army Coordinating Committee, special communiqué on the freeing of sister Assata Shakur, *Arm the Spirit* 36 (February/April 1980): 4.

2.B.7b.   Assata Shakur, "Statement from Assata Shakur," *Arm the Spirit* 36 (February/April 1980): 4–5, 15.

2.B.8.   "Letter from North American Political Prisoners," 1986. Document courtesy of Dan Berger.

2.B.9.   Rafael Cancel Miranda, speech to stop the Florence Control Unit, *Walkin' Steel: CEML Newsletter* 1, no. 1 (1991): 8. Reprinted with permission by Rafael Cancel Miranda.

2.B.10.   Laura Whitehorn, "Collectively Asserting Life over Death Creates Power!," in *Voices from Inside: Prisoners Respond to the AIDS Crisis*, ed. ACT UP/San Francisco Prison Issues Committee (San Francisco: ACT UP San Francisco, 1993), 35–37. Prisons box, Whitehorn materials, Interference Archive. Document courtesy of Interference Archive. Reprinted with permission by Laura Whitehorn.

2.B.11.   Bill Dunne, "Crack in the Federal Scheme: The October Rebellion of 1995," *Prison Legal News*, October 15, 2000, 16. Reprinted with permission by *Prison Legal News*.

2.B.12.   Safiya Bukhari, "Q&A on Jericho 98," in *The War Before: The True Story of Becoming a Black Panther, Keeping the Faith in Prison, and Fighting for Those Left Behind*, ed. Laura Whitehorn (New York: Feminist Press, 2010), 206–15. Reprinted with permission by Laura Whitehorn.

2.B.13   California Coalition for Women Prisoners, "Critical Resistance: Expanding Our Vision of What Is Possible," *Fire Inside* 9 (September 1998). Reprinted with permission by Diana Block.

2.B.14.   Brigette Sarabi, "Building the Prison Reform Movement," *Justice Matters* 2, no. 3 (2000): 10–11. Document courtesy of the Washington Prison History Project Archive, University of Washington Bothell/Cascadia College Library.

Section C. Fight for the City, Free the Land

2.C.1.   Yellow Seeds, "Unite to Fight for Democratic Rights," *Yellow Seeds* 2, no. 6 (1975): 5. Reprinted with permission by Mary Yee.

2.C.2.   Chester Hartman, "The Struggle for the I-Hotel: What We Won, What We Lost, What We Learned," *Common Sense* 4, no. 10 (1977): 1, 9. Reprinted with permission by Max Elbaum.

2.C.3.   James Yaki Sayles, "War for the Cities," in Sayles, *Meditations on Frantz Fanon's "Wretched of the Earth"* (Montreal: Kersplebedeb, 2010), 43–58. Reprinted with permission by Spear and Shield Publications.

2.C.4.   Association of Community Organizations for Reform Now, "People's Platform," 1978. Association of Community Organizations for Reform Now Papers, part 2, M94–006, box 9, Wisconsin Historical Society. Reprinted with permission by Wisconsin Historical Society.

2.C.5.   Willie Baptist, "Five Main Slogans: Lessons from the History of the National Union of the Homeless," flyer (1993). Reprinted with permission by Willie Baptist.

2.C.6.   James Boggs, "Rebuilding Detroit: An Alternative to Casino Gambling", in *Pages from a Black Radical's Notebook*, ed. Stephen Ward (Detroit, MI: Wayne State University Press, 2011), 341–46. Reprinted with permission by James and Grace Lee Boggs Trust/Foundation.

2.C.7.   Crips and Bloods, "Plan for the Reconstruction of Los Angeles: Give Us the Hammer and the Nails, We Will Rebuild the City," 1992. Reprinted with permission by Southern California Library.

2.C.8.   Eric Mann, *A New Vision for Urban Transportation* (Los Angeles: Strategy Center Publications, 1996), 1–3. Reprinted with permission by Eric Mann.

2.C.9.   Elizabeth Betita Martinez, "Be Down with the Brown!," in *De Colores Means All of Us: Latina Views for a Multicolored Century* (Cambridge, MA: South End Press, 1996), 200–226. Reprinted with permission by Tess Konig-Martinez.

2.C.10.   CopWatch Atlanta, "Atlanta '96: No Room at the Inn but Plenty of Room at the Jail," *North Ave Review* 23 (Fall 1995): https://smartech.gatech.edu/handle/1853/10644.

2.C.11. Queer to the Left, "Housing Is a Queer Issue," flyer distributed at Chicago Pride Parade, 2002. Reprinted with permission by Deborah Gould.

Part 3. Borders and Maps

Section A. Anti-Imperialism beyond Vietnam

3.A.1. Association of Arab-American University Graduates, "Statement Adopted at the AAUG Sixth Annual Convention," October 21, 1973, 1–3. Eastern Michigan University Archives, AAUG Collection, 018.AUUG, box 26. Reprinted with permission by Eastern Michigan University Archives.

3.A.2. Fuerzas Armadas de Liberación Nacional Puertorriqueña, "Communiqué No. 1," October 26, 1974, New York, NY.

3.A.3. US Out of Korea Committee, "When People Here Are Hungry, Should Your Dollars Go for War and Dictatorship in South Korea?," flyer for Rally to End US Intervention in Korea, 1977. Anar-Anti box, antiwar folder, Interference Archive. Document courtesy of Interference Archive.

3.A.4. International Indian Treaty Council, "Decolonization, Liberation, and the International Community," *Treaty Council News* (December 1977): 3–4. Inventory of the Roger A. Finzel American Indian Movement Papers, 1965–95, Special Collections and Center for Southwest Research, University of New Mexico Libraries. Reprinted with permission by Center for Southwest Research and Special Collections.

3.A.5. National Resistance Committee, "Resistance Statements," *Resistance News*, October 3, 1980. Document courtesy of Matt Meyer.

3.A.6. Women's Pentagon Action, "Unity Statement," *Social Justice* 27, no. 4 (82) (2000): 160–63. Reprinted with permission by *Social Justice*.

3.A.7. Armed Resistance Unit, "Communiqué from the Armed Resistance Unit, April 26, 1983." Anar-Anti box, antiwar folder, Interference Archive. Document courtesy of Interference Archive.

3.A.8. Palestine Human Rights Campaign, "No Vietnams in Central America or the Middle East," pamphlet, 1984.

3.A.9. Lesbians and Gays Against Intervention, "Principles of Unity" (1983). Reprinted with permission by LAGAI-Queer Insurrection (formerly Lesbians and Gays Against Intervention).

3.A.10. Marisa Pruitt, "Victoria Mercado Brigade," *Voices* 5 (Fall 1985): 13. Reprinted with permission by Amy Bank.

3.A.11. Committee in Solidarity with the People of El Salvador, "Convention Decisions," 1985 convention report. Nicaragua Information Center collection, BANC MSS 92–807, carton 10, folder 21, Bancroft Library Special Collections, University of California, Berkeley. Reprinted with permission by CISPES.

3.A.12. Witness for Peace, brochure, 1985. Nicaragua Information Center collection, BANC MSS 92–807, carton 9, folder 24, Bancroft Library Special Collections, University of California, Berkeley.

3.A.13. Pledge of Resistance, "The Pledge of Resistance: A Growing, Nonviolent Movement for Peace in Central America," flyer, 1986. Pledge of Resistance Collection, box 3, folder 35, Graduate Theological Union Archives, Graduate Theological Union. Reprinted with permission by Kenneth Butigan.

3.A.14. Rio Grande Defense Committee, statement regarding US policy in Central America and description of the Border Witness Program, 1991. National

Sanctuary Defense Fund records, 98-9-04, box 7, folder 1, Graduate Theological Union Archives, Graduate Theological Union. Reprinted with permission by Graduate Theological Union.

Section B. From Anti-Imperialism to Global Justice

3.B.1.   African Liberation Day Coalition, "Fight Imperialism and National Oppression from the USA to the USA," flyer, 1977. Printed Ephemera on Organizations, PE 36, African Liberation Day Folder, New York University Tamiment Library.

3.B.2.   Bay Area Free South Africa Movement, "Statement of Purpose," 1985. African Activist Archive, Michigan State University. Reprinted with permission by David Bacon.

3.B.3.   Africa Fund, "National Weeks of Anti-Apartheid Action Spark Spring Campus Upsurge," *Student Anti-Apartheid Newsletter* (Spring 1986): 1–2. African Activist Archive, Michigan State University.

3.B.4.   Justice for Janitors, "What Is Justice for Janitors?," strike flyer, 1990. Service Employees International Union, United Service Workers West Records, coll. 1940, UCLA Library. Reprinted with permission by UCLA Library.

3.B.5.   Lillian Galedo, "No One Is 'Illegal,'" *Bigayan* (Summer 1994): 2. Asian American Organizations and Newsletters (Filipinos for Affirmative Action), UC Berkeley Ethnic Studies Library. Reprinted with permission by Filipino Advocates for Justice (formerly Filipinos for Affirmative Action).

3.B.6.   Nora Rosenberg, "The Sweat-Free Campus Campaign," *Infusion: National Magazine for Progressive Student Activists* (December 1998–January 1999): 4. Jeremy Simer Papers, box 2, folder 6: Publications, 1992–98, University of Washington Special Collections. Reprinted with permission by Nora Rosenberg.

3.B.7.   Jessica Roach, "Strawberry Workers Fight to Organize," *Ruckus* 5 (April 1998): 4–5. Jeremy Simer Papers, box 2, folder 6: Publications, 1992–98, University of Washington Special Collections. Reprinted with permission by Jessica Roach.

3.B.8a.   Stephanie Guilloud, "Why Come to Seattle?," in *The Battle of the Story of the Battle of Seattle*, ed. David Solnit and Rebecca Solnit (Oakland, CA: AK Press, 2009): 109–10. Reprinted with permission by Stephanie Guilloud.

3.B.8b.   Direct Action Network, "Globalize Liberation Not Corporate Power: A Call to Action," in *The Battle of the Story of the Battle of Seattle*, ed. David Solnit and Rebecca Solnit (Oakland, CA: AK Press, 2009): 111–13. Reprinted with permission by Stephanie Guilloud.

3.B.9.   D2KLA, "Direct Action: Challenge the Republican and Democratic Parties This Summer in Philadelphia and Los Angeles," in "D2KLA Guide," 2000. Reprinted with permission by L. A. Kauffman.

3.B.10.   Catalyst Project, "Tools for Antiracist Organizing," 2002. Reprinted with permission by Catalyst Project.

3.B.11.   Farm Labor Organizing Committee, "Campaign for Legalization of Undocumented Immigrants Winning Support," 2001. Rosalinda Guillen Papers, University of Washington Special Collections. Reprinted with permission by Farm Labor Organizing Committee.

3.B.12.   Coalition of Immokalee Workers, "Consciousness + Commitment = Change," in *Globalize Liberation: How to Uproot the System and Build a Better World*, ed. David Solnit (San Francisco: City Lights Books, 2004), 347–60. Reprinted with permission by Coalition of Immokalee Workers.

Section C. Not in Our Name

3.C.1.   Confederation of Iranian Students, "Condemn Shah's US Visit; Free One Hundred Thousand Political Prisoners in Iran," 1977. Iran folder, H-I box, Interference Archive. Document courtesy of Interference Archive.

3.C.2.   Palestine Solidarity Committee, letter to supporters, 1980. Printed Ephemera on Organizations, PE 36, Palestine Solidarity Committee folder, New York University Tamiment Library.

3.C.3.   No More Witch Hunts, "No More Witch Hunts: A Day of Resistance," flyer, 1981. Printed Ephemera on Organizations, PE 36, No More Witch Hunts folder, New York University Tamiment Library.

3.C.4.   New Jewish Agenda, "New Jewish Agenda National Platform," in Ezra Berkley Nepon, *Justice, Justice Shall You Pursue: A History of New Jewish Agenda* (Oakland, CA: Thread Makes Blanket Press, 2012), 113–32. Reprinted with permission by Gerald Serotta.

3.C.5.   Joseph Gerson, introduction to *The Deadly Connection: Nuclear War and US Intervention* (Philadelphia: New Society Publishers, 1986), 2–8. Reprinted with permission by Joseph Gerson.

3.C.6.   Rachelle Marshall, "From Israel to America: The Women in Black," *Washington Report on Middle East Affairs* (February 1990): 8, 53. Reprinted with permission by *Washington Report on Middle East Affairs*.

3.C.7.   Out Now, *War Watch* special report, *War Watch* 5 (March 1991): 6–8. Reprinted with permission by Susan Davidoff.

3.C.8.   Roots Against War, "Queers Get RAW!," 1991. Queer Nation Records, Gay, Lesbian, Bisexual, Transgender Historical Society. Reprinted with permission by of Gay, Lesbian, Bisexual, Transgender Historical Society.

3.C.9.   Angela Davis, "Keynote Speech Delivered at CAAAV's Fifteenth Anniversary Fundraiser in New York City," in *Another World Is Possible*, ed. Jee Kim et al. (Chicago: Subway and Elevated Press, 2002): 49–54. Reprinted with permission by Billy Wimsatt for Subway and Elevated Press.

3.C.10.   Purvi Shah, Sakhi for South Asian Women, "The Rain of Sorrows," in *Another World is Possible*, ed. Jee Kim et al. (Chicago: Subway and Elevated Press, 2002): 107–9. Reprinted with permission by Billy Wimsatt for Subway and Elevated Press.

3.C.11.   Not in Our Name, "Pledge of Resistance," 2002.

3.C.12.   Retort, "Neither Their War nor Their Peace," broadsheet, February 15, 2003. Reprinted with permission by Iain Boal, T. J. Clark, Joseph Matthews, and Michael Watts.

Part 4. Utopias and Dystopias

Section A. Stopping the End of the World

4.A.1a.   Coalition for Direct Action at Seabrook/Clamshell Alliance, *Occupation/Blockade Handbook* (Seabrook, NH: Clamshell Alliance, 1980), np.

4.A.1b.   Blockade the Bombmakers, *Civil Disobedience Campaign Handbook* (New York: Civil Disobedience Campaign, 1982) 33–35, 13.

4.A.1c.   Livermore Action Group, *Livermore Weapons Lab Blockade/Demonstration Handbook* (Berkeley, CA: Livermore Action Group, 1982), 40, 58–60.

4.A.1d.   Unconventional Action, *Unconventional Action Guidebook* (Chicago: Unconventional Action, 1996), 26–27.

4.A.2a.   Clamshell Alliance, "We Can Stop the Seabrook Power Plant," 1977. Plowshares 8 Collected Records, Swarthmore College Peace Collection. Document courtesy of Swarthmore College Peace Collection.

4.A.2b. Clamshell Alliance, "Declaration of Nuclear Resistance," 1977. Plowshares 8 Collected Records, Swarthmore College Peace Collection. Document courtesy of Swarthmore College Peace Collection.

4.A.3. Clams for Democracy, flyer, 1978. Document courtesy of L. A. Kauffman.

4.A.4. Bruce Kokopeli and George Lakey, *Leadership for Change: Toward a Feminist Model* (Philadelphia: New Society Publishers, 1984), 10–11, 20–23. Reprinted with permission by of George Lakey.

4.A.5. C. T. Butler and Keith McHenry, "Why Food Not Bombs?," in *Food Not Bombs: How to Feed the Hungry and Build Community* (San Francisco: Food Not Bombs, 1992). Reprinted with permission by Keith McHenry.

4.A.6. Black Hills Alliance, Black Hills Alliance position paper, *No Nukes Left!* (Summer 1980): 17.

4.A.7. Southwest Organizing Project and others, open letter to the National Wildlife Federation, 1990. www.ejnet.org/ej/swop.pdf.

4.A.8. First National People of Color Environmental Leadership Summit, "Principles of Environmental Justice," 1991. www.ejnet.org/ej/principles.html.

4.A.9. Indigenous Antinuclear Summit, declaration, 1996. www.ienearth.org/indigenous-anti-nuclear-summit-declaration.

4.A.10. Laotian Organizing Project, *Fighting Fire with Fire: Lessons from the Laotian Organizing Project's First Campaign* (Oakland, CA: Asian Pacific Environmental Network, 2001): 36–37. Reprinted with permission by Asian Pacific Environmental Network.

4.A.11. Dave Foreman, *Ecodefense: A Field Guide to Monkeywrenching* (Chico, CA: Ned Ludd Books 1985).

4.A.12. Judi Bari, "The Feminization of Earth First!," *Ms.*, May 1992. Reprinted with permission by Lisa Bari.

4.A.13. George Katsiaficas and Paul Messersmith-Glavin, *Why Wall Street? The Case for Green Direct Action* (New York: Earth Day Wall Street Action, 1990). Reprinted with permission by Paul Messersmith-Glavin.

4.A.14. Rod Coronado, "'Spread Your Love through Action': An Open Letter from Rod Coronado," *Earth First! Journal* 15, no. 4 (1995): 8. Reprinted with permission by Rod Coronado.

4.A.15a. Earth Liberation Front, "Frequently Asked Questions," in *Igniting a Revolution: Voices in Defense of the Earth*, ed. Steven Best and Anthony J. Nocella III (Oakland, CA: AK Press, 2006), 406–8.

4.A.15b. Earth Liberation Front, "Beltane, 1997" in *Igniting a Revolution: Voices in Defense of the Earth*, ed. Steven Best and Anthony J. Nocella III (Oakland, CA: AK Press, 2006), 408–10.

Section B. Left Visions in Transition

4.B.1. John Trudell, "We Are Power," speech delivered at the Black Hills International Survival Gathering, July 18, 1980. Reprinted with permission by Poet Tree Publishing/Drive Media Publishing for the John Trudell estate.

4.B.2. Center for Third World Organizing, "Voter Registration: Will It Build the Power of Low-Income People, or Deliver Them to the Democratic Party?," *Third Force: Newsletter of the Center for Third World Organizing*, fall 1983, 1–2. Nicaragua Information Center records, BANC MSS92/807 cz, carton 9:29, Bancroft Library Special Collections, University of California, Berkeley. Document courtesy of the Bancroft Library, University of California, Berkeley.

4.B.3.   Youth Greens, "Summary of Youth Green May Gathering," 1989. Reprinted with permission by Paul Messersmith-Glavin.

4.B.4.   Prairie Fire Organizing Committee, "Crisis in Socialism: The Discreet Charm of the Bourgeoisie," *Breakthrough* (Winter 1990): 3–4. Document courtesy of Freedom Archives. Reprinted with permission by Mickey Ellinger.

4.B.5   Joel Olson, "Why the Masses Ain't Asses," in *Making Punk a Threat Again!*, ed. Profane Existence (Minneapolis, MN: Profane Existence, 1997), 113–17. Reprinted with permission by Audrey Creed.

4.B.6.   Mab Segrest, "A Bridge, Not a Wedge," in Segrest, *Memoir of a Race Traitor* (Boston: South End Press, 1993), 229–46. Reprinted with by permission by the New Press.

4.B.7.   Blue Mountain Working Group, "A Call to Defend Democracy and Plural-ism," in *Defending Democracy: An Activist Resource Kit*, ed. Political Research Associates (Somerville, MA: Political Research Associates, 2001), 43–52. Reprinted with permission by Political Research Associates.

4.B.8.   Love and Rage Revolutionary Anarchist Federation, "What Kind of Revolu-tionary Organization Is Needed Today?," in *A New World in Our Hearts: Eight Years of Writing from Love and Rage Revolutionary Anarchist Federation*, ed. Roy San Filipo (Oakland, CA: AK Press, 2003), 65–66. Reprinted with permission by Audrey Creed.

4.B.9.   Labor Party, "A Call to Economic Justice: Platform of the Labor Party," 1996. www.thelaborparty.org/d_program.htm.

4.B.10.   Black Radical Congress, "A Black Freedom Agenda for the Twenty-First Cen-tury," *Black Scholar* 28, no. 1 (1998): 71–73. Reprinted with permission by Tay-lor and Francis on behalf of the Black World Foundation.

4.B.11.   Gary Delgado, "The Last Stop Sign," *Shelterforce*, November 1, 1998, 18–20. Reprinted with permission by Gary Delgado.

4.B.12.   Andrew Boyd, "Truth Is a Virus: Meme Warfare and the Billionaires for Bush (or Gore)," in *Cultural Resistance: A Reader*, ed. Stephen Duncombe (London: Verso, 2002), 369–78. Reprinted with permission by Andrew Boyd.

4.B.13.   West Palm Beach Radical Cheerleaders, "Rebel," in *The Radical Cheerbook* (Grand Rapids, MI: Sprout Anarchist Collective, 2012).

Section C. Land, Decolonization, and Interdependence

4.C.1.   Akwesasne Notes, ed., *Voices from Wounded Knee* (Rooseveltown, NY: Akwe-sasne Notes, 1975), 55, 62–64, 247–48.

4.C.2.   "We Will Remember" Survival School, pamphlet, 1974.

4.C.3.   Native American Rights Fund/National Indian Law Library, "The Declara-tion of Indian Independence," *Announcements* 3, no. 2, part 1 (1975): 28–32. Reprinted with permission by the National Indian Law Library, Boulder.

4.C.4.   Michael Figures, "Opening Address—Minority Landowners Conference," 1976. Emergency Land Fund Papers, Amistad Research Center, New Orleans. Document courtesy of Alec Hickmott and Amistad Research Center.

4.C.5.   Governing Board of the National Council of the Churches of Christ, *Rural Crisis: A Call for Justice and Action*, 1983. Document courtesy of David Ostendorf.

4.C.6.   Akinyele Umoja, "Why We Say 'Free the Land,'" *By Any Means Necessary* (ca. 1984): 10. Reprinted with permission by Akinyele Umoja.

4.C.7.   Hawai'i Ecumenical Coalition on Tourism, "The 1989 Hawai'i Declaration of the Hawai'i Ecumenical Coalition on Tourism," in Haunani-Kay Trask, *From a Native Daughter: Colonialism and Sovereignty in Hawai'i*, rev. ed. (Honolulu:

University of Hawai'i Press, 1999), 245–50. Reprinted with permission by of University of Hawaii Press.

4.C.8.   Winona LaDuke, "We Are Still Here: The Five Hundred Years Celebration," *Sojourners* 20, no. 8 (1991): 00–00. Reprinted with permission by *Sojourners, www.sojo.net.*

4.C.9.   League of Indigenous Sovereign Nations, "Draft Declaration of Principles," 1991. Reprinted with permission by Center for World Indigenous Studies, www.cwis.org.

4.C.10. Bernice Lalo, "Sovereignty: A Western Shoshone Perspective" (1994). Western Shoshone Defense Project Records, Special Collections and University Archives Department, University of Nevada, Reno. Reprinted with permission by Special Collections and University Archives Department, University of Nevada, Reno, Libraries.

4.C.11. Ashanti Alston, "Beyond Nationalism but Not without It," *Onward* 2, no. 4 (2002), 10–11. Reprinted with permission by Ashanti Alston.

4.C.12. Katherine Whitlock, *In the Time of Broken Bones* (Philadelphia: American Friends Service Committee, 2001), 40–50. Reprinted with permission by Katherine "Peach" Whitlock and the American Friends Service Committee.

CONTRIBUTORS

Editors

Dan Berger is an associate professor of comparative ethnic studies at the University of Washington Bothell and the author of *Captive Nation: Black Prison Organizing in the Civil Rights Era* (University of North Carolina Press, 2014), among other titles.

Emily K. Hobson is an associate professor of history and gender, race, and identity at the University of Nevada, Reno, and the author of *Lavender and Red: Liberation and Solidarity in the Gay and Lesbian Left* (University of California Press, 2016).

Snapshot Authors

Lumumba Akinwole-Bandele is a Brooklyn-based educator and organizer with decades of local, national, and international experience of human rights work. Lumumba currently serves on the boards of the Caribbean Cultural Center African Diaspora Institute and the Center for Constitutional Rights and is senior community organizer at the University of Washington Bothell.

Umayyah Cable is an assistant professor of American culture and film, television, and media at the University of Michigan, Ann Arbor. Their research and teaching interests span the fields of ethnic studies, film and media studies, postcolonial studies, and queer theory, with a particular focus on the roles that art, film, and media play in the mobilization of Palestine solidarity activism in the United States.

Marisa Chappell is an associate professor of history at Oregon State University. She is the author of *The War on Welfare: Family, Poverty, and Politics in Modern America* and has written about social policy, social movements, and inequality in recent United States history for both academic and public audiences.

Jih-Fei Cheng is an assistant professor of feminist, gender, and sexuality studies at Scripps College. He has been involved in HIV/AIDS social services, media production and curation, and queer of color grassroots organizations. His current book project examines the science, media, and activism of AIDS in relation to the colonial history of virology and the historical transformations of global capitalism.

Norma Stoltz Chinchilla is a professor emeritus from the Department of Sociology and the Department of Women's, Gender, and Sexuality Studies at California State University Long Beach. She was an activist in the Central American solidarity and sanctuary movements of the 1980s.

Joseph Nicholas DeFilippis was the founding executive director of Queers for Economic Justice and the former director of SAGE/Queens. He is currently an assistant professor of social work at Seattle University. He is the coeditor of the three-volume book series *After Marriage Equality*.

Chris Dixon is a longtime anarchist organizer, writer, and educator. Originally from Alaska, he lives in Ottawa, Canada, on unceded Algonquin territory, where he is a member of Punch Up Collective. His most recent book is *Another Politics: Talking across Today's Transformative Movements*. Find him at writingwithmovements.com.

Alexander Dwinell is a Brooklyn-based artist, publisher, and editor. As part of the South End Press collective he published such authors as Vandana Shiva, Mumia Abu-Jamal, and Oscar Olivera. Currently part of Common Notions, his exhibitions include Smack Mellon, Temporary Agency, and Carriage Trade and publications include *Latin American Perspectives*, *Emergency Index*, and *Stencil Pirates*.

Keona K. Ervin is an associate professor of history at the University of Missouri-Columbia and the author of *Gateway to Equality: Black Women and the Struggle for Economic Justice in St. Louis*.

Sekou M. Franklin is an associate professor in the Department of Political Science at Middle Tennessee State University and is the author of *After the Rebellion: Black Youth, Social Movements Activism, and the Post–Civil Rights Generation*.

Bob Fulkerson has been an organizer for social and environmental justice issues in Nevada since 1984. He lives in Reno with his husband, Mike Perrier, a public school counselor.

Craig Gilmore is one of the founders of California Prison Moratorium Project and former coeditor of *Prison Focus*.

Amanda Joyce Hall is a PhD candidate in history and African American Studies at Yale University. She is writing a dissertation on the global grassroots movement against South African apartheid during the 1970s and 1980s.

Grace Handy is an anarchist scholar and creator interested in critical theory, queer potentialities, and poetics. Handy graduated from Wesleyan University in 2018 and has been involved with Palestine liberation and prison abolitionist organizing as well as soundscape and bookmaking projects.

Vernon Damani Johnson has been a professor of political science at Western Washington University since 1986. He is currently also the director of the Ralph Munro Institute for Civic Education there. He was a founding member of the Whatcom Human Rights Task Force (state of Washington) in 1994 and the president of the Northwest Coalition for Human Dignity from 2000–2003.

Joo-Hyun Kang is a long-time queer organizer and currently director of Communities United for Police Reform, a New York City campaign fighting to end police violence and decrease reliance on/power of policing in daily life.

Stacy Kono was inspired to work on garment worker organizing because her grandma was a seamstress for many years and taught her that workers, especially immigrant and women of color workers, deserve respect for their labor. Kono lives in Berkeley, California.

Brooke Lober is a feminist scholar, teacher, and activist. In collaboration with the Freedom Archives, Lober is the director of the Women against Imperialism Oral History Project and is documenting the work of several collectives that reshaped the meaning of feminist and queer activism through their years of Bay Area–based transnational feminist organizing. Lober is a member of the Abolition Collective, for which she is co-editing a special issue on abolitionist feminisms.

Scholar-activist **Paul K. Longmore** was professor of history at San Francisco State University until his untimely death in 2010. His wide-ranging work included *The Inven-*

tion of George Washington, *The New Disability History: American Perspectives* (coedited with Lauri Umansky), *Why I Burned My Book and Other Essays on Disability*, and the posthumous publication of his magnum opus, *Telethons: Spectacle, Disability, and the Business of Charity.*

Simmy Makhijani teaches in the Department of Race and Resistance Studies and the Department of Asian American Studies at San Francisco State University. Makhijani is also cofounder and former codirector of United Roots, a green youth arts and media center in Oakland, California, and continues to be active in multiple activist/organizing spaces.

Matt Meyer is secretary-general of the International Peace Research Association and a senior research scholar for the Resistance Studies Initiative at the University of Massachusetts, Amherst. The author or editor of numerous books, most recently *White Lives Matter Most: And Other "Little" White Lies*, Meyer writes extensively on issues of decolonization, revolutionary nonviolence, political prisoners, and pan-Africanism.

Luis Alejandro Molina has organized for over thirty years in the Puerto Rican diaspora in New York, Hartford, San Francisco, and Chicago around issues including Puerto Rican political prisoners and Puerto Rican self-determination. He currently sits on the coordinating committee of the National Boricua Human Rights Network.

Isabell Moore is a community organizer, teacher, and supporter of Siembra NC living in Greensboro, North Carolina. She is a PhD candidate in history at the University of North Carolina, Chapel Hill.

Lydia Pelot-Hobbs researches and writes on mass incarceration, racial capitalism, and freedom movements in Louisiana. She has long been involved in antiprison and antipolicing activism and was a cofounder of AORTA (Anti-Oppression Resource and Training Alliance). She is currently an assistant professor of geography and African American and Africana studies at the University of Kentucky.

Jessi Quizar researches race and urban land struggles in the United States, particularly urban agriculture movements and Black self-determination. She has been a community organizer, is a parent of four, and is currently an assistant professor in the Department of Ethnic Studies at Northern Arizona University.

Michael Rodríguez-Muñiz is an assistant professor of sociology and Latina/o studies at Northwestern University. Over the past twenty years, he has been deeply involved in the work of the Puerto Rican Cultural Center in Chicago. Most recently, he helped found the Puerto Rican Chicago Archive Project.

Loretta J. Ross is a scholar, organizer, and one of the principal creators of the concept of reproductive justice. She is a cofounder of the SisterSong Women of Color Reproductive Justice Collective and from 2005 to 2012 was the organization's national coordinator.

Tamara Lea Spira is an associate professor of queer studies at Fairhaven College and in the American Cultural Studies Department at Western Washington University. Her forthcoming book, *Movements of Feeling*, examines the vibrant call to remember the interlinked traumas of slavery, colonization, sexual violence, and state violence that came to preoccupy feminist and queer of color writers in the United States and Chile between 1975 and the end of the Cold War.

Suzy Subways coordinates the SLAM! Herstory Project, an oral history of the Student Liberation Action Movement. A member of SLAM! and Love and Rage in the 1990s, she is currently an editor of *Prison Health News* and the *Philadelphia Partisan*, an anarchist member of Philly Socialists, and a sometimes fiction writer.

Julie Sze is a professor of American studies at UC Davis. She is also the founding director of the Environmental Justice Project for UC Davis's John Muir Institute for the Environment. Sze's research investigates environmental justice and environmental inequality; culture and environment; race, gender, and power; and urban/community health and activism.

ethan ucker is a prison abolitionist organizer, researcher, and educator. He has worked in youth prisons, high schools, and group homes across Chicago to address harm through community-controlled practices of healing and accountability. He is the cofounder of Circles & Ciphers, a hip-hop infused restorative justice organization led by and for young people of color who are impacted by violence.

Lesley Wood is an associate professor and chair of sociology at York University. She is active in antipoverty and various other movements in Toronto. She is trying to understand how ordinary people change the world.

Elizabeth Yeampierre is an internationally recognized Puerto Rican attorney and environmental and climate justice leader of African and indigenous ancestry born and raised in New York City. A national leader in climate justice movement, Elizabeth is the cochair of the Climate Justice Alliance and director of UPROSE.

Patricia Zavella is a Professor Emerita at the University of California, Santa Cruz. Her most recent publication is *The Movement for Reproductive Justice: Empowering Women of Color through Social Activism* (New York University Press, 2020).

INDEX OF NAMES AND ORGANIZATIONS

See the introduction to this volume for guidance on where to find documents by subject, issue, or theme.

Indigenous Women's Network, 456
Inter-American Defense College (IADC), 257–58
International Brotherhood of Teamsters, 109, 110, 298
International Hotel campaign, 207–10
International Indian Treaty Council, 249–50, 345, 456
International Longshore and Warehouse Union (ILWU), 282
International Monetary Fund (IMF), 301–2, 312, 407, 408
International Socialist Organization (ISO), 297, 298
International Telephone and Telegraph Company (ITT), 66, 261
Iranian Students Association, 315
Iroquois Confederacy, 438

Jackson, George, 8, 166–68, 169, 177. *See also* Soledad Brothers Defense Committee
Jackson, Jesse, 13, 111, 400, 401
Jadallah, Huda, 321–22
James, Nathanial, 252
Jericho Amnesty Movement, 195–98, 452
Jewish Defense League (JDL), 70, 71
Jewish Women's Committee to End the Occupation (JWCEO), 326
Jobs with Justice (JwJ), 124–27
John Brown Anti-Klan Committee (JBAKC), 12, 69–72, 154, 452
Johnson, Vernon Damani, 89–91
Juhasz, Alexandra, 52
Justice Department. *See* Department of Justice
Justice for Janitors, 290–91
Justice 4 Youth Coalition, 430
Juvenile Detention Alternatives Initiative (JDAI), 430
Juvenile Justice Reform Movement (JJRM), 430

Kang, Joo-Hyun, 161–62
Karnataka State Farmer's Movement, 302
Katsiaficas, George, 388
King, Coretta Scott, 104–7
King, Martin Luther, Jr., 152, 154, 183, 217, 286
King, Rodney, 8, 223
Kiwi Collective, 92–95
Koch, Ed, 150–51
Kokopeli, Bruce, 13, 363–64
Kono, Stacy, 292–94
Korean Immigrant Workers Advocates (Koreatown Immigrant Workers Alliance), 91–92, 228
Kramer, Marian, 119–21
Ku Klux Klan (KKK or the Klan), 8, 69–73, 181, 182

Labor/Community Strategy Center, 159–61, 227–29

Labor Party, 13, 422–26
LaDuke, Winona, 455–57
Lakey, George, 13, 363–64
Lakota Nation, 345, 369, 392, 441; Oglala Sioux, 142, 438–39
Lalo, Bernice, 460
Landless Workers' Movement, 302
Laotian Organizing Project (LOP), 380–82
Las Vegas National Welfare Rights Organization, 96
Lavender and Red Union (L&RU), 40–41
LCLAA (Labor Council for Latin American Advancement), 307, 309
League of Indigenous Sovereign Nations of the Western Hemisphere, 458–59
Lebron, Lolita, 33, 245
Lee, Barbara, 333
Lenten Desert Experience, 376
Lesbian and Gay Asian Collective, 45
Lesbian Arab Network (LAN), 321
Lesbians against Police Violence, 138–39
Lesbians and Gays Against Intervention (LAGAI), 73–74, 262–65, 266, 321–22
Lesbian Schoolworkers, 139
Lesbians in Solidarity with the Palestinian People (LISPP), 322
Letelier, Orlando, 8
Lewis, John, 333
Lewisburg prison (United States Penitentiary), 180, 195
Lexington prison (Federal Correctional Institution), 190, 191; control unit, 185, 188–89
Liliuokalani, Queen, 452
Little, Joan (also Joann or Joanne), 35, 43, 181
Livermore Action Group, 355–57
Lober, Brooke, 188–90
Lockett, Gloria, 58, 59
Longmore, Paul K., 115–16
López Rívera, Oscar, 187, 188, 452
Lorde, Audre, 45, 156, 465
Los Angeles Coalition to End Hunger and Homelessness, 122
Los Angeles Police Department (LAPD), 159; Public Disorder and Intelligence Division (PDID), 148, 149
Los Angeles Unified School District (LAUSD), 224–25
Louima, Abner, 162, 230
Love and Rage Revolutionary Anarchist Federation, 163–64, 406, 419–22
Loy, Tana, 45
Lubinski, Barbara, 138
Lucas, Robin, 199
Lucky Sewing Company, 292–93

Magee, Ruchell, 167, 184
Makhijani, Simmy, 336–37
Malcolm X, 150, 151–52, 155, 183, 395, 449

CPSIA information can be obtained
at www.ICGtesting.com
Printed in the USA
LVHW030123130421
684323LV00008B/283

9 780820 357256